Date Due

GREEK THINKERS

GREEK THINKERS

A HISTORY OF ANCIENT PHILOSOPHY

By THEODOR GOMPERZ

PROFESSOR EMERITUS AT THE UNIVERSITY OF VIENNA, AND MEMBER OF
THE IMPERIAL ACADEMY ; HON. LL.D., DUBLIN AND CAMBRIDGE ; HON. PH.D., KÖNIGSBERG
CORRESPONDING MEMBER OF THE BRITISH ACADEMY FOR THE PROMOTION OF
PHILOSOPHICAL, HISTORICAL, AND PHILOLOGICAL STUDIES

AUTHORIZED EDITION

VOLUME IV

TRANSLATED BY

G. G. BERRY, B.A.

BALLIOL COLLEGE, OXFORD

LONDON
JOHN MURRAY, ALBEMARLE STREET

First published 1912
Fifth impression 1964

PRINTED IN GREAT BRITAIN BY
WILLIAM CLOWES AND SONS LIMITED, LONDON AND BECCLES

To the

MEMORY OF MY EARLY DEPARTED

BROTHERS

KARL AND RUDOLF

(1829–1851)   (1830–1851)

I DEDICATE THIS VOLUME

PREFACE.

In bringing to a close the publication of this work, begun more than a decade and a half ago, I find myself compelled to justify certain modifications of my original plans. The Preface to the second volume has already called attention to the impracticability, as it turned out, of including in that volume (Vols. II. and III. in the English Edition) the treatment of Aristotle and his successors. As the work progressed, however, a still more fundamental change of design has forced itself upon me. It became necessary to restrict the work, which had now reached its allotted number of volumes, within narrower limits of subject-matter. At the outset it had been my desire to carry the history of Greek philosophy down to the beginning of our era; but gradually it became manifest to me that with the first quarter of the third century before Christ a more appropriate terminus would be attained. This was an epoch at which the development of the special sciences reached a height which essentially changed their relations to philosophy. Though here and there an isolated writer appeared who took the whole of learning for his province, such as the Stoic Posidonius (first century B.C.), we are entitled to affirm that on the whole philosophy and the special sciences henceforth pursued separate paths. Universal science—the main object of this work—disappeared as such; the centre of gravity of scientific progress was transferred to the subordinate branches (cf. pp. 459 and 506).

The chronological limit thus indicated has on the whole been reached. The matter still wanting to its complete attainment, the description of the beginnings of the Stoic and Epicurean schools, and of the Sceptic movement, the author hopes to supply in a separate book, *The Philosophy of the Hellenistic Age*, in which anticipatory glances will also be cast upon the later periods.

TH. GOMPERZ.

VIENNA,
May, 1909.

ON August 29, 1912, when the last sheets of this volume were passing through the press, Dr. Theodor Gomperz died, almost at the moment when he had finished the revision of the final proofs.

It is matter for sincere regret that he did not live to see the publication of this English edition, on which he bestowed infinite pains, but which has been long delayed, owing to circumstances over which neither the author nor the publisher had control.

I am informed by his representatives that at the time of his death, Dr. Gomperz had not been able to make any considerable progress with the writing of the contemplated volume on the *Philosophy of the Hellenistic Age*, referred to in the last sentence of the foregoing Preface, and that therefore there is now no hope of its appearing.

JOHN MURRAY.

19th Sept., 1912.

CONTENTS.

BOOK VI.

ARISTOTLE AND HIS SUCCESSORS.

CHAPTER I.

THE OLD ACADEMY.

CHAPTER II.

THE LIFE OF ARISTOTLE.

CHAPTER III.

ARISTOTLE, THE MAN AND THE AUTHOR.

CHAPTER IV.

ARISTOTLE'S CATEGORIES.

CHAPTER XI.

ARISTOTLE AS AN INVESTIGATOR OF NATURE (INORGANIC NATURE).

CHAPTER XII.

ARISTOTLE AS AN INVESTIGATOR OF NATURE (CONTINUATION : ORGANIC NATURE).

CHAPTER XIII.

ARISTOTLE AS AN INVESTIGATOR OF NATURE (CONTINUATION : THE SYSTEMATIST, THE COMPARATIVE ANATOMIST AND PHYSIOLOGIST).

CHAPTER XIV.

ARISTOTLE AS AN INVESTIGATOR OF NATURE (CONCLUSION : EMBRYOLOGY).

xii   *CONTENTS.*

CHAPTER XV.

ARISTOTLE'S DOCTRINE OF THE SOUL.

CHAPTER XVI.

ARISTOTLE'S DOCTRINE OF THE SOUL
(CONTINUATION : THE PROBLEM OF WILL).

CHAPTER XVII.

ARISTOTLE'S DOCTRINE OF THE SOUL
(THE DOCTRINE OF NOUS, OR REASON : CONCLUSION).

CHAPTER XVIII.

ARISTOTLE'S THEOLOGY.

CHAPTER XIX.

ARISTOTLE'S THEOLOGY (CONTINUATION AND
CONCLUSION : ARISTOTLE'S ASTRONOMY).

CHAPTER XX.

ARISTOTLE'S ETHICS.

CHAPTER XXI.

ARISTOTLE'S ETHICS (CONTINUATION: JUSTICE).

CHAPTER XXII.

ARISTOTLE'S ETHICS (CONTINUATION: THE INTELLECTUAL VIRTUES AND WEAKNESS OF WILL).

CHAPTER XXIII.

ARISTOTLE'S ETHICS (CONTINUATION : FRIENDSHIP).

CHAPTER XXIV.

ARISTOTLE'S ETHICS (THE LAST BOOK).

CHAPTER XXX.

ARISTOTLE'S THEORY OF THE STATE (POLITICAL STATICS).

CHAPTER XXXI.

ARISTOTLE'S THEORY OF THE STATE (POLITICAL DYNAMICS).

CHAPTER XXXII.

ARISTOTLE'S THEORY OF THE STATE (CRITICISM OF POLITICAL IDEALS AND IDEAL STATES).

CHAPTER XXXIII.

ARISTOTLE'S THEORY OF THE STATE (THE PHILOSOPHER'S POLITICAL IDEAL).

CHAPTER XXXIV.

ARISTOTLE'S THEORY OF THE STATE (QUESTIONS OF REPRODUCTION AND EDUCATION).

CHAPTER XL.

THEOPHRASTUS OF ERESUS (CONTINUATION: THEOPHRASTUS AS BOTANIST).

CHAPTER XLI.

THEOPHRASTUS OF ERESUS (CONTINUATION: THE DELINEATOR OF CHARACTERS).

CHAPTER XLII.

THEOPHRASTUS OF ERESUS (CONTINUATION AND CONCLUSION).

CHAPTER XLIII.

STRATON OF LAMPSACUS.

GREEK THINKERS.

BOOK VI.

ARISTOTLE AND HIS SUCCESSORS.

"Is enim ut est diligentissimus in cognoscendis rebus singulis
quarum ingentem prorsus et prope incredibilem animo complexus
est scientiam, ut est acutus et ingeniosus in redigendis his singulis
rebus ad summas, quas distinxit, omnium entium categorias : ita
quum de iaciendis altissimis doctrinæ fundamentis et de confir-
mandis interque se conciliandis principiis agitur, plurimum relinquit
dubitationis."—HERMANN BONITZ.

CHAPTER I.

THE OLD ACADEMY.

1. PLATO'S successors drew their sustenance from the
heritage of his later years. The freshness and vigour—
the youthful vigour, we had almost said—of the great
philosopher's old age manifested itself in impulses which
for well-nigh a century dominated the activities of his
school. Even within this period, it is true, we can trace
the operation of that law, fundamental for the development
of the Platonic school, by which the master's different
phases of thought enjoyed successive supremacy. But
it was not till near its close that any real change took
place. From that point onward the teaching of Plato's
old age ceased to inspire the labours of those who succeeded to the headship of his school. The dialectics of
refutation, the Elenctic primarily due to Socrates, awoke
to new life after long repression ; and its reappearance

marks the beginning of the Middle Academy, which took
its rise with the Sceptic Arcesilaus.

Plato committed the direction of the Academy to his
sister's son Speusippus, who held it for eight years (347–
339). The figure of the nephew is to some extent lost
in the shadow of his mighty uncle; in ancient as in
modern times his significance has perhaps been rated
unduly low. It lies, if we are not mistaken, in his having
been the first to carry forward the line of thought entered
upon in the "Sophist" and the "Statesman." His chief
work consisted of ten books on "Similarities" (Ομοια)
in which, following the thread of analogy, he surveyed the
whole realm of plants and animals, endeavouring to set
like by the side of like, while separating those organisms
whose affinity rested on appearance only, and not on truth.
Expression is here given to the same classificatory instinct
which marks the two Platonic dialogues just named, and
which attained its richest development in Aristotle.

Speusippus may thus be regarded as Aristotle's predecessor. A further link between the two is the strength of
their common interest in the whole length and breadth
of the world of experience, not least of all in the sphere
of human affairs—a disposition of mind which brought
Speusippus into close relations with wide circles of Syracusan society, and led Timonides to address to him his
narrative of Dion's expedition (cf. Vol. III. p. 138). This
reinforcement of the empirical sense may be regarded as
the leading feature of his thought. Going a little further
into particulars, we may say that close study of the organic
world ripened in his mind the idea of development. This
is plain from what we are told by Aristotle. Speusippus
refused to set the principle of the Good at the head of
the world-process, and justified his refusal by pointing
to individual plants and animals which in the course of
their existence advance from a less to a more perfect
state. He thus came to discern, in the prime cause of
the universe, a formative principle akin to the vital forces
of the organic world, and by this attitude drew upon himself
the taunt of atheism.

With this empirical and inductive tendency there went (the reverse side of the medal) a renunciation of every kind of dialectic except the purely classificatory; nor did this kind escape profound modification. No reverence for his great uncle deterred Speusippus from rejecting the Platonic doctrine of Ideas. For all labours in the field of definition he showed as little respect as Antisthenes. Like the latter, he was manifestly unwilling to admit the distinction between essential and accidental attributes. " He who would define one thing rightly must know everything; for the definition of the one thing presupposes a knowledge of all the differences between it and everything else." In this connexion we gain a welcome glimpse into the peculiar character of his studies in natural history. Evidence which is above suspicion ascribes to him the rejection of "subdivision and definitions." This rejection, however, rested solely on the above objection to the possibility of adequate definition—an objection warranted by no less a person than Eudemus. The conclusion which we draw is as follows. Speusippus certainly did not abstain from any and every attempt at classification. So much is clear from the title of his main work, already referred to, as well as from the remnants, scanty as they are, of his writings. What he rejected was, as we infer, not classification at large, but that division of natural objects which is based on definitions of classes. He was, in other words, an opponent of what is now called technical or artificial classification, and the first advocate of that mode of forming groups which is called by antithesis the "natural system." He would have sided with Bernard de Jussieu against Linnæus. Of this method, triumphant in our own day, the following account has been given by Whewell, in his " History of Scientific Ideas ":—

" The class is steadily fixed, though not precisely limited; it is given, though not circumscribed; it is determined, not by a boundary line without, but by a central point within; not by what it strictly excludes, but by what it eminently includes; by an example, not a precept; in short, instead of Definition we have a Type for our Director."

In the fragments of Speusippus' work such terms as "resembling," "like," "similar," are of constant recurrence, while there is no trace of sharp delimitation or rigid definition. This agrees well with the conclusion stated above ; but when we come to the application in detail of the fundamental principles, we are left nearly as much in the dark as with regard to the arrangement of the subject-matter. Lastly, our hypothesis is confirmed by a book-title : "On the Patterns or Types of Genera and Species." In his endeavours after a natural system, in his opposition to the excessive use of twofold subdivision, Speusippus is a forerunner of Aristotle. Dichotomy, it is true, had already been abandoned by Plato in the "Statesman."

Close study of the endless multiplicity of organic structures could not possibly have been favourable to the hypothesis which identifies duality or the principle of differentiation with the principle of evil. We are thus not astonished to find the nephew here again in disaccord with the uncle. On the other hand, we cannot but be surprised by the records which represent Speusippus as nearer in some respects to the Pythagoreans than Plato himself. A great deal in these records is untrustworthy or inconclusive, but as much as this seems certain—Speusippus raised numbers to the rank of prime causes of things ; like the Pythagoreans, he carried into detail the analogies between geometrical and arithmetical relations, and among other things raised a hymn of praise which has quite a Pythagorean ring to the number Ten. But considerations which are not far to seek soon diminish our surprise. Plato's quest for fundamental principles, which led him into speculations on numbers, started from the point at which the Ideas passed into the background of his thought. We are thus prepared to find the same tendency accentuated in the work of a pupil, who not merely subordinated but abandoned the Ideas. For in abandoning them he did not at the same time lose hold of that fundamental premiss of the Platonic epistemology according to which knowledge would be impossible if there were

no entities transcending the world of sense. It must, moreover, be set down to the credit of Speusippus that he made
no total surrender to what may be called the analogism of
the Pythagoreans, but, in relation both to this and to the
corresponding tendency in Plato, put forth by no means
contemptible efforts towards sharper distinction of ideas.
Thus, for him, the point was not identical with unity,
but only of similar nature ; nor, again, did he identify
reason with unity and the good, but distinguished it
from them as something "specifically unique." His
numerous ethical writings exhibit him as moderate in
his claims upon life and free from visionary extravagance.
While reserving the highest place to the virtues, he did
not deny all value to health, wealth, and other external
goods.

2. The figure of Xenocrates is presented to us in less
shadowy outline. No favourite of the Graces ; needing
the spur, not the curb—such are the expressions with which
Plato himself described the ungracious, reserved, somewhat
heavy personality of his disciple. It was only by a " bare
majority " that the students elected him head of the
Academy after the death of Speusippus. To-day hardly
even a minority of competent judges would ventuie to
assign him the rank of a great original thinker. And
yet his scholarchate, which lasted a quarter of a century
(339–314), must not be regarded as wholly without significance for the destinies of the Platonic school. An ingenious
essayist has observed that among princely houses those
only have established themselves permanently in which
the founder was followed by an heir who proved a
diligent custodian of the newly acquired patrimony, and
administered it for a fair space of time. In philosophic
dynasties the same rule seems to hold good. Thus
Theophrastus was such an heir in the Aristotelian school
and Cleanthes in the Stoic ; in the school of Plato (after
the short reign of Speusippus) a similar part was played
by Xenocrates of Chalcedon, whose fidelity to the master
was greater than even that of his own sister's son. It is
true that in one respect, doubtless to the advantage of the

school, he trod other paths than those of the founder.
The alien settler in Athens found the democratic constitution of his adopted home more congenial than it had
been to the aristocratically-minded descendant of Attic
kings. He enjoyed the confidence of the people, and
after the unfortunate ending of the Lamian war was
elected a member of the embassy which treated with the
Macedonian regent, Antipater. During the occupation
of Munychia by a Macedonian garrison (B.C. 322) he
showed his patriotic grief by omitting the usual sacrifices
to the Muses at the Academy. Lastly, he refused the
grant of citizenship, offered him by Demades, on the
ground that it would be shameful for him to accept a
share in a constitution, imposed by Macedonian lances,
to resist whose introduction the people had deputed him
to Antipater.

Xenocrates was commended to the Athenian people
not merely by the warmth of his patriotism and the
universally acknowledged blamelessness of his life, but also
by the marked independence which he showed in his
relations to the great. When Alexander placed a considerable sum of money at his disposal, he invited the
messenger charged with the gift to the common table.
Pointing to the simplicity of the meal and the inexpensive
mode of life usual at the Academy, he declined the royal
bounty ; or rather, by accepting a small fraction of it, took
off the edge of a refusal that otherwise might have seemed
insulting or defiant. His attitude towards religion, too,
was such as to bring him nearer to the heart of the people.
He was a forerunner of the Stoic school (whose founder,
by the way, was one of his pupils) in what the ancients
called " adaptation " (συνοικείωσις), an abstract interpretation of mythical tales and symbols well suited to bridge
the gulf between philosophy and popular beliefs. Indeed,
he went so far as to modify the late Platonic doctrine of
numbers in an anthropomorphic sense by assigning to the
principles of unity and duality the characters, respectively,
of male and female divine principles—a new instance of
the tendency, which we have already noticed in the case

of the Megarian Euclides and the aged Plato, to an atavism by which metaphysical entities revert to the theological type (cf. Vol. II. p. 174 ; Vol. III. p. 173). Similarly, in the deification of natural forces, he went further than the star-gods of his master, and, lastly, he imagined countless hosts of dæmons mediating between the gods and men. In this demonology, following the precedent of the evil world-soul in the " Laws," he did not shrink from admitting spirits that plague and torment. Here, especially, we find him at a vast distance from the pride of intellect characteristic of true Socratism, and swayed by the ineradicable instincts of the popular mind.

Whether Xenocrates counted among the dæmons souls not yet incarnated or souls severed from their bodies, is a question that cannot be answered with full certainty. More important is his definition of the soul, applied by him to the world-soul as well as to the souls of human individuals : A number which moves itself. We rub our eyes on reading this marvellous definition for the first time. Well might Aristotle call it "the summit of absurdity." But at the same time he elucidated, aptly if not exhaustively, the currents of thought which brought it into being. On the "self-movement" we need waste no words. The reader is familiar to satiety with the doctrine of the " Phædrus " and the "Laws" that all motion is of psychic origin (cf. Vol. III. p. 45, *seq.*). Besides holding this doctrine, Xenocrates desired to lay emphasis on the cognitive function of the soul. Now, number was regarded as typically the most abstract, and therefore the purest and most exalted object of knowledge. Herewith was joined the ancient doctrine of the essential similarity between the knower and the known. Just as for Empedocles earth was known by earth and discord by discord (Vol. I. p. 246), so here it may be, some share in the nature of number was ascribed to that by which number is known. Perhaps, also, the following consideration may assist towards the understanding of this curiosity in definitions. If we suppose that Xenocrates wished to describe the soul as something that knows and that moves itself, he would have had a difficulty in specifying this something more precisely without at the same time suggesting erroneous ideas. It was important to prevent the soul being imagined as material, as extended in space, or even as a composite product into which body entered as well as soul; such words, therefore, as "thing," "living being," perhaps even "being," were hardly fit for his use. Turning his back on this region of terminology, he lighted on the word "number," which both commended itself by its abstractness, and promised to express the quantitative relation of the parts of the soul. In this latter respect the definition is no more absurd than the kindred conception of the soul as a harmony (cf. Vol. III. p. 43); both are open to Aristotle's objection that a harmony is a relation or a mode of composition, and presupposes elements which it relates or of which it is the synthesis.

This application of the concept of number is closely bound up with that product of Plato's old age which, under the name of intelligible or ideal numbers, has provided ancient and modern students with so much labour to so little purpose. The hint contained in the "Philebus" (cf. Vol. III. p. 215) was followed by a fuller exposition in a course of lectures "On the Good" which a well-informed ancient commentator described as "enigmatic." If the immediate successors of Plato were unable to solve these riddles satisfactorily, or even to make some approach to unanimity as to their solution, how should better success be possible for us, to whom the mere statement of the riddles is only known through dark and fragmentary allusions? Very little is known with certainty; for example, that those ideal numbers were distinguished from the numbers with which we calculate, and that there were not more than ten of them. Thus Plato cannot have been concerned with numbers in the mathematical sense, but with the principles of numbers. In these principles he believed he had discovered the fundamental causes of things. Preciser information is not within our reach, except with regard to the principles of unity and duality, also called the principles of indivisibility and divisibility, from the mixture of which numbers in the ordinary sense were supposed to take their rise—as "unity in multiplicity," to speak with a logician of the present age. With this exception, we discover nothing but vague analogies. The Pythagoreans had adduced parallels between arithmetical and geometrical ideas (point and unity, line and duality, surface and triplicity, body and quadruplicity, cf. Vol. I. pp. 104, 105) ; these were now supplemented by a parallelism dealing with the region of knowledge. Pure reason was assimilated to unity, knowledge to duality, opinion to triplicity, sense-perception to quadruplicity. Such is the account given by Aristotle of these speculations. A glimmer of light is thrown upon them when we remember that so far back as in the "Republic" Plato had paralleled the shadow-pictures of mere fallible opinion with the first superficial number, three (cf. Vol. III. p. 101). The equation of knowledge with duality seems to rest on the consideration that knowledge implies both a something that knows and a something that is known ; while pure reason is regarded as holding the two elements of subject and object in an as yet undivided unity, in the form, it may be, of divine self-contemplation. Two principles of arrangement seem here to be working at cross purposes. For, while there is a plain step downwards from reason to opinion, nothing of the kind is visible, at least at first sight, in the relations of opinion to sense-perception. Possibly, however, Plato might have met this objection by observing that in opinion, uncertain and deceptive as it may be, there is yet an element of active thought, a reflected flicker of reason ; while sense-perception plunges us fathom-deep in the world of the unreal, and, as one of the functions of the soul, takes its stand nearer to the corporeal and animal sphere than does opinion, which latter estimates and compares the impressions of sense. Analogies of this type may be spun out to whatever lengths we like ; but they will never furnish us, any more than they furnished Plato, with an Ariadne-clue to lead us out of the labyrinth of vague similitudes. Recent attempts to discover in these theories anticipations of the most modern school of logical mathematicians are, as we think, destitute of any tenable basis.

In this doctrine Plato indulged, to a greater extent than anywhere else, the craving for simplification natural to a speculative mind. We have noted how in the "Statesman," with a breadth of vision recalling Heraclitus, he sought to identify the powers that rule the moral sphere with those that rule the world of nature. In the "Timæus" we have seen ethics placed on a cosmic basis, while nature was ethicized, and, in the language of the ancient gibe, "mathematicized." We have witnessed the triumph which was won by mathematics in the arena of Plato's mind over a dialectic now held in lower regard because of its real or supposed misuse. Thus the tendency of thought which, at the inception of the doctrine of Ideas, made the reality of mathematical objects an inference from the irrefragable truth of mathematical propositions, moved on to complete victory (cf. Vol. III. pp. 4, 5). With the speculative forces we have named there was joined the Pythagorean conception of number as not merely the expression but the generator of universal law, as the source of all existence, as the highest reality (cf. Vol. I. p. 104). The last barriers are overthrown by which the several realms of Being were divided. Natural philosophy, ethics, epistemology are fused into a single whole ; and their highest concepts coalesce in the numerical principles which they have in common. At the summit of the pyramid of numbers, which is at the same time a pyramid of concepts, stands the principle of unity. We recall here that Platonic yearning for the unconditional unification of man and society which grew into a fierce hatred of all sundering differences, all Mine and Thine, all divergence of opinion, all individuality. In the universe, again, unity became the principle of salvation, of permanent subsistence, and so of the Good (cf. Vol. III. p. 215). To all this we have now to add the intellectual sphere, in which the principle of unity makes its appearance as self-thinking, universal reason, or as self-contemplating deity, drawing as yet no distinction between subject and object. We have already reached a point where more is surmise than inference. No glimpse whatever is afforded us of the manner in which Plato reduced the Ideas to numerical principles. All that can be said with certainty is that he associated each subordinate concept with its appropriate *summum genus*, or number-principle, the whole forming an arrangement in which the more general always ranked above the more particular (cf. Vol. III. p. 374). We can understand how a sober thinker like Speusippus, instead of falling under the intoxicating spell of these philosophic identities, found himself called upon to assert the specific differences which distinguish the fundamental conceptions of the ethical and physical, the intellectual and mathematical spheres.

Such sobriety was not among the gifts of Xenocrates. The magic of number held him in thrall. The sacred number three was discovered by him everywhere. It appeared in the composition of philosophy, which he subdivided primarily into physics, ethics, and logic. It was seen in the structure of the universe, to whose three regions there corresponded three forms of the Godhead, and three stages of knowledge ; while the threefold nature of entities —intelligible, sensible, and mixed—found a concrete representation in the three Parcæ. On fancies such as these there is no need to dwell. Nor is there much more profit to be won from the study of his physics. This was closely modelled on that of the "Timæus," with the distinction that the place of the primary triangles was taken by genuinely material particles. He would have nothing to do with an origin of the world in time, or a creation of the world-soul ; and accordingly he was one of the first, if not the first, to treat the expressions in the "Timæus" which set forth these ideas as mere devices of exposition. His ethics, which was contained in numerous writings, is known to us only in uncertain outline. One of his utterances which places the desire to do evil on a level with the accomplished deed, surprises us by the refinement of feeling it manifests. He did not entirely disregard bodily and external goods, and clearly was further removed from the Cynic position than his successor.

3. This was Polemon of Athens, a member of a wealthy family of ancient nobility, who was head of the Academy from 314 to 270. His youth was wild, even dissolute. He was once one of a company of revellers who rioted through the magnificent street of the "Potter's Market" in broad daylight. Intrigues which went beyond the limits allowed by Greek manners gave his wife occasion for a divorce suit. Intercourse with Xenocrates transformed him beyond recognition. His ideal came to be calmness and rigidity of mind carried to the extent of insensibility. In the theatre, when all around were in the grip of the keenest emotion, the little man with the hard stern features could not be seen to move a muscle. Not even the bite of a mad dog drew from him a cry of fear or anguish. From his pupils he received not only admiration, but the warmest devotion. Many of them, in order to be always near him, chose to live in the garden of the Academy, in which they erected small huts. In his teaching, dialectic and physics passed into the background ; his sole concern was with the Platonic ethics, which in his hands approximated to the Cynic type. He acknowledged nature as his guide ; and his commendation of the "life according to nature" contained germs capable of the richer elaboration which they subsequently received from Stoics and Epicureans. His professional labours were seconded by those of Crantor, a man of no slight importance, who, by expounding the "Timæus," opened the series of Platonic exegetes, though his interpretation of the dialogue followed lines traced by Xenocrates. In another direction, too, Crantor was a pioneer, for his celebrated book "On Mourning" founded the literature of consolation. Among other things, this work contained a review of the pros and cons of immortality which recalled Plato's "Apology." A precious fragment of it is extant, in which a profound understanding is revealed of the function performed by bodily pain as a guardian of health, and by mental pain as a preservative from brutish demoralization. A similar tone of moderation is shown in his "table of goods," in which virtue occupies the highest

place, while room is yet found for health and riches, and for pleasure between the two. The different goods were represented as appearing before a festival assembly of the Greeks and contending for the first prize—an idea which was carried out with the same grace and spirit that marked the work "On Mourning." Though Polemon's ideal of apathy or insensibility was not that of Crantor, the two men were bound by ties of the most intimate friendship. Indeed, their companionship grew into a complete community of life, in which they were joined by Crates, Polemon's successor in the headship of the school (270– ?), and lastly by the next head, Arcesilaus (?–241). Even the bones of the friends were directed to be laid in the same grave, a touch of sentimentality in which the spirit of the age proved stronger than the somewhat Cynically coloured ideal of Polemon. The latter would seem to have felt, dimly at any rate, the onesidedness of his nature and his consequent need of a complement. Otherwise, a man of his stamp, one who held aloof from all participation in state affairs, who avoided all gatherings of men, who entered the city as seldom as possible, would hardly have attached himself to Crates, who took an active share in politics and was even willing to undertake journeys as envoy. Crates, again, wrote a book on Comedy, while Polemon's favourite author was the tragic poet Sophocles. There was a still sharper contrast between Polemon and Arcesilaus, the fourth of the friendly band. While the former despised all dialectic, the latter awoke it to a new and vigorous life within the school of Plato. But with him we have reached the limits of the Old Academy. We cannot, however, take our leave of it without mentioning an accessory but exceedingly attractive figure, of whose manifold activities we must now give the briefest possible account.

4. The name of Heraclides is not new to our readers. They will remember the considerable share which he had in the progress of astronomical theory (cf. Vol. I. p. 121). But his many-sided intellect was not exhausted in this contribution. This native of Heraclea on the Black Sea

had become at home in the circle of Plato's pupils. It
would appear that he stood in particularly close relation
to Speusippus ; and he received instruction in rhetoric
from Aristotle during the latter's first residence in Athens.
Plato is said to have left him, during his last Sicilian
journey, to take his place at the Academy ; and, in any
case, his reputation in that quarter was so great that on
the death of Speusippus he nearly obtained the headship.
He was, however, second to Xenocrates, though by only
a narrow margin of votes, and his disappointment gave
him a motive for returning to his home. Unfortunately,
his literary and educational work did not satisfy his ambition. Like Empedocles, he was something of a *poseur*,
and the resemblance was heightened by his craving for
more than human honours. This presumption was visited
by a requital which may be called tragic. When his native
land had been suffering from persistent bad harvests, and
the Delphic oracle was consulted in the hope of obtaining
deliverance, he contrived, by bribing the envoys sent to
Delphi, as well as the Pythia herself, to have an answer
returned to the effect that the Heracleots would prosper
better if they were to crown Heraclides with a golden
crown as a benefactor of his country, and after his death
honour him as a hero. The sequel could not but impress
men's minds as a divine judgment. For while the response
of the oracle was being announced in the theatre before
the assembled people, Heraclides, who was in a state of
violent excitement, suddenly fell down dead, like that
Olympic victor who was seized with apoplexy at the
moment of his triumph. This touch of the charlatan in
his character has influenced in undue measure the judgments of men upon Heraclides the author. We do not
know, it is true, whether there is any justice in the charge
of plagiarism which was brought against him by a rival.
But if his dialogues were adorned with wonderful tales and
inventions of fantastic audacity, he was well within his
rights as an artist, and is no more blameable on that
account than was Plato for his vision of Er the Pamphyl-
lian, not to mention the marvellous realm of Atlantis.

The most remarkable of his fictions was probably that in which he represented a man as coming from the moon to the earth, perhaps with the same object as that which Voltaire had in view when he made his Micromegas leave his native Sirius to visit the earth and criticize the affairs of men.

This fashion of expanding the dialogue form beyond its original bounds by all manner of fanciful additions was by no means confined to Heraclides. Eudoxus composed "Dog-dialogues ;" and the "Panther" and the " Crow " of Diogenes are additional instances which imply an incursion into the realm of animal-lore. That which especially distinguished the dialogues of the Pontine philosopher was the rich variety of character depicted in them, the great extent of the narratives which formed their framework or were woven into their texture, and also the lifelike "medium conversational tone " for which they were famous. They were divided into tragic and comic, and embraced a wide gamut of subjects and modes of treatment. One of them, entitled "On the Apparently Dead," described a marvellous cure said to have been wrought by Empedocles. Another of his contributions to this class of literature introduced the reader into the world below, and yet another represented a Magus as arriving at the court of Gelo, and narrating the circumnavigation of Libya. Lastly, there was the " Abaris," in which Pythagoras appeared as an interlocutor as well as the Hyperborean wonder-worker whose name furnished the title. This work, which filled several volumes, would seem to have been simply a novel interspersed with dialogues.

Was Heraclides the author greater than Heraclides the philosopher ? One is inclined to conjecture that he was. For while the artistic form of his works receives repeated praise, and is imitated even by Varro and Cicero, the number of specific doctrines, apart from his great innovations in astronomy, that are attributed to him, is not considerable. Our authorities, it is true, often leave us in the lurch. We learn that he modified the

Atomism of Abdera, and that this doctrine, so modified, was retained by Asclepiades, the founder of the "Methodic" school of medicine (first century B.C.). But we have anything but clear information on the nature and extent of this transformation. In any case, Heraclides abandoned the old and largely misleading form of the doctrine by rejecting the conception of an atom and substituting for it that of a simple body. For it is obvious that his "unarticulated particles" can be interpreted in this and no other way. Testimony of unimpeachable credit forbids us to suppose that he tampered with what is fundamental in the atomic theory, the limitation of objective reality to the mechanical properties of the primitive particles. He may, however, have lopped off certain fanciful accretions to it; he may have denied the infinite series of simple kinds of body, and thrown the burden which this hypothesis was intended to bear on an assumed multiplicity of combinations by which varying effects are produced on our senses. This view of his teaching, which would thus have had affinities with modern chemistry, is suggested to us by the report, hardly susceptible of any other interpretation, that his atoms were liable to undergo changes, due, no doubt, to their action upon each other. The theistic disciple of Plato, moreover, can hardly have attributed to the world of matter that sovereign importance which it possessed in the eyes of Democritus, for whom the gods themselves were the products of linked atoms, incapable, as he thought, of exerting any influence on the processes of the world. The position of Heraclides may in this respect have resembled that of modern theologians, who no longer resist the doctrine of evolution, but regard that process rather as an instrument of the Divine purposes than as a prime cause in itself. That he attacked the Democritean theory of perception, we gather from the title of one of his books (" On Phantasms against Democritus "). His polemical activity was further directed against Heraclitus, as well as against his Eleatic antithesis, Zeno ; while the history of the Pythagorean school was a favourite subject with his pen. He filled many volumes with his writings.

on ethics and politics, mathematics and physics, and the history of music, in addition to his works of a mere purely literary character. The same tendency to the encyclopædic pursuit of knowledge is to be met with, on a much larger scale, in another and greater thinker, who, like the Pontine, sprang from the school of Plato, and, like him, failed to find a place within its bounds.

CHAPTER II.

THE LIFE OF ARISTOTLE.

1. APART from founders of religions, no single man has ever exerted so permanent an influence on the mental life of mankind as Socrates. But this influence was very largely indirect. It is to be perceived in quarters where the name of Socrates has never been heard. A very different destiny awaited the most illustrious of his intellectual grandchildren. The victorious march of Aristotle is without a parallel. Fifteen hundred years after his death he is spoken of by the great poet of the Middle Ages as the "Master of those who know." Ecclesiastical assemblies of Christian Europe penalize all deviation from the metaphysical doctrines of the heathen thinker : many a faggot blazes to consume his opponents. And the man whom Christendom delights to honour is no less the idol of Islam. In Bagdad and Cairo, in Cordova and Samarcand, the minds of men acknowledge his sway. The Crusader and the Moslem forget their strife while they vie in praises of the Grecian sage.

Truly the threads of fate are strangely interwoven here. Mediæval Europe owed the revival of Aristotelian philosophy to the Arabs. They in their turn drew their knowledge from Syriac translations, the makers of which were well fitted to mediate between their Greek brethren in the faith and their Arabian brethren of the Semite stock. Thus the dead Aristotle set up reciprocal influences of far-reaching compass between East and West, and contributed his part towards the realization of the ideal which his great pupil kept before his mind—that fusion of Orient and Occident after which Alexander strove in many a hotly contested fight.

This relation of pupil and teacher, which bound Alexander to Aristotle, the arbiter of the world to the arbiter of thought, strikes us as one of the most curious caprices of history. It had its origin in the connexion of the philosopher's father with the Macedonian Court. Nicomachus, an eminent member of the Asclepiad family, and not unknown to literary fame, stood in close relation to Philip's father Amyntas, as his physician and trusted adviser. Thus Aristotle spent his years of childhood at a royal court ; he was saved, however, from the enervating influences of court life by the bereavement which left him an orphan in his boyhood. He grew up in his native place, the humble Stagira, under the care of his guardian, Proxenus. At the age of seventeen he went to Athens and entered the school of Plato (367).

Here he abode for two decades, up to the death of the master. There were current in ancient days stories of the pupil's relation to the teacher, as to the truth of which we are in some measure able to judge. It is related that Aristotle made use of Plato's repeated absences to secure his own preponderant influence in the school, for which reason Plato charged him with ingratitude, and compared him to a colt that lashes out at his mother. Closely examined, this tale may be seen to be mere idle gossip. It is not only that in those of his works which have been preserved Aristotle displays the deepest reverence for his great teacher. For instance, there is the well-known passage in the " Ethics," where he prefaces a polemic against the Ideas by the fine saying that, difficult as he finds it to combat a doctrine originating in a friendly quarter, truth yet demands the sacrifice. " For if the choice is left to us between regard for truth and regard for a man, piety bids us pay the higher honour to truth." That which is most important is the simple fact that he spent all those years at Athens and in the Academy. Nor is it entirely without significance that a literary opponent, who assailed Aristotle during that period, could think of no more effective plan than to make the exclusively Platonic doctrine of Ideas the objective of his attack.

" He struck at Plato, wishing to wound Aristotle," says our authority. From this it is clear that he was at that time regarded simply as a member of the Platonic school, and that of misunderstandings between the two men outsiders at any rate knew nothing. The polemical writing referred to was the work of a pupil of Isocrates, Cephisodorus by name, and was connected with the rivalry which existed between Aristotle and Isocrates as teachers of rhetoric. For the Stagirite had already begun to give instruction in this subject, though not in philosophy ; and that he looked with some contempt on the pretentious superficiality of the older man is what we might have conjectured even if it had not been expressly attested. He meted out public chastisement to the inferiority of his distinguished rival.

In other ways, too, that period of his life saw him busy with his pen. The greater part, if not the whole, of his dialogues had been composed before he turned his back on Athens. This step was one which he could not bring himself to take till the aged master had drawn his last breath (347), just as for that master himself the execution of Socrates had been the signal for departure. Not only was the bond broken which had hitherto bound him to Athens ; it is clear that he could not see in Speusippus the man best qualified to direct the school. This is confirmed by the circumstance that when he left Athens he was accompanied by Xenocrates. For the new scene of their labours the comrades chose Assos, a city of Mysia. This city, together with Atarneus, was governed by Hermias, who had formerly been a slave of Eubulus, the sovereign of Assos, but who had risen to be his master's successor. He had at one time been a fellow-student of the two young philosophers at Athens ; he now acted as an out-sentinel of the Macedonian empire, which here came into collision with the Persian. This conflict claimed him as a victim ; for after Mentor the Rhodian, a commander of Persian troops, had enticed him outside the city on pretext of a diplomatic conference, he was taken prisoner and sent to the Great King, who had him put to a shameful death.

The two friends fled to Mitylene, the chief city of the neighbouring island Lesbos. At the same time, Pythias, a niece and adopted daughter of the fallen prince, likewise sought safety in flight. Aristotle felt himself drawn to her in her distress, and chose her for his wife. From Mitylene he was summoned (342) to the Macedonian Court, to which he was recommended by his literary achievements, the memory of the royal physician his father, and his close relations to Hermias, the unfortunate victim of Macedonian policy. With an unerring eye, Philip perceived in the rising scholar and author the right man to educate his son, then a boy of fourteen.

The kings of Macedon had always set store on "moral conquests" in Hellas. So far back as the first Persian wars, Alexander I. had sought to establish his claim to take part in the Olympic games by producing a pedigree which reached back to Heracles. At the present moment Philip was a member of the Delphic Amphictyony ; he had acted as president of the Pythian games ; he was already *de facto* the Protector of Greece. It was not to be thought of that an heir destined to still greater things should lack those means of education for the command of which Greek princes and statesmen strove at that time with the keenest rivalry. But, even apart from possible political complications, it may well have seemed undesirable to place him in the midst of Athenian democrats at the school of Isocrates or of Speusippus. The monarch seized upon an expedient which does the greatest honour to his pedagogic insight. He decided that Alexander should complete his studies in the peace of the country, far from the din of the court, under the guidance of the most eminent educational talent to be had. For this purpose he selected Mieza, a city lying to the south-west of the royal seat, at the foot of the wooded heights of Bermion, or rather not the city itself, but a shrine of the nymphs in its neighbourhood, not far from an extensive stalactite cave. There a kind of private university was established. To a late date tourists were shown the stone benches and shady avenues in which Aristotle can hardly have been the only teacher or Alexander the only pupil. We shall do better to picture the one at the head of a professorial staff, and the other surrounded by a company of fellow-students drawn from the highest Macedonian aristocracy. This university-life of Alexander lasted only two years. In the year 340 he was called upon to act as regent for his father while the latter was absent on a military expedition. This duty over, he may have continued his intercourse with the philosopher for a few years more, though not without frequent interruptions occasioned by participation in his father's campaigns.

To take the measure of the influence which Aristotle exercised over his ambitious pupil is, unfortunately, a task beyond the materials at our command. It is easier to indicate the point at which this influence failed. The Stagirite was filled with the consciousness of nationality steeped in national pride. The line between Greek and Barbarian was for him an inviolable frontier. Nature, he thought, had ordained the one to rule and the other to serve. The conqueror of the world, on the other hand, who in the far East assumed Persian dress, adopted Persian court-ceremonial, and entrusted Orientals with high office, mightily battered those barriers, and prepared the way for their final collapse. Whatever counsel Aristotle gave under this head was disregarded. It may be that we have here the source of that coolness which arose between the two men, of that growing estrangement whose traces were thought to be discernible in the tone of Alexander's letters. However begun, it was almost certainly enhanced by the embroilment of the king with a former fellow-student, Callisthenes, who was also a nephew of Aristotle. It is easy to understand that, in spite of all this, the royal pupil showed no remissness in bestowing honours on his teacher and providing financial support for his researches. Philip had during his lifetime accorded a full measure of favour to the tutor of his heir, and had entrusted him with the rebuilding of Stagira, which he himself had destroyed. A year after Alexander's accession Aristotle returned to Athens, and there, in the eastern part of the city, founded a school in connexion with the gymnasium known as the Lyceum, a name which was also borne by the school, and has passed into modern languages. A prodigious curriculum of philosophy and science was worked through in the lectures, to which the treatises preserved to us owed their origin.

Just as Alexander's accession opened his tutor's professional career at Athens, so his death set a term to it. All the hatred and ill will that Aristotle had ever aroused burst into activity on the death of his protector. Several circumstances combined to make this outburst as sudden as dangerous. The Stagirite had never been a practical politician. He had never lent the least assistance to Macedonian expansion. Indeed, wonderful as it may sound, the keen-sighted philosopher never suspected the momentousness of the world-change which was being accomplished before his eyes—perhaps for the very reason that the agents of it were only too near him. The idea that monarchical government was destined to prevail in Greece itself never occurred to his mind. No sentence in his " Politics " betrays a knowledge or even a presentiment of this transformation. His heart clung, as of old, to the Hellenic πόλις ; and his ideals, like those of Plato, were concerned solely with its development and renovation. It was as the allies, not the subjects, of the Macedonian kingdom that he pictured the Greeks of the future. But all this could not prevent a philosopher who had been the all-powerful ruler's tutor, who enjoyed his protection, and who had abundant cause for gratitude to him, from appearing in the light of a Macedonian partizan. For one thing, he stood in a relation of warm and unconcealed friendship to the vicegerent, Antipater. Again, Nicanor, the son of his guardian and assigned in his will as the future husband of his daughter Pythias, was an officer of high rank in the army of Alexander. In this capacity he had been entrusted, shortly before his master's death, with a duty which could not but arouse the liveliest antipathy against him and all associated with him. In the year 324 he was the bearer of a royal rescript, which he caused to be promulgated by herald's cry at the Olympic festival assembly. This document ordered, in a domineering tone, the restoration of all political exiles, and threatened recalcitrant states with immediate and severe punishment. The impression produced by this dictatorial act was profound. It was welcomed with loud shouts of exultation by the vast number of Macedonian *protégés* there present, who were now assured of a return to home and wealth and power. Exasperation and dismay filled the ranks of their opponents, especially the Athenians. Even the great orator Demosthenes, in spite of the patriotic zeal he had so often and so signally displayed, was severely censured for having caused himself to be elected leader of the festival-deputation in order to confer with Nicanor. The Stagirite's fatherly friendship for his guardian's son was well known. He certainly met him at Olympia on his return from long absence in the East, even if he did not receive a visit from him at Athens. The incident opened the flood-gates of a hatred which could not fail to break over Aristotle as well.

In the following year an indictment was laid against Aristotle, charging him, as usual in such cases, with offences against religion (ἀσέβεια). All the hostile interests here united themselves against him : religious orthodoxy, represented by Eurymedon, high-priest of the Eleusinian Demeter, and the rhetorical school of Isocrates, whose malice had been inherited by his pupil's pupil Demophilus, son of the historian Ephorus. Among the acts charged against him was his homage to Hermias, the dynast of Atarneus, who, as tyrant or unconstitutional ruler, as ex-slave, and as eunuch, seemed thrice unworthy of the honours which he had received from Aristotle, namely, a statue set up at Delphi, and a poem (which has been preserved) in glorification of his "manly virtue."

"Athens must not sin a second time against philosophy" —such are the words, we are told, in which the accused philosopher justified his flight. He turned his back on the city in which he had sat at the feet of Plato, in which he had ruled as the revered head of a school, and the constitutional development of which he had recorded with diligence and justice, even with affection. For a safe and convenient place of refuge he had not far to seek. At Chalcis in the neighbouring island of Eubœa, the home of his mother, he possessed an estate, inherited from her, the peaceful seclusion of which he was not to enjoy for long. He died there soon afterwards (322), at the age of sixty-two.

The will of Aristotle has been preserved, and affords us an instructive and pleasing glimpse of the disposition as well as of the personal and family circumstances of this extraordinary man. There is no mention in it of the school ; this and its appurtenances, together with the extensive private library, had been already transferred by Aristotle to Theophrastus, the successor chosen by himself, during his life-time, probably on the occasion of his migration to Chalcis. Antipater was named as executor. Nicanor, his son-in-law elect, was requested to take charge, "like a father and brother in one," of the two children, who were still of tender age. The daughter, as already mentioned, was named Pythias after her mother, Aristotle's first wife. Their marriage, contracted at the time of their common flight to Lesbos, seems to have been a particularly happy and high-toned union. Before her early death, the elder Pythias had expressed a wish that her bones might be laid with those of her husband. In his will he made provision for the fulfilment of that wish. It would seem, too, that he offered sacrifices at her grave as at that of a heroine. His second choice was a less romantic one. It fell on an obviously good-natured and sensible creature who secured for him the domestic peace and order which were demanded by his colossal aud unceasing intellectual labours. Her name, Herpyllis, occurs elsewhere only in the circles of the *hetæræ*. This is in accord with her status of housekeeper and concubine, which at Athens created no scandal, and to some extent enjoyed the protection of the law. She bore Aristotle a son, Nicomachus. In his will he praises her good conduct, provides for her sufficient maintenance, not forgetting furniture and service, and offers her for a dwelling-place the "hostel near the garden" of his Eubœan estate, in case she did not prefer to live at Stagira, where she, too, had been born, in the old and perhaps old-fashioned home. The gratitude and sympathy shown in these provisions are clearly differentiated from the fervent love and reverence which the philosopher manifests towards his own mother as well as towards his father's friend Proxenus and his family. A statue of his mother is to be set up at Nemea; others, of Nicanor and his parents, are to be commissioned; a votive-offering is to be presented in memory of a danger once fortunately escaped by Nicanor, probably in war or on the sea. The dispositions affecting the slaves of both sexes, none of whom is to be sold, show Aristotle as a kind master in death as in life.

CHAPTER III.

ARISTOTLE, THE MAN AND THE AUTHOR.

1. "MODERATE to excess"—such is the witticism (unintentional, as the context shows) in which an ancient biographer aptly summarized the character of Aristotle. The Greek ideal of measure, of an equipoise of harmoniously-developed powers, found expression in his personality as well as in his theory of ethics. Violent passions seem to have been utterly foreign to his nature. On the cancellation (clearly for political reasons) of honours previously conferred upon him for his services to the history of the Pythian games, he wrote to Antipater : "The situation as to the Delphic decisions is this—they neither distress me seriously, nor leave me altogether indifferent." It was just this kind of temper, not subject to violent perturbation, and yet with no leaning towards dull insensibility, that was thoroughly characteristic of him. A fundamental condition was thus satisfied for the immense and untiring activity of his mind. "Laborious" is the first epithet that falls from his pen, when he sings the praises at once of "Virtue" and of his friend Hermias. The labours of Heracles, too, receive prominent mention here. This pæan is not without its share of poetic inspiration ; but in another poetical essay, the elegy on Eudemus (Vol. II. p. 71), the level quickly falls. In the prose works it is but seldom that we come across outbreaks of strong feeling ; those which do occur are no doubt the more effective for their isolation. We may instance the tribute to truth already mentioned ; or the praise of justice as "perfected virtue," whose wondrous beauty "not the morning and not the evening star" can equal.

The numerous and extensive treatises reveal to us the
thought of their author much more closely than his will
and feeling. A few years ago a book was recovered which
brings the Stagirite somewhat nearer to us as a man.
The "Constitution of the Athenians" occupies a middle
position between the severely objective, not to say arid,
manuals and the highly personal utterances of the will,
the poems, and the epistolary fragments. It is a collection
of materials worked up into a readable book, one of many
preliminary studies for the comprehensive work on politics.
Aristotle here lets himself run on in an easy conversational
manner, so that his personal tastes are more clearly perceived ; and as his models and sources are at least in part
known to us, we gain a deeper view than elsewhere of
his relations to his predecessors and fellow-investigators.
The impression which we receive is throughout one of
benevolent dignity. He makes no parade of his laborious
researches. He silently corrects ancient errors and widespread misunderstandings. He wounds no contemporary,
he insults no predecessor. There is no breath of what
may be called the eristic spirit of the Stagirite, a spirit
which has sometimes given occasion for unjust judgments.
Some critics have detected, as they thought, a touch of
unchivalrous combativeness, especially in the polemics
against Plato. The disciple was supposed to have
concealed his dependence on his master in respect of
fundamentals behind discussions of minor details. This
charge we regard as unfounded. Dialectician as he was,
and, indeed, stronger by far in this than in any other
capacity, he no doubt indulged himself in dragging to
light even trivial offences against scientific rigour, and
in so doing employed a kind of criticism which must often
strike us as petty pedantry. The dialectical tourney
has an overpowering attraction for him. But he must be
acquitted of the disloyal motive just mentioned. The
lectures out of which the treatises grew were addressed
to youthful contemporaries, thoroughly familiar with Plato's
writings ; there was no reason why he should seize each
new occasion as it arose to remind them once more of

the debt of gratitude which bound him to his great teacher.

Another fundamental characteristic of his mind, specially prominent in the newly-discovered book, is his love of the particular. Anything in the nature of an anecdote has great charms for him. His delight in picturesque detail often leads him into digressions unnecessary for the main purpose of his exposition. Plato is said to have called the house in which he lived as a young man "the house of the reader;" and doubtless he belonged to the number of those whose appetite for reading has been insatiable during boyhood and youth. Like another great encyclopædist, Leibniz to wit, he wished to read everything; and the strength of his interest in general subjects increased rather than diminished with years. "The lonelier and more hermit-like I become"—so the ageing philosopher wrote to Antipater—"the greater pleasure I take in histories." It was not only that he loved to feast his imagination on the motley variety of events; his sense of humour was by no means weak, and drew rich nutriment from the perversity of human actions. The part of a crafty Ulysses so successfully enacted by Themistocles at the supersession of the Areopagus, the trick played on the Athenians by the exiled prince Pisistratus when he caused a Thracian flower-girl to pose as Pallas Athene escorting him back to his home, with the superstitious populace on their knees at her feet—this and the like of this is described in that book at remarkable length and with manifest enjoyment. We can almost see the roguish twinkle of the little eyes and the mocking smile playing round the lips. We no longer doubt the authenticity of the biting sarcasm attributed to him: "The Athenians have invented two things—wheat-culture (according to the myth of Triptolemus) and excellent laws. The only difference is that they eat the wheat, but make no use of the laws."

2. The judgments of the ancients on the artistic qualities of Aristotle's style are of a kind to cause us

considerable perplexity. The "golden ripple" of his language, the "richness of its colouring," its overwhelming "force," the magic fascination of its " grace "—for these we search the works of Aristotle in vain. We speak of him as an author who is nearly always monotonous and colourless, sometimes curt and sometimes prolix, not seldom obscure, occasionally negligent. The contrast of verdicts and impressions could not be more glaring. There must be a misunderstanding somewhere. It is as if we were describing that part of the moon's surface with which we are familiar, while our fellow-observers on some other planet had in view that side of our satellite which we never see. And such, indeed, is the fact. The Aristotle of the ancients is not our Aristotle, and ours is not theirs. Those of his writings which they read, or read by preference, have not reached us ; that which we have was in part entirely unknown to them, in part known in such a way that to make it the basis of a judgment on Aristotle's style would never enter their heads. Our part consists of the text-books, theirs of the dialogues. It is to the latter that the Stagirite refers when he speaks of his " published " works. Only a few sorry fragments of them remain. Contrary to the practice of Plato, the author introduced himself into them as one of the inter-locutors. They were not addressed to fellow-students of philosophy, but to the wide circles of the educated, to whose pampered and refined literary taste they gave full satisfaction.

It is far more surprising to be told that our Aristotle was not the Aristotle of the ancient critics and scholars. But this statement is supported by an authoritative piece of evidence, the list of Aristotle's works compiled in the Alexandrine epoch. One of the principal works best known to us is the " Metaphysics." It does not occur in that catalogue, while there are a number of book-titles that corre-spond to the contents of separate sections of that work. In order to understand this curious state of affairs we shall have to take into consideration both the origin of these treatises and the vicissitudes of their fortune. We have already spoken of them as text-books, and more than once we have intimated that they arose out of the lectures. To some extent evidence for this still exists in the titles. The work on physics bears even in our manuscripts the title " Lectures on Physics." The " Politics " was once at any rate headed by a similar phrase. Now and again we come upon the "hearer" when we expect to find the reader mentioned. The question presents itself whether what we have in our hands is the lecture as written down by the author ready for delivery, or as reproduced in the notes taken by his audience. The answer, it would appear, cannot be given either as simply or with the same generality as the question. Most of the systematic works are far too good to be merely students' notes ; much in them, on the other hand, is such matter as a practised teacher fittingly leaves to the inspiration of the moment, and does not bring with him, in black and white, into the lecture-room. Such, for example, is the address to the audience at the end of the course on logic, an apostrophe in which the creator of logic draws attention to the novelty of his subject and claims at once credit for what he has succeeded in doing and indulgence for any deficiencies. The process by which these systematic treatises came into being does not seem to have been in every case the same, and, generally speaking, was probably somewhat complicated. Most of them will have owed their origin to both sources—the lecturer's draft and memoranda made by the audience. In some cases the master may have himself worked up his original version with the aid of his pupils' notes, in others this work may have been done by others after his death, in one instance long after. The " Metaphysics," as a minute analysis has shown, was produced in the second of these ways. It is a work in which we find the same theme handled twice, first, it may be, in broad outline, and then immediately after in diffuse elaboration ; or, again, the two treatments may be barely distinguishable. The very name is due, not to the author, but to a late compiler, who placed the work after (μετά) the books on physics. Such an origin of the treatises, again, seems necessary to explain the remarkable oscillations between exaggerated compression and over-lucid expansion. Here we find an example hinted at with such enigmatic brevity that a severe effort is needed for its comprehension; another will be elaborated and explained with superfluous fulness. Both modes of treatment occur in the same book and in the same section of it. We are driven to seek the explanation in the varying exigencies of the lecture-room. Here time pressed, there it was only too abundant. Or again, what we have before us is sometimes the bare catch-phrase jotted down in the lecturer's notes; sometimes it is the detailed exposition into which he developed it in the lecture itself.

The history of these works, and of the component parts of some which were not yet extant as wholes, is so like a novel that the truth of the narratives containing it has often been called in question. Such doubts, we hold, are groundless, for the simple reason that both the beginning and the end of the story are vouched for by unassailable testimony—the first by the will of Theophrastus, the second by a statement of the geographer Strabo, who had been a pupil of the Tyrannion shortly to be mentioned.

Theophrastus bequeathed "all" his "books to Neleus," a friend and pupil who lived at Scepsis in the Troad. The heirs of Neleus thought only of the money value of this great collection of books, among which were those of Aristotle. But their very cupidity entailed severe injury upon the precious possession. That district of Asia Minor belonged to the kingdom of Pergamum, the rulers of which soon began to collect books in rivalry with the Ptolemies, and endeavoured to eclipse the Alexandrine library by their own. Fearing the loss of their treasure, the successors of Neleus buried it in a cellar-vault, where it remained secure from the prying commissioner, but all the more a prey to damp and insects. At length a rich buyer came forward, the bibliophile Apellicon, through whose agency an edition was prepared, an extremely defective one from a critical point of view, and disfigured by arbitrary restorations of the numerous *lacunæ*. At the capture of Athens, soon after Apellicon's death, the collection of books came to Rome as part of Sulla's loot, and the ill-treated text was subjected to a careful revision by Tyrannion, the librarian and writer on grammar. This revision formed the basis of the first complete edition of the works of Aristotle and Theophrastus, grouped according to their subject-matter, which was prepared by Andronicus of Rhodes (middle of the first century B.C.).

No doubt is permissible as to the actual occurrence of these events. But the case is different when we come to inquire into the range of their significance. Those who were concerned in the salvage and the preparation for public use of the long-lost aids to knowledge were naturally enough inclined to exaggerate the magnitude of these operations. Thus Tyrannion's pupil, Strabo, speaks of the older Peripatetics as almost entirely unacquainted with the works of their master. Clearly the unprejudiced Plutarch is far nearer the truth when he states that " most " of those works " were at that time not yet accurately known to the public." Modern research has carefully collected the traces of this knowledge, and has made an end of the idea that there were no copies of any of the text-books before the edition of Andronicus. As much as this, however, may be truthfully said, namely, that some of the treatises were entirely unknown, that some had appeared only in untrustworthy copies crowded with errors, and that there was no possibility of taking a comprehensive survey of them. It is, further, a manifest fact that the busy labours of the commentators did not begin before that epoch, and that the solid study of Aristotelian philosophy had no earlier representative than this same Andronicus, who expounded the works besides editing them.

3. Besides the works in finished literary style, mostly in dialogue form, and besides the text-books or treatises, there was a third class of Aristotelian writings which may be described shortly as preliminary studies and collections of materials. One portion of a work of this third class has already been considered by us, the " Constitution of the Athenians." The complete work, entitled " Polities,"

contained the description, in alphabetical order, of 158 constitutions of single states and confederations, with an appendix on the governments of tyrants or usurpers, to which was further added a monograph on the " Laws of Barbarians," and a separate study of the " Territorial Claims of States." It was long ago conjectured that in collecting and elaborating the vast mass of material, the master was assisted by his pupils. Among the circumstances which point in this direction, we may mention the varying accounts given in antiquity of the authorship of several works of this type. The law lexicon which appears among the works of Theophrastus is in one case expressly described as the joint work of teacher and pupil. It is only within the last few years that we have been in possession of strict documentary evidence of this state of affairs. We refer to the Delphic inscription, in which praise and public crowning (probably also privileges of some kind, cf. p. 27) were accorded to Aristotle and his nephew Callisthenes, mentioned above, for their list of the " victors in the Pythian games," and for their prefatory investigation into the origin of those games. Thus we can hardly doubt any longer that the edition of the " Iliad," primarily intended for Alexander's use, which is sometimes attributed to Aristotle and sometimes to Callisthenes, was produced by the kinsmen in collaboration. The Stagirite treated of the Olympian as well as of the Pythian victors, and in both cases provided a valuable aid to the study both of chronology and of the history of civilization. Of a similar character was his " Didascaliæ," a tabulation of dramatic performances based on inscriptions, forming an important preliminary study for his two books " On the Art of Poetry," the first of which has been preserved. Besides this, there were separate studies " On Tragedies " and " On Comic Poets," and again " On Difficulties " in Homer, Hesiod, Archilochus, Chœrilus, Euripides. Nor did he disdain to expound the details of costume-lore in casual passages of the three books of his dialogue " On the Poets." The three books, still extant, " On Rhetoric," and the lost dialogue, " Grylus," on the same subject, were similarly based on a preliminary study, the "Collection" of earlier theories of rhetoric. For the purpose of fixing his attitude to his philosophic predecessors, he wrote a number of monographs, on the Pythagoreans, on the philosophy of Archytas, and so on, down to special articles on separate Platonic dialogues. Lastly, the history of medicine was treated by his pupil Meno, certainly under his direction, and perhaps not without his help. These examples, drawn from the field of historical studies in the widest sense of the word, will give the reader some foretaste of the Stagirite's enormous activity in research. His treasures of knowledge would seem to have been acquired chiefly during his long student-time at Athens and in the years spent at Assos, Mitylene, and Mieza; while the dozen years embraced by his professoriate at Athens may well have been mainly occupied in the preparation of his courses of lectures. These succeeded each other in an order which, broadly speaking, corresponded to a progress from the general to the particular, from the simple to the complicated.

CHAPTER IV.

ARISTOTLE'S CATEGORIES.

1. WE often and rightly speak of the mystery of individuality. Not that the forces whose working is there to be traced are more enigmatic than any others. The riddle consists in the multitude and complication of the co-operating factors, of which we seldom gain a comprehensive and never a complete view. In the case of our philosopher, it must be added that the origin of his intellectual peculiarities is hidden behind a thick veil. There is only one point at which it may be lifted. An essential characteristic, the astonishing love of detail which we have already noted, must in any case rest upon an unusually great capacity for and enjoyment of observation ; and this may be confidently regarded as an inheritance from a long series of ancestors, members of the Asclepiad family. Herein, if we look carefully, we shall find the explanation of more than a little.

Two fundamental types of philosopher may be distinguished. In the one the preponderant element is the craving for fulness of knowledge, an insatiable quest for ever new and varied additions to the stock of facts ; in the other the more potent factor is the endeavour after inner consistency, after absolute logical rigour in the structure of thought. Obviously the distinction is one of degree ; neither element can be entirely absent where any considerable achievement in philosophy is aimed at. But none the less, there is a very real difference. A Descartes or a Spinoza building up, stone by stone, a compact and homogeneous edifice of thought, and a Leibniz or an Aristotle sporadically busy in every kind of special investigation present us with two widely divergent varieties of the same species. The encyclopædist engrossed in untiring detail work may strive as he will after strict unity in the fabric of his thought ; his labours will never be crowned with the same measure of success that awaits an intellect of equal calibre less stimulated and less distracted by the exigent instinct of the polymath. In the second case, moreover, the pursuit of clearness will follow a special direction. It will lead to efforts towards the arrangement and subdivision of the vast stock of knowledge. The encyclopædist will devise artifices for making his materials manageable, such as the conceptual language of Leibniz, or he will become the classifier *par excellence.* This latter was the great intellectual achievement of Aristotle. An inborn and, as we may conjecture, partly inherited capacity for observation was here combined with the training which the descendant of generations of physicians received in the school of Plato. When he first joined this school, the master's later phase was not far distant. The ceaseless exercises in classificatory dialectic, some residue of which remains to us in the "Sophist" and the "Statesman," formed a unique preparation for the future orderer and systematizer of the whole material of knowledge. Aristotle became a morphologist in every department of human cognition. His perception of similarities and differences, his sense of form in the highest sense of the word, was developed to incomparable power. His was a genius equal to the founding of new branches of knowledge, to the creation of sciences so widely divergent as logic and comparative anatomy, the comprehensive review in the one case of forms of inference, in the other of forms of organic life. It is true that some reserve is necessary. Even this light was not without its shade. The fondness for drawing distinctions was sometimes exaggerated to a mania ; the exquisite sense of form not seldom degenerates into a love of formulæ and their multiplication, into a formalism poor in content. The mill of his intellect grinds ever exceeding fine, but it is not always fed with a sufficiency of grain.

There is yet another fundamental characteristic which seems to belong to the great encyclopædist as such. He who moves and has his being in observation and the investigation of details can hardly fail fully to appreciate whatever is individual ; he is out of the reach of the temptation to merge separate existences in an absorbing universal, whether this be named Idea as by Plato, or Substance as by Spinoza. It is hardly a chance coincidence that the most eminent encyclopædist of modern times created the doctrine of Monads, and that his greater predecessor of antiquity found the type of complete reality in the individual thing (the τόδε τι). We learn this from the first glance into the work which both in the traditional arrangement and in the probable order of composition stands first in the course on logic : the little book on the Categories.

2. Hardly any other part of Aristotelian doctrine has met with so much honour and so much censure as his theory of the categories. The philosophic schools of Athens were not yet closed when the little work, now provided by commentators with endless annotations, and transformed by the neo-Platonist Porphyrius (232–304 A.D.) into a catechism, was translated into Latin, and, together with a few other elementary writings of Aristotle, formed the foundation of logical instruction in the West. At the same early date the Syrians became acquainted with these books, through them the Arabians, and gradually the whole of the Mohammedan East, in which to the present day the introduction of Porphyrius is the only text-book of logic. On the other hand, leaders of the most diverse, and indeed of opposite schools of thought, both in ancient and in modern times, have united in a single verdict of condemnation. We do not here speak of Stoics and Neo-Platonists, of an Athenodorus and a Plotinus. Even in the opinion of Kant, Aristotle jotted down the ten categories just as they occurred to him ; and Hegel says that he threw them together anyhow. The extreme of depreciation is reached with J. S. Mill, who remarks contemptuously that this enumeration "is like a division of

animals into men, quadrupeds, horses, asses, and ponies."
So uncompromising a condemnation of an eminent thinker
seldom hits the nail on the head. Far oftener it arises
from a misunderstanding of the object which he had in
view. How, we ask accordingly, did the Stagirite arrive
at that list of ten "kinds of statement" which runs : What
(also substance, being, or thing), Of what sort, How great,
Related to what, Where, When, Lying, Having, Doing,
Suffering ? Possibly the shafts of his assailants, particularly the last-named, were directed against some heaven-
scaling tower, but fly harmlessly over the more modest
structure which is really there. Some of the examples
used to illustrate the categories in the work devoted to
them show us clearly what kind of special case the author
had in his mind. Aristotle imagines a man standing before
him, say in the Lyceum, and passes in successive review
the questions which may be put and answered about him.
All the predicates which can be attached to that subject
fall under one or other of the ten heads, from the supreme
question : What is the object here perceived ? down to
such a subordinate question, dealing with mere externalities,
as : What has he on ? What equipment or accoutrements,
e.g. shoes or weapons ? Other questions are concerned with
his qualities and his size (white, instructed in grammar,
so many feet tall) ; under the head of relation (Related to
what) come answers in which a term such as Greater or
Less, Handsomer or Uglier, implies a reference to an
object or objects of comparison. The " When " is explained
by a Yesterday or To-morrow, the Doing and Suffering
by the sentences: "He is cutting or burning," "He is
being cut or burnt." The enumeration is intended to
comprise the maximum of predicates which can be assigned
to any thing or being. A maximum, be it observed ; for
it can hardly be by chance that the full number is found
in only two passages of the work, while the two which are
at once the most special and the least important, those
relating to Having, or possession, and to Lying, or attitude, are in every other case passed over without mention.
And indeed, what sense could there be in speaking of the

possessions of a stone or a piece of iron, or of the attitude of a sphere or a cube ? We further observe that several others of the categories are often lumped together under the one name of "Affections," while others are collectively designated "Motions."

What was the object at which Aristotle aimed in this enumeration and division ? To this question many contradictory answers have been given. Our opinion is that it is only allowable to speak of subsidiary aims in addition to the one supreme purpose which the orderer and systematizer of the whole material of knowledge kept here and everywhere before his eyes. The relation of subject and predicate had been elucidated by Plato (cf. Vol. III. p. 174). The question then naturally arose: How many kinds of predication are there altogether, and what are they ? What are the sub-varieties of these main divisions? Are there or are there not opposites within each region of predication ? These questions are all treated at length in the work on the categories. But there was also a subsidiary purpose to be served ; a new weapon was to be provided for that art of disputation, known as dialectic, of whose enormous vogue and importance in those days it is difficult to form an adequate idea, and a remedy was to be sought for the confusion which had been produced by the partly unconscious, partly intentional misuse of the idea of Being by the Eleatics and the Megarian eristics. The use of the word as denoting existence is therefore separated from its use as copula or connecting link, and the different applications of the copula are strictly bounded and defined. An adequate answer has to be given to the question : What *can* I mean whenever I say of a subject that it *is* something ? Here Aristotle, as his manner is, moves on a certain middle level of abstraction. He often suffers himself to be led by the forms of language, not always from inability to free himself from those bonds, but at least as often because the demands of dialectic will not allow him to quit its arena. An example will illustrate the external character of many of his distinctions. Cognition or knowledge is described as a relative concept, because we speak of the " cognition or knowledge *of some-thing.*" But the special departments of knowledge are not regarded as relative, because, for instance, the Greek words for "grammar" and " musical science " cannot have similar genitives associated with them. Thus a distinction is drawn between knowledge in general and the particular sciences, based solely on the fact that the objects of the latter are included in their names. Other and still more striking examples must be passed over just because they, too, are founded solely on linguistic distinctions.

3. We are now prepared to consider how far the above-mentioned objections of modern philosophers are justified. They are not altogether without foundation if we regard the Stagirite's achievement ; they are, if we regard his aim. This was not, or was not chiefly, directed towards the utmost conceivable simplification, the acquisition of supreme types of concept. Aristotle frankly admits that the cate-gory of "quality" cannot be distinguished with complete accuracy from that of "relation." It is enough for him that the separate instances of "quality" are not expressed by predicates in which "relation" is directly implied. Indeed, he does not shrink from the admission that sometimes one and the same predicate can be placed under both categories. His classification is frequently governed by considerations of linguistic expediency, a circumstance which, it must be allowed, ought to have restrained him from applying it occasionally to ontological purposes. It thus appears, when closely examined, to include here too much, there too little, the very faults which are set in so glaring a light by Mill's contemptuous illustration. In the course of the investiga-tion "quality" falls into two main divisions : (temporary) *states*, and (permanent) *properties.* Some may possibly be inclined to contend that these two varieties ought not to appear independently in the table of categories, because they can be comprehended under the higher notion of quality. For, according to Aristotle's own testimony, some-thing of the same kind may be said about quality with regard to the higher notion of relation. Mill is both right and wrong when he calls the distinction between " Where "

and "Lying" "a purely linguistic one." Right, in so far as the two categories are sub-varieties of a common genus ("spatial relation"); wrong, because they are yet sufficiently distinct to allow of mutually independent questions and answers. The question, "Where is A?" may be answered by "In this room;" the question, "What attitude is he in?" must have for answer, "Erect, bent, sitting, lying," etc. There is, however, not the remotest approach to truth in the statement that the ten categories, as a contemporary expresses it, are incapable of addition or diminution, much as the five regular solids. But while we find it surprising that Aristotle has here to a certain extent blended the necessary with the accidental, there are parallels, not far to seek, which mitigate our astonishment. Much the same kind of *rôle* which is here played by the unessential "Having" falls to the lot of "Song-composition" among the six components of tragedy. The author of the "Poetics" includes this operatic element simply because, whatever the difficulties of deriving it from the nature of drama, he finds it present in the Greek drama of his experience. It appears in his enumeration on an equal footing with those elements which are inseparable from the representation of an action by living performers. At the same time, he omits all mention of the gesture-language of the actor, which, equally with "diction," belongs to the means of dramatic expression, simply because it neither aroused his interest nor provided him with an opportunity for valuable discussions. Similarly, in the present case we may distinguish between the necessary items in the table of categories, those which are deducible from the "Principium" deemed absent by Kant, and the unessential ones which are gleaned from casual observation. Aristotle might have reasoned as follows: Concrete objects exist in time, and occupy measurable portions of space; their quality is not exhausted in the complex of properties which we regard as constituting their essence and forming the content of their names; lastly, they do not exist in isolation; on the contrary, they are bound together by a wide-spun net of reciprocal relations and interactions.

Accordingly, the whole range of statements that may be made about them falls under the heads of time, of place and spatial magnitude, of essence and quality, of relation, of the exercise and reception of influences. Had this been his procedure, he could not have failed to notice the subsidiary rank of the categories of " Having " and " Lying," and, according to the exigencies of his main purpose, he would either have excluded them altogether or admitted them under reservation, with an immediate reference to their unessential character and the limited sphere of their application. Here, however, just as in the " Poetics," he has obviously not worked on deductive lines ; he has been guided by the consideration, in the one case of the actual theatre, in the other of a supposed man standing before him ; questions of principle are introduced as an afterthought, by way partly of justification, partly of limitation.

CHAPTER V.

ARISTOTLE AS LOGICIAN AND DIALECTICIAN.

1. THROUGH the door of the categories we enter into the edifice of logic. From the theory of propositions, handled in the work "On Interpretation," we pass to the theory of inferences ("Prior Analytics"), from this to the theory of proof ("Posterior Analytics"). After this come the books on "Topics," which may be described as an art of disputation, of which the last book has the separate title "Sophistic Refutations."

Logic may be termed the least fruitful of all studies. To condemn it as absolutely sterile would be excessive and unjust. Such an injustice, indeed, is one into which we might easily be led by the reaction against the former over-appreciation of the science. Its founder is in curious contradiction with himself. At an enormous expense of original thought he investigated the forms of inference, distinguished them, and analyzed their finest ramifications. But in applying his genius to this great achievement his object was not exclusively, or even principally, to give an exhaustive description of a particular side of mental life. He believed, on the contrary, that he was constructing an intellectual mechanism of the first order, an "Organon" of all scientific investigation. And lo and behold! in all his numerous works, covering the whole domain of knowledge which was then accessible, he makes practically no use of the "kinds" (moods) and "figures" of the syllogism. He does not even shrink from the admission that all this great wealth of forms might be reduced to a few fundamental ones without loss in practice. We may add that subsequent research, greatly as it has developed and refined its instruments, confirms him in this ; that the figures and the moods (the latter greatly multiplied by his immediate successors) have remained a collection of curiosities, preserved by the history of science, but never put to practical use by science itself.

In spite of all this, an exceptionally high value ought, we think, to be ascribed to this formal, or Aristotelian, logic, and that not only as a training-ground for subtle thinking, but also as a means of promoting correct thinking. It is, however, not so much in the main result of Aristotle's labours as in a by-product that we recognize this value. We allude to the doctrine of fallacies, the distinction between legitimate and illegitimate processes of thought, which runs through all the parts of the " Organon," as the logical works are called collectively, but finds its chief exposition in the book of " Sophistical Refutations." The theory of fallacies supplies us to-day, as it has supplied our predecessors through a long series of centuries, with the means of quickly and surely discriminating between true and false inferences, correct and incorrect deductions. To use Börne's witticism, it saves us from the need of going to the ocean every time we want to wash our hands. This is an argument in a circle, that is an equivocation ; such and such a proposition contains an inadmissible generalization, such an other one an illicit conversion of a conclusion justifiable in itself ; here the negative is wrongly joined with the predicate instead of with the copula, there identity of kind or quality has been confused with numerical identity —if we are now able to frame judgments of this sort with rapidity, and compel their instant acceptance by our opponents, if we can promptly affix to false statements labels attesting their falsity, all this is due to that formal logic which, as a whole and in the majority of its parts, is the work of Aristotle.

The Aristotelian logic grew from a double root. It sprang, on the one hand, from the dialectical tourneys the sound of which filled the assembly of the people, the halls of justice, and the schools of the philosophers. On the other hand, its origin was in part due to the solitary

meditations of those researchers who founded and developed
the different branches of mathematics. The champion in
the war of words needed a rule and a measure by the aid
of which he might divide the good grain of reason from the
chaff of showy pretence, guard himself against deception,
and on occasion deceive his adversary in his turn. Mathematics, for its part, supplied model means of obtaining
universal truths. It already possessed definitions, axioms,
and theorems deduced from both, just as we find in Euclid's
" Elements." How much Aristotle learnt in this school
has not, to our knowledge, been anywhere duly recognized.
In his works we meet with definitions of geometrical figures
at every step ; one of Euclid's axioms, " When equals are
taken from equals, the remainders are equal," sometimes
occurs in his writings in a shortened form, as if worn down
by use ; the highest principles of knowledge seem to him
almost indistinguishable from the "axioms, as they are
called in mathematics ; " his standing examples of indubi-
table truths are taken from the theorems of geometry
(*e.g.* the sum of the angles in every triangle is equal to
two right angles) ; geometry, too, provides the constantly
recurring type of impossibility (the incommensurability of
the diagonal of a square with the side). It is clear that
one of the main motives which influenced the creator of
logic was a desire to extend to new and varied regions
of thought a scientific rigour which the mind of man had
already attained in one department of its activity.

2. The kernel and centre of the Aristotelian logic is
the theory of the Syllogism. In order to make its nature
clear, we adduce an ancient and traditional example, set
out in the form customary with Aristotle—

> All men are mortal ;
> N.N. is a man ;
> N.N. is mortal.

The three propositions, in the above order, are designated
the major and minor propositions, and the conclusion ; the
first two are also called premisses. The three terms or
concepts which occur are distinguished as major, middle

and minor. In our example, mortality is the major term, N.N. the minor, while humanity is the middle term which links them together. At this point a swift and precise thinker may perhaps interpose a series of objections. "How is it possible," such a reader may exclaim, "to conclude from the mortality of *all* men that of this particular man, who is in fact one among those all? Had I not been already convinced of his mortality, I ought not to have affirmed the major premiss, that *all* men are mortal. If, on the other hand, when I asserted that universal proposition I was in possession of full certainty with respect to this particular case of it as well as others, then I do not owe this certainty to the syllogism. The latter has thus revealed to me no truths that I did not know before." The syllogism is therefore so far from being the primary and fundamental form of all inference that, on the contrary, it yields no inference at all in the true sense of the word. It constitutes no advance from the known to the unknown: it is not a means to the acquisition of new truths. In all this, our supposed reader has said no more than was said of old by the Sceptics, and in modern times by a great number of thinkers, most emphatically, perhaps, by J. S. Mill.

The first thought suggested by the above considerations is that the syllogism is an empty hocus-pocus, a solemn farce. But this is not a conclusion to satisfy a thinker whose acumen is combined with caution. The syllogism, as J. S. Mill in particular has contended, though certainly no instrument for the acquisition of truth, is an exceedingly valuable instrument for the examination and the authentication of truth. In order to understand this verdict, let us return to our typical example. The mortality of N.N., who is now alive, is not and may not be inferred from the mortality of collective mankind, in which N.N. himself is included. His mortality, on the contrary, like that of all other men now living or yet to be born, is a consequence of the fact that hitherto all men have died, taken, it must be allowed, in conjunction with this other fact that these deaths belong to a class of phenomena within which absolute uniformity is the invariable rule. This proviso is indispensable. For there are other regularities as little subject to exception as the death of men and all living organisms (at any rate of the higher species), in the case of which, however, the possible report of an exception would by no means be necessarily received with absolute incredulity. For thousands and thousands of years our ancestors were acquainted with none but white swans; it was not till the discovery of Australia that black ones became known. A novelty of this kind is not in the least degree a breach of the order of nature. Black individuals existed side by side with white among men, horses, and dogs; the same difference might equally well occur in that particular species of birds. For, as numerous examples show, the presence or absence of a layer of pigment has little or no effect on the other qualities of a class of organisms.

The inference from past to future mortality is, in short, an *induction*, the certainty of which depends on the number of the observed instances, and in still higher degree on their nature—that is, on their inclusion in a field within which no deviation from the norm is to be expected so long as the present order of nature continues. That this order cannot change is more than we, as men, are able to affirm. We reach the maximum of certainty attainable by us when we trust experience in those regions where it has hitherto proved an absolutely reliable guide.

What, then, is the value and the function of such a syllogism as the one stated above? With Mill, we answer that its service is the bringing before us the context of propositions affirmed by ourselves or others in such a form as to facilitate in the highest possible degree the examination into their truth or trustworthiness. The inductions on which our knowledge of the nature of things is based are no doubt at bottom always inferences from particulars to particulars; but, so far as they are well-founded, they admit of universal formulation just because they rest on properties of whole classes of things, while these properties, in their turn, rest on relations of cause and effect which obtain without exception. Now, this general formula brings before our eyes the whole width and compass of the statements that must be true if we have any right to assume their truth in this or that individual case. A fanatical believer in race, regardless of appearances to the contrary, denies the possibility of a particular negro being susceptible of culture. He is refuted the moment we can compel him to give his denial the most general form, the syllogistic, and to found his argument on the explicit major premiss: "No negro is capable of culture;" for we can immediately bring up against him the numerous brilliant exceptions by which the actual facts contradict his alleged rule. In short: negligent thinking, limitation of the mental horizon, narrowness of outlook due to prejudice, acquaintance with only a small region of the facts concerned—all these are plentiful sources from which a constant and copious stream of ill-judged assertions pours into life and science. To compel the makers of these assertions to justify them against the most comprehensive conceivable objections, and for this purpose to clothe them in the most general conceivable form, is one of the most effective means of which we are in possession for aiding truth in the fight against falsehood. Now, it is the syllogism as exemplified above which preserves us from assuming the truth of a proposition in one case while ignoring or contesting it in a precisely similar case ; it is the syllogism that ensures for us rigour of thought and consistency of statement.

Rigour and consistency of thought—these are in truth the highest aims of the Aristotelian logic, at once its strength and its limitation. To preserve inward harmony among convictions already acquired is the great aim of the Stagirite's labours. It is true that above the syllogism there stands induction, whose function is to supply the knowledge which the syllogism utilizes and elaborates. Aristotle frankly admits as much, though he sometimes forgets the admission in the detailed exposition of his logical theories. But his treatment of the two main divisions of logic—and here we come to the main point —is altogether unequal. This inequality was due to the

different degrees of development which had been attained
in his day by the sciences which served as patterns in the
two departments. Formal logic finds its model in mathematics. In the time of Aristotle this was the only branch
of investigation conducive to the knowledge of nature
which had been pursued beyond the most elementary
stage. "In our day," so the Stagirite himself complains,
"mathematics has set itself in the place of philosophy."
Next to it came those subjects which had just then begun
to be treated mathematically: astronomy, optics, mechanics,
and harmony—subjects which Aristotle does in fact occasionally enumerate among the mathematical studies ; in
so enumerating them, moreover, he does not speak, as we
do, of "mathematical physics," but, with a significant
inversion, of "physical mathematics." The experimental
method, on the other hand, was still in its infancy. Of
the strictly scientific experiment, of minutely accurate or
numerically definite observation, hardly the first beginnings as yet existed. What more natural than that the
newly-created logic should follow the path, not of the
inductive and experimental sciences, but of deductive
mathematics?

3. Our use of the word "deductive" reminds us of an
important limitation which the above statement of the case
requires. The stock example from which we set out does
not exhaust all the possible applications of the syllogistic
form of inference. This latter is by no means exclusively
used for the subsumption of a particular case under a rule
already established. The syllogistic form does not in
itself require the major premiss to be of a more general
character than the minor. This mode of reasoning can
be applied to quite different, and, we may add, at least as
useful purposes. It may provide the bond by which we
join experiences to experiences, in order that we may so
reach conclusions as to the relations subsisting between
objective facts. The simplest case is that of what we may
call indirect comparison. Two objects, A and B, by reason
of their distance in space or time, or for some other cause,
cannot be compared by direct observation. We establish

the relation of equality between them, when this exists, by comparing each of them with a third object. This third object may be an instrument of weighing or measuring ; it may also be merely a numerical concept. $4 + 2 = 6$, $6 = 8 - 2$; therefore $4 + 2 = 8 - 2$: here we have an elementary piece of arithmetic in the form of a syllogism. A is greater than B, B is greater than C, therefore A is greater than C ; this inference, too, follows the same path. Further, the relation of magnitude that has to be ascertained need not be a relation of physical quantities ; relative values of every kind may be determined by the same indirect method. A is more beautiful, more praiseworthy, more serviceable than B, or the reverse ; the same relation subsists between B and C, and therefore also between A and C. Lastly, and chiefly : besides relations of equality and inequality, we must here include those of coexistence and succession, those relations, that is to say, of the knowledge of which our knowledge of the order of nature is compounded ; except that this form of inference is not always, as we might at first be inclined to think, applicable to the ascertainment of mere resemblance. A is like B, B is like C, therefore A is like C : here we have a fallacy. For since similarity is often equivalent to partial identity, it may well happen that the characters in which A and B resemble each other are not those in which B and C agree.

If the Aristotelian logic is directed in greatly preponderating measure to the establishment of purely notional relations, if the creator of the syllogism employs this instrument almost exclusively by way of subsumption, that which here betrays itself is the long-continued influence of the Socratic and Platonic philosophy of concepts. Another manifestation of the same influence is to be seen in the circumstance that much greater strictness is observed in the combinations of ideas than in the ascertainment of the facts from which the ideas are derived. Ill-founded theories of nature and inadequate observations (thunder is a sound produced by a flame at its extinction ; only broad-leaved plants are spared the loss of their leaves in winter, and so forth) are met with not infrequently in the books of the "Organon." The looseness of the premises is in striking contrast with the rigour of the deductions that are made from them.

Let us summarize. The syllogism is by its nature not only a valuable means of testing knowledge, but also a means of acquiring new information. The derivation of the word from a Greek verb meaning "to combine" allows us to cover by it every combination of pieces of knowledge already possessed by which new knowledge is produced. Stating the matter so, we are in exact agreement with Aristotle himself, although in his hands this instrument of investigation became almost exclusively a process of subsuming less comprehensive under more comprehensive notions, and thus seemed to issue in what has been recently described as the *emboîtement* of ideas.

4. Many a surprise awaits the reader of the "Topics." The first sections of this work arouse admiration and pleasure. The brilliance of the illumination which is shed on the subject, the masterly grasp and tireless manipulation of the material, delight even the most fastidious of readers. But before long misgivings make themselves felt, and occasionally even disgust. The examples weary by their monotony, and where they are absent the abstractness of the exposition is wearying in a still higher degree. As we have already remarked, the "Topics" is little else than a guide to the art of disputation. Had this work reached us anonymously, and without the hall-mark of the Aristotelian terminology, how severely we should have taken the author to task! And if this handbook of mental fencing had been presented to us under the name of a Megarian or a so-called "Sophist," the historian of philosophy would certainly have subjected it to some very rough criticism. The vague and general recommendation of Protagoras to "make the weaker cause the stronger" has a very innocent sound in comparison with this accumulation of the means of deception, this arsenal crammed with the weapons of eristic. If justice is to prevail here,

there are several points which must be considered. The conclusions to which our own reflections lead us will be found confirmed by explicit statements of Aristotle.

In the forefront we place the pedagogic motive, the endeavour to arouse and strengthen the pupil's acumen by practice and habituation. But this motive does not by any means stand alone. Aristotle also desired to equip his hearers and readers for the disputations which had acquired an astonishing importance and extent in the philosophy schools of that age. He who disdained participation in those contests created an impression not of superiority, but of the reverse. He appeared unequal to the difficulties of such exercises, and therefore anxious to evade them. Nor was it enough to show shrewdness and presence of mind in answering insidious questions, and in the unravelling of artful sophisms. He who stopped at defence won no more than a half-success. It behoved him to take the offensive and play the man for his own honour and that of the school to which he belonged.

It was with such aims as these that Aristotle, in early life as it would appear, composed this text-book of contentious dialectic, and included in it without scruple instructions on the means of deceiving the adversary. Of all the artifices adapted to win victory in the tourney of words and thoughts, none is despised by him ; he is not above the use of equivocal words, the prolongation of the debate beyond the time-limit, the distraction of the opponent's attention by new and unexpected questions foreign to the main issue. The defensive tactics recommended make an equally unfavourable impression on us. No verbal quibble, one might almost say no pun, is clumsy enough to be despised by the Stagirite as beneath his dignity. The exactitude in the use of words which he inculcates as a means of escaping dialectical snares and pitfalls is not seldom exaggerated into pedantry. In one passage we find him criticizing the definition of astonishment as an " excess of surprise " (instead of " excessive surprise "), on this ground among others that there can also be an excess of astonishment, which the definition would require us to describe absurdly as an excess of excess. In face of such subtleties we ask ourselves at times whether they are to be ascribed solely to the didactic motive, the desire to instruct the student and to equip him for the tournament of ideas, or whether they are not rather to be put down to the account of an eristic strain in the temperament of the philosopher himself. That there was such a strain can hardly be doubted, as other reasons show. Even in the works of his maturest years, to which the " Poetics " and the " Politics " belong, traces of a petti-fogging spirit are apparently to be discerned. But the zest with which the Stagirite on occasion criticizes even himself enables us to recognize the love of conflict as the essential factor in this supposed defect. For the rest, Aristotle was aware that the meaner devices of the dialectical duel leave the contestants in some danger of a permanent taint. He warns against this danger ; and we seem to discern behind his words an admission that he was not proof against it himself. Besides this, there are many passages in which an inward discord betrays itself. Thus in one place emphasis is laid on the necessity, when dealing with an unscrupulous assailant for whom all weapons are good, of using any and every weapon in the defence ; but elsewhere the recognition of the same necessity is accompanied by the reservation : " But it is not quite decent." The main impression with which we close the " Topics "—a work, by the way, which the historians of philosophy usually pass over in what might almost be called an embarrassed silence—is one of astonishment at the extraordinary mental agility and suppleness of its author. Results of which Plato had at best described the first dawnings are here used by the author as though familiar by long possession and thoroughly worked out in every direction. By the side of much that is diffuse and void of substance we find much that is refined and concentrated ; indeed, compressed and condensed up to the limits of intelligibility. At the same time, that other and less favourable impression remains, that Aristotle was only too often led into the misuse of his intellect, partly by the natural impulse to exercise his dialectical skill, partly by the eristic fashions of his day.

Near the close of the main work on logic, a fine image, and one of great significance, presents itself. As, when the tide of battle turns, first one stout-hearted warrior holds his ground, then a second, a third, and continually more and more ; so in the mind the first sense-impression of which a copy remains is joined by a second, then a third, and others in increasing numbers, till from the summation of retained perceptions there arises the completed structure of an experience. For out of perception there is first produced memory, while experience is the result of repeated memories. Out of experience, in its turn, or out of all the " universal that being a one as well as many, has become firmly rooted in the mind," there proceed art and science, where by " science" pure theory is meant, and by " art " theory applied to practice. In this context it is stated with express emphasis that it is " sense-perception" that generates universal notions, and that we necessarily obtain all our " first principles " by " induction." The Asclepiad in Aristotle has here gained the victory over the Platonist. We will now devote a little time to this polar antithesis in the mind of the Stagirite.

CHAPTER VI.

THE PLATONIST AND THE ASCLEPIAD.

1. WE have already spoken of Aristotle's power of and delight in observation as an inheritance from his medical ancestors. The extent of the field in which his curiosity disported itself is far too extensive to admit of a summary survey. His ruling passion is a craving for information. He excuses his faults by his "thirst for knowledge," just as a ruler or a warrior might justify his misdoings by the overwhelming force of his impulses to action. It is after his own image that he figures his deity, whose life is pure contemplation ; just as among human lots he sets the contemplative life in the foremost place. "We prefer the spectator's pleasures to almost all others:" it is thus that, thinking to describe human nature in general, he strikes the keynote of his own character. From boyhood he must have been an earnest watcher of the heavens ; otherwise he could not have written : "For more than fifty years we have only twice seen a lunar rainbow." At the same time, he is familiar with all trades and crafts, with that of the embroiderer who confuses his colours by artificial light, and with that of the gardener who sprinkles his plants, not only with water but with an admixture of earth as well. He has noticed that at some distance from a boat in motion we do not hear the stroke of the oar till after we have seen the oar leave the water. Here, however, we have to make an important distinction.

By the side of observations which astonish by their refinement and certainty, which move a Cuvier or a Darwin to enthusiastic praise, we meet with malobservations which are still more astonishing. It was not till the century just past, that Johannes Müller rediscovered, in the body of the smooth pike, the yolk-sac resembling a mammalian placenta, which is described by Aristotle. A chorus of admiration naturally arose from the zoologists. But their praises are silenced when they learn that the same Aristotle believed the brain to be cold and to act as a refrigerating apparatus in opposition to the heart; that he affirmed the number of the teeth to be dependent on sex, and to be greater in man than in woman. Thus we are confronted by inaccuracy in extreme degree as well as by malobservations which, unlike many others, are not to be explained by the imperfection of the ancient processes and instruments. The explanation of the remarkable contrast can hardly be other than the following. The universal student and encyclopædist over-rated his own powers. He must have derived his knowledge as often, nay, much oftener, from books and popular tradition than from his own observation. He did not by any means always judge rightly of the worth or the worthlessness of these written and oral statements. He repeatedly censures the worthy Herodotus as a "teller of tales;" but the reproach recoils on an author who tells of the hen-partridge being impregnated by a breath of air blowing on her from the male; or of ravens, sparrows, and swallows turned white by cold; or of the reddening, though to ever so slight a degree, of a mirror breathed on by a woman at the time of her indisposition.

Such failures on the critical side are probably not unconnected with a peculiar feature of our philosopher's mental physiognomy, one which is not at all the product of shallowness. He does not, as a matter of principle, adopt too sceptical an attitude towards popular opinions. Following the law of reaction, he stands in a certain opposition to the representatives of the storm and stress period of enlightenment. He accordingly loves to find the results of his speculations prefigured in the naïve beliefs of the people, and he frequently seeks corroboration for his conclusions in current opinion, in popular proverbs, even in etymologies, which are sometimes of the most venturesome

type. Indeed, he goes on occasion so far as to identify
popular belief, when purged of its inner contradictions
and, so to speak, brought into inner harmony, with
objective truth. To the same origin may be ascribed his
constant references to linguistic usage, the ever-recurring
"We say so-and-so"—an appeal to that general opinion
in which he finds, no doubt far in excess of what is
admissible, a residue of reasoned conviction. All flat
contradiction and trenchant negation is abhorrent to his
inmost nature, a temper which is at the root of much that
is good and much that is bad in his mode of thought.
" That is true in one sense, false in another "—" In one sense
these men are right, in another they are wrong "—phrases
of this kind recur quite frequently, and testify unmistak-
ably to the fineness of his sense for shades of thought, to
his dread of crude one-sidedness. We are reminded now
and then of a very modern writer, Ernest Renan, who for
his part stands on the shoulders of Hegel, and shows a
germ of Heraclitean thought carried to full development.
This peculiarity of Aristotle's mind, as operative in the
sphere of mental science, both saved him from many
grave errors and impeded the development of great
originality. In the sphere of natural science, the same
tendency exercised an influence on his investigations
which seems to have been entirely injurious. It led him to
renounce the triumphs which the boldness of a Pythagoras
or a Democritus had gained over the appearances presented
to the senses and over agelong habit. It may be set down
to his lack of scientific courage that he contented himself
with the revived popular physics of Empedocles, including
the four elements, and that he even replaced the earth in
that position at the centre of the universe from which it had
long before been ousted.

2. In spite of all these impediments, the inductive
spirit had gained great power in Aristotle, or at least had
received his cordial recognition. An anthology of expressions might be compiled in which the Stagirite presents
the appearance of a rigid empiric, of a researcher wholly
devoted to the cult of facts and filled with the deepest

distrust of mere dialectical speculation. What could sound more Baconian than the saying with which he closes his discussion of the process of generation among bees : " The facts on this subject have not yet been sufficiently ascertained ; if ever they are, it will be necessary to trust our senses more than our reasonings, and the latter only when the results are in agreement with the phenomena." No one could set a higher value on the new " eye " that experience provides us with. Repeatedly he takes up the cause of the Atomists, against Plato no less than against the Eleatics. It is not that he merely champions one particular theory in preference to another ; in both cases he pierces through to the fountain-head of truth or of error, and once more the antithesis of facts and notions, of observation and reasoning, occupies the foreground of his thought. He contends that, measured by the standard of facts, the Eleatic doctrine, plausible as its arguments may sound, borders on insanity. Certainly the expressions he uses with reference to his master are not quite so strong. But he frankly accords to the Democritean methods precedence even over the Platonic. He describes a preponderant concern with notions as an actual danger to the investigator of nature, inasmuch as it estranges him from the contemplation of reality, perpetually confines his outlook to a narrow circle of facts, and thus leads him to the construction of inadequate theories (cf. Vol. I. p. 319). This, too, the refrain continues, is the way we distinguish between the investigation of nature and mere ratiocination : he who lives and works in the observation of nature is able to frame hypotheses which bind together wide circles of facts —that is to say, fertile hypotheses, the exact opposite of the " random " hypotheses of which we shall soon hear. It is by following up the paths opened by Democritus and Leucippus, he says, that a methodical and systematic explanation of natural processes has been found possible. Such explanation has been based on a real foundation, and has not involved doing violence to the facts of sense-perception after the manner of the Eleatics ; it has not required the denial of generation and destruction, of the

motion and the multiplicity of things. Nor are the works
of our philosopher lacking in expressions of humble self-
depreciation and resignation in which reference is made
to the "limited resources" of research and to a more
fortunate time to come. Even "small successes," he says,
must suffice in respect of the "great riddles." Should
others some day succeed in devising stricter methods and
more cogent proofs, to such men abundant thanks will be
due. But at the present time—so he declares emphatically in two different passages—it is right for us to say
what we think to be true. If our investigations go wide
of the mark, we are not on that account to be charged
with presumption ; we ought rather to be praised for the
zeal which has carried us away into error.

3. We now turn to the other side of the picture. Such
expressions as those just cited have not failed of their
effect. Taken in combination with the truly great services
rendered by Aristotle to certain branches of biology, they
have created a widespread belief that he was an investigator
of nature in the modern sense. Nothing could be further
from the truth. We have already noted that his researches
often rested on an altogether insecure basis of fact. But
his interpretation of the facts, whether real or presumed,
is frequently quite arbitrary and governed by preconceived
opinions. We are amazed by the inexhaustible resources
of his extraordinary ingenuity ; but the impression produced is very far from being that of a disciplined mind
controlling its fancies and bowing beneath the hard yoke
of facts.

"This must necessarily be so ;" "that is impossible "—
such authoritative *dicta* are especially frequent in the
physical works. In most cases they are simply the expression of old habits of thought which prevent him from
acquiescing in new theories, though they may be perfectly
correct and well founded. Two memorable instances of
this kind of supposed *reductio ad absurdum* may con-
veniently be mentioned here. The first is directed
against the hypothesis of empty space, the existence of
which was affirmed by the Atomists. In a vacuum, so

Aristotle argues with perfect justice, all bodies would necessarily fall with equal velocities : that, however, is impossible ; therefore empty space is non-existent ! This refutation strikes him as so convincing that he cannot refrain from following it up with a gibe : " Thus their supposed void turns out to have nothing in it." Secondly, the theory of respiration arrived at by Anaxagoras, Democritus, and Diogenes is repudiated on the strength of, among others, the following argument : If aquatic animals breathed, there would have to be air in the water, which is among the impossibilities.

This glaring contrast between purpose and execution, this continual backsliding of the professed empiric into the bad *à priori* habits which he himself detects so readily and condemns so severely in the case of the Eleatics, the Pythagoreans, and his own teacher, Plato (cf. Vol. I. p. 110) —all this, combined with the suspicion which now and again seems to flash through his mind, that his labours were in vain, presents us with an almost tragic picture. But the feelings so aroused ought not to lead us to gloss over or disguise the truth of the case. This can hardly be made plainer than by a study of Aristotle's doctrine of the elements, an account of which will now be given for the sake of greater completeness in the delineation of his intellectual character which we are now attempting.

CHAPTER VII.

THE PLATONIST AND THE ASCLEPIAD.—(*continued*).

THE ARISTOTELIAN DOCTRINE OF THE ELEMENTS.

1. ONE-tenth experience, nine-tenths speculation—it is thus that we may not unjustly describe the contents of the works which Aristotle devoted to physical and cognate subjects. By the word "speculation," be it observed, we do not mean the legitimate application of the deductive method, the drawing of consequences from well-established premisses. That would have been mathematical physics, the foundations for which were in Aristotle's time only being laid. What we have in mind is rather the *à priori* method in the bad sense, which proceeds from arbitrary assumptions or natural prejudices, and thence spins its unending web by means of a dialectic which impresses by its ingenuity and energy, but yields no results of real worth. The Stagirite is truly unsurpassable in wealth of expedients, in dialectical agility. But for one who sought to explain Nature this was a fatal endowment. Far better, for a worker in this field, is the simplicity and directness of mind that clearly and surely perceives the opposition between fact and hypothesis, that does not seek time after time to blunt the edge of such contradictions by ingenious auxiliary assumptions or shifting-hued comparisons, thus freeing itself from the spur which would otherwise drive it on from failures to half-successes and thence to wholly successful solutions. If Aristotle had had less ingenuity, and if his intellect had been of a less forensic character, then—as we have good ground for conjecturing—his explanation of Nature would have been far more valuable.

He himself falls under the censure which he applies to the Pythagoreans : " It is not difficult to set up random hypotheses, to spin them out to great length, and to weave them together."

2. In his doctrine of the elements Aristotle follows Empedocles, except that, like Philolaus and like Plato in his old age, he adds a fifth element, the "ether" or heavenly substance. In one of his expositions he refers only to ether, fire, and earth, supporting this trinity of elements by the following speculative considerations. There are two fundamental geometrical forms, the circle and the straight line. To these must correspond the fundamental forms of motion, and that, too, in such a way that each fundamental substance has a mode of motion of its own. For the heavenly substance this is motion in a circle ; is it not in a perpetual circle that we see the celestial sphere revolve ? The straight line, however, has two directions. To the one of these corresponds the ascending element of fire, to the other the element of downward-falling earth. We note that the words " up " and " down " are not here used in the traditional sense, but denote movement from and to the centre of the universe, the motionless earth. In the system so constructed no room was left for water and air. It is not till later, and then, we may almost say, with reluctance, that Aristotle admits these two elements, as supposed " necessary " intermediate stages between fire and earth.

In another work we find a different construction, in which the heavenly substance is omitted and the existence of the four remaining elements supported by the following argument. The numberless qualities of matter may be reduced, it is claimed, to four fundamental qualities. These are those favourites of ancient natural philosophy : the warm and the cold, the dry and the moist. Now, out of any four terms there can be formed six combinations, two at a time (*ab, ac, ad, bc, bd, cd*). In the present case, however, two of these six may be ignored ; for opposites like warm and cold, moist and dry, cannot be combined. There remain, then, four pairs : the dry-warm, the dry-cold, the

moist-warm, the moist-cold. Thus the quaternion of elements (fire, earth, air, and water) is obtained and justified.
Aristotle does not spare his predecessors the reproach that
none of them had proved that there *could* only have been
just this number of elements, no more and no fewer. We
need not once more tell our readers that this Empedoclean
doctrine of the elements is a mere outgrowth of primitive
popular physics, that it takes the three modes of aggregation (the solid, the liquid, and the expansive), together with
a phenomenon associated with the third, for fundamental
substances, and declares them to be the only fundamental
substances. On the other hand, there is in this revival
of the Empedoclean theory hardly any mention of the
really valuable contribution contained in it, the anticipation, fanciful in details but fundamentally sound, of the
modern doctrine of chemical proportions or equivalents
(cf. Vol. I. pp. 230–234).

3. The attentive reader will not have failed to observe
that both in the doctrine of the elements itself, and in the
theory of "natural places" on which it rests, Aristotle is
a docile pupil of his master, Plato (cf. Vol. III. pp. 84, 223,
224). If both of them here rejected the views to which the
Atomists had won their way, **if** the Stagirite eagerly assailed
the theory of "displacement" or of "expulsion" (ἔκθλιψις)
which Democritus had already arrived at, they blocked up
for themselves the path which might have led them to
the right understanding of the most fundamental natural
phenomena. Closely connected with this rejection is their
return to the old delusion which regards the earth as resting at the centre of the universe. It is true that mitigating
circumstances may be urged in excuse of this grave lapse.
But still it was a long step backwards, retrograde even in
comparison with that doctrine of the central fire and the
earth's revolution round it, which, though arbitrary in
details, yet cleared away the fatal error of a central and
motionless earth (cf. Vol. I. pp. 113 *seq.*). Thus, to use
the language of Schopenhauer, "a truth of the highest
importance, already once acquired, was lost again to mankind for nearly two thousand years."

The doctrine of "natural places" entangled Aristotle not only in errors of the greatest magnitude, but also in irreconcilable contradictions with other theories of his, also derived from Plato—contradictions which may more readily be excused in the poet-thinker than in the systematist who boasts so loudly of his logical precision. Elsewhere he followed the path trodden by Plato in the "Phædrus" (cf. Vol. III. pp. 45, 46), and allowed matter no motion except what comes to it from without. The question thus forces itself upon us how this depotentialization of matter, if we may call it so, this denial to matter of all innate impulse towards motion, can be reconciled with the supposed upward striving of fire, the downward striving of earth, the tendency of air and water to the middle regions. To this question we never receive any satisfactory answer. A possible expedient would have been to explain the "natural" or peculiar "places" of the fundamental substances as their original home, the habitation assigned to them by the Deity at the beginning of things, from which they had later been in part dislodged by "violent" or "unnatural" motions. Their striving would then have been at most a reflux or return to the order of things instituted by the Deity. But this expedient was barred, because Aristotle acknowledged no Cosmogony, or origin of the world in Time. There is one single passage in which we meet with what seems to be at any rate an attempt to solve the difficulty. But the attempt is miserably inadequate. It sounds almost like a play on words when what we may call the circulation of matter (earth becomes water, water becomes air, and *vice versâ*) is connected by the philosopher in the vaguest manner with the circular motion of the heavens, and thus (so we may complete his thought) with the Deity, which, as "First Mover," is the immediate cause of that unceasing rotation of the celestial sphere.

This attempt is made a little more intelligible to us by the reference which follows it to another circular motion, that in the oblique circle of the ecliptic, and to the varying relations which the sun, by travelling in this path, is caused

ɔ the different parts of the earth. The alternate
d diminution so occasioned in the sun's heat
...ᴄᴄᴛs, as it is hinted, in the course of the changing seasons
a transition of one form of matter into another. By progressive cooling fire becomes air ; water, earth ; the reverse
changes take place in consequence of progressive heating.
The transformation of the substances thus brought about
removes them in the first instance from their " natural
places," and then awakes their slumbering tendency to
return to their homes. Now, so far as the motion of the
sun in its path is to be referred, like all other movements
of the heavenly bodies, to an impulse received from God as
the First Mover, to this extent the divine activity enters
into the cause of these transformations and movements of
matter. Still, with whatever good will we follow up (as
we have done above) the hints of the Stagirite, the unsolved, and, as we think, insoluble question remains : " How
is the *nisus* of the elements towards their natural places to
be harmonized with that absolute passivity of matter which
is elsewhere so emphatically asserted ? "

4. So far we have spoken of "elements" just as
Aristotle himself does. But the true content and the full
value of the doctrine of the elements were lost to him.
The earlier nature-philosophers, men whom Aristotle
treats with an undeserved contempt, had believed in the
changeless persistence of the fundamental substances or
elementary bodies ; they had denied all genesis and
destruction in the strict sense, resolving these processes
into composition and separation ; in this connexion, too,
they had distinguished between primary and secondary
qualities. For views of this kind we may search the
physical writings of Aristotle in vain. Instead, we shall
find a frank and emphatic repudiation of these attempts
to make the course of Nature intelligible. The main argument on which he bases this rejection is the following.
The mere separation and combination of qualitatively unchangeable fundamental substances—such, approximately,
is his statement of the case—cannot be reconciled with
the facts. Dark comes from light, and light again from

dark ; this would be impossible if fire could not become
water and water fire. There is here a change, not of
merely accidental conditions, but of essential properties ;
the notions of genesis and annihilation are therefore
indispensable. In criticizing this argument we have to
distinguish between two things. It is quite in accordance
with the general bent of Aristotle's mind that in dealing
with the world of matter, as in other departments of
thought, he keeps to the solid ground of ascertained facts
instead of endeavouring to penetrate beyond the surface of
appearances by the aid of hypotheses. It is far more surprising that he should have retained the already-mentioned
error of Empedocles and the popular physics, by which the
three states of matter and the accompaniment of one of
them were identified with primary substances, that in
distinctions based on imperfect views of natural processes
he should have imagined frontiers drawn by Nature herself,
and that, consequently, he should have regarded the change
of these forms as a true transmutation of elements. Two
very different motives thus impelled him to abandon
valuable conquests of his predecessors and to reject a
theory of Nature which had already been in their hands a
fruitful aid to investigation and which was destined in the
course of time to wear the same character in ever-increasing
degree. But, while he rejected it, he did not do so without
vacillation and hesitancy, or even, we may perhaps add,
without an inward struggle. On repeated occasions he
takes his stand, as we have seen, on the side of the
Atomists. He defends their doctrine against objections
of the more superficial order ; he praises their method, as
we have also seen, in opposition to the mere investigation
of concepts ; and the blow which he thus aims at Plato
falls upon himself. But in the main and in the end he
recedes from their position. It seems " impossible " to
him that the truth should be what the Atomists had rightly
surmised—that all genesis and destruction are such only in
appearance, that the facts behind the names are simply the
combination and the separation of material particles. He
does not, indeed, go so far as to believe in an absolute

origination of matter ; but he revives the long-exploded notion of its magical transformation. To use the technical expressions of our own times, he denies the qualitative but not the quantitative constancy of matter.

In thus contrasting Aristotle's praise of investigation on the lines of experience with his flagrantly opposite practice, we have given, we think, the best possible illustration of the dual character of his mind. Our purpose was especially well suited by his doctrine of elements, founded as it is on speculative and arbitrary assumptions, inconsistent and thoroughly retrograde in its development. We must, however, be on our guard against illegitimate generalizations. The psychology of Aristotle is not so retrograde as his physics. Far more favourable are the impressions that await us as soon as we turn from the inorganic to the organic world. And even where his subject overlaps the domain of physics, in his theory of the senses, he displays a fineness of vision which had been denied to his predecessors, even to the greatest of them, Democritus.

It is not here, however, that the mind of Aristotle is seen at its best. The brightest display of that lucid intellect is rather to be sought for in the chapters on the highest principles of proof, which are subjoined to the logical works. The thought which there finds expression is irreproachable in its rigour and marred by no discords. It has learnt extreme wariness in the school of debate, and the whetstone of dialectical practice has sharpened its edge. To this part of his work we now turn, thus resuming a thread which we dropped at the close of an earlier section.

CHAPTER VIII.

THE PRINCIPLES OF PROOF.

1. ARISTOTLE designates these principles by the name
of "axioms," an expression which he borrows from the
mathematical text-books of his day, and employs in a
generalized sense. He does not attempt an exhaustive
enumeration of them, and it is only one of their number,
"the most certain of all," the so-called Principle of Contradiction, that he treats with anything like completeness.
In this he had been preceded, so he tells us, by "some
of the nature-philosophers," we do not know which. His
object is to forestall dialectical trickery by a careful and
cautious formulation of the principle which will secure it
against misuse. "It is impossible," so runs his enunciation,
"that the same [predicate] should at the same time and in
the same relation both belong and not belong to the same
[subject]." The qualifying phrases "at the same time" and
"in the same relation" are followed, in the original, by
references to other limitations, the nature of which is not
fully stated, but which are also intended to cut away the
ground from captious dialectic. Certain utterances of
Heraclitus, which we need hardly recall to the reader's
memory, served Aristotle as concrete examples of the
opposite thesis. As types of that revolt against sound
common sense it is clear that he has in his mind such
propositions as : "We are and we are not," or "Good and
evil are the same" (cf. Vol. I. p. 68). The purpose of the
qualifications in the formula becomes at once apparent.
To Heraclitus and his followers Aristotle was ready to
reply that a thing is not "good and bad," but good in one
respect or at one time, bad in another respect or at another

time. The river is not the same and different; it is the
same in one sense, as fed from the same source or occupying the same channel, and different in another sense,
as a continually renewed body of water. To deny this
fundamental principle with full consciousness of its meaning
is, he says, impossible; if Heraclitus professes disbelief,
then "what a man says is not necessarily what he really
believes." Those pointedly paradoxical utterances, however, do not seem to Aristotle so dangerous as their source,
the doctrine of flux itself and the cognate doctrines of
other nature-philosophers touching growth and change.
Hence arise doubts as to the existence of unchanging
objects of knowledge and fixed truths. Were these doubts
well founded, the seeker after truth would be like a boy
snatching at birds and butterflies.

Another principle which he treats with less fulness but
equal emphasis is that which has become famous under the
name of the Excluded Third or Middle. According to his
statement of it, "Everything must be either affirmed or
denied." That is to say, a given predicate either applies
or does not apply to a given subject; between the two
assertions no room remains for any third or middle course.
The two principles may be combined in the following
enunciation: "It is *impossible* that A should simultaneously be *b* and not be *b*; it is *necessary* that A should
either be *b* or not be *b*." Perhaps the simplest way of
expressing them is to say: "Of two contradictory assertions only one *can* be true; moreover one of them *must* be
true and the other false." The principle of the excluded
middle gives rise to objections which are worth closer
consideration. The peremptory "either—or" is sometimes revolted against, not always unjustly. Extreme
judgments, it may be urged, are mostly erroneous; the
truth is often in the middle; the most important thing is
to hit the precise shade, the individual character, which in
no two cases is the same. Considerations of this kind do
indeed narrow the field within which the axiom may be
applied; but they do not diminish its legitimacy, which
can only be lost by misuse. This occurs when the negative

proposition ceases to be the mere strict negation of its companion positive, or when the latter is insufficiently definite. A negation which simply annuls the corresponding affirmation, and does not replace it by the faintest shadow of a new positive statement, gives rise to what the logician calls "contradictory" opposition, as distinguished from "contrary" opposition, by which is understood the relation between positive states or qualities shown by experience to be mutually exclusive. Nor is the principle of the Excluded Middle affected by the instances which may be adduced of a subject and a predicate which cannot be joined together in any intelligible sense, where, therefore, the denial of such union gives the impression not merely of an idle but of a meaningless utterance. Let us suppose that some one takes a fancy to link together phenomena belonging to fundamentally different and entirely unconnected regions, and that we reject the combination by a negative proposition. We should then have confronting each other two such statements as: "The high C is violet," and "The high C is not violet." It might be (and has been) objected that in such instances the affirmation and the negation are equally void of meaning, and that therefore the necessity which the axiom postulates of accepting either one or the other ceases to exist. Such a judgment seems to us to take insufficient account of the distinction between contradictory and contrary opposition. The pure and simple denial is justified even in this instance; it is far from being meaningless, though it may be misleading. It will mislead, will, indeed, drive us full sail to the realm of nonsense, if with as much as a hyphen we join the words "not" and "violet," thus giving the impression that in denying a particular colour to a sound we are thereby ascribing to it some other colour.

The highest degree of this misleading quality is found in those instances where not merely is the combination of the subject with the predicate void of meaning, but the subject itself is a figment or non-entity. To questions such as: "Is the man in the moon bearded?" even the negative reply seems at first incorrect, because the sentence,

"The man in the moon is not bearded," seems to include a recognition of his existence. But even this objection, we think, is not really valid. The true import of such a negative assertion is nothing more than that the supposed predicate does not apply to the supposed subject, even if for the simple reason that the subject does not exist. The two principles, as we hold, remain intact ; and it is a pleasure to add that Aristotle himself, by sharply distinguishing the different kinds of opposition — contrary, contradictory, and, not least of all, privative—did his best to guard against their misuse.

Such misuse is exemplified by the metaphysicians who have imagined themselves enabled by the principle of the Excluded Middle to overstep the bounds of experience and penetrate into the realm of the transcendental. Thus in the last century Sir William Hamilton armed himself with this magic disjunction, and set before transcendent entities (such as matter in itself or the Deity) the alternative of possessing either such and such a definite quality, or else its opposite, both in those cases where we are able to decide one way or the other, and in those where we must leave the question open. All such audacities come to an end when it is recognized that the principle of the Excluded Middle offers us the choice, not between contrary opposites, but simply and solely between a positive statement and the pure negation of it, the latter to contain no jot or tittle of affirmative meaning. Thus we are altogether unable to assert that because motion is not an attribute of a particular entity, that entity must therefore abide in eternal rest ; rest and motion may possibly be categories which have no application whatever to the entity in question. Aristotle himself recognized this truth, and gave it emphatic expression—a fact which in our opinion is greatly to his honour.

2. But if we abstain from all ontological misuse of these principles, what is left of them? Without doubt they possess the highest universality ; the question is whether their fruitfulness stands on the same level. They are the recognition of self-evident truths, against which no serious

doubt has ever been raised.   That every one tacitly admits these principles the moment he speaks, were it only with himself, that he cannot violate them without rendering all intelligent discussion impossible, without indeed becoming a mere "block" instead of a thinking and speaking being —these are facts which the Stagirite not only admits, but which he makes the basis of those maxims which only "want of education" would attempt to demonstrate. What value, then, can attach to the express recognition of a truth which it has never occurred to any one to deny? In the first place, we answer, it has for Aristotle the value of a dialectical weapon. The adversary having been driven into a corner, how is a confession of defeat to be wrung from him? By compelling him to express in clear words the incompatibility of his thesis with some truth of which the denial has already been made impossible to him. Thus the seal is set on the dialectical triumph, and the unsuccessful disputant is robbed of the last refuge which might have remained to him if his contradictory statements could have passed unnoticed.

The principle of the Excluded Middle, more especially, carries on its front clear evidence of its origin in the dialectical tournament.   It is hardly an effect of chance that its author enounced it in a form which obliged us to translate it into objective language before presenting it to the reader. "That one must either affirm or deny everything"—such words strike us as being primarily an instruction to the participants in a debate.   And this, no doubt, was the source from which Aristotle drew the rule. Whether a thesis has to be maintained or an opponent's case to be destroyed, nothing is more fatal to the success of the logical duel than that the adversary should refuse to commit himself, that, using such phrases as "yes and no," or "I do not know," he should evade giving the answer which was meant to lead on to new questions and answers, so forming an essential link in the intended chain of argument.   In reality, of course, such evasion is by no means necessarily a mere trick of dialetic; it may be the simple and natural result of ignorance or of doubt;

and these states of mind play a large and legitimate part
in human thought, not only as products of insufficient
education or unfamiliarity with the matter in hand, but
as derived from the imperfection of human faculties in
general and their inadequacy for the solution of the world-
riddle. Temporary or permanent doubt on the one hand,
the nature of things on the other, resisting as it does the
hard-and-fast alternative by its infinity of gradations—
these combine to restrict the principle of the Excluded
Middle to the narrowest possible field of application. And
yet, even apart from its primary importance in the dialectical struggle, this principle is not altogether destitute of
objective value.

In what—we now ask—does the true import of these
principles consist ? They enlighten us, it has been
answered, on the scope and significance of such words
as "no" and "not." This is not quite exact, as we are
here concerned not with the meaning of words, but with the
actuality of the relations expressed by them. We might
accordingly be at first inclined to regard the Principle of
Contradiction as giving information on incompatibilities
subsisting in the nature of things. This would be right if
the principle related to contrary pairs of opposites, such as
heat and cold, rest and motion, sound and silence, and so
forth. But it is wrong, since, as we have repeated quite
often enough, the principle relates merely to a positive
assertion on the one hand and the pure negation of it on
the other. To say that a phenomenon is incompatible
with its own suspension has in strictness no meaning ; the
denial of A means nothing more than just that A is absent,
though it sometimes appears to bear a different or larger
meaning in consequence of the habit which the mind has
of passing insensibly on from the pure negation to an
affirmative associated with it in experience. Here, it may
be, we have reached the inmost kernel of the matter, the
fact, of constant recurrence throughout our experience, that
we have to reckon with the absence of phenomena as well
as with their presence. Since all our knowledge relates to
phenomena, or at most to their essentially unknowable

vehicles as well, it is to this that the Principle of Contradiction comes in the last resort. It means nothing else than that the antitheses of presence and absence, of occurrence and non-occurrence, of possession and lack—to use some of the commonest expressions—traverse our whole experience. The principle of the Excluded Middle, on the other hand, regarded as a principle of cognition, and not as a rule of dialectic fence, expresses our conviction that this duality divides the whole world of phenomena ; that only imperfect insight and insufficient exactness in framing the question prevent us from solving the alternative in each possible case.

3. Aristotle, to whom we now return, likewise referred these maxims to their source in experience. He represents νοῦς, or mind, as the agent by which we obtain the knowledge of them ; but the instrument with which it works is here, as in the case of all " first " truths, induction. That the fact is as we have stated it, and that all idea of *à priori* knowledge is in this connexion entirely foreign to the mind of the Stagirite, has been maintained, with equal fervour and success, by George Grote, the immortal historian of Greece, whose work in this field also is worthy of the highest consideration.

In answer to the objection that an induction never in reality includes all the instances, but only those known to us, and that it gives us no sufficient guarantee against the possibility of new instances breaking through the rule, Aristotle was accustomed to refer to universally accepted beliefs and to the proofs by probability which dialectical discussion supplies. He might have added here that inductions which extend uniformly over all departments of experience and nowhere meet with any exception, strike back to fundamental ordinances of nature, and are perceived by us only in virtue of fundamental human attributes. Without memory, indeed, and without the faculty of discriminating primary impressions from their secondary copies, we should certainly be unable to distinguish between the presence of a phenomenon and its absence.

The third of the principles under consideration, the Principle of Identity, is mentioned by Aristotle only in passing, if at all. It appears in his writings as the reverse side of the Principle of Contradiction, from which it is hardly to be distinguished. It is so, for example, in the main passage, which runs as follows: "It is false, namely to say that the existent is not, or that the non-existent is [Principle of Contradiction]; it is true, on the contrary, to say that the existent is and that the non-existent is not." We have thus no need to dwell on what later became the stereotyped formulation of the principle: $A = A$. This formula has long been recognized, not merely as an empty tautology, but also, by the keener-sighted, as an absurdity. To compare a thing with itself is an impossibility; in every case what happens is that a reflexion or reproduction of the thing is set by the side of the thing itself and note taken of the similarity, sometimes rising to indistinguishability, between copy and original. If, however, I escape this illusion, then I am comparing, not the thing with itself, but successive states of it with each other. But that these must be absolutely similar is anything but an axiomatic truth. Indeed, in this world of change, the contrary affirmation would seem to have a better claim to the title.

The principles which we have been considering are not laws at all in the scientific sense, but they are so in the sense of practical rules and precepts. He who thinks or speaks may profitably bring or keep them before his own and others' attention. They are useful as timely reminders, be it only of the self-evident. Even the Principle of Identity, poor as it is in content, may be thus employed in dealing either with a pupil or with an adversary in debate. The latter is, so to speak, clutched by the coat-tails the moment he seems likely to escape us. He is recalled to the exact point in dispute when on the point of substituting for it some other which is like it in appearance but different in reality. Similarly, the pupil may be reminded of the subject under consideration when he is in danger of losing sight of it and replacing it by something else, whether ambiguity of language, looseness of thought, or the interposition of a long chain of argument be the cause of his distraction.

CHAPTER IX.

THE ARISTOTELIAN ONTOLOGY.

1. WE turn from the *principles* to the *object* of knowledge. And at once we are faced by what we have met with so often already—the deep cleavage which runs through the spirit and the teaching of Aristotle. Again the Asclepiad is in conflict with the Platonist, or, to put it differently, the investigator of nature with the investigator of concepts. The first takes the individual, the concrete, the second takes the universal, the abstract, as the true object of knowledge, as the type of full reality. In different passages of his "Metaphysics" Aristotle has, in truth, adopted fundamentally different attitudes towards this question ; he has defined the truly existent, or οὐσία, now in the one, now in the other sense. The contradiction is glaring, and, in fact, generally recognized. No attempt to minimize its significance could possibly succeed. Followed into its consequences, the conflict is between the recognition of the world of experience on the one hand, and the transcendental world on the other. The mention of this latter, the sum of metaphysical entities, recalls Plato's doctrine of Ideas ; and the question at once presents itself as to how Aristotle ranged himself with regard to this fundamental doctrine of his master. His attitude, it must be answered, was one of unceasing and violent opposition. He took every suitable and many an unsuitable occasion of combating it ; and thus—the statement is paradoxical, but incontestably true—he proved that he never wholly overcame it in his own mind. A man who has hewn through the trunk of a tree does not go on hacking at the branches. When once the main principle of a doctrine

has been recognized as baseless, that doctrine is set aside as done with, and we pass on to something else. But Plato's pupil never wearies of attacking Plato's chief doctrine ; he thus himself testifies to its vitality, and betrays, we may add, its survival within his own breast. We are reminded of the Hydra, with its heads growing ever anew ; and the impression proves to be fully justified. The more deeply we study the "Metaphysics," the more surely we recognize that the author retains the premises out of which Plato's doctrine of Ideas grew, and that his struggles against accepting the conclusions which flow from those premises are vain though violent. "As by an irresistible fate," justly remarks a recent writer on the subject, "he is driven further and further along the course which he would fain avoid."

This contradiction, too, is only one special case among several. Through the whole field of ontology Aristotle's investigation moves almost without exception along the same lines. All the leading thoughts are borrowed by the pupil from the teacher. Plato supplies these thoughts : what Aristotle does is to elaborate them, to trace their ramifications, to enrich them with distinctions and refinements. Finally, he gives a summary of the whole, which on examination appears for the most part self-contradictory and full of gaping flaws. Three reasons may be assigned for this unsoundness of the metaphysical conclusions. The contradiction is sometimes contained in the Platonic doctrine itself : we may instance the depotentialization of matter (a subject cognate to our present theme) and the doctrine of natural places (cf. p. 65). In other and more frequent cases the strongly developed sense for reality of the observer of nature has revolted from the idealistic philosophy of concepts, and purposely watered down the conclusions which flow from it. Side by side with this conflict, now so familiar to us, a third process is at work with still greater danger to the consistency of Aristotle's teaching. Its origin is to be found in a tendency of his mind which likewise is well known to us already, one which, in its normal and healthy manifestation, may be

variously described as the historical sense, as hatred of
extravagance and respect for common sense, but which
not seldom degenerates into an almost superstitious over-
appreciation of traditional opinions. This tendency, too,
brings diluted conclusions and inconsistencies in its train.
Thus both the initial and the final stages of these reasonings seldom or never bear witness to the power and
originality of Aristotle's thought. His strength is much
more clearly revealed in the middle region of the investigation, where the ordering, sifting, distinguishing, classifying
activities of the dialectician find their appropriate arena.
He is at his strongest when he is criticizing Plato's doctrine.

There are four main arguments which Aristotle marshals
against Plato's doctrine of Ideas. The first of these contains a germ which a leader of the mediæval Nominalists,
William of Occam, developed into the formula : " Entities
are not to be multiplied unnecessarily " (" Entia non sunt
multiplicanda præter necessitatem "). This objection is
expressed by the Stagirite in a manner which borders on
scorn : the authors of the doctrine of Ideas " desired to
ascertain the causes of sensible objects, and therefore
added to them an equal number of other objects. Just
as if one who had to count a set of things were to think
himself unequal to his task till he had doubled their
number." The second objection is to the effect that the
arguments adduced in support of the doctrine of Ideas
prove too much. If they were valid, there would have
to be ideas of negative and relative concepts. It is precisely these " more accurate grounds of proof" that are
said to lead to the hypothesis of the "third man " (cf.
Vol. III. p. 151). Thirdly, the doctrine is barren. It
contributes nothing to the understanding of the world.
The Ideas, too, are not the causes either of any movement
or of any change. If they are explained as patterns upon
which things are modelled, this is " empty talk and mere
poetic metaphor ; what, then, is the active principle which
works with an eye on the Ideas fashioning things in their
likeness ? " And again, for one and the same thing not
one pattern would be required, but several ; *e.g.* for the

individual man we should need the Ideas of "living being," of "biped," and of "man." Fourthly and lastly, it must be held impossible that the essence of a thing and the thing of which it is the essence should subsist in separation from each other. This objection to "separation" or transcendence is at the same time the bridge which leads to Aristotle's transformation of his master's doctrine, his theory of the immanence of the Ideas.

2. It is just at this point that we are presented with a most astonishing spectacle. The pupil who here attacks his master with the utmost keenness and emphasis remains none the less a pupil; his efforts to free himself from the old teaching are ardent but unavailing. The fundamental thesis—we may as well say at once the fundamental error —from which Aristotle cannot break loose, may be formulated as follows. The things of sense are a countless multitude, perishable, vowed to everlasting flux ; therefore they cannot be the object of genuine solid knowledge. Such knowledge would thus have to be renounced were there not, in addition to individual things, something abiding and imperishable : the hyperphysical object of real knowledge. To this two replies might have been made. A sound theory of matter, like that of the Atomists, be it or be it not the last word of Science, has in any case proved the most powerful lever of scientific progress. The Democritean doctrine of atoms and not the Heraclitean doctrine of flux was the right starting-point to choose ; in this direction salvation was to be hoped for. But, secondly, even on the soil of Heraclitean theory, good fruit might have grown if only the universal reign of law which the Ephesian proclaimed with the greatest imaginable emphasis had not been grudged the central position which was its due. Let the things of sense be in themselves never so incapable of appearing as the object of scientific knowledge, the regularities of nature are none the less of exceeding strictness ; the laws of nature might have been for Plato and Aristotle what they are for us, a type of scientific precision and scientific certainty. We note with ever renewed surprise that this point of view remained

foreign as well to the founder of the Academy as to the most illustrious of his disciples. But our astonishment diminishes when we recognize in the failure a defect rooted in the evolution of ancient science. One feature of this evolution was that the sciences which deal with the co-existences of things arrived at a high degree of perfection much earlier than those which, primarily by physical experiment, determine the successions of things. Hence the words which correspond to our "law of nature" are used in this sense by the Greeks and Romans only in isolated cases, and are far more frequently employed to denote a typical stock of qualities. Conceptual types and cogent reasonings were largely taken to be the characteristic elements in scientific knowledge, not empirical determinations of the succession of phenomena. Socratism, in particular, united with mathematics to create an ideal of science which at that time and place may well have seemed incapable of full realization outside the purely descriptive field. In the result thought fled for refuge to the region of the supersensual and often supramundane forms, types, or Ideas ; and Aristotle is as often to be found resisting this flight as taking part in it. His utterances on these matters contradict one another most glaringly ; but, in spite of this, they deserve the most careful examination.

A part, indeed, of these utterances is worthy of our full attention for its own sake. For sterling matter and luminous expression, this part ranks with the best that Aristotle has left us. So clear and so sound are these thoughts of his on the origin and function of general concepts, that it appears at first incomprehensible how, after once gaining the shore, he could have slipped back into the vortex of doubt, and allowed himself to be engulfed in the depths of Platonic mysticism.

There is a highly noteworthy passage in the "Meta-physics," the character of which is stamped upon it by the incessant repetition of a little Greek word, variously translated by "as," "*qua*," "in so far as." It runs thus : "Concerning things which move much may be affirmed and known which applies to them not as moving but merely as bodies, much else in which they are involved only so far as they are surface or line. Other propositions deal with things *qua* divisible or *qua* indivisible, and located in space (point) or merely *qua* indivisible (unit). . . . If the objects of mathematics have the attribute of being perceptible to the senses, while yet that science does not treat of them in so far as they are so perceptible, the branches of mathematics do not thereby become sciences of sensible objects ; but just as little can they be said to have for their object separate entities subsisting in addition to the things of sense." Here the transcendentality of metaphysical entities is denied ; a few sentences earlier their immanence is included in the same condemnation. "Although there are many propositions about moving things as moving (independently of their other attributes and their general nature), it is not necessary on that account that there should exist a moving somewhat, *separate* from the things of sense, or that a determinate entity of that kind should be found *in* them."

Here, then, we have a repudiation both of transcendent entities, subsisting in addition to things, and of immanent entities residing in them—that is, of all metaphysical entities whatever. It would be impossible to make this rejection of ontology more decisive or more complete. This is done, it is true, only within a limited field, that of mathematics. The hostility to ontology breaks out in the course of the fight against Plato's assumption of particular mathematical entities. It is to the heat of this conflict that the philosopher owes the surprising clearness of vision, the extraordinary maturity of thought which he displays on this occasion. There is hardly another passage where Aristotle expresses himself with equal lucidity on the *rôle* of abstraction in science, on the origin and function of universal concepts. Things themselves (thus we may generalize his exposition) present many sides to our contemplation. For the purposes of investigation it is expedient to close our eyes now to this aspect, now to that ; we do well always to concentrate our attention upon some one aspect, and for the moment to give heed to it alone. It is acknowledged that this mental isolation of one side of things is apt to engender the illusion of its separate existence; but, with the fairness born of superiority (a fairness, however, not too common in Aristotle), he admits that the artifice which leads to this illusion is harmless, and indeed helpful to research. "Every object"— such are his words—"is best viewed when that which is not separate (that which has no independent existence) is posited in separation (as an independent object), just as is done by the arithmetician and the geometer."

In this connexion the outlines of what we to-day call, with Comte, the "hierarchy of the sciences" (cf. Vol. III. p. 83) is sketched with wonderful clearness and conciseness. The most abstract sciences are at once the most difficult and the most exact, both from the same reason; they lie at the greatest distance behind sense-perception. The greater the number of added determinations, that is, the concreter the object, the more knowledge suffers in clearness and exactness; such, for example, is the relation of applied to pure mathematics. To all this we moderns may also subscribe, more or less in the words of d'Alembert: "It is chiefly to the simplicity of their object that they (the mathematical sciences) owe their certainty." At the most we should draw a sharper line between, on the one hand, the sciences of coexistence, and, on the other, those sciences of the succession of phenomena in which the decrease of exactitude runs parallel with the multiplication of co-operating and interacting forces, as well as with the superposition of new factors upon old. We should also justify the unconditional rigour of the mathematical sciences upon somewhat different grounds, by pointing out that they are not concerned with realities at all, but with "assumptions" or "conventions"—the first of these expressions is due to J. S. Mill, the second to Poincaré— which remain clear-cut and precise till they are plunged by their applications into the turbid waters of reality.

3. Sharply contrasting with the calm and security which distinguishes these wonderful expositions, other passages

occur which reveal the innermost wrestlings of Aristotle's mind, and betoken the never-ending struggles of ontology and the ontologists. Who can fail to detect a note of helplessness bordering on desperation in such passages as that which follows ? " One question there is which has ever been, now is, and always will remain an object of unceasing search and constant doubt." The question meant is that as to the nature of Being or substance, which " some hold to be one, some many ; some limited, others unlimited." It is exceeding strange that the main source of these perplexities, the ambiguity of language, is touched upon in this connexion, but not made in anything like adequate degree to contribute towards the solution of the riddle. " Being," says Aristotle, is a term with several senses ; the words " substance " or " essence " have at least four.

The Stagirite's way out of the difficulty may be fairly stated somewhat as follows. The essence or the essential is the concept ; " science is concerned with essentials ; science must be concerned with reality ; consequently . . . the concept is something real." Here Aristotle seems to have once more arrived at that Platonic doctrine of Ideas which he has so vigorously combated. But this he cannot for a moment admit. He saves himself from the threatened relapse by substituting immanence for transcendence, by allowing the " concept or form " to subsist in things instead of by their side. But although the formula so obtained, the " one in many," seems to be absolutely correct, in correspondence with the facts, free from all the wild imaginings of ontology, Aristotle can yet find no lasting peace in it. Passages are not wanting in which "the notion or form" appears yet again as something independent, separable from things. So glaring are these contradictions that in the most recent times it has been possible to publish the conjecture—without doubt an erroneous one—that the confusion is chargeable not on the author, but on the arranger or editor of the metaphysical books. We shall come nearest the truth if we term Aristotle's doctrine a diluted Realism or Platonism.

"The concept or form"—in this identification we have the most characteristic feature of Aristotle's ontology. For him the concept is the principle which gives form to things, and thus the agent which provides each one of them with its unity and determinate individuality. Sometimes we have to do with a principle of structure and organization, at other times we should speak rather of the highest function, the work or purpose of the object considered. As a type of form we have the hollow sphere into which wax is melted. A house is a union of matter and form, as contrasted with the stones and bricks of which it is composed ; so too is a statue relatively to the bronze or stone of which it is made ; the seeing eye and the animate body are yet other examples in regard to which vision and the soul, or life-principle, play the part of form. To this active and formative principle matter is opposed and subordinated as its passive and formless object. Matter, in our sense of the word, is regarded as altogether inert and characterless. For Aristotle here follows the precedent of Plato, as set in the "Philebus" rather than in the "Timæus ;" and behind the elements, in which a union of opposed characters is already contained, he posits an absolutely featureless and purely passive primary matter, void of form till form is impressed upon it. This ultimate substratum, it should be observed, is conceived by him as prior to all else, not so much in time as in thought. And it is only in this sense, as we may here remark by way of anticipation, that the Aristotelian philosophy can be called a philosophy of development; the Stagirite had no conception of a true evolution, in Spencer's or Darwin's sense, as a process accomplished in the course of time.

4. It is highly noteworthy that what for Aristotle is matter in one regard is form for him in another. The material elements, indeed, are among the things so treated by him. As contrasted with all other bodies they are matter ; they are form relatively to that truly primary matter just mentioned. Here is a surprising breadth of vision, worthy of Heraclitus ; homage is paid to the principle

of the unity of opposites. But there is shade beside
this light, namely, the vagueness of an analogism which
refines away fundamental distinctions and issues in abstractions which, where not contradictory, are poor in content.
We are reminded of those essays towards a philosophy of
identity which we met with in Xenocrates (cf. pp. 7–11).
Thus the antithesis of form and matter is discovered in
the world of thought, in the material universe, in the realm
of life. It is claimed that the subordinate species is related
to the comprehending genus, the elements which rule in
the upper regions to those which are found below, the soul
to the body, the male to the female—each as form to its
correspondent matter. Still more luxuriant growths occur
in a closely-related region.

With form and matter is associated another pair of
ideas, the antithesis of the real and the possible, the actual
and the potential. While the first pair of opposites applies
to the division of a thing into two parts or aspects, the
second is concerned with events and processes, and with
the states and qualities which they produce.

That this pair of ideas comprehends very much that is
bound together by the threads of analogy rather than
embraced under a strict definition is what Aristotle himself
informs us when he appends a warning against seeking
logical rigour everywhere. Such a warning is in truth
necessary if one category is to cover such disparate instances
as the following propositions supply. Hermes is potentially in the wood, that is, the likeness of the god is present
as a possibility in the material from which his image is
to be carved ; similarly, the half of the line is contained
potentially in the whole from which it may be cut off;
the same antithesis is further illustrated by the relation of
the builder resting to the same builder at work on a house,
of the man with closed but not blind eyes to the same
man looking at something ; with others of the same kind.
A rising scale is thus constituted, the apex of which consists
in the full realization of the powers and faculties latent
in a being, and is called its "entelechy." Even within
the entelechy itself, that which is state or condition is

distinguished from what is actual operation, and called the first entelechy (that is, the lowest of the upper stages). Such, for example, is intelligence as a quality distinguished from the actual process of understanding things. With the fuller realization of capacity there goes hand in hand a sharper impress of the form, so that the highest actuality becomes at the same time the complete triumph of form over characterless matter. Accordingly, form is identified with the realization of concepts, matter with their merely potential existence ; and the two pairs of opposites coincide in this application of them. The soul, in fact, is sometimes called the entelechy and sometimes the form of the body.

Even this short survey is enough to show that the true home of these categories is the realm of nature, and more particularly that of organic life, which both in the gradation of species and in the development of individuals exhibits a progressive realization of rudimentary germs and merely indicated possibilities. The vague analogism, on the other hand, which employs the instances first mentioned by us, replaces the ideas of capacity and germ by that of mere possibility. In this manner a distinction by no means barren in itself is expanded to a breadth hurtful to its fertility, the more so as that antithesis of actual and potential energy which is so important in modern physics could by no possibility have played any part in Aristotle's system. From the barren to the wrongful employment of such categories is but a step. Just this step has been made more than once by the dialectician when under the intoxication produced by the widest abstractions ; and he has thus exposed himself to the censure of even the most benevolent of his interpreters, Hermann Bonitz. It is an apt description which this sound commentator gives of the distinction between form and matter, the actual and the potential, as "a medicine ever at hand to cure all wounds of the system."

All these distinctions have rendered plentiful service not only as cloaks to cover the inner rifts of the system, but also as ministering to that love of compromise which

we have already noted in Aristotle. The Stagirite is often
unwilling either to reject common opinion or to condemn
an antagonistic view championed by eminent predecessors.
At such times his efforts to uphold conflicting judgments
simultaneously find useful allies in the division of a thing
into form and matter, the division of a process or a state
produced by it into the actual and the potential. One
subject is in this manner regularly made into two ; with
the one part may be joined the predicate A, and to the
other the predicate not-A, without any manifest infringement of the principle of contradiction.

This easy and airy manipulation of the notion of the
potential as something parallel to and of equal rank with
the actual prompted Aristotle's Megarian opponents—men
of rigidly logical thought eagerly spying out the joints in
his harness—to engage in that polemic on which we have
already touched (cf. Vol. II. p. 203). Whenever I treat—
so they evidently contended—of that which a human or
other being has the power to make or do, I must not forget
the fact that such production or achievement, like any other
future event, may indeed depend on some one factor in
preponderant degree, but hardly ever exclusively. The
predominance of the one factor very easily comes to be
regarded by us as its unshared sovereignty. Against this
illusion we ought to be on our guard ; we should remember
that the artist, for example, is not wholly independent of
his material, or of those who give him commissions, and so
on ; that, in short, every real event needs the co-operation
of numberless conditions from among which we are only
too ready to single out the most important or the most
decisive and treat it as if it stood alone. This seems to
be the central aim and true meaning of that attack which
the author of the " Metaphysics " describes and parries as if
it were a denial of potentiality, falling, as he does so, into
the most serious contradictions.

5. We have passed in review the chief ontological
doctrines of Aristotle. Let us now consider them critically. First of all, the conviction forces itself upon us
that in our exposition one point has so far enjoyed a

preponderance to which it is not fairly entitled. That Aristotle does not fully free himself from the Platonic tendency to objectify abstractions, that he wrestles with this temptation, seems at one time to have conquered it, and then again succumbs,—all this is true, but it is not the crucial consideration in the appraisement of Aristotle's metaphysics. Not to be able to occupy one's self continuously with abstractions without at least occasionally falling into the illusion that lends them an independent being, without at least lapsing into what is technically called the hypostasy of abstractions, this is a defect and a weakness of the human mind which cannot be taken as characteristic of one particular application of its powers. It is a pitfall of language into which the physicists with their " forces " and the physchologists with their "faculties" have more than once fallen.

Much more important is the question as to *which* abstractions we employ in explanation of the world-process In this connexion it is characteristic of Aristotle in the highest degree that he regards the concept as the form-giving, or, in the widest sense, the constitutive principle of things. The pupil of Plato thus continues to walk in the path which his master had followed, which Socrates had opened, and which has proved as useful in supplying a preliminary training for philosophy as incapable of making the world intelligible. " Form and active force "— this combination of words occurring in the " Metaphysics," throws a flood of light on the spirit of the Aristotelian ontology. Where we speak of natural forces and the laws governing their operations, there Aristotle treats of concepts. This is the point at which his path diverges from that of the founders of a genuine natural philosophy capable of development. From his investigation of concepts there is no thoroughfare to the root-principles of the investigation of nature. Not from such a starting-point could any one ever have travelled to the foundation-laying experiments by which Archimedes created the science of statics or Galilei that of dynamics. In one passage of the " Metaphysics " we read the highly significant words :

" The Why is in the end reduced to the concept of the thing." This is a typical expression of that illusion by which we imagine ourselves able to deduce the real connexions of things from the relations of the concepts applicable to them. What we should say is really the reverse : after observation or experiment has enlightened us on the *nexus* of phenomena, we then accommodate our ideas to the knowledge so won ; empirical knowledge is the first stage, the corresponding formation of concepts the second.

This reversal of the true relation leaves its impress on the numerous illusory explanations, and no less on the illusory problems of which these books are full. Having once raised the question : " Why is fire hot ?" Aristotle would certainly not have considered it sufficiently answered if he had been initiated into the chemical process of combustion. He would continually have passed on to another Why ; he would have demanded an explanation of the connexion, in its very nature inexplicable, between particular movements of molecules and the particular sensation of heat ; and he would have found peace at last in a supposed notional explanation, that is, in a tautology which extracts from the meaning of a word what experience has first placed there, and then puts it forward as the true ground of the empirical fact. But there is something worse than tautology. What is a concept ? Far too often it is merely a piece of old knowledge, stiffened and compacted into a shield on which new knowledge beats in vain. How arbitrary and misleading this conceptual analysis can be in the explanations of nature, appears from a section which we have already considered in advance, that in which Aristotle lays the foundation for his doctrine of the elements and in so doing brings out two flatly contradictory results. Another typical example will be supplied us by the theory of the "First Mover," which really comes to nothing more than a postulate of concept-building, and might be condensed to the following formula : Out of three conceivable combinations two are realized in nature ; why should the same not also hold of the third, and on the most comprehensive scale?

In other cases an old doctrine is retained, but attenuated to a mere shadow by being emptied of its content. That contraries condition each other was a profound discovery of the ancients, particularly Heraclitus. It was the same with the discovery that contraries often pass over into each other. In the two theorems taken together there lay a recognition of the vastly important part played in nature and mental life by the coexistence and the succession of contraries. Physical polarity, that play of antagonistic forces, which so promotes the health of individuals and societies, the protection thus afforded against what Plato calls in the "Phædo" the "lameness" of a one-sided process (Vol. III. p. 42); add further the danger of re-action and reversal inherent in all extremes—all this was contained in the contributions of Plato and Heraclitus to this theme, while the older and cruder appreciations of elementary oppositions (such as water feeds on fire, fire on water, and so on) had formed a kind of prelude. Now, the heir of all this wisdom might surely have been expected at once to acknowledge the value of these generalizations, and to reduce them to their proper measure. But what Aristotle really does is something very different. He does not reject those theories, in which he is right; and he does not limit them, in which he is wrong. He can no more pierce to the root of these extravagant generalizations than in the case of the Platonic theory of ideas or the mystic doctrine of numbers. He clearly rejected all such pro-cedure as too radical; and he adopted another method, better adapted to reconcile his excessive respect for tradi-tion with the demands of his critical intelligence. He desires to put the doctrine of elementary opposites on a rational basis. But while he is at work on this task contradictory opposition usurps unperceived the place of contrary opposition ; what the doctrine thus gains in certainty is lost in significance, till in the end it becomes nothing more than a bald assertion of the self-evident. "White," so we read in the chief passage of the "Physics," "arises out of the not-white, but not out of all such [the exclusion, as the preceding matter teaches us, applies to

such entirely disparate fields of thought as the musical],
but from black *or from one of the intermediates,*" by which
is understood the totality of other colours! Thus of the
pretentious and often overworked doctrine of the older
thinkers nothing is left beyond the absolutely tautological
assertion that the acquisition of a quality involves its
previous absence. This may sound like exaggeration,
but it is the literal truth ; and the most wonderful thing
about it is that Aristotle never ceased to regard this
watered-down or rather washed-out doctrine of opposed
principles as a fundamental law of nature. It hardly
seems worth while to point out that the truism here promulgated as an august principle of nature has not even
received a rigidly accurate formulation. For not every
"arrangement or composition," as there stated, proceeds
from non-arrangement and non-composition. Arrangement may be merely rearrangement ; composition may
be transposition. Take, for example, cases of chemical
affinity, in which the combinations AB and CD are transformed into the new combinations AC and BD ; take the
changing configurations of the kaleidoscope or the chess-
board, or again the chorus in a Greek play, divided fivefold
for its entry, threefold for the performance.

6. The theory of Becoming here touched upon appears
to other expositors in a much more important light than
it does to us. In combination with the distinction between
the actual and the potential it is supposed to have solved
a problem on which Plato had made shipwreck. The
truth is that the Stagirite had intended to reconcile the
dictum of the nature-philosopher : "Nothing proceeds from
nothing," with the popular view that things begin to be,
by allowing the thing itself to abide while such of its
properties as are considered accidental pass into and out
of existence. It comes to this, that in the realm of matter
the first principle of constancy (cf. p. 67) is admitted, and
the second at the same time denied—a denial by which
Aristotle renounces, if not an established truth, at all
events a heuristic maxim of uncommon fertility (cf. Vol. I.
pp. 173 *seqq.* and 324-5). Outside or above the realm of

matter his doctrine is not open to the same objection. His reconciliation of the conflicting theses: "Nothing comes from nothing," and "Something comes from nothing," may be regarded as a statement, perhaps too pretentious in tone, of the self-evident proposition that an object abides and its states change. For example, the day breaks ; herewith an in itself unaltered portion of the globe, which before was dark, is now illuminated. But consider the typical Aristotelian instance : if a man receives a musical education, the substratum, the man, abides ; he does not become man from not-man ; but in so far as a musically-uneducated has become a musically-educated person, in a certain sense *something has come from nothing*, and at the same time what was present only in germ has become actual. The poverty in content of these assertions appears still more glaring in the light of an obvious reflexion. If we sum up a situation by saying "first there is nothing, then there is something," our words can as a rule (since explosive changes are rare exceptions) be true only of the minimal increments by whose gradual summation the great majority of all changes take place. The paradoxical ring of the statement, "From the uneducated comes the educated," is in any case lost when we remember the stages of transition and the continuous progress from quarter-educated to half-educated, and so on. And in the last resort can even that accumulation of increments be justly compared with the production of something out of nothing ? To vary Aristotle's example a little, let us imagine some one learning to dance. By a convenient transcription of the facts it may be said that a dancer has come from a non-dancer. But the transcription is by no means so appropriate as it is convenient. Rightly regarded, the facts are something like this: the person's sense of rhythm has been strengthened by exercise, so have some of his muscles ; habit has made it easier to perform certain movements simultaneously and to refrain from certain other movements which are undesirable ; and so we might go on. It is only an arbitrary convention that accords the name of dancer to one who has reached a particular stage in this progress and denies it to another who is perhaps a poor fraction of a step behind. Is it not at bottom a misuse of language to call one point of this path a something and to identify an immediately preceding, hardly distinguishable, point with nothing?

We gladly turn from this explanation of becoming and happening, which in our opinion explains little and solves no serious difficulty, to Aristotle's treatment of the chief law of all happening, the law of causation. The first question which here presents itself is whether the Stagirite did or did not admit exceptions to this supreme rule. We believe it possible to answer this question in the negative, and to prove the contrary assertions of eminent predecessors to be in error. It is a pleasure here to see the mind of our philosopher moving, up to a certain point dictated by his peculiar characteristics, along the path opened up by his great forerunners, above all by the Atomists.

CHAPTER X.

OF CHANCE AND NECESSITY.

1. A TREATMENT of the Greek thinkers' conception of chance is made not inappreciably more difficult by the fact that the Greek terms denoting this idea and its modifications do not altogether cover the same ground as those used in modern languages. One of the expressions concerned must, as a preliminary, be separated from the others, as not being, like them, in any way bound up with the question of cause. We refer to the word which denotes the "accidental," as opposed not to that which is causally determined, but to that which is essential. But in order to eliminate the notion in question we have first to assign it its place in the general family of such notions; and for that purpose we must also pass these others in review. The necessity here arises of distinguishing the Aristotelian terminology from common Greek usage in respect of some of these words. "A drop of luck is worth a cask of sense." In this line, ascribed to Menander, the idea of luck is expressed by τύχη ; in another line from the same source man is warned not to forget "the common τύχη," that is his dependence on the whims of fate. Thus τύχη became an embodiment of the haphazard, whether helpful or hurtful ; it was also worshipped as a goddess, and the rolling sphere, the symbol of inconstancy, was her attribute. For Aristotle, the word τύχη signifies as a rule the concurrence of two events bound by no causal connexion, but yet presenting the appearance of such a bond. I have dreamt something, and the dream comes true ; I dig up my field and light on a treasure. These are a few types of what is here meant, of chance in the widest sense of the

word (A). A subordinate variety of this genus is provided by those cases in which the appearance of a causal *nexus* is limited to cases of apparent purpose. An action performed with quite different intentions is followed by a result of so striking a nature that the impression is produced of a designed result (*a*). A sub-variety of this sub-variety comprehends those instances in which purpose was not merely absent but was bound to be absent by the very nature of the agents, which, being lifeless and soulless, or in any case void of reason, are removed from the possibility of purposeful action. To designate this group Aristotle uses a word which elsewhere and incidentally has another and a wider meaning, for it then denotes that which arises "of itself" or spontaneously, as distinguished not merely from what is purposed but from what is in any way causally conditioned: this word survives in our "automaton" (*b*).

2. Besides τύχη and its varieties we have an idea not always strictly separated from it and sometimes subsumed under it, that expressed by συμβεβηκός, literally that which accompanies. The word "accident" might be used for both, but for the sake of stricter separation we prefer to represent τύχη by "chance" or "haphazard," συμβεβηκός by "accident." The common element is the lack of inner connexion between two things (events or qualities); but this lack is generally expressed by the first word when events or processes are in question, and by the second in respect of qualities or states.

For Aristotle every quality is an accident which is not deducible from the concept of the object, even though it may be as inseparably bound up with that concept as (to cite his favourite example) the possession of angles amounting to two right angles is bound up with the notion of a triangle. From this kind of necessary or demonstrable "accident in itself" or attribute, the other kinds of accident are distinguished; and according as they lie nearer to or remoter from the conceptual or essential heart of the thing they are distributed along the degrees of a scale. Thus the white grease-paint, which a man may apply to himself for an occasion is a more remote accident for him than the white colour of his skin that he has had from birth. A remarkable and quite sound application of this category is its relative use. If, for example, a physician is for once a patient as well, then it is said the possession of medical skill is an accident for this patient; while for the physician as such the being a patient is also an accident. But we are somewhat taken aback when in the application of the whole theory to the sculptor Polycletus we are informed that for the sculptor not merely musical education, but also the white colour of his skin, and even the circumstance that he is a man or a living being at all, is an accident. We are reminded of the tendency, noticeable elsewhere as well, towards the sharp separation of what is in thought separable but in fact bound up together, a tendency already exemplified by the logical distinctions of form and matter, of the actual and the potential. We note the great pleasure that Aristotle takes in conceptual distinctions, so that he even dwells on the monstrous idea of a sculptor who is neither God nor man nor any other kind of living being, and we ask whether this temper can be of service for the sound understanding of things. Must not the immoderate fondness for distinctions divert the mind from the perception of actually existing connexions which are often important for the understanding of causal relations? Are not isolating boundary-stakes often thereby planted where the important and desirable thing is really an unimpeded view of the whole field? And is not this one-sidedly logical or formalistic mode of viewing things partly to blame for the Stagirite's scant success in explaining phenomena by their causes, for his remaining in all departments of knowledge so much more of an anatomist than a physiologist?

3. There are two favourite examples by which Aristotle illustrates chance and its subdivisions. One is that of the creditor who is pressing for payment of a debt, but obtains it unexpectedly and by chance, when, having gone to the market on quite other business, he there lights on the debtor with the requisite sum in his possession (*a*). The second illustration is afforded by a horse which has

lost its rider in the battle, and in the evening of the same
day (driven, we are to suppose, by hunger, thirst, or
instinct) returns to the camp, and is thus restored to its
owner (*b*). The most important point is that in the section
of the "Physics" devoted to this topic the existence of
chance in the absolute sense is emphatically denied, and
a merely relative validity accorded to the notion. In thus
refusing to see in chance and haphazard a limit to the
universal sway of cause he walks in the footsteps of his
great predecessors. He approaches here the position of
such a thinker as Leucippus, the founder of Atomism, from
whom we have received the precious saying (Vol. I, p. 317):
"Nothing happens without a cause, but everything with a
cause and by necessity." For Aristotle the automatic or
self-moving is just as little an independent factor intro-
ducing a disturbing element into the realm of knowledge
and purposeful action based on knowledge as it is for the
author of the work "On the Art" (cf. Vol. I. pp. 423 and
467), that sophist powerful in thought and speech who
penned these memorable words : "The spontaneous or
automatic, when grappled at close quarters, turns out to
be non-existent. For in the case of everything that
happens it is possible to discover that it happens through
something ; but in this 'through something' the automatic
loses its existence and becomes a mere name. Now, the
art of healing (any other art or reasoned practice might
have been named here) has and ever will have its being
in the region of that which happens through something
and can be foreseen."

    4. Occasionally, it is true, a suspicion arises that
on this matter, too, the consistency of the Stagirite is
not irreproachable. His excessive respect for traditional
opinions, and the special circumstance that Plato in the
"Timæus" had postulated an "erratic" cause in addition
to those that work according to law, might incline us to
see in some of his utterances an occasional lapse from the
position which he proclaimed as a general principle with so
much vigour and clearness. It cannot be denied that here
and there a passage occurs which *could* be so interpreted ;

but in no single instance does such interpretation seem to us unavoidable ; and this once, to our thinking, it will be better not to call Aristotle's consistency of thought into question. Let one example suffice for many. The occasional occurrence of wintry cold in the dog-days is described as an accidental phenomenon, and therefore inaccessible to scientific explanation. It looks here, at first sight, as if a particular sphere of action had been assigned to freakish chance. But this impression may be corrected simply by a consideration of the word (συμβεβηκός) used for "accidental." What Aristotle meant to say may very well have been merely this: If cold sets in during the dog-days, in spite of the sun's altitude and the now long-continued warming of the earth's surface, the fault is with the north wind, in the prevalence of which no regularity is discernible. Certainly, supposing he had desired to forestall the misunderstandings of a distant future, he might have added the reservation, "perhaps such regularity may some day be discovered." But it was far more natural for him to omit qualifications of that kind, and, though fully convinced of the universal reign of cause, to regard a possible law of the north wind and the law connecting the earth's temperature with the seasons as two parallel chains of cause and effect touching each other only in quite isolated instances. The abnormal temperature— he may have thought—is just as accidental for the dog-days as, for example, some bodily abnormality, such as a birthmark, would be for the sculptor or the general.

We therefore see no inconsistency even in the raising of the question whether the universe does or does not owe its origin to chance. On a superficial consideration of the matter, it may seem as if merely to ask the question was to recognize chance as an independent and active factor. But, apart from the fact that Aristotle himself answers the question in the negative, and therefore did not necessarily approve of the implication it may have contained, the question itself expresses no more than a doubt as to whether, on the one hand, divine purposes or natural tendencies directed towards ends are the foundations which support the structure of the universe, or whether, on the other hand, blindly operating forces are here supreme. Is the appearance of purpose in the Cosmos founded on fact, or is it not? Such a question might well be asked even by one in whose thought there has never been room for an event without a cause.

We will dwell yet a moment on this point, because men of mark, held by us in the greatest esteem, have entered the lists for the view we reject, moved by the consideration rather of isolated passages than of Aristotle's teaching as a whole, and misled by a certainly odd laxity of linguistic usage. The author of the "Metaphysics" severely censures the nature-philosophers before Anaxagoras, because, in explaining the world, they employed only material factors, and sought for no ground of the well-ordering of the Cosmos. His words are: "They have also not done well in leaving so great a matter to automatism and fate (τύχη)." From this passage J. S. Mill inferred, to all appearance very rightly, that Aristotle rejects chance and spontaneity "as not sufficiently worthy causes for the order in the universe; but he does not reject them as incapable of producing *any* effect, but only as incapable of producing *that* effect." But this inference falls to the ground as soon as we recall its almost verbal echo in a passage of the Nicomachean Ethics. Aristotle is there combating the view of life according to which happiness consists in the possession of external goods rather than in a particular state of the soul; and in so doing he makes use of the following words: "To assign what is greatest and best to chance would be the height of absurdity." Can any one believe that when Aristotle wrote these words he supposed the acquisition of money, power, honour, and other external goods to be exempted from the law of cause and effect? Chance is in these passages the antithesis, firstly of action guided by purpose, secondly of the independence enjoyed by those whose happiness rests on the qualities of their own souls. It denotes in the one instance the play of natural forces operating, not without rule, but blindly, not directed

towards any goal ; in the second, it applies to the influence
of factors which are just as far from being without rule,
but which act without choice ; for even the unworthy (this
is the Stagirite's thought) may and not unfrequently do
win power, honour, riches, and the other gifts of fortune.

We return to the problem which may with approximate
correctness be termed the problem of the cosmogony.
Although in this connexion Aristotle escapes, as we have
seen, the reproach of inconsistency, yet the manner in which
he treats the problem provides us with a typical sample
of what we may venture to call his wholly unproductive
metaphysical method. Having arrived at the point where
the crowning proof is to be given of the dogma that the
universe has its origin in purpose, he proceeds as follows.
The decision is to be extracted from the *concepts* involved
in the question. Since chance and automatism include the
negation of end, of purpose, and so of mind, it follows that
these last-mentioned concepts are the more primitive and
the first-named derived from them. On the one side are
ranged chance, haphazard, automatism ; on the other, purpose, with the intelligence revealed in it, as also natural
tendencies directed towards ends. The second set of ideas
has entered into the formation of the members of the first
group and helped to determine them. From this relationship of the concepts an inference is drawn as to the relationship of the things themselves. The more primitive factor
must have begun to act at an earlier time than the derived
factor. "Thus, however true it might turn out to be that
automatism is the cause of the heavens, mind and nature
must have begun to operate earlier still." Who does not
see here the fundamental vice of the metaphysical method,
the inference from the order of human ideas to the order
of natural facts, disdaining every veil and flaunting itself in
unabashed nakedness ?

5. We have now considered the charge brought against
the Stagirite that by his use of the notion of chance he
has cast suspicion upon his faith in causality, and we have
found it untenable. How is it, we have now to ask, with the
second count of this accusation, founded on his distinction

between laws of causation that admit no exception, and those that hold only in the majority of cases, between the necessity and the probability of events ? We must here consider somewhat closely both the period of scientific development into which Aristotle's life was cast and his own individual peculiarities. Here, as elsewhere, he takes his stand on the ground of known facts, of what has been perceived in the course of experience ; he is an observer, not an experimental researcher. He could not, therefore, have been familiar with a view of causation which is hardly capable of thriving elsewhere than where the experimental dissection of natural processes has gained ascendency and exercised a permanent influence on men's conceptions of causal relations. For example, the law of gravitation is rigorously valid only in a vacuum ; when its operation is modified by the frictional resistance of the air we moderns say that the law is all the same universally valid ; we regard it, however, only as a tendency which does not in all circumstances become equally manifest. Now, the elements of this view are by no means foreign to Aristotle. He is familiar with the notion of tendency, for he more than once speaks of what nature aims at or desires without being able in every case to achieve ; he is equally well acquainted with the impediments which a tendency may encounter, as he mentions on occasion the conflict of move-ment-impulses which mutually check and, in the extreme cases, destroy each other ; he is aware, lastly, that the motives of human action are related to each other in just the same way. But to form by generalization out of these elements a comprehensive theory of causation in which they should all come by their rights was a feat which it perhaps did not lie in his genius to perform. His mind was much more inclined to the contemplation of the facts as given than to the analysis of them into components which for the most part are inferred and not perceived. The genius of the Atomists appears herein superior to his own ; though we are certainly unacquainted with the mode in which they carried out their supreme causal principle in particular cases or came to terms with the facts which opposed their main theory. It is in keeping with the contemporary phase of science that Aristotle is so much more frequently led to inquire into the causes of given effects than into the effects of given causes. This was another reason why the notion of probability was bound to assert itself by the side of necessity and occupy a considerable space in his expositions. "If a woman is pale," he once asks, "can I thence infer that she is with child? No; for there are other causes of paleness." In the backward argument from effect to cause that particular factor comes into play which has been named the "plurality of causes."

When, therefore (so we may summarize our reflexions), Aristotle set out from causes to discover their effects, he had not, as a rule, to deal with the simplest causes, such as generally only the hand of the experimenter can isolate; resistances, interferences, modifications of every kind thus entered of necessity into the regularities under observation and seriously impaired their universality. But in the second and commoner case, when the why of a phenomenon was in question, that is, when the cause or causes of an effect were to be ascertained, a strictly universal answer, not subject to any exception, still more rarely rewarded his search, owing to the "plurality of causes." Must we therefore suppose that Aristotle postulated or accepted as a fundamental principle a distinction between causal laws, which are in themselves universal, and others whose nature it is to be only partially valid, between factors which always work in the same way and others which work now this way, now that? This must be at least allowed to be extremely doubtful. In very many cases where a rule suffers exceptions the circumstance responsible for the exceptions could not possibly have remained hidden from him. If the same quantity of wine intoxicates many persons but leaves others sober, if the same rocking of a ship makes some passengers sea-sick while others escape, our philosopher could not doubt for a moment that the differing susceptibility of different subjects to the same influence is here at work. A thinker who appraised the power of practice and habit so high as to call habit "second nature," could at least not have failed to recognize the part which use and hardening play in modifying natural disposition and aptitude.

As with physical, so with psychical stimuli, he must have recognized that the effects vary according to individual receptivity. We ought not really, therefore, to be in the least surprised when we find the author of the "Poetics" assigning a place to probability by the side of necessity whenever he speaks of the laws governing human action. It would indeed have been sheer folly to have represented all external events as acting by necessity, that is, always in the same manner and always with the same intensity on all individuals. That, on the contrary, different individuals react in the most diverse ways to the same stimulus, that the insult which one will forgive moves another to take a bloody revenge, that one will stake his life for a pleasure on which another looks with contempt— who needs to be told all this? But while these individual differences are truly countless in number, they may yet be grouped under a few main types, of which some occur with greater and others with less frequency. For this reason it is allowable to speak of probability in this connexion. Even where he is demanding the strict observance of cause in respect of dramatic motive, Aristotle cannot avoid including probability as well as necessity. To admit the latter alone would have been permissible only on the supposition that the minds of the characters lay like an open book before the spectators. Consider Iphigenia, Alcestis, Macaria, who went to their death joyfully for the sake of kin and country—did it not tax the full poetic power of an Euripides to make such a victory over human and feminine weakness seem even probable?

We have dwelt so long on this special point because it has been made a subject of wonder that in these discussions Aristotle so often sets probability by the side of necessity. The truth is that in these and many kindred instances he could not help looking at the question of cause with the same eyes as ourselves and modern science.

One and the same tendency constantly prevailing on the side of the causal factor, resistances or manifold modifying influences occurring on the side of the objects affected—in wide provinces of nature and human life this state of things must have seemed to him exactly as normal as it does to us moderns. It is only when we come to ask whether he advanced so far as to generalize this perception into a fundamental principle admitting of no exception, that some measure of doubt arises. The stage of development at which contemporary science stood was not favourable to such a generalization; and he was in any case not driven in that direction by the special qualities of his own mind. It remains, then, not fully established that the distinction between the necessity and the probability of an occurrence was regarded by him as merely subjective, based on the incompleteness of our knowledge, or that he was prepared to admit what the Atomists, in virtue of their presuppositions, were hardly able to deny—that in every case where we knew the total conditions of an event with exhaustive completeness, we should never speak of probability but always of necessity.

The foregoing remarks need to be supplemented. This will be done when we come to consider Aristotle's treatment of the problem of will. We shall find this treatment comparatively free from inconsistencies, though it as yet falls short of that iron rigour with which the Stoic Chrysippus a century later laboured towards the solution of that problem with almost unsurpassable success.

Be this, however, as it may, the fact (which, after all is only a conjecture) that Aristotle's faith in causality fell short of unconditional strictness, gives us no right to look down on him. The postulate of exceptionless uniformity in the working of causes or causal tendencies has possibly been the salvation of scientific progress up to now. It may be allowed to be a heuristic maxim of the very highest value. But there is nothing intrinsically incredible in the possibility, first emphasized by Laplace, that neither is any particle of matter ever indistinguishably like its neighbour nor any one causal sequence to any other; that the appearance of absolute identity, so far as it actually presents itself, is due to our insufficient knowledge both of the fundamental processes and the ultimate components of the physical world. The weakness of our senses and the imperfection of even our most perfect instruments of precision may condemn us to work ever with the mere averages yielded by vast accumulations of particles and processes, while countless deviations from the mean, more or less trivial in amount, escape our perception.

6. Aristotle would hardly have been Aristotle if he had brought the exposition of any of his doctrines to a well-rounded definite conclusion. On the subject now before us the Megarians had invented a puzzle to which he failed to give a fully unambiguous and satisfactory answer. Or, to be more accurate, what he failed in was not so much decisiveness in rejecting the Megarian conclusion, as exactness in solving the root-difficulty. What we refer to is the Megarian denial, already known to the reader (cf. Vol. II. p. 200 *seq.*), of contingency, or the possibility of things being otherwise than as they are. This denial also took the following form. Of two assertions relating to a future occurrence, one positive and the other its contradictory negative, it was argued that one must be true and the other false. If, then, the truth of the one prediction is a fixed and objective fact, how can the will or deed of man exert any influence on the course of things? This question, be it remarked by the way, has not the remotest connexion with the problem of the freedom of the will. The point here is not how a volition is produced, but how it can itself produce any change in the march of events; in this connexion the spontaneous actions of animals might have been mentioned equally well with human acts of will. But further—and here is the kernel of the problem—if one of the two predictions must be right, the other must be impossible, and all futurity is withdrawn from the region of May-Be : it is necessary ; chance and haphazard have the ground cut from under them. The precision with which the paradox is stated and developed leaves nothing to be desired. But the reply is not so satisfactory. It is merely

an appeal to the obvious : we see that resolves and actions
are not so void of effect as the argument would make
them ; we see, too, that in this changing and inconstant
world there is no lack of room for the application of the
ideas of possibility and impossibility. " The possibility of
being cut to pieces remains for this cloak, even if it never
is so cut, but is first worn out by use. And should the
cutting take place, there would still have existed for it the
possibility of not being cut."

What we miss in this reasoning is the reference to the
wider and narrower fields of survey, a distinction which
in truth affords each of these standpoints its justification.
For a mind which embraced the totality of causes, all their
combinations and interactions, there would, as we have
already had occasion to point out (Vol. II. pp. 201, 202),
be no such thing as chance or a possibility which failed to
be realized. These are ideas which correspond to the
limitation of our horizon, and are therefore suited to the
demands both of practical life and of science as it actually
exists, and as alone it is attainable by man. The confusing
effect of the paradox is due, we think, to the fact that
neither of the two points of view, each quite possible in
itself, is maintained with complete strictness.

All further study of Aristotle's theory of causation presupposes a knowledge of the fourfold meaning in which the
word "cause " was used by the Stagirite. With these
distinctions we hope to gain a familiar acquaintance in the
survey which we are about to make of our philosopher's
chief physical doctrines.

CHAPTER XI.

ARISTOTLE AS AN INVESTIGATOR OF NATURE.

(INORGANIC NATURE.)

1. THE physical doctrines of Aristotle are a disappointing chapter in the history of science. They display to us an eminent mind wrestling with problems to which it is in no wise equal. In no wise. For, strangely enough, the excellences of Aristotle's intellect proved hardly less adverse to the success of his efforts than its defects. The Platonist and the Asclepiad are not here in conflict with one another. They are allied, to the double prejudice of scientific progress. How little that progress had to gain from the mastery of dialectic learnt in Plato's school, the reader has been able to judge from the glaringly contradictory constructions of the theory of elements; and an important part of the Platonic heritage, the doctrine of "natural places," has already been seen to be a serious impediment to the sound understanding of physical things. But at the same time, that naïve faith in the senses which is the foundation of the taste for observation and of exactness in observation was—however paradoxical it may sound —rather hurtful than helpful to Aristotle's researches in this province. For the great classifier was led by this bent of his faculties to linger in the field of observed facts in cases where the truth was to be sought and found not *in* these facts but only *behind* them. In what we might call the pre-experimental age no other path led to a deeper understanding of physical processes than that which had been trodden, first by the nature-philosophers, and then,

with growing audacity and increasing success, by the Atomists.

Invisible movements, invisible particles, their varying configurations and distances from each other,—these and kindred assumptions supplied the window through which the human mind has sought to spy into the inner machinery of phenomena, and has in fact been enabled to do so to better and better purpose. If a drop of water freezes, then melts, then evaporates, we have a process in which Anaximenes surmised, while Leucippus and Democritus detected with certainty, a closing together followed by a drawing apart of the same particles of matter. For the Stagirite the different states of aggregation were different elements, their interchange a transmutation of mutually alien substances defying every attempt at explanation. He stood here on the same ground as the men of a hoary past, the authors of the Homeric poems or of the Book of Genesis.

No less primitive in character is his theory of the heavens. In this connexion, too, he censures the nature-philosophers and the Atomists for opinions in which modern science declares them to have been perfectly right. That the farthest fixed stars harbour the same substances as our earth is to-day no longer a speculative assumption, but a fact established by the spectroscope. Just as little does any contemporary investigator of nature cherish the slenderest doubt that heavenly bodies come into and pass out of being ; in other words, that the constant regrouping of matter is equally the rule in all parts of the Cosmos ; that there is no privileged region exempt from the universal law of change. Just these very doctrines had already been familiar to the old Physiologists, and had by no one been formulated with greater strictness than by their advance guard, the adherents of Leucippus and Democritus (cf. Vol. I. p. 366). It is very different with Aristotle. So firm is his conviction that the universe is divided into a perishable and an imperishable part, that he uses a really wonderful argument in censure of his predecessors. He complains that their hypothesis of the similarity of matter in all regions of the universe leaves that division unexplained! Indeed, strictly taken, it does away with the possibility of assuming here (in the sublunary world) change and decay, there (in the regions above the moon) eternal constancy. For him, as we have already remarked, the ether was the fifth element, occupying the "highest heavenly regions." In other respects, too, he is so far from regarding things celestial with the sober eye of the natural philosopher, that he calls the sun, moon, and stars "divine bodies," the appearances in the sky "the most divine of phenomena," and does not shrink from representing the celestial spheres as being turned round in space by spirits or gods of the second order. Indeed, his astronomy is tinged so deeply with theology that it can be treated and understood only in connexion with his doctrine of the "Unmoved Mover."

The Stagirite's theory of the heavens fell behind that of his predecessors, not only in its main outlines, but also in details. Thus while Democritus had already detected in the Milky Way a collection of a great number of stars, Aristotle took it for a mass of vapour thrown off and ignited by the motion of the heavens. He gave essentially the same explanation of comets, the right understanding of which, however, was denied equally to his predecessors and to his successors up to Seneca. Nero's tutor, in fact, was, if we may take his own word for it, the first to see in comets, not "suddenly blazing flames," but "stars with an exceedingly long period of revolution."

2. It is not our fault if we are continually travelling from Aristotle back to Democritus. The comparison with Atomism forces itself upon us at every step. For it is not only in cases where the facts speak in unambiguous language that the Democritean doctrine of nature manifests an incontestable superiority over the Aristotelian. Even in matters which modern means of research have not finally cleared up, the paths trodden by Leucippus and Democritus have proved much the safer and more profitable. The unitary nature of ultimate matter, that heirloom which passed from the old nature-philosophy to the

Atomists, has continually gained in credibility with the more modern progress of chemistry. Moreover, the so-called mechanical explanation of nature, that is, the attempt to derive all the changes that we perceive from changes in the positions of immutable portions of matter, or, more accurately, to connect the former with the latter, is winning new triumphs of greater and greater importance every day ; and these triumphs abide, no matter with what epistemological reservations we may prefer to hedge the atomic theory. The Aristotelian doctrine, which abandoned all these conceptions, was smitten with sheer sterility. The science of the Renaissance period was obliged to shake off the fetters of his authority before it could return to the paths of progressive and fruitful research (cf. Vol. I. p. 349).

Since for us the kernel of Aristotle's nature-theory is to be found in his repudiation of his predecessors' acquisitions, it is worth while to pursue a closer acquaintance with the arguments by which he sought to justify that reversal. In the very passage in which he accords to the Atomists the far-reaching praise of having more than others striven " to explain the processes of nature in a methodical and uniform manner " (cf. p. 59), he raises the following objection against the main principle of their teaching : " Why, then, should the property of indivisibility belong to the small bodies (atoms) any more than to the large ones ? " It was clearly because the distinction could be supported by no reason drawn from the inner nature and the pure notion of body, that the Stagirite deemed the hypothesis untenable. The adherents of atomism might, however, have justly replied to him : " We assume the actual indivisibility of those small bodies because this assumption, unlike your assimilation of them to the larger bodies proved by experience to be divisible, renders service towards the explanation of phenomena. But such opponents as yourself do exactly what you have lately reproached the Eleatics for doing : like them, you thrust the facts on one side and proceed as if dialectic were the only guide." Presently the atomic theory is blamed on the point in

which it is most indubitably right. Changes in the state
of aggregation cannot, it is urged, be explained by changes
in the position of the smallest parts. Why? Because
" the *whole* body, being continuous, has been first fluid and
then hard and rigid." Here Anaxagoras might have come
to the help of the Atomists, and reminded their adversary
of the "weakness" of our senses (cf. Vol. I. p. 211 *seq.*).
Further, the increase or decrease in the volume of a body
cannot, it is urged, be due to the accession or withdrawal
of smallest particles, "for every part would not (in this
case) have become larger (or smaller)." As if we had no
right to assume, behind all the particles which we can
perceive, other much smaller particles inaccessible to our
senses.

When Aristotle notes the absence from the Atomists'
writings of a strict separation between the ideas of mechanical mingling and true mixture (which clearly comprises
our " solution" and " chemical combination "), we are
unable to judge with full certainty whether his complaint
is well-founded. All we know is that Leucippus' division
of sensible qualities into primary and secondary made it
possible for the creator of the atomic theory and his successors to wrestle with the difficulties of such problems
much more successfully than their opponents. Their
doctrine placed at their disposal many aids towards the
solution of the problem as to how the same particles of
matter can act upon our organs of sense or on other bodies
differently according as they are joined in intimate union
or merely form juxtaposed masses. The different kinds
of arrangement and situation, which Democritus called
"contact" and "turning" (cf. Vol. I. p. 323), further, the
manifold modes of distributing the intervening spaces
empty of matter supplied them in this regard with many
an expedient (cf. Vol. I. p. 330). That a being with quite
other senses than ours, or with vastly acuter senses, would
receive from the same aggregation of matter impressions
very different from those received by men, that a Lynceus
would see sharply sundered particles where we perceive
unbroken continuity,—these and similar propositions must

have seemed to them the legitimate corollary of their presuppositions, and they could never have found in them a stone of stumbling as Aristotle did when he deduced such conclusions from their premises. It is a main feature in our philosopher's treatment of these subjects that he seeks absolute differences where only relative ones are to be found. He holds that the union of two substances ceases to be a mixture when one of them obtains an immeasurable preponderance over the other, as when, for example, a drop of wine is introduced into 20,000 quarts of water. To this, of course, there is no objection to be made if it only means that in such a case the colour, the taste, or the intoxicating effect of the wine ceases to be perceptible by us. But Aristotle speaks of a loss of the "form" of wine, and obviously understands by the expression an objective and absolute, not a subjective and relative change. Where would he have drawn a boundary-line of this character if he had been acquainted with tests which disclose clear traces of the presence of a substance long after it has lost the power of affecting our senses—tests, moreover, which by no means justify the assumption that final and impassable barriers are to be met with, even at the vast distances here suggested? But the atomistic hypothesis, we may add, was fundamentally in harmony with the revelations which we owe to the reagents and instruments of precision used by modern science, auxiliaries thousands of millions of times more powerful than our own senses.

At this point let us indulge in a digression. Even the history of science is not without its humour. It treats us sometimes to the most amusing surprises. Such a surprise has been provided in connexion with the truly Aristotelian hyperbole just mentioned. The Stagirite loves to replace a long-drawn-out chain of reasoning by a drastic instance, which beats down all opposition by its extravagance. Thus when he is contending that to be beautiful a thing must be capable of being seen all at once, he illustrates the point by a supposed animal 10,000 stadia long, which would be too big to be beautiful, since its size would mock every attempt at a comprehensive survey. In another passage he speaks of a ship a span long, which, just because of its diminutiveness, would cease to perform the function or to deserve the name of a ship. The drop of wine in 20,000 quarts of water is clearly to be understood in the same sense. It is a hyperbolical expression, intended to illustrate, in a telling and picturesque fashion, the impossibility of detecting a small amount of matter which is lost in a mixture. It is thus highly diverting to learn that the auxiliaries of modern science have proved more than equal even to so extreme a case. A drop of wine in the quantity of water mentioned means a dilution of not quite $1\frac{1}{2}$ millionths of a gramme to the litre. The almost thirtyfold greater dilution of sodium vapour in the atmosphere has been detected by the spectroscope; and the electrometer has revealed a not much lower dilution of silver iodide in water. It has long ago been remarked that the paradoxes of yesterday are the truisms of to-day. It might be added that the "palpable impossibilities," stamped with the seal of absurdity, of one age, are the acknowledged, assured, and exact truths of another.

3. One of the points of controversy between Aristotle and the Atomists brings us back to the theory of cause. Our readers remember the refusal of Democritus to seek a ground or cause for the original beginning of things. "So it always happens," or "So also it used to happen before" —such a pronouncement always seemed to him a sufficient answer to the Why of those causal connexions which we call fundamental laws of nature. That in acknowledging ultimate facts, which are only to be established empirically and admit of no further reduction, Democritus took up a position which is also that of the science of to-day, is a view which we have already sufficiently laboured to expound and to establish (cf. Vol. I. p. 340). Equally familiar to us is the exactly opposite opinion of Plato, which regards all that is given merely in experience as an impediment and a barrier, which nearly everywhere gives to the analysis of concepts precedence over the ascertainment of facts, and which, in addition, insists on viewing the

knowledge of nature from the standpoint of the "better," or of teleology (cf. Vol. III. pp. 40 and 88). The same direction was followed by Aristotle in the investigation of causes ; his intellectual temperament was influenced by his great teacher in a far higher degree than is generally supposed.

4. The Aristotelian method of research is acquainted with four kinds of cause. Three of them, however, the formal or notional, the motive or efficient, and the final cause, are sometimes comprehended into a unity and opposed to the fourth, the material cause. Other group-ings, too, are not wanting ; and reciprocal relations of the following kind are acknowledged : bodily exercise is called the efficient cause of good health, while this latter is the final cause of exercise. But that twofold division, which, so to speak, distinguishes a higher and a lower region in the realm of cause, is the commoner and the more charac-teristic. In regard to matter, Plato's pupil completed the breach which his master had opened with the hylozoism of the older thinkers. The essential attribute of matter is, according to him, pure passivity. It is the medium in which the purposes of nature find their realization ; but it is a refractory medium, resisting the impress of form. Matter supplies the justification of all that we now call "dysteleo-logy ;" it is the vehicle of what recently has been aptly termed Platonic Manichæism. It contains, too, the ultimate root of that which is opposed to purpose, but also of the purposeless or indifferent, among which things are reckoned all individual varieties found among organized beings, and incidentally also, though without logical justification, their sexual characters. Another inconsistency of this theory, its relation to the doctrine of natural places, has already been treated by us in anticipation.

This deanimation of matter, this view of it as merely passive and receptive, is greatly predominant with Aristotle and full of far-reaching consequences. Predominant, we must say, but not sole sovereign, for here, too, contra-dictions are not wanting. In particular passages the old Hellenic spirit breaks forth with moving ardour, and bursts the bonds of system—that spirit, we mean, for which all nature is alive and the All endowed with soul. But the rule is the depotentialization of matter, as we have called it, such as we have found prefigured in Plato's teaching and discussed in connexion with Atomism (cf. Vol. I. p. 343). The observation which we there made on the probable motive of such depotentialization, on the preponderant direction of the researcher's eye to bodies of moderate size, needs here some modification. It is true that the movements of the smallest particles, which played a leading part in the Democritean system, and which modern physics, too, sees no reason for attributing to external impact, are not to be found in Aristotle's picture of the universe. But the celestial motions, on the bare ground of the perfection of their supposed circular form, are ascribed to a purely spiritual being, the First Mover, as their author. His agency, operating on the celestial sphere, which, despite his immateriality he is supposed to "touch," one knows not how, and to "move, as a loved object" moves the lover, forms according to Aristotle's teaching the ultimate source of all heavenly and earthly motions (cf. p. 65). These motions themselves, however, apart from the pressing of the elements towards their "natural places," are entirely occasioned by material contact ; they are propagated exclusively by impact and pressure. To this extent the Stagirite's universe resembles a piece of mechanism in which there is nowhere to be perceived any source of motion, but only the transmission of motion ; and as an infinite regress is counted among the impossibilities, we are again referred to a First Mover as origin and starting-point.

5. By "movement" it should also be noticed that Plato's disciple understands change in general, quantitative as well as qualitative, together with the coming into and the passing out of existence (so far as these are admitted at all). But in spatial movement or change of place he recognizes a condition of those other kinds of "movement ; " for quantitative change implies an accession or withdrawal of matter, and qualitative change, of which

destruction and its opposite are only extreme cases, the local congress of an agent and a patient.

Thus in respect of motion a double series of considerations is presented to us. On the one hand, we have the discussions on motion in the widest and most general sense. It is called by our philosopher the "actuality of the potential," the realization of what is in itself merely possible, an "incomplete reality," because with the attainment of its aim it always ceases to exist, a something which is ever accomplishing itself in contradictions. We have already pointed out the emptiness of this last definition. But that such definitions do enrich our knowledge and increase our insight, that they are more than "a scholastic husk with no kernel inside," we are as little inclined to doubt as an eminent contemporary with whom we do not often find ourselves in agreement. In respect of that movement in space which conditions all other kinds of movement we do not, it is true, meet with either ascertainment of facts, which could only have been gained by experiment, nor with their anticipation by means of great hypotheses such as the genius of the age of enlightenment had produced. But the endeavour after clearer fundamental notions on these subjects bore valuable fruit, and still more often assisted the progress of thought indirectly, by the precise statement of questions and the distinct formulation of answers.

6. Since change of place is like every other change a process in time, the concept of time is in this connexion entitled to the first position. The Aristotelian definition of time may be rendered thus: "Time is a continuous magnitude, more particularly it is the magnitude of events in respect of their order of succession." The word "magnitude" here represents the Greek word for "number." The substitution is intended to avoid misunderstandings which have actually occurred, and which the Stagirite himself foresaw, as he showed by expressly pointing out that the word "number" did not here denote the means but the object of counting—the "counted" or "countable." If we have further replaced "movement" by "event," our

justification is that in this section the former word bears
its most comprehensive meaning, and applies to every
conceivable physical or psychical process. It is so in
the memorable passage which runs: "For even when it
is dark (and still), and we receive no impression through
the body but some movement (=emotion) arises in the
soul, we have at once the impression of the lapse of time."
Finally, to our "order of succession" there corresponds in
the original the combination of words "earlier and later,"
a combination which we cannot reproduce without producing an appearance which is both false and very
derogatory to Aristotle's exactness of thought. For
nothing could be more obvious than the objection that
in the expression "earlier and later" the notion of
sequence or temporal succession is already contained, that
the definition therefore revolves in a circle, assuming in
the explanation the thing which is to be explained. But
this is by no means the case. The expression concerned
is in Aristotle very far from being exclusively appropriated to relations of time; it is used, on the contrary,
and primarily so in the present instance, in a spatial sense
(fore and rear); and the idea involved is only secondarily
applied to movements or processes through the mediation of the idea of magnitude. To the local coexistence
of material magnitudes there corresponds the temporal
succession of processes or movements.

The treatment of the concept of time is followed by
the remarkable question whether time, which is a number,
or rather a numerable, would continue to exist in the
absence of a soul capable of counting and its power of
thought? The answer, if we understand it rightly, is to
the effect that the question leads back to another and
deeper question, in which it disappears: whether that
which is the basis of time—namely, movement or process—
is possible without a perceiving soul? This reminds us
of another equally isolated utterance, which also might
be described as a fore-gleam of the Critical philosophy:
"The soul is in a certain sense the totality of all things."
This pronouncement is justified somewhat as follows: All

that is knowable is an object partly of perceptive sensation, partly of the thinking intelligence ; but both of these are in a certain sense identical with their object, for, if not the stone itself, yet the form or notion of the stone is present in the soul.

The discussion of time also becomes an occasion to raise the problem of infinity, a problem which the Stagirite has treated with penetrating acuteness and perfect clearness of thought. All the more surprising is it to find the infinity of time supported on a ground which, whether valid or not, in any case admits of an equally just application to space. This equivalence is completely overlooked by Aristotle, who asserts that time is unbounded, but space bounded. Beyond every "Now"—that is, beyond every individual moment whatsoever—he argues that there must exist another Now ; why, we cannot but ask, must there not be another "Here" beyond each particular Here, beyond any given point in space ? We do not undertake to defend this inference : it is simply an appeal to our powers of mental representation. But how could we represent to our minds that which, whether objectively real or not, has never entered the horizon of our experience either directly or by the mediation of any analogy whatever ? This is no less true of any possible boundary of time than of a boundary of space.

7. He also undertakes to prove that the three dimensions of bodies and the space which limits them are the only dimensions possible. This proof proceeds by an appeal to the doctrines of the Pythagoreans touching the trinity of beginning, middle, and end, and to linguistic usage, which, in the case of two things, speaks of "both," and reserves "all" till three is reached. The three dimensions of space are said to correspond to the only three natural movements—from the centre, to the centre, round the centre ; here the scheme of three elements already known to the reader (cf. p. 63) is again drawn into connexion with the argument. A similar *a priori* character belongs to many of the numerous objections which Aristotle marshals against the existence of empty space. Even the

fiction of "natural places" is employed as a weapon in this battle. He contends that the different directions of motion have been, so to speak, disposed of by the elements; what, then, remains for empty space? Whither should a body situated in such space move? The most valuable part of this discussion is, in our opinion, the indication of how it is possible for a body to make way for another even without an empty space; an allusion is here made to vortices. This is the expedient used by Plato to explain the process of breathing, and is naturally only applicable to rotary motions which return upon themselves (cf. Vol. III. p. 224). It makes little difference to the advantage possessed by the Atomist in the treatment of this fundamental question, that the most modern physics substitute for perfectly empty space a space occupied by matter of extraordinary tenuity, and supposes the interstices filled by an absolutely elastic medium.

If empty space was for the Stagirite an absurdity, an infinitely vast, empty space must have seemed to him doubly impossible. For infinite greatness and infinite smallness are equally rejected by him as realized or completed magnitudes; it is only as becoming, as increasing or decreasing, that he admits the infinite at all. "The infinite," so runs a wonderfully pregnant little sentence of his, "does not subsist, but becomes." Unlimited addition, unlimited division, are the modes in which the two species of it arise. An example of the first kind, one, be it noted, raised above all doubt and all the contentions of the schools, is provided by the series of natural numbers. Why should we not, were eternal life our portion, go on counting for ever, continually reaching higher and higher numbers? To this unlimited addition is opposed the process of unlimited division, the diminution of unity by splitting it up into ever smaller fractions.

The question now presents itself whether the matter which fills space is also infinitely divisible, and whether it is similarly capable of indefinite increase. Aristotle answers the first part affirmatively and the second part negatively. He reaches these results by long, winding arguments, conducted with all the power of his subtle mind. In respect of the infinite divisibility of what fills space, he first of all takes up the standpoint of Zeno in one of his paradoxes, and of Plato nearly at the end of his " Parmenides." If matter were infinitely divisible, it would be possible, by going on dividing it, to "crumble" it away to nothing ; we should then have to say that magnitudes are built up out of what has no magnitude, bodies out of the incorporeal. Thus the verdict is for those who hold the existence of ultimate irresolvable units or " indivisible magnitudes." Though up to this point Aristotle is on the side of the Atomists, what he is really contending for is the existence, not so much of ultimate bodies possessing definite form and magnitude, such as Leucippus and Democritus postulated, but of spatial units having the nature of points, such entities as the " philosophical " atoms devised by Boscovich. But now comes an abrupt turn. It is accomplished by means of arguments which, so far as we know, have never been fully explained by any interpreter. The heart of them is probably to be found in the thesis, maintained elsewhere, that just as little as a *continuum* of time can arise out of the separate indivisible instants of time, out of what the Stagirite calls the " Now," so little can a *continuum* of space arise out of separate points or spatial units. The defence which was to be raised against a supposed breaking up or crumbling away of the matter filling space appears on closer examination to be inadequate, and to leave its purpose unfulfilled. While Aristotle (perhaps for good reasons) omits an explanation of the *continuum*, the difficulties of the Atomistic theory which we have just described seem to him in any case to outweigh those of the contrary hypothesis.

Coming now to the counterpart of spatial division, that is, spatial enlargement : in this regard, too, says Aristotle, no limit is set to our thought. But thought is one thing, fact another. Nothing hinders us from imagining the bodily measurements of any one of us multiplied indefinitely. "But yet no man has ever been known whose limbs reached from one gate of the city to another."

8. As we have already noticed, Aristotle's denial of empty space paved the way for his denial of an infinitely extended universe. An infinite space full, and uniformly full, of matter, presents enhanced difficulties from which even eminent thinkers of our own time have been unable to find an escape. But Aristotle needed no such aggravation of difficulty to induce him to reject the idea. His arguments against the existence of spatial infinity form a remarkable mixture of the subtle and the crude, the valuable and the worthless. The great majority of the old nature-philosophers are here described by the Stagirite as his opponents. And it cannot be denied that those thinkers, on occasions where they really desired to speak only of vast numbers and huge spaces exceeding all possibility of human measurement, used the words "infinite" and "infinity" with a careless indifference to the consequences which might be drawn from those terms. Aristotle drew those consequences; and it was not difficult for him to show that spatial infinity, strictly taken, is quite incompatible with many of our notions derived from finite experience. We cannot, it may be added, expect to tamper seriously with the fabric of our experience at a vital spot and then find the remainder of it intact. But our philosopher goes further, and draws conclusions, the nullity of which need not detain us, from the incompatibility of the hypothesis in question with a number of arbitrary theories, such as are the assumption of a centre of the universe, the geocentric hypothesis, and the doctrine of natural places. What most astonishes is, however, the length to which he is carried by his reaction against the youthful and exuberant audacity of his predecessors. The illustrious thinker here falls a victim to the crudest illusions of the senses. The visible sphere of the heavens, which overarches our heads, is for him the whole universe. He even sets himself to prove, seriously and emphatically, that there can be but this one heaven. Every thought of the possibility of other stellar systems, of a true universe, of other stars situated outside this hollow sphere in the most varying planes and distances,

is either alien to him or combated by him. All the
matter that ever was, so he thinks, has been used up
and exhausted in the formation of this one heaven. An
excess of matter is so little to be found beyond that
hollow sphere as a space bereft of matter. And as with
the absence of matter every possibility lapses of any and
every motion or change, so beyond that boundary—thus
he concludes with an in itself admirable courage and
consistency of thought—there can also be no time, for
time is only a magnitude of events or processes.

9. The hymn of praise which Aristotle chants to the
honour of the " one, only, and perfect " heaven, which
is also " without beginning and imperishable," rests on
foundations which, though certainly unsound, by no means
lack all plausibility. At first, indeed, the Stagirite has
to fight down a difficulty which he has himself called
to life. Against the uniqueness of this heavenly sphere
of ours an objection may be raised whose sources lie at
a considerable depth. Are we ever justified in believing
in anything unique? Have we a right to suppose that
a generic type, a " form," is ever realized in one sole
exemplar? It is not only from the standpoint of Plato's
doctrine of ideas that such an hypothesis seems inadmissible. But here an important distinction is necessary.
This inadmissibility is said to exist for all forms which
are impressed on matter and for the renewed impression
of which new matter is ever ready; the exhaustion of
all matter, of all " physical and perceptible body," in the
formation of this one heaven brings about an exception
to the general rule, and justifies the uniqueness of that
exception.

Much greater depths are reached by the demonstration
which is intended to confirm the eternity of the celestial
sphere. It rests in the last resort on the empirical
connexion which obtains between coming into and passing
out of existence on the one hand, between both these
and qualitative change on the other. Here we may first
call to memory a profound saying of the Eleatic Melissus :
" If the universe were to change in ten thousand years

by as much as a hair's breadth, it would be destroyed in the course of all time" (cf. Vol. I. p. 188). This reminiscence is all the more in place, as in the very passage we are considering, Aristotle refers to the views of his predecessors both more copiously and more benevolently than is his wont. In so doing he lets fall a fine saying. The reader ought to examine the claims of conflicting theories before he gives his verdict, in order that he may not appear to convict the rejected opinion unheard, and as it were by default; further, he who desires to come to a true decision should put himself rather in the position of an umpire than in that of a litigant.

Out of the demonstration, which is spun to considerable length, we may perhaps extract, as forming the kernel of it, the following propositions. It will not do to hold, with Plato, that the heavens had a beginning but will have no end, for experience teaches the contrary, that whatever has a beginning perishes. It is also clear that the components which have united to form a whole, and which therefore were previously able to exist apart from such combination, must possess the capacity for independent existence, and therefore be able to return to it. Again, the beginning as well as the end of things is coupled with qualitative change, and the same causal factors which produce change of quality also bring things into and out of existence. Now, for our philosopher the qualitative changelessness of the stars and other bodies enclosed in the celestial sphere is a fact firmly established by experience—an experience, we may remark, of which the many centuries old astronomical observations of the Egyptians and Babylonians play by no means the smallest part. But causal factors — here we come to the last link in the argument—which during vast intervals of time have not revealed their presence by the slightest trace, may be taken as non-existent; the possibility as well of their past as of their future operation, and so of their cumulative production of great total effects, may thus be regarded as excluded.

Plausible as all this sounds, it is devoid of probative force. It is much as if one were to reject the theory of descent on the ground that a gradual transformation of species cannot be proved to have occurred within the historical period. Here again the great Atomists have seen much further than Aristotle (cf. Vol. I. p. 366). They had the same facts before their eyes. But the absence of a vision-clouding veil permitted them to recognize the truth where the unsuspected agency of prejudice and superstitious opinion (perfection of the spherical form, existence and power of star-spirits, neighbourhood of the First Mover) hid it from the gaze of the Stagirite. To this was added a remarkable difference of endowment. That supple and well-developed faculty of imagination which is the instrument of genius no less for scientific discovery than for artistic creation, was certainly possessed in lower degree by Aristotle than by Leucippus and Democritus. Those who like stronger language may speak of his fancy as dwarfed and weak in the wing. At all events, there was lacking in him that strong impulse of the mind which has both the craving and the power to press on far beyond and above the facts presented to the senses.

10. The comparative narrowness of Aristotle's world-scheme was also antagonistic to another fundamental doctrine of the old nature-philosophers, that of alternating cosmic periods. It is true that his speculation did not succeed in altogether leaving the groove, already worn so deeply, of cyclic theories. But he confined this mutation exclusively to the history of the earth and the history of mankind conditioned by it. The bold constructions of his predecessors, among whom he refers to Heraclitus and Empedocles, while he might also have named Anaximander and Plato himself (in the "Statesman"), are altogether foreign to his thought. His system comprehends no Cosmogony, no Zoogony, no Anthropogony. And not, as might perhaps be thought, because scientific caution restrained him from such adventurous enterprises. From adventurous recklessness even his own cyclic doctrine is

not free.   It is to the effect that the human race has from
eternity resided on this earth, which likewise is without
beginning and without a preliminary history.   The author
of the "Politics" and the "Poetics" acknowledges a progress, an ascent from lower to higher forms of social
organization, of science, and of art, as accomplished by
our species.   Here, we may remark by the way, is the only
instance of true development, gradually realized in the
course of time, that is to be met with in the teaching of
Aristotle.   This movement has already reached its goal
times without number, and has as often been compelled
to ebb back to its starting-point.   For secular catastrophes,
repeated with immeasurable frequency, have laid the earth
waste, destroyed the race of mankind down to a small
remnant, and then allowed that race to rise anew and enter
upon and retravel its ascending path of civilization again
and again and again.

This doctrine is at once the weakened reflex of an old
Pythagorean faith (cf. Vol. I. p. 140 *seq.*), and the consequence of the assumed eternity of the earth and the
human race combined with the fact that the Stagirite, no
less than ourselves, was acquainted with peoples of primitive rudeness and savagery.   This last circumstance necessarily leads—apart from hypotheses of degeneration—to
the surprised question why civilization has in so many
instances not yet advanced beyond its rudiments.   The
answers which we are accustomed to give to this question :
the gradual cooling and solidification of a gaseous earth
projected into space immeasurable ages ago ; the late
appearance upon it of the human race, with an interminable pedigree of brutish ancestors ; historical accidents of
every kind, now hastening and now retarding the rise and
the progress of civilization,—all these answers were either
unknown to him or deemed untenable.   From these difficulties and perplexities a means of escape was provided by
the circulatory theory of social progress, preparation for
which had been made by the cyclic doctrines of his predecessors and the records of great floods and kindred
catastrophes.

11. We have now, without noticing it, entered the region of the Aristotelian geology. Our philosopher knows and uses here the principle, formerly taught by Xenophanes, of the summation of minute effects (cf. Vol. I. p. 162), as well as that of the periodicity of alternately recurring changes. Thus he admits for the history of the earth modes of explanation which he rejected in the case of the Cosmos. It is true that he lays distinct and particular emphasis on the fact that he is treating only of partial, not of universal, changes. But even with this limitation, his admission conflicts with a wonderful argument which he adduces in support of the changelessness of the Cosmos, and which we permitted ourselves to overlook in that connexion because of its manifest unsoundness: A cause which remains eternally like itself, as does the Godhead, cannot act now in this way and now in that. Applied with full strictness, this argument would hold good against the alternation of day and night, the circle of the seasons, all change, all processes, even the march of time itself; it would, in fact, call a halt to the universe. This would make Aristotle the natural philosopher into one of those " unnatural philosophers " for being which he so severely lashed the Eleatics (cf. Vol. I. pp. 166 and 552).

Warming and cooling are represented as producing in the earth's interior changes which are comparable to the different ages in the lives of plants and animals, and which bring in their train a periodic alternation of sea and dry land. The gradual drying up of rivers and the final disappearance of springs transforms the sea into land ; the water-courses thence dislodged reappear in other regions and there convert the dry land into sea. The way in which this transformation is conditioned by the sun's journey and the revolution of the heavens is suggested with great obscurity. Full clearness is accorded us only on the one point that these alternating processes are accomplished in periods compared with which the life of men is pitifully short. But in spite of this, Aristotle claims to detect in the Homeric poems, comparatively young as they are, traces of a less advanced stage in the desiccation of Egypt as well as of some districts of Greece. He proceeds, not unjustly for once, to censure the ancients—among whom, it is true, Herodotus and Thucydides are not to be reckoned (cf. Vol. I. pp. 263 and 512)—who, because of their "limited survey," generalized these partial processes, and, on the ground of the observed facts, pronounced in favour of a progressive increase of land-surface.

12. We have been able to describe as justified the above expression of blame, which is directed chiefly against Anaximander ; the reverse is the case with the reproaches which in a neighbouring passage Aristotle levels against Anaximander's immediate successor. The dart of poisoned scorn which the Stagirite aims at Anaximenes recoils upon himself. At the point where he is about to treat of the winds, then of rivers and the sea, he makes an astonishingly pretentious opening remark. None of the older writers, he says, has produced anything on the subject which might not have been contributed by the man in the street. And immediately afterwards he proceeds to rebuke those who see in the wind "nothing else but air in motion," who therefore regard all the different winds as essentially the same and only distinguished by the regions over which they have blown. The context of the passage allows no doubt that among those on whom the Stagirite here pours the vials of his scorn, Anaximenes occupies the foremost place. He himself explains the cause of the winds to be what he calls "dry exhalation," a species of which smoke is a sub-variety, and from which stones and other non-fusible minerals have derived their origin. On a level with this application of an obscure fiction, or with his polemic against those who derive all springs from atmospheric precipitation, is his confident explanation of a phenomenon before which modern research halts helpless and unable to do more than acknowledge a primordial fact—the saltness of the sea.

Confidence in the false is an attribute of Aristotle the physicist and metaphysician which greatly outweighs his occasional fits of modesty. It is a characteristic which sometimes we may find amusing ; but in truth it teaches an impressive lesson in the duty of self-criticism, and supplies an urgent warning against intellectual arrogance. Near the end of the twelfth book of the "Metaphysics" there is an accumulation, such as perhaps can nowhere else be found, of expressions of satisfaction with his own achievements and of the depreciation which he thinks the due of all his predecessors, including this time Plato himself. Nearly all the fundamental problems of natural philosophy are there passed in review, and continually the same refrain occurs: "On this subject no one says anything that is right." And the general summing-up is given in the words: "No one can produce anything sound on the subject unless he says the same as we do."

And how slender was the foundation for this self-confidence! The acumen of the brilliant dialectician certainly did not fail him even in these regions. His physics, indeed, may be described as misused dialectic. But his infatuation with *à priori* and superstitious prejudices, his excessive trust in the supposed kernel of truth contained in widespread and ancient opinions, his fear, due to deficient imagination, of bold hypotheses that far transcend the bounds of the sensible, and finally a preference, partly an old Greek heritage, partly a personal characteristic, for comparatively narrow and circumscribed horizons, a preference which we shall meet with again in his political theories,—all these factors co-operated to dwarf the Stagirite's achievement in this field, and to stamp it with the seal of retrogression.

The task which now presents itself of discussing the second pair of causes gives us a welcome opportunity to enter a region in which the intellect of our philospher has left a far deeper trace, the region of organic nature and biological research.

CHAPTER XII.

ARISTOTLE AS AN INVESTIGATOR OF NATURE.

(CONTINUATION : ORGANIC NATURE.)

1. WERE Aristotle not known to us as a philosophic encyclopædist of universal range, we might almost have been tempted to take him for a specialist in zoology ; so remarkable is the depth of his studies in this field and so astonishing the magnitude of his achievement. The compass of his main work on zoology is to that of his writings on inorganic nature (" Physics," " On the Heavens," " On Generation and Corruption," " Meteorology ") in the proportion of about three to two. It is almost equal to the compass of his anthropological works, using the term in its widest sense (" On the Soul," " Ethics," " Politics," " Rhetoric," and " Poetics," the second lost book of which last we suppose as long as the first), and again about equal to that of the works on general philosophy, fundamental for all subjects alike (the books of the " Organon " and the " Metaphysics "). The other main division of organic life evidently occupied the Stagirite much less persistently. The extant tract " On Plants " is no doubt spurious, and gives us no right to draw conclusions ; but the fact that his successor Theophrastus treated botany in two extensive works, which have come down to us, clearly indicates that the master had left the pupil much to do in this direction.

Was it a taste inherited from his medical ancestors that moved Aristotle to this preferential treatment of animal life ? Or was it as being the next thing to man that the beast so particularly engaged the interest of one who probed all sides of human existence with never-failing ardour ? In any case he was, even according to his own view, least of a specialist in mathematical and astronomical matters, in dealing with which he so often appeals to the "expert" and the "competent judge." It agrees with this that he cultivated the neighbouring field of physical and chemical studies with far less success than the biological field. We might almost describe him as one who was a humanist in his natural philosophy, one whose intellect grew in penetrative power the nearer his subject approached to that other pole of all knowledge, the science of mind and the soul.

Aristotle has, moreover, himself declared the grounds of his preference for the organic world in memorable words. "Here, too, there are gods"—it is thus that, like Heraclitus, he apostrophizes the student about to enter this department of research. In it more than elsewhere he sees the rule, not of blind chance but of purpose, rooted in the beautiful (of the "ideal," we should say). If any one were inclined to sniff at this employment upon the bodies of animals for the reason that blood, flesh, mucus, etc., are not exalted objects of contemplation, he could hardly think otherwise of the study of man. But in each case the important thing is not the matter, but the way in which it is compounded, and the whole being. Truly the imperishable bodies revealed to us in the vault of heaven are infinitely higher than all earthly things ; but their vast distance places them out of the reach of accurate inspection. We must therefore content ourselves with little, just as the lover prefers a glimpse accorded him by the object of his love to the full view of any other face. In respect of the animal world a kind of compensation is given us. Though these perishable beings may not be comparable in value to the eternal stars, yet even the ugliest and meanest of them, just because they are nearer and more familiar to us, afford "unspeakable pleasures" to be enjoyed by those "who are not devoid of the philosophic sense and are devoted to the study of causes."

2. In what precedes, we have already found ourselves obliged to refer to the idea of purpose. In entering the

region of organic nature we have reached the true home and principal workshop of the fourth of Aristotle's causes, the final cause, which, besides, makes so near an approach to the third, the notional or formal cause, that the two not seldom coincide. For the Stagirite shows himself a true disciple of Plato in this, that he makes things receive their definiteness from their generic types, though these no longer confront them from without, but reside within them as immanent. But the question is not hereby solved as to where those qualities have their root which vary from individual to individual, instead of being common to a whole species, *e.g.* the brown or blue colour of our eyes. The goal-seeking character of nature is now paralleled with the technical skill of man, to which it is regarded as cognate. If houses were natural products—he says in a noteworthy passage of the " Physics "—they would be like the houses actually built by human art. It is a fundamental rule for him that " Nature does nothing in vain." Not, it is true, that even this rule is without exceptions. That the ideal or natural purpose does not everywhere and at all times win through and arrive at full realization is a patent fact to which the Stagirite was anything but blind. He acknowledges in such cases the victorious power of recalcitrant matter (ὕλη), which, elsewhere, it is true, he describes as mere featureless potentiality. Here, too, his mind travels in the grooves cut by Plato. In particular he compares monstrosities, the occurrence of which in the animal world claimed much of his attention, to the failures which arise in all technical pursuits, to the scribe's slip of the pen, the physician's or apothecary's undue dilution of a drug.

Aristotle's teleological interpretation of the universe outgrew the cramping bounds by which that conception had been confined in the thought of Xenophon, perhaps of Socrates. It is not man and the profit that he draws from the well-ordering of the universe that stands in the foreground of his contemplation. It is rather the well-ordered beauty of the Cosmos itself that determines his judgment, wherein he resembles Anaxagoras, Diogenes of Apollonia, and Plato. The occasional and isolated accomplishment of a result—somewhat to this effect runs a passage on the subject in the " Physics "—passes with us for an accident ; but where a process or agency achieves its result with exceptionless regularity, or even in the great majority of cases, there we have a right to assume an effort directed to an end. Whoever at the time of the Trojan war had observed the advantageous disposition of the Greek army and the subordination of its movements would have been well justified in supposing a guiding purpose behind what he saw ; and so would any one who watched a ship speeding through the high seas to the haven with sails full-spread to the favouring wind. Such are the examples with which in one of his popular works the Stagirite illustrated the purposefulness of natural processes. Foremost in this connexion he places the structure and the activities of organic beings, including the arrangements which provide for the preservation of the species, such as the nest-building of birds, the performances of bees and ants, and so on. He is acquainted with Empedocles' attempt to explain the purpose-serving character of organic forms by the mere survival of the fit ; but he mocks the attempt in a manner which is not without humour. If these hybrid creatures which Empedocles supposed to have appeared spontaneously, and to have perished because of their unfitness, *e.g.* " bovine bodies with human heads," had ever come actually before our eyes, we should have regarded them just as we regard the monstrosities which even now occur in the animal world, namely, as deviations from an already established rule, not as phenomena preceding the establishment of one.

We ourselves have no right whatever to look slightingly on Aristotle's teleology. The purpose-serving character of organic forms is still one of the problems whose solution we long for, but in spite of Lamarck, Wallace, and Darwin, have by no means yet found. The chief question that forces itself upon us here is this: Does the hypothesis of purpose in nature serve more to hinder or to help the progress of biological research ? This question, so far as

we can judge, admits of no simple and peremptory answer.
If the beholder of a machine has rightly grasped its function
and purpose, his eye for the details of its construction and
working has no doubt become keener and surer. To this
extent it is certainly just to speak of the heuristic value
of the teleological way of looking at nature. But against
this advantage there are to be set two disadvantages. The
pursuit of assumed final causes may divert the researcher's
aim from the ascertainment of immediate causes, easily
and safely accessible to human discernment. And again,
the work or function of an organ may be misunderstood, and the erroneous teleological interpretation may
cloud our perception of the facts themselves, may support
or help to produce inexact observations and hasty conclusions. The first of these dangers was well known to
Aristotle, and he laboured with much care, but assuredly
not with uniform success, for its obviation. " Zeus," he
says somewhere, " does not send rain that the plants may
grow, but of necessity. For the rising exhalations must
cool ; when cooled they must become water and sink downwards." It is surprising to find the mechanical explanation
here taking the place of the teleological one. The reason
is to be found partly in the immediately following reference
to the damage done by excessive or unseasonable rains—
visitations which for once preserve our philosopher from
teleological optimism. Partly, too, the obvious character
of these physical processes counts for something ; the teleological interpretation usually makes its appearance in Aristotle, as elsewhere, when the ordinary means of explaining
nature deny their aid. As a principle, it is true, he does not
hold with neglecting the Why of things while attending
to their Wherefore. There is a passage full of meaning
in which he describes the mechanical causes as the servants
and instruments of the final causes. But it is one thing
thus to acknowledge a principle and another to carry it
out consistently in practice. Aristotle's attempt to do
so, as can well be understood, is frequently wrecked on
the difficulty, if not impossibility, of discerning the connexion of the proximate or mechanical causes, especially in

biological matters. Thus, in point of fact, nature is for him broken up into two spheres, in one of which necessity reigns, and in the other purpose. For the rest he has equal censure for those who assume purposes of nature where mere mechanical necessity is at work, and for those who, like the Atomists, discard altogether the question of the Wherefore or purpose, and who judge precisely as one would do who at the tapping of a dropsy should describe the physician's lancet, and not his desire to cure the patient, as the cause of the operation. Telling as this comparison seems, it really is anything but convincing. For while many human purposes, like that of the operator just spoken of, are plain to be seen, our endeavour to learn the purposes of nature is exposed to the severest deceptions, and is led astray by subjective interpretation of the facts. A flagrant example of such error may find a place here. Inexact observation had led Aristotle or his predecessors to assert that the number of sutures is greater in the human skull than in that of other creatures, and greater in the male skull than in the female. Straight on the heels of the malobservation comes an interpretation that blocks the way to its correction. Those sutures, it is suggested, serve to ventilate the brain, and must therefore be most numerous where the heart and lungs are richest in blood, and give the brain (fantastically conceived as a refrigerator) the greatest amount of work to do.

3. There are three great works in which the Stagirite expatiated over all the provinces of animal life. The first and most extensive, the " History of Animals," treats the phenomena (his own expression) of animal life ; while the second does not, as its title, " On the Parts of Animals," would suggest, serve a purely anatomical purpose, but together with the organs of animals describes also their functions, and is therefore termed by its author an exposition of causes. The third main work, " On the Generation of Animals," is intended to instruct us on their origin, and accordingly covers the ground of reproduction and development (embryology).

A chorus of enthusiastic voices sings the praises of

these works. Some of the most eminent biologists, zoologists, and philosophic naturalists of the nineteenth century
have outbid each other in admiration of the "great
Stagirite." Cuvier and the son of his opponent, the
younger Geoffroy St. Hilaire, Sir John Herschel with
his deistic tendencies, and Blainville so highly esteemed
by the positivists, are here found in unanimous agreement.
No less a person than Charles Darwin affirms somewhere
that he has always looked up to Linnæus and Cuvier as
to gods, but that by the side of the man who wrote the
"History of Animals" they seem to him like schoolboys.
On the other hand, George Henry Lewes, the biographer
of Goethe, and the author of "Seaside Studies," has
penned some severe, perhaps not seldom unduly severe,
criticism of Aristotle's achievement in his "Aristotle, a
Chapter from the History of Science." But he fared like
Balaam ; his reprimand more than once veered round
into a hymn of exuberant praise.

Let us contemplate, first of all, the reverse of the
medal. "Aristotle," so Lewes exclaims in one passage,
"knew nothing of the muscles, not even of their existence.
He knew very little indeed of two or three nerves, and
absolutely nothing of the nervous *system.* He did not
distinguish between arteries and veins. Thus the three
most important parts of the organism . . . were wholly
hidden from him." We might go further. The brain,
which had already been recognized by Alcmæon, who
had been followed by a great Hippocratic and Plato
(cf. Vol. I. pp. 148 and 313), as a central organ, was
deposed by the Stagirite from that rank, and explained
as being, like the lungs, an apparatus for cooling the
blood ; the heart, on the other hand, was in accordance
with old-time popular physiology restored to its position
as the seat of consciousness. The reproductive act was
seriously misunderstood, as there was ascribed to the
male element merely a stimulating and quickening influence ; while the hypothesis of spontaneous generation
was extended to organisms of quite complex structure.
How is the recognition of such grave defects and errors,

which partly at least arose from the rejection of knowledge already won, to be reconciled with an extravagantly high estimate of Aristotle as a biologist? If we
wish to give a just answer to this question, if we wish
within the limits of possibility to give this great man his
full rights, to appraise his merit not too high and not
too low, it is first of all necessary to cast a rapid glance
over his predecessors, the means of research at his disposal,
and the methods he employed. In this way—to state our
verdict in advance—we shall learn to know and admire
the unprecedented greatness of his undertaking, the
astonishing width of his survey, his choice of valuable
methods despite the temptations of his own dialectical
skill, finally, certain generalizations of great if not universal
application, and the marvellous and many-sided gifts which
made these triumphs possible.

4. An opinion formerly widespread and hardly as yet
contested a quarter of a century ago, to the effect that
Aristotle, so to speak, created zoology out of nothing, did
our philosopher at once too much and too little honour.
It credited him with a more than human achievement, and
it charged him with the responsibility for countless fallacies
and malobservations of others. It is not even to-day
possible to draw a clean line of separation between what
is original and what is borrowed either in his triumphs
or in his failures. But we know at least that in none of
the fields here concerned Aristotle was without predecessors. Our author himself seems to us to distinguish,
here and there with some care, between what he has seen
for himself and what he takes on the authority of others.
Not seldom an emphatic "we have observed" contrasts
with "it has been seen," or "it has been noticed." There
is no lack, too, as has always been sufficiently evident, of
appeals to specialists. For example, the Cypriote Syennesis, the Hippocratic Polybus, and Diogenes of Apollonia,
are made use of and criticized in the section descriptive
of the arteries, just as Leophanes (or Cleophanes), the
putative author of the pseudo-Hippocratic treatise "On
Superfetation," is utilized on the subject of reproduction.

In addition to scientific specialists there also appears a
host of "practical specialists" outside the guild of learning,
among whom fishermen, bee-keepers, shepherds, all kinds
of hunters, fowlers, stock-breeders, and veterinary surgeons
receive particular mention.   Frequent reference is made to
the doctrines of the old and the new nature-philosophers,
sometimes laudatory, more commonly the reverse ; and
the harshness of his criticism does not spare even Plato's
"Timæus."   In the field of descriptive zoology, the number
of his predecessors seems smaller.   It remains a question
how far Democritus is included among them, as of his
work in three books on the problems of animal life only
scanty remnants are in our hands ; in any case, Aristotle
discusses his views on animal physiology with unnsual
frequency.   Speusippus, too, from what we know of his
book "On Similarities" could not possibly be absent from
the list ; a Herodorus of Heraclea is once mentioned and
censured in connexion with a special question ; and in the
same passage reference is made to an error of which
"many" have been guilty.   Other writers, with whom
we shall soon have to concern ourselves, had preceded
him in the fields of classification combined with description,
of comparative anatomy, and of embryology.

Next to the literary and cognate aids to study come
the available means and opportunities of independent
observation.   As early as the time of Herodotus it was
possible to enjoy the sight of a variety of exotic beasts
in the park of the Persian king's palace at Susa ; and in
the Egypt of the Ptolemies even municipal zoological
gardens were to be found in the cities.   But we have no
record of any similar institutions in Macedon and Greece.
Still, at Athens, single specimens of rare animals were
kept by fanciers and exhibited for pay.   Indeed, there
were even menageries in which trained lions and bears
and so on showed off their tricks.   The narratives of the
ancients respecting the support given by Alexander to
his tutor by consignments of animals from the Far East
deserve little credence, if only because of the fabulous
numbers mentioned.   In any case, such gifts could only

have been received in the last lustrum of our philosopher's life, while the composition of his zoological works belongs, certainly to an advanced, but not to quite the latest stage of his scientific activity. In this respect, therefore, his resources can hardly have exceeded those possessed by his contemporaries ; and the exacter knowledge (in some instances the uncommonly exact knowledge) which specialists find in his works, of about five hundred species of animals (a three-thousandth part of the species now known over the whole globe), is, under all the circumstances, an amazing result of his restless research and his devoted zeal in collecting. This knowledge extended from the lowest shell-fish, which he himself calls a "middle thing between plant and animal," up to man.

5. It is not a little strange to learn that the knowledge which Aristotle possessed of physical man stands at a far lower level than that which he acquired of organisms much lower in the scale of life. Thus he has never seen either the human kidneys or the human uterus. He himself does not shrink from the confession that the inward parts of man are " the least known of all," and that such knowledge must be based on the examination of other forms of life— a foundation on which his own anatomical diagrams rested. Indeed, the already-mentioned absolutely false assumption as to the number of the cranial sutures shows us, as has rightly been remarked, that he never once took advantage of any of the many opportunities that must have presented themselves of carefully examining the skulls of the dead and comparing them with each other as well as with animal skulls. If, on the other hand, as we may remark in passing, such easily avoidable shortcomings are not to be laid at the door of the great encyclopædist himself, but of the writers whom he consulted, we lose the right of giving him, rather than the authorities, the credit of the strikingly exact observations which are so much admired in other passages. Take, for example, the observation that the male cuttlefish sometimes inserts an arm in the female mantle and leaves it there—a phenomenon which even Cuvier interpreted falsely, for he regarded the arm as an intestinal

worm.   In both sets of instances we shall do well to put
the responsibility on the incomparable acuteness of the
senses and the ever-active curiosity of the ancient Greeks
in general, as also on their lack of strict objective exactness and scientific training.   But to return to man : what
hindered the exhaustive knowledge of his bodily con-
formation was that shrinking from *post-mortem* examina-
tions which was first overcome by the great Alexandrine
physicians.   There was only one quarter in which this
shrinking had no effect.   The human fœtus was opened
and dismembered by Aristotle's contemporaries and by
himself ; and this branch of research, assisted as it was
by the frequency at that time of deliberately induced
abortion, gave students a much exacter idea of man in
the make than of the completed product.

The anatomist followed in the train of the butcher, the
sacrificing priest, and the cook.   Here, as elsewhere, real
or supposed need smoothed the way for science.   Animals,
too, were prepared in an ingenious manner for purely
external inspection ; thus they were kept without food in
order that the course of the blood-vessels might be better
traced in their emaciated bodies.   If a dead animal was
preferred for examination, it was killed in such cases exclusively by strangling, so that the emptying of the vessels
by loss of blood might be avoided.   When the legend exhibits
to us Democritus surrounded by the opened bodies of
animals (cf. Vol. I. p. 316), it brings before our eyes a
faithful picture of what the state of knowledge at that time
shows to have been the only form of anatomical research
then in use.   It is not open to doubt that Aristotle performed many dissections of animals ; and it must be considered as at least highly probable that he considerably
enlarged the horizon of contemporary research in this
respect.   If the minute examination of the lower animals
had been no novelty, the Stagirite would hardly have felt
any need to undertake an emphatic defence of this branch
of research against its despisers ; he would have had no
occasion to chastise the "childish reluctance" which objected to the investigation of "meanly regarded animals."

He may well have fared like the founder of English surgery, John Hunter (1728–1793), who was laughed at by his short-sighted colleagues for "wasting his time over flies and frogs." Nothing was accounted by the Stagirite as too mean or too remote: not the ovary of the oyster, nor the bladder of the tortoise, nor the posture of mating hedgehogs. Although in this province, too, he has committed numerous errors of detail, his high appreciation and his advancement, if not foundation, of the practice of animal-dissections, to which, according to Tiedemann, we owe "almost all the most important discoveries in anatomy and physiology," constitute merit of the highest order.

6. We come to a question of importance both in itself and for the purposes of the present work—the question as to the temper of mind in which Aristotle minted the treasures of his own and others' observation and drew far-reaching inferences and general views from the raw material of facts. Here we are at once surprised by a remarkable contrast. In treating of the books on physics, we were entitled to speak of "misused dialectic." No one would ever think of employing such a term to characterize the biological books. In no part of his writings does the Stagirite stand at so great a distance from the author of the " Topics " as in the works which now occupy us. Loose, merely dialectical proofs are most decisively repudiated. The deduction of conclusions from the " specific principles " peculiar to the object of study is inculcated repeatedly and with the greatest emphasis. " Too far-fetched explanations " are severely condemned. At the same time, to be sure, the adroit dialectician cannot always deny himself the pleasure of inventing ingenious pseudo-demonstrations. But he does not here, as so often elsewhere, set them in the van of his argument to be followed by weightier and more cogent reasons ; on the contrary, he expressly designates them as "empty" or "null," and draws the most definite possible distinction between such sportive exercise of the mind and the kind of proof which he judges truly valid.

It is so in respect of a question which, from the time of
Democritus onwards had formed the theme of much discussion, that as to the sterility of mules. He begins by
an attempt to prove it impossible that these animals should
breed. For what kind of young could they have? From
the union of two animals of unlike species there is produced
offspring different from both, while from that of individuals
of the same species like offspring is derived. Neither of
these suppositions can be admitted here. The young
cannot be different, because the male and female belong
to the same species, as being both mules ; but just as little
can such a union produce like offspring, because both
parents, as mixtures of horse and ass, are themselves
different. It is plain enough that the words implying likeness and unlikeness of species are not used in the same
sense in the two parts of the argument ; in the first case,
the reference is to the *nature* of the two animals themselves, and in the second to their *origin*. In point of fact,
Aristotle adduces the argument only to condemn it, and
that as being "too general and therefore vain ;" as being
a mere show argument, which, for the rest, proves too much
the unfruitfulness of all bastards without exception.

Here, no less than elsewhere, he falls a victim to the
fever of universal explanation. The biological works are
crammed with desperate attempts at explanation which
have their origin in deficient knowledge and in unsound,
sometimes we might say superficial, interpretations of the
phenomena. That wise reserve which abstains from the
explanation of enigmatic processes and relegates them to
a future better prepared for the task (cf. p. 60) is the
rarest of exceptions. The greatest harm is done by his
leaning to over-simple explanations, such as make specifically biological phenomena depend immediately upon
merely physical causes. We might almost speak here of
premature attempts to establish the "unity of natural
forces"—a tendency towards which the Atomists were
impelled by the exclusively mechanical presuppositions of
their doctrine, while even our philosopher, with his greater
endowment of biological insight, was led in the same

direction by defective knowledge of the higher regions
of organic life, more especially by his total ignorance of
the functions of brain and nerves. An instance of this
occurs when he proposes to deduce the palpitation caused
by fear from a cooling of the upper part of the body
brought about by emotion, and a consequent sinking and
contraction of the vital heat, an occasional result of which
is the extinction of that heat and the death of the
frightened animal. Another instance is his theory that
the exceptional size of some animals' hearts is the cause
of their shyness and timidity—a theory based on the
ground that the warmth of the heart when spread over
a large space has less effect than if it were compressed
into less room, much as the same fire that warms a little
chamber leaves a large hall cold. Other examples are
supplied by the fantastic attempt to explain the fair hair
of the Sarmatians and the rough wool of the Sarmatian
sheep as equally due to northern cold. Again, the breaking
of a boy's voice and the shrill tones of a eunuch are
deduced from fundamentally false anatomical premisses ;
baldness is ascribed to the coolness of the brain, etc., etc.
Georges Pouchet, the best exponent of the Aristotelian
biology, might well exclaim, in view of such aberrations,
"Lucky philosophy to be able to reconcile all contradictions so well and to give a reason for everything!"
But by the side of such expressions of justified impatience
the following consideration may also perhaps find a place.
This irritating intrusiveness of Aristotle's passion for
explanation may well have been an indispensable servant
of his polymathy. The mind of the all-embracing encyclopædist could hardly have preserved in security the same
immense store of knowledge if it had remained for the
most part a heap of unconnected data and problems. His
essays in explanation, premature and presumptuous as
many of them were, wove a net whose meshes were
adapted to hold the vast unwieldy mass together and
save it from falling to pieces.

7. Our philosopher's wealth of resource—that at once
so valuable and so fatal dowry—assumed, as we see, very

different forms at different phases of his activity; it wears
one shape in his physical, and another in his biological
works. In the latter he is as far removed as possible from
the empty apriorism of the former. We are inclined to
imagine a progressive maturity, a clarification of his mind
accomplished in the lapse of time. And, in point of fact,
the three main works treating the subjects of zoology,
anatomy and physiology, and embryology, imply the
previous composition not only of the four chief physical
works, but also of the books "On the Soul." There is,
however, a great deal that restrains us from making the
progress of years alone responsible for this change in
method. What we have in mind is not so much the part
played by dialectical sham-proofs in the "Rhetoric," a
work of still later date, whose subject and purpose connect
it closely with the much earlier "Topics," as the heap-
ing up of sound and unsound proofs that occurs in the
"Poetics," a work written not long before the "Rhetoric."
For example, the superiority of tragic over epic poetry is
there maintained with an astonishing muster of looser and
stricter arguments mixed together. To the same category
belong those violent adjustments by which the whole of
the virtues, including truthfulness and justice, are forced
into the framework of the "mean." The difference of
subject may have meant still more than the difference
of age. In physics, a lack of at once assured and fruitful
fundamental knowledge, a lack for which no doubt (as
in his rejection of the Democritean theory of displacement)
he was sometimes himself to blame, threw him into the
arms of empty thought-constructions like his doctrine of
elements (cf. pp. 63, 64). But in the biological field a countless abundance of valuable facts were at his command.
Here, we might say, he is as much at home in the concrete
as there he was in the abstract. The excessive mobility
and adaptability of his mind drives him, not now to
unsubstantial thought-building, but rather to a premature
acceptance of supposed connexions in matters of fact.
From these excrescences of the quest for causes one
branch alone of biology remains fully free. It is that

branch in which the mind of the investigator must be content with observation and comparison, where his whole task consists of arrangement, classification, the ascertainment of similarities and of widely comprehensive laws of coexistence. It is here that Aristotle—so much may be confidently maintained—did his best work and showed his full mastery as an investigator of nature.

CHAPTER XIII.

ARISTOTLE AS AN INVESTIGATOR OF NATURE.

(CONTINUATION: THE SYSTEMATIST, THE COMPARATIVE ANATOMIST AND PHYSIOLOGIST.)

1. To classify is to arrange by means of generalizations and at the same time to provide a graduated scheme of such generalizations. Out of the abundance of data in the nature of facts (phenomena, processes, things) the mind selects elements connected by common features, and with them constructs a general type. With these general types the same procedure is continued, each new set of ideas is subordinated to another set, until the narrowing pyramid finally ends in a point—one or several generic notions of the highest order. In the case with which we are concerned, such generic notions are those of plant or animal, of organic being, or even of entity in general. Though this construction serves the ends of scientific perspective, it is by no means originally a product of the scientific sense or even of conscious effort. The truth rather is that in its first stages the process goes on, as we may say, automatically. What happens is not so much that the common element is recognized in different things, but that the differences are overlooked, neglected, or forgotten. It is so that the Polynesian proceeds at the present day; if a new quadruped is imported into his country, he assimilates it to the only quadruped he knows, calls it by the same name, and by the transference acquires the general notion of quadruped. The strong impression made on a child by the barking of the family dog leads him to regard all other animals that bark, though the

differences between them may be no less than that between a lapdog and a greyhound, as belonging together, and to greet their appearance by an imitative bark. In such processes we may see the beginnings of, or at any rate the first steps towards, the formation of classes. At a later stage it is principally the relation to human purposes that supplements the most striking differences of size, form, and habitat as a basis of classification. We speak of wild and tame, of useful and noxious animals, of domestic animals and game, of large and small stock, of flying and creeping creatures, of sea-monsters, with many other like distinctions.

Occasionally superstition has led to a more careful separation of animal groups, such as is found in the dietary prohibitions of the Old Testament. We refer to the recognition of the class of ruminants, and their partial identification with the group of cloven-hoofed quadrupeds —an isolated gleam of illumination, since a little further on such widely different species as the lizard and the mole are coupled together.

2. We are as yet unacquainted with the first beginnings among the Greeks of a purely scientific division of animals, a division, that is, which disregards all points of view foreign to the subject itself, and which accurately emphasizes the essential features. That in this field, too, Aristotle did not lack predecessors might be conjectured simply in view of the restless scientific activity of that age. Some of the names given by Aristotle to the leading groups (outside universally known terms like "fish" and "bird") are found in earlier writers, namely, the great physician Diocles, known as the "Second Hippocrates," and also Speusippus. Probably Democritus had already spoken of the great class of "blood-possessing" animals, and others again had alluded to the sub-group of the "single-hoofed." At the end of Plato's "Timæus" some principal members of the animal series are mentioned in connexion with that theory of descent which so well deserves the name. A searching analysis of the second of the pseudo-Hippocratic books "On Diet" has also enabled a contemporary of ours to

treat of a "Coan" system of animals, which in its main features agrees with that of Aristotle.

It is quite possible that Aristotle was not himself the first to define any single one of the chief animal-groups which occur in his writings. Can we acknowledge this possibility and yet retain a right to commemorate him as a pioneer who rendered the most eminent service to this branch of knowledge? Most certainly we can; for, with the contemporary just alluded to, we may regard the essential merit of his achievement as lying not so much "in the special arrangement of the material" as "rather in the development of the logical principles of classification." But not in this last alone. For all specialists are unanimous in declaring that systematic zoology itself did not progress a single step between Aristotle and Linnæus (1707–1778). And even the author of the "Systema Naturæ" stood in several matters to the rear of Aristotle; thus in ten out of the twelve editions which he personally prepared he numbered the whales among the fishes, while Aristotle placed them among the "viviparous" animals, as he called them—that is, the mammalia.

3. A first step in this exhibition of the true principles of systematization is the Stagirite's decisive rejection of dichotomy. This mode of procedure, which undertakes to build up a classification by repeated division into two, was the earliest and most obvious method of didactic partition. On such lines were the attempts at classification in Plato's "Sophist." But increasing maturity of thought soon led the author of that work, as we learn from the "Statesman" and the "Philebus," to discover that this principle of division does not admit of anything like universal application. Such could not be the case—we may add in explanation—unless the upper division always fell into no more than two lower divisions, related to each other as contrary opposites, much like white and black. But since black may be also contrasted with blue, green, red, etc., the twofold division can be maintained erect in such cases only by balancing black against not-black, which latter must be afterwards broken up into its sub-varieties.

It is obvious from this example that the contradictory antithesis provides a merely artificial and altogether unfruitful principle of division. Aristotle, who seems to have been preceded in this by Speusippus, discussed the matter thoroughly, with unmistakable allusion to the attempts at classification in the "Sophist," and came to the conclusion that dichotomy is untenable as an exclusive principle of division, and that its employment is "partly impossible, partly nugatory."

His first and chief objection is the sterility of negation as a ground of division. The footless, the wingless, and so on, give no handle to further division ; there are no subvarieties of the merely negative. To this first disadvantage a second is added whenever the dichotomy separates things closely connected with each other, as happens not only in the case of the subdivisions of a common genus, but also in that of the members of one and the same kind or species. This drawback attends the dichotomy "land-animals and water-animals," or the antithesis of "winged and wingless." In the first case aquatic birds, for example, are separated from their near relations, the land-birds ; the first are thrown into a class along with the fishes, the second with land-mammals and reptiles. But the opposition of winged and wingless even tears apart creatures belonging to the same species ; it parts the winged ants that possess sex from the wingless neuters, the winged male glow-worm from the wingless female.

Thus Aristotle was led, without noticing it, to discover and to proclaim with emphasis those principles of natural division which in our century have won their final victory. Lewes, indeed, credited the Stagirite with no more than a "dim perception of the natural method." But he might have learnt better from the thorough treatment of the subject by Jürgen Bona Meyer in his "Zoology of Aristotle." Over and over again Aristotle points out that whatever distinguishing marks we divide by, we should never use one alone, but always a number of them. And among these marks those are placed in the second rank which rest upon "functions" or "performances," conditioned as these so

often are by the habitat of animals and their mode of life.
The precedence is thus transferred from the physiological
to the anatomical characters ; original or structural features
are preferred to those depending on adaptation. "Animals
differing in species are distinguished in most of their parts
(their presence or absence, their position and arrangement),
. . . groups (on the other hand) whose parts show only
differences of degree are combined into a common group."
Without dreaming of the theory of descent, Aristotle did
preliminary work towards it by choosing for his guiding-
lines in the systematization of animals those characters
which have the greatest permanence and therefore the
greatest probative force for family relationship. In this
he resembles Cuvier ; and the praise given to this latter,
e.g. by Louis Agassiz in his "Essay on Classification," is
by others bestowed in almost the same terms on Aristotle.
The "vertebrates" of Cuvier correspond precisely to the
Stagirite's "blood-animals," with their subdivisions : the
mammalia (called by him "viviparous"), the birds, the
reptiles and amphibia (four-footed or footless egg-layers),
and fishes. He was not here guided by the possession of
this one attribute alone ; but the presence or absence of
blood was for him the accompaniment and index of a large
number of other important qualities. The other "great
class" of bloodless animals he divided into soft animals
(our cephalopods), soft shell-fish (our crustacea), shell-
skinned (mussels and snails), and insects, including spiders
and worms—the least sharply defined of all the classes.

Man is sometimes considered as forming an order by
himself, sometimes reckoned in the first of the above-named
divisions of the "blood-animals." The reason why this
last is not the regular procedure is to be found in the
defective nomenclature, which sometimes, but not invariably, adds to the term "viviparous" the name of "quadruped ;" for Aristotle was by no means fanatically exact
in his designations. For example, while he usually sub-
ordinates "species" to "genus," there yet occur passages
in which the two terms are used without distinction. The
strict thinker is a somewhat lax author. His favourite

literary garb is a comfortable *deshabillé*. He uses the
same words, without always warning the reader, now in a
narrower, now in a wider, and again in an altogether
different sense; so in the "Poetics" he uses the word
"metres" in most cases for the poetical rhythms themselves, but also occasionally to denote the parts of the
drama written in verse but not meant to be sung. It is
thus intelligible that his animal-system also fails to exhibit
a strictly articulated structure throughout, and that the
inclusion of the lower in the higher divisions has often to
be inferred from casual and not always consistent indications. It is obvious, too, that he desired to make no
more than a very limited use of palpable innovations in
language; hence the frequent remark that such and such
animals do, in fact, form a group, but that the group has
no name.

4. Precisely this namelessness of many important
groups of animals speaks for the view that in at least the
greater part of these cases Aristotle stands on his own legs
and does not simply make free with the inheritance left
him by some predecessor. Still more definite evidence
to the same purpose is given by the particular nature of
his labours in classification, which are distinguished by
two features: the sense for similarity, for "relationship of
form"—this is his own highly characteristic expression—
and an uncommonly keen eye for what has been called the
correlation of parts. That sense for identity, the foundation of the Stagirite's general mastery of morphology,
forms the root of his knowledge of comparative anatomy,
concerning which we shall have more to say later on. In
isolated passages it also gives him an occasion for genetic
considerations, which beat against the barriers imposed by
the exclusive observation of coexistences. "A variation"—
so runs an extremely noteworthy passage—"which affects
a small organ in an animal can be clearly seen to produce
a great change in the qualities of the whole body." An
experimental verification, as we may call it, of this assertion
is supplied by the case of a castrated animal, in which the
removal of "a small organ" has for its consequence a

change " to the female nature." We here light upon a
thought which it was not his fortune to pursue to its ultimate goal, the transmutation of species, a thought, therefore, of which he makes no really serious use.   In spite of
appearances to the contrary, he does not really go even
as far as Anaximander, who brought land and water
animals into a relation of kinship (cf. Vol. I. p. 54).   He
has a much deeper perception of the reciprocal dependence
of the marks united in one and the same group of animals,
as in the case of the plurality of stomachs and the imperfectly developed dental system of the ruminants—a
case, to be sure, in which the teleological connexion which
he clearly detected lay on the surface.   But "his highly-
developed sense for organic correlations" (to use Georges
Pouchet's expression) permits him to discover much more
deeply hidden connexions, as that between the nature of
eggs and the nature of the animal that lays them, on which
occasion he cannot help putting birds and reptiles close
together, in agreement with modern zoology.   Here, too,
we should take an instance of knowledge which aroused
Cuvier's admiration, the knowledge that all two-horned
beasts are double-hoofed, but not conversely, or that no
bird with spurs has curved claws, and conversely.

   5. A highly important part of this general principle is
the rule, rediscovered by Etienne Geoffroy St. Hilaire and
Goethe, and named by them "the balance of organs."
Aristotle formulates this law of compensation as follows :
"What Nature takes from one part she everywhere gives
to another. . . . She cannot go to the same expense on
two sides. . . . She cannot possibly use the same material
in many places at the same time."   With these one may
at once compare the cognate expressions of Goethe : "If
the formative *nisus* tends to expend more under one head,
there is no absolute hindrance, but it is at once compelled
to leave something missing under another head ; thus
Nature can never run into debt or go bankrupt."   Examples
of this " housekeeper-like economy in giving and taking "
(Goethe) are supplied, for Aristotle, by, among other things,
those species of crabs which have fewer pincers but more

feet than other kinds; similarly by birds of heavy flight, in which the material otherwise used on the wings has been applied to the thickening of the skin. He finds another manifestation of the same parsimony in the fact that Nature "adapts the bodily parts common to all animals to many different uses by modifying their form;" thus the mouth serves all for the reception of food, most for breathing, many for fighting, some again for communication, and man for speech. But far as Nature is from prodigality, she yet does not fall into the opposite fault of "stingy provision" or niggardliness. This last thought is developed by the Stagirite in a manner that connects his biological and his sociological theories by a close and very interesting bond.

"Wherever it is possible"—so we read in the work "On the Parts of Animals"—"to use two things for two purposes. . . . Nature is not accustomed to work like the metal-worker, who, for the sake of cheapness, makes a spit that will also serve as a candlestick." And again, in the "Politics," the use of women for slave-work, a common thing among the barbarians, is opposed by the following argument: "Nature makes nothing penuriously, as the cutler makes the Delphic knife"—probably a bread-knife which the pilgrim could also use as a weapon on his journey—"but for every end she appoints a special means. For every instrument can only then achieve its greatest perfection when it is used not for many services but for one alone." And in pointing out exceptions to the rule he makes in both departments of study the same reference to occasional limitation of means, and even employs the same illustrative comparison. Those authorities which in a very small state are called upon to perform a variety of functions are compared with just those "spit-candlesticks" that we have been mentioning. Nor is it to be wondered at, we may remark in passing, that a leading thought of Plato's "Republic," the division of labour and the specialization of functions, should have made a deep impression on Plato's pupil, and should therefore recur on a variety of quite different occasions.

6. We reach here a new and still more important point of view. We should not have spoken above of exceptions so much as of lower stages of perfection in the realm of organisms. For progressive specialization of activities, and still more of their instruments, is only another expression for the increased complication of structure and the enhanced inner wealth of living beings. This "more multiform and more richly endowed" structure is also the condition of the greater "unity" of an organism. Thus it is set down to the credit of the "best-made" animals that they cannot be cloven or mutilated and still survive like many species of lower grade, an individual of which "rather resembles a complex of individuals than a single one." Thus—to use the language of a contemporary highly competent in this subject—we arrive at that "gradation of all living beings which forms the foundation" as of the Aristotelian, so "of our modern classification" or systematization.

At this point a false path opens which not all have been able to avoid. The Aristotelian system of graded types has been half involuntarily identified with a succession in time; and the Stagirite has been credited with a theory of development and descent totally foreign to him. Necessary as the warning is, however, against entrance upon this false path and the confusion of either Aristotle's or Goethe's theory of types and grades with Spencer's theory of evolution or Lamarck's and Darwin's theories of descent, the doctrines named are undeniably connected by inner ties of kinship. Moreover, it was necessary to learn how to distinguish lower from higher organisms before the thought could possibly arise that the latter had followed or had actually proceeded from the former; in short, that the morphological series coincides with the chronological or, indeed, with the genealogical series. But for Aristotle—and this is a truth to be kept carefully in sight—the organic world contained merely a juxtaposition of higher and lower, not a succession, and still less a derivation of the one from the other.

There is nothing to contradict what has just been said

in the fact that the form of expression, with our philosopher as with any other thinker and author, fails to hold these two fundamentally distinct thoughts strictly apart. It lies in the very nature of human thought and speech to reproduce and image forth connexions and relations by means of successions and processes, rest by means of motion. It is so in the case of geometrical figures, that is, spatial coexistences, which the mind prefers to make more readily intelligible by purely genetic constructions (cf. Vol. III. p. 210). If, then, the question in hand is entirely one of ranks or gradations in a series, it is difficult to keep the picture of progress, growth, increase, or conversely of regress and diminution, entirely at a distance. Aristotle's use of such expressions might, in some instances, lead even to the altogether erroneous impression that he had been inclined, at a certain stage of his mental development, towards the theory propounded in Plato's " Timæus " of a deterioration or degeneration of organic beings. In truth all idea of an actual evolution, whether of upward or downward tendency, is entirely absent from his mind. It is only within the circle of human civilization that he knows anything of real progress, of development actually accomplished, and that only to be in the end annihilated by catastrophes and brought back to the starting-point.

7. The scale of ranks of which we have been speaking extends beyond the animal world, and, in fact, embraces the totality of earthly things, beginning with the inanimate world and ending in man as the summit. Nothing in the exposition of this idea is so worthy of notice as the strong emphasis laid on continuity, and the conviction that qualitative differences even of the most striking kind rest in the last resort on quantitative differences or differences of degree. We are reminded of Xenophanes (cf. Vol. I. p. 162) and his doctrine of minute processes producing great total effects by their gradual summation. The assumption of continuity is the same in Aristotle, although it is only in a metaphorical sense that he speaks of progress or transition in passages like the following : " From inanimate things Nature passes on to animals so gradually that

the continuity of the change blurs the boundaries and often leaves us in doubt how to class the intermediate links.   First comes the realm of plants, within which the same variation by degrees is exhibited, but which as a whole seems almost endowed with soul in comparison with the rest of the physical world, but void of soul as compared with animals.   The transition from plants to animals is again continuous."   A reference is here made to those middle beings which entirely lack the power of spontaneous movement characteristic of the animal world, and which show dim, if any, traces of sensation.   Shell-fish, sea-anemones, and especially sponges, are named in this connexion.   "After these comes a gradual succession of beings, each with more life and movement than the last." The case is the same with the functions of living beings ; thus to the tasks of self-preservation and reproduction common to plants and animals, there is added the rearing of the young, which process again exhibits higher and lower stages according to its duration and the degree of "socialization."   But even in regard to mental and moral qualities the relevant passages in the biological works recognize little more than differences of degree between animals and man.   This relationship is most clearly discernible in the comparison of children with animals ; for in the former only a "kind of trace or germ" is to be found of the qualities displayed at maturity, and "the child-soul is as good as indistinguishable from the animal-soul."

8. The Aristotelian doctrine of what we now call the "natural series" has been censured as containing several contradictions, or, at least, as lacking in systematic exactness.   The accusation seems to us unfounded.   It is not Nature's exponent but Nature herself which in this case displays a want of strictness, perhaps one might say of pedantic consistency.   The true state of the case may perhaps be best brought before the mind by such an illustration as the following.   The world of organisms is like a rising succession of terraces, the different levels of which are thickly planted with trees.   But these trees have not everywhere the same power of growth.   It may happen,

accordingly, that individual branches shoot higher than their fellows, and perhaps even tower above the topmost foliage of trees rooted far higher up. Thus the point of view which Aristotle brought out with so sure a touch certainly does present us with a graduated series ; but its scheme does not include every detail, every quality that characterizes every group of living beings. The insects, for example, as members of the "bloodless," or (as we have called it since Cuvier's time) the invertebrate class, certainly stand lower on the whole in intellectual development than the blood-animals, or vertebrates. But that does not prevent certain families of insects, the bees and ants, from being superior in intelligence to many members of the vertebrate class. Aristotle was entitled, even bound, to notice these anomalies ; and if any blame at all attaches to his recognition of them, it can only relate to his tendency towards referring the facts before him to insufficient causes. It is not a defect but an excess of the spirit of system that we have to reproach him with, an excess which now and then even clouded and prejudiced his apprehension of the facts. He was right, for example, in holding the division into two sexes to be a characteristic of the higher organic forms, an instance of that specialization of functions which he understands so well, but which he here supposes—ungallantly enough—to be reinforced by Nature's effort to separate the higher from the lower, the form, as it were, from the matter. It is not without justification that he uses this principle as a kind of presumptive evidence against the self-fertilization of fishes, which many had affirmed, since sexual reproduction had been already sufficiently established in the case of many lower animals of the bloodless, or invertebrate class. But the charge of ignorance made against the defender of this error recoils upon the accuser when, on the ground of the same presumption, he maintains that throughout the vegetable kingdom every individual is two-sexed, thus lagging behind the common Greek opinion as embodied, for example, in the expression " male palm." The division of the sexes in the date-palm at least had, in fact, been known even to the ancient Babylonians, just as it is now to every Arabian child.

9. False generalizations of the above kind, or, more correctly, the confusion of mere tendencies with universally valid laws, can naturally be encountered not unfrequently in these products of an early stage of research. Occasionally a generalization, which thus overshoots the mark, occurs in connexion with a problem which the Stagirite has stated with correctness and characteristic acumen, but the true solution of which was placed beyond his reach by unavoidable gaps in his knowledge of the facts. Take, for example, the theory that the air taken in, in breathing, serves to maintain the vital heat within the body. This wonderfully apt guess at the true state of things is opposed, in the work "On Respiration," chiefly on the ground that, if the hypothesis were true, a product of combustion would be formed, and would be obliged to leave the lungs by the same passages by which the exciter of combustion had entered them. That this is the actual fact could not possibly be known to Aristotle, to whom oxygen, the exciter of combustion, and carbonic dioxide, its product, were equally unknown. But he overdid things when he rejected *à priori* an hypothesis which exactly corresponds to the reality, with an appeal to the supposed universal experience that the reception of nutritive material and the ejection of its residue never take place by the same channel.

Although here and elsewhere biological generalizations, and the method of comparison by which they are governed, have led Aristotle astray, this method nevertheless remains the foundation of his researches in physiology and anatomy, and at the same time of his most remarkable successes. Comparative biology, in particular comparative anatomy, provides one of his least-contested titles to glory. In this field he left his predecessors—for predecessors he certainly had—far in the rear. Among them we should give first mention to the genius who produced the work "On the Joints," contained in the Hippocratic collection. This writer, a man raised a heaven's breadth above all charlatanism, noble in temper and indefatigable in research (cf.

Vol. I. pp. 314, 315), could not, without the most thorough and comprehensive preparatory study, have written down such sentences as those in which he compared the abdomen of man with "that of all other animals," or affirmed the human ribs to be "the most curved of all."

10. After anatomical come physiological generalizations, which also were no novelty in principle. We recall the discussion of breathing by Empedocles and Plato, the theories of nutrition and growth propounded by the Hippocratics and Democritus, together with Alcmæon's attempt to discover a general cause for the death of organisms. In point of systematic fulness, it is true, none of the earlier writers came near him.

There is, to begin with, no little significance in the fact that the word " organic," in its modern and specific sense, makes its first appearance in Aristotle. Thus he calls the ψυχή, or soul, "the first entelechy of an organic physical body." He holds that whatever is capable of or destined for life must, as a fundamental condition, possess organs, of which the plant has few, the animal many, and the more the greater its perfection. These organs he distinguishes, as being composed of " unlike parts," from the structures composed of "like parts " which make up the organic body ; it is a distinction precisely corresponding to that made by modern science between organs and tissues. The homogeneous components are discriminated by their quali·ties, their hardness or softness, moistness or dryness, and so on ; the heterogeneous by their function, their operation and performance. In the treatment of these subjects we note the workings of a strongly-marked sense for similarity and sameness of kind, which ranks high, if not highest, among the virtues of the scientific investigator. As an example of a tissue, he comprehends under a single common notion, citing with approval a line of Empedocles bearing on the subject, such things as hairs, feathers, the hedgehog's spines, and—here, to be sure, no longer borne out by modern science—the scales of fishes and reptiles. Similarly, in the department of organs, he associates together the human arm, the fore legs of quadrupeds, and

the wings of birds ; while the human hand is paralleled
with the crab's pincers and the elephant's trunk. The last-
named, indeed, is almost too closely fitted by the charac-
terization which Aristotle gives of the human hand.   The
devotee of teleological thought, who regarded this "one
instrument in place of many" as given to the "living being
capable of most kinds of skill" for the sake of this skilful-
ness—in opposition to Anaxagoras, who had made the
intellectual precedence of man the result of his possession
of hands—ought properly to have answered the question
as to a similar purpose of the elephant's trunk in much less
pretentious language.

It is true that Aristotle did not advance to the distinction between mere analogy and strict homology resting
on essential similarity of interior structure. His faith in
what has been called "functional unity" in the organic
realm continually leads him to seek equivalents to the
tissues, organs, and functions of one class of animals in
all the others.   To the inner framework of bones he
compares the outer shell of the testaceous animals ; to
the blood of the animals which possess it corresponds the
nutritive fluid of the bloodless class ; even the heart and
the brain are matched by analogous structures. A remarkable instance is furnished by the assertion, confirmed by
modern research, of the exceptionless universality of urine-
like excretions, which Aristotle detects even where the
outward appearances are so different as they are in the
case of birds and snakes.   Naturally enough, right views
are here often mixed with errors.   Sometimes the two
are found in immediate neighbourhood, as when gills are
recognized as equivalent to lungs, but not (we have noticed
this already, see p. 61) as instruments of respiration.   The
link between gills and lungs is for Aristotle the common
task which he mistakenly assigns to them of cooling the
blood, in the one case by means of air, and in the other
by means of water.

This analogism takes its boldest flight in the passage
where the Stagirite brings into prominence the likeness
and at the same time the difference between animals and

plants by a memorable figure. He here utilizes Plato's theory of degeneration, and supposes an animal to become a plant by retrograde modifications ; its generative organs move upwards, its head and mouth downwards, and the latter finally becomes a root, drawing nourishment from the earth. In this way is reached the last stage of this reversed development, the governing fact of which is a decrease of vital warmth. For Aristotle did not, as we do, draw a strict distinction between warm-blooded and cold-blooded animals ; but he fancied he could trace a more and less of warmth throughout the animal series, in which warmth by its physical operation expanded the animal body, erected it, and increased its mobility, while cold exercised a dwarfing effect. Here we have a generalization, based on one-sided physical considerations, which clearly over-shoots the mark, and which, moreover, was not regarded by its author as free from exceptions. Its foundation probably lay in the perception that warm-blooded animals are the most perfect, and the bloodless animals on the whole, "all but quite a few," smaller than the animals with blood.

But while the numerous threads of analogy running through all stages and classes of organic beings thus apply to the means which serve the performance of like tasks, a residue is left over for which such connecting purposes are no longer demonstrable. When faced by such whims of Nature as the nipples of male mammalia, we speak of rudimentary or evanescent organs, anomalies to which the key must be sought in the theory of descent. Aristotle, to whom this resource was denied, speaks in such cases (just as Schopenhauer did so much later) of parts which are only present "by way of indication," as if the formative spirit of Nature were unwilling entirely to dispense with an element in its design which has often proved service-able even in those cases where it answers no purpose.

11. Some leading points of Aristotle's physiology we have already been obliged to touch on ; a summary account of his teaching in this department will bring once more before our eyes the weakness of his investigation of causes.

Food must be mixed in order that the parts of the body, composed as they are of all elements, may be enabled to replace their loss of substance at every point. The reception of nourishment is followed by its transformation, its digestion or elaboration, which Aristotle is not the only one to describe as a "cooking." On the contrary, the term is a piece of primitive popular physiology. The ripening of fruit under the influence of the sun's heat ; the preparation of the ripened fruit or other food at the domestic hearth ; lastly, its further softening or dissolution within the warm animal body,—here are three phenomena which the Greeks, like other peoples, had from the first been inclined to regard as three stages of essentially one and the same process. Indeed, the same word ($\pi \acute{\epsilon} \psi \iota \varsigma$, preserved in our "pepsin," "dyspepsia," etc.) denotes cooking in the proper sense just as much as digestion ; while the nearly-related $\pi \epsilon \pi \alpha \acute{\iota} \nu \omega$ is applied to the first of these stages, the ripening of the fruit. The Latin *coquo* is used in the full compass of the three meanings. It is a little different with the German *kochen*, "to cook," the extended use of which is found only in poetical or technical language. Thus fruit ripened by the Arabian sun is spoken of by Schiller, in his "Spaziergang," as "that which Arabia cooks," and a digestive trouble of Martin Opitz is specified by the statement that "his stomach soon ceases to cook." The more backward physiologists of even the nineteenth century still spoke of digestion as a cooking ; for example, take a passage in Hegel's "Encyclopædia." That which is here peculiar to our philosopher seems to be only the following. In this cooking, or transformation by animal heat of the crude and ignoble into the refined and perfected, he believes himself able to detect different gradations. Thus phlegm or mucus seems to him the product of a first or provisional cooking ; on the other hand, of all the nutrient fluids, it is the blood which is produced by the last definitive stage of the process.

The products of incomplete cooking and the residues left over at each stage of the process form, in contrast with the blood, the means of building up and keeping in repair the less noble portions of the body. For each of the nutrient fluids reaches the part which needs it: the blood, as the noblest of the fluids, goes to the noblest of the tissues—a title which is awarded to the "flesh and the substance of the other instruments of sense." In regard to these matters the body is compared to a household in which the best food is given to the free inmates, the inferior food and the leavings of the best to the servants, while the least valuable part goes to the domestic animals. The blood, of whose circulation Aristotle knows nothing, is prepared in the heart, which he names "the source of warmth and of sensation," the "hearth," and, because of its sheltered position, "the acropolis of the body." From it as centre the blood flows to all parts in ever finer and finer division, much as in a well-tended garden a similar purpose is served by "watercourses starting from one head and spring, but parted into a continually increasing number of channels."

Aristotle, of course, could not have given the highest rank in the organism to the flesh if he had not been unacquainted with the nerves and their functions as well as with those of the brain. Concerning this ignorance, there can be no doubt: we have already alluded to it several times (cf. pp. 57 and 143): the only question that remains is whether he simply lumped the nerves and the sinews together (in accordance with the root meaning of the word, as it survives, *e.g.* in *nervus rerum*), or whether he distinguished some of the former from the latter. This ignorance of the nerves is associated with a similar ignorance of the muscles and their functions: he had no separate acquaintance with them, but comprehended them under the general term "flesh." He neither supposed sensory stimuli to be conducted from the periphery to the centre by nerves—a task which he seems rather to have assigned to the veins—nor regarded motor stimuli as conveyed by nerves from the centre to the periphery and there taking effect through the muscles. On the contrary, he imagines those impulses to arise in the heart and to be communicated to the bones by the tendons and sinews themselves. Thus his intrinsically apt comparison of the skeleton to marionettes is only half correct in its working out. To the wood and metal of the puppets there correspond, rightly enough, the bones; but to the governing strings merely the sinews and tendons. We shall be led back to the question of the mechanism of sensation and the organs of sense by the Stagirite's theory of the soul; in the mean time, however, we must pass in survey that part of his physiology which stands at a much higher level than these rudiments of a doctrine of nutrition and movement, namely, his doctrine of reproduction and development.

CHAPTER XIV.

ARISTOTLE AS AN INVESTIGATOR OF NATURE.

(CONCLUSION : EMBRYOLOGY.)

1. THE work "On the Generation of Animals" forms the conclusion of the biological writings preserved to us, even including the psychological treatises. And as this whole group of books follows the "Organon" and the whole collection of physical works, we might expect to find here a culminating height of intellectual maturity. This expectation is not disappointed. We light, first of all, on an extraordinary piece of self-correction. Fire is removed from the series of elements, and now conceived as a phenomenon accompanying processes of which any of the three remaining elements may be the seat. That the unnatural may also be the natural in its own kind, and unnatural only in the sense of being an as yet incompletely triumphant tendency, that in general there is nothing truly irregular or fortuitous, that, on the contrary, all exceptions to valid rules are in truth merely the outcome of conflicting causes,—this is a series of thoughts to which Aristotle has here given either precise expression or a nearer approach to precise expression than anywhere else in his works. With this agrees the more frequent and emphatic protest against inadequate observations, against illicit generalizations and "empty" generalities, against too far-fetched explanations, against the preference of reasoning to fact, against the arbitrary substitution of plausible conjecture for the actualities of perception.

There is, in truth, an abundance of actual observations collected in these books. The author appeals to ocular evidence with unusual frequency and unusual emphasis. It is no diminution of his merit that he owes the fundamental "method of embryological research which up to our own times has been the most fertile in results" to a predecessor, the author of the book "On the Origin of the Child," contained in the Hippocratic collection. This method is described by its originator as follows: "If a man will set twenty or more eggs under two or more hens, if he will take away and break an egg each day, beginning from the second and going on till chickens are hatched, he will . . . find everything correspond to my description, so far as a bird can be compared with a human being." This "conception worthy of genius" rested on the fact that in truth "it is possible to draw inferences from the development of the chicken to that of the mammals." Thus comparative embryology was founded and a path entered upon which in antiquity was trodden by Aristotle alone, which still remained choked up during the Middle Ages, and which was first reopened and pursued further by a great Italian of the Renaissance, Ulisse Aldrovandi (1522–1607). What chiefly distinguishes the achievement of Aristotle is, in the language of the contemporary just quoted, "the universal vision which seeks to comprise in one view the embryological relations of all known species of animals," and which, by the side of many malobservations, brought to light an astonishing number of facts, some of them destined not to be rediscovered till the nineteenth century, relating to the development of the most diverse species of animals, notably the Selachii (cf. p. 57) and the cephalopods.

Aristotle's sense for correlations finds here again a wealth of opportunities for exercise. We meet with observations bearing on this point which arouse the astonishment of modern embryologists. Thus Aristotle knows and describes that replacement of the placenta by lobes (termed by him "cotyledons"), which is associated with the characters of the ruminants and the porcine family of mammals. The most pleasing effect is produced when in such cases Aristotle does not enounce dogmatic judgments steeped in the spirit of system, but cautiously weighs the facts, and only comes to a decision with some hesitation. Thus the position of the pig causes him, justly, as our specialists know, considerable perplexity: for the sow's young are both several in number and fully developed —several as is the case with the many-toed animals, fully developed as is the case almost solely with the single-hoofed and double-hoofed animals, to which the pig in truth belongs. Is, then, the pig's place in the system to be determined by the one or the other analogy? Aristotle decides for the second alternative, and, at the same time, attempts to account for this exception to the conditions prevailing in the double-hoofed class by considerations founded on the smallness of the animal and its abundant nourishment (presence of a considerable surplus available for reproduction). This example may in addition serve to illustrate the influence which Aristotle as classifier allows to the facts of development as well as to anatomical facts.

2. Perhaps the most noteworthy masterpiece of Aristotelian subtlety and indefatigability in research and reflexion is provided us by his discussions on teratology. This theory of monstrosities or malformations evidently rested on foundations supplied by the observations of soothsayers and sacrificing priests. To these may well have been added facts noted by animal-breeders of all kinds. Yet no one would ever have expected from the all-embracing encyclopædist so thorough a treatment of this special branch as he actually gives us. For example, that extremely rare monstrosity, the two-headed snake, is not unknown to him; he is aware that malformations do not occur among bees and wasps; and the only mistake he makes is in naming these particular species instead of the general class of insects in which they are contained.

Still more astonishing, though perhaps of much more doubtful value than this extensive knowledge of the facts, is the wealth of points of view applied to the explanation of them. Thus the question is raised whether there is not a connexion between the larger or smaller number of young produced at one time and the occurrence of superfluous or defective limbs. Evidently there is here a dim perception that excess or defect of structural material may be acknowledged as the common cause in the two cases. Again, the crowding to which the eggs of many oviparous animals are subject is taken into account as endangering the unimpaired development of the young. Yet another point of view is the following. Malformations are represented as most frequent among those animals whose young come into the world before they are fully developed; the imperfect development and the incomplete resemblance to the parents are already steps on the road towards monstrous formations. Then the supposed greater frequency of malformations in the male than the female sex—a supposition, as our specialists assure us, exactly contrary to the truth—is immediately referred to a cause with that facility of explanation which is already familiar to us, and which is so often fatal: the fault is said to lie with the greater warmth and consequent greater liveliness and mobility of the male embryo, which is thus exposed to greater risk of injury than the female.

Since, with our philosopher, monstrosity passes for an extreme case of dissimilarity between offspring and parent, the problem of atavism or reversion becomes very closely connected with the teratological problem. The fact that children "resemble remote ancestors" is well known to him. By way of explanation he points to the circumstance that the parents are not merely such and such definite individuals, but also representatives of larger groups in which they are included. As soon, then, as the tendency towards the reproduction of the parents (primarily of each parent) is from any cause weakened, it is supplanted by the in themselves weaker tendencies towards the reproduction of the more distant types, of the ancestors (we might add, of the people or race), of humanity, finally of the animal type in general.

3. Here it deserves to be noticed that in our days Charles Darwin coupled in exactly the same way the tendency to reversion with the tendency to dissimilarity

or variation, and this last with the occurrence of monsters. But there are two momentous differences. For Darwin, as the advocate of a theory of descent, reversion always means the recurrence to an ancestral and never to a merely generalized type. But further—and here it may be doubtful whether the ancient or the modern investigator comes nearer the truth—Darwin seeks to explain atavism by the hypothesis of pangenesis, while Aristotle employs the atavistic phenomena themselves as weapons against that hypothesis, which had already been championed by the Hippocratics. If the reproductive material (it is somewhat after this fashion that he expresses himself) is to contain contributions from all the parts of the body, solid as well as liquid, etc., and if this is the cause of the resemblance between parent and offspring, what are we to say of such a case as that reported from Elis, in which a Greek woman had relations with a negro, but the negro-type did not appear till the second generation? How is such a re-emergence of the negro characters to be explained by material transportation? Where were the particles that served for such transport in the intervening generation? They were present, we should answer, with Darwin, in this one generation, and often in a long series of generations, as latent germs, and owed their final development to favouring conditions which are unknown to us. This, however, is not the Stagirite's only argument against the hypothesis. Children resemble their parents in gesture as well as in feature: what transference of particles can have produced such resemblance? A beardless youth begets a son who in time becomes a bearded man, though no part of his father's as yet non-existent beard could have gone to the making of him.

4. What are the circumstances which determine whether the child to be born shall be a boy or a girl? This problem, at the present moment still unsolved, gave early and frequent employment to natural philosophers and physicians. The practical interests as well of parents as of stock-raisers, and the enigmatic nature of the process itself, roused in equal measure a desire to let in some light

upon this darkest corner of nature's life. But nothing was available except hypotheses, which, for the greatest part, were crude and fantastic, and bore, in addition, the stamp of the *à priori*. The right and the left—as the worthier and the less worthy sides of the embryo, or of the reproductive chamber and mechanism, the greater or less warmth of that chamber—such were the factors which did chief duty as explanations both in philosophical and medical literature, and which even brought practical measures and maxims in their train. Aristotle discusses these theories with great exhaustiveness, and in part at least, it may be added, with great success. To preconceived opinions he opposes ocular evidence, the result of numerous dissections of animal and human embryos ; he is also acquainted with cases of amputation which contradict the theories in question. There is much point in his reference to the occurrence of twins of different sexes in cases where those theories would exclude one or the other sex altogether. He is more successful in his polemic against Anaxagoras, who had followed Parmenides (cf. Vol. I. p. 183), against Leophanes and also Empedocles, than he was against Democritus. The latter had laid the responsibility for the result on the preponderance of the male or the female generative material, a theory which, in attributing generative material to both sides, was at least in better correspondence with facts now established than the Stagirite's objection based on the supposed merely stimulative and formative influence of the male element. His own answer to the much-discussed question is to the effect that the production of a girl is the result of insufficient nourishment of the embryo, and that this insufficiency depends on the age of the parent or parents— his exposition varies on this point. The epoch of full maturity is, he holds, reserved to the propagation of boys, the preceding and the following time to that of girls. As late as half a century ago there were not wanting statisticians and men of science who imagined that the general average of the facts of experience sufficiently supported this theory. The researches of the last decade seem to have finally established the inadequacy of this as of every other yet propounded attempt at explanation.

5. There is still another part of this field in which the authority of the Stagirite has continued to make itself felt for an astonishingly long period of time. We refer to the hypothesis of the spontaneous generation of comparatively highly-developed animals. Many kinds of insects, all shell-fish, and a not inconsiderable number of vertebrates, namely fishes, were supposed by Aristotle to come into being spontaneously—an error which a highly gifted Italian (Francesco Redi, 1626–1697) was the first to escape in his "Experiments on the Generation of Insects." It was imagined that plants and animals might spring partly from mud, partly from wet sand, partly from putrefying matter, under the influence of the "vital or psychic warmth" bound up with an air-like substance ($\pi\nu\epsilon\hat{\nu}\mu a$). We are reminded of Anaximander's doctrine of the origin of organic beings (cf. Vol. I. p. 54), which, like the doctrine of the primary vortex, became the common property of the nature-philosophers. Aristotle is in truth here under the yoke of hylozoism; thus, in speaking of the universal dissemination of the vital or psychic warmth contained in all fluids, he cannot refrain from drawing the inference: "So that in a certain manner everything is filled with soul." We ask in amazement how the same man who achieved so many triumphs in this department of research was able to fall at the same time into such grave errors. The answer to this question will be somewhat as follows: The knowledge of a few fundamental facts of sovereign importance in this field was first acquired by means of the microscope. With the ignorance of these facts was coupled a hardly avoidable misunderstanding of many ambiguous experiences, a misunderstanding illustrated by precise and apt parallels in even the most recent past. The extreme teleological view of nature and the, so to speak, atavistic tendency to assume the animation of all matter operated in the same direction. In these influences we may recognize the factors whose product, so long as it is not analyzed, is so well calculated to rouse our astonishment.

Thus Aristotle knew nothing of the fusion of the male and the female generative products. The mammalian egg was unknown to him. As we have already remarked, he grossly misunderstood the mode in which the male element operates. The motive and formative power which he made the sole function of that element was thus readily attributed to a different source of energy and heat. If he went on to regard the sea-slime as the origin instead of the mere nursery of the life with which it teems, his error was no worse than that committed by the eighteenth and nineteenth century defenders of spontaneous generation. They pointed to two vessels kept in the same place, one of which showed no trace of organic life, while such life swarmed in the other, this having been filled with an infusion serving as they thought for the generation, but really only for the nutrition of low forms of life. Spallanzani (1729–1799) and Pasteur (1822–1895) were the first to carry Redi's demand for the exclusion of all organic germs to such a pitch of stringency that the old error collapsed. Again and again experimenters had believed themselves entitled to deny the presence of germs, where in reality all that could rightly have been affirmed was in the one case the absence, in the other the presence, of conditions favourable to their development. This same confusion of favouring circumstance with originating cause is illustrated in Aristotle by an instance of almost amusing *naïveté.* All shell-fish, he teaches, are generated spontaneously, and that out of frothy slime. Thus localities previously free from shell-fish are found tenanted by them as soon as loss of water has made them slimy. By way of *experimentum crucis* the two following instances are adduced. When a fleet had lain for some time at anchor off Rhodes, and the potsherds which during this stay had been thrown in large quantities into the sea became coated with slime, numerous oysters were found attached to them. But that oysters do not themselves produce any generative substance is proved by another incident. Some sea-travelled Chians wished to lay out an oyster-bed on the coast of their native island. They employed for this purpose oysters from the bay of Pyrrha, which was almost land-locked and exceedingly rich in all species of marine delicacies, a kind of Lesbian *mare piccolo* (cf. Vol. II. p. 259). The attempt failed. For though the shell-fish transplanted to the coast of Chios increased considerably in size, little or no addition was made to their numbers. What this incident really teaches is the fact, for which there are also other grounds of belief, that the conditions sufficient for the thriving of the adult specimens are not always adequate to ensure the breeding of oysters. One of these conditions, the sheltered situation, was, as Aristotle reports, known and heeded by the Chians. Their choice may have fallen on the spot where the strait between the island and the mainland is still further narrowed by the adjacent group of the " wine-islands." Other conditions, such as the presence of numerous objects affording a hold for attachment (such as the potsherds in the former instance, shells, fascines, etc.), or again the greater saltness of the sea-water, were probably unknown to them. Thus the young fry, which modern oyster-breeders often transfer to a special basin of the oyster-farm, did not succeed in attaining full development.

The thought, too, that countless invisible organic germs swarm everywhere, only waiting for a combination of favourable circumstances to enter upon development and growth, must have remained even more alien to Aristotle, who seldom looked beyond the immediately perceptible (cf. p. 108), than to many of his predecessors. If among these Empedocles (cf. Vol. I. p. 243), and to a certain extent Anaximander, did not disdain to employ transformational hypotheses to explain the adaptation of organisms to purposes, Aristotle, with his strong confidence in the purposefulness of Nature could not believe himself in need of such aids. Thus in respect of this great question he not only failed to advance beyond Anaximander, Empedocles, Anaxagoras, Archelaus, and Democritus ; he even remained in a measure behind them. But while we record and endeavour to explain this surprising mistake, we must not omit to notice that it was not one of fundamental principle.   The origin of life is a problem which the science of the future, too, will continue to investigate.   The fact that all attempts so far made at explanation have proved without result by no means excludes the possibility of the simplest forms of life being some day produced in the laboratory, or of proof being obtained that the necessary conditions for their production were present in an earlier stage of the earth's history but have now ceased to exist.   Not many will be content with Fechner's hypothesis that organic life was the original condition of matter, while all inorganic substances are the refuse or waste products of what once was alive.   And when we come to the view advocated by no less a person than Helmholtz, that the first germs of life reached our planet from some other cosmic body (enclosed in meteoric stones), even this postponement of the problem will hardly yield permanent satisfaction.

If in the course of this exposition we have been several times obliged to mention Aristotle's "vital or psychic heat," we have involuntarily brought to notice the close connexion which for our philosopher obtained between biological and psychological phenomena—a connexion which will appear in a still clearer light from our account of his theory of the soul.

CHAPTER XV.

ARISTOTLE'S DOCTRINE OF THE SOUL.

1. WE have already encountered Aristotle's conception of the soul. Psychic, organic, living—these are ideas between which there reigns the closest possible connexion. The "organic physical body" is for him the "potentially alive," while endowment with soul is the "entelechy" or realization of the potentially alive or organic. Thus the essential thing in the psychic is not, as with us, consciousness or sensation ; and when, for example, Aristotle speaks of the vegetable soul, we are not to understand him as merely extending and transferring what is found in the animal world to the subordinate realm of organic life. The meaning attached by the Stagirite to the word "soul" is best understood when we comprehend under it the whole set of properties which characterize the organic or living beings. But he is in the habit of designating by the expression not only the totality but also particular groups of these properties. As a rule, he distinguishes three such groups, and names them the nutritive, the perceptive, and the thinking soul. From the perceptive soul the appetitive soul is not sharply discriminated. But on occasion nutrition is divided, according as it subserves the mere preservation or the growth of the being concerned, and accordingly at this lowest stage of the soul-system two souls sometimes appear in place of one. In the ascending scale of beings the lower soul is as it were absorbed into the higher and more comprehensive soul ; " as the triangle is contained potentially in the quadrilateral " (in virtue of its divisibility by the diagonal), "the nutritive soul is contained potentially in the perceptive."

Plato's scheme of truly separate substantial souls, attached to different parts of the body, is wholly foreign to his pupil.

The vital force of the organism is compared to the visual power of the eye ; the one, like the other, is called the form of the corresponding matter. The soul is for Aristotle neither a species of body, like, for example, the spherical soul-atoms of Democritus, nor yet anything detachable from the body and capable of surviving it. The Greek language allows him to express the connexion between soul and body much as we should if we could say : " The soul is something of the body." It is, so he wishes to assert, something attached to the body, not something which can be separated from it. When the body is bereft of its soul, the latter ceases to exist, but so does the organic body itself, as a hand hewn off or hand of stone is not or is no longer capable of any function, and so in the true sense is no hand at all. Of the one limitation to which, according to Aristotle, the mortality of the soul is subject, we shall have to speak later on.

The definition of the soul as the "first entelechy of an organic physical body" has already become known to us. But the reference to "the first entelechy" still needs a word of explanation. Here, as elsewhere (cf. p. 86), it emphasizes a capacity as distinguished from actual exertion, somewhat as knowledge not in use may be contrasted with knowledge present to the mind, or the latent possession of qualities during sleep to their actual manifestation in waking hours.

2. Before expounding his own doctrine of the soul, Aristotle passes in review and examines the theories of his predecessors. The most remarkable feature of this polemic, which occupies the first of the three books " On the Soul," is perhaps the zeal and decision with which the close connexion between body and the soul is defended. Thus the Pythagorean thesis that any soul goes into any body is despatched by the rough retort that one might as well say that the carpenter's art goes into flutes. On the contrary, he urges, every exercise of art must use its specifically appointed instrument ; and for this purpose it

is not enough that the soul should simply use the body, rather must this particular soul be united with this particular body. This is a subject of which the Stagirite can never have enough ; he recurs to it again and again, meeting the opposite opinion sometimes with reasons and sometimes with ridicule.

In this battle against older views there is much that is very apt to give a false impression. For the polemic is directed, not only with Aristotle's accustomed dialectical acuteness, but also with special emphasis, against opinions which in their deepest root are near enough to his own. It is clearly this endeavour to mark the frontier between his own doctrine and a kindred but not coincident doctrine that produces the appearance of a deeper discord than actually exists. The doctrine, probably due to Philolaus, that the soul is a "harmony" of bodily factors, is one which we have already (in treating of Plato's "Phædo," Vol. III. p. 43) reduced to its true kernel, the principle that "psychic processes are a function of bodily factors." From thence it is not a long journey to Aristotle's formula : "The soul is an entelechy of an organic body." In the one case as in the other (remember the Aristotelian phrase : "The soul is something of the body "), there is a rejection of the hypothesis which demands a special, supernatural and incorporeal vehicle and generator of the psychic functions. It thus also becomes easy to understand how Peripatetics such as Aristoxenus and Dicæarchus could labour to bring that old doctrine into new vogue.

3. We return to the carefully cultivated field of the theory of sensation. There is great significance here in the recognition of the necessity of a medium for sight as well as sound. Whatever the nature of this medium may be, whether light is such a medium for the eye, or whether air serves this purpose for eye and ear alike, in any case Aristotle considers it established that "the movement propagated in this medium is that which causes sight." His teaching on this subject thus towers high above the crude views of the Atomists. While even Democritus explained sensation as a detachment of exceedingly thin husks and

films from the perceived objects and a penetration by them
of our organs, so that all intervening objects appeared as
impediments to the process, the Stagirite was perfectly well
aware that without such supposed impediment no perception was possible at all. Even an ant creeping on the vault
of heaven—Democritus thought—would be clearly visible
to us if only there were an absolutely empty space stretch-
ing from earth to heaven. Quite on the contrary—Aristotle
answers—if that intervening space were perfectly empty,
occupied by no medium, we should lack, not merely clear
vision, but all vision whatever, just as much as when there
is no intervening space at all and the object is held pressed
against the eye.

In the sense of touch Aristotle recognized a number
of different senses collected under a single name; for he
found included in it not only the contrast of hard and
soft, but also those of dry and moist and of warm and
cold (temperature-sense), together with others not expressly
named. When he divides the instruments of sense into
organs of mediate and organs of immediate perception,
he places the organ of smell in the first class along with
the ear and the eye, while the senses of touch and taste
at least appear to need immediate contact with the
perceived object. But this appearance, he maintains, is
deceptive. The true difference is only one of degree. It
is a question whether the contact is really immediate,
whether skin and flesh really are the seat of the sense
of touch. A sensation of touch passes unimpaired through
a membrane spread over our limbs (through a glove, to
suggest an example). Why should it not also pass through
the flesh, if not this but an organ lying behind it is the
true seat of the sensation? One might almost say that
Aristotle has here divined the *papillæ* of touch. In any
case, he was unwilling to dispense with an exact analogy
between the different departments of sensation.

The example of the tongue, which conveys to us
sensations both of touch and taste, shows, he says, how it
sometimes depends on an accident whether we distinguish
several senses or lump them together without distinction.

Had the same combination occurred over the whole surface of the body, taste and touch would have been fused for us into a single sense ; and if all our organs of sense were enveloped in a layer of air permanently attached to us, we should imagine ourselves to perceive sound, colour, and smell by the same organ, and these senses would appear to us as only one.

4. These acute and fertile thoughts are sometimes in conflict with touches of a barren spirit of system. The attempt to reconcile the five senses with the four elements had already occupied his predecessors. He himself begins by treating these efforts with gentle raillery ; but in the end he arrives at such a reconciliation by (strangely enough) not only restoring the unity of the sense of touch, but by also joining taste to it as a sub-variety. The result is an artificial parallelism, on which it is hardly worth while to linger. The eye (because of its partly fluid contents) is made to correspond to water, the ear to air, smell (because its object is a " smoke-like exhalation ") to fire, and, lastly, touch to earth.

On the other hand, it is a pleasure to note comprehensive generalizations, based on an abundance of observed facts, such as the following. Sensation is in abeyance when strong emotion (violent fear, for example), when absorption in thought or a strong sensory stimulus exerts a counteracting influence. In such conflicts, not only the feebler, but also the stronger stimulus is weakened. If, however, both impulses have the same intensity, they annul each other, and the net result is nothing. The same principle is at work in mixed impressions, which have less power than the simple ones. Here, too, we should place Aristotle's acknowledgment of the opposition between the emotional effect of sensations and the clearness of the information they give. This rule is exemplified on the one hand by the human sense of smell, the impressions on which have little accuracy (a small number of shades), but are continually accompanied by painful or pleasant feeling ; on the other hand, by those animals whose lidless eyes seem to convey to them few distinctions of colour, but strong emotional impressions (fear, and so on). Lastly, the Stagirite does not fail to recognize that our sensory mechanism has an upper as well as a lower limit to its receptivity, that there are thus stimuli of excessive as well as of insufficient intensity, and that the excess not only impairs perception, but in extreme cases may destroy the organ of sense itself.

In the scale of the senses touch takes the highest place. It was regarded by Aristotle as at once the most indispensable, for which reason it is not wanting in any animal, and as the one which has reached its highest refinement in man—a refinement which has the closest possible connexion with mankind's possession of under-standing. We are reminded of Diderot's saying, " Le toucher est le plus philosophique des sens." Even within our species higher intellectual endowment goes hand in hand with greater fineness of skin—a remarkable observa-tion, the soundness of which has to the present day been neither established nor disproved. Aristotle ascribes higher intelligence, or at least a higher capacity for intellectual development, to the blind from birth than to deaf-mutes, because the latter are denied access to oral instruction. But against this accidental advantage possessed by the sense of hearing is to be set the greater wealth of informa-tion which the sense of sight affords concerning the objects of the external world, clothed, as they universally are, with colour ; so that this sense yields the most important contributions towards the construction of the world of concepts.

5. In the special part of Aristotle's theory of the senses nothing is so remarkable as his endeavour to make the results obtained in one particular field do service towards the understanding of the whole province. It was by this analogism, as we have seen, that he was led to presume a medium of sensation even in cases where its existence can only be conjectured. Similarly, he sought to repeat the acoustic discoveries of the Pythagoreans—this time in the field of optics, and even in that of taste-sensations. The beauty of colours and the agreeableness of tastes

were supposed to rest, like the harmony of sounds, on a basis of numerical proportions. The analogy, indeed, was somewhat vague. The combinations of sounds which please the ear had been traced back to the length-ratios of the strings producing them by their vibrations. The Stagirite, however, is not concerned with the harmony of simultaneously perceived colours, but with their production by the mixture in different proportions of two colours which he assumed as fundamental—black and white. Similarly, the manifold variety of tastes was supposed to arise from different mixtures of two fundamental tastes— sweet and bitter. The pleasing effect of these combinations was conditioned by the simplicity of the combination-ratios. But mixture was not the only origin of colours. They were also produced by the clear shining through the turbid, or *vice versâ*; as, for example, the sun is white in itself, but appears red when seen through smoke or mist. This reduction of optical diversity to the duality of light and darkness, as the supposed effect of their shining through each other, recurs in Goethe's theory of colour. The attempt to explain beauty of colour was resumed by Schopenhauer, further developed by him and defended against attack. The difference between the two theories consists in this—that while Aristotle treats of the proportional shares of light and darkness in producing a single colour, Schopenhauer speaks of the "qualitative division of the retinal function." Thus red and green are declared to be "the two exactly equivalent halves of the retina's activity . . . orange is two-thirds of this activity," and so on.

6. Starting from sense-perception, the road leads through after-images (which were well known to our philosopher), then through the permanent residues of sensation or secondary images to the higher functions of opinion and rational knowledge. On the first of the stages, more particularly, he expatiates with all the clearness that could be wished. He is acquainted both with the continuance of a strong sensation after removal of the object which excites it, and with the occurrence of

complementary colours or negative after-images ; both of
these phenomena he is inclined to compare to the continued
operation of a mechanical impulse once given. But these
transitory after-effects are of less importance than the
permanent "residues of actual sensation" which remain
preserved in the images of memory. In the treatise
devoted to this subject our surprise is first aroused by the
elaborately illustrated exposition of the two fundamental
laws of association, the law of similarity, and the law of
contiguity. He is here following his teacher, Plato (cf.
Vol. III. pp. 46, 47), but he outstrips him by perceiving
that the bond of association acquires special strength from
emotion. For this is what it comes to when we are told
than even a "small resemblance" will cheat the coward
with the vision of an enemy, the lover with that of his
beloved. And the greater the individual tendency to such
emotion, the smaller is the degree of similarity necessary
to effect the illusion, that is, to rouse the associated idea.
These expositions are weakest in their attempts at physiological explanation. Those who are most distressed by
failures of memory are supposed to have an excess of
moisture in their organ of perception ; and, again, persons
of dwarfish size and disproportionately large in the upper
part of the body are said to have specially bad memories,
because the organ of perception, the heart, is pressed upon
by a heavy load. These errors, however, should be judged
leniently. They are only excrescences ; and that out of
which they grew, the endeavour to bring psychic qualities
and processes into close relation with physical, is altogether
worthy of respect. Thus, in proof of the close connexion
asserted, reference is made to the fact that a memory which
a persistent effort has failed to recall to the mind often
presents itself unexpectedly after the attempt has been
abandoned. Those efforts at recollection had set up a
physical process which the wearied searcher had no more
power to check than the man who has thrown a spear or
ball can stop it when once it has left his hand. Aristotle
distinguishes between those who firmly retain the impressions they have received, and those who can reproduce

them quickly and easily—a distinction which recurs in modern psychology under various designations, such as "exactness" and "readiness" of memory. It is at first surprising to learn that while memory is common to man and animals, recollection is peculiar to man. Here, however, Aristotle is distinguishing, as Plato had done before him, between, on the one hand, the continuance of an impression, or its reappearance as the direct result of repetition, and on the other the recovery of an impression by the help of one or more intermediate ideas, generally as the result of conscious effort. Whether the higher animals can be justly contrasted with man in this respect is perhaps as little certain now as it was then.

The product of memory is compared, quite in modern style, sometimes with a "picture" or "image," more often with the "impression of a seal." The remark is added that the earliest youth and the latest age are alike lacking in strength of memory. With the very young, impressions are all too fugitive; applied to running water, the seal leaves no impression. In the very aged, on the other hand, the receptive organ is as it were hardened, so that the impression has no depth or sharpness. Innate differences of mental qualities produce the same effects as differences of age. The too great quickness and the too great slowness of intellectual processes affect the sharpness and depth of the seal's impression in a precisely similar way.

7. Memory-pictures and dream-pictures are grouped together under the common name of "phantasies," or "phantasms." When they are memory-pictures, they are so by their relation to the primary images of experience. The emergence of sensory residues in the stillness of night and sleep is explained by the suspension of that which overpowers them during waking hours, the pressure of immediate sensation. We are familiar with the illustration of this thought by the image of the sun putting out the stars; and Aristotle makes a close approach to it when he speaks of a weaker flame being invisible by the side of a stronger. The first is not perceived till the second is extinguished. A comparison peculiar to the Stagirite is

that which has reference to an ancient toy—artificial frogs, which bobbed up in a dish of water when a layer of salt sprinkled over them was melted. In all the cases alike the disappearance of an obstacle permitted the emergence into the light of something previously suppressed.

The treatment of sleep and dreams is again weakest at the point where physiological explanations are attempted. The exhalations arising from the food and forced upwards by the vital heat, the loading of the head by them, and the consequent feeling of sleepiness, the cooling of the exhalations by the brain, the sinking of them so occasioned, followed by the cooling of the heart and the stoppage of its vital activity—on all this silence is more profitable than speech. On the other hand, we ought specially to notice that Aristotle deduces sleep from the refusal of the exhausted central organ to perform its office, on the ground that, if this were not the case, the separate organs of sense, being tired at different times, would sleep by turns. The purpose of sleep is, in his view, the preservation of life ; for all things made for motion are unable to move un-interruptedly, but must have intervals of rest.

Aristotle is here so little governed by the spirit of system that he readily admits the existence of certain con-tradictory phenomena of dream-consciousness. There are many cases in which it is observed that external stimuli reach persons even in sleep, that they even answer ques-tions addressed to them, that at least they experience sensations of sight and sound, touch and taste, "though in a weakened degree, and as if the object were at a dis-tance." It is admitted, further, that objectively weak stimuli are sometimes felt as unusually intense ; a slight noise may be taken for thunder, and so on. The first set of instances is explained on the principle that the sleeper's re-ceptivity for sense-impressions is at best greatly diminished. The explanation of the contrary phenomenon comes as a corollary to that of dreams in general. In waking hours the phantasms are drowned in the stronger sense-impres-sions, and the same thing occasionally happens to indivi-dual primary impressions of low intensity ; others, again—

favoured, we must suppose, by such circumstances as local proximity—are heightened because they are relieved of the usual competition with other and stronger stimuli. The first of these categories includes more particularly the sensations originating in the body itself. Such sensations occasionally come into prominence during sleep, having been to a certain extent suppressed during waking hours by stronger external stimuli. This latter phenomenon gives our philosopher a welcome opportunity to indulge that taste for compromise which we know so well.

The significance of dreams had been roundly denied by the champions of enlightenment. Aristotle makes an attempt to justify within certain boundaries even this piece of old and widespread popular belief. On the one hand, he contends that sometimes in the dream-state threads of consciousness are started which persist into the waking state. It may thus happen that now and again dreams become "signs and causes" of the actions that follow in the waking state ; more correctly it might be said that the true "causes" or beginnings are taken for the "signs" of actions because their influence upon the latter has remained unperceived. The second part of this attempted apology is of greater interest. "Eminent physicians" are said to have set a precedent by recognizing that "dreams are by no means unworthy of our attention." Suppose, for example, that a man dreams he is going through fire and is burnt by it. It is advisable to examine the parts of his body burnt in the dream. The cause of the dream may be a "slight heating," due to morbid changes, which escapes observation in the waking state for reasons rendered above.

8. But while certain classes of dreams are thus not entirely divested of significance, Aristotle's attitude towards this question is preponderantly that of the Enlightenment. Against the hypothesis of "god-sent dreams" he raises the objection, among others, that the dream-messages appearing to bear this character are not vouchsafed to the "best and most intelligent," but to "ordinary persons." We are reminded in a measure of those opponents of spiritualism

who at the present day express their surprise that the supposed "spirits" have hardly anything more to say than any chance circle of gossipers in any market town. On the other hand, the Stagirite is not entirely adverse to the belief in telepathy. He assumes a specially close relation in this respect between intimate friends and kinsfolk ; "movements"—which he does not particularize—proceed from human beings, and are most readily perceived by those who in the waking state concern themselves most about them. Still more obscure than this attempt to explain mysterious facts (real or supposed) is the reference to those persons, subject to the ecstatic state, who are so much the more impressionable by the "movements" coming from others as, by in a manner getting outside themselves, they lose the ballast of their own "movements." For the sake of completeness we note the not quite relevant fact that Aristotle is acquainted with the phenomena of somnambulism, that he gives a short account of them, and that in a lost passage of his "Problems" he tried to explain them.

9. "Phantasies" or "phantasms" are, as we have seen, the common names for secondary images of all kinds, whether those of memory or those perceived in dreams. We ask what is Aristotle's judgment on truth and error in this field. His utterances are here not without self-contradiction, but it is a contradiction which appears rather in the words than in the thought. In one place emphatic prominence is given to the point that phantasy is fundamentally distinct from affirmation and denial, that is, from assertion in general; that it is consequently taken out of the categories of truth and error. Again in another place "the majority of phantasies" are called "false" or untrue. The following is a probable solution of the contradiction. The single phantasy does not constitute an assertion which might conform to or conflict with the facts. Thus such a mere mental picture can deviate very widely from a judgment founded on knowledge and insight without actually contradicting it. For example, side by side with our conviction that the sun is larger than the earth, we retain

an image in our minds of the sun as "a foot in breadth."
But although the mental image puts forth no claim to
express a judgment, nothing prevents the percipient from
comparing its nature with the reality which in any wise is
mirrored by it. Thus the condemnation referred to, over-
severe as it is, becomes intelligible to us. For the secondary
image is mainly a "weakened sensation," that is, a copy
which in any case differs from its original in degree or
quantity. There must be added the combinations and
interlacings which arise among these copies, compared by
Aristotle with reflexions in water which a little undulation
will cause so to run into one another that all resemblance
to the originals is lost.

10. If the secondary images are thus steeped in error,
how is it with the primary impressions themselves? On
this point, too, Aristotle's pronouncements are somewhat,
but not too far, removed from full strictness of thought.
In more than one passage the veracity of sensation is
emphatically maintained, in a manner reminding us of the
Cyrenaics and of Plato's declarations in the "Theætetus"
(cf. Vol. II. pp. 233, 234; and Vol. III. p. 158). The sense-
impression is described as veracious so long as it remains
"on its own ground." For example, I see white; that is a
fact on which no doubt is admissible; but that the white is
a man's face may be true or false. Pleasing as it is to
find the actual sensation thus strictly separated from the
inferences thence drawn, it is a pleasure which we do not
enjoy for too long. We soon find that Aristotle did not
apprehend in its full generality or retain permanently the
thought which has here come to the surface. For though
he once describes sensations as true without exception, at
another time he speaks of the "error which attaches to
them," even though it be "in very slight degree."

This contradiction hardly seems to admit of any but
the following solution. In the one passage Aristotle considers merely the illusions depending on the incorrect
interpretation of received impressions, and refuses to see
in them any diminution of the truthfulness of those impressions. In the other passage he remembers those

differences of sensations which rest on individual anomalies
(the bitter taste of honey for the jaundiced is the typical
instance in ancient writers), and he is led thereby to limit
the universality of his former assertion.   He might have
classed both sets of cases under a common head.   The
man instanced by him as imagining himself to see a white
human face may possibly be mistaken only in his interpretation of the sensation he has received, or again, his error
may have begun still earlier, and, being colour-blind, he
may have seen as a greyish white what appears to others
as red.   It is no matter ; even in the second case we
cannot speak of the impression as false in the strict sense,
because, as Democritus aptly remarked, questions of true
and false are not decided by numbers (cf. Vol. I. p. 360).
A just judge will not lay much stress on the inconsistency
of the Stagirite.   He has on the one occasion neglected a
practically unimportant class of errors which at another
time he is not willing, for the sake of completeness, to
ignore entirely.

He is, in any case, excellently informed on the means
of overcoming the sense-illusions referred to, whether they
rest on abnormal or on normal misinterpretation, whether
they arise from physical and physiological or from pathological causes.   One sense—somewhat to this effect he
writes in a particular passage—corrects the messages of
the others ; thus sight, for example, corrects the error of
the sense of touch produced by crossing the fingers (cf.
Vol. II. p. 232), just as the sense of touch corrects the
numerous optical illusions.   It is a short step to the
thought that only the co-operation of several senses can
inform us on the objective qualities of things.   It is only
by this road that the general qualities (permanent and
variable) of sensible objects can come to our knowledge—
their form and magnitude, their number, rest, and motion.
Here one of Aristotle's familiar exaggerations (cf. p. 113)
makes its entry.   Having to establish the advantage which
a plurality of senses brings to their possessor, he does so
in drastic fashion by putting an extreme case.   Suppose
we had only one sense, and this was responsive to only

a single class of sensations. Suppose, for example, that we had no sense but that of sight, and that white was the only colour we could see,—a white, it must be added, containing in itself no differences of brightness, nor any variety of shades whatever. A very little consideration will show that all external objects would in that case blend indistinguishably ; separate things or forms, even rest and motion, would be no more.

It may here be fittingly observed that in numerous passages referring to the specific objects of the senses colour alone is spoken of as corresponding to sight, just as exclusively as smell corresponds to the olfactory sense. Aristotle seems as firmly convinced as Berkeley that distance, size, and form are perceived by the aid of sight only mediately, in a manner depending upon inference. The detailed elaboration of this theory must have been contained in a lost treatise on optics which was extensively laid under contribution by the great Aristotelian, Alexander. So far as the preserved works go, Aristotle speaks only of the co-operation of sight with other senses in cases where Berkeley expressly treats of inferences drawn from impressions of light or colour. Fundamentally, the two come to the same thing, namely, that all advance beyond the specific sense-impression is possible only by means of comparison and combination ; that is to say, by inference.

11. From " phantasy" two paths diverge, one leading to the thought that works with concepts, and the other to desire. Of the first, as the active exercise of reason or Nous, we shall speak later on. Here we merely note the significant fact that Aristotle always regards thinking in concepts as bound to and conditioned by the presence of mental images or representations. We fare in thinking much as we do in drawing. So little as we can draw a general triangle, being always compelled to give our drawing a definite size, just as little can we treat of the general properties of a triangle without summoning before the mind's eye a quantitatively definite triangle, though we may afterwards entirely disregard its special attributes. Without phantasy or mental images, again, desire is impossible.

We are specially concerned here with deliberative or consultative phantasy.

In order to understand the *rôle* assigned to this last, it is advisable to consider, first of all, the other two ways in which the Stagirite conceives actions to come about with the help of knowledge or experience. In the one case, desire appears and "says to the living creature: 'Let us drink.' Perception adds: 'Here is something drinkable.' Forthwith the creature drinks." In the other case, the road followed is that of the syllogistic procedure. "Men must walk; I am a man; I must walk." Naturally our philosopher is well aware that man is not always like a thinking-machine. He hastens to follow up examples such as the above by the remark that the "manifest" or self-evident part of such an argument, the minor premiss: "I am a man," is frequently suppressed in practice. We must not be too surprised that he does not go a great deal further and abandon altogether a view of human action which is, to put it shortly, untrue to life. The man who had discovered and systematized the syllogism could not be expected to put it on half-pay, so to speak, with no duties but those of revision. It is thus extremely instructive and highly pleasing to learn that this more correct view did at least casually dawn upon him. Between the instinctive action first mentioned above, and the syllogistic action governed by general notions, there comes the already-mentioned "deliberative" or "consultative" phantasy, which in a passage of the work "On the Soul" is described as follows. A living being is confronted with a choice which cannot be made without comparison and the discovery of a common measure. But the kind of consideration involved—this is roughly what we are told—is of so primitive or simple a kind that "it does not seem to bear the character of an 'opinion;' indeed, it lacks the syllogistic form." Here, obviously, we have a confession, let slip half involuntarily by the Stagirite, that there is another sort of thinking besides that which works in concepts, that, as we say now, there is in reality an inference from particulars to particulars. This middle stage is not assigned to man only, but to some of the higher animals as well, seeing that "beings," in the plural, are spoken of as deliberating. Doubtless these animals are conceived of as often remaining at the lowest stage of instinctive action ; and we shall hardly go wrong if we attribute to Aristotle the thought that the undeveloped man (child or savage) frequently acts at this lowest level, and even the fully-developed man sometimes, when he is swayed by emotion or led by blind custom.

CHAPTER XVI.

ARISTOTLE'S DOCTRINE OF THE SOUL.

(CONTINUATION : THE PROBLEM OF WILL.)

1. WE have now reached Aristotle's discussion of the problem of will, concerning which we have already made the anticipatory remark that it would appear "comparatively free from inconsistencies." Comparatively, it may be, but not completely. One might almost be tempted, were the subject not entirely incapable of numerical statement, to say that the Stagirite was nine-tenths determinist, one-tenth indeterminist. It was, as we have seen, quite without justification that his treatment of the notion of chance has had read into it an attack upon universal causation. With equal injustice he has been supposed to be defending freedom of the will as something morally valuable in passages where what he has in view is only spontaneous action, such as is common alike to men and animals, to children and adults. The main point in his teaching is that characters, dispositions of will, moral qualities, belong to the mature human being ; they are modes of action which have become fixed by habit. We are certainly not bound for that reason to regard them as absolutely unalterable ; but still they cannot be discarded or fundamentally changed at mere pleasure, by an arbitrary resolve. Each single act of a man is the outcome of his character at the time. There is a passage in the "Ethics" where it is said that we can at will strike a fellow-man or offer him money ; no external coercion compels us to perform or to abstain from either act. So far they are voluntary actions, standing in our power.

But the elements of character from which these actions spring, the brutality that comes to light in the blow, or the corrupt purpose manifested in the offer of money, are conditioned by our past life : they are the result of habit and education. Aristotle declares with full emphasis, and almost in the words of a modern determinist, that " we cannot, indeed, directly will to be different from what we are." The vicious man can no more shake off his vice by an act of will than the sick man his sickness. But this comparison by no means carries with it the thought that every moral malady, any more than every physical malady, is incurable. The systematic treatment which in the one case devolves upon the physician is in the other case a matter of training and education, which latter may quite conceivably be self-education.

Hitherto, the Stagirite's thought moves entirely on the lines of modern determinism, which was developed in an earlier age by the Stoics. But at this point he enters upon a new and unexpected path. Responsibility, and that for virtuous actions much more than for vicious, demands a justification. Aristotle provides one, as he thinks, by attaching responsibility not to the ready-formed character, but to the character in the make. Admitted that the individual act is the outcome and result of a well- or ill-formed character, that this formation proceeds chiefly through habit, and that each new repetition of an action strengthens and confirms in ever-increasing degree the disposition of mind from which it springs : the *choice* of character is yet represented as having been originally in our own hands. We are reminded of the choice of destinies in Plato's " Republic " (cf. Vol. III. p. 105). Great is our astonishment, and many are the objections which throng upon our mind. How, for example, can the criminal's child, born with vicious dispositions and bred to vice, have full freedom in such a choice ? But while Aristotle thus saddles himself with many an impossibility, he would not have been the powerful thinker that he was if he had simply stopped here. He could not acknowledge so generously the power of habit, and at the same time entirely overlook the

influence of the still more potent factor of natural endowment which is presupposed in habit. While considering
natural endowment, he obviously falls into perplexity
about his own doctrine, and brings against it an objection
of the following form. As against the assertion that we
choose our character, it may be urged that all creatures
strive after that which seems to them to be good (that
is, in this case, profitable, healthful, or pleasurable). If,
then, an individual assigns this quality to a particular end,
he does so on the strength of a mental representation or
"phantasy." Thus the former thesis cannot be maintained
erect unless we concede the power of choosing not only
one's character, but also one's mode of representing things
to the mind. Our philosopher evidently finds it extremely
difficult to reconcile himself to such a concession. He
cannot forget that natural endowment here counts for
something, and indeed plays a decisive part. An anxious
suspicion may well have insinuated itself into his mind,
that his position involves a circular argument: choice of
character depending on presentations, presentations depending on character already acquired. He falls into
bewilderment, and cannot come to a real decision. To
the adverse thesis he gives the most forcible formulation
possible: "For the good as for the bad, the supreme end
of life is fixed by natural bent or some other such cause,
and is permanently regarded as such." But presently he
recoils from the consequences of this admission ; he yields
himself prisoner to the widespread popular opinions which
he is unable to coin afresh, and he exclaims: "If all this
is true, how could virtue be any more voluntary than vice?"
He is afraid of endangering free-will, and with it, as he
thinks, the value of virtue ; for this reason he breaks off
the whole discussion, and abandons arguments the validity
of which he is unable to destroy. The investigation which
he has spun out to such great length, often with great
refinement and depth, has thus been all in vain. Or
perhaps it has not been wholly fruitless. In cutting the
knot Aristotle may have hoped to convince his hearers and
readers: he did not convince himself. This is betrayed

by his tone, which from sentence to sentence becomes
more timid and uncertain ; it is proved by the constant
accumulation of qualifications, limitations, and parentheses.
At the beginning of the discussion man is described as
the "author" of his disposition ; presently he is so only
"as it were," then "to a certain extent," and lastly he is
only "in a manner the co-author" of his character. Just
such language might be used by a convinced determinist,
—might, in fact, have been used by the Stoic Chrysippus,
who neither denied the effectiveness of "intense volitions"
nor detached them from the general network of causes,
but recognized them as intermediate links of the utmost
importance and indispensability.

2. That Aristotle's peculiar doctrine of freedom struck
no deep root in his soul may be inferred, we think with
certainty, in another way. From that doctrine there flow
consequences in the field of criminal responsibility which
Aristotle was far removed from drawing. If the evil-doer's
responsibility were confined to his choice of his own
character, the habitual criminal would escape with little
or no punishment, while the youthful offender, who has
just chosen his character, would have to be punished with
great severity. But with our philosopher there is no trace
of any such inference. His judgment on the punishment
due to an offence is not determined by any regard to that
original freedom of choice, its nearness or remoteness, but
simply and solely by considerations of social "utility,"
which he emphasizes in explicit terms. He confines himself entirely to the lines of a rational criminal jurisprudence
which regards the infliction of evils as justifiable only so
far as it serves to prevent the commission of future mis-
deeds. In this he even goes further than the majority
of modern criminalists. He refuses to accept drunkenness
as a mitigating circumstance. He cites with approval that
law of Pittacus which enacted severer punishments for acts
of violence committed in the drunken state than for similar
acts committed by sober persons. His aim was to produce
a deterrent effect on the drunkard by attaching a penalty
to his vice itself as soon as it led to the injury of others.

Legislation, says Aristotle bluntly, should aim at encouraging the one class of actions (those serving the general good) and at restraining the other class (those to the common hurt). If in such contexts he uses words like "voluntarily" or "in our power," he is not in the least thinking of that remote original choice of disposition, but merely excluding actions caused by "external force" or by unavoidable "ignorance." Possibly he does not always strictly maintain the distinction between the two meanings of those expressions.

We may add that the theory of punishment built on this foundation is in entire harmony with Aristotle's prevalent determinism. Punishment may follow, as subsidiary aims, the restraining of private revenge, the rendering criminals harmless, or their reformation (though with the short-term imprisonments of antiquity this last result was not much thought of); its main purpose is and remains, whatever may be said, that of intimidation. The lawgiver who aims at this may very well cherish the determinist view of human will. To the social motive proved insufficient he adds a more efficient motive; he seeks to weaken antisocial tendencies by throwing into the opposite scale a new factor, the fear of punishment—a fear which in the worst case is calculated to produce a wholesome effect, if not on the hardened soul of the criminal, yet on the more plastic soul of the onlooker.

3. The deterministic view which thus prevails with Aristotle is apparently broken through at a point on which we have already touched (cf. p. 106). But the object of his attack is there not in reality determinism, but the distinct, though cognate, fatalistic principle. If anything happens by necessity—so we are told in that passage of the work "On Interpretation"—no room is left for human action and the deliberation which precedes it. The fact that human deliberation and the actions which spring from it do often interfere with the course of things moves the Stagirite to a protest against the mechanization of the whole sum of happenings. It must not be overlooked that Aristotle is not here speaking strictly of human will; that

which he emphasizes in opposition to fatalism is not so much the so-called freedom of the will as the capacity for deliberation, for taking counsel with one's self and acting accordingly. Had he been required to enlarge his survey he would certainly not have denied that these deliberations have in each case a previous history, that they are conditioned by the deliberator's stock of know-ledge and power of thought, and not least of all, as our philosopher elsewhere emphatically acknowledges, by his emotions. But on this occasion the distinction between, on the one hand, what a later thinker (Epicurus) calls "automatic necessity," or the causal linkage of purely material processes, and the intervention of human thought and corresponding action on the other, has produced so deep an impression on him that he has lost sight for a moment of the common causal foundation underlying both kinds of processes. An earlier philosopher, for whom Aristotle professed no exaggerated esteem, might well have been here recalled to his memory. We have already said, in praise of Heraclitus, " that he constructed compre-hensive generalizations comprising both realms of human knowledge, as it were, with a mighty bow " (Vol. I. p. 63). He recognized, and the recognition took a high place in his system, the universal sway of order and law governing both spheres alike. The late successors of Heraclitus, the founders of the Stoa, may for their part have only too often overlooked the deep - rooted distinction in their acknowledgment of what was common, and so have leant towards fatalism ; Chrysippus, the true shaper of the Stoic doctrine, will ever be remembered as the first to discriminate strictly between the deterministic theory which acknowledges the exceptionless rule of cause, and the fatalistic theory which, in addition, ignores or eliminates the part played by acts of human will.

CHAPTER XVII.

ARISTOTLE'S DOCTRINE OF THE SOUL.

(THE DOCTRINE OF NOUS, OR REASON.—CONCLUSION.)

1. WE enter upon the second of the paths which lead from the lower ground of "phantasy" to the higher forms of human mental life (cf. p. 189). Or, to be more accurate, we have already trodden this path more than once. In treating of Aristotle's "principles of proof," we were introduced to induction as the instrument for the acquisition of these as of other "first" truths (p. 75). Still earlier we came upon the stages by which the soul climbs from the first fixation of a received impression up to art and science, that is, to pure theory and theory applied to practice (p. 55). These stages were declared to be first memory, then experience, which arises from the frequent repetition of similar impressions, and which comes to be nothing else than a "multitude of memories of the same object." Out of experience, again—or better, out of all the "universal that being a one as well as many has become firmly rooted in the soul "—we saw art and science take their rise.

The separate members of the series of living beings take a lower or a higher place in the animal world according as they share only in the lowest of these activities, or in the less elementary as well. To some animals, at the bottom of the scale, sense-perception alone is allowed ; to others, memory ; and to others again, the faculty of learning. This last is represented as conferred through the intermediacy of the sense of hearing—a sense extremely serviceable to the development of intelligence, though not unconditionally requisite, as the example of the bees shows.

True understanding is peculiar to man ; he alone has the power of forming general concepts, by means of which he mounts to the summit of knowledge.

It is, if not a directly authenticated fact, yet a highly probable inference, that in these lines of thought the founder of the Peripatetic school followed in the footsteps of an original thinker whose acquaintance the reader has already made, Alcmæon of Crotona, a physician with Pythagorean leanings (cf. Vol. I. p. 150). Thus we are once more confronted by the Asclepiad in Aristotle (cf. ch. vi.). The Platonist in him, the complementary opposite of the empiric, will appear in his doctrine of Nous, with its tinge of mysticism.

2. This doctrine, which can be traced back finally to Anaxagoras, is one of the most debated portions of the Aristotelian system. Theophrastus, Aristotle's immediate successor in his school, vainly wrestled with its difficulties. That he failed to gain a complete understanding of the doctrine is, indeed, more than we can affirm. But he was in any case at a loss how to answer certain obvious objections to it, or how to defend it successfully against attack. A precious fragment of his writings is preserved to us in which he sets out so many difficulties with so much emphasis that we seem to hear the voice of an opponent rather than of a disciple. There is, at any rate, one inference which we may draw with tolerable certainty from this state of things, and that is that the author of the Nous doctrine did not expound it, somewhere outside the works known to us, with clearness and fulness sufficient to ensure its comprehension and acceptance.

We are reminded of Plato, and Plato in the last phase of his speculation, by the part of Aristotle's teaching which bears upon the continuance of the principle of Nous, or reason. While elsewhere the soul is for our philosopher, not indeed corporeal, but something inseparably attached to an organic body, the rational principle in man receives from him the same prerogative which the Platonic "Timæus" accords to the "reasonable head-soul" (cf. Vol. III. p. 38). Even this immortality, it is true, is not for

Aristotle a personal thing. The rational principle implanted in man before birth returns after his dissolution to the place whence it came, to the ether of the celestial regions—that ether which is immaterial because divested of all physical qualities except those of filling space and moving in it. In this respect Aristotle stands on the ground of an ancient and popular belief, which we have met with both in Epicharmus and in Euripides, and which was quite the predominant opinion at Athens about the end of the fifth century (cf. Vol. II. p. 84 ; Vol. III. p. 10). Aristotle has thus compromised between the teaching of his master and the current belief of the age. He took from the first the limitation of immortality to the rational part of the soul ; from the latter, its return to the heavenly element and the extinction of individual consciousness.

3. For the motives of this innovation we have not far to seek. Definitely and emphatically as Aristotle asserts the intimate union of the individual soul with the individual body, decisively as he repudiates the "entrance of any soul into any body" (cf. p. 176), the grounds of this anti-Pythagorean attitude do not reach as far as the point at which the soul appears as a purely intellectual factor. The greater or smaller susceptibility to particular emotions might seem to be connected by experience with the physical constitution of the individual; the same might appear to be true of the obstacles which impede intellectual activity; the irascibility of one or the stupidity of another might be charged upon their bodily peculiarities : the faculty of thought itself, as soon as and as long as it is actively exercised, displays the same features in all alike. There are no individual differences in A's and B's manner of proving the Pythagorean theorem. It thus becomes intelligible that the vehicle of purely intellectual activity should be regarded as a factor common to all men, emancipated from the limits of individual and physical particularity, and just for that reason delivered from the curse of mortality—as a factor whose origin is directly associated with the Deity, and which is endowed with only that kind of materiality which is furthest removed from the cruder

forms. We thus find ourselves in a position to understand our philosopher's celebrated asseveration that Nous alone enters into man from without, and is alone divine ; that its activity is in no way affected by the activity of the body. In immediate proximity to this statement is another in which the soul in general is spoken of as " more divine than the so-called elements," and its seat declared to be the heat enclosed in the breath of life ($\pi\nu\epsilon\hat{\upsilon}\mu\alpha$). But while this vital warmth is only " by analogy" regarded as the matter of which the stars are formed, Nous is itself clothed with the heavenly substance or ether, and is therefore alone of truly divine nature. Parallel with these gradations is the progressive refinement which leads from pure matter to pure form. This rising scale has its beginning, as we saw (cf. p. 86), within the series of the elements them-selves. As among these fire has most of the nature of form, so clearly the principle of life or of soul is in the same way pre-eminent over fire ; while the heavenly ether, as the garment of Nous, receives the highest place in this scale, and is described as pure, immaterial form. This analogism may perhaps strike us as somewhat sportive ; still, it is intelligible that the part of the soul which stands highest and at the greatest distance from the crudely material, is regarded as the vehicle of the most refined mental functions, as the cognitive principle to which man owes his knowledge of the highest and most general abstractions. Thus Nous is termed, on the one hand, immaterial, or all but immaterial matter ; on the other, " the form of forms."

4. These deliverances have certainly offered many a handle to criticism. As early a critic as Theophrastus asks why Nous, which enters ready-formed into the embryo, waits so long before manifesting itself in activity. Why does the child exhibit a lack of understanding ? What are the conditions and what the accompaniments of reason's awakening ? We should have expected so obvious an objection to have been known to and even anticipated by the author of the doctrine. Any one who likes high-sounding phrases may describe what appears to be

Aristotle's answer by saying that he substitutes the principle of adaptation for that of development. He compares Nous to the eyes of nocturnal animals which are blinded by the light of day ; and the comparison at least suggests the thought that only by gradual habituation to the glare of the highest truths can we become enabled to perceive them. For since Aristotle cannot possibly deny to the Nous in man the power of seeing these truths, it can hardly be idle conjecture if we attribute to him the thought that their full knowledge is conditioned by the training and adaptation of the cognitive organ. According to this view, Nous would not, properly speaking, become stronger during the period of growth, but would fare like an eye which gradually becomes accustomed to a brilliant light and so learns to bear it.

Another of Theophrastus's puzzles relates to "the origin of forgetting, deception, and falsehood." How is it possible —such, clearly, is the point of his question—to reconcile such loss and such clouding of the truth with the presence in us of an essentially divine, imperishable, and unchangeable principle of knowledge ? But here the statement of the difficulty is followed by at least the rudiment of a solution. Theophrastus adds doubtingly : " Or is it perhaps through mixture ? " In these words he points to a main element in the doctrine on which we have not yet touched. The Nous in man is delared to be twofold, or, when we consider it more accurately, of threefold nature—active, passive, and the mixture of the two. It is properly the first which is the divine and eternal principle ; it is wholly and absolutely energy and actuality ; it is unceasingly active, even though we are not always aware of its activity. (We are here, by the way, reminded of Lichtenberg's and Heinrich von Kleist's expressive saying : " It thinks in us.") This active principle is matched with a receptive or passive element comparable to matter and potentiality as opposed to form and actuality. It might be termed a mediator between the strength of the divine nature and the weakness of the human. The active Nous effects everything, the passive Nous undergoes everything ; the first is immortal, the second is not.   In regard to its particular nature, Aristotle is still more sparing of words than in the case of the active Nous.   It may be conjectured, not without reason, that he conceived its function only in shadowy outline, and that his thought lacked clear and full development for himself as well as for his reader.   In a certain sense, so Theophrastus tells us, the two kinds of Nous are two entities, but in another sense only one, just as one object is compounded of form and matter.

5. The whole theme is treated mainly by way of indication, and is full of enigmas.   How are we to understand the identity which Aristotle asserts between Nous and its object ?   We can, indeed, discover, with more than approximate certainty, how it is *not* to be understood.   Aristotle may not be credited with a confusion between a function or activity and its object.   Just as little can he have intended to maintain the mere subjectivity of the truths apprehended by Nous.   Thus, other considerations apart, he compares active Nous with light, which makes visible and lifts into true actuality those colours which, though previously only potential, were still objectively present. The following we imagine to be the true interpretation of that asserted identity.   If I cognize a sensible object, then besides the cognized form there is the matter united with it, which remains over as the mere substratum of it, given in point of fact but not penetrated by the mind, a kind of opaque residue.   This is not the case where knowledge relates, not to the concrete thing, the compound of form and matter, but to the pure form itself.   This object of knowledge is wholly cognized, wholly penetrated by the mind, wholly taken up into it.   In so far as this is the task of Nous, which is itself pure form—indeed the "form of forms "—Nous may be spoken of as identical with its object.

Further, how can Aristotle have arrived at the view that the active Nous is unceasingly at work in us, while our consciousness bears no witness to this uninterrupted activity of the processes of thought ?   It would be an insufficient answer merely to presuppose that there is no sleep without dreams, and thus no intermission of conscious life. For it is one thing to assume that our imagination or "phantasy" never takes holiday, quite another to suppose that the true intellect, the higher faculty of thought, exercises its powers absolutely without interruption. A better way out of the difficulty might seem to be provided by the observation that after beginning a piece of mental work, one sometimes finds one's self suddenly in presence of the result, without any consciousness of the path by which it has been reached. But even here it is not made an easy matter for us to rest satisfied. We have already seen how Aristotle found an exit from an at least similar *impasse* without assuming unconscious thought (cf. p. 182). The unexpected emergence of a memory for which a search has been begun and then abandoned, was explained as due to the continuance of a physiological process set up by the search. But it is quite possible that this solution, while sufficient in what he deemed a lower sphere, may have seemed to him inadequate where the functions of the true intellect were concerned. The most probable explanation is perhaps that the belief we are considering followed immediately from his conviction that the vehicle of thought is immaterial, seconded, possibly, by the analogy of the heavenly bodies, themselves moving without cease, which, like Nous, are "divine," and which occupy the celestial spaces whence Nous proceeds.

The Nous now lodged in our bodies is existent, active, and living from all eternity, but we have no recollection of this former life of it, any more than of its uninterrupted working in ourselves. This discrepancy between the theory and the testimony of consciousness needed explanation. The following consideration would seem to have opened the way for one. The mental faculty which preserves impressions is identical, or at least closely kin, with the faculty which has received them. But the receptive element in the soul, just because of its receptivity, must be something dependent, more of the nature of matter than of form, passive, and therefore vulnerable and perishable. In its vulnerability and perishability the ground is to be sought for the absence of all memory touching the previous history of the active Nous, or rational principle, at work in each one of us. We shall hardly err, we think, if we interpret Aristotle's hints as indicating that this was the road by which he arrived at the division of Nous into an active and a passive part.

But this division, when once accomplished, was bound to prove serviceable towards other ends as well. Just as that highest thought-principle, precisely because of its immateriality, could admit no suspension of its activity, so, too, it was subject to no enfeeblement or corruption. Where such undeniably appears, it is attributed, firstly, to the subordinate passive principle of reason, then to the body which for the time being houses it and the associated organs of the soul. Just as the man who is blind through senile weakness would have his full power of sight restored by a change of visual organs, so a change of the soul's instruments would restore the full power of thought to the psychically enfeebled. Aristotle thus seizes upon the expedient which is always ready to hand for those who, despite contradictory appearances, stand forth as defenders of the indestructible and invulnerable soul. The musician is in perfect health, his power unimpaired ; but from strings out of tune he can draw no sound that pleases, and from broken strings no sound at all.

6. Before we proceed, we have to bring into prominence an important distinction which hitherto has been mostly overlooked. Aristotle speaks of Nous sometimes in a narrower and sometimes in a wider sense, and, as his manner is, he does not inform the reader of the fact. Sometimes the term means for him the power of thought in general, that "by means of which the soul fashions thoughts and sets up hypotheses ; " sometimes it is used as the antithesis to all mediate knowledge, to all proof and all reflexion (*logos*). In these cases the function of Nous is represented by him as a "touching ; " it is compared with the physical senses as being, in a manner, a new sense of higher order, as a capacity, we might say, for intuitive rational cognition. This Nous, in the narrow sense, is the organ for the apprehension of concepts.

It is difficult, if not impossible, to compass here a full agreement with that version of Aristotle's theory of knowledge which we have found at the close of his main logical work and also in some passages of the " Metaphysics " (cf. pp. 55 and 82). In the form of the Nous-doctrine which now occupies us there is no mention of the decisive *rôle* which was there assigned to sense-perception and induction in the formation of concepts. The empirical element which stood in the forefront of the theory of knowledge both there and in the doctrine approximating to Alcmæon's (cf. p. 198), has now retreated somewhat into the background ; we are reminded of that residue of Platonism which Aristotle never fully overcame (cf. p. 78). It is thus desirable to ascertain the limits of this discrepancy with all attainable precision, but at the same time to avoid all exaggeration with the greatest possible care.

7. This intuitive cognition by the reason, or intellectual apprehension, is applied by our philosopher only to the formation of concepts and to those judgments called analytic or elucidatory (Kant's expression), not to the synthetic judgments which add something to what is already contained in the subject. The first of these categories includes more especially definitions or delimitations of concepts. In this region Nous is said to be as infallible as the senses in their own province (cf. p. 187). The oft-mentioned "immediate propositions" are certainly in preponderant measure the statements or the developments of definitions. They include a portion of the *material* out of which syllogisms are constructed, but this is true only in small measure of the axioms or *rules* by which the structure of syllogisms is governed. The function of Nous in its narrower and higher sense reaches thus far and no farther ; it apprehends its objects, concepts, no otherwise than as the organs of sense apprehend sensible objects. It has not the capacity of acquiring new truths, new combinations (syntheses). The apriorism which we have so often met with, especially in the physical works, is, we see, an occasional if not infrequent abuse, not a method followed as a matter of principle.

There is one real contradiction which critics have believed themselves to have discovered within the doctrine of Nous On the one hand, Aristotle persists in an earnest endeavour to represent Nous as a mere capacity, as a force which previous to or apart from its exertion is nothing, which before such exertion has no more content than an " uninscribed tablet." On the other hand, it is observed, Aristotle assigns to Nous such predicates as "free from admixture," " separable," " incapable of being acted upon," which one does not feel justified in applying, except to a substance or entity. And just this word ($o\dot{v}\sigma\acute{\iota}a$) does occur sometimes in connexion with Nous. To any one who sees in this a want of clearness and consistency, it can only be answered, as we have remarked already (p. 89), that we have before us " a fault and a weakness of the human mind which cannot be taken as characterizing a special employment of it," still less a particular hero of the intellect. In any case, when Aristotle appended to those very predicates the designation "in its essence pure energy," he was conscious of no contradiction.

We shall again meet with Nous and its intuitive character in the ethical doctrines of Aristotle. For the present its oft-extolled godlike or divine nature leads us on to the consideration of that which, in his dialogue " On Prayer," Aristotle represents as "itself Nous, or else something raised above Nous," namely, the Deity.

CHAPTER XVIII.

ARISTOTLE'S THEOLOGY.

1. RELIGION comes before theology, that is, systematic reflexion on divine things is preceded by surmise and emotion. Religious feeling was by no means lacking in Aristotle. It finds expression in his writings after a manner which is often affecting, and sometimes rises to fervour. Nor should this surprise us. Though the depth of his character does not reach to that of his master Plato, his nature was not flat and shallow enough to be blind to the wonders of Nature's ways, to be obtuse to the secrets of the world's workings, or not to look upward with reverent eyes to a " Higher, Unknown." But as soon as he undertakes to condense his surmises into propositions, and to mould their content in definite forms, it becomes uncommonly difficult for him to reconcile the demands of his religious feeling with the claims of his scientific thinking. If he did not succeed in the attempt to create a self-contained and rounded-off theological system, we have no cause for wonder. Much more remarkable is the deep earnestness with which he conceived the problem and laboured to bridge the yawning gulf between the conflicting claims of emotion and intellect.

The attitude which the Stagirite assumed towards the great riddles of the universe may be described as a monotheism inset with touches of pantheism. Following, as he did, in the footsteps of Xenophanes and Plato, he was impelled to presume *one* Director of the universe mainly by his conviction of the strict unity of all nature. We have noticed the zeal with which he maintains the unity and uniqueness of the heaven—a zeal which leads him as far as to identify the visible celestial sphere with the universe (cf. p. 123). He distinguished, indeed, between the four elements of the sublunary region and the one element of the celestial region above, between the changefulness of the first and the unchangeableness of the other. But he regarded the distinction as no infringement of the supreme unity, because the region of our world is only "a small, evanescent part of the All." He illustrates this unity by a twice-repeated comparison taken from the province of dramatic art. Nature, he says, is not "episodic, like a bad tragedy," one, that is to say, in which the separate acts and scenes are only loosely ranged in series, not inwardly connected with each other. It is quite consonant with all this that, in reviewing the doctrines of the nature-philosophers, Aristotle awards the prize to Anaxagoras, with the emphatic words: "Nous was now named as the author of order in the whole of nature, as well as in the structure of living beings ; and he who affirmed this seemed like a sober man after the wild words of his predecessors." The most deep-going of his theological discussions ends in an approving citation of the Homeric line—

" Bad is the lordship of many ; let one be your ruler and master."

2. Just this mention of Anaxagoras should remind us of the limits set to our philosopher's monotheism, in spite of the emphasis with which he professes it. Part of these limits he has in common with the sage of Clazomenæ, part is peculiar to himself. Both of them wished to impose upon the scientific spirit, which demands the recognition of a permanent orderliness, inherent in things themselves, no greater sacrifice than appeared absolutely necessary for the benefit of their God or Spiritual Being. Accordingly, Anaxagoras supposed a single, spatially limited intervention of Nous, at the beginning of the rotary movement ; Aristotle, a permanent but likewise spatially limited attraction exercised by the "First Mover" on the outermost celestial sphere ; and each attached to such primary influence an interminable vista of consequences. But these

consequences could be produced, whether by Nous or the " First Mover," only on condition that the peculiar tendencies of matter itself, its weight and lightness, or *nisus* towards the "natural places," should co-operate with those impulses to motion or be set at work by them (cf. Vol. I. pp. 214, 215). Each set of primordial tendencies is of the highest teleological significance as the foundation of all purpose-serving distribution of matter ; at the same time, they are original and ultimate facts, independent of all directing or shaping activity of Nous or the Deity.

For the rest it is possible to detect a noteworthy difference between the two systems, the exact opposite of what on prior grounds one would have been inclined to expect. Anaxagoras, who came so near to the Hylozoists both in point of time and in his conception of primary Being, is freer from their influence in regard to his conception of nature than is the comparatively late thinker Aristotle. Of the two, Anaxagoras is more of a mechanical physicist. For Aristotle is not without his relapses into the hoary theory of soul-endowed matter which as a principle he denies ; he is moved in that direction by a kind of atavistic tendency, which causes him to imagine " all things in a manner filled with soul "—while yet for him soul is a something that operates in accordance with purpose (cf. p. 171). And that the Deity is not for him the sole source of order and design is no more than what he says expressly himself where he mentions the final tendencies of Nature itself, sometimes using the very expression, " This is what Nature wills." But while Nature sometimes appears in the place of God, in such words as, " Nature does nothing in vain," there are other passages where God and Nature are presented in a combination reminding us of Spinoza's " Deus sive Natura." In " God and Nature do nothing in vain," the two are set side by side as factors of equal rank. It will be seen that we have not without reason spoken of the pantheistic features which are to be observed in Aristotle's representation of the way in which God is related to Nature and the world.

We have, indeed, understated the case by saying that in the last-cited passage God and Nature are placed on an equal footing. Strange as it may seem, we ought to have spoken of a preponderance assigned to the nature-principle. " God and Nature " means for Aristotle the forces at work in nature, which are reverenced as divine, not Nature on the one side and on the other a self-existent and independently active Godhead. This is so for the simple reason that Aristotle most completely and emphatically denies to the pure and absolute Deity all work and action, and indeed all endeavour towards action, all will and therefore all good and purposeful will. Efforts have been made to weaken the force of utterances which run so counter to ordinary religious ideas ; but the artificiality and nullity of such explanations have been demonstrated in the most convincing manner.

For one thing, the grounds of these paradoxical deliverances are not unknown to us. That which seems to us a limitation of the Deity and of the divine power is regarded by Aristotle as a consequence of perfection. That which is absolutely perfect cannot work or act, because prior to and corresponding to all work and action there must be desire and longing, prior to desire and longing there must be defect and need. Human actions are means to obtain ends ; the Deity, perfect in itself, can strive after no goal or end outside itself. Again, in reviewing the series of virtues or moral excellences, Aristotle arrives at the result that in the being of the Deity there is no room for their exercise, nor therefore for their existence. This is true, not only of courage and continence—that is, the overcoming of dangers and temptations which could not exist for a perfect being—but also of justice, for the curious reason that this virtue implies the exchange of goods or some other business transaction. Indeed, goodness itself, which Plato had identified with the divine principle, has no place in this ideal, at any rate in the sense of benevolence or love. Everything which provides human virtue with exercise and expression must be termed " unworthy and petty" when measured by the standard of the highest Being. We shall presently learn what remains over as the sole content of the divine life.

First of all, however, we may here find place for the remark that Aristotle's theism, important as it may have been for the history of theology, has meant little or nothing for the religious life of mankind. It elevates the Deity to a height from which scarce a path leads down to the lowlands of humanity. Nowhere in this teaching about God is there any mention of a loving and compassionate father, of a rewarding and punishing judge, nor even of a provident architect of the universe. In his desire to remove his God from even the remotest contact with human weakness, Aristotle condemns Him at the same time to complete sterility. That such a God does nothing and achieves nothing is true in yet another sense, a sense which one might almost say is fatal to Him as a living reality.

3. But whence, we ask, comes this contradiction between execution and design? " One lord and master " is set upon the throne of the universe. But the result is hardly other than if the throne had been left empty. *Le roi règne, mais ne gouverne pas*—even this formula of constitutional monarchy does not fairly represent the position assigned by Aristotle to the supreme ruler of the world.

Two motives seem to have co-operated in producing this great contrast : the dread of any disturbance to the regular course of Nature, and the repugnance to all anthropomorphism. These are two highly estimable motives, the first of which, however, need have led no further than to that " denial of supernatural intervention " and that view as to the " divine source " of orderly natural processes which we have already met with among the Hippocratics (cf. Vol. I. p. 311). But the two taken together and followed up with the utmost strictness lead beyond all theology and issue in agnosticism. Herbert Spencer's " Unknowable," the " neither knowing nor knowable One " of Plotinus (cf. Vol. III. p. 268), are the appropriate designations of a God conceived as emptied of all anthropomorphic qualifications. Aristotle has gone too far or not far enough. If he had proceeded in a less radical or in a still more radical manner, he might equally in either case have avoided an exposition which stamps his theology with the seal of the grotesque.

On all mythology he boldly turned his back. He knows it only as a "mythical addition" or as a "mythical envelope" of the truth. But truly not much kernel is left out of all that husk; for in every kind of doing, working, and willing, and in every kind of moral excellence, he detects a residue of anthropomorphism, and removes it with resolute, if gentle, hand from his picture of the Deity. Even the little that remains would not have been left if Aristotle had not here fallen short of strict consistency, had not, indeed, bidden defiance to his own definite declarations. All doing is denied to the Godhead, yet one kind of doing ($\pi\rho\acute{a}\tau\tau\epsilon\iota\nu$) is yet conceded to it, namely, a reflective contemplation that fills it with beatitude. All action and production ($\pi o\iota\epsilon\hat{\iota}\nu$) is withheld from it; yet it is the ultimate source of all heavenly and earthly movement, by exerting an overwhelming attraction while itself remains at rest. It is true that it is said to move the universe only as a loved object moves the lover (cf. p. 216). Thus Aristotle breaks through the self-imposed barrier at two points, more violently in the one case by removing "contemplation" from the category of doing, in the second case more surreptitiously. It is only by such ways as these—underhand ways, we might almost call them—that he gains the vision of the divine nature forbidden him by his own declared principles.

4. Though we have here been unable to refrain from a somewhat trenchant criticism, we are yet very far removed from any desire to disparage the great thinker. His weaknesses and inconsistencies appear, on closer examination, to be the hardly avoidable results of powers at war with each other. The scientific spirit was strong in Aristotle; so, too, was his religious need. The two currents could not but run counter to each other. The formative impulse of his religious sense was opposed by the disintegrating force of his critical sense. It was inevitable that the conflict should

come to some kind of an issue ; and it speaks well for Aristotle's psychical equipoise that neither contestant was forced to concede everything. If logical rigour suffered on the whole comparatively little, while the religious impulse was severely repressed, this is no more than was to be expected in a man who was a thinker first and an architect of religion afterwards. On the other hand, this arrest of religious developments, this impoverishment of the notion of God, make it easy for us to understand why the transcendental Deity towards which Aristotle's aim was directed came to be largely overgrown with elements of pantheism. Just because in Aristotle's system the Ruler of the world is so estranged from the world, because He is bound to it by only the faintest ties, because between Him and it, as has been rightly said, an " icy coldness " reigns, He can afford no adequate satisfaction to the philosopher's religious need. That is why he does not disdain to seek satisfaction where the systematic course of his thought, directed as it was towards the rooting up of Hylozoism, should have prevented him from seeking it—in Nature itself, its materials and its productions, conceived as governed throughout by divine forces, and animated with purpose.

But in order to be completely just it is necessary to distinguish, still more carefully than we have yet done, between the object willed and the result achieved. Aristotle's God was very far from being intended as a stop-gap. He was meant, on the contrary, to crown the edifice of thought, to form a bridge between ontology and natural science. In Him the notional or formal cause, the final cause, and the motive cause, were to meet in unity. As the most eminent historian of ancient philosophy has aptly remarked, the eternity of the world was to be combined " with its dependence upon an extra-mundane Deity," while a reference of the world's existence, order, or motion " to definite acts of the Godhead," conceived as events in time, would conflict with the principle that the world had no beginning. But when we ask how these great aims were carried out, Aristotle's utterances afford no satisfactory reply. To begin with, it is hard to understand how this Being, which, on the one hand, excites spatial movements, and, on the other, lives on in beatific self-contemplation, could be the supreme final Cause. Difficulties of no less seriousness are suggested by the assertion that the impulse to motion just spoken of has its origin in a yearning of the corporeal after the divine. The word "attraction," which we have used in this connexion, is to a certain extent misleading. For when we moderns speak of a physical attraction, the clearest-headed of us, at any rate, are consciously using a metaphor which is intended to describe the facts, not to explain them. It is otherwise with Aristotle. Explanation is his aim in all such cases. It is thus that at least Theophrastus, his successor in the school, understood the words "as a loved object" (p. 116). For, so understanding the expression, he could not withhold the searching objection : " If a desire, especially when directed towards the best, does not come into being without an activity of the soul, then the bodies so moved must be themselves endowed with soul." Thus the intimate friend and disciple of the Stagirite charged him at that early date with the relapse into the theory of animated matter which has just been the object of our criticism.

Belief in the gods was derived by Aristotle from two sources : he had regard to the impression produced upon early man partly by the celestial phenomena, their regularity and subservience to purpose, partly by psychic phenomena. In connexion with the latter, he draws attention in his popular works to dream-messages and to revelations received by the soul at the point of death, at a time when it is severed from the outer world, and even from the body itself, to a greater degree than in sleep. Such messages, he says, have been acknowledged as the outcome of divine inspiration. This defence of theism is not met with in his systematic treatises. We have thus to choose between two alternatives. It may be that we have here a mere conjecture as to primitive theology, based, it may be added, on passages in the Homeric poems. Or else the view in question is one approved by the philosopher himself, though only at an early phase of his speculation, as is shown by the rationalistic conception of dreams in the formal treatises. We ourselves cannot accept this second hypothesis, though it is propounded by an author for whom we entertain the greatest respect.

5. We are not sorry to have the present opportunity of calling attention to certain rules of method which are only too often left out of sight, especially when modern expositors desire to find their favourite views in Aristotle's writings. In cases of conflict, the treatises ought always to be preferred to the dialogues, which, precisely because they are popular works, often accommodate themselves to received opinion, and which are preserved to us only in fragments and without any indication of the persons speaking. Again, within the treatises themselves we ought carefully to distinguish between the systematic, conscientious development of a theme and *obiter dicta*, assertions and allusions interspersed in alien contexts, and thereby, likely enough, considerably altered in meaning. Nor can the Stagirite always bring himself to dispense with an argument favourable to the thesis he is for the moment defending, on the ground that the premisses from which it starts do not fully harmonize with his personal convictions. Sometimes, it is true, he silences his critical conscience, if we may say so, by the hypothetical form of his argument ("if, indeed, it is the fact that . . ."), or by an added qualification (" as people think," or " as it appears to be "). But whether he does so or not, his joy in the accumulation of proofs (cf. p. 114), his pleasure in the exercise of his dialectical skill, a wish to bury an opposing view under the number as well as the weight of objections, lastly, his respect for everything traditional, in which he so readily detects at least traces and rudiments of the truth—all this combines to make him not too fastidious in the choice of arguments, and causes him not infrequently to change his point of view.

There is thus no more certain method of barring the way to an understanding of the genuine Aristotle than to forget completely all the circumstances just enumerated, to take all his utterances, however casual, and lay them on the scale, follow them to their extreme consequences, and then, in case of discrepancy between this mode of exegesis and Aristotle's plain and unambiguous statement of principles, to decide for the former. The monstrous results to which this negation of method may mislead are well illustrated by an example taken from this very province of theology which is our present subject. By way of proving that Aristotle does *not* deny all doing and working to his Deity, reference has been made, among other things, to a sentence in the " Rhetoric " which runs thus : " The dæmonic is either a deity or the work of a deity ; he, therefore, who believes in as much as one dæmon necessarily assumes the existence of gods " (notice the plural). This is simply an abbreviated repetition of an argument by which Plato represents Socrates as defending himself and his dæmon ; Aristotle merely adduces it as one among many examples of a particular mode of proof, that by definition. To draw from such passages inferences as to the content of Aristotelian doctrines may well be called the height of arbitrary caprice.

6. Of the proofs which Aristotle gives for the existence of God, one, the teleological proof, or proof from design, has already been treated by us in advance. We have said enough already of the inadequate way in which it is worked out, and of the contradiction between the task laid upon the Deity and the insufficiency for that task of the divine nature as conceived by Aristotle himself. But apart from these blemishes, this proof is doubtless the most important of them all (cf. Vol. I. pp. 364, 365).

Aristotle entered upon another path when he endeavoured to prove the existence of an Absolute contrasted with the relative which is alone encountered in human experience. Where there is a better—so runs the most forcible of his arguments on this point—there must also be a best. Since, then, the totality of existing beings reveals to us a rising scale, a progress from the less to the more perfect, we have the right to infer a culmination or final term of this series, an unconditionally best. Here the philosopher has taken that step out of the world of relativity, the legitimacy of which will be contested by all those who believe human knowledge to be confined to that relative world, and every glimpse of the Absolute denied us. We notice, in passing, an objection which very readily occurs to the mind. There is just as much reason, it may be urged, to infer an absolutely bad as an absolutely good. If there is a scale of goodness, a similar scale of badness is equally undeniable ; and the existence of absolute evil is as much proved by the one as that of absolute good by the other. The same line of proof which, followed upwards, leads to the Deity, followed downwards, leads to an evil world-principle, whether we give it the name of devil or any other name. Aristotle is here opposed, not only by the adherents of dualistic religions such as Zoroastrianism, but also by his own master, who in at least one phase of his development set an evil world-soul by the side of the good (cf. Vol. III. p. 213).

A third argument has no direct connexion with the Absolute ; the nucleus of it is rather an attempt to solve the problem of the origin of motion. The existence of an Unmoved Mover is supported by a proof which, though not entirely without plausibility, has little strictness, and is only put forward by Aristotle himself under reserve. It is, says he, a " probable, not to say necessary, assumption," that of the three hypotheses which are possible in relation to this matter, not two alone are realized, but the third as well. Experience acquaints us with moved movers and moved non-movers ; how, then, should the third feasible combination (the purely negative unmoved non-mover being legitimately ignored), that is, the Unmoved Mover, be lacking ? The following examples may be added as explanatory of the first two cases. We set a sphere in motion ; while rolling it strikes another sphere, and puts an end to its previous state of rest. Or we may cause the first sphere to rotate on a fixed axis, when without exerting any appreciable influence on anything else it will be itself in movement. In Nature winds and streams play the first of these parts ; rotating heavenly bodies the second. In addition, then, to the moved mover and the moved non-mover, so illustrated by us, the realization of the third possibility, the Unmoved Mover, is demanded— in the interests, so we shall best suppose, of thought-construction. The demand is satisfied, on the large scale, by Aristotle's God. The high-pitched requirements of the Stagirite were obviously not met by such instances on a small scale as the attraction of a magnet, which he regarded as a mere curiosity.

7. The Unmoved Mover is presented to us not merely as a postulate of logical symmetry, but also as an indispensable aid towards the physical explanation of the world. "God keeps as still as a mouse, and therefore the universe revolves round Him:" so wrote Gottfried Keller in jest; and the words might supply a motto for the doctrine of the First Mover. The universe being conceived as without beginning or end in time, the motions which go on in it without ceasing must depend upon some ultimate mover, unless an infinite regress is to be assumed, and this is deemed impossible. Conceivably the ultimate cause of motion might be self-moving; this hypothesis is stated and discussed at some length, but finally rejected without strict disproof. For it can hardly be considered as refuted by a reference to the ideal distinction which in the case of the self-moving can be drawn between the active and the passive factor. In all this Aristotle is under the influence of Plato, from whom he borrows his leading thought that the origin of all movement is psychic; he desires, however, to formulate this thought more sharply, and at the same time to materialize, in a certain sense, the psychic factor which is in question. Evidence of such a desire appears in his attempt to localize the Unmoved Mover in a particular part of space, whereby His purely spiritual nature, maintained elsewhere by Aristotle with so much earnestness, suffers a manifest infringement.

This attempt, however, to prove that ultimate origin of motion enters into ultimate connexion with the thesis, which we have already discussed, that the combination of ideas Unmoved Mover, must be represented in the

Cosmos equally with the other two kindred combinations which are there realized on a large scale. It is not surprising that the two lines of thought lead to the conclusion that in the Unmoved Mover we have to recognize that first source of all motion which was vainly sought elsewhere. This result needed, on the one hand, to be supported by considerations of still more comprehensive generality; on the other, to be followed into its consequences. The two operations sometimes proceed simultaneously.

The highest generality is found in the doctrine that all becoming—in Aristotelian terms, all transition from potential to actual existence—is effected *by* something actual. As examples, the generation of one human being by another is mentioned, and also the training to professional skill, as of one musician by another. This doctrine is then applied to the supreme principle of the universe. It is inferred that the essence of this principle must be complete actuality or pure energy. For if its nature included in addition any merely potential element, that is, any element conditioned by and dependent on other things, then its complete efficiency and unceasing operation would be endangered. If, then, that supreme world-principle is identical with the first cause of motion, the latter, too, must be divested of all potentiality if it is to act without failure or intermission. In order, therefore, not to be tainted with potentiality, the essence of the Unmoved Mover must be free from any material element. Hence, too, it follows that it must also be free from multiplicity. In this is included the non-possession of parts ; in other words, it must be pure spirit. His life is thought ; but this thought can only be directed towards the best, that is, Himself ; and this self-contemplation fills Him with the highest bliss. What we men feel once and again, in favoured moments, that and more is felt by the Deity perpetually. The long-spun-out proof becomes finally a hymn of praise, and ends with the asseveration : "On this Supreme Principle heaven and the whole of Nature depend."

8. But more than one reader has, perhaps, long been

ready to interrupt us with a string of questions. What about the starting-point of this long chain of proofs? Whence the philosopher's confident certainty as to the effects which he finds himself compelled to ascribe to so extraordinary a cause? Granted that only the Unmoved Mover could guarantee us the eternity of the celestial movements which we perceive, how do we know that these movements have, in fact, existed from all eternity, and that they will endure for ever? Aristotle's mode of justifying this affirmation is certainly not one which we moderns would be likely to follow in a similar case. He believes in the revolution, without beginning or end, of the one heaven, which revolution is caused by the Unmoved Mover, and in its turn causes all the movements which occur in the universe. But this one heaven and its revolution are of equally fictitious character. In the place of that one heaven modern science gives us individual heavenly bodies, groups and systems of stars, lying in the most diverse planes, and situated at the most varying distances from us and from each other. But this transformation of Aristotle's picture of the universe, however important in another respect, has no decisive bearing on the question before us. It has, at any rate, no significance beyond the fact that, whereas Aristotle speaks of one eternal and uniform motion, we are acquainted with nothing of the kind, but find multiplicity taking its place in this field, as in so many others.

The telescope and the spectroscope have resolved the one heaven into countless worlds, and replaced its changeless, homogeneous character by a variegated succession of changing states. We believe we can distinguish between worlds now in the make from worlds made long ago and not subject to perceptible change during the present period; these, again, we distinguish from worlds now coming to an end. But though the barrier between Aristotle's unchanging heavenly region and his everchanging sublunary world has thus been broken down, the true heart of the problem under consideration remains untouched. The question of the origin of movement compelled Aristotle to venture on the boldest of hypotheses simply because he chose to raise it. We set narrower bounds to our curiosity. Motion—the molecular motions of which Aristotle knew nothing, as well as the motion of perceptible masses—is included for us in the primal endowment of matter. We do not, indeed, answer the problem as to the origin of movement; but neither do we count it a special or peculiar mystery. It remains for us shrouded in that same impenetrable obscurity which envelops the whole of the problems relating to this subject, which are alike inaccessible to human intelligence.

We do not ask how the movement of matter originated, any more than we inquire into the origin of matter itself or of its other attributes. The position of the Atomists was the same, and so too, in essentials, was that of all the earlier nature-philosophers. But in course of time, misled by the deceptive appearance of rest presented by material objects of moderate size, and forsaken by the genius which had prompted the surmises of a Heraclitus or a Leucippus, thinkers tore asunder what, in fact, is always linked together—matter and its endowment of force. Then, and not till then, thought found itself faced by a problem which could only be answered by the most reckless conjectures (cf. Vol. I. pp. 343, 344). We have arrived at a stage of greater maturity and moderation; with more humility and less pretension we decline to pronounce one part of these riddles more capable of solution than another part; and we do not assign to human wisdom the task of lifting the veil which covers all ultimate beginnings.

We have already referred in general terms to Aristotle's localizing of the Unmoved Mover, and also to the manner in which the latter was supposed by him to generate the cosmic movements. If we wish for more accurate ideas on these two points, it is necessary to take into consideration the astronomical doctrine of our philosopher. As, for Aristotle, the Deity is hardly anything more than the First Mover, while the latter operates through the medium of the star-spheres and the subordinate gods or spirits which guide them in their revolutions, we are not, in turning to this new subject, leaving the field of his theological doctrines.

CHAPTER XIX.

ARISTOTLE'S THEOLOGY.

(CONTINUATION AND CONCLUSION: ARISTOTLE'S ASTRONOMY.)

1. IN astronomical as in mathematical subjects Aristotle does not regard himself as a specialist. When he treats of them he refers oftener than elsewhere, as we have already remarked, to the judgment of " experts " or " competent authorities" (cf. p. 131). In this field, therefore, he has less of the glory of a path-finding discoverer than in any other. His failures in this province will be viewed differently according as attention is directed to their causes or to their effects. It is difficult to repress the feeling of resentment which rises when we observe that errors previously attacked and shaken were, mainly by Aristotle's authority, established anew and maintained in existence for thousands of years (cf. pp. 58, 122, and Vol. III. p. 265). But we shall find ourselves moved to greater lenity of judgment when we realize the difficulties which oppose the introduction of an isolated, even if highly progressive, innovation in the general fabric of science. What we have here in mind is the geocentric theory, which had been abandoned by the later Pythagoreans and by Plato in his extreme old age (cf. Vol. I. pp. 113, 114; Vol. III. p. 221), but which was revived by Plato's pupil.

One is at first surprised at the magnitude of the self-contradiction into which Aristotle falls. He by no means bars his mind against the progress made by specialists' investigations. He knows and approves of the calculations which estimate the earth's circumference at four hundred thousand stadia—an amount of roughly fifty thousand miles, somewhat less than double the true figure. But this circumference, to use his own words, is "small in comparison with the magnitude of the other heavenly bodies,' and "means practically nothing in relation to the whole fabric of the heavens." Thus, in regard to this subject, he expresses himself almost exactly as we are accustomed to do when we speak of our abode as a speck in the universe. He cannot refrain from mordant irony when he alludes to the opinion of those who in older times "supposed the rest of the heavens to have been built up around this place because of its dignity." Yet, in spite of all this, he held with absolute rigour to the central position of the earth, and to its condition of rest, denying to it even the rotary movement round its own axis. The impression produced upon us at first is that an heirloom of the earliest science has been retained, though the foundations on which it rests have been abandoned. We can hardly believe our eyes when we see Aristotle applying the same severity of censure, first to the immoderate exaggerations of the earth's circumference previously current, and then to the inference drawn from the opposite view, "The earth is a star among stars."

This remarkable polemic must engage our attention for a moment. It is directed, half against the aged Plato, and half against the Pythagoreans. The late Pythagorean doctrine last mentioned by us, one of the boldest feats of emancipation ever achieved by human genius, is quoted by a great thinker merely to be condemned. And this adverse judgment is founded upon the consideration that its authors "have set reasoning above facts." A stronger instance of unconscious self-directed irony can hardly be imagined. This is the language of the man who in his own scientific practice has so often placed dialectic above experience, whose favourite indulgence — remember his doctrine of the elements—is the building of the most reckless *à priori* constructions. What a warning is supplied by the following judicial sentence which so heavily recoils upon the judge! The opponents of the geocentric theory are said to deny the central position of the earth " because they do not think the earth worthy of it ; they believe the most dignified position due to the most dignified body ; and this is not the earth, but fire." *A priori* inferences of this kind may sometimes serve the interests of the most salutary truths ; in any case, it ill becomes Aristotle to despise them, for he continually operates with prejudices of precisely similar character. He applies this very predicate of dignity to movement in an upward direction ; he is never tired of basing theories on the perfection of the circle and the sphere. The strangest thing, however, is the fact that this sage, who is raised so high above the fundamental presuppositions of the geocentric doctrine, undertook to defend that doctrine, and indeed to found it afresh.

It was natural and even inevitable that the earth should be assigned a position of special privilege at the centre of the universe so long as the stars were regarded as sparks in the heavens, and the heavens themselves as a cover for the earth—so long, in brief, as the " infinite earth " was everything and the heavens as good as nothing. But when this relation was replaced by its contrary, how absurd it seems to us that any one should continue to imagine the immeasurably great as circling round a central body of comparatively insignificant size !

2. But here it is fitting to recall the " mitigating circumstances " (cf. p. 64) which are calculated to modify our judgment on this sin against science. In the first place, while for many centuries Aristotle's authority was the main bulwark of the geocentric delusion, he was not alone in falling under its spell. His great contemporary, Eudoxus of Cnidos, one of the most eminent astronomers of all time, shared that error ; nor could his belief have been due to the influence of the philosopher, who in these matters was not to be regarded as more than an educated outsider. This circumstance by itself is enough to prove that the geocentric theory possessed an intrinsic and powerful vitality, independent of all individual caprice. The same conclusion is indicated with still greater clearness

by a fact of uncommon significance in the history of science, to which we may be allowed to make here an anticipatory reference. A century after Aristarchus of Samos, who, as the creator of the heliocentric theory, may rightly be named the Copernicus of antiquity (cf. Vol. I. p. 98), Seleucus of Seleucia revived that doctrine, which had so far met with scant respect, and supported it by a series of proofs of whose nature we are ignorant. But he, too, failed to receive his just reward. The true doctrine, which had now been twice enunciated, but not yet strictly proved, was again condemned, and that by Hipparchus (*circa* 150 B.C.), the most famous astronomer of the day. The heliocentric theory was now regarded as finally disposed of. It was buried, and remained entombed till at last the immortal capitulary of Thorn awoke it from apparent death to new and imperishable life.

The true strength of the geocentric view rested on the circumstance that the opposed theory, to use the language of Paul Tannery, " involved an immeasurable step forward from the point of view of mechanics and physics, but offered no real advantage from the geometric point of view, beyond which the astronomy of the ancients did not advance." Whether the earth was to be allowed to revolve round the sun or the sun round the earth made no difference to the relative positions of the two bodies. Suppose I am sitting in a railway train, watching another on the adjacent track. Whether the truth be that my train is moving in one direction, or that the other train is moving in the opposite direction, the result is absolutely the same as regards the relation of the two trains to each other, though very different when we consider their relation to the surrounding country. Thus the scientific imagination found itself called upon to perform an unheard-of feat, while no sufficient reward was held out for the effort. But suppose the effort made, great as it must necessarily be, and the bonds of sense-illusion broken through, another and no less difficult task remained. In obedience to the demands of thought, the rest which the senses show us has been declared a mere appearance, and a motion, non-existent for the senses, has been proclaimed as the reality. Still obeying the same demands of thought, we now look for the appropriate consequences of motion—and we do not find them. Suppose a fixed star viewed even at different seasons and thus from widely separated points of the earth's presumed orbit, no sensible or measurable change was to be observed in the angular distances (absence of an annual parallax). The magnitude of the distances cancelled the effect of the change of position. This explanation is possible to us now that the perfected instruments and methods of the present day have succeeded to some extent in overcoming the difficulties which here present themselves. But for the majority of the ancient astronomers, who did not see so far as Aristarchus and his small band of followers, the inference was almost irresistible that the observer is always at the same point of space, in other words, that the earth remains eternally at rest. How far removed was such a view from an acknowledgment of the reality—the restless threefold movement of our planet, which turns on its axis, revolves round the sun, and journeys through space in company with the whole solar system and a number of neighbouring stars !

3. Turning now to Aristotle's attempt to *explain* the celestial phenomena, we must endeavour, in the first place, not to recall modern analogies, but to keep them out of sight. For not a few ancient thinkers, and for none of them more than for Aristotle, there yawned an impassable chasm between the things of earth and the things of heaven. By an explanation of celestial phenomena we understand the referring of them to universal forces which prevail on the earth as elsewhere. Such a thought was alien to the mind of the Stagirite. Suppose that in his day the necessary conditions for Newton's great intellectual feat had been fulfilled, that, indeed, the feat had already been performed, and its result made known to our philosopher. Even then he could hardly have reconciled himself with the Newtonian doctrine. For his aim was not the identification of celestial and terrestrial forces, but

rather their widest possible severance. But while to this extent his attitude was the precise opposite of the modern scientific spirit, the same cannot be said of his endeavour to set regularity in the place of irregularity, order in the place of apparent chaos. His mind here moved in the paths which had been opened up by the Pythagoreans and trodden by Plato. According to trustworthy records, the last-named philosopher formulated the fundamental problem of astronomical research in the question : " By what hypothesis of uniform and orderly movements can the actually observed movements of the planets be accounted for ? "

In this statement of the problem there lay a summons to consider movements conflicting with the canon thus set up as compound, and to analyze them into factors which should not so conflict. We moderns would add that the investigation ought to proceed tentatively, and be continued till it led to combinations of which the elements are known effects of known forces, already exemplified elsewhere. But a reservation of this kind, springing as it does from the desire to assimilate celestial processes to terrestrial, had no influenee upon the ancients ; indeed, the sound canons of research were for them still further falsified by the intrusion of a peremptory prejudice in favour of purely circular paths. It became, then, their main preoccupation to devise arrangements and modes of action by which, out of strictly circular motions there might arise motions not strictly circular. These endeavours were the main source of the sphere theory (cf. Vol. III. p. 221). This theory was bound to undergo ever-increasing elaboration. As observation improved in exactness, and as at the same time the discovery of apparent anomalies (*i.e.* real irregularities as well as mere deviations from strictly circular paths) became more frequent, the more exacting grew the demands made upon the combined action of the spheres, and the greater the number of them. Eudoxus was satisfied with twenty-six planetary spheres, but Callippus required as many as thirty-three ; while Aristotle found himself unable to manage with fewer than fifty-five, though he was prepared, on certain suppositions, to abate the number to forty-seven. Thus the theory became more and more complicated, and finally collapsed under the weight of this superstructure. Aristotle, as we have just seen, contributed his share to this result. We have now to describe his relation to the theory as a whole.

4. Aristotle was influenced not only by the example of his master and of eminent specialists, but also by peculiar considerations, sometimes of truly wonderful nature. Free motion in space was, he supposed, impossible for the heavenly bodies because of their spherical shape, which by a legitimate generalization had been deduced from the phenomena of the lunar phases and of eclipses. Nature "does nothing in vain and without a cause"—indeed, in some passages on the subject, he even ascribes "foresight" to Nature. If, then, the stars had been intended to move freely, Nature would have provided them with organs of motion—with extremities, we may suppose! But while the spherical form is the most unsuited to forward motion, it is the fittest of all for rest and for the rotation of a body on its own axis. Strangely enough, the possibility that a rotating body may at the same time roll is ignored in this discussion. Now, the great instance of rotation is supplied by the heaven of the fixed stars ; and the other celestial spheres are to be conceived as formed after its pattern. To these spheres are attached the seven wandering stars, that is, the sun and moon, as well as the five planets visible to the naked eye. The order is : Saturn, Jupiter, Mars, Venus, Mercury, Sun, Moon.

Aristotle was not a specialist in astronomy ; and it was not without hesitancy and reservations that he put forward his proposal to increase the number of the spheres. That which led him to this step was one of the fundamental thoughts of his cosmical dynamics : that the motive impulse proceeds from the "Unmoved Mover" residing beyond the celestial spheres, and is propagated to the centre. To make this possible, the totality of the sphere-groups must be materially connected and linked up into a mechanical unity. But this postulate created for him a difficulty unknown to his predecessors. Each inner group of spheres is turned round by the nearest group outside it. Some of the impulses so received help to explain the observed facts ; others are in contradiction with them. In order to nullify this second set of impulses, some means must be devised of eliminating them. Such a means was found by Aristotle in additional spheres, invented for the purpose, which he called " backward-rolling," or " retrograde," and to which he assigned the office of annulling or compensating the superfluous or obstructive impulses communicated by each outer to the next inner group of spheres. It is not necessary for our purpose to enter into the details of this supplementary theory.

5. At this point, however, a riddle presents itself which it is extremely difficult to solve. What are we to make of the fact that the predecessors of Aristotle did not know or did not heed the difficulty which called forth the theory of accessory spheres? Some of the most eminent specialists of our day answer the question as follows. For Eudoxus and Callippus the planetary spheres were not what they were for Aristotle, material, if transparent, bodies. They used them solely as an aid to imagination, as a means of illustration. Their sphere-theory—so it is contended—meant nothing more than that the movements of the stars are performed in the same way *as if* each of the wandering luminaries were fixed within a group of spheres, and received through their medium the motive impulses presupposed in the theory. If their account of the matter had been anything more than a mere device of exposition, if it had involved an assumption as to the facts, then, it is thought, those inquirers must have been confronted by the same difficulty as Aristotle, and driven to similar attempts at a solution. But what they aimed at, so we are now told, was not in any degree an explanation, but a description, a means of representing the play of forces upon each planet. Their doctrine was purely geometrical till Aristotle interpreted it as a physical hypothesis, or, in other words, grossly misunderstood it.

We should be glad to bow to a decision proceeding from high contemporary authority ; but we are unable to overcome certain weighty objections which present themselves. Admitted, what indeed is not easy to admit, that the Stagirite was capable of so gross a misunderstanding; admitted, that the man who in these discussions so frequently appeals to the judgment of the specialists, of the "mathematicians" who are the "stronger" in this branch of knowledge, took in truth so little pains to discover their true meaning ;—even these far-reaching admissions by no means settle the question. The men whose theories he so completely misunderstood were his contemporaries, companions, and fellow-students, bound to him by close personal ties (Callippus is spoken of as one of his quite intimate friends), and yet we are to suppose that not one of them was both willing and able to set him right. Again, there was one of his immediate pupils, Eudemus, whose knowledge of these subjects was almost unequalled. The learned author of the "History of Astronomy" was, next to Theophrastus, Aristotle's favourite pupil ; and a credible tradition states that he narrowly missed being nominated by the master as his successor in the school. He, too, we are asked to believe, never ventured on a word of remonstrance against Aristotle's misconception, or, if he did, failed to make the slightest impression. Again, the sphere-theory, in all the forms in which it was stated, met with vigorous censure and penetrating criticism. Among its active critics was Sosigenes, the contemporary of Julius Cæsar and his helper in the work of calendar-reform. Concerning this astronomer, we learn from an extensive fragment of the Commentary of Simplicius (*circa* 530 A.D.) that he subjected the sphere-theory, as set forth by Eudoxus, Callippus, and Aristotle, to severe, perhaps too severe, judgment. We know, too, that he made a special study of Aristotle's "retrograde spheres," and composed a monograph on the subject. But he did not refer by as much as a syllable to any misunderstanding on Aristotle's part. We need not dwell, be it remarked by the way, on the question whether Aristotle misunderstood his master

Plato along with the others, or whether Plato himself may be supposed to have wrongly interpreted the hints which he possibly received from Eudoxus. We come to the last and most important consideration. Not long after Aristotle's time the doctrine of concentric spheres was radically modified by Apollonius of Perga (born about 260 B.C.), and again, about a century later, by Hipparchus (excentric spheres, epicycles). But the planetary spheres survived, still conceived as actual physical objects. Nor was this only in popular belief and in the pseudo-science of astrology. Here, indeed, we might with some show of justice urge the possibility of crude misconstruction, though all the probabilities are against the hypothesis. But exact science and the history of exact science adhered immovably to the same view. This fidelity was shared even by Claudius Ptolemæus (about 150 A.D.), who gathered together and gave final form to the astronomical and geographical researches of antiquity. This great systematist treats the doctrine of the celestial spheres with great thoroughness. He enters into long discussions of their nature, their relative positions, their mode of attachment. But he lets fall not the slenderest hint that the planetary spheres had ever been understood in a different and purely ideal sense. However highly we appraise the influence of Aristotle's authority, it would be attributing impossibilities to it to suppose that by its means an earlier and fundamentally different view of the subject concerned was wiped out for all future time without leaving a trace behind.

The following is the most we feel able to concede to the distinguished specialists whom we here find ourselves obliged to contradict. It may be a legitimate supposition that with other great virtues of a researcher Eudoxus combined an unusual measure of modesty. He may possibly have regarded all that he seemed to have discovered about "celestial mechanics" as valid only under reservation ; he may never have fully overcome doubts that rose in his mind touching the absolute certainty of his conclusions on particular objective facts. He may then

have silenced such doubts by the reflexion that even if
it be denied to the human mind to achieve unconditional
certitude on the mechanism of celestial motions, still the
correct representation of the motive impulses acting on
each separate planet must possess and retain an independent value. Thus the sphere-theory which he elaborated
may have come to be regarded by him in a great and
perhaps preponderant degree as a faithful portrayal of the
forces at work, though, as an explanatory hypothesis, it
remained subject to a residue of scepticism. For the
ascertainment of exhaustive truth on the co-operation or
counter-operation of the different sphere-groups connected
with each planet may conceivably have remained for him
a problem hardly capable of solution. In the transition,
further, from Eudoxus to Aristotle, from the precisely
calculating and soberly critical mathematician to the
philosopher in quest of a full and absolute understanding
of the universe, some shifting of accent, if we may use
the term, may have taken place with regard to these
questions.

6. We return to the fundamental ideas of Aristotle's
cosmical dynamics to which we have already referred.
The original home and source of all motive forces is to
be found, according to him, beyond the sphere of heaven.
This source, the Deity, as Unmoved Mover, must be conceived as at once a purely spiritual being and as occupying a residence in space. For "beyond," in connexion
with objects situated in space, must have a spatial meaning ;
though Aristotle will not admit this, and insists that the
existence of space is limited by the celestial sphere. It
would be labour lost to endeavour the solution of this
inconsistency. The Stagirite has simply failed to effect
a satisfactory reconciliation between the primeval ideas of
popular religion, which he cannot bring himself to sacrifice,
and his own more refined comprehension. Instead, he
assigns to his *one* spiritual God, in whom the "gods"
dwelling in the "broad heaven" have been absorbed, not
altogether without residue as we shall shortly see, a place
corresponding to his own cosmological system. Coming

now to the operation of the First Mover upon the sphere of heaven or of the fixed stars, we find it not a little strange that this influence is based upon contact. We cannot understand, in the first place, what meaning is to be given to the word "contact" when it is applied to an immaterial being. The difficulty, too, is not made any the less by the representation of this contact as one-sided— the Deity touches the heavens, but the heavens do not touch the Deity. But we have little need to dwell on this point, since Aristotle has left no room for doubt as to what was his real aim. It is clear from his explanations on this head that the expression borrowed from the realm of matter was in this context intended merely to denote the share possessed by local proximity in the operations of the Unmoved Mover. Greater difficulties are reserved for us by the question, which now arises, of how this operation, compared as it is with the influence exerted by a loved or desired object upon the lover or desirer, can cause the rotary movement of the celestial sphere. We cannot at first resist the impression that, in this case, as in any other, the loved or desired object must be the goal of the motion which it provokes—that this motion, in other words, must be one of approach to its exciting cause. But the rotation of the celestial sphere leaves every part of it just as near to and just as far from the Unmoved Mover as it was before the impulse to motion was received. That impulse may be said to have failed of its original aim.

We moderns are here reminded of the scientific explanation of planetary movements, of that co-operation by which tangential momentum and the force of gravitation produce a resultant curve. There is, in fact, one point of agreement between the two explanations. In both cases a pair of forces come into play. But Aristotle is by no mean thinking of two motions so compounded as to give rise to a third. What he has in his mind is rather this. The influence of the First Mover—which, by the way, has not been exerted once for all, but is permanently active and ever renewed—consists in an impulse or stimulus towards motion. The rotation is the response to this stimulus.

There are two reasons why this is so. The heaven, possessing the most perfect, in Aristotle's opinion, of all forms, the spherical, possesses with it a tendency to move in the most perfect of plane figures, the circle. Forced from the state of rest, it passes to the one kind of motion which is in accordance with its nature. But, apart from the spherical form of the heaven, the same result is arrived at by the following consideration. The stimulus in question can primarily produce only a movement in the widest sense of the word—that is, a change, But, of all changes, change of place or motion holds the first or highest rank, and, of all movements, movement in a circle. The heaven, there-fore, as the most august of corporeal things, must, if acted upon at all, engage in just this kind of movement. It is thus, we believe, that we have to understand Aristotle's theory of the First Mover and the rotation of the heaven of the fixed stars effected by him. We base our view partly on Aristotle's explicit statements in this connexion, partly on a consideration of his general teachings.

7. While the sphere of the fixed stars receives its impulse to motion direct from the Unmoved Mover, the remaining spheres receive theirs through the mediation of special beings, who may be called subordinate gods, dæmons, or better, sphere-spirits. This hypothesis makes a breach in the monotheism towards which Aristotle pressed, and, indeed, reminds us of fetichism. How, we ask, did he arrive at it? The answer to this question is supplied by his general view, derived from primitive ideas, of celestial things, which he sets in sharp contrast with all that is earthly and subject to change, and in discussing which he by no means avoids the use of the word "divine." Thus he expressly censures the view which holds the stars to be purely corporeal entities. For him they are beings endowed with soul. In plain terms, he attributes to them life and also activity, so distinguishing them at once from the purely passive inorganic world of matter, and from a Deity ever at rest. The star-souls, or star-gods, so postu-lated, became for him sphere-souls, or sphere-gods, probably for the reason that each of the wandering stars concerned

receives its motive impulses from the joint operation of several spheres, and it seemed illegitimate to represent different and in part conflicting impulses as proceeding from one and the same god-like being. Thus the sphere-spirits are simply the star-spirits, or star-gods, each resolved into a plurality. To us this blend of science and fetichism seems highly odd; but not all ages have judged in this way. As late as in the "Cosmographia" of Johannes Kepler, the "spirits that move the planets round" are still playing an important part!

But while each planetary sphere is presided over by its own sphere-spirit, the unnumbered hosts of the fixed stars, being all served by one sphere, must dispense with the aid of these minor divinities. The resulting want of symmetry in the distribution of the spheres and the divine agents which control them—here a vast multitude of stars attached to a single sphere, there each separate star moved by several spheres and sphere-spirits—great as it is in itself, becomes still more extraordinary when we go into further detail. It was not even possible to assert or represent as tenable the hypothesis that the number of spheres increases continually from the periphery to the centre. Quite the contrary: the observed facts of astronomy made it necessary to assign the greatest number to the planets of the middle region, and the smallest number to the innermost and furthest removed from the circumference, namely, the sun and the moon. Not a little pained astonishment is hereby caused to our philosopher. These anomalies gravely offend his sense of symmetry and harmony. But even here, as so often elsewhere, the inexhaustible resources of his dialectic do not leave him in the lurch.

Very simple and speedy is his method of overcoming the first of the objections which here present themselves. The sphere of heaven, which carries and moves the countless fixed stars, is placed nearest to the "best," that is, to the Unmoved Mover. The force exerted by the latter—so we may read Aristotle's thought—is therefore here at its strongest. It reaches this sphere as yet intact, having lost none of its power on the way; here, therefore, it may be supposed to perform the mightiest of its tasks. The second difficulty is removed by a comparison borrowed from the province of human hygiene, a comparison in respect of which it is not easy either for author or for reader to maintain strict seriousness. The wandering luminaries are compared to different types of human beings. Some of these (corresponding to the outer planets which are near the heaven of the fixed stars) have constitutionally so large a measure of health and activity that they need little, if any, help from dietary rules or athletics—say, a short walk taken regularly. Others, again (with whom the middle planets are compared), must be at pains to remedy the sluggishness of their bodies by strenuous exercises, by running, wrestling, gymnastics, and so on. Lastly, we come to individuals who would find even the combined application of all such aids towards lightness of movement quite inadequate, who would therefore renounce the attempt, and who in no circumstances could rise above imperfect achievement. This part of the comparison has reference to the innermost of the celestial wanderers, the sun and the moon, which are nearest to the eternally motionless earth, and which are described as inferior in speed of movement to all the other planets.

We take our leave of this uninspiring portion of Aristotle's doctrine with the confession that much in it remains for us utterly obscure. Admitted that the predicates " life " and " activity " here applied to the stars were really coined for the benefit of the star-spirits, this can still hold only of the planets. What, then, are we to think about the fixed stars ? They, too, are assuredly not meant to be conceived of as without soul. But movement, the highest of the functions of soul, is denied by Aristotle to the stars of all kinds, and only conceded to the spheres to which they are attached. A comparison of the stars with plants and animals is still less of a help to clearness, since genesis and corruption, nutrition and excretion, all forms of growth or change, are expressly banned from the celestial realm. Finally, even contemplative activity is never ascribed to the star-gods, but solely and exclusively to the Supreme

Deity or Unmoved Mover. This last article of Aristotle's divinity must now engage our attention.

8. God thinks—God thinks Himself—God thinks only Himself—this self-thinking of the Deity forms is supreme blessedness : such are the propositions in which Aristotle's theology terminates. They are based upon the following considerations. Thought, excluding all doing or working, is the one activity worthy of the highest being. The value of each thought is determined by its object ; therefore the object of the divine thought, were it other than the Deity Himself, would at once degrade Him to unworthy depths and divest Him of His majesty. Finally, thought, as the one activity which is completely free from external influences, is also the only source of the highest happiness.

Even in our own days this doctrine has not lacked enthusiastic panegyrists. But " the most elevated doctrine to which the mind of Aristotle soared " has, since the Scholastic period, succeeded in maintaining this position only when the attempt has been made to empty it of its true content by an illegitimate reconstruction. Thomas of Aquino (who died in 1274) imagined himself to be merely playing the part of an interpreter while in reality he was labouring to give the fatal narrowness of that doctrine an inadmissible extension. " In knowing Himself," so affirms the great Scholastic, " God knows all other things " of which the Deity itself is the cause and first principle. This addition was intended to bar an inference which all truly unprejudiced interpreters have been unable to avoid drawing, and which the latest successor of Saint Thomas and of Duns Scotus (died 1308) has sarcastically expressed by the phrase, " the all-ignorance of God." But precisely this " all-ignorance " must be acquiesced in unless we allow ourselves simply to explain away whatever in Aristotle's teaching displeases us. Quick-witted, but by no means superficial Frenchmen, from Pierre de la Ramée (1515–1572) down to our own contemporary, Jules Simon (1814–1896), have taken an especial part in subjecting this doctrine to severe criticism. The first, who expiated the audacity of his attack on Aristotle in the Massacre of St.

Bartholomew, speaks of the " peacock-like vanity " involved in that beatific self-contemplation lasting through all eternity; while Jules Simon is amazed at the " lonely God of Aristotle, who is declared at once to be the cause of the harmony of the universe and to lack the knowledge both of that universe and of its harmony."

That the eternal sameness of this divine self-contemplation could only mean the most utter tedium is an obvious criticism, to which the reply might possibly be made that it attributes too much to human weakness, which always seeks after change, for which, indeed, change, or at least interruption, is a fundamental condition of all perception (cf. Vol. I. p. 118). We have no right, it may be urged, to exalt our own imperfection into a measure of the psychic life of the Deity. The objection is sound, but it is not raised in the right place. Just as little as we are entitled to transfer the limits of human perception, human feeling, human happiness, to the Deity, so little is it open to us to assume that what makes men happy has the same effect on a supernatural being. So long as differences of degree are alone in question, we may draw admissible inferences by way of analogy from the states and experiences of less perfect to those of more perfect natures. But where we are concerned with the fundamental conditions of psychic life, not merely with regard to their degree, but their nature, all ground is lacking for any conclusions whatever. Once let us assume enough similarity between the psychic life of man and any other psychic life to justify the smallest inference by analogy, and we are faced by the fundamental fact of unceasing change and contrast. A changeless feeling, remaining continually the same, is something totally unknown to us, accessible by no bridge of analogy. The Stagirite, however, has fashioned his Deity after the image of man, or, more accurately, not after that of man in general, but after that of the philosopher devoted to the contemplative life. His teaching on the preeminence of this type of life above all others will soon meet us again as the crowning point of his theory of ethics.

CHAPTER XX.

ARISTOTLE'S ETHICS.

1. THE ethical teachings of Aristotle have been handed down to us in threefold presentment. Strangely enough, the work in two books, which appears under the most pretentious title, the " Great Ethics," has long been recognized as a mere extract, a handbook for school use. The other two works, the " Nicomachean " and the " Eudemian Ethics," the first in ten books, the second in seven (of which, however, Books IV.–VI. have been lost and replaced by the corresponding books of the " Nicomachean Ethics "), are worked-up versions of Aristotle's course of ethical lectures. These lectures were delivered by him to his maturer pupils, and are expressly described as unsuited to the too youthful " hearers." We have before us two editions of the same course, one compiled and published by Aristotle's favourite pupil Eudemus, the other perhaps by his son Nicomachus, who died early, but may have had the assistance of Theophrastus. The Eudemian version exhibits certain individual peculiarities, especially a stronger emphasis on the religious element; the Nicomachean version is that one with which the half-dozen quotations from himself made by Aristotle in his other works are found to correspond exactly. It is rightly regarded as the more authentic of the two versions, just as it is the more complete. The fidelity of the reproduction seems to shine out in many peculiarities specially characteristic of lectures (cf. p. 32). Sometimes we have desultory remarks, in part raising anew questions settled in much earlier sections, sometimes remarkable and almost verbal repetitions. Some

points are treated at length, others again with such curt
mention that we can hardly avoid supposing the editor to
have been here deserted by the pupils' note-books and
compelled to utilize the mere outline-sketches of the teacher
himself.

2. We begin with the structure and general content of
the work. The first is faultless, and shows no lack of
unity. The doubts which arise on a superficial view vanish
before a more careful scrutiny.

The introduction treats, among other matters, of goods
in general, of the distinction between those which are ends
and those which are means, of the subordination of the
auxiliary arts to the master arts, and of all arts to that
art or reasoned practice which pursues the actual goal of
life. This last art, which may be named politics or statecraft, is represented as including ethics, since in the welfare
of the State or community—we should here distinguish
between the State and society—that of individuals is
comprehended. Accordingly, as we may pause to observe,
throughout this course of instruction the word "politics"
is used for ethics as well, by a figure which sets the whole
in the place of the part. To seek closer acquaintance with
the supreme end cannot, says Aristotle, be without its
use. Would not the archer have a better prospect of
making a bull's-eye if he knew the target than if he did
not? The investigation must renounce the highest exactitude. For so great is the divergence of opinion on what
is honourable and what just, that doubts have actually found
expression as to whether these distinctions are not wholly
artificial, resting not on nature but on convention. The
ultimate foundation of these doubts is the uncertainty of
consequences—we should rather say the enormous complication of human life. Not merely a virtue, like courage,
but even a good, like wealth, has proved a source of ruin
for many. We must therefore content ourselves with
approximate generalizations, with the knowledge of what
happens "as a rule;" just as in every department of
knowledge only the appropriate measure of exactness is
to be professed. It would be equally foolish to expect

merely probable reasoning from a mathematician and rigorous demonstration from a statesman.

What, then, is the goal of life or the highest good? By name it is known to us all as welfare (εὐδαιμονία). Herein the great multitude is of the same opinion with the "more refined persons." With the attempt at closer definition the ways part; for the mass of mankind understand by the term something "tangible and on the surface," such as riches, honour, pleasure. (Even at this early stage it becomes clear that the conception of εὐδαιμονία has, as it were, an objective side. If it meant mere happiness it would almost inevitably have been apprehended as a sum of pleasurable feelings or at least of permanent pleasurable states. It comprises rather what one might call the normal or healthy condition of the whole soul.) To begin with, Aristotle proposes to extract the knowledge of εὐδαιμονία from a comparative examination of the main types of life.

Of these there are three: the life of pleasure, the contemplative life, the political life. The rejection of the first is pronounced without any real logical ground, but rather, one may say, on the strength of an estimate brought ready-made to the discussion, and manifesting itself in such vituperative expressions as "brutish," "servile," and so forth. The appraisement of political life reaches greater depths. The prize is denied it because of the dependence of honour—the presumed goal of the politician —on those who pay honour. But the highest good, it is urged, must be independent and hard to lose. Further, men desire to be honoured for their virtue; and this very desire acknowledges that virtue is the higher aim. One who has learnt this might now be inclined to think virtue the supreme end; but this would be a mistake. For it is conceivable that a possessor of virtue might slumber away his days, live a life without deeds, and in addition be afflicted by all kinds of disappointment and adversity. In such a life no one would discover εὐδαιμονία, unless it were a disputatious dialectician—a proviso which sounds like a premonition of the paradoxes yet to come (the wise man is happy even in the bull of Phalaris, and so on).

This examination is based on premisses which are partly tacit, though not arbitrary, such as: the highest good must be permanent, and independent of external influences ; honour is not so high a thing as that for which honour is paid. But in part, too, the premisses are far-fetched and arbitrarily assumed. To this number belongs the hypothesis of a "virtue" which could slumber for a life-time as a latent capacity, without enforcing any active manifestation of itself, and yet without rusting from disuse.

There follows a polemical digression against Plato and his doctrine of Ideas, from which is derived the since proverbial "Amicus Plato, sed magis amica veritas" (cf. p. 19) ; and then the problem of the supreme good is resumed. In every case, it is now urged, that object is more perfect which is sought after as an end ; that object is absolutely perfect which is always an end and never a means. This holds good pre-eminently of εὐδαιμονία. The same result is obtained by an investigation which sets out from the idea of αὐτάρκεια (self-sufficiency). The perfect good must possess this character, and εὐδαιμονία does in truth possess it ; it makes life worth living even when denuded of all other goods. There follow attempts to define εὐδαιμονία more closely. It is declared first of all to be the peculiar "function" of man, which is found in the "activity of the soul according to reason, or at least not devoid of reason," or in the "activity of the soul according to the highest and most perfect of the virtues." An activity in accordance with virtue, not virtue itself—the distinction is one on which Aristotle lays considerable stress. Among other illustrations of it there occurs the fine saying, "At Olympia it is not the best-built and most powerful men who are crowned, but the contestants." So, too, it is only those who act rightly, not (as we may complete the thought) those who merely have good dispositions, to whom a share of the good and beautiful in life is granted. This kind of life does not need "plea-sure" as an external addition or "appendage," but rather includes it in itself.

By this desire to prove human happiness as independent

as he possibly can of external circumstances, to found it on
inner worth and its practical manifestation, the philosopher
is here and there led to the brink of exaggerations from
which he is immediately recalled by his sense of measure,
his clear vision of the realities of life. Among external
requisites first mention is given to a "full," that is, not too
short, span of life, for "one swallow does not make a
summer." A moderate degree of outward wealth is then
pronounced desirable. Straitened circumstances are said
to be not indifferent, chiefly because they rob us of the
instruments of beautiful and noble action. Nor can
complete εὐδαιμονία be the portion of one who is exceptionally ugly, of the low-born, of the isolated, of the child-
less : it is still more emphatically denied to one whose
children have turned out downright failures, or have turned
out well and died. Still, even the lot of a Priam does not
in itself necessarily make a man wretched ; though to one
so afflicted the name of happy could no longer be applied.
The language of this discussion is at once warm and
elevated in tone ; it bears witness to the inner feeling of
the author, who would have even "many and grievous
strokes of fortune" borne in a temper springing "not from
mere obtuseness, but from nobility of soul and high-
mindedness." Lastly, the permanence of εὐδαιμονία, its
independence, within large limits, of fate, are based upon
the fixity of a character once acquired. Its continuance
is more assured than that of intellectual acquisitions.
Exercise and constant translation into act here make anything corresponding to forgetfulness an impossibility. Yet
we seem to have before us rather the expression of a wish
than the statement of a fact when we read that the "most
valuable" habits of life are at the same time the "most
permanent," just as if there were no hardened evil-doers,
no "habitual criminals."

3. Two characteristic details now claim our attention.
The question is glanced at whether εὐδαιμονία is obtained
from teaching, by practice, or how else. The exclusively
religious view of the matter is here rejected gently and
considerately, but no less decisively. To those who hold

εὐδαιμονία "a gift of the gods," he answers that it is in any case one of the divinest of possessions, even if it is not actually conferred by the gods. A mere gift of the gods—it is hinted—could only be the privilege of a few elect, while in truth εὐδαιμονία, as the goal and prize of virtue, is accessible to all who in this respect are not, so to speak, "crippled." We admire here that union of candour with delicacy which surrenders no right of philosophy and yet avoids giving unnecessary offence to religious feeling.

In a neighbouring passage, on the other hand, Aristotle goes further than we should expect on the road of concession to popular opinions. The question mooted is whether we are affected by events happening after our death, by the fate of our posterity and friends ; whether the title "happy" is to be withheld from a life now ended on the ground that those nearest and dearest to the departed may yet be visited by grievous calamity. As the Stagirite wholly denies the immortality of the individual human soul (with the sole exception of the intellectual element, which is not here in question), the answer to this problem was clearly marked out for him. But he cannot bring himself to give this answer. The bare negative seems to him "too heartless," too sharply "opposed to current opinion." He accordingly contents himself with a compromise which we can hardly describe otherwise than as weak. The influence alluded to is not denied, but reduced to a minimum. It is said to be "slight and weak," both in itself, since external events have little effect on εὐδαιμονία, and also in regard to the dead as such, This is one of many instances from which we can learn a useful lesson. Sometimes Aristotle consciously and deliberately adopts popular opinions, and draws the consequences that flow from them. Sometimes he expresses his own convictions. But it is by no means possible, as it may perhaps have been thought, to draw with certainty the boundary-line between the two cases. It is not a rare thing for him to slip down from the higher region to the lower. Occasional lack of scientific courage is a fault which we have already found in him (cf. p. 58), and loth as we are to repeat the charge, this is not altogether avoidable.

With εὐδαιμονία the course of ethical lectures both begins and ends. The intermediate part is occupied with discussions of the means which subserve this highest end, and as this end has been discovered to be an activity of the soul in accordance with virtue, most of the matter relates to the virtues or excellences of the human soul. Now, a man who wished to investigate the excellence of the eye would first make himself acquainted with the eye itself and its functions ; just so he who wishes to discover the excellence of the soul must first learn to know the soul itself and its operations. Thus ethics is referred to a basis in psychology. From this basis is derived the distinction between intellectual excellence and ethical (in the narrower and proper sense). We have to notice that for Aristotle this distinction signifies anything but a strict severance. Quite the contrary. The rule of reason has no less important a part to play in moral than in intellectual virtue or excellence, while the former figures as a main condition of the latter. But however close the relationship of the two branches, and however intimate their interaction, a separate treatment of them seems absolutely necessary.

4. With this distinction the second book opens. It treats firstly of the different modes of acquiring the two main kinds of excellence of the soul. Instruction and experience on the one side are paralleled by habituation and practice on the other. Here we note with some surprise the wide interval which separates Aristotle's teaching from the Socratic intellectualism. " From youth upwards to be accustomed to be good "—this is for Aristotle the alpha and the omega of moral education, the goal on which the legislator, too, is bound to fix his eye. The connexion between habituation and its consequences is illustrated by physiological parallels. Generous nutrition and vigorous practice confer bodily strength ; every advance in bodily strength qualifies in its turn for the reception of still more generous nutriment, and the practice of still more vigorous exercises. So habituation to the

contempt of danger makes us brave, while every advance in courage increases our self-confidence, and enables us to face still greater dangers. But now we come to a puzzle. How can we become just by practising justice, seeing that it is impossible to practise justice without being already just ? The difficulty is solved by a comparison with the learning of music or the art of writing ; the first steps are taken half by accident or under the guidance of others. Those who in philosophy content themselves with theoretical knowledge are compared with patients who listen eagerly to the physician's words, but absolutely refuse to follow his prescriptions.

The exposition approaches nearer and nearer to the governing theory of the mean. No absolutely fixed, easily definable standard exists with respect to the beneficial effects of food or of bodily exercises ; just as little is there such a standard where objects of fear, desire, and so on are concerned. In all these departments there is a too-much on the one side, and a too-little on the other. An excess of sensuous desire is called dissoluteness ; a defect, insensibility. He who is terrified by the rustling of a mouse is rightly held a coward ; he who challenges tenfold odds is with equal justice deemed foolhardy. Excellence is attributed to a quality equally removed from defect and excess. We have, however, to distinguish the objective mean from the relative. Midway between the numbers 2 and 10 we have the number 6, which differs equally from both. But if food costing 2 minæ (£8) a year is too little for a person, while food costing 10 minæ is too much, it does not follow from this that a yearly outlay of 6 minæ will provide him with the most appropriate and desirable quantity. The right amount of food for him will lie somewhere or other between the two extremes, but at what point of the interval is to be determined by experience and judgment.

5. There now follows the definition of ethical excellence or virtue as a disposition of will "which abides in a relative mean having reference to us." To the question how this mean is to be ascertained, he answers that its determination

is left to the wise. The looseness of this answer has moved posterity to mockery which refuses to be silenced. Since wisdom is represented as on the one hand the standard-setting factor or regulator of virtue, and on the other as itself depending on ethical virtue, Aristotle has not been spared the reproach of arguing in a circle. But though the form of the exposition may justify this reproach, which has been urged particularly by the logically rigorous Herbartians, the kernel of the doctrine, as we think, is not touched by it. We believe that the true defect of the theory of the mean lies elsewhere—in its undue extension, in its application to excellences, such as truthfulness and justice, which cannot without violence be forced into its framework (cf. p. 144). The true and valuable kernel of the doctrine, on the other hand, is to be found, we think, in the recognition, in the affirmation, as we may perhaps call it, of the totality of human nature. No element of that nature—here Aristotle's ethical teaching bears a genuinely Hellenic aspect—is absolutely rejected and pronounced wholly bad ; of each just this is demanded, that it should fill no more than the space which is its due. What this due space is, Aristotle certainly leaves to be decided by the judgment of the " wise," or, as he expresses it with at least equal frequency, of the " respectable " man. He was thus anything else rather than a radical reformer of morals or society. On the contrary, he makes it as clear as possible that in questions of the conduct of life he takes his stand on the ideals of his age and his people, or perhaps of a cultivated circle forming part of it. Herein lies the secret at once of his strength and his weakness (cf. pp. 57, 58). He is preserved from violent onesidedness and exaggeration such as we have met with among the Cynics, and may meet with again amongst the Stoics and Epicureans ; but he renounces the privilege of supplying one of those leavens which have influenced the moral progress of mankind, sometimes beneficially, sometimes hurtfully, but always with permanent effect (cf. Vol. II. p. 166 *seq.*).

Misuse of the doctrine of the mean is sought to be provided against by the remark that not every action and not every feeling admits of a praiseworthy mean. For there are feelings and actions the very name of which implies blame ; and in their case no middle region of commendability may be spoken of. Here Aristotle is in danger of paying more than due regard to the traditional opinions incorporated in language. We are reminded of Bentham's warning against " question-begging names." The remainder of the book is occupied by a preliminary exemplification of the doctrine of the mean. Many subtle remarks are interspersed in this portion of the work. We are told that we have to be on our guard against nothing so much as against pleasure and the pleasure-giving. In face of these we are like corrupted judges. We may take for our pattern the old men who looked down from the wall of Troy, who were powerfully moved by the superhuman beauty of Helen, and who added to their expression of admiration the wish—

" Yet, though so lovely she be, let her sail away home to her kindred."

6. Since the ethical virtues have been affirmed to be particular conditions of the will, Aristotle finds himself compelled, before treating them in detail, to review the questions to which the human will gives rise. The first half of the third book is devoted to this subject.

The first place is occupied by the distinction between the voluntary and the involuntary. The springs of involuntary action are said to be force and ignorance. Of forced actions, one kind consists of those performed under pressure of threats or other dangers. Examples are supplied by the command of a tyrant who has our dearest in his power, and by the storm which necessitates the lightening of a ship by throwing valuable goods overboard. Actions performed in such times of stress are of mixed nature ; still the voluntary element in them preponderates, since our freedom of choice is not annihilated. Some might perhaps be inclined to expand the notion of force to such an extent as to include under it even the pleasurable and the morally admirable, on the ground that both are outside us and exercise constraint upon us. To such it may be answered that there would then be no action but forced action; since whatever we do is done from motives of this kind. Accordingly, the notion of "force" is limited to cases of true compulsion, in which the origin of the action lies outside ourselves, and we contribute nothing to it.

With regard to ignorant action various subtle distinctions are drawn. The involuntary agent is not the same as the non-voluntary, for the former produces effects contrary to his intentions, not merely foreign to them. In the same way action *through* ignorance is distinguished from action *in* ignorance. In the first case the ignorance relates to the end, and there is a mistaken view of the purpose of life; in the second case the ignorance relates to the means of execution, as when drunkenness or rage dictates the act and the darkened intelligence errs in the choice of means. The view that actions prompted by emotion are in themselves involuntary is combated by the argument, among others, that it would then be necessary to deny all voluntary action to animals and children. Thus the name of "voluntary" is here given to merely animal spontaneous acts. A higher stage of voluntary action is found in resolution accompanied by reflexion ($\pi\rho o\alpha i\rho\epsilon\sigma\iota\varsigma$), which is more exactly defined as "a deliberate striving after that which is within our power." A detailed account of the investigation would require too lengthy a consideration of linguistic differences. We content ourselves with the result: the object of the wish is the end or goal; the object of deliberation and the consequent resolve is the means; the actions directed towards such means are purposeful and voluntary. This applies to manifestations of virtue as well as of vice. In an earlier section (pp. 192–7) we have described the way in which Aristotle wrestles, not altogether unsuccessfully, with the difficulties of the problem of the will. The two paths which start from "phantasy," and lead, the one to logical thinking, the other to desire and striving ($\ddot{o}\rho\epsilon\xi\iota\varsigma$), conducted us to this culminating point of Aristotle's psychology. The philosopher himself took so little pains about systematic arrangement in these subjects that he reserved these purely psychological discussions of the will-problem for his work on ethics ; while the doctrine of the emotions, which equally belongs to psychology, was brought by him into a somewhat external connexion with rhetoric, and incorporated in his course of instruction upon that art.

The second half of the book passes on to the detailed consideration of the ethical virtues and vices. At the head of them is placed courage, which (in obviously intentional contrast to Plato's extension of this notion, cf. Vol. II. p. 297 *seq.*) he prefers to understand in the original and popular sense. Special fruitfulness cannot be claimed for this discussion, nor yet for the section on the next cardinal virtue, temperance ($\sigma\omega\phi\rho\sigma\sigma\acute{\upsilon}\nu\eta$), to which, moreover, a return is made in the seventh book. That which is worthiest note in these chapters is, perhaps, the statement that cowardice is of more pathological nature than profligacy.

7. The fourth book treats of moral excellences and defects in a manner which is highly characteristic, partly of ancient sentiment and partly of Aristotle himself. Our philosopher has already shown how small a part business played in his conception of life by slurring it over when discussing the chief types of human existence. It is true that together with the life of pleasure, of politics, and of contemplation, he also mentions the life of business ; but it is only to dismiss it immediately with the remark that material possessions are a means for other ends, but not an end in themselves. Quite in keeping with this aristocratic rather than bourgeois temper is his estimate of moral qualities relating to money matters. He explains "liberality" as the right mean between "prodigality" and "meanness." Indulgent consideration is here meted out to the prodigal, whose extravagance is attributed in most cases to faults of education, while it is held to be a task of not too great difficulty to lead him back by suitable training to the correct medium. "Meanness," on the other hand, is pronounced incurable ; it is an inheritance of the many which grows with the increase of years, and is aggravated by every other

diminution of power. Some of the touches employed in this description remind us of comedy ; for example, the "cummin-splitter," who is taken as the type of the niggard and skinflint.

A higher stage of liberality is known as "magnificence," a term which fails to coincide with our "munificence," since it denotes the grand style in money matters rather than the disposition to incur great expense for the benefit of others or for public purposes. Thus it is described as manifesting itself in the appointments of a man's own house. The two extremes are "pettiness" (differing from "meanness" rather in degree than in kind) and "swaggering ostentation." These last words denote not so much an exaggeration of "magnificence" as the display of it in the wrong place and on unsuitable occasions, as when a man entertains his clubmates on a scale appropriate to wedding-feasts, or when a choir-leader in a comedy wears a purple cloak. The man of "petty" mind, on the other hand, will spoil the effect of the greatest expenditure for the sake of a trifling economy ; he undertakes nothing costly without hesitation and reluctance, and yet is always afraid that he has overstepped the limit of what is necessary. In discussing these faults, Aristotle uses the word which denotes vice in the true sense, but he distinguishes them from such vice by the remark that they do not hurt others and are not really disgraceful.

The same qualification recurs in the treatment of "mean-spiritedness" and "conceit," the two extremes between which "magnanimity" is represented as lying. With this crown and "ornament of all the virtues" we reach that point in the Aristotelian and ancient morality which represents the maximum of self-assertion and thus the greatest divergence from Christian self-denial. Kindness is certainly an element in this assured, deep-seated sense of distinction. But it is the kindness of superiority, partly of pride. Thus the magnanimous man greatly prefers conferring benefits to receiving them. To bear malice is as foreign to his nature as to dissemble his feelings ; the second is contrary to the fearlessness, the first to the dignity, of his nature. His feeling towards the many is one of contempt, and his intercourse with them marked by irony. The central element in magnanimity is that the possessor of this quality knows himself worthy of the highest honours and seeks them, though without haste or eagerness. Even princely power and wealth are regarded by him as means, not ends. Among the external marks of his character are measured bodily movements and a composed voice, far removed from all shrillness—tokens, we may add, of the secure possession of power, such as are to be found particularly in the great ones of the East. And indeed the type here described might perhaps be best named as that of the *grand seigneur* equipped with all the virtues. The " magnanimous " man, lastly, is worthy of the honour which he claims ; while the pretensions of the " mean-spirited " are over-modest, and those of the " conceited " immoderate.

"Ambition" is related to "magnanimity" just as " liberality " is to " magnificence " in money matters. It signifies the desire for honour, not on a strikingly great scale, but in a manner which hits the correct medium in respect of the sources and the degree. It has to be confessed that there is no settled linguistic usage, as the same word is sometimes employed in a sense which conveys reproach. On the other hand, men are sometimes called "unambitious" by way of praise ; for where the correct mean has no separate name, the extremes often usurp the vacant place.

8. We now come to gentleness. This term relates to the emotion of anger ; it denotes not so much the true mean as a point below it, but is still recommended as a name for the mean itself. One of the extremes, blameworthy " irritability " or " irascibility," is described much as we should describe it ; the delineation of the too-little is much more characteristic. We are here enabled to measure the deep gulf which separates the Aristotelian way of thinking, which is also that of the Greeks in general, both from Christian humility and from Cynic " freedom from emotion." He who is not angry when there is need,

or not in the needful measure, "gives an impression of insensibility, and of not being in a condition to defend himself." The man, further, who "takes insults quietly, whether offered to himself or to his connexions, shows the temper of a slave," not of a free man. These thoughts were spun out to further length in the Peripatetic school, and illustrated by apt comparisons. The emotion of anger is required not only for defence, but for castigation ; he who would abolish it cuts through the sinews of the soul ; without anger and cognate emotions reason resembles a general without soldiers.

Some of the types of character now discussed belong to the sphere of social intercourse. Such, for example, is the case with the quality, not possessing a separate name, which lies in the correct mean between "obsequiousness" (which is called flattery when coupled with selfishness) and the opposite extreme of "peevishness" and "contentiousness." We, perhaps, should call this excellence "urbanity," in the highest sense of the word. Similarly, we have the adroit master of graceful and sociable wit, distinguished on the one hand from the "buffoon," or "vulgar jester," and on the other from the "boorish and wooden" fellow. The Old and the New Comedy are cited in illustration. Broad comic effects were produced in the former by coarse abuse ; in the latter the place of this is taken by innuendo. Legislators have already forbidden certain things to be reviled ; perhaps they would have done well to protect them also from being made fun of. For he who takes pleasure in listening to something is soon ready to do it himself. But here the man of really refined feeling, who has nothing of the slave in him, ought to be a law to himself.

Some attention is here given to "shame," though the subject does not, as he says, properly belong here, since this word signifies either mere emotion or the mastery over us of an emotion, not a quality of will. Shame, being fear of evil reputation, is closely akin to the fear of danger, which it further resembles in its influence over the body. It makes us blush, just as the other kind of fear causes us to turn pale. It is becoming to youth, upon which it acts as a

wholesome corrective of the manifold errors due to passion.
But it ill befits maturity ; for at this stage of life it is not
for a man either to be actually guilty of any act for which
he need feel shame, or to be seriously perturbed by the
imputation of such an act. Nor is any difference to be
made here between what is truly disgraceful and what is
so by convention, " for both are to be avoided." This little
clause, be it remarked in parenthesis, could not have been
written by any Cynic, nor yet by Plato, who showed so
little respect for tradition, for example, in questions relating
to women. Utterances of this kind teach us how great
was the philosopher's dependence on his *milieu,* and how
vain the attempt is to distinguish rigorously between the
cases in which he expresses personal conviction and those
in which he merely represents current opinion.

If in treating of shame Aristotle abandons the formula
of the mean, the subject of truthfulness leads him to a not
very happy application of it. Granted the necessity of
forcing this virtue somehow into the framework of the mean,
it was open to him to take for one extreme the thorough-
paced liar, and for the other the fanatical lover of truth
who refuses to lie even if his own life or the safety of his
country depends upon it. The types which he adduces,
namely, of the " boastful " man on the one side, and the
" ironist, or self-depreciator," on the other, are indeed more
in keeping with real life ; but they are concerned with only
a small portion of the subject, and impose a corresponding
limitation on the virtue which lies between them. It is
true that, in addition to the statements here in question,
those relating to the merits of the utterer, Aristotle also
mentions others, namely, those having to do with contracts
and promises ; but it is only to refer them to the sphere of
justice. No one need be told that these two classes taken
together are far from exhausting the whole province of
truthfulness.

In treating of boastfulness our philosopher exhibits
once more a trait in his character which we have already
noted—his contempt for money-making. In so far as
boasting has a purpose, it is said to be less blameworthy

when it aims at fame and honour than when its object is pecuniary profit. Self-depreciation, or irony, is regarded as objectionable only in its cruder forms. Sometimes, as is subtly remarked, the one extreme assumes the garb of the other. Thus the excessive simplicity of Spartan costume appears, superficially regarded, as self-depreciation ; in truth, it is disguised vain-glory. We are reminded of Plato's saying, " The vanity of Antisthenes peeps out through the holes in his cloak."

CHAPTER XXI.

ARISTOTLE'S ETHICS.

(CONTINUATION : JUSTICE.)

1. THE inadequacy of the theory of the mean is nowhere more clearly exhibited than in the treatment of justice. One whole book, the fifth, is devoted to this virtue. But it is not only by its exceptional compass that this section is distinguished from the others. Here for the first time altruism makes its appearance without disguise. Let us not be misunderstood. We do not here speak of altruism in the sense of Christian charity, or of Comte's "vivre pour autrui." Just as little do we wish to hint that the duty of caring for others' welfare was unknown to the Hellenes before Aristotle. No assertion could be more foolish. In the Homeric poems the gods often appear as the guardians of justice ; the most striking passage is that in which rich produce of the fields, fertility of fruit trees and flocks, are mentioned as rewarding the just judgments of a god-fearing king. Nor will the reader need to be reminded of the great part which justice plays in Plato's ethics. But at the same time, he will not have forgotten the artificial nature of the reasoning by which Plato connected justice with the welfare of the just person. By a strange limitation of its content this virtue was identified with the harmony of classes in the state, which harmony in its turn was represented as the counterpart of harmony reigning in the individual soul. Such is the wide circuit by which Plato reached the proof that just actions are demanded by the interest of the agent. Act justly, else thy inward peace is endangered—such, reduced to its

tersest expression, is Plato's mode of basing the chief social virtue on a foundation of individualistic ethics. There is nothing of this in the moral philosophy of Plato's pupil. Without any circumlocution, justice is declared to be a virtue aiming at the good of others. That such a virtue does exist, one which is not directed to the good of the agent, but to another (πρὸς ἕτερον, *ad alterum*), Aristotle expressly remarks ; and he notes the fact not without a certain surprise. He does not trouble himself about any eudæmonistic foundation. Indirectly, he rejects Plato's attempt to supply one by cutting away the ground on which he built, the identification of political justice with the subordination of one class to another, contrary to the principle of equality. We are thus entitled to say that altruism here appears for the first time in Greek philosophy without any support from the agent's quest of happiness, no longer masquerading as something else, but standing firm on its own rights.

Two cases of "justice" are distinguished—a wider and a narrower. The narrower kind of justice, as we shall presently see, is in its turn subdivided into several species. The wider justice is identified with moral virtue or excellence in general. This is done in the following way. Obedience to the laws is in a manner just, and disobedience to them unjust. Since, then, this positive law, or justice, commands the exercise of all other virtues and sometimes punishes the neglect of them (for example, cowardice in war or assault in peace), Aristotle finds it possible, not without some violence, to bring all the other virtues and vices under this head, by the aid of the mediating concepts of lawfulness and unlawfulness. This is done with the reservations that the virtues concerned are here to be regarded from the standpoint, not of one's own but of another's welfare. The philosopher thus claims to have confirmed the truth of the proverb—

" Verily all of the virtues are comprehended in justice,"

as well as that of the assertion that justice is perfected virtue. For it is far harder, he says, to maintain moral excellence in dealing with others, than merely in following one's own interest. The exposition of these thoughts terminates in the burst of fervour to which we have already alluded (p. 27). Not the morning and not the evening star is so wondrous fair as justice, which, lastly, is also called the foundation of every political or social community.

2. Justice in the special sense, to which we now come, has two sub-varieties. These are distributive justice and corrective, as it is generally called, though perhaps the term "directive," employed by the Schoolmen. is preferable. The sphere in which this latter operates is that of transactions, especially commercial transactions, such as sale, hire, giving security, and so on. By the side of these voluntary transactions are set others which (regarded from the side of the passive party) are involuntary. This somewhat artificial heading comprises all imaginable aggressions upon life and property, honour and freedom ; and these are further subdivided into secret treacheries and acts of open violence. It is only in respect of these involuntary transactions that directive justice can be regarded as also corrective or penal.

Distributive justice is said to consist in allotting to each person according to his worth or desert—a definition in which political privileges are preponderantly, though not exclusively, held in view. The standard of worth is said to be different in differently ordered states : in a democracy, it is freedom (that is, every one who is not a slave has the same due) ; in an oligarchy it is riches ; in an aristocracy of birth, it is descent ; in true aristocracy, it is virtue. All strife and confusion is said to spring from the inequality of the equal or from the equality of the unequal.

In reality, it is said, distributive justice rests on a proportional equality. In every case the proportion involves four terms, or three if one has a double employment. It makes no difference in principle whether the proportion runs as $a : b$ so $b : c$, or as $a : b$ so $c : d$, or again as $a : c$ so $b : d$. The point always is that performances must in each case correspond to rewards, duties to rights. The doer of injustice receives more, the sufferer of injustice less, than the amount to which the proportion leads. This applies to cases where goods are in question ; with evils the reverse relation holds. This more and less now provides the handle by means of which the doctrine of the mean is introduced into this branch of justice. It was impossible for Aristotle to apply the theory to justice directly or in any other way. No pair of extremes can here be named like those of cowardice and foolhardiness, insensibility and dissoluteness, between which courage and temperance strike the happy mean. The only contrast to justice is injustice. Aristotle is fully aware of this distinction, and he gives it frank expression in the remark that the mean does not here come into play " in the same manner as in the case of the other virtues ; " it now relates to the "object"—we might say the purpose or intended consequence—of the action. This object or result is represented as an equality, which certainly lies in the middle between two extremes, a more and a less. But on occasion the philosopher allows himself to be betrayed into a form of words which again obscures the distinction, and, if taken literally, amounts to an absurdity. Of this nature is the sentence: "Justice is a mean between the doing and the suffering of injustice." Or is there any intelligible sense in which we can say that honesty in business is a mean between overreaching and being overreached ? This could in any case be said only of honesty combined with prudence, the second of which saves us from the loss sustained through being over-reached by others, while the first withholds from us the profit which we might gain by overreaching others. Here, however, it is merely a case of looseness in expression, though, no doubt, besides simple negligence, there comes into play, perhaps in preponderant measure, a half-unconscious desire to mask in some degree the fundamental difference between the idea of the mean in its application to justice and the same idea applied to the other virtues.

This double use of the same notion, firstly, with respect to the agent's disposition of mind, secondly, with respect to the results of the action, depends on a merely external similarity, and may be regarded as an attempt at subtlety. The great dialectician has for once allowed himself to be caught in the meshes of his own dialectic. The true basis of that theory of the mean is the fact that human nature is endowed with instincts which crave satisfaction and press for active manifestation, but which at the same time have to be prevented from encroaching on the sphere of other instincts and needs possessing equal or greater claims. This is the case, for example, with the instinct of self-defence no less than with the impulses of the sensuous order. It is in these regions that we have to seek the root and the justification of the theory of the mean, wherein we see a scientific expression of that law of moderation which played so eminent a part in the popular naturalistic morality of the Greeks.

3. The eye of our philosopher being thus one-sidedly fixed on the equality which is disturbed by excess or defect and restored by just dealing, it becomes possible to understand, what would otherwise be incomprehensible, how he comes to regard penal justice, at least in one leading passage, as exclusively a matter of readjustment. The judge, who is "justice personified," seeks to effect this adjustment by taking away unjust gain from the gainer, by compensating the loser for unjustly inflicted loss. The best modern interpreter of the "Nicomachean Ethics" refused to credit the author of it with the "childish doctrine" that the awarding of damages is the only task of legal procedure. He also urges that Aristotle could not have possibly failed to observe that the relations between the doing and the suffering of injustice is by no means always of the simple nature supposed ; that, on the contrary, the injustice with which the one party is chargeable often far exceeds, but sometimes falls far below, the damage sustained by the other party. To this we have to answer that while so narrow a conception of a judge's duties and the failure to perceive the objection just raised are not faults with which one would expect Aristotle to be guilty, yet the wording of his statements leaves no other interpretation open, and that the error in question is the

legitimate offspring of another more fundamental error, the illegitimate transference of the theory of the mean to a region where it does not apply.

It is a pleasure to add that in another passage of the same book Aristotle clearly detects and powerfully combats a kindred error. On this occasion, no doubt, his vision is sharpened by the stimulus of a controversy. The Pythagoreans, as our readers know (cf. Vol. I. p. 106), had identified justice with a square number, because the notion of exact requital, like for like, reminded them of the genesis of a number from two equal factors. This presupposition of theirs, the *lex talionis*, is attacked by Aristotle with objections of great force. If a man in authority strikes a subordinate, justice does not require him to be struck in return ; and, in the reverse case, if the subordinate strikes the superior, mere requital, the repayment of the blow, is not enough ; it is necessary—doubtless in the interests of discipline—to inflict a heavier penalty.

4. After a few remarks on the mere analogue of justice presented by the relations of master to slave or householder to family, Aristotle turns to that far-reaching distinction, now so well known to us, between natural and conventional justice (cf. Vol. I. p. 402 *seq.*). Persons are not wanting— the reference may well be to the Cynics—who banish all political justice to the second category, founding their opinion on the following reason. Everything natural is invariable : fire, for example, burns alike everywhere, in Greece as well as in Persia. Thus the conventional origin of justice is proved by its variations from place to place and from time to time. Not so, answers our philosopher. The natural is not necessarily the unchangeable. For example, the right hand is naturally the better hand ; and yet by custom and training the left hand can be brought to equal perfection. So, too, in political justice we always have before us a mixture of the unchangeable with the changing. We see that the compromise which Epicurus hit upon between the two theories of the origin of language (cf. Vol. I. p. 398), was anticipated by Aristotle in the similar controversy on the origin of justice.

The subject of just and unjust action leads to a resumption of the problem of voluntary agency, which is now discussed with greater exactness than before (cf. pp. 249, 250). An act is voluntary when a man knowingly and not in ignorance performs that which it is within his power to do or to forbear. Here the knowledge and the ignorance may extend to the object acted upon as well as to the instrument and the purpose of the action. (An example is given of ignorance as to the object: A strikes B without knowing that B is his father; the action then falls into a different category from that which would apply to it if he had known.) Voluntary action, again, is subdivided into deliberate, that is, preceded by reflexion, and unpremeditated. That injuring of others which springs from passion is indeed unjust; but the agent is not thereby proved to be unjust and bad. Of involuntary offences some are and some are not pardonable. The unpardonable wrongs include those that are done in ignorance, when the ignorance is neither natural nor human, that is, when it is caused by a bestial passion.

5. The most important of the still remaining sections treats of equity and its relation to justice. Since equity is regarded as something praiseworthy, and yet relates to the same object as strict justice, there is a difficulty. How can the just and the equitable be both worthy of praise, seeing that they conflict with each other? The solution of the difficulty is to be found in the view that the equitable is indeed just, but not the justice corresponding to the law. It is rather a correction applied to legal justice or positive law. Every law has a character of universality; still cases arise which clash with the general rule. In such circumstances the law really means the majority of cases, not the totality of them; the error of generalization is not imputable to the law and the law-giver, but to the nature of the thing legislated about. The law-giver, supposing him present and aware of the facts, would himself correct the error. An ancient expositor supplies an illustrative example. In time of war a stranger is found upon the city wall. The law dooms him to death, as gravely

suspected of an understanding with the enemy. It appears, however, that the stranger has given the defending forces a signal which was to their advantage. The letter of the law decrees his death ; equity, taking into account the special nature of the case, awards him thanks and honour. In addition to individual cases such as this, there are naturally also exceptions from the primary rule of law which can themselves form a class and become the object of a new rule.

There are two countries, Rome and England, in whose jurisprudence the principle of equity plays a considerable part. The development which the *jus æquum* or *æquabile* has received in the English courts of equity, corresponds fairly closely to the thoughts here expressed by Aristotle. This appears from the treatment of the subject by one of the most illustrious philosophic lawyers of modern England, John Austin. Referring to a supposed case that needs to be decided on the principles of equity, he writes : " It is certain that the case . . . was not present to the mind of the law-giver when he constructed the law. But since its provisions *would* have embraced the case, if its author had pursued consequentially his own general design, the judge . . . completes the defective provisions actually comprised in the law ; and supplies the defective intention which its maker actually entertained from the predominant purpose or end which moved him to make the statute." Aristotle paid chief attention to the negative side of the question, the representatives of English legal development to the positive. Yet the former or negative aspect is by no means alien to the modern science of law. It is emphasized, for example, by Hugo Grotius, who remarks that a law is interpreted according to the demands of equity when it is *not* applied to a case covered by the letter of the law but not by its governing purpose. A distinction is accordingly drawn between the " extensive " and the " limitative " interpretations of the law. The following is a simple illustration of both. Relatively to the command in the Decalogue : " Thou shalt do no murder," and its penal sanction, the imitative interpretation would require impunity for homicide

in necessary self-defence, and the extensive would require punishment of negligent homicide. According to
Aristotle, the "equitable" or broad-minded judge always
deserves preference over the pedant who is faithful to the
letter of the law.

6. The discussion of suicide is noteworthy, not so much
for what it contains as for its omissions. Aristotle does
not hint by so much as a syllable at the Platonic and
Pythagorean conception which regards suicide as a wilful
desertion of the post assigned to us by the Deity, and
therefore as a mutiny against the Divine will. Just
as little is there any recognition of the view that a man
has no right to deprive society of his self and his
capacities, since by so doing he repudiates an obligation.
Nor yet is suicide acknowledged to be an offence against
a man's self, because no one voluntarily does himself an
injury. When, finally, the State is recognized as the party
wronged by suicide, the nature of the penalty approved by
the philosopher, seems to show that he here stands on the
ground of traditional opinion. For as penalty he names
"a certain kind of infamy;" and at Athens the legal
punishment for suicide was in fact a kind of infamy,
consisting in the separate burial of the culprit's arm as the
offending part of his body. Evidently the ground of this
was the pollution of the community by bloodshed.

But while Aristotle here gives effect to the current
notions of religious expiation, he does not make piety, as
one of the moral virtues, the subject of a particular
investigation and exposition. Was his standpoint possibly
that reached by Plato through the discussions of the
"Euthyphro:" piety has no separate sphere of operation,
but is a disposition of mind accompanying our acts in
general (cf. Vol. II. p. 363 *seq.*) ? It would still have been
open to him to contrast his own opinion on things divine
with that of the generality in a special section of his work.
Nor need this plan have involved any detriment to the
theory of the mean. It offered, indeed, an enticing opportunity for representing true faith as the right mean between unbelief and superstition. Perhaps considerations

of prudence restrained him from concentrating to a focus
theological views so likely to give offence as were his own.
To do this would have been to provide material, in the
handiest form, for an indictment of impiety, which, even as
it was, he did not in the end escape. How far, occasional
relapses apart, his principles were removed from popular
belief, may be learnt from his condemnation of the whole
mass of mythology, which he pronounced mere " accretion " and " husk," and of polytheism except for the
star-gods. Even from the purified theology of his master
Plato he is separated by a wide gulf, wide almost beyond
belief in the light of chronology. Between the close of
Plato's labours on the last work of his old age and the
delivery of the lectures from which the " Nicomachean
Ethics " sprang hardly two decades can have intervened.
And yet the second of the heresies which in the " Laws "
are proscribed under penalties rising as high as death, the
denial of Divine interventions in human fortunes, is now
treated as though it were a self-evident truth (cf. Vol. III.
pp. 255 *sqq.*). Indeed, it is affirmed that the Godhead exerts
no influence whatever on the course of the world, and hence
none on the fates of men.

The discourse now takes a polemical turn ; the object
of attack is Plato himself and the theory of justice which
he is here said to have based on a mere analogy or
" similarity." This ends the book, and with it the section
on the moral virtues.

CHAPTER XXII.

ARISTOTLE'S ETHICS.

(CONTINUATION: THE INTELLECTUAL VIRTUES AND WEAKNESS OF WILL.)

1. AFTER the ethical virtues come the intellectual, that is to say, the excellences of the intellect so far as they serve the interests of action. The road from the old subject to the new is opened by the reflexion that hitherto the mean has been recommended for choice, and that the term has designated whatever the "right rule" pronounces to be the mean. Hence it becomes of interest to consider this right rule more closely. The investigation begins with a logical division of wide range. The soul has on the one hand an irrational, and on the other a rational, part. Again, the objects of intellectual cognition are of twofold character: they are necessary or contingent, according to the impossibility or the possibility of their being otherwise than as they are. Objects of the first kind are apprehended by strictly scientific knowledge, those of the second by knowledge which may be called reflective and calculative, sometimes also deliberative. In order that an action may be performed, three elements are necessary; besides the faculty of thought there must be present in the soul both perceptive sensation and an impulse or desire, and all these must co-operate. The last-named element may also be negatively directed. Just as in theory we have affirmation and negation, so in practice we have pursuit (or desire) and avoidance. The source of the action is purpose, and this again arises out of impulse or desire together with knowledge relating to an end. Purpose is thus represented

as a combination of reason and desire. " For reason alone
sets nothing in motion "—a highly important saying, which
limits the intellect to its appointed sphere, and which
shows Aristotle's great superiority both over ancient in-
tellectualists such as Socrates, and over modern rationalists
such as Samuel Clarke or Henry More.

The different species of knowledge are now passed in
review ; here we confine ourselves to essentials, because
of the lack of exact correspondence between ancient and
modern terminology.   The realm of the contingent comprises the objects of making or production and of doing
or action.   The first are the concern of art, and the
second of prudence, that is, of practical wisdom dealing
with what is useful or hurtful to man.   As an example
of this prudence Pericles is named.   Here, evidently,
Aristotle has followed the traditional estimate of this
statesman *par excellence*, rather than his own, which, as
the " Constitution of Athens " shows us, was decidedly
unenthusiastic.   Nous, or " reason," is spoken of as originating the knowledge of principles.   " Wisdom " is taken
in two senses.   On the one hand, it is attributed to the
most excellent artists, and here means nothing else than
" the perfection of art."   On the other hand, says Aristotle,
we also speak of the " wise " without any limitation to a
special sphere.   We then understand the term as referring,
not merely to the knowledge of that which is deduced from
principles, but also to the knowledge of the principles
themselves.   In this sense wisdom includes within itself
both reason and science.   Its objects are stated to be " the
things which are most august by nature."   This preeminence is elaborately justified by an appeal to the
relative character of prudence or practical wisdom, which
is restricted to human affairs.   It would be vain to impugn
this order of precedence on the ground that man is " the
highest in rank of terrestrial beings."   True, but a glance
at the universe is enough to show that there are other
beings, far diviner in their nature than man.   We pause
here to ask whether Aristotle's judgment on the relation
of man to the universe is not sounder than that of those

almost contemporary thinkers who, like Comte or Feuer-
bach, desired to substitute the " religion of humanity " for
the veneration of universal powers. Far sounder, we
think, in spite of that belief in the absolute changelessness
of the stars which the progress of science has disproved.

2. The achievements of philosophers such as Thales or
Anaxagoras are rewarded by mankind with all possible
titles of honour ; they are said to be the works of genius,
magnificent, wonderful, but at the same time unfruitful,
since their authors have not striven after " human goods."
These latter are the aim of practical wisdom, a quality in
which special experience is often worth more than knowledge of the universal. If, for example, a man knows that
light meat is digestible and therefore beneficial, but does
not know what kinds of meat are light, he is inferior in
practice to the man who has no knowledge of the general
rule but is acquainted with the wholesomeness of poultry.

Aristotle goes on to say that among the objects of
practical wisdom a leading place is taken by politics. The
" architectonic " or governing art in this sphere is legislation,
with which is contrasted politics in the narrower sense, the
provision of ordinances and decrees to meet the needs of
the moment, a craft which serves as an instrument in the
larger life of the State. Mention is made of the widespread
opinion that practical wisdom principally concerns the
individual, so that the man whose mind is fixed solely on
his own private advantage is regarded as the true example
of this kind of wisdom. In opposition to this view, Aristotle
hints his conviction that man is intended by Nature for the
life of the family and the State, so that when isolated and
pursuing his private advantage he does not gain even that.

The investigation returns to the theme already glanced
at : the chief object of practical wisdom is detail, the individual thing. Occasion is taken to draw a significant distinction between that knowledge which is accessible to
inexperienced youths and that which requires a richer
experience and therefore a longer space of time before it
can be acquired. Geometry and other kinds of mathematics
are placed in the first category ; but even natural science,

still more political wisdom and prudence in the affairs of life, need a riper experience. The possibility of reaching a high level in mathematics even during boyhood is explained by the clause : " perhaps because these are matters of abstraction." That is to say, a minimum of experience is here sufficient ; for in Aristotle's view even mathematical knowledge grows in the soil of induction. We note that the history of science has amply corroborated this observation of Aristotle. It records instances of early maturity and even creative power by which this department of research is distinguished above all others. Abel, Bolzano, Eisenstein, Galois, Gauss, Lord Kelvin, Newton, Pascal— all these before the age of twenty, or just after reaching it, had already done mathematical work of importance, some of them, indeed, as pioneers. Truths the knowledge of which depends on comprehensive experience may, it is said, be " repeated " by the young, but " they lack belief " or inner conviction. In another context the same thought is expressed perhaps still more aptly : beginners " string propositions together without understanding them," even when there is no lack of verbal comprehension ; for the mind, so Aristotle continues, " must grow into unity with the object."

There follow somewhat lengthy disquisitions dealing with particular terms such as " judiciousness," " good sense," " intelligence," for the most part written with a polemical intention directed against Plato. These we pass over, partly because of their slender fruitfulness, partly of the lack, to which we have already alluded, of precise correspondence between the Greek termino- logy and our own. But in spite of this difficulty, we must dwell a little on what is said of Nous (cf. p. 207). Its intuitive character is here brought into so great prominence that even the gulf between the most general principles and the most particular perceptions disappears in comparison. Direct intuition, indeed, is described as characteristic of both the extreme points of all knowledge. Immediate certainty is ascribed on the one hand to the supreme principles of reason, that is, the logical axioms, and on the other to individual perceptions, which make it possible to apply general propositions to particular cases. Both alike are contrasted with all mediate knowledge. The individual perceptions complete chains of reasoning which issue in practical application by supplying them with their last links in the form of such propositions as : this particular thing is "of such and such a nature," that is, it possesses the marks or generic qualities which condition the applicability to the case in hand of general propositions already won. Thus if reason and sense-perception sometimes change places in this discussion, it comes to much the same as our use of the word " see " in respect of knowledge far removed from the sphere of sense perceptions, as when we say : " Any one can see . . ." or, " Who can fail to see that . . .?" and so on.

3. The closing section of the book consists of a dialectical tourney in which Aristotle first piles up objections of every kind, and then clears them away. Which of these objections are his own and which not, it is impossible to decide with certainty. The first question relates to the utility of practical wisdom or prudence and of the higher wisdom. The second is said not to be concerned with any becoming or beginning to be, and therefore not with the conditions of happiness. Practical wisdom does indeed possess the advantage of being so concerned, but what need have we of it if we admit that, although this kind of wisdom deals with what is just, good, and profitable to man, yet the knowledge of all these things makes us none the more able to do them ? And yet there is now a unanimous opinion—in the circle of the Platonists, that is—to the effect that the virtues are habits or qualities of will. And if any one urges that practical wisdom favours the acquisition of these qualities, it would still remain useless alike to those who possess the qualities already and to those who lack them. In respect of this second class of persons it is observed that it makes no difference whether we possess the desired qualities of will ourselves or obey others who possess them. We all wish to have good health, but we do not therefore all of us study medicine.

Lastly, it seems odd that practical wisdom, while inferior
to the other wisdom in value and dignity, is at the same
time superior to it, as having sovereign authority over
every department of life.

Now begins the series of replies. In the first place, the
two excellences under consideration would still be worth
pursuit as the perfection of one of the two parts of the soul,
even if they led to nothing further. But they do lead further.
Wisdom, in fact, does not resemble the art of medicine
which produces health so much as health itself ; it makes
the same kind of contribution to happiness. It is a part
of complete virtue, and as such blesses those who possess
it and practise it. This practice or active exercise is always
strongly emphasized by Aristotle, particularly in opposition to Xenocrates, who regarded happiness as guaranteed
by the mere possession of virtue. It is this tacit polemic
that is responsible for the violent hypothesis of a man
possessed of virtue slumbering away his life (cf. p. 243).
Further, the task set us is accomplished by practical wisdom
in combination with ethical virtue. The latter ensures
that the right goal is pursued, the former provides the
appropriate means.

The discussion which follows provides an apt criticism
of Socratic intellectualism, running, it is true, on lines
which Plato had already opened up in the " Statesman "
(cf. Vol. III. p. 184). It was but a half-truth which Socrates
stated when he affirmed the virtues to be knowledge, or
varieties of practical wisdom. Such wisdom is not the
essence of virtue, but an indispensable condition for its
existence. It is impossible to be perfectly good without
wisdom, but it is also impossible to be perfectly wise
without the virtue of the will. In our opinion a bright
light is here shed on the connexion between character and
intellect, on the ruin which comes to the mind when moral
disorder fills the soul with falsehood. The indispensability
of wisdom seems, it is said, to be contradicted by the fact
that there is a kind of natural virtue, that there are
dispositions and temperaments which incline towards the
good, as may be noted in the case of children and even of

animals. But they all need the guidance of reason, just as a powerful human or animal body, if bereft of the light of the eyes, falls all the more heavily—an illustration which can hardly fail to remind us of the Cyclops blinded by Ulysses. The intellectual element, too, supplies the bond which gives the virtues their unity—a unity on which it is easy to be led into error by the observation that hardly any one is equally favoured by Nature in respect of all of them. That skill in the choice of means which results from practical wisdom deserves our praise when the end is good ; in the contrary case, " capacity for everything " ($\pi\alpha\nu o\nu\rho\gamma i\alpha$) is hardly to be distinguished from knavery. There still remains the solution of the last puzzle on the relations of the two kinds of wisdom. It is just as false, we are told, to say that the higher wisdom is subordinate to practical wisdom, and consequently a higher part of the soul to a lower, as it would be to say that health is subordinate to medicine. Medical precepts are not addressed to health, but issued for the sake of health ; practical and theoretical wisdom are related in just the same way.

Any one who gives the book an impartial reading, equally avoiding both censoriousness and blind worship of the author, will hardly deny that it is rich in fine observation, ingenious thought, and subtle demonstration, but that it yet fails to perform the promise with which it opens. This book was to have cleared up the mystery of the mean. The "right rule" mentioned at the beginning is indeed once more alluded to towards the end, but only in the statement that we have to act not only *according to* it but also *with* it. In other words, we must not merely conform to the rule, but have it fully present to our consciousness. It will hardly be maintained by any one that either this statement or the other contents of this section can be regarded as providing the doctrine of the mean with an unassailable basis, or as giving it any other significance than an appeal to the tact and experience of the "excellent" or "practically wise" man.

4. Of what use is all the power of the directing intellect if the executing will refuses its services ? This unspoken

question forms the bridge between the sixth book and the seventh, between the doctrine of the intellectual virtues and the doctrine of the feeble will to which we now pass on. Aristotle himself speaks of making a " new beginning." He returns, in fact, to the ethical virtues already dealt with, and adds a postscript in which he treats a particular subject, self-control, more thoroughly than had been feasible in the former summary review. Three things, he begins, are worthy of reprobation in the ethical sphere: badness, lack of will-power, and brutality—the last, to be sure, being somewhat rare. The first has been sufficiently treated already, the third will be touched on afterwards ; it is now the time to speak of weakness of will and the opposite quality. A remark of far-reaching importance follows on the subject of method. First the facts are to be stated, then the puzzles or difficulties which present themselves are to be discussed, and the commonly held opinions, or at least the chief of them. When the difficulties have been solved and the current opinions are left established, then a sufficient account of the subject has been given. We have here a revelation, more undisguised than any to be found elsewhere, of the strongly conservative strain in Aristotle's mind to which we have already referred in passing (cf. p. 57). Current opinion, when purged or corroborated by the settlement of real or apparent contradictions, is identified with absolute truth so far as concerns questions relating to the conduct of life. The rule, to be sure, is not applied to all cases without exception. It was impossible, for example, to establish in this manner the superiority of the contemplative life, not merely to the little-esteemed life of pleasure, but also to the highly regarded life of politics. But whatever the range of validity accorded to the rule, the mere fact that it is set up at all is above measure characteristic of its author. A vast gulf separates him from the champions of revolutionary moral reforms. The Cynics, indeed, so far from starting with a presumption in favour of common opinion, did rather the reverse : they contended that generally recognized standards were delusion and empty vapour.

5. Our readers will remember the fundamental doctrine of Socratic intellectualism. It denies the existence of what is usually called the victory of desire or pleasure over wisdom ; according to it no one ever acts against his better knowledge : to acknowledge something as right and give the acknowledgment no sequel in act is outside the power of the mentally sound, it is nothing else than a form of insanity. We have already endeavoured (Vol. II. p. 67) to extract and do full justice to the element of truth "contained in this exaggeration." What Aristotle here considers is a modification of the Socratic doctrine, the work, probably, of Academics. The invincibility which Socrates affirmed was now said to be the property of true knowledge, not of the mere opinion which so often takes its place. Opinion is a feeble thing when pitted against the strength of desires ; no wonder, then, that pleasure gains the victory in the contest.

This is the first of the six puzzles ; the second cannot be reproduced without some straining of language. The abstinent person is said to be at the same time the healthy-minded person (σώφρων, cf. Vol. II. p. 300). And yet his abstinence can manifest itself only in conflict with strong and evil desires, whereas it is foreign to the nature of healthy-mindedness to have any evil desires at all, and still more so to have them in excess. If, on the other hand, the desires which the abstinent person overcomes are not evil but good, the quality in his character by which he resists them is bad, and if so all abstinence would not be praiseworthy. Nor is any special praise due to the conquest of desires which, though evil, are weak.

Thirdly : if strength of will (this is now the shade of meaning which is borne by the Greek word which we have just been obliged to render "abstinence") causes a man to hold stubbornly to his opinion, it is a bad thing when that opinion happens to be false. And if the contrary quality, weakness of will, makes us inclined to abandon our opinions, there will similarly be a praiseworthy kind of weak will, such as that exhibited by Neoptolemus in the " Philoctetes " of Sophocles. The son of Achilles deserves praise for being

moved by his sense of truth to revolt against the conviction which Ulysses had implanted in his mind, namely,
that it was incumbent on him to beguile Philoctetes into
sailing for Troy.

The fourth of the puzzles is called "sophistic" by
Aristotle himself.   It is an argument to prove that
weakness of will coupled with want of understanding is
not a vice but a virtue.   In such a case, it is urged, the
understanding makes a bad choice and the weak will
corrects it.   The underlying assumption may be illustrated
by the instance of a conspirator who through weakness of
will fails to perform his promised part in an assassination,
or by that of a religious fanatic who holds it his duty to
kill the heretic but lacks the will power necessary for
the act.

The fifth difficulty is supplied by a transference to the
present subject of a paradox which we have already
encountered in the "Lesser Hippias" (Vol. II. p. 291 *seq.*).
Which is the better, it is asked—the man who indulges his
desires from perverse convictions or the man who succumbs
to them from weakness of will?   The first, it is answered,
because there is a possibility of changing his convictions,
and by this means he may more easily than the other be
led to abandon the false paths.

Finally we have this question: If self-control and
weakness of will are to be found in every sphere of action,
who is the man that is to be called weak-willed absolutely,
since all the varieties of weak will can hardly be found
united in any one person?

6. Aristotle now proceeds to the solution of these
puzzles.   He begins by contesting the relevancy of the
distinction drawn in the first paradox.   Not only knowledge but mere opinion as well—so his thought may be
stated—is often maintained with extreme stubbornness.   A
weakly founded opinion need not be a weakly acting
opinion, incapable of powerfully affecting the holder's mind.
Heraclitus is mentioned as an instance, the suggestion
being that the tone of oracular certainty with which
the Ephesian proclaimed his tenets is sorely out of

proportion with their objective basis. Aristotle might have gone further, he might have adduced the madness of fanatical crowds and the "fixed ideas" of the insane. But even so he would have proved no more than that the objective justification and the subjective certainty of a conviction do not necessarily run parallel. Outside the province of authority, tradition, and religion there are wide fields within which such a parallelism does in fact exist. Temptations triumph over vacillating, confused, or inconsistent opinions much more easily than over such items of knowledge as that twice two are four or that prussic acid kills. To assail this position would have been vain labour.

Further attempts at solution greatly expand the questions under discussion. The special problem : How is it possible to act against one's better knowledge ? gives place to the more general problem : What influence has knowledge on will ? Intelligibly enough, the creator of logic is not content to use such ideas as "knowledge" or "cognition" without subjecting them to a careful analysis. He firstly points out the ambiguity of these words, they denote on the one hand the mere possession of dormant or latent knowledge, on the other its active exercise, the having a thing before the mind here and now. Secondly, distinctions are drawn between the different objects of knowledge, the different kinds of propositions or complexes of propositions. It is possible to know a general rule but not its applicability to a special case. Again, this ignorance may sometimes be caused by ignorance of the minor premiss, sometimes by mere unacquaintance with a particular object. Here is an example of this second case. Dry food is wholesome ; food of such and such a quality is dry : both these propositions may be known to me, but I may still fail in judging whether the food before me has or has not that quality which indicates dryness.

The third argument distinguishes two kinds of potential knowledge. On the one hand we may have knowledge which is simply not actual ; but on the other, knowledge may be impeded in its actuality—sleep, drunkenness, madness are impediments of the kind considered. The emotions, too, have their place here. Aristotle reckons persons swayed by violent emotions among the number of those who cannot wake and use the knowledge slumbering within them ; he even represents their bodily organs as being moved directly by the emotions ; and thus he makes a very near approach to the Socratic standpoint which he has previously censured.

The next and fourth attempt at solution seems, in Aristotle's opinion, to be the one which really settles the question. It leads to the paradoxical result that the process named by us a victory of the desires over the intellect is itself not without an intellectual element. Weakness of will is said to be in a certain sense "a product of opinion and reflexion." Our mind harbours at one and the same time two syllogisms leading to contrary conclusions. For example: "All sweet things are to be enjoyed ; the thing before us is sweet ; therefore we are to enjoy the thing before us." And on the other hand : "That which is sweet is not wholesome ; this thing is sweet ; therefore this thing is not wholesome." Desire, having predominance within the mind, now causes us to mistake our way, when we set out to make a choice, and reach the hurtful instead of the helpful syllogism. It seems to us that we have here a culminating example, hardly to be surpassed, of a tendency which characterizes Aristotle, though he sometimes happily overcomes it, namely, the tendency to see in man a syllogistic thinking-machine (cf. p. 190). The idea does indeed contain an element of truth. The pleasure-giving objects which at any given moment solicit our will, as also the feelings of pleasure or the reverse which are to be expected from them, may be assigned to definite categories, known to us from previous experience ; and this is a truly intellectual factor in the process of choice. If Aristotle further represents this act of classification as performed by aid of the strict forms of the syllogism, it may quite well be supposed that his intention was to supply a description which should be schematic and transparently clear rather than absolutely true to nature. We have been unwilling to pass over in silence this last way out of the difficulty, although we are hardly able to rest satisfied with it as a final account of the matter.

In any case the third of the solutions offered by Aristotle appears to us to stand higher than the fourth. In order to make it a complete solution nothing more is lacking than an explicit reference to a phenomenon which, as far as our knowledge goes, John Locke was the first to set in the foreground of the discussion. In the majority of the cases with which we are here concerned our action is not determined by any kind of anticipation of the consequences. We act under the stress of "a present uneasiness" which, at the moment, has the predominance in the mind. This pressure may be strong enough to outweigh all expectations of the future ; it may compel us to forbear all calculation of the pain or pleasure which may afterwards arise out of our action. The lamp of the intellect is not covered over or dimmed, it is absolutely extinguished. Socrates was right to speak of madness ; he ought only to have added that this psychical anomaly is not a rarity and an exception but an everyday occurrence.

7. At length Aristotle turns to the second of his puzzles. That the abstinent person must be at the same time "healthy-minded" is merely a postulate of linguistic usage, which confounds two neighbouring but by no means identical qualities. For the abstinent person truly cannot be fully free from the possession of evil desires, while healthy-mindedness excludes the possession of them. Perhaps we shall come nearest to Aristotle's thought if we say that two phases are here to be distinguished in the formation of character, two stages of development which because of their similarity, are easily confused. The abstinent person is not yet healthy-minded, and the healthy-minded person is no longer abstinent. For the first, evil pleasures have still a charm, which he is able to resist ; for the second, they have lost their charm altogether.

Fine distinctions again serve for the solution of the third puzzle, in which it is asked whether strength of will or persistence may not in some circumstances be an evil. "Obstinacy" or "indocility," as well as "opinionatedness," are marked off from the domain of will-power. Concerning the opinionated it is said, not without wit, that they resemble the weak-willed and self-indulgent, that is, those who are ruled by pleasure and pain, more than the abstinent and the strong-willed. For the contentious person's love of debate and victory, his dread of defeat in the conflict of opinions, assign him to the first rather than to the second category. Returning to the example from Sophocles, Aristotle remarks that Neoptolemus certainly was induced by pleasure to break his promise to Ulysses, but it was by a noble pleasure, the pleasure of truthfulness. An answer is at the same time provided for the question which that example illustrated, whether there is not a "praiseworthy weakness of will." The existence of such a quality is denied on the ground that the essence of weak will is not the being overcome by pleasure in general but by ignoble pleasure.

Aristotle clearly did not think it necessary to discuss separately the fourth of his puzzles, which he described as "sophistical" in his preliminary statement. He might have remarked that while want of courage or perseverance may in special cases turn out to be profitable instead of injurious, this does not affect the truth that the vast majority of cases verify the tendency of these qualities to injure their possessor.

The fifth puzzle raised the question as to which is the better—the man who is vicious from conviction, or the one who succumbs at times to the allurements of vice. In the first statement of the paradoxes the former was preferred ; this preference is now withdrawn and impugned. It may be said that in first propounding the problem Aristotle regarded it from the purely intellectualistic standpoint. The firm but false conviction can be corrected by instruction, and is thus more curable than the lack of conviction. But now he exchanges the intellectualistic for the properly ethical standpoint ; instead of convictions amenable to instruction we now read of habits which harden the soul. It is habit that governs the " profligate " man, cuts him off from remorse and prevents his reformation. But his counterpart, the man who errs from weakness, is subject to remorse and therefore capable of improvement.

The sixth of the puzzles and the answer to it both seem somewhat strange to us. Undoubtedly weakness of will is not like a smooth surface free from all irregularity. The man of strong character seldom shows his strength equally in all directions, and similarly the weak-willed man is as a rule more susceptible to temptations from one quarter than from another. But this two-fold fact need not prevent us from speaking of some individuals simply as strong-willed and of others as weak-willed. Aristotle's mode of distinguishing between universal and partial weakness of will can hardly be deemed above reproach. He contends that where the pleasure supplying the motive is not one of those given us by nature, the predicate " weak-willed " is applied only with a qualification, limiting it to the special field concerned ; it is so, for example, with ambition or avarice. On the other hand, the qualification is dropped where natural or bodily pleasures form the motive. Yet it may very well be objected that even in this latter case there is no lack of individual differences ; gluttony, for example, is distinguished from drunkenness. So much at most seems to be true, namely, that according to the nature of the case, we find ourselves emphasizing now the strength of the predisposing impulse, now the weakness of the resisting factor of will. It is, in fact, to cases of the latter kind rather than to others that we as well as Aristotle are inclined to apply such terms as " self-indulgence," " want of moderation," or " profligacy." This last reproach—to quote one of the remarks here let fall —is more fully deserved by the man who inclines to excess though his desires are weak than by the one whose desires are violent in themselves. " For what could he be expected to do if he had violent desires ? " Here, too, we have a division of inclinations into those which are by nature noble, those which are the opposite, and those which lie between, arising as they do out of bodily needs. Even the first class, we are told, admits of an excess which is blameable, though never, to be sure, absolutely vicious ; reference is made, by way of illustration, to Niobe, whose love for her children led her to challenge Leto. In the second category are placed the inclinations peculiar to bestiality or brutishness, as well as those which depend on morbid disposition or habits.

We are further told that it is less disgraceful to be overcome by anger than by sensual desires. For anger, though it often misunderstands the voice of reason, does in a measure listen to that voice. It is compared with those over-zealous servants who before they have exactly caught their master's commands hurry off to perform what they suppose to be his bidding. Thus the passionate man receives the impression that an insult has been offered him ; and immediately, without previous careful reflexion, he sets about defending himself and retaliating. Thus he does in a certain sense listen to reason ; but the sensual man listens only to desire. There is another ground for judging more leniently the excesses of passionate anger, and that is its freedom from concealment and intrigue. For the aristocratically minded philosopher the frank and fearless emotion of defiance is the nobleman in the slavish crew of sly and deceitful desires. He even thinks it worth while to quote the words of a poetess who called the goddess of love "craft-weaving."

8. This is not the only application of poetry to be found in this part of the work. Quotations, anecodotes, even scraps of folk-lore, follow each other in variegated succession. This unusual opulence, and at the same time the striking negligence of the style, provoke the conjecture that this section of the lecture course lacked more than others the sifting and revising care of an editor.

This superfluity finds a contrast in the curtness and baldness of the closing chapters of the book. Here we have the one portion of the work the genuineness of which has been questioned with some show of reason. It is a treatise on pleasure ; and the lengthy discussion devoted to the same subject in the tenth book seems to ignore it altogether. There we find no backward glance, here no anticipatory hint. As even the ancients saw, this is not a little surprising. We are entitled to infer that the two sections were written down each without any regard to the other. But this is as far as we have any right to go. For the contradictions which have been supposed to exist between the contents of the two sections are merely apparent. Take the polemic directed against despisers of pleasure, such as Speusippus, and without doubt Antisthenes as well. We must not for a moment lose sight of the predominantly dialectical character of the discussion. Referring to certain arguments used by the other side, he says, " This does not show that pleasure is not the highest good, much less that it is no good at all." But it does not in the least follow that the author (who could not then be Aristotle, nor Eudemus either) represents pleasure as the highest good. We regard these chapters as a preliminary sketch. This matter was perhaps inserted here by the editor, just as the rough students' notes had been before, in order to fill a gap in the text (cf. p. 241). We shall return to some of the matter here contained when we come to treat of the last book. For the present it will suffice to draw attention to a thought of great refinement and extensive application. It is not enough, we read in a certain passage, to confute an error ; we must know and state its cause. Putting this sentence in its tersest form : " Men refute only what they explain," we are reminded of Comte's profound words : " Men destroy only what they have replaced." But it is now time to pass on to the eighth and ninth books, which treat of friendship.

CHAPTER XXIII.

ARISTOTLE'S ETHICS.

(CONTINUATION : FRIENDSHIP.)

1. TWO books out of ten, one-fifth of the whole work on ethics, are devoted to friendship. To us the disproportion seems so striking that we can hardly forbear inquiring the cause of this preference. Granted that under the term "friendship" many things are here comprehended to which we are not accustomed to give that name, in particular the sense of unity among fellow-citizens, still the principal theme of the two books is friendship in the proper sense, friendship between men in all its grades, from mere sympathy without deeds up to self-sacrificing devotion. There is hardly a mention of the erotic bond between men which Plato made so familiar to us. Aristotle, who like the whole of that age was clearly influenced herein by the Cynics, regards the love of boys almost solely as an unnatural inclination, and in speaking of "brutishness," adduces it in company with other flagrant abnormalities. In his mind it is clearly divested of every touch of ideality or romance. But the result which we might have expected does not follow. We do not find that the process which we have described as the depreciation of woman (cf. Vol. II. p. 382) is at once reversed, or that the sentimental love of woman steps into the place left vacant. It is true that indications are not wanting which mark the first beginnings of this change ; we may remind the reader of the manner in which our philosopher's will mentioned his first wife (cf. p. 25). But these beginnings were all that as yet appeared. In the didactic works of Aristotle

which have reached us, the love of woman is regarded in one of three aspects—as an impulse towards the satisfaction of a natural need, as a blameable excess in the profligate, as a motive for encroachment on the rights of husbands. The marriage relation itself is assigned a highly dignified but modest position in the circle of friendships. A few lines suffice to set forth its character as an association that goes beyond the immediate aim of nature, that promotes the common welfare of the couple by the exchange of specifically different services, that in addition produces joy as well as benefit by means of the excellence (when this is present) of both parties. Truly an unpretentious niche in the splendid temple of friendship! A change of taste was clearly coming over the age which may be tersely summed up in the remark that the sentimental love of boys was now extinguished, but that the sentimental love of women had not yet been kindled.

The world, however, had not long to wait. A year after Aristotle's death, Menander, the leader of the New Comedy in which the love-match holds supreme place, gained his first dramatic victory. He had probably been preceded by Philemon. The change was assisted by the decay of public spirit and the corresponding growth in importance of private interests. This social change obviously had its effect upon Aristotle as well as others, and in combination with the other causes that have been mentioned caused a greater space to be devoted to the cultivation of friendship, though this relation was not yet marked by the fervour and emotionality which it was destined to exhibit in the circles of the Epicureans. Still, both this glance forwards and a glance backwards to the celebrated Pythagorean brotherhoods (cf. Vol. I. p. 147) indicate to us the source from which Aristotle's intensive cultivation of friendship may well have sprung. He spent by far the greater part of his life as a member of two Societies which have been rightly named " federations of men:" first the Platonic Academy, then the Peripatetic School founded by himself. These were associations which for many men lasted from youth to old age, which, beginning for them as students' corporations, gradually became transformed into societies of researchers, akin to our academies, but far surpassing them in the warmth and intimacy of their common life. Now and again Aristotle involuntarily betrays the origin of his ideals by letting slip, in passages purporting to treat of friendship in general, such phrases as " community of studies and thoughts."

2. One word on the position occupied by these two books, relatively to the others. In our opinion it is the best conceivable, indeed the only appropriate one. It has been objected that the treatment of friendship would have been more suitably placed immediately after that of justice as the social virtue. The idea is not a bad one, but there are weighty objections to it. The author of the " Ethics " clearly attached great importance to the plan of treating all the " virtues " together, and, in particular, bringing the two main classes of them into close conjunction. Nothing but this wish could have led him to leave " weakness of will " till after the intellectual virtues instead of taking it immediately after the moral virtues. Supposing, now, that he had placed his exposition of friendship next after that of justice—that is, between the fifth and sixth books— he would thereby have driven a great wedge between the two main groups of virtues, and so gravely impeded the presentation of the theory of virtue as a compact and connected whole. Thus, since according to Aristotle's own words friendship is rather an accompaniment of the virtues than one of their number, the treatment of this subject was necessarily placed after that of the virtues but before the discussion of their goal, happiness, towards the realization of which this same friendship renders the most signal service.

3. The exposition begins with a tribute of the warmest praise to its subject. Friendship is exalted even above justice, on the ground that where friendship is present justice is not needed, whereas the just cannot dispense with friendship. At this point a remarkable saying occurs. He who has found his way back to human habitations after being lost in the wilderness gains, we are told, a

sense of the nearness and kinship of man to man. Neither the distinction between Greek and barbarian, nor that between bond and free, perverts the pure human feeling of this passage. It is something almost unique in Aristotle, an all but isolated touch of cosmopolitan sentiment. A ray of that new light which had been kindled by Hippias and the Cynics, and which was destined shortly to shine with such brilliance in the Stoa, has strayed even into the soul of our philosopher.

Here follows the customary dialectical skirmishing, or discussion of puzzles. Two old questions are touched upon. The first asks whether the need of an unlike complement, or the attraction of like to like forms the chief motive for friendship, the notion of which is expanded in the cosmic sense familiar to us from Plato's "Lysis" and "Symposium" (cf. Vol. II. p. 385 *seq.*). The second concerns the loveable, which is reduced, in the last resort, to the good and the pleasant.

Friendships contracted for the sake of advantage or pleasure are declared to be of uncertain continuance ; and it is added that the first species preponderates with the old, the second with the young. The most perfect kind of friendship is that of good men. It is permanent, but rare, since few possess the requisite qualifications for it. After the friendship of the equal comes that of the unequal, as between parents and children, husband and wife, the holder of authority and the subordinate. In regard to equality there is a notable difference between friendship and justice. Proportional equality is predominant in the second, absolute equality in the first. This thought is illustrated by an extreme case. The wide interval prevents friendship with one who is very greatly the higher in rank, especially with the gods. Now comes the strange question whether one friend can wish that the other may become a god. A negative answer is given. For the consequence would be that the two would cease to be friends, and the one who was raised to divine rank would be deprived of a good thing, namely, friendship. (Perhaps this problem, which at first seems extremely artificial and far-fetched, arose out of the philosopher's relation to the deified Alexander.) Cases, however, arise in which equality in friendship is dispensed with. It is so with flatterers, who condemn themselves to inferiority, and in dealing with whom men are ready to bring their own superiority into prominence. Again, men often prefer to be honoured rather than to be loved, for example, in their relations to the powerful. To stand high in the regard of such opens up a prospect of help or favour in case of need ; and a man accepts this situation as a kind of symbol of his own prosperity. Men desire, further, to be honoured by those who have high character and know-ledge in order that their own good opinion of themselves may be strengthened. But while the being honoured is thus often sought for as a means to other ends, the being loved is an end in itself, and therefore something higher. If, however, the desire to have one's love returned is strong, the impulse to manifest one's own love in action is still stronger. By way of illustration we are referred to those mothers who—clearly under the stress of circum-stances, such as crushing poverty or illegitimate parent-hood—allow their children to grow up abroad, but yet rejoice in their prosperity and love them dearly, even when no sign of love or respect reaches them from their estranged offspring.

4. We come now to what seems at first a somewhat strange digression on political constitutions and their degenerate forms. This leads, partly to a comparison of the different types of friendship with the different types of government, partly to a discussion of the influence which is exercised on the private relations and characters of the citizens by the form of the political community under which they live. We may mention, as coming under the first head, the apt and familiar comparison of original patriarchal monarchy with the relation of parent to child, more particularly with paternal authority. We note, too, in the same connexion, the "aristocratic" character which is here said to attach to the relation of husband and wife, a predominance of the higher element which

degenerates into " oligarchy " when the husband encroaches on the sphere of activity proper to the wife, and so grasps total authority for himself. In regard to the second head, nothing is perhaps more remarkable than a saying about democracy, to the effect that under this form of government friendship is promoted among the citizens because " many things are common to those who are equal." Fraternity, we might say, is here deduced from equality. We, perhaps, should be inclined to expect the same result from Cæsarism, which resolves society, as it were, into its component atoms. But Aristotle ascribes precisely the opposite effect to tyranny, possibly on account of the frequent and successful practice by Greek tyrants of the motto " divide et impera."

Next, we have a lengthy treatment of the following theme : friendship directed towards profit is a fruitful source of discord, and the same is in general true of friendships based on inequality. For example, the superior friend and the needy friend will raise conflicting claims, the one pressing his superiority, the other his need, and both striving to gain the greater share of the profit which the friendship yields. The paradoxically sounding decision is arrived at that both sides are right. Each deserves a preference, but not both the same preference. The friend who is inferior in position may rightly claim the greater share of profit, the higher-placed friend is entitled to a greater share of honour. The State acts on this principle when it pays higher honour to the more efficient, but provides more ample succour for its needier members.

5. Kindred problems continue to occupy the opening portion of the ninth book. Among other things, the erotic relation between males is considered, but only in its more mercenary form. It thus appears as a variety of that " friendship " which is directed towards pleasure and profit, —that is, to something accessory and fleeting—not to the permanent and central elements of the personality ; it is therefore of short duration.

There follows what has been called the casuistry of friendship. There is no absolutely universal standard, we are told, by which to decide between the conflicting claims which may be made upon us by parents, it may be, on the one hand and by possessors of special knowledge on the other, or, again, between the claims of benefactors and those of comrades. As a rule, the requital of benefits received has precedence over the demands of mere comradeship. Fanciful cases are not excluded from the discussion. A has ransomed me from robbers ; must I do the same for him, supposing the opportunity presents itself, irrespectively of what his character may be ? Or if he asks reimbursement for his outlay, must I comply without regard to the circumstances ? Ought I not rather to use the money to pay my own father's ransom ? Yes, says Aristotle, with an ingenuity not altogether above suspicion, for I would have preferred my father's liberation even to my own. Again, if some one has lent me money, it may sometimes be permissible for me to refuse the like favour in return. Such a case will arise if the other man has lent to me in the full assurance that he will be repaid, knowing me to be a man of honour, while I, because of his untrustworthiness, cannot hope to see my money again.

The next subject is the dissolution of friendship. This takes place when the object of the friendship was gain or pleasure, and these are no longer yielded by it. But if any one has wrongly supposed that he was being loved for the sake of himself, the author of the deception deserves the severest censure. Deceit of this kind is worse than the offence of coining, since the counterfeited object is of so much more value than money. But how are we to demean ourselves towards a friend who has become bad ? The friendship cannot be maintained ; but it is only when the badness is incurable that an immediate breach is imperative. If the friend remains capable of amendment, then more help should be given to him, for the sake of his moral rehabilitation, than would be given to the financially unfortunate friend for the sake of restoring his position. Now comes a difficulty of a cognate kind : suppose that the one party has not become worse, but that the other has become very much better. Here, again, we have a barrier that will hardly allow the friendship to continue; the ties which it severs are most commonly those formed in childhood. Yet we ought so far to be affected by the past as to entertain greater good will towards our onetime friends than towards mere strangers.

Passing from the friend, who is a "second self," we come now to the first self, and consider a man's communion with his own soul. Two types are contrasted. On the one hand we have the man who is inwardly at one with himself, who knows little if anything of remorse, and who therefore willingly lives in memories as well as in anticipations. On the other hand, we have the picture of the bad man, who has fallen out with himself. Though it is impossible to feel pleasure and pain at the same time, yet this condition is approached as near as human nature can approach it, by the man of divided personality who wills one thing and wishes another, who now pursues a pleasure and at once repents it. Such persons do not live in friendship with themselves; on the contrary, they flee from themselves and seek refuge in distraction and self-forgetfulness, even if they do not go to the length of self-destruction.

6. We now come to certain feelings which, though akin to friendship, yet have to be distinguished from it; of this nature are good will or sympathy on the one hand, and concord on the other. The first is deficient in intensity; it lacks the ardour and the intimate association which characterize friendship. A typical example is the preference which we entertain for one among the participants in a contest (of poets, actors, athletes). We wish him the victory, but have no thought of helping him towards it. (Aristotle knew nothing of the passionate partisanships which afterwards centred round the arena.) Sometimes, however, sympathy of this kind is a first step towards friendship, just as pleasure in the sight of a person is often the first step towards love. Concord, again, is something higher than mere agreement in opinion, the subject of which might be any set of astronomical or mathematical

propositions. Its field is practice, more especially politics. Such community of thought and feeling unites men, while egoism separates them by causing each to strive after a greater share of advantage, a smaller share of efforts and sacrifices. Where this latter temper prevails, each man opposes and watches over his neighbour; indeed, it is only by this constant checking of each other on the part of its members that such a community is saved from destruction.

We are conducted to much greater depths by a question dealing with the relations of benefactors and benefited. Why do the first seem to love the second more than the second love the first? Aristotle begins by stating a popular attempt at an explanation: the two parties are comparable to creditor and debtor. The creditor has an interest in the solvency, and so in the welfare, of his debtor; while the latter would like to see creditor and obligation disappear together. But this is looking at life too much from the bad side, as Epicharmus would say. A much better comparison would be that with artists. An artist loves his own work much more than he would be loved by it, were it alive. This is especially true of poets. They cherish the warmest affection for their creations, love them as parents love their children. ("Marian is in the next room, crying over the distresses of her young people" —so writes Lewes, referring to George Eliot. Dickens says, in a letter to a friend: "I am breaking my heart over this story, and cannot bear to finish it.") The case is similar with benefactors. The ultimate reason is that we all love existence; now, we exist in our activities. "The work in a manner is the worker in his full actuality." Then, too, we have to consider the ideal element in the benevolent act. For the benefactor, this is, so to speak, embodied in the recipient; while the latter often reaps no more than a passing advantage. The discussion ends with the reflexion that all things laboriously produced are valued the more highly on that account. Thus we prize the possessions which we have acquired for ourselves more than those which we have inherited; thus mothers love their children more than fathers. The same appears to hold good of benefactors.

7. The book ends with the treatment of a number of controversial points. Men are sometimes reproached with "self-love;" on the other hand, we are advised to love our best friend best; but who is nearer to me than my own self? It is necessary to distinguish self-love in the ordinary sense from another and much rarer kind. The first is subservient to the desires, the emotions, in short, to the irrational element in man; the second renders homage to the ruling element in the soul,—that is, to reason; this homage, moreover, may be termed self-love, since in man, as in the State, and any other complex, the ruling element may fitly be identified with the whole. The practice of this self-love is fraught with the highest blessings for both community and individual. This thought is developed by Aristotle in fervid language bespeaking genuine enthusiasm. The man so minded—this is roughly what he says—will surrender money and goods and honours; he will sacrifice everything for the sake of the "beautiful"—that is, the ideal—and this he will prefer above all else. He will even leave to his friend the doing of great deeds, thinking it nobler to be the cause of his friend's achievements than to be himself the achiever. An attempt is made to justify this self-sacrifice on quasi-hedonistic principles; "a short but intense joy," to give the gist of the argument, "is preferable to a long-enduring but placid satisfaction." We, too, might admit that one year of consummate happiness is worth more than many decades of a half-enjoyed life. But to make considerations of this kind a ground for justifying the sacrifice even of life itself can hardly seem to us other than artificiality. From the hedonistic standpoint there can be no immediate justification for self-sacrificing death, though there may be for the filling of life with a rich content, for a devotion to ideals, which may entail such death as a consequence. The judgment of Aristotle here seems to us less sound than that of J. S. Mill, who answers the same question in these words: "It can be shown that on the whole more

happiness will exist in the world, if feelings are cultivated which will make people, in certain cases, regardless of happiness."

It is next asked whether the happy or the unhappy person has the greater need of friends. This question is at first discussed with the help of considerations which arise naturally out of what precedes. The unhappy man needs a benefactor; the happy man needs some one on whom he may confer benefits. The common opinion, that we need friends most in adversity, is explained as due to the vulgar utilitarian conception of friendship. As against this view reference is made to the social nature of man, to the fruitfulness of combined action as contrasted with the rapidly wearying efforts of the solitary worker, and lastly to the fact that only the possession of good friends makes it possible for us to contemplate actions which are at once excellent in themselves and connected with us through the doers of them. At this point there comes a turn of language which in Aristotle not seldom marks the transition to the profounder and more decisive arguments ("It lies more in the nature of the case that . . ."). Of all the purposes which friendship serves, by far the most important, so it now appears, is the expansion of a man's own self, the extension of the acquired or "secondary ego," as Theodor Meynert calls it. The intermediate link is the conception, not reached without a certain effort, of self-consciousness: "We feel that we feel; we know that we know." This knowledge of our mental states includes the consciousness of our own existence, a consciousness which is in itself pleasurable, though not to the bad. Feeling of this kind, as also the pleasure bound up with it, is greatly enhanced by fellow-feeling, and so becomes the consciousness of a widened existence.

Should we, then, desire to multiply indefinitely so desirable a possession? Aristotle proves, by arguments which lie ready to hand, that in the case of friendships grounded on utility this is impossible. But is there also a limit of this kind for the more ideal type of friendship? Much in the same sense—so, curiously enough, he continues

—as there is for the population of a city. " For a city cannot consist of ten inhabitants nor yet of a hundred thousand." All sorts of reasons are given for this limitation. It is not possible to share a common life with a great number of others and divide one's self, as it were, among them all; my friends, too, must be each other's friends, and this is the more difficult the greater their number; further, the more numerous one's friends, the oftener is it necessary at one and the same time to rejoice with one and mourn with another. Finally, it is suggested that high intensity and wide extension of the feeling of friendship are incompatible. The friend of everybody is rightly regarded as the friend of nobody. Allusion is made to pairs of friends celebrated in story and to the exclusiveness of the kindred passion of love.

We still have to mention a chapter on the relations of friends to each other in prosperity and in adversity. Our misfortunes are alleviated by the sympathy of our friends; is this alleviation to be regarded as the distribution of a load among several shoulders? Or are the presence of friends and our consciousness of their sympathy things pleasant in themselves and so calculated to lighten our pain? The question is left undecided. Manly natures avoid allowing their friends to participate in their sorrow ; women and womanish men take delight in common lamentation. Friends are to be called in chiefly when a maximum of satisfaction to us is coupled with a minimum burden on them. We ought, further, to visit the sorrowing even without an invitation, but we should only seldom accept the hospitality of the prosperous. Still, in the declining of invitations we should carefully avoid anything that might give an impression of boorishness.

CHAPTER XXIV.

ARISTOTLE'S ETHICS.

(THE LAST BOOK.)

1. THE last book gathers together with powerful hand the threads started in the previous nine. It begins with a discursive treatment of pleasure, a subject which Aristotle discusses with great thoroughness and many a polemical side-glance, and that not only in the present book or even in the course on ethics. We give our attention first to the results, on which the theory of happiness is based.

There is a passage of capital importance, in our opinion the most valuable in the whole work, which states that pleasure is the perfection or crown of activity, in the same way as beauty is the crown and flower of youth. The thought thus wrapped up may be put more clearly as follows. Just as the organism does not strive after beauty, but after preservation and development, while beauty accompanies the attainment of this aim, so by nature and instinct we strive after all normal exercise of our powers, after the full development of our capacities, and in so doing we harvest the pleasure which accompanies that exercise and that development. Aristotle himself supplied in advance a commentary on the passage referred to when he wrote : " Every perception, as also every exercise of thought and contemplation, is accompanied by pleasure. The most pleasurable, as well as the most perfect, of all these activities is that of which the subject is in a normal state, and of which the object is the most excellent of all the things included under the category concerned." There is here only one thing to give us pause. What is said of the production of pleasure clearly has a quite general application, and covers all activity or exercise of powers ; explicitly, nothing is mentioned but varieties of intellectual activity. Now, the author himself lived the contemplative life ; he purposed presently to extol contemplation as the summit of happiness ; it was thus natural that he should employ the speculative activities as the representatives of activities in general, or, more accurately speaking, as a starting-point from which to pass on to the others. This transition is made immediately after the settlement of a preliminary question, one of which the justification may be read between the lines : *"How comes it*—since our faculties are in constant exercise—*that we do not enjoy pleasure without ceasing ?"* For answer, reference is made to two fundamental facts of human nature, fatigue and the dulling of the soul's faculties by use. As a result of this second factor the intensity of the exertion relaxes, and at the same time the lustre of the accompanying pleasure becomes " dimmed."

2. Now the horizon widens. Instead of the merely contemplative operations we now have life itself : " All strive after pleasure because all desire life, and life is an exercise of powers." This exercise differs with different individuals according to the objects towards which the powers are directed and the instruments which each person uses by preference. One question is mentioned only to be dropped immediately, the question, namely, as to whether we choose pleasure for the sake of life or life for the sake of pleasure. Are not the two inseparably connected ? There follows a wearisome discussion of the specific differences between pleasurable feelings which depend on the specific differences between the activities determining them. The object is the severance of valuable from reprehensible pleasures—a region of ethics which has frequently been the arena of arbitrary dogmatisms. Aristotle knows nothing of Plato's untenable distinction between " true " and " false " pleasures (cf. Vol. III. pp. 190, 191). But he has no scruple in taking the feelings of the " excellent " man and raising them to the rank of

sole valid standard. With an unmistakable allusion to the Protagorean dictum touching the "measure of all things," he replaces "man" in general by "virtue and the good man." In dealing with the pleasure of the abnormal and the corrupt man (such is the tenour of his remarks), we say that it is a pleasure solely *for him* and his like ; but when we come to the normal man—who in an earlier section has also been described as the man who is at one with himself, untroubled by the inner war of the different parts of the soul—we say that his pleasure is pleasure in the absolute sense. The philosopher's sense of the relativity of all things human is here subjected to some strain, but a measure of compensation is afforded by the recognition of a scale of pleasures, widely differing in value, which lie in the interval between the two extremes of the unconditionally praiseworthy and the unconditionally reprehensible.

Several subtle observations are made in the course of this discussion. We may instance what is said on the effect of pleasures on the activities which they accompany and on what we may call the interference of different pleasures with each other. An unpleasant feeling impairs the corresponding activity, as, for example, when one who is sick of writing writes worse in consequence ; at the same time, a pleasure alien to the occupation in hand produces a similar inhibitory effect. The lover of the flute can with difficulty follow a conversation when he hears flute-playing. On the other hand, when the acting is bad in a theatre, there is an increase in the consumption by the public of the fruit and confectionery offered them by vendors of refreshments. An activity is maintained, enhanced, and perfected by the pleasure peculiar to itself, impeded by the pleasure with which it has no connexion.

3. Now comes the transition to the closing section, of which the subject is εὐδαιμονία or happiness. This position, we are told, is the due of that which is the end or goal of all human action. By reasoning which is already known to the reader (cf. pp. 243 and 272), it is proved afresh that happiness is " an activity according to virtue," and not, say, a mere " quality." Since εὐδαιμονία is not a means

but an end in itself, occasion arises to introduce the subject
of play, which likewise serves no end outside itself ; and
the claim for the first place thus suggested is examined
with what to us is a surprising fulness.   It was not a
difficult matter to prove that all the toil and labour of life
is directed towards a serious purpose and not to mere
sport and entertainment.   For the Greeks, the proof was
made easier by the close bond which their language wove
between the ideas " boy," " game," " jest " (παῖς, παίζειν,
παιδιά), and by the thought thus readily suggested that the
characteristic occupation of boyhood cannot possibly form
the highest task of maturity.   That which invited Aristotle
to linger over this subject was the circumstance that the
mode of life to which he awarded the highest prize is,
equally with play, directed to no external aim, and that
both, consequently, were often comprehended under the
common generic notion of " entertainment " in the widest
sense.

The highest prize is awarded to the contemplative life,
in whose praise and honour a fervid hymn is raised.
" Wonderful pleasures, wonderful in their purity and their
permanence, are afforded by philosophy or science."   Before
we enter upon the proofs by which it is sought to establish
this assertion, we cannot forbear a remark.   Judge as we
may as to the validity of the arguments here adduced,
they are absolutely cogent in respect of one thing—the
feelings of the man who devised them.   How great a tide
of happiness must have flooded the soul of one whose life
was filled with scientific research, and who extolled the
beatific power of such a life with so much enthusiasm !

The demonstration to which we have referred has the
following form.   If the highest end of life, εὐδαιμονία, is
an activity according to virtue, the virtue or excellence
concerned must be the highest of all, it must be an active
manifestation of the best in us.   But this best can only
be Nous (reason) or whatever else is ordained to bear rule
and exercise guidance and likewise possess knowledge of
beautiful and divine things, whether this element be itself
of divine nature or only that in us which stands nearest

to the truly divine. This conclusion, we are told, agrees with the teaching of predecessors and with the facts. Then, too, contemplative activity is the most continuous of all ; we can occupy ourselves with it for a longer time without fatigue than we can with any other kind of exertion. Further, there is another requisite of happiness, self-sufficiency (αὐτάρκεια), which is in a high degree characteristic of the speculative life. Even the cultivation of the practical virtues, justice, courage, temperance, always implies the presence of persons with reference to which they may be exercised. No doubt it is also profitable to the pursuer of wisdom not to lack fellow-workers, still he does not absolutely need them. Another argument starts from the antithesis of leisure and "occupations." All of these latter, including the occupations of politics and war which are distinguished by their importance and honourableness. serve as means to other ends. No one chooses war for the sake of war. We fight that we may have peace ; *we sacrifice leisure in order to gain leisure.* But when we look for something which is an end in itself, for the manner of enjoying complete leisure, we come to the contemplative life, the excellence of which is further attested by the fact of its not producing any result outside itself. Thus contemplation, provided only that it fills a human life of full span, contains perfected well-being. Such a life is superhuman. But we ought not to listen to the poets who warn us to respect the barriers set to the sons of earth and to content ourselves with what is on a level with man. We should rather desire to share, so far as is by any means possible, in the immortal life of the gods.

4. To criticize an outburst of fervour like this is a somewhat thankless undertaking. A thoughtful reader hardly needs to be told that some limitations are necessary here ; that the argument from self-sufficiency is not wholly free from artificiality, since the means of research cannot without exaggeration be represented as dispensable, while there is violence in the separation of the man in the researcher from the researcher as such ; that the argument from leisure bears a suspicious resemblance to a *circulus in*

probando, since it overlooks the fact that a born statesman
or general, a Pitt or a Napoleon, does not by any means
prefer political conflict or the clash of battle merely as a
means to other ends. It is more important to point out
that the lack of the necessary limitations exposes Aristotle's teaching to a criticism that overshoots the mark,
and impedes its just appreciation. It is so very easy to
say : The Stagirite was born to be a thinker and investigator above anything else ; what else should he do but
generalize his individual preference, elevate his personal
ideal to the rank of an ideal for all humanity ?

We may be permitted to answer with a parable. Let
us suppose that by the seashore there stands a lonely
house, which the numerous inmates are not permitted to
leave during life. The majority of them devote themselves
to routine occupations in the subdued light of the rooms.
Some see to the housekeeping, others compose the frequent
quarrels that arise within the house, others prepare to
defend it against attack from without. There are just a
few who renounce all but their indispensable share in the
produce of the common labour. That part of their time
which is not taken up with their duties to the community
they prefer to spend chiefly sitting in a bay-window from
which there is an endless prospect. Here they delight
themselves with the rich variety of pictures offered them
by the changeful clouds, the star-spangled firmament, the
face of the sea now bright and calm, now lashed with the
storm. They are alone in their preference. Among
the others, one has too weak sight to bear the full brilliance
of the sun, another has too sensitive an ear to bear the
roaring of the breakers. Such defects in their perceptive
faculties, perhaps also the greater strength of muscles that
permit and demand severe exertion, lastly, the higher
measure of their physical needs, subject them to the yoke
of everyday work. It would certainly be an error to maintain that this, by far the largest, class would do well to
set the contemplation of nature's wonders above the pursuit
of their useful occupations. But who will deny that the
better lot has fallen, that the fuller and richer existence

has been vouchsafed, to those who from their narrow and stifling bounds reach out towards the immeasurable distances, who greedily treasure all the stupendous impressions which come to them from the universal life ? Even such a contrast is to be observed within the frail and ephemeral race, animal by nature though at the head of the animal series, which peoples our tiny planet. On the one hand, the great mass ; on the other, that fraction which has chosen for its life's aim the vision of the "never-ageing order" of the infinite universe and of the forces which pervade and govern it.

5. Less elevated strains are employed in the praise of that contribution to well-being which is supplied by the exercise of the practical virtues. These have their root in the "composite" nature of man, who is a being compounded of spirit and body. There is a significant reference to the close intertwining of the intellectual with the ethical. From the intellect ethics borrows the notion of rightness or correctness ; the ethical virtues, on the other hand, are the foundation of practical reason. (We may remark that the stronger this conviction was, the less could it meet with the Stagirite's approval to separate two so closely allied themes by a section as long as that which deals with friendship ; cf. p. 286.) Aristotle now returns to the work of justifying the preference which he has accorded to the speculative life. He insists with increasing emphasis on its independence of external factors. For instance, he had previously said of the just man simply that he needs persons with whom he may deal justly ; he now speaks also of goods, by means of which the just man may make restitutions, and so forth. The same holds good of the liberal man. Similarly, too, the brave man needs material instruments of prowess ; and the temperate man must not lack the possibility of excess, for otherwise—so we have to add in thought—his temperance would be enforced. Debate as one may whether the purpose or the execution is the more important in the practice of virtue, the perfection of virtue cannot be attained without both ; the acts, however, require many external

aids, and the greater and nobler acts need them in ampler abundance. But he who is devoted to contemplation needs nothing of the kind ; indeed it may be said that such aids can only distract him. It must be admitted that in so far as he is a man living among men he will exercise the practical virtues as well, and that to this extent he will not be able to dispense with materials outside himself.

The last and highest trump is now played out. It is an argument which, starting from the absolute inactivity of God or of the gods (cf. p. 211), and from the supreme blessedness denied them by none, infers that their happiness, and therefore also whatever approach to it can be made by man, must consist solely in contemplation. We note that the reason is easily discernible why Aristotle speaks now of his one Deity, and again of the plurality of gods recognized by the popular faith. He cannot *prove* the blessedness of his Supreme Being ; instead, he sets out from the universally accepted belief (" We all assume," etc.), and then he quietly substitutes the one God of the philosopher for the many "blessed gods" of popular religion.

6. The concluding remarks of the " Ethics " prepare the transition to the " Politics," and also contain a reference to the great preliminary study for this latter work, the " Polities," the most important section of which was not many years ago recovered for us (cf. pp. 28 and 33, 34). This allusion appears in the form of a polemic against Aristotle's old opponent Isocrates (cf. pp. 20 and 24). In one of his speeches the latter had casually expressed the thought that the legal reformer need not necessarily produce anything new, that it rather behoves him to collect the numerous existing laws and choose out of them those which have proved best, " a task which any one who likes can perform easily." To this Aristotle replies with words of bitter censure. His critical sense is sharpened by profound antipathy, perhaps, too, by the consciousness of having solved, at a great expense of laborious investigation, the alleged easy problem of "collecting constitutions

and laws." His most decided contradiction is called forth by the eclectic procedure which Isocrates seems to have recommended. For everything depends (as he points out both here and in several other passages with much emphasis) on the agreement of a country's laws with each other and with the given conditions—as we should say—with the state of contemporary society.

The way to the " Politics " is opened up by the reflexion that the great majority are restrained from evil far more by fear of punishment than by a sense of shame. It is therefore pre-eminently necessary that not only education, which, as it were, prepares the soil for the seed, but also the "conduct of life " itself should be regulated by law, which alone has "compelling power." In this connexion reference is made to the pattern state, Sparta. A contrast is then drawn, with an obvious reference to Plato's " Statesman," between regulations which level all and individual treatment (cf. Vol. III. p. 183). But, whichever of the two we prefer, the active politician will always need general principles, which yet will indispensably need to be supplemented by empirical routine. The polemic against Isocrates, which we have already mentioned, was intended to prove the insufficiency of the treatment of this matter by sophists and rhetoricians. The course on ethics closes with an announcement of the main content of the " Politics " as the proposed completion of the "science of human things " and as the immediate continuation of the present work.

But before we step through the open door, we have still to return to a main and fundamental doctrine of the "Ethics," which is now to be surveyed as a whole and supplemented by Aristotle's teaching on the subject as found in his other writings.

CHAPTER XXV.

ARISTOTLE'S ETHICS.

(Conclusion : The Doctrine of Pleasure.)

1. Self-preservation and self-development are objects which are striven after by the human organism as by all others. Man strives further after the unfolding and the exercise of the faculties innate in the human soul. With every phase of this self-realization sensations of pleasure go hand in hand. These sensations, accordingly, are not primarily the goal of our strivings, but phenomena accompanying their success.

It is true that, once tasted, pleasure becomes in addition an immediate object of desire. As such it needs our unceasing and vigilant supervision. Not only are these secondary aims, when pursued for their own sakes, liable to interfere most injuriously with the primary aims (consider the dangers of incontinence or gluttony), but even the primary aims themselves, directed towards the realization of our faculties, need constant regard to the conditions of life (consider the dangers of foolhardiness) as well as mutual limitation. Without such regard and without such limitation the exertion of powers leads to a harmful excess. At the other extreme stands inadequacy of development, lagging behind the standard ordained by Nature. Here lies the root of the theory of the mean. Moreover, self-realization meets with many impediments and interruptions due to the action of external factors, and the overcoming and removal of these is again a main source of pleasure, which to this extent may be termed a phenomenon accompanying a return to the normal condition.

But the obstacles and disturbing influences which beset the struggle towards full and many-sided development are not all of external origin or caused by the disproportionate strengthening of particular elements in our composite nature. Even the merely temporary predominance of particular powers is felt as painful by the others which for the moment suffer repression. Such a predominance of one part is "something in a manner unnatural for the remainder of our nature." On this rests the necessity of change, which is counterbalanced by the desire for the repetition of the accustomed.

These are the main lines of Aristotle's doctrine of pleasure, gathered together from scattered utterances, with here and there a missing link supplied. His attitude towards both the true Hedonists and the despisers of pleasure is at once obvious. But since his treatment of the subject includes a certain amount of polemical writing which is not without independent value, a few points must be specially considered.

Aristotle allows some excuse to those who describe pleasure as an unqualified evil, and thus appear to be guilty of a palpable absurdity. These philosophers, Speusippus and the Cynics, probably do not go so far in their own minds ; in view, however, of the excessively pleasure-loving tendency of the majority, they feel themselves called to champion the opposite extreme, trusting in this manner to lead the world back to the commendable medium. "But just here lies their error." In these questions men look rather to deeds than to words. If the two are found flatly contradicting each other, the theory, including the element of truth contained in it, becomes discredited, and its advocates fall into contempt. He who denounces pleasure, and yet on occasion is seen to pursue it, creates an impression that he is wholly devoted to it. "Fine distinctions are outside the province of the great majority."

The philosophers who pronounced pleasure an evil had been answered by some with the following argument. The opposite of pleasure, that is, pain or suffering, which all desire to escape, is manifestly an evil; this alone proves that pleasure is a good. Aristotle does not think this demonstration quite convincing. In his view there is nothing intrinsically impossible in the supposition that both the extremes are evils, and that the corresponding good—the thought is natural enough to the author of the theory of the mean—is the neutral state lying between the two extremes. This, he says, would not be logically impossible, but it is false to the facts.

2. Leaving the despisers of pleasure, and passing on to the Hedonists at the other end of the scale, we note once more that Aristotle does not name, as the representative of this school, a man like Aristippus, whom he despised as a "sophist" (cf. Vol. I. p. 421). He prefers to direct his polemic against Eudoxus of Cnidos, a personal friend of his, who was celebrated for the strictness of his morals as well as for his work in astronomy. This choice of an antagonist alone indicates that Aristotle was far from adopting the attitude of uncompromising hostility to hedonism which was assumed, for example, by Plato in the "Philebus." The opinion which we thus form in advance is corroborated by the sentence in which Aristotle summarizes his investigation: "Pleasure is not identical with the good, and not every pleasure is to be chosen: some kinds of pleasure, however, deserve to be chosen merely for themselves; they differ from those which do not deserve such choice partly in their nature, partly in their origin."

The two philosophers approach the subject from a common starting-point. This is not to be found in postulates or imperatives of any kind, but in facts—facts of human nature, or rather of the whole animal creation. The thesis of Eudoxus, together with the proof on which he based it, is recorded for us in what are probably the original words: "All beings, rational as well as irrational, strive after pleasure; and their moving in that direction makes it plain that pleasure is the best thing for them. For every creature is able to find what is best for it, just as it knows how to choose its own food. But that which is good

for all, and after which all strive, is the universal good."
He contends, further, that the most desirable thing of all
is that which is pursued or craved without reference to a
reason or purpose outside itself. But this is the case, as
all allow, with pleasure. No one who is enjoying himself asks to what end he does so, since every one takes
for granted that pleasure or enjoyment is intrinsically
desirable.

Now, nothing can be more noteworthy than the fact
that in entering upon the discussion of this teaching
Aristotle ranges himself absolutely on the side of the
Hedonist Eudoxus. "It is absurd," he exclaims with
unusual emphasis, "to object that what all strive after is
not therefore necessarily good. Of that which appears to
all to be true we have a right to say that it *is* true. Those
who would rob us of this guarantee for our opinions will
hardly put a better in its place." But—so many a reader
will, perhaps, ask with surprise—does not Aristotle here
speak like a Protagorean, like a defender of the dictum :
" Man is the measure of all things " ? Certainly he does,
and that not in the present passage alone, where he might
have been influenced by a wish to defend a doctrine which
he respected, though he did not accept it, against invalid
objections. He does so, likewise, at the beginning of his
treatise on ethics, when he is laying the foundations of
the subject. He there adopts as his own a definition
already given by others, probably by Eudoxus himself :
" The good is that after which all beings strive." We
think this " subjectivism " well justified and greatly to
Aristotle's credit. Nothing could have been further from
him than the folly of identifying the opinions or inferences
of the great majority with objective truth. (Such a
misinterpretation, by the way, is less readily suggested by
the Greek original than by the word " seems," which we
have used in translating it.) The saying does not relate
to derived or secondary knowledge and volition, but to
that which is original and primary in both the knowledge
and the endeavours of man ; the same is true of the underlying principle, namely, that in the phenomena concerned

we have an ultimate source of knowledge and an ultimate basis for all codes regulating the conduct of life.

3. The point at which the paths of the Stagirite and the Cnidian part is not now unknown to the reader. In the opinion of the former human instincts and impulses are primarily directed, not towards pleasure, but towards the fulfilment of Nature's purposes—a fulfilment which pleasure accompanies as a subsidiary result. Our philosopher, however, gives full recognition to the close bond which couples original instinctive action with pleasure ; and he makes abundant use of it when he sets about framing regulations for the conduct of life. But—it may be asked —does not this bond snap at the point where individual, self-regarding morality makes way for social morality ? On what foundation, then, does Aristotle rest that social virtue, or justice, which he prizes so highly, seeing that it seems to have so little to do either with Nature's aims and natural instincts or with the considerations suggested by the parallelism between pleasurable feelings and instinctive actions ?

Aristotle might, indeed, quite conceivably have renounced every attempt to build a bridge between the demands embodied in justice and the self-interest of the individual. On the one side, society with its needs and the claims which spring from them ; on the other, the individual, whom praise and blame, reward and punishment press into the service of those needs, and render subject to the resulting canons. But that such was not in reality the Stagirite's attitude towards these problems is plain from more than one disclosure of his sentiments. For how, in the case supposed, could he have recognized a natural law in addition to positive or statutory ? Still less could he have written that fervid eulogy of justice, now so well known to us, in which he describes it as perfected virtue, endowed with wondrous beauty (cf. p. 27), Nor could he have identified justice with the whole of virtue (cf. p. 258), if in the philosopher's mind an impassable gulf had yawned between those virtues which are enforced, as it were, upon the individual from without and those which constitute his own personal happiness. This, however, is far from being the case. On first thoughts, one might be inclined to see a natural basis of social virtue in that which was said to be a product and an aim of friendship—the expansion of the individual self, the enhancement of the joy of existence by sympathy with others, and the share so gained in their life (cf. p. 294). The same result which "friendship" in the true sense brings about, with higher intensity but narrower extension, must also follow the cultivation of social sentiment in general, but this time with a wider extension and a corresponding total effect. The thought can hardly have been wholly absent from Aristotle's mind. But he does not dwell on it any more than he does on the possibility which we have had occasion to refer to (Vol. III. p. 131) of an artificial "rooting-up of the social feelings." His mind was at home in concrete reality, and he never employed it upon such academic questions as these. Man was for him first and foremost a being designed for "life in common," a "social being." The family, the municipality, the state—these are the enchanted circles within which he sees every individual constrained to move ; membership of such groupings is for him a fundamental law of human nature, which can evade these bonds only at the price, not merely of outward decay, but also of inner maiming. Thus he found the natural basis of social feelings and social morality in the social character of man, which he regarded as a fundamental fact, needing no further justification, open to no cavilling doubt. But the relation of man to the different stages and forms of the social tie is explained and described in the lecture-course on " Politics," to the consideration of which we now turn.

CHAPTER XXVI.

ARISTOTLE'S THEORY OF THE STATE.

(THE PRELIMINARY STUDY, THE STRUCTURE OF THE WORK, AND THE INTRODUCTION TO IT.)

1. WE have just learnt to know man as a member of *society;* immediately afterwards he becomes the centre of the doctrine of the *state.* The Greek language does not distinguish the two ideas, and the linguistic defect is one of considerable importance historically. We write sometimes "state," sometimes "society," as translations of one and the same word, πόλις, with its congeners, which at bottom means neither the one nor the other. So emphatically, for the Hellene, was the "city" the type of all social as well as political combination. Aristotle even uses the word "political" to describe the family life of animals and their co-operation for common ends, no matter (as he explicitly adds) whether the animal community lives, like the bees, under the rule of a single head, or whether, like the ants, they have no such head, and thus present in its weakest form the analogy with human political life.

The fact that the Greek knew the state only in the form of "city-state" exercised a lasting influence on the growth of his civilization, and was also responsible for the early destruction of Hellenic independence. But when we say that a boundary between state and society hardly existed, that the state, in fact, set itself in the place of society, that is only another way of expressing the fact that the provinces of law and morals, of the compulsory and the voluntary, were anything but strictly separated. This, again, appears clearly from the use of one word for two ideas. The Greeks gave the name of νόμος to *customs,* even the most indifferent and the most void of sanction, such as a particular mode of wearing the hair or beard ; they gave the same name to the most severely enforced *laws,* such as that which forbade murder under the penalty of death. Least of all was such a distinction to be found in the ideals of a Plato or an Aristotle. Sparta, with its Lycurgean discipline, served them as a pattern state, as the most serious attempt yet made to realize approximately their ideal of universal regulation. Not to go back so far as to Plato's " Republic," we have only just learnt that Aristotle desired the whole " conduct of life," and not education alone, to be directed and controlled by the state. Wholly foreign to him is the thought that individual freedom, including freedom to err, can be among the number of desirable things ; that not only is the power of the state always wielded by fallible hands, but that, apart from this, spontaneity of action and the diversity of characters and situations bound up with it, are in themselves of incalculable value. The vision of these truths was reserved for the Athenian Demos, its leader Pericles, and the philosopher among historians, Thucydides (cf. Vol. II. pp. 38–42).

2. Aristotle did not set about creating a theory of the state without elaborate preparations. Perhaps it would be more correct to say that his deep interest in history and politics kept him continually busy in collecting, comparing, and digesting the facts bearing on the subject, and that a part of these labours was turned to account in the " Lectures on Politics " (cf. pp. 33, 34). This does not apply to his chronological researches, which related to the history of the holy places and of the national games ; still less does it apply to his historico-geographical study on disputed territory (" The Territorial Claims of States ") ; but it is eminently applicable to the great compilation entitled " Polities," of which we may note that an appendix on barbarian states brought Rome and Carthage into the field of study. The structure of this work, as appears from its most important section,

which was not long ago rediscovered (cf. p. 28), was actually the same as we moderns employ in writings of similar character. It is customary to distinguish an historical portion from one which is statistical and antiquarian : the first deals with the growth of institutions, the second with the full-grown product. In the same way the " Polity " of the Athenians falls into two sharply divided sections. The first of them expounds the constitutional history of Athens, with easy-going diffuseness and no anxious endeavour to remain within the bounds of essential matters. The second main division describes existing political institutions, including details of the functions of administrative and judicial authorities. Some of the lost popular works were also among the fruit borne by all these historical and political studies, and by the speculation which they fostered. In particular, we may name a portion of the long dialogue " On Justice ; " another dialogue entitled " The Statesman," and giving the model of one ; a treatise " On Monarchy," in the form of a letter addressed to Alexander ; and a dialogue, perhaps similar in character, with the title " Alexander, or on Colonies." Less importance attaches to the few pages which make up the first book of the " Economics," matter of which the genuineness has been doubted, as far as I can see, without decisive reasons.

3. The structure of the " Politics " presents some peculiarities. The traditional arrangement of the books is not entirely in unison with the anticipations and the backward references which they contain. The following is the hypothesis on which we think the anomaly may best be explained. Aristotle repeated the course on politics, and did not in every case deliver the lectures in the same order as before—a change which has left traces in the gradually compiled notes.

The " Politics " falls into three main parts. The first comprises books i.–iii. ; the second, books iv.–vi. ; the third and last, the two remaining books. This division is plainly indicated by the work itself, and is borne out by the hints of the author. At the beginning of the fourth book he refers to the first group of books (spoken of as the

" first investigation "), and again at the beginning of the
seventh book he mentions the " first sections."

The first book is of the nature of an introduction.   In
treating of the elements of the state, it enters on a discussion of slavery, the completion of which is to be found
in many other passages both of this work and of the main
work on ethics.   A treatment of economic theory is also
naturally included in these fundamental chapters.   Some
surprise is produced by the announcement, made at the
end of the book, of the subject to which the second book is
to be principally devoted.   The author proposes to speak
of those " who have given their opinions on the best state."
And in point of fact, Plato's ideal state provides the first
material for exposition and criticism.   After it come the
projects of less eminent theoretical legislators, and then the
political systems regarded by philosophers as models,
namely, those of Sparta and Crete, while that of Carthage
is added as a supplement.   It is not easy to say what led
the author to adopt this order.   The question is complicated with another and much more difficult one.   The
third book begins with a kind of postscript to the introduction, dealing with the fundamental ideas of the whole
subject ; it goes on to describe the main forms of constitution, normal as well as degenerate, and treats exhaustively
of monarchy, which, in a certain sense, ranks highest
among them.   The reader is thus led to expect the
remaining forms to be presently passed in review, and
this expectation is actually satisfied in the fourth book.
But the lecture-course did not always exhibit this natural
and reasonable arrangement.   The continuation promised
at the end of the third book is not what we have indicated,
but a description of the " best state "—that is, of Aristotle's
ideal.   And again, soon after the beginning of the fourth
book, the reader is referred for a description of aristocracy
—the second best of constitutions—to an earlier section,
where it is not to be found.   There was thus a time when
the lecture-course was arranged very differently, and, we
may add, in a much less satisfactory order.   It seems
legitimate to assume that the lecturer originally developed

his ideal of the State merely in a sketch of slight extent. Now, however, the exposition of that ideal, which still lacks completion, and indeed is not carried further than the education question, occupies the whole of the last two books, almost a quarter of the entire work, Here we have what must have been for Aristotle a sufficient reason for removing this exposition to a later position than that first intended for it; while the editors of the lectures omitted to expunge those forward and backward references which had now become misleading.

But what can have been Aristotle's purpose when he originally chose so early a stage of the lecture-course in which to treat both his own ideals of State and society and, consequentially perhaps, the ideals of other authors and the pattern constitutions approximating to them ? We cannot answer this question with certainty. Perhaps here, too, he showed himself his master's pupil. Plato, as the reader will remember (cf. Vol. III. pp. 90, 91), was at times inclined to bring the "order in rank" and the "order in time" of constitutions into a somewhat fantastic connexion, to represent political systems of less than the highest excellence as being invariably degenerate lapses from original perfection, and for the purposes of such representations, tacitly to replace his own ideal state, which had nowhere been realized, "first by patriarchal monarchy, then by the corresponding type of aristocracy." Might not Aristotle also at one time have been guided by similar thoughts ? For in this field, as in others, he was a Platonist before the Asclepiad in him gained the victory. In this second character, that of empiricist, he put diagnosis before treatment : he began by reviewing the imperfect constitutions presented by history, criticized their defects, and left till last of all his own suggestions for improving and perfecting them.

Books iv.–vi. are bound together in the closest union. The survey of different forms of constitution in the first of these books does not stop at the main types, but extends to manifold sub-species and varieties. It ends with a comparative account of the powers of the State, and the forms which they assume under different constitutions. The fifth book contains what may be called political dynamics, in contrast with the statical mode of treatment which prevails elsewhere. How constitutions change ; how they fall into decay and become ripe for destruction ; how, on the other hand, they may be saved from catastrophes and maintained in existence ;—such are the questions treated in this book and its continuation, the sixth. (This last book returns to a point of view developed in the fourth book, that of the manifold differentiation of the main constitutional forms. Occasion has hence been taken to propose the transposition of books v. and vi. But not only is there an absence of valid reason for such a step ; it cannot be taken without the most violent interference with the traditional text.) Nowhere in the " Politics" is the author so much of a relativist as in these two books. With an impartial objectivity that reminds us of the author of the " Prince," he studies the nature of the various political systems, and searches out the means by which each of them may be provided with inner coherence, and protected against the dangers that threaten it. Even the " tyrant," though regarded with manifest aversion, receives his share of good advice, and of recommendations profitable for the maintenance of his autocratic power.

The spirit that breathes in these expositions permits us to judge how difficult it must have been for the Stagirite to set forth his own ideal of the State. We are tempted to say that the contents of book vi. explain why the section consisting of books vii. and viii. remained imperfect. The excellences and the defects of Aristotle's mind here worked in unison. He was too rich in adaptability, too poor in original fancy, to shine as a star of the first magnitude among the creators of new ideals.

4. The work begins with a polemic against Plato. The latter had given prominence (in the " Statesman ") to the common element in the ideas of the king, the statesman, the master, the father. Aristotle, in reply, emphasizes the specific differences between the groupings concerned. Here, as elsewhere, clearness is sought from analysis, from the

" breaking-up of the compound into its simplest constitu-
ents." The primary element of the State is found in the
married couple, united by the instinct of reproduction. To
this is added a second antithesis, that of master and servant,
which coincides with the first only among barbarians, with
whom the element fitted for command is wanting (cf. pp.
153, 284, and 288). From these two combinations the family
springs ; from the family, the village ; from the fusion of
several villages, the city or State. With this last the goal
of complete self-sufficiency is reached. It comes into being
for the sake of life, but maintains its existence as a means
towards " well-living." This form of community is a product of Nature. The man who belongs to no State is either
a bad man or more than a man. Man is a " political
creature," in a higher sense than bees or other society-
forming animals. For Nature, which does nothing in vain,
has given to man, above and beyond a voice expressive of
pleasure and pain, language which enables him to distinguish between the useful and the hurtful, and between
right and wrong. Interwoven with this exposition is an
excursus on the world of gods, who have been fashioned
in the image of man, and on primitive times. Nothing
could be more intelligible than that monarchy is the oldest
form of government. For it was the mode of rule which
men brought with them from the patriarchally governed
family—in support of which view reference is made to the
Homeric description of the Cyclops " ruling wife and
children."

This genetic mode of treatment is supplemented by
its antithesis, which operates with concepts. Though the
State is later in point of time, yet " it exists by nature
before " the family and the individual, just as in general
the same may be said of the whole in relation to each of
its parts. The paradoxical saying is soon provided with
an explanation. If a hand be deprived of its peculiar
functions by separation from the body, it is only in name,
not in its true being, that it remains what it was. The
dead hand is no more a hand than is a hand carved out
of stone (cf. p. 176). Just as man in the State reaches the

highest perfections, so, when severed from justice and law, he is the worst of creatures. Is not well-equipped injustice the most dangerous of all?

5. Aristotle does not, like Plato, derive the origin of the State from the economic need of the individual (cf. Vol. III. p. 64). But he is soon obliged to fix his attention on the subjects of industry and finance. He begins by enumerating the different modes of life, starting from the distinctions observable in the animal kingdom (herbivora, carnivora, and their subdivisions). The list includes huntsmen in the widest sense of the word (including fishers, fowlers, and—slave-hunters), then come tillers of the soil and nomadic shepherds who "pursue a sort of living agriculture." Mention, too, is made of mixed modes of life; but we notice the absence of any reference to industry in this connexion. The object of financial knowledge is stated to be trade, for which there is no room in the first stage of the community, the self-sufficing "house," while in the more developed forms division of property appears, and with it the need for the reciprocal "completion" of individuals by each other. A fully satis-factory account is given of the advance from barter to the discovery and use of money. But although the indispensability of money as an intermediary is clearly discerned, the class of men by whose agency it works is treated from the first with ethical disfavour. Contemptuous words, similar in nature to our "huckstering," serve to designate trade, both on the large and on the small scale. There follows what might be called a condemnation of mercantilism. Some, it is said, hold riches to be a "store of gold"; others, whose view receives manifest preference, teach that gold is "empty trash," and that its value is arbitrary, seeing that it is affected by every change in the monetary standard: while it is even possible for a man to have gold in excess and at the same time, like Midas in the story, to lack the most absolute necessaries.

Another reason for the unbridled race after money is found in the fact that man is more concerned about life than about well-living, and is even prone to identify the latter with abundance of bodily pleasures. Thus it has come about that every human faculty is employed upon an unnatural purpose—the gaining of money. Reference is made to the art of war, at that time much practised by *condottieri*, and to medicine. The first of these aims at victory, the second is devoted to the restoration of health ; yet both are pressed into the service of mere profit-making. A current of thought is here observable which has since been revived in Emil Steinbach's attempt to separate professional remuneration from the hunt after wealth. When Aristotle goes on to speak of the financial side of business science as "rightly held in evil repute," because the gain thereby promoted is "not of natural growth," we are reminded of modern socialists and their onslaught on the parasitic middleman. It remains, certainly, somewhat hard to understand why direct exchange is justified by the economic need for complementary services : while the business of intermediate trading, which fulfils the same purpose in the interests of persons at a distance from each other, is, together with its ancillary financial transactions, described as "hated for the best of reasons." Here, too, we find a condemnation of interest, based on an astonishing argument (since wittily ridiculed by Bentham), which is drawn from the Greek word denoting the idea. This word primarily signifies "offspring." As animals produce young, so lent capital produces its interest. This mode of employing money is accordingly censured as unnatural, because it "makes the currency itself into a means of gain, perverting it from its true purpose," and because "interest is coin begotten of coin," which in reality is sterile. The analyzer, who elsewhere displays such keenness of perception, here overlooks the fact that, though money usually supplies the garb in which a loan-transaction is clothed, it by no means constitutes the essence of it. For what is in the main quite the same transaction may be concluded where as yet the natural system has not been displaced by the use of money. Thus a well-to-do farmer may lend seed-corn or implements of husbandry to his distressed neighbour, and for the temporary deprivation

of these means of production he may claim compensation,
consisting in a share of the produce obtained by their use.

If these arguments have little convincing force, they
reveal to us all the more clearly the deep-rooted aversion
which Aristotle felt for the immoderate pursuit of gain.
Friend as he was of the old Greek order of life, which was
based on the preponderance of landed property, he justly
saw an influence hostile to those ideals in the growing
importance of movable capital.   Nor was the reproach of
unnaturalness wholly without foundation.   It did not,
indeed, apply to the intermediate agency of the trader, or
to the receipt of dues for loans, but to that insatiable greed
of gain which loses sight of all relation between the accumulation of money and the satisfaction of human needs.

6. After these exhibitions of emotion, the passionless
classifier has another turn.   He begins by dividing practical
finance into its sub-species.   These are the theories (1) of
cattle-breeding, (2) of tillage, (3) of bee-keeping and of
the management of other useful animals.   Reference is
here made to special treatises, such as then existed on
agriculture, on the culture of the olive and the vine, and so
on (cf. Vol. I. p. 386).   The finance which deals with exchange comprises (1) trade in its three branches : com-
merce by land and by sea and retail selling ; (2) the
money-lending business ; (3) wage-earning, which is again
subdivided by the aid of the distinction between skilled
and unskilled labour.   A middle position between
"natural" finance and that which relates to exchange is
assigned to the theory of those products of the soil which
are not consumed like the fruits of the field, but are put to
use in other ways : wood-cutting and all branches of mining
come under this head.   The exposition of the subject concludes with the mention of clever financial tricks, such as
the oil-monopoly which Thales once obtained in Ionia
(cf. Vol. I. p. 47), and a monopoly of iron which a wide-
awake merchant once procured for himself in Sicily.

Leaving the details of material gain, which he calls
" wearisome," Aristotle returns with a good will to the
ethico-political part, as it may be termed, of domestic

economy. He considers the position of the father, the husband, and the master. Paternal power is justified by a reference to " the greater age and the greater maturity " of the parent. This rule is spoken of as " monarchical," but the predominance of the husband is expressed by words which remind us of the position, now of a " constitutional " superior official, now of a " protector." Nor are the exceptions to this general rule forgotten ; the abnormal phenomena of the virago on the one hand, and the womanish man on the other, come under consideration. The Socratic belief in the complete equality of man and woman, and therefore of the moral demands to be made on both, is held by Aristotle for an illusion which dissolves the moment we leave the domain of vague generalities and fix our gaze on particulars. A woman, for example, would be thought bold if her modesty went no further than that of a reputable man ; a man would be esteemed a coward if his courage were no greater than that of a brave woman. In opposition to Plato's gibe about the " swarm of virtues " (cf. Vol. II. p. 367), full justification is allowed to the attempt of Gorgias the sophist to assign special virtues to men, women, children, and so on. But the question of the slave's virtue, and of his master's general relations to him, leads us to the great problem of slavery, the treatment of which claims a separate section.

CHAPTER XXVII.

ARISTOTLE'S THEORY OF THE STATE.

(THE QUESTION OF SLAVERY, GREEKS AND BAR-
BARIANS, BANAUSOI.)

1. WE have already seen that in enumerating the chief
occupations of men Aristotle mentions slave-raiding, or
man-hunting, among the varieties of the chase (cf. also
Vol. II. p. 205). Nor does he, as one might have conjectured, accompany this mention with a cry of horror.
Quite the contrary ; he expresses his full approval, so far
as the lot falls upon those "who are designed by Nature
to serve, and who resist this their destination." For then
subjugation is a blessing even to the captives themselves !
And here, it is to be observed, he is not concerned
exclusively with men of another colour or marked by
strong racial differences, circumstances which might help
to explain, if not justify, such an illusion. The great mass
of the slaves in Hellas drew their origin from Asia Minor
and the countries round the Black Sea. Typical slave-
names, such as Manes and Daos, direct us to the Thraco-
Phrygian division of languages, and thus, so far as
community of language implies affinity of race, to the
Iranian branch of the Indo-European family. When a
man of the lofty intellect and the humane sentiment which
the Stagirite elsewhere exhibits is found to be so deceived
as to confuse the low state of civilization attained by many
peoples with an incapacity for attaining it, as, in particular,
to mistake the effects of slavery for its causes, and to
discover in them adequate justification for violence and
man-stealing, how urgent an admonition to modesty and

self-criticism is conveyed to us by this monstrous error!
It is an error which seems all the more noteworthy when
we reflect that the legitimacy of slavery had long been
contested, that in the schools of philosophy, and even on
the stage, the question had often been debated whether
that institution rested on natural law or on mere convention and arbitrary practice (cf. Vol. I. p. 404; Vol. II.
p. 15 *seq.,* 151). Nor did the author of the " Politics "
remain untouched by these doubts any more than by the
cognate movement towards a cosmopolitan spirit and a
sentiment of universal humanity. Nothing, therefore, could
be more instructive than to follow out the conflict which
was waged within the mind and heart of our philosopher
by these fundamentally opposed opinions and feelings.

The arguments of the advocates of slavery and those
of its opponents are marshalled against each other. The
former launch out into long-winded reflexions on the
universal occurrence, in external nature as in the human
soul, of superior and of subordinate elements, the first
bearing rule, the second doing service. The opponents—
so this rhetorical tourney teaches us—had already made
some use of the weapons supplied by what was known
later as natural law. In opposition to the positive right
possessed by the slave-owner, they appealed to a higher
and inalienable right of humanity. For this is what it
comes to when Aristotle makes them raise the "objection of illegality" against the existing law. These words
refer to a form of legal process by which at Athens it
was possible to contest the admissibility of a project of
law or the legality of a measure already voted in the
assembly of the people by proving its incompatibility
with some more general principle of law. Much in the
same way, at the present time, the Supreme Court of the
United States is entitled to annul a special law which
violates a principle of the constitution or a fundamental
right of the citizens. It is a revolting idea (so the
philosopher makes the advocates of human rights protest)
that mere superiority of power should suffice to justify the
theft of liberty. For in the last resort it is solely the right

of the stronger, the excess of force manifested in battle, by virtue of which the one has become the master, the other the slave.

Here Aristotle makes an admission. Besides natural slavery there is also, as he allows, a slavery based merely on convention, that, namely, which depends on no distinction of worth between two classes of men, but only on the changes and chances of war. But he hastens to qualify this concession by detecting in conquest a moral element on which, possibly mindful of a Heraclitean saying (cf. Vol. I. p. 72), he lays considerable emphasis. Superior power, he urges, is an outward advantage which is usually based on inward excellences, so that force is not as a rule destitute of every nobler element. On the other hand, he admits, it cannot be denied that the origin and occasion of a war may be unjust, and hence, so we may add, that the title accruing from it may be of slender validity. And again : though the vanquished may have proved their inferiority by the mere fact of their defeat, it by no means follows that their descendants share this inferiority, and are therefore unworthy of freedom. The inheritance of qualities is indeed the rule, but not a rule without exceptions ; Nature possesses the tendency, but cannot realize it with rigorous exactitude.

2. The advocate of slavery, we see, has not made his task a particularly easy one. Neither the haphazard of the battle-field nor the accident of birth—descent from prisoners of war—is accepted by him as deciding beyond objection who are to be slaves. The test of outward appearance, too, often leaves us in the lurch. It is, indeed, the *intention* of Nature to distinguish by external marks those who are fitted for menial tasks and those who are capable of higher things. But this tendency, again, is among those which cannot always be fulfilled. Where, then, are we to seek the distinctive sign which infallibly and unambiguously separates those "destined by Nature to slavery" from those appointed to freedom? We are almost ashamed to record the answer. After all the subtle distinctions, after all the ingenious pleas and counterpleas, nothing results except the crude pronouncement : " Let the alien serve the Hellene ; they are bondmen, we are free." This line of poetry (cf. Vol. II. p. 19) is quoted with approval, and its import reduced to its simplest expression : " Barbarism and slavedom are by nature identical."

I know not what may be the effect of this utterance on others ; on myself it is one of petrifying astonishment. The whole of mankind, with the single exception of the Greeks, doomed to slavery, and that, apparently, in perpetuity !

It is true that, in proclaiming his own people the most excellent of all, Aristotle was not merely exercising an ordinary right. It needed no national prejudice to recognize that in art and science the Hellenes took by far the foremost rank ; that the combination of even approximately equal merit with free political institutions was nowhere else to be found. But it raises a smile to read an elaborate generalization such as the following :

" The peoples of the cold North and of Europe are courageous, and therefore remain in undisturbed possession of their freedom ; but they lack intelligence and skill in the arts ; for this reason they have no good political institutions and are incapable of ruling their neighbours. The Orientals, on the other hand, are distinguished by their intelligence and their skill in the arts ; but they lack courage ; hence they are perpetually dominated and enslaved. But just as Greece occupies a middle position, so the Greek people shares the advantages of both. [Notice here the attempt at anthropo-geographical deductions, on which compare also Vol. I. p. 311, and the allusion to the doctrine of the mean.] This people is at once courageous and intelligent. Hence it preserves its freedom, possesses the best political institutions, and would be able, could it attain constitutional unity, to rule over all."

That the peoples of Europe were not completely and for ever bereft of the capacity for ruling over their neighbours ; that the Greek climate and the national character supposed to result from it gave no guarantee against conquest and alien rule ;—all this would have been learnt by the Stagirite, could he have cast a glance upon a sadly near future, which was to transform proud Hellas into Achaia, a sorry province of the Roman Empire. The most remarkable point about this in every respect remarkable utterance is the confident expectation that the Greek people would gain dominion over the world if it renounced its constitutional disunion. Now, the only way to approach this goal, or, at the least, to preserve the national freedom, was to construct a federal state. So, at any rate, we should have expected a philosopher to think, for whom the permanent union of Greece under monarchical rule was out of the question, for whom the rise of a monarchy seemed excluded by the levelling culture of the age. It is thus truly astonishing that although in the " Polities " Aristotle treated fully of federal constitutions as well as those of separate states, in the " Politics " the federal state hardly receives even the most casual mention.

3. But, to return to our main theme, that which is maintained and ostensibly proved in the passage just cited is the claim of Greece to political predominance, not the claim to hold in slavery any section whatever of barbarian, that is, not-Greek, humanity. The more carefully we reflect upon it, the more incomprehensible does the claim become. Let us make the largest possible allowance for national pride and conceit ; there remains the discrepancy between this wholesale condemnation of the barbarian world and the cordial acknowledgment which Aristotle himself makes of "barbarian" achievement. As an instance of these take the Carthaginian constitution ; so highly does he rate it that he places its description immediately after that of the two Greek pattern-constitutions (the Lacedæmonian and the Cretan), that he speaks of the three constitutions as "standing near to each other" and as "far surpassing" all others, that he freely uses expressions of praise such as "good," "excellent," "well-ordered," and devotes a whole section to the exposition on which this verdict rests. Yet in spite of all this, each individual member of that highly commended state is to be regarded

as unfit for the free disposal of his own life, as appointed by Nature to slavery, as absolutely lacking the "capacity for reflexion," indeed, as an "altogether contemptible being."

Still more glaring, if possible, is the contradiction in which Aristotle entangles himself when he is considering the most effective means of educating slaves. This, he holds, is to be found in a prospect which should be held out to them of a reward for good behaviour ; and this reward is—emancipation. How, it has long ago been asked, can the philosopher propose to take those whom Nature has destined to slavery and part them from this their destiny ? how, on the other hand, can he detain in servitude till the tardy hour of emancipation those exceptional beings who here and there break through the general rule ? Possibly Aristotle might have replied by giving a weakened version of his doctrine, somewhat to this effect : " If I have called the non-Greek a born slave, my intention was to state a general presumption. But still this presumption may be rebutted in particular cases especially where a lifelong education comes into play ; and this conditional promise of emancipation counts among the most successful means of imparting such an education." This milder form of the principle seems to derive considerable support from Aristotle's acknowledgment, already noticed by us, of a slavery based on mere convention, in addition to that based on Nature, as well as from the further admission, to which we have also called attention, that the offspring of slaves may sometimes fail to inherit the inferiority which robbed their progenitors of freedom and at the same time made them unworthy of it. If the author of the " Politics " had in both instances merely referred to Greeks to whose lot slavery had fallen, he would certainly have said so explicitly, and he would have protested, in words as unambiguous as Plato's, exclusively against the enslavement of Greek prisoners of war (cf. Vol. III. p. 107).

4. In any case we have to acknowledge a certain looseness of expression ; and this may well be utilized for the solution of the otherwise insoluble contradiction. Such

looseness is by no means unparalleled in Aristotle's writings. Thus, to take one of the most flagrant instances, he uses the significant technical term "unwritten law" sometimes in the sense of customary, and sometimes in the sense of natural law, though the first is a part of positive law and the second the antithesis of it. So, again, the words "barbarian" and "barbaric" are sometimes employed by him with exclusive reference to primitive peoples and institutions, destitute of progressive civilization and lacking all refinement. For example, when he treats of the servile position of women among barbarians and of its cause (cf. p. 317), or when he speaks of archaic laws as "too simple and barbaric," he cannot possibly have in his mind civilized nations such as the Carthaginians and the Egyptians, the Persians or the Assyrians. Yet he takes no pains to discriminate this sense of the term from its other and more usual meaning. Indeed, this looseness of language paves the way presently for a more truly deplorable looseness, that of thought. As the less civilized peoples supplied the main contingent to the body of slaves then present in Greece, and as the state of servitude is in itself not a little apt to corrupt character, the reprehensible qualities due to want of civilization and those engendered by slavery were compounded by Aristotle into a single mass of badness which he called sometimes "slavish," sometimes "barbaric," and of which, in addition, he sometimes spoke as if it were common to all non-Greeks without exception.

" Low," "unmanly," "slavish,"—these are expressions which were used as equivalents even before Aristotle. But they merely incorporated the results of observation and naive prejudice; no one claimed to find here a ground and justification of slavery. Just as little was the popular use of the term "barbarian" as an inclusive term for all men except Greeks intended to convey a philosophic theory and a scientific basis for the dichotomy of mankind. Aristotle, however, puts forth this dichotomy, and by so doing drew upon himself the severe censure of the great Alexandrian scholar, Eratosthenes, who followed him about a century later. It would be better, he said, to class men according to their excellences and defects ; many among the Greeks are uncultured, while among the barbarians many are refined and in possession of admirable institutions. But it was precisely in this interval, the reader will perhaps urge, that the Hellenistic epoch had opened. The consequences of Alexander's victories, in particular the foundation of cities with mixed nationality, such as Alexandria, had cut away the ground from the theories of Alexander's tutor. True as this may be, it is not the whole truth. There were profounder minds which had no need to wait for this ocular demonstration before they broke through the spell of national self-conceit, chastised this spirit with biting scorn, and indeed attacked the " dichotomy " of our race with the same words and the same earnestness as Eratosthenes. How illegitimate it is to " give to nations which do not know each other, which have no intercourse with each other and agree in nothing, the one name of ' barbarians,' and then, on the ground of this one denomination, assume that they form a single class. . . . Just as the Greeks contrast all others with themselves, might not some other race of intelligent creatures, say the cranes, become inflated with pride, and balance themselves against all other living beings, lumping into one mass all that are not cranes, men included, and dubbing them all alike ' beasts ' ? " These are the words of Plato in the " Statesman."

It may well surprise us that the pupil overlooked such a warning as this from his master. But the cause which held him to the low levels of hereditary prejudice was not this time his tendency, now so familiar to us, to accommodate himself to tradition. Pride of race was here enlisted on behalf of a defence of slavery, and slavery was subservient to an ideal of the State.

5. Aristotle's ideal of the State included a body of citizens with an abundance of leisure permitting them to devote themselves entirely to State-business ; and such a body, in spite of its large numbers, necessarily constituted an aristocracy, requiring as its complement at least a

"banausic" class. What he meant by this term was a mass of persons destitute of political rights, dependent on the citizens, and looking to them for protection, consisting of farmers and mechanics, supplemented as a rule by a number of alien traders whose presence was tolerated in the State. Both for Aristotle and for Plato (in the "Republic"), such a class formed the necessary foundation on which to build the superstructure of a free and noble body of citizens. Falling far short of this ideal, but still not wholly unacceptable as a makeshift, was such a democracy as the Athenian, in the midst of which Aristotle lived. Here the banausic element had a share in the government ; but for truly menial tasks even this company of artisans and "market-folk" was deemed too good. Slavery, so daily experience seemed to teach, no less than philosophic speculation, is an indispensable institution. So long as we live in the real world, and not in a world of dreams and fairy-tales, so long, he judged, services must be rendered the rendering of which is incompatible with the position of a politically or even personally free member of the State. It would be otherwise if the creations of poetic fancy were realities, " if the statues of Dædalus and the tripods of Hephæstus moved of themselves, if looms wove of their own accord, if, in general, every tool and implement fulfilled its task at, or in anticipation of, the word of command." The modern reader can here scarcely fail to be reminded of the triumphs of applied science, and of that world of machinery which has transformed into a reality what to one of the wisest of the Greeks seemed a type of the impossible. And, with this contrast before us the hope may perhaps insinuate itself into our minds that the progressive liberation of men from purely mechanical tasks, as well as from those which demand mere bodily strength, combined with the expedients (unknown to antiquity) of representative government, may make more and more possible the fruitful participation of the masses in political life.

When an institution appears to be the necessary foundation on which the social order rests, every age has proved able and ready to defend it by arguments of every kind, good and bad. Slavery itself, and not only in that mildest of its forms, the domestic slavery practised among the Islamic peoples, but even that negro slavery which lends itself at times to such fearful and violent misuse, has found eloquent and fiery defenders as late as in our own days. In the year 1845, J. H. Hammond, the ex-Governor of South Carolina, published " Two Letters on Slavery in the United States," in which he condemned the anti-slavery movement as the fruit of a hateful rationalism which sets human reason above the Word of God. There lies before me a manifesto, signed by nearly a hundred ministers of the most diverse Protestant denominations, which, though it appeared in the midst of the American Civil War (1863), explicitly disclaims all political bias. "We consider Abolitionism," so declare the "Clergy of the Confederate States," "as an interference with the designs of Divine providence. It does not possess the signs of the Lord's blessing. . . . We declare in the sight of God that the relation of master and slave, much as we deplore abuses in this as in other human institutions, is not incompatible with our holy faith." Indeed, threats are held out with fearful explicitness of a "massacre of the blacks in case" the public safety absolutely demanded such a measure ; and the responsibility for this "darkest chapter in the history of human misery" is laid on the northern states which opposed slavery !

6. Aristotle, to be sure, is far removed from such hideous consistency. His inconsequence, indeed, seems to us to be, in this connexion, his highest title to honour. Apart from the inconsistencies which have already been mentioned, and which may possibly lie rather in the words than in the thoughts, there is one particular flaw which visibly runs through the whole of our philosopher's handling of this question. On the one hand, the slave is for him a mere thing and tool—" one tool in place of many," an "animated tool," not differing from a domestic animal, "a horse or an ox"—he needs but "little virtue," his master's advantage is his highest law, a friendship

between bond and free is held to be as impossible as one between the artisan and his implement, or, it may be added, between gods and men (cf. p. 287). But on the other hand, all this is said to be true of the slave only *as slave*, not *as man*. " For it does not appear that there can be a total absence of right and justice in the relations of any man to any other who is capable of any share in law and contract ; thus the slave, so far as he is a man, may have a share in friendship as well."

To us this distinction seems a mere artifice. On both occasions the subject of discussion is the possibility or impossibility of a friendship ; it is not a distinction such as in an analogous case might be drawn in something like the following terms : The monarch has chosen a subject to be his private friend ; the latter, *as subject*, owes him unconditional obedience ; *as friend*, he owes him unreserved candour, and therefore occasional contradiction. The case is different with the distinction between the purely legal situations which arise when the slave is considered, first as such, or secondly, as being also a man. As slave, the Stagirite may have thought, he owes his master, in return for lifelong protection and maintenance, his whole capacity for work and service ; the man in the slave, however, has a rightful claim to be exempt from additional exploitation, from the infliction of wilful injury to his health, from cruel maltreatment, from erotic abuse, and so on. But even between these two regions it would not be easy to draw the line with certainty. In making use of his slave's powers of work, is the master to be guided solely by his own interest ? May he go as far as the mechanic does in the use of his tools, as the ploughman or the rider does in exploiting his ox or his horse ? or should regard for the man come into play here so as to exert a moderating influence ?

Aristotle would scarcely have been able to return an unambiguous answer to these questions. We at least are inclined to the view that he was carried now hither, now thither, by varying currents of thought, that he vainly sought to harden himself against the humanitarian tendencies of the age, and that these left clear traces in his theory just as they entirely governed his practice. In his treatment of the question of slavery, much appears to be harsh and cruel, but that all this had its origin in his head and not in his heart may be learnt from the provisions of his will (cf. p. 25), which bestowed freedom on many, if not the majority, of the members of his extensive household.

7. From slavery to the banausic condition there is but a step. Aristotle makes this step by calling the latter a "limited slavery,"—limited because this condition, unlike true slavery, does not affect the life and being of the individual from birth onwards and throughout its whole compass. "No one is a cobbler by nature," whereas "slaves"—apart, possibly, from the rare exceptions which he mentions—"are destined by Nature to slavery." In his contempt for bread-winning occupations, our philosopher is at once the faithful disciple of his teacher and the interpreter of the universal Greek sentiment—a sentiment which was most strongly marked in warlike Sparta, least strongly in busy Corinth, but which was nowhere entirely absent (cf. Vol. I. p. 417, and note). Even the language embodied this manner of thinking; for it branded paid occupations with the stamp of "slavishness," and pronounced them "illiberal," that is, unworthy of the free man.

Contempt for the mechanical went so far among the Greeks that even the practice of the fine arts did not remain exempt from the stigma. The wide difference between ancient and modern feeling in this respect receives astonishing illustration from such a pronouncement as the following of Plutarch's : No well-disposed young man, he says, however he may admire the plastic works of a Phidias or a Polycletus, the poetical and musical creations of an Archilochus or an Anacreon, would ever wish to be one of these men. "Just in the same way we enjoy the magnificence of purple garments and the fragrance of unguents, while we deem the dyers and the makers of unguents to be illiberal and banausic." According to an anecdote, which is also found in Plutarch, Alexander was

once playing the lyre artistically at a banquet when
King Philip called out to him : " Are you not ashamed to
play so well ? " If this is true, the prince's philosophic
tutor was in full accord with his royal father. He
might, perhaps, have seconded Philip's warning with a
learned observation which we find in the " Politics " :
" None of the poets has represented Zeus as himself singing
or striking the lyre." But more than this : his own widely
extended learning might have brought him under the
suspicion of being banausic himself, and that, too, on the
ground of his own principles in relation to these matters.
In the " Gorgias " of Plato we have noted (Vol. II. p. 334)
the warning of Callicles against the " immoderate " pursuit
of philosophy. We seem almost to hear the same voice
again when the great polymath detects a danger for body
and soul in the study of even the "liberal sciences."
When this goes "beyond a certain measure," and strives
after too great perfection, the " free man," he says, runs a
risk of becoming " banausic." One is inclined to believe
that he was afraid of hearing similar reproaches from the
lips of his aristocratic friends. He forestalls them, at any
rate, by distinctions of the same kind which Plato had used
in order to divide, as by ditch and rampart, his own educational activity from that of the sophists and rhetoricians
(cf. Vol. I. p. 418). A strange spectacle. One of the
greatest, if not the greatest, among the scholars of all time
cannot bear to be a scholar by profession. He would
rather pass for a dilettante and man of the world, who
researches, teaches, and writes for his own and his friends'
pleasure ; anything on earth but a professional who cultivates the sciences "for the sake of others," that is, in the
exercise of a calling and for reward. So great is his terror
of all that is banausic, of all that "robs the mind of its
freedom and strips it of its majesty."

8. Property was still less a protection than education
against the banausic stigma. The author of the " Politics "
complains that in oligarchies, in which there is a high
property-qualification for positions of authority, while wage-
earners are excluded from citizenship, the same does not

apply to banausic persons in general, many of whom attain great wealth. And yet it is as impossible for the one class as the other "to devote themselves wholly to the requirements of virtue." For civic virtue is possible for him alone "who is not only free-born, but also free from all modes of work which serve the needs of daily life." That he is here not thinking merely of manual labour of the meaner kind is proved, not only by the remark just alluded to concerning the wealth of *parvenus,* but also by many other utterances, in which wage-earners and banausic persons in the narrower sense, that is, manual labourers, are found in company with the whole class of those engaged in trades and crafts, and in which the life of all these classes is pronounced "evil and forsaken of virtue."

To enter into this way of thinking is no easy task for us moderns, who everywhere see riches surrounded with social regard, and in many cases distinguished by political privileges. In order not to be unjust to the philosopher and the view of life which he represents, it is well to remember that false generalizations of a similar kind are not unknown among ourselves. It is certain that independence of character is not wholly absent from the class of man-servants. Yet we do not scruple to use a word like "flunkeyism" to describe character which is the opposite of independent, on the simple ground that the position occupied by those belonging to this class is only too well calculated to impair self-reliance and manliness. If Aristotle had known merchant princes who promoted culture, as the Fugger family and the Medici did, or even modern traders willing, like Schliemann or Nobel, to employ their acquired wealth in the service of the common welfare, assuredly his judgment on "market-folk and retailers" would have had a very different sound. But the majority of traders in ancient Hellas doubtless provoked the same disagreeable impression which we receive to-day in Southern lands from great numbers of importunate and untrustworthy chafferers — men who now artfully cheat their customer, now impudently overreach him, a haggling and screeching multitude.

The sharpest possible contrast to all this must have been supplied by the members of a community like Sparta. Freed from that care for daily needs which harasses and so easily narrows the soul, free, too, from the dodges and tricks of petty profit-mongering, trained to the extreme of fearlessness, both by a discipline imposed on youth for that express purpose, and by the incessant practice of war, animated by the most punctilious sense of honour and filled with proud reserve, accustomed to face death for the fatherland,—such were at least the majority of that lordly race ; and though their failings in other respects may have been many and great, they represented a type which stood out in bright relief from the dark background provided by the other class which we have described. Let us remember, finally, that the " virtue " which Aristotle, like his countrymen and his philosophic predecessors, held high above all else, was the virtue of sturdy self-assertion, of manly pride, of devotion to the common weal, and, in far lower measure, that of gentleness, of humility, and what have been called the " huckstering virtues " ; his position will then appear to us far more intelligible than one is inclined to think at first.

In this discussion of the State's social basis, constitutional questions have already presented themselves more than once. We must now devote our full attention to them, but first of all to the fundamental question of the function and purpose of the State as such.

CHAPTER XXVIII.

ARISTOTLE'S THEORY OF THE STATE.

(THE CONFLICT OF FORMS OF STATE.)

1. No contrast is more glaring than that between Humboldt's and Aristotle's views on the purposes and the boundaries of the action of the State. The first regards the State as an evil to be confined within the narrowest limits, the activity of which is only justified by necessity. The second objects against even the chief of the pattern-constitutions, the Lycurgean, that it does not go far enough in the tutelage of the citizens. In the one case there is an all-absorbing anxiety to maintain intact the individuality of the citizens and to promote its most powerful development; in the other there is as little concern about this aim as if that imperishable programme of individual freedom, the funeral oration of Pericles, had never been spoken (cf. Vol. I. pp. 5, 6; Vol. II. pp. 40, 41). The European and American society of the present day includes two parties, of which one would give the State nothing, the other all. The broad middle stratum professes neither of the two extreme opinions, but probably holds a position much nearer to that of the ancient Greek sage than to that of the German who was almost our own contemporary.

Ever louder and louder rises the cry for the extension of benevolent institutions, for greater protection of the economically weak ; less and less do we hear the counter-cry warning us against that weakening which is inevitably suffered by personal initiative when its place is taken in ever-increasing measure by the fostering care of the State.

Yet whatever is destined to be the outcome of these cross-currents of opinion, there are certain highly important distinctions now familiar to us, which were overlooked by anti-State radicalism—the distinction between the coercive power of the State and its helpful activity, making no use of force, but working partly by encouragement and partly by instruction : and then again within the coercive sphere itself, between that coercion which does, and that which emphatically does not, tend to stifle or to misdirect individual powers. What a gulf yawns between the forcible imposition of faith, thought, or even morality, on the one hand, and the use of compulsion to obtain statistical information on the other! It makes the greatest difference conceivable whether we choke up a stream at the source, or place a momentary obstruction in its course in order that it may turn a mill-wheel for us.

Was antiquity quite without advocates for that which the modern world has become accustomed to speak of contemptuously as the " policeman state " ? or were there even then thinkers who like Humboldt, and like Mirabeau whom Humboldt quotes, conceived the sole task of the State as the providing of security, both by the protection of the law and by defence against external enemies ? An affirmative answer to this question might be gathered from certain polemical utterances of the Stagirite, which will soon engage our attention. But besides this he reports a saying, a very curt one it is true, of Gorgias' pupil, Lycophron, which we can hardly interpret except in this sense. We have already made the acquaintance of this Sophist as a theorizer on knowledge, who proposed to overcome the difficulties arising from the idea of Being by the radical method of absolutely avoiding the use of the copula (cf. Vol. I. p. 493). In the province of social science, he showed his radicalism chiefly in this, that, contrary to Aristotle, he denied any and every value to illustrious descent, and placed the low-born on an absolute equality with the nobly born. When, therefore, we learn that he spoke of law based on contract as " the mutual guarantor of rights," and when we find this definition coupled with a repudiation of all educational activity on the part of the State, we have good cause for regarding Lycophron as a champion of the legal State in the narrowest sense of the expression. Considering the unqualified Laconizing tendency both of Plato and of his disciple, considering, too, the imperfect distinction between law and morality throughout antiquity, and the predominating inclination to invest the administrative authority with nothing short of omnipotence, the attempt to discriminate between essentially different spheres must be regarded as meritorious, in spite of its onesidedness.

2. Neither a tariff union nor a military convention makes a state out of the districts which it binds together ; just as little can this end be achieved by a joint-stock company. We have here somewhat modernized the garment of language, but faithfully reproduced the thought. The author of the " Politics " desires to illustrate his positive conception of the State by the contrast with instances which on a superficial consideration appear as analogous to it. But " for him who looks deeper " it is not an association for war or for trade, neither a company formed for gain, nor a mere provision for security. First and foremost, we are told, it is an educational institution. More precisely, it is " a community of good life, embracing both families and tribes, intended to promote full and independent existence." One necessary condition for this, in addition to the reciprocal right of free intermarriage, is residence in the same place. But this is not the essential ; if it were, the activity of the State would be limited to the provision of security, and the State itself would be merely an " alliance," differing from ordinary alliances only by the local contiguity of the parties to it. Stress is again laid on full and independent existence, which is now identified with happy and (morally) beautiful life. Hence those who excel in political virtue contribute more to the community and have more claim upon the State than those who lag behind in this respect, even though they have the advantage of free or noble birth, or of riches. The transition to the question as to the seat of sovereignty

is assisted by the remark that the advocates of the different forms of government propound wh ᐞ are merely half-truths.

3. The "element of the State," the citizen, has already been treated of. Naturally, he is not absolutely identified with the resident in the State-territory. This class comprised also the immigrant and the slave. After a few fruitless attempts, the distinctive mark of the citizen is found to be his participation in the acts of the State and his exercise of official authority. In spite of the appearance to the contrary, the juror and the member of the popular assembly must be regarded as officials, although their tenure of office is not for a specified period. (The Athenian, for example, supposing him to be of unblemished character, entered upon those functions on attaining a certain age without further preliminaries.)

This definition, as Aristotle admits, applies most strictly to the members of a democratic community. (It is noteworthy here that the philosopher is sufficiently influenced by his Athenian surroundings to take this form of government as a starting-point, in spite of the depreciation of it which followed from his principles.) For other forms of the State the definition must be modified, since the powers of government are now wielded by persons with a limited, instead of an unlimited, period of authority. Here, therefore, the name of citizen must be given to those who are not excluded from access to the functions of deliberation or decision. But a difficulty arises from the fact that for practical purposes the citizen is defined as the descendant of citizens—as the son, grandson, or great-grandson of one who had that quality. How, it is asked, can the first member of such a series have been himself a citizen? The answer is simple enough. If the men who founded such families possessed citizenship, in the sense of eligibility to office, then they were citizens, even though their ancestors were not. The case is much the same with persons raised to citizenship from the status of slaves or immigrants—as was done on a large scale by the Athenian Clisthenes (cf. Vol. II. p. 39).

A more important question relates to the identity of the State. Is this extinguished by a revolution, and do the obligations incurred by the old government necessarily bind the new one? No general answer is given to this question. The identity of the State depends chiefly, it is contended, on the identity of the constitution, and is as little affected by the change of the population as the identity of a river is by the incessant renewal of its water. In this discussion, it is to be observed, the distinction between the city and the State (cf. p. 311) is touched upon though in the further course of the work it is again lost to view.

4. The question as to the seat of sovereignty coincides with that as to the different forms of government and their several values. These forms are now named and divided into two fundamentally distinct classes. On the one hand are the "right" forms of State, which seek the welfare of the whole commuity. On the other hand are the caricatures of, or at any rate the "deviations" from, them. Monarchy, or the rule of one man conditioned by "a certain order," is opposed to the arbitrary rule of a king, or tyranny. The rule of the best, otherwise aristocracy contrasts with oligarchy, or the rule of the richest ; and the constitutional State in the narrower sense, with democracy or mob-rule (cf. Vol. III. p. 183). One would now naturally expect a full description of all these forms, or at least of the "right" ones, to precede the comparison of them and the appraisement of their relative worth. But Aristotle pursues a different course. He enters upon a criticism of the fundamental claims put forward by the partisans of the different constitutions, and seeks to prove that these claims are all based on half-truths. Once more we have one of those dialectical tourneys in which Aristotle is so fond of displaying the peculiar wealth and flexibility of his mind.

The question as to the justification of oligarchy and democracy is governed by the idea of equality. The one side holds equality, the other inequality, to be the true and just basis. But here they overlook the relativity of the idea. Equality is a right, but only for equals ; so also is inequality, but only for the unequal. Again, partial equality, or inequality, is mistaken for total. The oligarchs think that, because they are unequal (that is unequal, or superior to the mass) in one point, namely, in property, therefore they are unequal, or superior, in everything; the democrats, on the other hand, imagine that because they are equal in one point, as being free-born, they are equal absolutely. The oligarchical claim pleads the injustice of a man who has contributed only 1 mina having the same share in 100 minæ as the man who has contributed the other 99. The inference is sound so far as relates to the partners in a trading concern. But this the State emphatically is not; in it civic virtue and its gradations mean far more than the different degrees of material wealth.

Suppose, however, the claim of the democrats allowed, so that the majority becomes the sovereign: how if the propertyless persons who compose this majority divide among themselves, first the estates of the wealthy, and then, when these are exhausted, the substance of the moderately well-to-do? Would that not be unjust? It may be contended that an act performed by decree of the sovereign must be legitimate, and therefore just. But obviously the act considered is destructive of the State, and that which destroys the State cannot possibly be just; consequently—so we are bound to infer—the authority which decrees such an act cannot be the rightful sovereign. Perhaps, then, the "respectable" people alone ought to possess the whole of official authority and full sovereignty. In that case all the remainder would suffer a loss of honour in being excluded from official positions, which we regard as always honourable. And, again, if we travel further on the same road, all office will in the end come into the sole possession of one man, the most competent of all; and thus the loss of honour will be universal. It may be objected, however, that we ought to have for sovereign, not a man, who necessarily is endowed with human passions, but the law itself, which is impersonal and dispassionate Very good; but even so the difficulty is not overcome. For if the law were a democratic or an oligarchic law, we should come round by another circuit to the same evil consequences as before.

5. In treating this fundamental question, Aristotle is unable to satisfy himself. A new argument is adduced in favour of the sovereignty of the people, an argument which "perhaps includes the truth within itself." It depends on the distinction between the ideas "collective" and "distributive." Possibly no one individual out of the many may be entirely competent, and yet, taken all together, they may be better than the best. (We are reminded of the French saying: "Il y a quelqu'un qui a plus d'esprit que M. de Voltaire, c'est tout le monde.") The total achievement resulting from the many contributions is likened to a picnic, which often turns out better than a meal prepared by a single person. It is a comparison to which Aristotle has recourse a second time; clearly he thought it more than a mere dialetical makeshift. The multitude thus comes almost to be an individual with many hands, many feet, and many organs of sense; may not the same hold good in respect of character and intellect? For the multitude judges better than any one critic the merits of musical and poetical compositions. We may here remark that Aristotle can scarcely have been thinking of anything else than the awards made at Athenian prize-competitions by judges chosen from the general public by lot. He must have approved of their decisions on the whole, in spite of the censure with which he occasionally visits the musical fashions of his age. Thus the artistic taste of the highly cultured philosopher was, mainly at any rate, in unison with that of the average Athenian. His admission that this collective ability, though certainly not to be found everywhere, does yet occur in one or the other demos, must be interpreted in favour of Athens, the democracy of which, as we shall see, is judged by Aristotle with remarkable leniency.

With this the controversy appears to be decided. But presently a new doubt emerges, relating to the admissibility of the mass to the highest offices of state. Such admission gives rise, it is urged, to well-founded anxiety. But, on the other hand, the exclusion of the many is highly objectionable, since it threatens to multiply indefinitely the enemies of the State. For this reason Solon and some other legislators had recourse to the expedient of giving the multitude a share in the election of magistrates and in the holding to account of officials, while prohibiting their personal exercise of office. In combination the many may possess sufficient understanding ; and so far they may be compared with a foodstuff of inferior value which is mixed with a superior kind (as, for instance, bran with flour), and makes the whole more productive. Again, reasons and counter-reasons are played off against each other, but with a result not unfavourable to the advocates of democracy. The Solonian expedient is attacked by an objection based on what may be called the Socratic and Platonic appreciation, or over-appreciation, of professional knowledge : as a physician ought to render account only to physicians, so, too, ought those who practise other arts to be controlled only by their like. To this it is answered that, apart from the collective capacity of the multitude, there are many things the goodness of which is better appraised by the user than by the maker ; thus the quality of a banquet, for example, is better judged by a guest than by a cook. Finally, the collectivity argument is employed in a new way. Suppose that, even in democracies, many important positions of trust may only be filled by a large tax-payer, while the man who pays little or no taxes may help to elect him, there is here no real inconsistency. It must not be forgotten that the individual elector is a member of a great whole, the electorate, which collectively owns a taxable capital equal, and indeed superior, to that of the eligible candidate.

In view of the imperfection which necessarily attaches to the holder of supreme power in the State it is once more declared desirable that this supremacy should, as far as possible, reside in the laws themselves ; it should be exercised by personal rulers, whether one or many, only so far as the laws are unable to exhaust the abundance of individual cases. Reference is here made to the intimate connexion between laws and constitutional forms; "the former must be adapted to the latter." Just laws are possible only within the right forms; in those of the contrary kind there is no room for them.

6. The lecturer now makes a fresh start. The problem of equality gives him no rest. He feels the need of working out more amply than had at first been possible, the fruitful subject of the danger of confusing partial with total equality and inequality. It is not every inequality or superiority which can rightly confer a privilege. The privilege must rest upon an excellence which has some connexion with the favoured activity. A drastic instance is given. Suppose that flutes are to be distributed among flute-players of equal excellence: ought some of these, because they are of noble birth, to receive more flutes than the others? Certainly not. "For they blow the flute none the better for that."

Nor again is it practicable to set up a scale of inequalities or superiorities and maintain their commensurability throughout. For example, it may be thought that virtue is worth more than stature; but a certain extraordinarily high measure of stature may be worth more than a certain very low degree of virtue. A competition of this kind is free from such absurdities only where we have to do with the true elements of the State. Thus wealth may claim privilege because the community cannot consist entirely of the propertyless; the rich, too, are generally better trusted in ordinary business matters. Nobility, again, denotes noble race; we may reasonably expect that the descendants of the better will themselves be better. The claim of virtue is also well-founded; for justice, which is indispensable for the welfare of the community, in a certain sense includes all the other virtues within itself. Lastly, the claim which the majority founds upon its collective superiority is by no means void. Here, however, an objection presents itself which applies to all political privileges alike which rest on such foundations as these. Granted that wealth supplies a title to privilege, how if one single man (or a very few) is richer than all the rest put together? The same difficulty appeared in the case of noble birth, and again in that of virtue, and even in that of physical strength, if strength be regarded as justifying the rule of the many. On each of the hypotheses the one who surpasses all others (or the few who do so) would have to be the sovereign. Thus pushed to extremes, all the criteria considered prove unsound.

7. The supposition which was made originally for the sake of a *reductio ad absurdum* is still kept in sight. The thought that a single person may surpass all others in value, though it seemed at first a mere dialectical artifice, has gained a more serious significance by being dwelt upon. Such a person would move through the world "as a god among men." Legislation, however, can deal only with persons of approximately the same character and strength; exceptional natures are "a law to themselves." Attempt to bring them under the yoke of a common standard, and their language will be that which Antisthenes makes the lion use when the hares delivered political speeches and preached universal equality. Observe the resurrection of the superman, whose cause was pleaded by Callicles in Plato's "Gorgias," not without the author's sympathy (cf. Vol. II. p. 333); his type, the king of beasts, is likewise not forgotten.

The difficulty which arises in respect of exceptional natures moved democracies, so we now read, to the introduction of ostracism (judgment by potsherd). Here, it must be admitted, the idea of the exceptional or superman has undergone a modification; it is no longer a question solely of exceptional personal excellences, but also of the mere excess of power which results from wealth, from the size of a man's following, or from political importance otherwise acquired. It is confessed, further, that in practice the employment of ostracism has often been determined by party considerations. For our part, that institution seems most comparable to the banishment of pretenders and to other similar measures, harsh, but often indispensable, which have been taken against persons cf excessive influence. Aristotle couples with ostracism the Athenian mode of dealing with those members of their maritime confederacy which, like Chios and Samos, became dangerous by their power ; and he adds the Persian treatment of refractory nationalities, such as the Medes and the Babylonians. Yet another example is drawn from the sphere of plastic arts : " No painter will leave in his picture a foot which exceeds the measure of symmetry, no matter how beautiful it may be." This defence of levelling tendencies concludes with the remark that it would certainly be better to have the constitution so framed from the first that remedies like these should not be necessary. The next best thing, however, is to seek a readjustment by the use of the appropriate corrective. In spite of these concessions, it still remains an open question how the State with the best constitution is to act towards those who stand above the rest, not in bodily strength, or riches, or number of adherents, but in virtue. No one would advise that such a man should be expelled, or even temporarily excluded, from the State territory. But just as little may he be subjected to authority. That would be much the same as if the rotation of office were to be carried so far as to place Zeus himself under orders. Nothing then remains but "joyful obedience" to these men, the truly royal natures.

8. An easy transition now leads to the next section, in which first monarchy and then the other forms of government are discussed. We, however, need, before we pass on, to glance once more over the dialectical tourney which we have witnessed, for the sake of comparison and criticism. The arguments which have been propounded vary enormously in excellence and perhaps even in seriousness. Samples of high statesmanlike wisdom stand side by side with trivial, one might almost say sophistic, reasonings and quibbles, worthy of the law courts.

The deepest depth is reached by the argument relating to the "taxable capital." If, even in advanced democracies, certain important positions of trust were guarded by a high property-qualification, the purpose of this was to secure a twofold guarantee. In case of loss through the carelessness or dishonesty of the official, the State could indemnify itself out of his property ; besides, there was less probability of misconduct in the case of a man whose material situation saved him from many a temptation.　There was not much relevance in the objection that the numerous poor members of the popular or tribal, assembly take part in the election of such officers, and that thus property is subordinated to the lack of property.　But what connexion is there between this objection and the remark that the total property, or taxable capital, of the many is as great as, or greater than, the amount which the official is required to possess ? This summation of trivial amounts seems to us an entirely illegitimate artifice, since property in a state of extreme subdivision can produce none of the effects of which it is capable when concentrated under a single hand.　Nor, in our opinion, does the pic-nic comparison run on all-fours.　Perversities of opinion, as well as true perceptions, enter into the general stock.　More exactly, while it may be true that one purely intellectual error is often com-pensated by another, and that common sense, or the sound average judgment of a great number, prevails over individual whims and aberrations, the argument is still anything but convincing.　It overlooks the infectious force of temporarily predominant tendencies, all that is included under the head of fashionable folly and the contagion of masses.　It fails us altogether in cases where anti-social interests come into play rather than want of intellectual clearness.　Aristotle was acquainted with the communistic tendencies, as we may briefly call them, which result from the ordinary situation of the great majority, and he described them as the greatest of the dangers inherent in the rule of the many.　But this objection is not removed by the pic-nic argument ; it seems rather to have become lost for a time to the philosopher's view.　We come to the special claims which wealth, moral excellence, and so on, seem to be justified in raising.　When these are met by an appeal to extreme cases (the richest of all, the justest of all, would then obtain exclusive sovereignty) this argument, too, appears to us not unanswerable. When a principle of practice does not stand the test of an extreme application, that is nothing against its goodness, but only against its exclusive validity. It only proves that other principles share the field of its applicability, that these also demand to be taken into account and cannot be neglected with impunity. But Aristotle appears to have meant much more than this.

We are more favourably impressed by what Aristotle has to say on the participation of the multitude in the election of officers, and the holding of them to account. He is attempting to overcome the objection that by this means the State becomes dependent, in regard to its most important interests, upon that very multitude which is judged incompetent to manage them. This objection certainly appears well founded, for by this road the State drifts surely, if slowly, into democracy. But the circumstance favourable to Aristotle is this, that the author of this innovation, the wise Solon, by no means intended to create a democracy, and did not directly create one. It was thus possible, temporarily, at least, to allow the Demos this far-reaching power without making it immediately and absolutely the master of the State. But the culminating point of these arguments is to be found, we imagine, in a thought which is far removed from Socratic doctrinairism, and its embodiment in Plato's "pedantocracy"—the thought, namely, that in things political it is not always and everywhere professional training and expert knowledge that is required, that, on the contrary, here and elsewhere the user of an object, and not the producer, is the truly competent judge.

9. This contest between forms of government to which we have devoted so much space provides us with a beacon well fitted to illuminate the remainder of our journey. It is permeated by the thought that the champions of the different forms of State are in no case able to put forward more than partial or half-truths. We are thus prepared to find the author of the "Politics" bestowing on none of these forms unstinted praise and unqualified recognition.

The truth lies in the mean.   This fundamental note of the
" Ethics" is struck once more in the treatise devoted to the
sister science.   We may expect, accordingly, that Aristotle
will prefer the tempered to the pure forms of State, the
mixture of principles to the ruthless following out of any
one principle.   We shall not be surprised if suggestions of
compromise frequently emerge, nor even if the passion for
compromise becomes at times almost a caricature of that
manysidedness which we found so characteristic of the last
phase of Aristotle's master (cf. Vol. III. pp. 176, 235).

But our critical examination of that dialectical tourney
was more particularly intended to pave the way for another
and more important consideration.   We had to point out
contradictions, chiefly in order to prepare for their explanation.   The lack of consistency in Aristotle's judgment upon
democracy may be traced back to its origin in a twofold
source : theoretical reflexion and personal experience.   The
democracy in the midst of which he lived, that of Athens,
presented to him, on the whole, a much less unpleasant
picture than the one which he had deduced from general
and *à priori* principles.   His treatment of monarchy, to
which we now pass on, will produce in us an almost
exactly opposite impression.

CHAPTER XXIX.

ARISTOTLE'S THEORY OF THE STATE.

(MONARCHY.)

1. THE praise of monarchy is sounded in resonant strains. It is named the best of all forms of government. The precedence due to it is said to be made evident even by the contrary character of its degenerate form, tyranny, since everywhere the best becomes the worst when corrupted (*Corruptio optimi pessima*). Who that reads such words can doubt that Aristotle was a convinced, an enthusiastic adherent of monarchy? There is but one difficulty. With what purpose did Aristotle take such pains over the elaboration of his own "best constitution," if the best of constitutions was already in existence, barely admitting of a final touch in details, and certainly not requiring to be modelled anew? The truth of the matter is this. That monarchy which is praised above all else is no monarchy known to history; it is a Utopia in the true sense, a fabric without date or place, one which, so far as Aristotle knows, has never and nowhere subsisted in fact, unless perhaps as an isolated accident of the rarest kind. This will be understood as soon as we consider the demands made upon this monarchy. The king must satisfy the most extraordinary expectations. He must "be sufficient to himself, possess all goods and advantages, so that he may need nothing and desire nothing for himself, but pursue exclusively the welfare of his subjects." All this is altogether out of harmony with the impressions which our philosopher received from the rulers of his day. For proof, we might cull an anthology from his references

to court-life. "Virtue and reason are not at home on thrones;" "the possessors of power need only two kinds of companions—unscrupulous tools and entertaining society-men" (we might almost say *bravi* and clowns); "private persons are superior, not inferior, to princes in respectability."

But here an objection may be raised. We shall perhaps be accused of indiscriminately citing expressions of blame which refer to tyrants or usurpers as much as to legitimate kings. But Aristotle himself has not attempted or accomplished a clear demarcation between the two. Many of the terms which he uses in these passages are of quite general import; he speaks of "rulers," "princes," "possessors of power," without noticing in the slightest degree the origin of the authority. At all events we nowhere find in any of his works one word of warm praise for a contemporary monarch. It is always kings of the legendary age or of the earliest historical period who are praised, in contrast with the present state of affairs, as "benefactors" of their people ; and, indeed, the boundary between ideal monarchy and the monarchy of the heroic age is anything but sharply defined.

2. The true king can thus only be one of those heaven-favoured exceptional natures that may be compared with Zeus himself. The monarchy, however, which distantly approaches this ideal, and which is not practicable in contemporary Greece, has a task which is thus stated : Keep watch over the rights of the propertied as well as over those of the mass, so that the second may suffer no grievous wrong, and the first no spoliation. Such kings were once raised to the throne for their virtues, their deeds, or the deeds of their kindred, by the higher classes desirous of preserving their privileges. In addition, services to civilization, the foundation of states, or the liberation of them by war have gained the royal dignity for the men by whom they were accomplished. Besides heroic monarchy, mention is made of barbaric monarchy (which in most cases is not wholly unlimited), of a monarchy which is elective instead of hereditary (such

a king is called an "æsymnete" or dictator), and, lastly, of the Spartan monarchy, which with its extraordinary limitations came to little more than an hereditary generalship. After elimination of those forms of state which are monarchies rather in name than reality, the question as to the advantages and disadvantages of kingship is reduced to this : What gain or loss comes from the unlimited or almost unlimited power of a single man ?

"The best of all constitutions" does not emerge altogether unscathed from the dialectical cross-fire. The discussion opens by asking which is preferable, the rule of the best man or the rule of the best laws. The advocates of monarchy appeal to the impossibilty of laws, which are quite general, doing justice to all the particular cases which come under them. This admitted, the new question arises whether these inevitable gaps in legislation are rather to be filled by the best one than by many good. The simile of the pic-nic reappears, and with it another, and as we think, less questionable comparison : a large body of water is less exposed to corruption than a small one, and the same holds good of a large number of men. Aristotle shows his seriousness in this argument by his re-employment of it in the "Constitution of the Athenians." He there justifies the Athenian Demos in reserving to itself judicial decisions which had formerly been within the competency of the "Council" by remarking that "the few are easier to corrupt by money or favour than the many." Here, the place of the many is taken by a number of honest citizens. To the objection that party divisions may reign among these, the answer is made that "even they, if they are as good as the one man, will not be led into evil by their divisions." Thus aristocracy, the rule of a great number of excellent citizens, is preferred to monarchical rule. Men have only suffered themselves to be governed by kings because in past ages, especially in states of limited extent, the desired number of good citizens was lacking. A greater degree of historical correctness will probably be allowed to the sketch, which now follows, of political development. The exploitation of official position for the purpose of enrichment has converted aristocracies of the kind described into oligarchies. With the growing narrowness of an oligarchy, the opposition to it of the excluded multitude has also increased. Attacks on the oligarchic government have led, first, to tyranny, and, through this, to democracy. What the philosopher had here in his mind was perhaps mainly the true thought that the power of the multitude was earlier sufficient to support a usurper's bid for authority than to defend its own interests independently.

3. After this historical digression, the inherent disadvantages of monarchy are enumerated. In the forefront stands the undiscriminating haphazard of inheritance. Then comes the danger of a misuse of military power. Next, unlimited monarchy is termed contrary to nature, because it conflicts with the equality which by nature befits equals. The exceptional natures which tower above the generality are here tacitly ignored, and with perfect justice, since the discussion is concerned with monarchy as a permanent institution. For equals, the taking of turns in ruling and obeying may be recommended ; but so far as it is advisable to grant larger powers to individuals, these should be appointed, in every case, as guardians and servants of the laws. Provision, too, is made by the law for a political education which makes it possible to trust an official to decide individual cases justly. The rule of law is the rule of reason and of God ; he who adds man adds also the beast that dwells in the human breast.

The advocates of monarchy are credited with the assertion that the ruler, like other men, needs freedom of judgment ; to hold him unconditionally to the law would be much as if one were to insist on the physician curing "by the book" (according to the letter of scientific precepts), as indeed is actually done in Egypt within certain limits. To this Aristotle replies that the two cases are not of like nature ; the interest of the physician coincides with that of the patient ; it is otherwise in politics, where one man does much for the sake of pleasing or annoying another. Besides, when a physician comes under suspicion

of being in league with the patient's enemies, that repudiated " treatment by the book " will be greatly preferred.
And if personal intelligence stands higher than the letter
of the law, it does not possess the same superiority over
the truly fundamental laws embodied in the customs and
character of a people. Yet again, the single ruler is absolutely unable to supervise everything himself; he will
always need many helpers to share the work of government with him. What difference, then, does it make
whether this partition of power exists from the beginning,
or is left to be made by the ruler? Lastly, if the good
man as such has a claim to authority, two good men are
still better than one. The opponents of monarchy do not
deny that in many cases a personal decision is necessary.
They only desire that this decision may be shared by
many instead of being restricted to a single person. Why
should two eyes and two ears, two hands and two feet,
perceive and do more than many persons possessed of
many organs and many limbs?

4. It is difficult to pass by this chain of arguments
without a word of criticism. It applies, not only to
monarchy, but to every strong executive, even in a republic. The idea of executive power failed to attain
sufficient sharpness and distinctness in our philosopher's
mind, probably because the division of powers in the
Greek commonwealths was very imperfect. He altogether
overlooks the tremendous advantages of unity and continuity of will. It makes in reality the very greatest
difference whether the many helpers are nominated and
directed by the head of the Government or whether they
enjoy collateral authority. It is the difference between
the strict administration of French prefects or Prussian
presidents and the loose fabric of the modern Chinese or
the ancient Persian empires with their half independent
viceroys and satraps. If two good men are better than
one, even in political matters, why should not the former
dual government of Japan by Mikado and Shogun be an
accepted model? And yet such dual government has
always been noted by history as an exception. In the

case of Sparta, with its highly limited monarchy, it was, perhaps, of little moment, though Aristotle himself censured it indirectly ; and it was only in Rome and Carthage that it failed to produce the most disastrous consequences.

5. Following upon this long series of attacks upon monarchy we meet with only a slender supply of arguments in its favour. Really there is only one, an appeal to that exceptional case, now so familiar to us, of a single man whose excellences of character and intellect raise him high above his fellows. " The soil in which monarchy grows "—so runs the conclusion—" is a population willing to submit itself to a family marked out by its virtues for the control of the State."

Here, to be sure, there occurs a notable variation. Instead of the one favoured and exceptional nature a whole "family" is spoken of. But clearly the "virtue" of a royal house cannot have so high claims made upon it as that of a single superman who ranks almost as a miracle. On the other hand, the persons whose claims have to be satisfied are not now men in general, including the Greeks, but only the barbarians, who are " by nature more inclined to serve."

All doubt may be regarded as excluded. The author of the "Politics" had absolutely no idea of the revival of monarchy in Greece itself. We have already referred to that levelling of culture which was deemed hostile to monarchy (cf. p. 325) ; still more significant is the expression of an expectation that "in view of the growth of cities and their population there will hardly be room in the future for any constitution but the democratic." For the moment, indeed, it being necessary to reckon with the situation created by Alexander's victories, Aristotle did not disdain to address to that monarch the counsel and the request that he would "exercise a protectorate over Hellenes, but rule over the barbarians as an absolute king." But nothing suggests that he ever contemplated more than a passing subordination of Greece to "barbarian" Macedonia.

Had he been able to read the signs of the times, had

he been even dimly conscious that the days of the Greek
republics were coming to an end, and that the future
belonged to monarchy, he could not have regarded the old
city-states as a necessary and eternal feature of the Greek
world. But he went on, partly drawing his political
doctrines from Plato, partly shaping them afresh in the
academic contest with Plato and his followers. He did
not perceive that a fusion of East and West was in progress, initiated by his own pupil; and he deemed his
fellow-countrymen to be now as ever privileged, permanently and exclusively destined and qualified by nature
for freedom. All this has a serious lesson for us. We
touch the bounds of Aristotle's mind, indeed we become
filled with a wholesome mistrust of the farsightedness of
great thinkers in general. The political foresight of
Aristotle stands on a level with Alexis de Tocqueville's
supposition that "equality of conditions" was the permanent economic norm of North America — that land
which a few decades later witnessed accumulations of
wealth unprecedented in history, which became the home
of the mammoth trust and the multi-millionaire.

CHAPTER XXX.

ARISTOTLE'S THEORY OF THE STATE.

(POLITICAL STATICS.)

1. THE main, central portion of the " Politics," consisting of books iv.–vi. treats of what in our time has been called political statics and dynamics. This last subject, the theory of political changes, as also of the decay of constitutions and the means by which they may be preserved, is naturally preceded by an account of the different constitutions themselves, one of which, namely, monarchy, has already been treated. The chief thoughts in this description are the following. " There is not merely *one* democracy or oligarchy," but a great number of varieties of these fundamental forms. These differences depend on the varying social conditions of the populations concerned. Political theorists, despite the excellence of their work in other respects, have hitherto erred by not observing this connexion. They have thus always sought merely the best constitution in the abstract, and not that constitution which for a given people, under given conditions, is the most advantageous, or even the only one attainable. The absolute side of the question is not without its value— indeed, Aristotle himself does not forego the quest of an ideal state—but it ought to be supplemented by a relative treatment. This will be directed towards the solution of two closely cognate problems: what type of constitution, or what variety of such type, corresponds to a given state of society ; and, again, what particular constitutional rules and laws correspond to that type, or that variety ?

The work hitherto done in this field is marked, in

Aristotle's judgment, by three defects. The multiplicity of real conditions is often sacrificed to an abstract uniformity ; the question of the relatively best is constantly put second to that of the absolutely best ; lastly, the details of legislation are judged without due regard to the type or variety of the constitution to which they belong.

This transition from the general and abstract to the particular and concrete is accompanied by a change of method. Dialectical jousting gives way to a more copious employment of historical examples and an abundance of practical suggestions in matters of detail. We have already referred to De Tocqueville. The change just described is like that which appears when we compare the later, matter-crammed work of this master-hand, " L' Ancien Régime," with the ofttimes thin-spun deductions of his " Démocratie en Amérique," or at least of its second section. We may conjecture that a considerable interval elapsed between the composition, or the delivery, of the " first investigation," to which book iv. looks back, and this continuation of it.

2. Emphatic stress is laid on the economic basis of the different forms of State. Mere numerical proportions have only a secondary importance. Suppose a city has thirteen hundred citizens, of whom a thousand are rich, and three hundred poor. The rule of the thousand would not then be democracy, nor that of the three hundred oligarchy. No doubt differences of descent, of education, of capacity must be taken into account as well as differences in wealth, According to the predominance of one or more of these elements qualitative differences show themselves in the constitutional forms. What makes a democracy is the sovereignty of free men without property constituting a majority ; oligarchy is the rule of nobles and wealthy men who form a minority. The process of further differentiation is illustrated by a zoological example. The number and character of the possible animal forms might be determined almost *à priori* by reviewing successively all the conceivable combinations of organs having this or that quality (such and such a mouth

combined with such and such an abdomen, and so on). Similarly, we may group those elements which are now called social in whatever manner we choose, and thence deduce a vast number of varieties. Poverty and wealth must always be the chief pivots of the differentiation; according to the relative power of these two elements, the first of which is in practice generally represented by a majority and the second by a minority of the citizens, we have a democracy or an oligarchy. The sub-varieties of these two main types, however, are based on the social distinctions already treated of. In a democracy, the special type depends on whether the Demos consists of peasants, of artizans, of tradesmen, of sailors, or of day-labourers; while oligarchies differ according as acquired or inherited wealth, nobility of birth, education, or capacity takes the foremost rank.

3. A particularly fine saying points to the distinction between the mere constitutional form and the spirit in which it is worked. Aristotle was perhaps the first to call attention to the significant and often overlooked truth that factors which have been suppressed or vitally weakened by political revolutions may yet long retain a firm footing in "education and custom," that characters do not alter with the same speed as laws. A political right is one thing, the moral or social power of a class is quite another. In Athens the social influence of the nobility survived its political privileges—we may call to mind Nicias or Alcibiades—and the case is similar in modern England, where a constitution that becomes more and more democratic proves eminently reconcilable with the regard for the aristocracy which is rooted in the national character. At the present time even radical parties have for their leaders chiefly scions of the old families, and the Lower House itself contains but a very slight infusion of the proletariate.

A superficial consideration of democracy, Aristotle goes on, not seldom leads to serious error. The equal share of all in the government may seem to be the full realization of the principle of equality. But since the

great mass constitutes the majority, and the decision of
the majority controls the State, this rule of the equality
becomes really the rule of the Demos. As stages in the
advance towards democracy we have, first, the enforcement
of a property qualification, low in amount, then the inclusion in the governing body of citizens with an unblemished
character. After this, all the citizens alike share in the
government, but subject to the law ; lastly, the multitude
rules and no longer the law, the place of which is taken by
decrees or resolutions of the people. The Demos thus
becomes a " many-headed sole ruler." As with a monarch,
so with the Demos flatterers, now called demagogues,
stand in high honour. They induce the people to decide
everything in the assembly, and they themselves control
the decisions. Such a democracy might be denied the
name of constitution altogether, for a constitution can
never be wholly void of law. Indeed, we may go farther.
By ceasing to be constitutional, such a state of things
ceases even to be a democracy, seeing that democracy is
always reckoned among the constitutions.

To a somewhat cursory reader of the " Politics " it may
perhaps seem a confusion of ideas, if not a mere arbitrary
assumption, when the author identifies universal participation in the government with despotic quality of the
government and the negation of the sovereignty of law.
One might be inclined to imagine that he confused the
unlimited power of the people with the unlimited exercise
of that power. His true opinion, however, appears from
the considerations which he devotes to the different
varieties of democracy. He manifests a decided preference
in treating of that variety in which an agricultural and
moderately well-off population holds the helm. Such a
population does not lack a sufficient livelihood, but it does
lack the leisure which alone makes possible a large share
in the direct work of government. Here, therefore, the
people allow the law to rule, and limit themselves to the
indispensable number of assemblies. The case is similar
in other varieties of democracy, till at last the growth of
states and the great increase of their revenues bring about

a change. Government now for the first time falls into the hands of the mass, whose participation is rendered possible by the fact that the unpropertied now receive pay and gain the leisure they would otherwise lack. Indeed, the multitude has in this case the most leisure of all. Their leisure, unlike that of the rich, is not encroached upon by care for their private concerns. Thus only those who have no property are entirely without hindrance in attending the popular assembly and filling the office of juror. Obviously, Aristotle takes it for an axiomatic truth, hardly worth the trouble of justifying, that when the mass has arrived at the full possession and direct exercise of political power, it is unable to restrain its varying caprices or to resist the seductive arts of the demagogue.

4. In order not to be misled here, it is necessary that this apparently unconditional condemnation of democracy, and that, too, of democracy in precisely the form which won at Athens, should be read in the light of other and far more lenient judgments pronounced by the Stagirite. While tyranny is for him the worst of the degenerate constitutional forms, just because it is the corruption of the best (cf. p. 351), democracy is, for kindred reasons, "the most tolerable of them all," and oligarchy is allowed a middle station between them. Other utterances in which the democratic form of government is justified or approved have already presented themselves to our notice (cf. pp. 344 and 353). Athens is not in our philosopher's mind when he charges the propertyless mass with an inclination to plunder those who have means (cf. p. 342). The work, "On the Constitution of the Athenians," has not a word of complaint on the score of the undue burdening or the spoliation of the rich. The author of the "Politics," too, is entirely at one with Demosthenes, that champion of the popular party, in censuring the care of the poor at Athens as unsuitable and insufficient, not at all as excessive. It is still more worthy of note that the personal friend of Macedonian potentates takes occasion to praise the "customary lenience" of the Athenian Demos, though often

enough it allows itself to be deceived and befooled, but
soon wakes from its stupor and punishes its seducers.
But when he touches on the behaviour of the Demos, after
the conclusion of the Civil War, his eulogy of its high-
mindedness has a ring of genuine enthusiasm. Not only,
he remarks, was the amnesty observed with scrupulous
fidelity and the tribe of informers kept down with a
ruthless hand ; the people went far beyond the obligations
assumed under the treaty of peace by taking up the debt
incurred by the defeated oligarchic faction in Sparta, and
paying it off with the greatest speed possible. Thus,
dissatisfied as he was with the rule of the demagogues,
Aristotle by no means failed to recognize the incorruptible
heart of goodness in the noble people among whom he
worked. What he really has to charge it with is its
disposition to take sudden leaps, and that political short-
sightedness which so often sacrificed future welfare to the
interests of the hour. Besides this lack of stability and
foresight, the rough tone which tanners and lampmakers
(a Cleon or an Hyperbolus) had established upon the
orators' tribune repelled the dignified man of the world.
Little, then, as the Athenian democracy corresponded to
his ideal, he was not altogether out of humour with it ;
and the vehemence of his invective did not exclude warm
affection for the people against whom his censure was
directed.

5. Oligarchy, like democracy, runs through several
stages, until it passes into a government by dynasts
which no longer aims at the general welfare, but pursues
the interests of the rulers with arbitrary lawlessness. The
stages of this process are distinguished as, first, the
establishment of a property qualification which opens State
offices to every person of means while excluding all the
poor ; secondly, a high property qualification combined
with co-optation ; lastly, the hereditary transmission of
office. The first of these phases corresponds to a fairly
even distribution of wealth ; in the second, the number of
qualified persons shrinks ; a continuation of the process is
still for a while compatible with the reign of law ; at last

a stage is reached which may be regarded as the precise opposite of extreme democracy.

What Aristotle calls "polity," or the truly constitutional state, is only sketched in shadowy outline. It is represented as a mixed form, a combination of democracy and oligarchy. Such a mixture may be effected in various ways,—for example, the oligarchic principle of election may replace the democratic method of casting lots for office, while democracy contributes the principle of dispensing with property qualifications. Aristotle's love of system has here produced remarkable fruit; for this hybrid is at the same time presented to us as that "right" constitutional type of which democracy is the corruption or degeneration —observe how a mere mongrel type has been raised to the rank of an independent species. Plato had been content to recognize three types of constitution, and to distinguish between the good, or lawful, and the bad, or lawless, manipulation of each (cf. Vol. III., p. 183). Aristotle goes further: the forms of state which to him appear failures must in every case be regarded as the deteriorations or corruptions of commendable types. In the relation of tyranny to monarchy and of oligarchy to aristocracy, this idea received adequate support. But when the turn came to democracy it failed, and could only be saved by the assignment to the mixed form called "polity" of a higher significance than was its due. The third in the company of constitutional failures, namely, tyranny, is described as the government, resting on force, of a sole ruler, not directed to the welfare of the governed.

6. The best constitution—that is, the best in a practical sense, not a "dream-state," not an ideal which could only be realized by an extraordinary accident or a radical transformation of existing conditions—is declared to be the rule of the middle class. This reminds us of the ethical theory of the mean; and there is, in truth, an intimate connexion, which Aristotle himself recognizes. If the middle mode of life is the best, it follows that a medium endowment with the good things of fortune must also be the most desirable. The chief reason is that in such a

situation obedience to reason is easier than in any other.
Both superfluity, whether in beauty, in wealth, or in nobility
of birth, and also the direct opposites of these, destitution,
the lowest depths of ignominy and weakness, are alike
difficult to enlist in the service of reason. The first
extreme engenders lawlessness and crime on the grand
scale, the second rascality and petty wrong-doing. But
here we have the two main sources of all evil.

It is further explained how the first-named class are
unable to obey—they show this incapacity even as children
at school—while the second class go too far in submissive-
ness. The two together do not unite into a political whole;
they form a combination of slaves and masters, the first
filled with envy, the second with contempt. The middle
class ought to be stronger than the two extremes together,
if possible, in any case it ought to be stronger than either
alone. It thus becomes, and chiefly so in a state of considerable extent, a guarantee against insurrection and
revolution. Tyranny, indeed, springs as often from extreme
democracy as from unmixed oligarchy. Besides, the best
legislators have been produced by the middle class.

7. This discussion opens up the question as to the
relation of political forms to social conditions. In its most
general expression, the solution is as follows : that element
which has an interest in preserving the form of the State
must in every case be stronger than the element of which
the reverse is true. The application of this rule requires a
twofold examination of any particular case. There are in
every state qualitative as well as quantitative factors. Such
are freedom, wealth, education, nobility ; the quantitative
factor is arrived at by counting heads. Now, it may happen
that quality is to be found on one side, quantity on the
other. This is illustrated by an example. The noble or
the rich may be surpassed in numbers by the plebeian or
the poor, yet not in so high a degree as they themselves
enjoy a preponderance in respect of quality. Where the
numerical advantage of the propertyless is not compensated
by the qualitative superiority of their rivals, there is the
place for democracy, and for one or another variety of it

according to the predominance of each particular kind of
Demos. Thus in one case, where tillers of the soil pre-
dominate, we shall have the first, most moderate form of
democracy (cf. p. 361); the last or extreme form will
correspond to the predominance of mechanics and day-
labourers. The case is similar with the intermediate forms.
On the other hand, when the qualitative superiority of the
propertied and socially higher class is greater than their
quantitative inferiority, then oligarchy will come to its
rights, and each particular variety of this type according to
considerations similar to those already adduced.

The reconciliation of opposing factors, that main task
of a legislator aiming at a middle line, is sometimes assisted
by artifices which, without infringing on the equality of
political rights, affect their practical exercise either by
facilitating or by impeding it. Those who lack property
may be induced to take part in the public assembly by the
payment of fees, the propertied, but these alone, by the
threat of punishment (compare what is said in Vol. III. pp.
243, 244, on compulsory voting in Plato). If the equilibrium
of the two main factors is not hereby secured, one possibility—and this is what Aristotle himself recommends—is
to limit the payment of fees to that part of the lower class
which does not exceed the wealthy class in numbers ;
another expedient would be to eliminate the excess by
casting lots.

In this connexion there occurs also a passing reference
to the possibility of popular representation. The idea is
suggested by the awkwardness and unwieldiness of mass-
meetings. The popular assembly is here replaced by a
body whose members are chosen, either by vote or by lot,
from the several divisions of the people.

8. Other modes of reconciliation, partly historical, partly
new-invented, are adapted to tempered forms of government.
One of these, penally enforced attendance at the popular
assembly, has already been mentioned. This compulsion
pursued a threefold purpose. It was intended to promote
the balance of power ; it was intended to retain in the service
of the State that wisdom and expert knowledge which the

aloofness of the upper class threatened to withdraw from it ;
above all, it was intended to prevent the members of this
class from sullenly turning their backs on the State,
becoming estranged from it in their minds, and so more
inclined for violent revolutions. (A part of these dangers
may now, or might till recently, have been discerned in
North America.) The same tendency towards compromise
produces a variety of suggestions applicable to oligarchic
States. The "preparatory authority" may well associate
with itself a certain number of additional members, taken
from and chosen by the Demos, or again, the decisions of
the "preliminary advisers" or "guardians of the laws" may
be reserved for confirmation by the people. The aim is
here to avoid alienating the masses (as in the former
instances the upper class) from the State. But in order
that the power of the masses may not assume dangerous
proportions, Aristotle puts forward for consideration a
number of precautionary measures. The people should be
entitled either simply to confirm the "preliminary resolution" or at all events not to enact what is absolutely
contrary to it. Again, the voting on a measure may be
open to all, but the discussion confined to the magistrates.
Lastly, the people may be empowered to reject a "preliminary resolution," but not to substitute another in its place,
being required, in such cases, to refer the matter back to
the authorities. Applied to modern circumstances, this
last proposal, one that well deserves consideration, would
take the following form : Parliament may not impair the
unity of a law by amendments ; it must be in a position to
safeguard the general interest in the most effective possible
way, but not to substitute its own ignorance and impetuosity
for the expert knowledge and careful consideration of the
Government.

9. We have already entered upon the discussion of the
division of powers. The ideas which are so familiar to us,
imperfectly realized as they were in the public life of
Greece, could not be developed without an effort. This
remark has the least applicability to the "judicial," a little
more to the legislative (here called the "deliberative"),

and most of all to the "ordering" or executive power. Under this head offices of all kinds are named, including the office of a priest or of a choregus, till at last there is a dawning perception that the "ordering" authorities are "authorities" in a stricter sense than the others. The distinction, however, still remains imperfect, because the supreme deliberative body is invested with the right of decision in certain cases—for example, in questions of war and peace or the conclusion of treaties—which in modern States (the North American Union excepted) are reserved to the executive. Other matters, too, are dealt with by the deliberative body which now almost without exception fall within the competence of the law courts—we may instance the death-penalty, banishment, and confiscation of property. If, further, the selection of high officials and the holding them to account on retirement are assigned to the assemblies corresponding to our Parliaments, there is no lack of analogies, at any rate in the Republican States of the present day.

Besides the abundant illustrations of the possible ways in which the three powers may be modified, we notice once more the relativity of the standpoint ; the author inquires which of the different modifications harmonize with, or are advantageous to, the different forms of State. The most important points relating to the legislative power in this connexion have already been dealt with. In regard to the executive, the mode of nominating officials comes under consideration ; it is asked whether they are to be chosen by vote or by lot, whether the right of election —active or passive—and that of eligibility by lot are to be universal or limited. It is possible, again, that one part of the offices should be filled by election, another by lot. The unit recognized in the elections, or lot-drawing, may be either the whole body of citizens or a smaller combination, such as a tribe or township (Deme). Yet again, a limited active may be combined with an unlimited passive right of election, as well as with either a limited or unlimited participation in the lot-drawings. The absence of all such limitations is democratic, and so is the mixture

of the two systems. The double limitation of the right of
election, and the single limitation of the right to share in
the lot-drawings, are peculiar to oligarchy. Lastly, similar
distinctions are drawn in respect of appointments to
judicial work.

CHAPTER XXXI.

ARISTOTLE'S THEORY OF THE STATE.

(POLITICAL DYNAMICS.)

1. THE dynamic treatment of politics is as it were embedded in the static. The two are united by a practical point of view. In order to ensure the continuance of a state of things it is necessary to search out the dangers by which it is threatened. Aristotle addresses himself to this task. Having gained the requisite knowledge, he goes back to the starting-point of his investigations, and now at last is able the more accurately to set forth the measures which can arrest the decay or destruction, first of the main types of constitution, then of the subordinate varieties. This is the bond, one often misunderstood, which connects book vi. with book v. and both with book iv.

He begins by enumerating the " sources of sedition," among which misunderstood equality (cf. pp. 341, 342) takes the first place in oligarchy no less than in democracy. The attack may take a threefold direction : it may be aimed at the form of the constitution or at the persons in power, or it may seek to modify the political system in operation by exaggerating or softening its characteristic features. Special cases arise when it is desired to change a part of the constitution, for example, to raise or lower the status of a particular authority. The troubles that arise within a democracy are not so bad as those to which an oligarchy is subject ; for here the battle with the enemy (the Demos), is apt to be complicated with internal faction.

Among the more general causes of civil broils two are placed in special prominence. The first is the unequal development of the constituent elements in the community. This latter is compared—a truly Aristotelian exaggeration —with an organism which remains two spans high, while one foot alone attains a length of four ells. Equally dangerous is " heterogeneity," the building up of the State from elements not sufficiently akin. A fine image is used by way of illustration. In war the crossing of irrigation- channels, however small they may be, disturbs the coherence of the lines ; similarly the unity of the citizens is impaired by every sundering distinction. Differences of character and occupation are mentioned here as well as defects in national homogeneity. Those who live in our large modern States cannot fail to be struck, and indeed amused, by the emphasis which, in this connexion, Aristotle lays on the difference between Athens and its port-suburb, the Piræus. He holds to this point of view so exclusively here that he seems to forget his own polemic against Plato, whom he had accused of excessively " unify- ing" the State, and so reducing it to the level of an individual (cf. Vol. III. p. 118). For the moment, too, he loses sight of the historical fact that in many instances the successful foundation of colonies was due to the co-operation of several cities and nationalities, and their prosperous development to the union of Greeks and barbarians. It may almost be said that he counts upon his readers being able to remedy his occasional onesidednesses.

The enumeration of grounds and occasions which lead to political strife is preceded by a weighty saying : " Civil conflicts arise, not for small objects, but from small occasions." Having made this reservation, however, he enters upon an extraordinarily copious account of these small occasions—fear of punishment, personal rivalry, contempt provoked by maladministration, election in- trigues, deeds of violence, and even including love troubles, contested inheritances, rejected offers of marriage, and family quarrels of all kinds. The amplitude with which special instances are described, the manifest joy in anecdote,

call to mind perhaps more than any other part of the
" Politics," the rich colouring which distinguishes the
" Constitution of the Athenians."

But while in general it is the excessive power of one
social factor that threatens civic peace, at times the exact
opposite occurs.   Conflicts may be delayed till the two
parties are nearly in   equilibrium, since the obvious
superiority of the one side renders an attack much too
hazardous in the eyes of the other.   Such, moreover, is
the situation of those who necessarily feel "equality" as
most oppressive, and who are the readiest to raise special
claims, that is, those who are superior to the rest in
personal character.   "They are a very small company
in comparison with the whole."

2. The theme, hitherto treated generally, is now
expounded in detail. Demagogy, the chief factor in
revolutionary movements within democracy, is described
in its varying forms.   Often originally identical with the
military commander, the demagogue in past times frequently
pushed his way upwards till he became tyrant. Now
rhetoric is his most effective weapon.   The remedy
proposed for demagogy is the substitution of voting by
districts for collective voting, a means, we may add, which
would free the smaller interests, in particular the agricultural, from the domination of the city mob assembled
in the market-place.

Demagogy occurs also under oligarchic government,
particularly where the passive right of election is narrowly
limited but the active right common to all citizens capable
of bearing arms or to all without restriction. Here the
oligarchs have ground and occasion to flatter the people.
On the other hand, oppression of the masses is a frequent
cause of revolution in this form of government, but equally
so is the progressive narrowing of the oligarchy, which
increases the number of discontented outsiders. These not
seldom call in the help of the people, with a result which
often goes far beyond their intentions. A united oligarchy
cannot easily be destroyed from within. But if individual
oligarchs are ruined by extravagant living they may seek

to make themselves or others tyrants, or they may lay hands on public property, and in either way they may indirectly fan sedition. Further causes of revolution or usurpation are the employment of mercenaries in war or the appointment of arbitrators to judge between parties in peace—two consequences of mistrust felt by the oligarchs for the people or by each for the other. To these and many other causes of an accidental and personal nature such as the resentment aroused by insults or unjust judgments, there is added a type of what may be almost called automatic revolution. The form of the constitution may remain inviolate while its substance undergoes a change. Thus with the growth of national wealth and the general rise of values occasioned by a long peace it may happen that the property qualification fixed by law may lose it's exclusiveness and admit to political privileges a far wider circle of the public than in former times.

This is the place to mention a means by which, as Aristotle suggests, not oligarchies alone may guard against the automatic lowering of the property-qualification in the manner described above. He recommends that the tax-register should be examined at regular intervals, in order that the property-qualification may be revised accordingly, doubled, for example, if the amount of taxable capital is found to have been doubled. The qualifying amount thus forms a constant fraction of the whole taxable capital, and is protected against a rise in the value of commodities, or what comes to the same thing, a fall in the value of money. Protection is equally afforded against the opposite danger. There is one obvious objection to this plan. Nothing could be more undesirable in Aristotle's view than a diminution in the number of those entitled to political privileges. But this might easily be the result if his proposed adjustment of the property-qualification to the rise or fall of the total assessment were carried out without regard to the distribution of the assessed property. The changes occurring within a period might include a great concentration of wealth, so that, for example, a number of tenfold millionaires might be found to have taken the place each of a hundred men worth a hundred thousand drachmæ. Thus in order to keep the level of the property-qualification in harmony with changing social conditions, it would be necessary, we think, to take into consideration not merely the sum-total, from time to time, of the national wealth, but also the manner of its distribution.

We return for the present to the study in political dynamics. The chief cause of dissolution in the case of "polities" and aristocracies is the violation of their constitutional basis. Such in a "polity" is the principle by which the power of the people is blended with that of the upper class ; in an aristocracy the combination of these elements with that of personal capacity. There are two directions which a change of constitution may take : firstly, the tendencies already present in the constitution may be followed still further ; but another possibility is a revulsion towards the opposite type. Account is taken not only of developments accelerated by force, but also of changes which take place gradually and imperceptibly. As soon as any one part of the constitution is abandoned the way is opened for the abolition of another more important part, and so for the destruction of the whole. Along with tranformations operated from within, those also are considered which are effected by external influences. Such influences proceed, sometimes from a neighbouring State, sometimes from one situated at some distance but possessing superior power. The chief example of this is furnished by the Peloponnesian War, in the course of which Athens everywhere overthrew the oligarchies and Sparta the democracies.

3. From now onwards the static point of view gains the upper hand. Nothing is to be more guarded against in well-ordered constitutions than illegalities, small ones not least of all. For the evil creeps in unperceived, just as in a household small excesses of expenditure, by accumulating, eat up the family means without attracting notice. In both cases the judgment is overpowered by the same fallacy : if the individual item is small, so is the total. Many a constitution is indebted for its permanent subsistence less to its own intrinsic goodness than to the skill which the

heads of the State show in dealing both with those outside the privileged pale and with their fellows in authority. They treat the first class considerately, avoiding so far as possible everything which wounds their feelings or subjects them to loss ; indeed, they admit the most capable of them to a share in the government. With all the possessors of full citizenship they consort on terms of democratic equality.

It is also advisable for oligarchies and aristocracies to borrow particular institutions from democracy ; for example, short-termed, even half-yearly tenure of office, in order that all may have their turn, and that those dangers may be avoided which arise from a long continuance in office of the highest authorities. There is yet another point of view. Sometimes it is not the remoteness but the nearness of dangers which guards the constitution. For the effect of a threat is that men busy themselves all the more anxiously with the defence of the thing threatened. It is therefore profitable to instil such fears into the minds of the citizens ; they will then rally round the constitution and keep watch over it day and night, suffering no more intermission of this vigilance than they would in the case of sentry duty. Another step to be recommended is the setting of legal limits to quarrels within the governing classes. No one man should be allowed to rise too high, and, above all, too quickly; should this, however, happen, the too rapid fall of such a man is a thing to be guarded against. If purely personal affairs are not to open the way to undertakings which imperil the State, strict supervision must be maintained over private life, especially within the governing classes.

4. Once more we encounter the specifically Aristotelian endeavour to reconcile opposites and pare away extremes. It is possible, he says, to combine, in a certain measure, aristocracy with democracy. For this purpose it is necessary, before everything else, to provide against the officials becoming unduly rich. For in that case the mass does not feel too keenly its exclusion from positions of authority ; indeed, men are rather pleased to be able to go about their

private business undisturbed, so long as suspicions of the kind here suggested are not aroused. But when that kind of suspicion does gain ground, the resentment thereby caused is twofold: men miss the honour, as well as the profit, of office. In the opposite case, access to office may be granted to the masses without their making any actual use of the concession. But those who are well-to-do, having no need of these illicit gains, will be ready and willing to hold office rather than be governed by the first comer.

In democracy it is important to spare the rich: not their capital only, but also their income. Indeed, one may go further, and even prohibit their undertaking costly but useless services to the public such as the maintenance of choruses, or the organizing of torch-races, and so on. In an oligarchy, on the other hand, it is necessary to take much thought for the poor; the more lucrative offices may be reserved for them; the right of testamentary disposition may be limited in order that property may remain in families; there may be a prohibition against one man inheriting from several. The same equalizing purpose is served by the counsel to allow to the factor which is the less favoured by the constitution—to the well-off in democracies, to the unpropertied in oligarchies—the greater share in those offices which are not the actual seat of the sovereign power.

For the judicious filling of these last-named offices three requisites are named: loyalty to the constitution; the greatest possible degree of specific capability; lastly, virtue and justice. Which of these qualities is to govern the choice when all three are not to be had together? This difficulty, it is said, must be settled by considering which of them is met with the more commonly and which the more rarely. In appointing a general, for instance, more depends on the rare talent for military command than on the commoner qualities of virtue and loyalty to the constitution. But in the case of an office coming under the head of police or finance a higher than the average degree of integrity is demanded, while the requisite technical knowledge is "common to all" (!). But virtue and strength of character are necessary for the reason that the possession of knowledge and love of the constitution are as insufficient in politics as knowledge and self-love alone are for the conduct of private life.

Aristotle returns once more to his leading point of view, the maintenance of the correct medium. It is possible, especially where a constitution in itself deviates from the true mean, that the exaggeration of its special features may produce a progressive deterioration which in the end leaves it no constitution at all (cf. p. 361). A more important point than any yet mentioned, one, too, on which hitherto no thought has been bestowed, is *education in the spirit of the constitution.* He who is so educated will not do what is desired by or pleasing to the friends of oligarchy or of democracy, but that which affords them the possibility of maintaining erect the system of government which they favour. But it is the opposite of this that happens. In an oligarchy the sons of those in power live extravagantly, while those of the poor acquire by labour and exertion both the will and the strength for revolutionary undertakings. On the other hand, in those democracies which are counted the most democratic of all, "freedom and equality" are interpreted as denoting merely individual caprice.

5. The turn now comes of monarchy, the causes of its decay and the means for its preservation. Much of what has been said about republics applies to this constitution as well. For of the two kinds of monarchy, true kingship corresponds to aristocracy, while tyranny is as it were a compound of extreme oligarchy with democracy. In order to give the more point to this antithesis a statement is made which is unaccompanied by any corroborating historical example and which, perhaps, rests on mere deduction. This statement is to the effect that kingship was instituted for the protection of the higher against the lower classes, while tyranny—here we are on solid historical ground—was often intended to protect the masses against their superiors. Not that this was anciently the case, for then tyranny arose

partly out of kingship through the extension of the royal
powers, partly out of the higher offices of state, partly also
out of oligarchy.   Presently the deduction of which we
have spoken is abandoned, and kingship is regarded as a
bulwark against one-sided class-rule in general.

The causes of revolution which have been named in
connexion with other forms of government, such as the
suffering of injustice, fear of anticipated evils, contempt,
and the like, are so far modified, in the case of monarchy,
that the injustice and the contempt appear as the fruits of
arrogance, which for its part falls again under a number of
heads such as insult, bodily maltreatment, erotic abuse,
and so on.   Historical examples are adduced in prodigal
abundance.   The fact that Philip of Macedon and his
murder by Pausanias are mentioned in this connexion
should give pause to those who are undiscerning enough to
read a glorification of that monarch out of Aristotle's work.
In the passage where ambition is mentioned among the
motives of conspiracies, that particular kind of ambition is
not forgotten which is solely concerned to accomplish,
perhaps only to attempt, some deed of desperate daring.
In this category is placed Dion of Syracuse, of whom an
utterance is quoted implying slender hope for the success
of his undertaking (cf. Vol. III. pp. 138 *seqq.*).

6. There now follows a discussion in which the king
and the tyrant are distinguished.   The fall of tyranny is
brought about from outside as soon as it is opposed by a
hostile political form which has greater strength ; such
enemies are democracy, aristocracy, and kingship.   Ruin
comes to tyranny from within when the members of the
princely house quarrel with each other.   Of the two chief
causes of enmity, hatred and contempt, the first is inevitable, but the destruction of the tyranny is not generally
brought about till the second is added as well.   Thus the
founders of tyrannies have as a rule been able to keep
them, but their successors have commonly lost their power
after making themselves contemptible by a life of pleasure.
It is inquired whether in such cases hatred or anger is the
more powerful factor.   Anger certainly incites to action

with more immediate force, but its characteristic lack of reflexion renders it on the whole less dangerous.

Kingship is the form of government most rarely overthrown by external forces ; it is, therefore, long-lived. Its internal corruption occurs in one of two ways : through strife within the dynasty, and through the attempt to render the Government more despotic. But "*no new kingdoms come into being now.*" For already men are too much alike, there is too great a lack of individuals who tower above their fellows to allow of that willing subordination which belongs to the essence of kingly rule (cf. pp. 325 and 356). We are astonished here by the philosopher's blindness to the historical transformation which was then approaching, nay, had actually begun. He speaks as though Hellas were at the close, rather than the opening, of a monarchical era. And he who so spoke was the tutor of Alexander, the friend of Antipater (cf. p. 23), and, without doubt, of many others among those generals of Alexander who divided the world among them after his death. Aristotle, we may say, sat at table with monarchy without knowing it. And let it not be answered that he was thinking only of Greece and not of the surrounding countries. For among the subjects of the Ptolemies, of the Seleucids, of Lysimachus, there were very many Greeks. And if no new monarchy arose in Greece itself, yet its permanent subjection to the Macedonian monarchy is a fact which in the spirit, if not in the letter, most decisively contradicts the pseudo-prophecy we have quoted. Nor will it avail to range the monarchies of the Diadochi under the category of tyranny rather than that of kingship. A monarchy like that of the Ptolemies, one which made continuity its aim, which took so serious account of custom and tradition, which, in consequence, lasted for so long, is wholly out of keeping with the picture which Aristotle gives of tyranny —a Government based on craft and violence, and, therefore, as certainly short-lived as monarchy is solid and enduring. But, did any doubt remain, one consideration is decisive— the tireless care with which Aristotle elaborates his projects of amelioration for the republican constitutions. How could such plans have come into his mind if he had as much as dreamed that the old order was at an end, that the republican forms were henceforth to clothe no weightier substance than paltry municipal affairs? It is highly profitable for us to dwell on such great errors of mighty intellects. They inspire us with a very wholesome mistrust. Who knows how gravely the intellects of the day, great and small alike, may be in error when they see more than a transitory phase of historical development in those institutions, such as universal franchise, which in recent times have been so keenly fought for, and, in almost all cases, so triumphantly won?

7. To the causes of decay are opposed the means of preservation. The chief means of preserving kingly rule is its own moderation. In the case of tyranny, two precisely opposite paths are open. The first is the traditional one, which most tyrants tread. They seek to inspire their subjects with mistrust of each other, to hold them powerless, to crush their spirit. This purpose is served by forbidding the assembling of men at common meals or in clubs, everything, in fact, which brings men together and facilitates co-operation, by fostering spies and informers, by egging on one class against another, by bleeding the people —a point of view from which the great architectural works of tyrants are somewhat one-sidedly regarded. There follows an apt saying, which still more forcibly reminds us of Cæsarism and Napoleonism: " The tyrant is a fomenter of wars," with the object, that is, of keeping his subjects busy and making his leadership indispensable. Here Aristotle, the devotee of cool reason, treats the influence of imagination and the thirst for glory with the same undue neglect with which in the immediately preceding case he had treated the increase of prestige. Tyranny, like extreme democracy, welcomes woman-rule and the insolence of slaves, for these are classes from which the tyrant has no more serious danger to fear than the demagogue. Finally, the tyrant loves to consort with persons of bad character, with foreigners in preference to natives, while in every man distinguished by fearless candour and dignified bearing he sees a menace to and a diminution of his power.

The nature of the second path may be inferred from the causes which lead to the decay of kingship. If the latter is ruined by modification in the direction of tyranny, then tyranny must be benefited by an approach towards true kingship—it being always understood that the ruler's independence of his subjects' will must remain unimpaired. For the tyranny which surrenders this surrenders its very self. With this reservation, it is profitable for the tyrant sometimes to act as a true king would, sometimes to simulate such action successfully. For this purpose it is particularly necessary that he should be careful about the finances of the State. He will not take the money which the people has earned by hard work and squander it on favourites (*hetæræ*, aliens, artists) ; he will even follow the example of certain tyrants and render public account of his revenues and expenditure. He will seek to inspire reverence rather than fear. He must, therefore, in no respect lay himself open to reproach, neither he himself, nor his *entourage*, nor, in particular, the women of his household. He is advised to be moderate in pleasures of all kinds, and, above all, to keep up an appearance of such moderation. For it is not the vigilant and sober man, but the drunken sluggard, who provokes contempt and invites attack. He should also make a show of piety, for thus he will create public confidence both in his own justice and in the continuance of a power which is likely to receive divine protection. But all this must be without weakness. It is further advisable for him to distinguish those among his subjects who have shown merit, in order that they may not expect greater honours from their free fellow-citizens than from him. And while reserving for himself the bestowal of such rewards, he should leave punishments to other authorities, particularly the law courts. There are two kinds of arrogant insolence from which the tyrant should specially guard himself, cruel corporal punishments, and attacks on sexual honour. If, after all, dishonour has been inflicted, it must be compensated by honours in other directions.

The tyrant is in the best case when both the main classes of society believe their welfare dependent on his authority. If this cannot be brought about, he should attach the more powerful party to himself. His rule is thus established, and he need have no recourse to unpalatable measures, such as liberating the slaves, or disarming the citizens. Taking all in all, the tyrant is recommended to play the part of a protector and guardian, to avoid all excess, to court the upper classes by affability, and the masses by a policy of social beneficence. In this way his position becomes in a measure consolidated, and his personal character at the least half virtuous. Finally, an historical survey tests the correctness of these considerations.

8. The sixth book of the " Politics," which, obviously, was at first intended to form the conclusion of the work, accordingly contains, as one might expect, not a few summarizing repetitions, which need not detain us. It is characterized by many a formulation, in more general terms, of thoughts previously expressed less comprehensively. We may instance the advice not to pursue consistency to extremes, and not always to attempt the realization of the whole body of characters belonging to a particular constitution. Or, again, "we must not give the name of democratic or oligarchic to that which makes the State more democratic or oligarchic than it would otherwise be, but to that which allows it to preserve its special form of government the more successfully." We are reminded of J. S. Mill's profound remark that it is no recommendation of a political measure to say that it follows from the principle of the constitution actually in force. The presumption is much rather in favour of institutions which are calculated to mitigate the disadvantages inseparable from every form of state. The wise quest for constitutional mixtures which had been bequeathed by Plato here takes concrete form in definite proposals. Once more a *reductio ad absurdum* is brought to bear upon the exclusive application either of the democratic principle of counting heads or of the oligarchic favouring of wealth (cf. pp. 342, 346, and 348). For the first principle may lead to the spoliation of the rich minority, and the latter, if the

concentration of wealth is carried to its extreme degree, may end in absolute tyranny.

A way out of the difficulty is provided by the principle of estates or electoral divisions, which appears in two modifications. For the election of officials and judges a procedure is recommended which accurately corresponds to the Prussian system of electoral classes. The class which consists of those who pay the highest taxes is to appoint the same number of direct electors as the class of the less highly taxed. Thus, for example, the five hundred at the top, whose contribution equals that of the remaining thousand, are to choose as many representatives as the latter. In respect to the resolutions of the popular assembly, the same principle is applied in the following manner. The two electoral classes are to meet separately, and no decision to be held valid unless both parts concur in it. In case they fail to agree, that vote is to carry the day which contributes the greater amount of taxes. In order to carry out this system, it is necessary to combine the majority of the one class with the minority of the other, and see which of the two totals so formed has the preponderance. Thus, if A and B are the majorities, a and b the corresponding minorities, the choice will be between $A + b$ and $B + a$. A formal analogy to this is presented by the Austro-Hungarian delegations, which vote in common session if repeated interchange of messages has failed to remove a disagreement between them. Here, too, the issue is decided by the accession of numbers which the majority of one body gains from the minority of the other. There is, however, one difference between the two cases. In the modern instance, votes are simply counted ; according to Aristotle's proposal they were also in a manner to be weighed. For if his declared object was to be obtained, if not a mere majority of votes but a preponderence in property or taxable capital was to prevail,—then, keeping to the numbers of the above illustration, no fewer than one hundred votes of the second class would be required to balance fifty of the first. But, difficult as it is to ascertain the true principles of equality and justice, it is still more difficult to carry them out in practice, "since it is always the weaker, not those who for the time being enjoy the superiority, who trouble themselves seriously about equality and justice."

9. The concluding portion of the book is mainly devoted to static considerations on the individual varieties of the different constitutional types. After praising agricultural democracy, the picture of which reminds us chiefly of the primitive Swiss cantons and the States of the Union in old colonial times, Aristotle goes on to commend certain measures by which it was formerly endeavoured to perpetuate that healthy condition. Among these were the prohibition against the accumulation of landed property, either absolutely or (after the example of Solon) in the neighbourhood of urban centres, and another prohibition which was directed against the sale or excessive mortgaging of the original lots of land; in some cases, too, political privileges were restricted to those possessing at least a certain minimum of landed property. The democracies which are composed of industrial and commercial elements stand much lower in Aristotle's estimation. Not every community can bear the last and extreme form of democracy. In order to preserve itself—this is perhaps said with an eye on Athens—it needs quite particularly wise institutions and customs suited to it. From the standpoint of this extreme democracy, no disapproval is expressed of a mode of strengthening the masses by adding bastards and half-breeds until the number of citizens reaches the necessary magnitude. Clisthenes is held up as a model because of his endeavours to fuse all classes together, and to link up the old groupings of the people by new ones (cf. Vol. II. p. 39). The same purpose is served by the concentration of religious interests by the reduction of their number, and by raising many private rituals to the rank of public observances. In this kind of democracy, as in tyranny, it is profitable to allow greater licence to women and slaves, and, in general, to avoid restraints on private life.

Aristotle turns to the struggle against those abuses which most injuriously affect the permanence of extreme democracy. Among these are included the confiscation of property in favour of the State or people. The goods of the condemned should preferably be assigned to the gods. The deterrent force of the penalty would be as great as ever, but the motives for procuring condemnation would be diminished. Political trials should be as rare as possible, and the bringing of frivolous charges severely punished. As in democracies of this kind the system of allowances to ecclesiasts and jurors can hardly be dispensed with, economy should be sought by the utmost possible limitations of the number of popular assemblies, and by the shortest possible sessions of the law courts served by large juries. This last measure will also promote the interests of judicial administration, since those who take part in it will include a larger proportion of the well-to-do. The system now in vogue— at Athens, we must add—of dividing surpluses among the people is compared to the sieve of the Danaids. The kind of relief demanded by the interests of the democracy, which needs to be preserved from decay, and also, indirectly, by the interests of the rich, is permanent assistance. The needy man should be supplied with a small capital, varying according to the different sections of the population, which will enable him to buy a small estate, set up a business, or take up a farm on lease.

10. In the first and best variety of oligarchy there should be a graded property-qualification, a lower for the less and a higher for the more important offices. The number of those totally excluded from power will be reduced to a minimum, just as in democracy it was necessary to attract the higher classes in the greatest possible numbers into the work of government. The next type of oligarchy must be organized in a similar spirit, though with a somewhat tightened grasp of the oligarchic principle. Finally, the rule of dynasts, that form of oligarchy which contrasts with extreme democracy and approximates to tyranny, needs the greatest care of all, precisely because it is the worst of these varieties, just as ailing bodies or badly built ships must be guarded from danger more anxiously than others.

Even in treating of the different departments in an army or an administration Aristotle manifests once more that love of reconciling opposites which has become so familiar to us. Although the cavalry service is naturally recruited chiefly from the wealthiest class, and the heavy-armed division from those of moderate means, while the great mass enlist in the fleet or the light-armed infantry, it is yet advisable that the sons of oligarchs should be trained in this last branch of the service, in order to counteract the preponderance of the light-armed troops in case of civil war. Various measures enable persons from the ranks of the people to be admitted to the oligarchic citizenship; at Massalia, for example, this admission is granted to the worthiest of those below the property-qualification. On the other hand, in order to keep the people at a distance from the more important offices, these may have attached to them burdensome public services which are also calculated to disarm ill-will—costly inaugural sacrifices, and especially votive offerings and the erection of buildings to adorn the city. Other provisions are intended to diminish the unpopularity connected with the execution of judicial sentences and other duties coming under the head of police administration, in order that the reluctance of better-class persons to assume these functions may be to some extent overcome. This purpose is specially served by a strict division between the authority which pronounces and the authority which executes sentence, as also by short-term tenure of these distasteful offices and a distribution of them which prevents one man holding several at once. We note the contrast, perhaps more glaring and palpable here than anywhere else, between a strong and firmly-established body of officials, nominated and protected by the executive, and its exact opposite, directly dependent on the will and favour of the people.

CHAPTER XXXII.

ARISTOTLE'S THEORY OF THE STATE.

(CRITICISM OF POLITICAL IDEALS AND IDEAL STATES.)

1. WE shall do no injustice to Aristotle's original purpose if we take his criticism of other thinkers' ideals immediately before the ideal which he himself began to construct, but left unfinished (cf. p. 314). Part of this criticism has been already anticipated (cf. Vol. III. p. 118). We have seen how Aristotle laid a sure finger on the weak places of Plato's communistic proposals with regard to property and the family.

That criticism may be summed up in three words: lack of intensity. Lack of intensity in the love of kin, which is watered down by its extension over vast circles, and, what is almost more important (cf. Vol. III. p. 120), lack of zeal and care in the administration of properties which are owned by all and therefore by no one in particular. There would be a revival in a new form of the old experience that one is served worse by many servants than by few. Quarrels and unpleasantnesses, such as arise so easily among temporary travelling companions, would break out with heightened force in a life permanently lived in common. Perfect equality in services and enjoyments would soon be recognized as a chimæra. The abolition of private property would also choke up a source of many indescribable pleasures, not only those which legitimate self-love brings, but all manner of kindnesses which men constantly show to their friends, acquaintances, or guests. There are even two virtues, continence and liberality, from the practice of which the ground would be cut away. But the "fair face" which the Platonic ideal shows, is due partly to the fact that men fix their gaze on the evils springing from private property and overlook the constant occurrence of the similar evils, quarrels, lawsuits, and so on, among joint possessors of property, such as partners in a trade. An illusion is caused here by men comparing the comparatively few cases of the second kind with the countless numbers of the first, without attending to the relative frequency of the situations and occasions which give rise to them. All persons, according to Plato, should give the names of Mine and Thine to the same objects. But the Mine is one thing in the sense of exclusive possession, and quite another in the sense of a fractional interest in a piece of common property.

Of the "many inconveniences" which marital communism would bring in its train, a few are singled out for mention. In spite of all precautions, the real facts of relationship would often betray themselves, especially by the resemblance of children to their parents; they could not remain wholly concealed under a system by which transferences of the nature of adoption would be made from one class to another. If, however, they did remain unknown, nothing would prevent the occurrence of murders, assaults, and love affairs between blood-relations of a kind which would outrage every feeling of piety.

2. In Aristotle's criticism of the "Laws" nothing seems so strange to us as the astonishment he expresses at the size of the standing army demanded by Plato. Five thousand men, with camp-followers in proportion! How is the State to feed so many non-workers? It would need a territory as fertile and extensive as Mesopotamia. The second charge is that Plato proposes no means of regulating the increase of population. Without this, all levelling of property would remain useless. Plato's prohibition against dividing up the lots of land could only make the situation worse, at the expense of the surplus citizens. This negligence is contrasted with the wise care of Pheido the Corinthian, who provided for the maintenance of a constant number of citizens and a constant number of

families, even though the original lots of land were unequal. The censure which falls on Plato applies equally to another reformer, Phaleas of Chalcedon (cf. Vol. I. p. 409), who combined the same levelling tendency with the same lack of precautions. Moreover, that all should possess equally is not so important as that each should possess the right amount. The salutary effects of equality in property are commonly exaggerated. The greatest crimes are not committed for the sake of necessaries but of superfluities. No one ever grasped at a throne to save himself from cold or hunger. Mere equality of possessions is of little profit for the further reason that "superior persons" imagine themselves entitled to something more than equality. The remedy is not to be found so much in levelling as in causing the better sort not to *wish* for an advantage over the rest, and in making it *impossible* for the worse sort to obtain one.

3. A searchingly critical account is given of the reforms proposed by Hippodamus (cf. Vol. I. pp. 409, 410), and occasion is taken to raise the general problem of how far it is legitimate to assail the existing order by innovations. Primitive customs and institutions must in many respects be crude, imperfect, even childish. Historical examples are adduced bearing out this assertion. In other departments of human practice, in medicine, gymnastics, and so on, the need of progressive improvements has been proved ; why not also in statecraft ? Still, Aristotle recommends the observance of "great caution" in political innovations, chiefly because the advantage obtained in detail is often run hard by the loss sustained through the blow dealt at the authority of the laws. Here we come to a passage which holds valid for all time—golden words that might have been written by a Burke : "The example drawn from the arts is illusory. Changes in an art do not stand on the same footing as changes in the law. The law's power of procuring obedience rests wholly on the force of custom ; and custom is the growth of time. Thus to pass lightly from old laws to new is a sure means of weakening the inmost essence of all law whatever." Patience is therefore recommended in face of many abuses and mistakes on the

part both of legislators and magistrates.   If Aristotle had
pursued this train of thought further, it might have led
him to perceive the profound contrast that often appears
between the direct and the indirect consequences of revolutionary innovations.   The first may be calculable and
salutary ; the second are generally incalculable, and not
seldom disastrous.   Particular advantages, outweighed by
more general disadvantages ; universal ideals, which lose
their applicability in the special case—these, without doubt,
are the fatal dangers of all radicalism.   Aristotle, as we
have seen, recognized the first of these ; Goethe had the
second in view when he left us the memorable saying :
" Universal notions and great conceit are ever on the way
to work fearful harm."

4. This examination of political ideas is followed,
naturally enough, by a criticism of the work of those
legislators who have either not attempted, or not permanently established, constitutional reforms of their own
devising.   The second category includes Solon, the first
Zaleucus and Charondas in Lower Italy, Dracon at Athens,
and Phildaus of Corinth who gave laws to the Thebans,
and whose regulations with regard to adoption were
intended to preserve the number of lots of land unaltered.
This somewhat summary discussion is preceded by a criticism of the constitutions which Aristotle, like Plato, regarded
as models, namely, those of Sparta and Crete.   There is
one point in particular at which our critic finds the legislation of Lycurgus open to censure, and that is its failure to
extend to women the stringent discipline which it provided
for men.   He is also displeased by the way in which
Spartan institutions favoured the unequal distribution of
wealth.   They did so by allowing freedom of testamentary
disposition, and by placing no restrictions on the marriage
of heiresses, or on the right of giving daughters rich dow-
ries.   These omissions were due, we think, to the weakening
of tribal and family bonds, which was caused by the strict
military and political unity of Sparta.   Aristotle is not
satisfied by the manner in which the problem of serfdom
was solved.   " The Helots are continually on the watch

to turn every difficulty of the State to their own advantage."
The insular position of Crete, he remarks, has greatly
reduced that danger. Aristotle offers no positive proposals
for the reform of this institution, nor yet for that of the
ephorate, whose advantages and disadvantages he is content
to set side by side. It is a bad thing that five casual citizens,
often extremely poor and thus not seldom corruptible,
should occupy a position of such importance, one raised
above that even of the kings themselves. On the other
side, "this office holds the city together." The Demos,
which has access to it, receives as much satisfaction there-
from as the kings do from their position of honour, and the
higher classes from their representation in the Gerusia, or
council of old men. It is clear that Aristotle here finds
his ideal of the reconciliation of opposites in a measure
realized (cf. Vol. III. p. 234).

After a number of pronouncements on details of the
Lacedæmonian form of government, he rises at last to a
general point of view. He expresses agreement with Plato,
who had declared the fundamental defect of the Spartan
constitution to be its adaptation to only one form of virtue,
namely, that of the soldier. " For that reason they flourished
so long as they were engaged in wars, but soon slipped
down from the height they had reached because they had
not learned to live at leisure." Aristotle has remarked
elsewhere that while imagining themselves to have escaped
all taint of the banausic, the Spartans yet did in a certain
sense acquire that quality as a consequence of mechanical
military drill. We need not enter into the details of Cretan
institutions and their critical examination by Aristotle,
which opens no new point of view. The tone of sure knowledge in which Minos and the Cretan maritime supremacy
are spoken of finds in the discoveries of recent years a
support which it had hitherto lacked.

With a notable want of consistency (cf. p. 326), the constitution of Carthage is placed after those of Sparta and
Crete as a third model of political organization. It is
praised for its great stability ; but disapproval is expressed
of its plutocratic tendency, which leads even to the sale of

offices. Highly admirable is said to be the manner in which the Demos is kept quiet by the perpetual founding of new colonies. This is the great remedy for constitutional dangers, yet one which, in great calamities, may easily prove ineffective.

CHAPTER XXXIII.

ARISTOTLE'S THEORY OF THE STATE.

(THE PHILOSOPHER'S POLITICAL IDEAL.)

1. ARISTOTLE'S political ideal! "Surely," so many a reader may be ready to exclaim, "we are already familiar with that!" Tempered, instead of absolute, forms of government, the rule of the middle class—such are the features which we have by now learnt to recognize as characteristic of the political institutions which he favoured. "In his treatment both of ethical and political problems," it might be added, "we have met with no trace of that idealistic and youthful courage, that Titanic confidence, which enabled Plato to reject the whole existing order of things and rebuild social as well as political life on entirely new foundations. So bold a work of construction as that contained in the 'Republic' will not be expected of our philosopher by any one. Nor, indeed, are the conditions here present for a much less original creation, such as that presented to us by the 'Laws.'"

If we are not mistaken, doubts of this nature were not wholly absent from Aristotle's own mind. It is a highly remarkable fact that, though he began, he never finished his sketch of the "best State." The usual assumption, that he lacked time, seems to us hardly tenable. The lectures on "Politics," at the close of which he placed the sketch in question, were followed by at least the course on "Poetry" and that on "Rhetoric." The inference seems unavoidable that Aristotle purposely delayed the completion of that task. May not this postponement, which finally became definitive, have been occasioned by his consciouness of the unpromising nature of the undertaking, a consciousness which grew as the work progressed ?

An attempt to rival or even outbid the master, in this field as well as others, was urged upon the pupil by the special character of his ambition ; the venture might, indeed, have been required of him by his *entourage*, much as every head of a school was expected to draw up a particular " drinking-code," or " rules for the table " (cf. Vol. II. p. 274). His indefatigable reflexion on social and political subjects might also very easily have inspired him with the illusion of being equally qualified for that supreme and comprehensive labour. But this self-deception, we are inclined to believe, melted away when he approached the heart of his task, and perceived, perhaps not without astonishment, that he had nothing of decisive moment left to say. The fierce anger which flamed up in Plato against tradition, the abysmal contempt with which he looked down upon laws actually in force and customs actually observed, were not shared by his disciple. The latter was not unprepared with suggestions for the improvement of inherited institutions ; but it was not given to him to press on towards revolutionary innovations. Lacking great originality, he also lacked that capacity for illusion which alone could have given him faith in a possible rebirth of the State and of society. As we have seen, his survey was bounded by the limits of the conditions obtaining in his own day, so much so that he could conceive no other future for the populous city-states of Greece than a continuance of democracy (cf. p. 356), a form of polity which only needed to be freed from its worst excrescences. A contemporary who weighed all this could hardly have cast a favourable horoscope for his undertaking. The " best State " of Aristotle was bound either to turn out a colourless medley, lacking all strongly marked individuality, or else to remain what, in fact, it did remain—a torso.

The first glance at that part of the project which was actually executed bears out these impressions. We have already spoken of Aristotle's love of compromise (cf. pp. 349, 350). It has left its stamp on this part of his work. One subject of controversy was the mode of building a city. Is the chess-board pattern introduced by Hippodamus (cf. Vol. I. p. 387) to be followed ; or shall the ancient irregularity be observed ? The answer is : Take a mixture of both. Is communism in landed property or private ownership to prevail ? Half one and half the other. Are there to be private slaves or State slaves ? The two are to exist side by side. Compromise has been justly called the soul of all practical politics ; but it is much too easy an expedient to solve any and every conflict of principle by a Solomon's judgment. The use of it as a guiding canon for the construction of an ideal State shows clearly enough that the thinker who thus employs it is not the right man for the work.

2. The treatment of the theme begins with a lengthy prologue—devoted to ethical principles as applied to political life. The first task is to ascertain the proportion of the three factors : external, bodily, and spiritual goods. Our goal should be to obtain, not a minimum of these last, such as satisfies the great multitude, but a maximum. For everything external serves only as an instrument, and is therefore tied down to a definite limit, beyond which it ceases to be useful or even begins to be injurious. It is otherwise with the goods of the soul, the possession and active exercise of which is decisive for happiness. This truth is attested by the Deity, whose blessedness is founded, not on outward possessions, but on inner qualities. As with individuals, so also with combinations of them ; among States, too, only the best are happy. The parallelism here assumed brings the Stagirite face to face with a difficulty of some magnitude. For the individual he had maintained the superiority of the contemplative life. Was the State, therefore, to live like a philosopher ? The champions both of the active and of the contemplative life are brought forward to defend their respective standpoints. They arrive, finally, at an agreement in which the contemplative ideal is reconciled with the active. This agreement is obtained by accepting each type in a weakened-down form. The contemplative life, in the sense of one " detached from

everything external," is not held up as a complete ideal even for the individual. On the other hand, peaceful states, which "live for themselves," and which are sharply contrasted with those whose aim is conquest and robbery, make a near approach to the individual given up to contemplation. The latter is not denied a share in all "doing"; for such is not necessarily directed towards the external. For among men of action we hold those the most active who guide the actions of others by their thoughts. The contemplative ideal which was enthroned in the "Ethics" suffers, as it will be observed, some curtailment, now that individual and State have to row in the same boat; the practical ideal, however, is subjected to still greater limitation. "Practice" is taken to include the mere internal action and reaction of the parts, whether of a State or of an individual. "Otherwise"—that is, if this inward could not replace outward action—"God and the universe could not prosper, for they lack the power of acting on anything beyond themselves."

3. There follows an investigation of the external conditions for the ideal State, of the raw material, as it were, which the legislator must have at his disposal. In the front rank stands the question as to the size of the territory and the population. We are here more astonished than ever at the narrow bounds which hem in the philosopher's survey. He cannot look beyond even quite external peculiarities of the ancient city-state. The citizens must not be so numerous that the herald, who speaks to them all when assembled together, would need the voice of a Stentor. The obvious thought does not occur to him that several heralds might be employed in place of one, or that the necessary communications might be made with the help of writing. And this is the same Aristotle who, in the province of poetry, can so easily break down the barriers of tradition that he boldly detaches tragedy from its mythical or heroic basis. Again, though elsewhere, as we have seen, he prefers election by districts to direct election; he now considers the mutual personal acquaintance of all the citizens as an indispensable requisite for the election of authorities.

The self-sufficiency (αὐτάρκεια) of the State supplies the fundamental standard by which are to be measured both the number of the citizens and the extent of the land occupied by them. The danger for internal order which comes from maritime intercourse is not rated so high by Plato's pupil as by Plato himself in the "Laws" (cf. Vol. III. pp. 237, 238). He thinks that it may be overcome by limitations of personal intercourse with foreigners. Nor does he fear over-population as a result of sea-traffic, for the citizens will only be required to man the fleet, while the mercantile marine may be recruited from immigrants and serfs. Though laying emphasis on the commercial as well as the military advantages of a maritime situation, he has no intention of allowing his pattern-state to descend, through greed of gain, to the level of a mere market for foreign peoples.

4. What is to be ordained with regard to the different activities of the State: the conduct of war, "deliberation on what is for the public good," "the decision upon justice and injustice"? Are these functions to be divided or combined? In a certain sense, both, runs the answer; for they will be entrusted to the same persons, but at different ages. The ages will be different, because fresh vigour dwells with youth, mature insight with fulness of days. The full citizen must be a man of means, but not self-made. Those who belong to the class of peasants, of mechanics, or of traders, are stringently and decisively excluded from all participation in the guidance of the State. The truly civic classes, we are inclined to exclaim, are to forfeit all civic rights! The members of the ideal State are *rentiers*, who in youth perform military service, in middle life hold offices of State, and in old age are invested with the priesthood. So much in these chapters is said on the cultivation of "virtue," so incessantly does the subject recur, that we can hardly forbear a question. How, in a thoroughly peaceable community of limited size, one which is to wage none but defensive wars, and which must on no account become a commercial emporium or a seat of extensive production—how, we ask, in a little State, so

sunk in the placid life of contemplation, is material to be
supplied in any abundance for the exercise of the political
virtues ?

Looked at closely, the master-element in Aristotle's
ideal State is seen to consist of peace-loving Spartans or
Cretans maintained by the labour of peasants and artisans
held in serfage. Is it too much to say that the Stagirite
retains an ideal based on war and conquest, while rejecting
its aims and fundamental principles ? He finds it matter
for censure that in the State built up by Lycurgus everything was organized with a view towards war ; and yet it is
from this very community and others akin to it that he
borrows his political and social ideal. One is inclined to
call this "best State" an unwarlike Sparta, a name that
carries sufficient condemnation with it. We may go further.
Our reformer's immediate model was the "Republic" of
his master. But in his class of rulers or guardians the
latter provided the study of the sciences with a sure refuge,
or rather, with a position of commanding eminence. Was
Aristotle's aim directed towards anything resembling this ?
No word of the "Politics" admits of being interpreted in
such a sense. So far as these chapters carry us, the
professional votaries of the sciences, no less than of the arts,
are denied civil rights, unless they happen to belong to the
class of landowners, the ruling caste, which does not live by
its own labour (cf. pp. 333, 334). Among liberal callings
none in Hellas had from of old enjoyed higher social consideration than the profession of medicine. But one asks in
vain how even the most worthy successor of the man named
by Aristotle "Hippocrates the Great" (cf. Vol. I. p. 282)
could have become a full citizen of the philosopher's ideal
State.

5. We have exchanged exposition for criticism. Our
justification is that we have arrived at the end of what·
is set forth on matters of principle. The remainder consists
of all kinds of discussions and proposals, which, as they
leave the social and political structure of the community
untouched, have no more to do with the best State than
with any other. In support of the institutions of his

Utopia Aristotle makes a few historical references to the
Egyptian caste-system and to the common meals of men,
which he knows to have been customary in Italy as well as
in Sparta and Crete. He now turns to the question of site.
What is most noteworthy here is the high value placed on
the abundance and goodness of the water-supply, and the
recommendation to separate, when necessary, the drinking-
water from that used for other purposes. The preference
of open cities to fortified, in spite of the model Sparta and
the praise given to it in the "Laws" for this feature, is
pronounced a piece of old-fashioned simplicity, especially
in view of the progress in ballistics. Besides, the defenders
are always free to meet the attacking force outside the
protection of the walls. Questions relating to generation
and marriage, the care and education of children, now
come to the front, and demand a chapter to themselves.

CHAPTER XXXIV.

ARISTOTLE'S THEORY OF THE STATE.

(QUESTIONS OF REPRODUCTION AND EDUCATION.)

"BREEDING and education are the two cardinal pillars of society." An English contemporary, the author of a dialogue that may be called truly classical, has placed these words in the mouth of one of his characters; and they may serve as a motto for this chapter.

In what is said on the first of these subjects, maxims of prudence are combined with physiological assumptions that are very far from being borne out by modern science. Among the former are the following observations. The generative capacity of both parents should become extinguished at nearly the same time; the difference of age between them and their children should be neither too great nor too small. In the latter case, filial reverence may suffer; in the former, the parents may easily fail to profit by the active gratitude of their children, and the children may not receive a full measure of support from their parents. The main consideration, however, is that of the bodily and mental excellence of the offspring. The experience of stock-raisers proves that the pairing of very young specimens tends to produce imperfect and weakly young, mostly of the female sex only; this is confirmed by what is observed in many States where early marriages are the rule. Other reasons adduced are the severity of child-birth, the greater laxity of conduct on the part of women who are humoured and indulged at an early age, and the unfavourable influence on the growth of youthful husbands. The age of marriage is therefore recommended as eighteen years for girls, thirty-seven for men. The bodies of those who contract marriage should have been already strengthened by gymnastic exercises, but not of a violent character like those practised by contestants for athletic prizes. This applies to both sexes. Women with child are to be protected from excitements, but they must neither be kept on low diet nor allowed to spend their time in slothful inaction. The legislator may therefore prescribe for them a daily visit to some sanctuary in the neighbourhood. Over-population and the rearing of the unfit are provided against by anything but gentle means. Deformed children are to be exposed ; all excess over the prescribed number of children is to be checked by abortion induced at the right time, that is, before the commencement of life and feeling. The age of procreation is also bounded by an upper limit since the offspring of elderly parents are apt to turn out badly both in body and mind. For this reason men beyond the middle fifties are no longer to practise marital intercourse with the intention of begetting and rearing new offspring. Extra-marital intercourse, wherever a marriage-bond exists which is more than a name, receives unqualified condemnation, and within the years assigned to procreation is punished by the withdrawal of certain privileges.

2. In dealing with the care of children Aristotle recommends a diet rich in milk, the avoidance of wine, moderate bodily movements, no interference with crying, which he considers a kind of gymnastics, the use of mechanical means for securing straightness of growth, and early habituation to cold. The period from weaning to the age of five is devoted to play, which should consist chiefly in the imitation of the serious occupations of life. The preservation of children from harmful influences, including a too intimate contact with slaves, is made the duty of State-appointed overseers ; these, however, are to control only the home-care which children of that age require. With this comes the prohibition of unseemly, that is for the most part, indecent, words or pictures—a prohibition which is to be enforced by penalties graduated according to the offender's age. A remarkable exception is made in

connexion with certain religious ceremonies. But this exception applies only to adults ; while the youth are to be debarred from seeing comedies performed or from hearing recitations of satirical verse, a kind of carnival-amusement then in vogue.

The importance of early impressions is emphasized by a detail concerning the celebrated actor Theodorus. He would never suffer any one, even a rival of no pretensions whatever, to appear on the stage before himself. The first impression is overwhelming and decisive. It is thus imperative that the fresh receptivity of the youthful soul should from the very beginning be placed beyond the reach of all that is evil or ugly.

3. The theme of the eighth book, instruction and the training of the mind, is led up to by three questions. Is there to be a State system of education ? Is the system to be administered by the State ? What is to be the nature of the system ? The first two questions are answered affirmatively. Emphasis is once more laid on the necessity of educating the citizens in the spirit of the constitution (cf. p. 377). Again, the practice of virtue, like that of every art, and like the exercise of every other faculty, needs preliminary instruction and training. Lastly, that which is the common concern of all must be under the management of the community, A right care for the well-being of each individual member—and every citizen is a member of the State, not an independent unit—must keep in mind the good of the whole.

The fundamental treatment of educational questions begins with a reference to the differences of opinion which prevail in this field. One point of controversy is whether the training of the intellect or that of the character deserves precedence. Nor are men agreed whether practical utility, the acquisition of virtue, or lastly, the higher culture, should be placed in the forefront. Each of these standpoints has found champions. There follows a warning, such as we are now sufficiently familiar with (cf. pp. 333, 334), against all that is banausic. The process of instruction should begin by children aged from five to seven being present while others receive the teaching which they themselves are to receive later on. The most usual and indispensable means of education are next enumerated. These are the elementary subjects (reading, writing, arithmetic), gymnastics, music, and drawing (cf. Vol. I. pp. 413, 579). The last-named subject of instruction, we may remark in passing, is warmly recommended, not only for the sake of its utility, but also with an eye to the training of our "feeling for the beauty of forms."

Aristotle accompanies his praise of gymnastic teaching by a number of reservations. He blames the States which brutalize the youth and injure their growth by too violent exercises. A point of great importance is that the body and the mind ought not to be worked hard at the same time. Greater demands may be made on physical strength, and a corresponding diet supplied, at a later age, some three years after puberty is attained. In this connexion mention is made of the interesting fact that in the Olympic games the same contestant rarely won prizes both as boy and as man. The infant prodigy, in this department as in others, would seem to have come as a rule to an early halt.

The last chapters of the book, and of the work in its present arrangement, are devoted to music. But as the author of the "Politics" does not here limit himself to the educational importance of music, but takes into consideration its influence in other directions as well, it appears advisable to treat his remarks on the subject in connexion with his general teaching on art. Already, as we shall presently see, he has made casual incursions into this more comprehensive province.

CHAPTER XXXV.

ARISTOTLE'S THEORY OF ART.

1. "THE young should not look at the pictures of (the crudely realistic) Pauson, but at those of (the idealist) Polygnotus." This precept, in which the pedagogic influence of the plastic arts is recognized in addition to that of the others, occurs in the closing section of the "Politics," from which we have just passed on. It shows how great an effect upon the formation or deformation of character is ascribed by our philosopher to these arts, which present to us, as he says, no true "copy" of objects, but "signs" of qualities of the soul—their corporeal clothing, as it were. The influence of poetry upon the growth of the soul is rated by Aristotle still higher. We learn this not only from his exclusion of one whole species of poetry, comedy, from contact with the youthful mind, but also, and in still higher measure, from his attempt to deduce the classification of poetry, especially the drama, not, as one would have expected, from distinctions between poetic gifts, but from differences in the characters of poets. "Those who incline more towards the elevated have depicted noble actions and the actions of noble persons ; those who lean more to the trivial have presented us with the doings of mean persons." It is thus that the authors of tragedies and comedies are distinguished from each other. Clearly the distinction must reproduce itself in their works and become manifest in influence exerted upon the mind of receptive youth. A more lasting influence is ascribed to dancing, which, so far as it is not mere bravura-dancing, "imitates characters, emotions, and actions by gesture-rhythm ;" but still more to music. This art presents to

us qualities and passions of the soul, immediately embodied in rhythms and melodies ; and, according as we find pleasure in one kind or another, in courage or in gentleness, in anger or in love, our souls themselves grow to one or another character. From these peculiarities of the different musical modes Aristotle deduces without hesitation their importance for an education which is to begin early but last through life.

2. The cultivation of music is, however, not to serve exclusively this highest end, as Aristotle conceives it. There are three subsidiary aims which also are to be pursued by its aid : incitement to immediate action, which is the concern of "practical music ;" entertainment or recreation ; and, lastly, catharsis, the purging of the soul or the discharge of emotion. The second of these objects gives Aristotle occasion to relax the severity of his demands, and to allow some room for the lighter forms of music. For those who possess a "soul out of joint," so to speak, that is, as he expressly adds, " for a public consisting of banausic persons, proletarians, and such-like," a kind of music is to be allowed as a means of recreation which is little suited to the truly " free and well-educated." It is much as if, side by side with the elevated and solid grand opera, we were to allow an independent, though subordinate, place to the frivolous operetta, coupled with that kind of opera which deals in unmeaning flourishes and embellishments.

The subject of " catharsis " is treated by Aristotle first of all in a few pregnant sentences : " We see, in the case of the sacred songs (by these are meant chiefly certain melodies ascribed to the mythical singer Olympus), that while usually their effect upon the mind is a sort of intoxication, yet when they are heard by persons in ecstasy, these are calmed, as though they had gone through a medical cure and a 'catharsis' (that is, relief)." This alleviation, he adds presently, comes to them "accompanied by feelings of pleasure " ; and here he includes those who incline to such emotions as fear and pity and who are acted upon, not by music, but by tragic poetry.

This (pleasurable) discharge of fear and pity is then described in the definition of tragedy as nothing less than its main effect and supreme end. It is now hardly necessary to speak of the chaos of misunderstandings which has clustered round these teachings. It has been supposed that the process was one in which, instead of the soul finding relief and being purified of its passions, the passions themselves were cleansed and clarified. Pierre Corneille incorporated this error in his teaching ; Lessing strove with it in vain ; the intuition of Goethe gave the first blow to its authority ; Jakob Bernays, by his systematic investigations, achieved its final dispatch. The "truth and error" of this theory, too, have been dealt with in our own time, with decisive finality, as we think. Two kinds of "catharsis" have been distinguished. One is more especially the privilege of youth, which is prone to work off a surplus of energy by a bout of violent emotion ending in assuagement ; the other, more characteristic of advancing years, consists in a discharge of old, unspent, emotional tensions, which finds its occasion, rather than its material, in the contemplation of tragic events. This second kind of "catharsis," it may be mentioned, was anticipated by Plato in a memorable passage of the "Republic." The "sympathy" with the hero, as it is imagined to be, has been aptly compared with the emotional state of those maids of Achilles, who, according to Homer, seemed to be weeping for the dead Patroclus, while in reality they were bewailing their own sad condition.

But is the enigma of "pleasure in the tragic" hereby solved ? Clearly this was Aristotle's opinion ; for he was emphatic in placing "catharsis" at the close of his definition, and he altogether omitted to seek for any other cause of the mysterious pleasure caused by the poetic representation of painful happenings. But the new æsthetic, rightly, as we think, has not followed him in this. The Frenchman Dubos (1670–1742), the Swiss Sulzer (1720–1779), Lessing himself most clearly of all, have expressed the thought that the painfulness of the tragic impression may be outweighed by its intensity, that by the violence of our feeling we become "conscious of a higher degree of our reality," and that, to end with the language of a contemporary, "enhancement and extension of our consciousness is in itself a kind of happiness." The correctness of this interpretation receives proof, if we are not mistaken, from those tragedies, such as Shakespeare's *Cymbeline* and Lessing's *Nathan*, which act upon us quite in the same way as powerful tragedies, though their content is not tragic in the usual sense of the word.

3. But if Aristotle thus mistakes the part for the whole, an accessory phenomenon for the heart of the matter, the depth of his psychological vision still deserves our full admiration. Even here, however, a great surprise awaits us. Astonishing as it is to find "catharsis" recognized so early and placed in so emphatic prominence among the ingredients in the effect produced by art, it is hardly less so to find that process ignored in the field where it plays its most important part—that of artistic creation itself. Nothing is more familiar to us than the view of lyric poetry as a means by which the poet sets himself free; Aristotle gives no hint of having had even the remotest perception of this. But, it may be objected, our familiarity with this idea is due to Goethe's self-revelations, and this late discovery cannot justly be demanded from the earliest thinker who gave any sustained attention to the philosophy of poetry. The objection is well-founded, but does not end the matter. It is not only that Aristotle knows nothing of any self-liberation on the poet's part; he almost absolutely ignores that whole branch of poetry which takes its peculiar character from this self-liberation. It is not too much to say that he had no sense whatever for lyric poetry. This assertion has so bold a sound, the question is so important and so well fitted to introduce us to the innermost essence of Aristotle's conception of art, that we have no choice but to dwell upon it for a while.

The fact that lyric poetry finds no place among the divisions of poetic art may well surprise us, but is not necessarily of decisive importance. Verse written to be sung and indeed composed by the older poets simultaneously with the melody, might possibly have been accounted a part of music, and treated under that head. But this supposition does not remove our difficulty ; for Aristotle does not treat lyric poetry at all. The few exceptions from this rule are quite of the kind by which a rule is proved. Some species of lyric poetry are indeed known and named by Aristotle ; but how and where ? In the historical part of his exposition he mentions "hymns and songs of praise," and with them "songs of invective," as preliminaries and rudiments of the higher branches. Another and perhaps more notable exception is the class of poetry called "dithyrambic," half lyric and half dramatic, which is not passed over in the enumeration, and is also mentioned a few times elsewhere. In the passage which distributes the embellishments of language among the different kinds of poetry written in the higher style, the dithyramb is not sent quite empty away, while purely lyric poetry receives not a word of mention. It is only in the discussion of real and supposed errors of art that a linguistic observation is to be found which has been referred with probability to a line of Pindar. The same silence, finally, is observed in that portion of the "Rhetoric" where a survey is given of the different forms of "procemium" found in different species of poetry. Once more the dithyramb appears, and once more the works of even the masters of Greek lyric are entirely ignored.

4. This silence does not stand alone. The negative fact is matched by positive ones of almost still greater force. For the author of the "Poetics" the successful reproduction of the objective is the beginning and end of all exercise of art. He places the theory of "plot-construction" almost in the forefront of his undertaking. But in the case of a satirical song by Archilochus, a love-song by Sappho, or a drinking-song by Anacreon, is it legitimate to speak of a plot at all ? From the very beginning our philosopher's gaze is rivetted on the epic and the tragedy, the subjects of his first book ; while the second and last book was devoted to the other main branch of the drama, comedy. It is true that the task of all musical art is stated to be

the representation, not only of actions, but also of "dispositions and emotions." But this process of expression is far from being one of self-expression. We perceive this most clearly from the passage where the poetic endowment is spoken of and reduced to two main types. To compose poetry, he tells us, is the work of a nature which is either particularly intellectual or particularly emotional. The "plastic flexibility" of the first, the want of inner steadfastness and the tendency to "ecstasy" on the part of the second, permit them to transport themselves with ease into the emotions which the subject of the poem requires to be represented. In the one case, the intellectual genius adapts himself easily to the emotions concerned; in the other, the man of emotional temperament easily falls into them. But there is not the most distant allusion to self-representation, to the streaming out of moods and feelings actually present in the poet's mind. We are accustomed to seek the sources even of many dramatic productions, a "Tasso" or a "Faust," in the poet's inner experiences; but this point of view is essentially foreign to the Stagirite; indeed, it could hardly have been intelligible to him. For it reduces the dramatic to something lyrical, the pragmatic or objective species of poetry to a subjective form.

The author of the "Poetics," as we have seen, had no true feeling for subjective poetry. But this attitude of depreciation was not long maintained. Even among Aristotle's pupils, there were two, Chamæleon and Dicæarchus, who, by devoting monographs to lyric poets, testified to the value which they placed on this branch of the art. The same course was pursued by the great art-critics both of the Alexandrine school and of the Græco-Roman epoch. Dionysius of Halicarnassus, for example, carefully analyzes an ode of Sappho. How different from Aristotle, who cites the lyric poets only as witnesses to historical facts, as the authors of ingenious and profound sayings, at most as patterns in the employment of rhetorical artifices, never once as bearing upon the theory and rules of poetic art! Lyric poetry and its masters had then won a position of equality with the other branches of poetry and their

representatives. Aristotle's failure to recognize this equality
might have been inferred beforehand from his predominantly intellectualistic conception of art. He goes, indeed,
so far in this that he puts in the foremost place those
effects of art which have least to do with feeling or fancy.
There is a cardinal passage in which he actually reduces
the pleasure received from art to the pleasure of learning.
"Imitations," he tells us, "are contemplated with satisfaction
because they give occasion for learning and for reasoning
out what each of them means ; in the case of a portrait,
for example, that it represents such and such a person."
And this character of the cool reasoner it maintained, not
only in dealing with the enjoyment of art, but also in
judging artistic production itself. It is so especially where
he investigates the relative ranks of the different elements
which enter into tragedy, for him the supreme form of
poetry. The first place is here given to the "plot," or
"construction of the events," precisely that element which
is entirely a product of artistic reason.

5. There are three roots from which artistic creation
springs—the love of beauty, the craving for emotional
liberation, the formative impulse. Of these, the second is
ignored by our philosopher, and it is only the third, known
to him as the imitative impulse, which he considers with
any exhaustiveness. In regard to the conception of beauty,
he follows the path opened up by his master, who had for
the first time brought the elementary æsthetic feelings to
light (cf. Vol. III. p. 192 ; also Vol. II. pp. 353, 354). He
is successful in detaching the Beautiful from its old entanglement with the Useful, less so in separating it from
the Good in general. As elements of beauty he names
(in the "Metaphysics") "order, symmetry, limitation,"
and again (in the "Poetics") a middle magnitude which is
equally removed from the diminutive and the inordinately
large ; the "innate sense of rhythm and harmony" also
appears here among the factors which govern the production
and the enjoyment of art. With these rudiments of a
philosophy of the beautiful is coupled a strong emphasis
on the imitative impulse or mimetic element in artistic

creation. In this last particular an ancient Greek could only be expected to follow the line marked for him by the national endowment of lucid vision and plastic talent. But the exclusiveness of this emphasis was certainly calculated to narrow the Stagirite's æsthetic horizon in a serious degree.

Truth to nature in the imitation, beauty in the copy— what is the relation between these two requirements? Not a few pronouncements of Aristotle teach that the second must invariably have the precedence. The poet should " do as good portrait-painters do, make the picture like, and at the same time embellish it." A saying of Sophocles is quoted with approval, in which he claimed that " he depicted men as they ought to be, Euripides as they are." A critic had complained that Zeuxis " had painted men such as could never exist in reality." Aristotle replies: " But that is the better course, for the ideal should always surpass the real." Thus everywhere the preference is given to the higher, the more perfect, the more beautiful. But this demand is never justified from first principles, or deduced from the supreme aim of artistic creation. That aim remains throughout " mimesis," or imitation ; the demand for beauty, though made with great emphasis, as we have seen, was yet added as a casual after-thought— smuggled in, one might almost say. No one will deny that Aristotle's theory of art is here marred by a great inconsistency. And yet he was well-advised not to torment himself with the quest for a single principle of beauty to serve as the starting-point of his deductions. Such an abstraction would have been exceedingly difficult to reach, and when won would have been certainly unfruitful, because poor in content.

6. The time has come to speak of the uncontested and brilliant excellences of the " Poetics." These are chiefly to be sought where the strength of that intellect is generally to be found, in the masterly skill of the divisions, in the freedom, acuteness, and unerring certainty of the vision. To bring likes together, to set unlikes apart, even where external appearance, tradition, and habit make such juxtaposition and such severance matters of the uttermost

difficulty,—this is the task for which Aristotle has abilities
with hardly a parallel, and in accomplishing which his
intellect, distinguished as it is pre-eminently by the
amplest fulness of knowledge and the supple flexibility of
thought, reaches the height of true genius. It was thus
reserved for him to free the concept of poetry from the
external marks of versification, and to bring under that
category, not only artistically composed dialogues like
those of Plato, but also prose *geure*-pictures, such as were
painted by a Sophron and a Xenarchus (cf. Vol. II. p. 265).
No error in antiquity was more widespread and more per-
sisted in than the confusion, or at least the mixture, of
poetry with ethics on the one hand, and with science on
the other. Hardly anything redounds more to our author's
honour than the sure steadfastness with which he avoids
all such errors of delimitation, keeps the specifically poetic
value of a composition unwaveringly in sight, and shows
that he has learnt to make abstraction of the moral or
other didactic purpose served by a poem. While recognizing the poetical character of an artistic piece of literature
which lacks the form of verse, he excludes from this
category versified works of didactic substance : " Homer
and Empedocles have nothing but the metre in common."
In sharply pointed antitheses he contrasts the ethical with
the æsthetic valuations. If for the first the purpose is
everything and the execution nothing, for the second the
reverse is the case—in art the purpose counts for nothing,
the execution for everything. How little inclined he was
to allow the artist's intentions, be they never so noble and
elevated, to be reckoned as an excuse for artistic impo-
tence ; how poor a substitute, too, all learning and all
knowledge seemed to him for specifically artistic endowment ;—all this may be deduced with rigorous consequences
from one pregnant sentence of the " Poetics." A saying of
Schopenhauer, " In art, . . . as the very word indicates,
power [1] alone is of any importance," might serve as a
motto for the " Poetics."

---

[1] In the original, *Kunst* and *Können*, corresponding etymologically to
" cunning " and " can."—Tr.

Aristotle's eye for the essential is as well shown in the strictness with which he insists upon canons drawn from the nature of the subject-matter as in the laxity with which he abandons a rule so soon as its violation yields greater gains for poetry than its inflexible enforcement. He goes so far in this that he even advises the poet to sacrifice truth to nature, if by this means he can succeed in producing a more powerful effect than would otherwise be attainable. "An error has been committed, but it was right to err." Such is his manner of expressing this thought. Here we may pause to mention the old error which made Aristotle the author of the pedantic rules, so cramping to dramatic poets, of the three unities. In reality, he demanded only the unity of the action,—a demand, to be sure, which he made with the utmost emphasis, and which he applied to poetical compositions of all kinds, epic as well as dramatic, refusing at the same time to accept as a substitute the mere unity of the person, the hero of the poem. The unity of time was not recommended by him, but tacitly assumed, because it was the governing rule in the ancient drama, seldom violated, and still more seldom in any serious degree. It was the same with the unity of place, which, it may be noted, is not mentioned in the "Poetics" at all.

7. The necessity and the sufficiency of strict unity in the action are themes to which Aristotle constantly recurs. The poet is advised to keep this ideal firmly before his eyes, not to lose himself in the accessory matter which cannot be dispensed with, especially in epic, not to be content with brilliance and charm here as a substitute for excellence in the main point. As a protection against this danger, it is recommended that he should strip the central heart of his story free from all that is subsidiary, so as to bring it clearly before his mind. Preliminary practice for this operation is to be gained by analyzing in a similar manner poems already in existence ; and a few models of such work are offered for his guidance. The essence, for example, of the story of Iphigenia is given as follows : "A maiden was appointed to be sacrificed ; but without the

fore-knowledge of the sacrificers she was removed to a distant
land, where it was the custom to sacrifice foreign new-comers
to the goddess of the country. She there became a priestess
of this goddess, and after long time it so happened that her
brother came there too ; the oracular response which sent
him, the occasion of it, and the purpose of it are irrelevant.
Having arrived, he was seized, and would have been sacrificed, but that a recognition took place." Here, again, is
the kernel of the voluminous " Odyssey : " " A man lived for
long years lonely in a strange land ; meanwhile, at his
home, other men consumed his substance and sought his
son's life ; at last he returned, tempest-tossed ; was recognized by a few persons ; and so ventured on the attack
which brought happiness to himself and destruction to his
enemies."

For our philosopher, the daughter of Agamemnon, the
most powerful among the Greek princes, is thus merely a
" maiden ; " Ulysses is not a hero and a mighty warrior
before Troy, but simply a " man." How, then, could he
be expected to hold with unyielding exclusiveness to the
traditional material, derived from heroic legends and from
history ? For even the familiar subjects, as he aptly objects,
" are familiar to only a few, but none the less give pleasure
to all." We are thus not surprised to find him professing
his faith in the capacity of tragedy for a further development, a profession which necessarily leads our thoughts to
the *bourgeois* tragedy, at that time either non-existent or
known only in isolated experiments.

From this comparatively low estimate of the traditional,
of what is actual fact or at least held to be true, it is but
a step to those famous words which have so highly pleased
our classics : " Poetry is a more philosophical and a more
serious matter than history." The justification of the
paradoxically sounding utterance is given by the author
of the " Poetics " himself. " The first," he continues, " busies
itself more with the general, the second with the particular.
It is a generality that a person of such and such a character
necessarily or naturally does or says such and such a thing ;
and this is what poetry aims at telling us, though it gives

its heroes (individual) names. But what Alcibiades has
done or suffered is particular." These important thoughts
may perhaps be transcribed thus : The poet, who must have
a profound knowledge of human nature, presents us with
a single chain of causation ; he shows how external events
affect the soul of the agent ; then, how such influence, in
its turn becoming a cause, leads to further consequences,
reactions, and interactions, the whole series being displayed
to us in all its purity and independent unity. On the other
hand, the facts of actual experience continually interrupt
this ideal sequence ; instead of an orderly, because isolated,
chain of causes, we ever again come upon chance, that is,
the complication of one causal chain with several. The
hero of a poem drains to the dregs the cup of his own
filling ; the curse or the blessing that falls upon him answers
strictly to his actions. In real life an apoplectic fit may
intervene between the most momentous of actions and the
whole train of its consequences. Tell may miss the apple ;
Romeo may fall from the rope-ladder. Lastly, the pre-
dilection of ancient poetry for typical characters lent to
Aristotle's pronouncement a higher measure of truth than
it possesses for us. Modern poetry, dealing as it often does
with complicated characters, worked out in their individuality, makes to that extent an approximation to the
tangle of real life, in which law and regularity are so much
harder to discern than in fiction.

8. This breadth and comprehensiveness of vision, however, does not diminish the loving care bestowed on detail.
The " Poetics " is full of what may be called studio-wisdom,
of important technical hints and observations springing
from a range of experience which arouses our admiration.
The author may well have received here the expert assistance of a professed poet, probably the rhetorician and
tragedian Theodectes of Phaselis, a disciple who was highly
honoured by his master and who died early. These very
interesting details will be the more easily found by the
reader in the book itself, the more accurately we make him
acquainted with its structure and divisions.

The little work opens with the separation of poetry

from the group of musical arts to which it is most closely
related. Then comes the division of the poetic art into its
sub-varieties. After this follows the genetic consideration
of these species, or at least of those recognized by Aristotle.
By this means the way is imperceptibly prepared for the
establishment of an order in rank, and so of an order in
treatment, of the three main branches—tragedy, epic, and
comedy. The investigation of tragedy leads to a discrimination between its several (internal) components or elements,
and then to the arrangement of these in a series according
to their rank. The elements are then treated in that order.
First comes the "fable" or plot, which is discussed with
great exhaustiveness, in accordance with the pre-eminent
importance attached to it by Aristotle. It is next the
turn of the second main element, the "characters." But
here the sequence is seriously disturbed. The author
returns to a particular ingredient in the "fable," recognition. This deviation from methodic rigour can be
adequately explained in perhaps only one way ; it is a
later addition, introduced by the lecturer when repeating
his course, and not transferred by the editor to its appropriate place. There follows a long series, not very systema-
tically arranged, of particular hints and observations, partly
relating to the tragic poet's process of creation, partly
betraying a desire to have done with the treatment of
tragedy and to reserve for further discussion only two
more of its six components ("reflection" and "diction").
That is to say, two of the components, "scenic apparatus"
and the "song-composition" of the choral portion are
only mentioned for the sake of completeness, and are
relegated to the lowest position in spite of their "fascinat-
ing charm" and their high importance as "seasoning."
The intention so indicated is realized to this extent that
"reflection" is referred to the domain of rhetoric ;
"diction," however, is made the subject of a discussion
which arouses the reader's astonishment not solely by its
excessive length. For it is also very surprising at first
to find that the author treats this and only this component
of tragedy at a point where, by appending a long series

of desultory observations, he had shown his intention of bringing his theory of tragedy to a conclusion. The two circumstances are very closely connected ; and we shall now show in what way.

In Aristotle's age the theory of language had hardly progressed beyond its first beginnings (cf. Vol. I. pp. 441, 442 ; Vol. III. p. 187). It did not provide matter enough for an independent treatise. What wonder, then, if an encyclopædist of universal range took the first occasion which presented itself to make public some part of what he had to say on the subject ? Such an occasion was supplied by the necessity of stating his views on the requirements of poetic diction. It was, too, repugnant in itself to the Stagirite's systematic intellect to treat of the means of poetic expression without first passing in review the means of linguistic expression in general. He had thus to begin by discriminating the different parts of speech or kinds of words. But from words the road leads downwards through the syllable to the speech-sound, upwards to discourse or the combination of words. (The syntactical remarks on this last subject are reserved to the "Rhetoric.") Hence the great extent of this chapter on language ; hence also the position, so strange at first sight, which it occupies. In truth, this position was most carefully chosen. At any earlier point the excessive length of this section would have seriously injured the symmetry of the exposition. But there was another consideration which weighed still more heavily. "Diction" may be what Aristotle calls it, a "component" of tragedy ; but it is just as much a component of epic and of every other form of poetry It was thus quite a happy thought to place these chapters at the close of the part of the work which deals with tragedy, and just before the beginning of the sections which treat the remaining branches of poetry, beginning with epic. The arrangement of the last chapters is not less well-considered. Two of them are devoted to the epic as such ; the last but one discusses the theme of "problems and solutions," the matter of which is taken, not exclusively but in far preponderant measure, from heroic poetry. For it was the pattern epics of Homer on which the acumen of critics and expositors had from early times been accustomed to exercise itself. In this section, a curious guide to the dialectics of poetical questions, occasion is taken now and then to extract principles of fundamental importance and to apply them to tragedy as well as to epic. The conclusion is a comparison of the two forms of poetry which alone receive treatment in the extant first book, and is intended to supply a final justification for that preference of tragedy over epic which has already been amply indicated.

9. Two reasons for this preference are clear and convincing—the vigorous compression and the lifelike embodiment in which it presents its characters. The value of this "embodiment" is appraised so high by Aristotle that he even praises Homer because "he alone did not fail to recognize what the poet has to do in his own person. . . . The others (epic poets) . . . represent by way of imitation only isolated details in isolated cases ; but Homer, after a short introduction, brings on a man, a woman, or some other being, etc." The Stagirite here travels in the footprints of his master, who in the "Republic" awards the same praise to the "poet," and alludes to the speeches of Chryses and Agamemnon at the beginning of the "Iliad." "The poet," Aristotle continues, "should say as little as possible in his own person ; for to that extent he is not an imitative portrayer." Here, to be sure, we must not press every word. For as these dramatic episodes, in which the characters of the heroic poem are introduced as speaking, form only a part of the two Homeric epics, the author of the "Poetics" would, strictly interpreted, allow Homer the character of an "imitative portrayer" only within this limited range ; outside it he would lose this character and with it that of poet. But obviously he only desired to enforce a distinction of degree, and insisted upon it with more than due emphasis.

As we have already once remarked by way of anticipation (cf. p. 144), Aristotle's mode of establishing his thesis of the precedence of tragedy before epic is by no means free from one-sided violence. It is even claimed as an advantage for tragedy that it may make use of the heroic metre—in reality an occurrence of the greatest possible rarity—while the epic is tied down to one metre, the hexameter. Certainly this argument is merely a small item in a far more comprehensive plea: tragedy has everything which belongs to epic, and surpasses it by possessing a greater abundance of artistic resources. But a well-considered objection was raised against this statement by so early an æsthetic as that of the Epicureans, and an undeniable, if not very momentous, defect of Aristotle's theory of poetry was laid bare at the same time. As the subject of poetry, Aristotle had named "agents;" and that by these only men could be understood appears at once from the immediately following division of these acting beings into "noble" and "common," into persons who reach the average moral level, rise above it, or fall below it. What, asked Philodemus the Epicurean, has become of natural objects and processes in the external world, of the (superhuman) gods and the (infra-human) animals—themes which are practically unknown to Aristotle's favourite, the drama, but quite accessible to epic? Thus, in reality, as he contends, these two branches of poetry stand in precisely the opposite relation to each other.

Aristotle the Eristic has now for some time been lost to our sight. But here we meet him once more, just as we are about to enter upon one of the chief fields of his activity, the province of rhetoric.

CHAPTER XXXVI.

ARISTOTLE AND RHETORIC.

1. FAR back in the Homeric age the phrase, "To be a speaker of words and a doer of deeds," testifies to an ideal the like of which is difficult to find in the early period of other peoples. In the democratic communities the practice of oratory grew to be of cardinal importance (cf. Vol. I. p. 382). But it was in the island of Sicily that the theory of rhetoric found its first cultivators in the persons of Corax and Tisias (cf. Vol. I. pp. 228, 229). The man who transplanted Sicilian rhetoric to Athens, Gorgias of Leontini, has long ago been introduced to the reader's acquaintance (Vol. I. p. 476). Handbooks of this art were composed in so great number that a quite general term (τέχνη), denoting arts and crafts of all kinds, was appropriated to this special meaning. The hostile attitude of Plato towards that older practice of rhetoric has been shown to us in his dialogue "Gorgias," which was primarily directed against that sham art, as he held it to be (cf. Vol. II. p. 327), We know, too, how after repudiating this art root and branch, Plato attempted in the "Phædrus" to re-establish it on new foundations, and to replace empirical routine by a scientific system based on dialectic and psychology (cf. Vol. III. p. 21). According to this ideal, the orator would need such a knowledge of his subject-matter as would enable him to analyze it into its finest and minutest divisions ; he would also need to know the souls of his audience, both comprehensively and individually. While still a young man, Aristotle was engaged in the teaching of rhetoric (cf. p. 20). He was so familiar with the host of text-books already referred to that he did not disdain

the task of giving a compendious account of them. During his second Athenian residence he delivered a course of lectures on rhetoric ; out of these he formed a work of three books, the contents of which will now occupy our attention.

2. The fundamental motive of the first two books (the third is mainly devoted to diction) may be taken to be that of carrying on towards realization the ideal set up by Plato in the "Phædrus." We agree with the verdict of the great historian of Greece that this ideal was in truth unattainable, partly because of its severity, partly because of internal contradictions by which it is affected. To allow for individual differences within the audience is a feat which the orator's tact may attempt with approximate success ; but to comprehend this infinite variety in general precepts may well be accounted an impossibility ; moreover, perfect knowledge of the matter in hand, far surpassing the level of the auditors, would raise, as Grote pointed out with a reference to passages in the "Gorgias," an almost impassable barrier between the speaker and his hearers. But be this as it may, Aristotle believed himself to be making an approach to that high aim when he incorporated in his manual on rhetoric sections of psychology and descriptive ethics, in particular the theory of the emotions and an account of the types of character which correspond to different ages and stations in life. We have not disturbed this arrangement in order to give the reader as true a delineation of the book as is possible. In summarizing its contents we shall hardly be able to avoid interspersing critical comments.

Rhetoric is spoken of as a counterpart to dialectic. With both there is an absence of any limitation to a separate profession. All are in a measure qualified to practise both the one and the other. Hence it must also be possible to discover the causes of their occasional success ; and that this is the concern of an art, no one will dispute. The authors of handbooks have busied themselves only with secondary matters, not with the main problem, the creation of conviction. The arousing of emotions is something subsidiary and unessential; it is entirely forbidden to plaintiffs and defendants by the legislation of all well-ordered states, for it is a deliberate warping of what should be the straight rule in the hand of justice. A party to a suit has merely to prove or disprove some matter of fact. But to judge the quality of a fact or an event, to say whether it is great or small, just or unjust, is the affair of the judge himself, so far as the law entrusts him with the decision. Good laws, by the way, leave to the decision of the judge as little as possible, and that for three reasons. It is easier to find one or a few wise (legislator or legislators) than many; the legislator judges at leisure and not on the spur of the moment; lastly and chiefly, the decision of the law is general and delivered in advance, not special and concerned with matters of the immediate present. When the latter is the case, love and hatred interfere too easily, private prejudice does its share, and all together cloud the faculty of judgment. We notice how the forensic oration has imperceptibly taken the place of oratory in general, not exclusively, indeed, but preponderantly. As Aristotle himself tells us, the labours of his predecessors had been concentrated upon this special province—the less harmless one, he adds, since he who judges on political questions, has only to decide concerning his own interests, while the judge in the law courts gives decisions affecting the interests of others. (This position, it might be replied, can be maintained only where the body of citizens possesses strict unity, and where the interests which are severally at stake are always those of the community, and not merely of a party.)

3. Thus the true subject of rhetoric is the means of convincing, and these again are the means of proof. To be familiar with these, to possess even the power of proving opposites in order to be on guard against the misuse of them, is a kind of defensive efficiency more important and more worthy of humanity than endowment with bodily strength. The objection that the power of speech may do as much harm when unjustly used as good when justly, applies in no higher degree to this than to any

other good thing, with the sole exception of virtue. Here Aristotle stands on the side of Gorgias and Polus against Plato (cf. Vol. II. p. 328), and at the head of a long series of writers, chiefly Stoic, Epicurean, and Sceptic philosophers, who have unweariedly discussed the pros and cons of this question.

The task of rhetoric is not to convince, but to discern the means of convincing, which are present in each special case. The means of gaining assent are divided into "artful" and "artless." It is only the first that we create; the second we merely use, *e.g.* depositions of witnesses, business documents, and so forth. Certain means of persuasion are mentioned which are relative to the character of the speaker; along with these, remarkably enough, we find those which at the outset were so flatly repudiated, those, namely, which are based on the emotions of the hearers. Three demands are now made upon the orator. He must possess the power of drawing inferences, the power of judging about virtues and characters, and, with regard to the emotions, the knowledge of what each of them is, what are its qualities, how and by what means it is aroused. Those who participate in the deliberations here referred to, the juror and the ecclesiast, are regarded as "men of simple mind," and as incapable of "reaching a conclusion through a number of intermediate steps and drawing long-spun inferences;" hence in this department (the political and judicial department, on which the author's attention becomes more and more focussed) abridged and effective forms are to be used, both of the syllogism and of induction. These forms are, on the one hand, probable reasonings and inferences from marks (enthymemes); on the other, the example. These arguments may be sound or the reverse. A sound argument from marks, for example, is the following: So-and-so is feverish, therefore he is ill; or again: Such and such a woman has milk, therefore she has borne a child. But it would be unsound to reason thus: So-and-so is feverish, for he is breathing rapidly; for his manner of breathing may be due to another cause (*e.g.* violent running). The "example" may

be used to prove that Dionysius of Syracuse is aiming
at a tyranny ; he has, in fact, demanded a body-guard,
which is what others did before him.   Pisistratus at
Athens, Theagenes at Megara, when they sought to
become tyrants.   Enthymemes are now divided into those
which are deduced from general truths, valid in all regions
of knowledge, and special truths, limited to particular fields.
This distinction is intended to pave the way for the lengthy
treatment of the subject which follows later.   But first
the subject-matter of rhetoric is divided into its three
branches : deliberative, forensic, and display-oratory.

4. The deliberative, or political, speech aims sometimes
at suasion, in other cases at dissuasion ; the forensic speech
may be inculpatory or defensive ; the show-speech, finally,
has for its subject praise or blame.   The first species is
concerned with the future, the second with the past, the
third mainly with the present, but not exclusively (we
may instance funeral and memorial speeches)   For the
orator of the first kind the chief point of view is that
of the useful (which he commends), or of the harmful
(against which he warns) ; other points of view, such as
those of the just and the unjust, the praiseworthy and
the blameable, also play their part.   In the forensic speech,
the question of justice and injustice takes the supreme
place, and it is the others already mentioned which enter
in as accessory.   For the orator who deals in eulogy or
invective, the laudable and the blameworthy occupy the
forefront.   In the law court the defendant does not always
deny that he did the alleged deed, or that the alleged
damage was caused, but he never admits his guilt (or at
least the full guilt).   The deliberative orator, again, will
never avow that he is advising what is injurious or unprofitable, and that he is dissuading from what is salutary,
whatever other concessions he may make to his opponent.
In panegyric and invective, finally, the same holds of
the noble or morally good, and its opposite.   From all
this it follows that the orator must be ready with propositions relating to the possible and the impossible, the
real and the unreal, in the past as well as the future,

and so on. It also follows that since everything often turns on degrees of utility and harmfulness, of justice and injustice, of good and bad, both in the absolute and the relative sense, orators must also have at their disposal propositions about greatness and smallness in general, and particularly on the determination of which is the greater good or evil, which the greater or smaller guilt.

The subject-matter of deliberation is now stated to be the contingent, as distinguished both from the impossible and the necessary ; within the contingent it is further limited to that which lies within our power. The detailed treatment of these subjects of deliberation, the encroachment of merely formal rhetoric on the domain of the objective studies, particularly politics, is repeatedly and emphatically disallowed. But this does not prevent the author from entering somewhat fully into the questions which form the matter of political deliberation. He names five of them as the most important : taxation, war and peace, defence, imports and exports, legislation. He expatiates on these points, and, *apropos* of legislation, touches on themes which have been discussed in the " Politics," such as the different forms of constitution and the question of what tends towards the preservation and what towards the destruction of each. Throughout, the political orator is required to enlarge his survey to the greatest possible width, and to gain an extensive knowledge both of historical facts and of contemporary parallels to them.

5. The different points of view indicated above are now considered in greater detail. Nothing is here so noteworthy as the way in which the author of the " Rhetoric " takes his stand almost entirely on current opinions, often strangely conflicting with his own ethical doctrines. He starts from the deliberative or political speech, the gist of which is persuasion to or dissuasion from some measure. In either case the orator has to do with what men choose or avoid. The first is essentially well-being or happiness. In conformity with popular opinion the elements of

well-being **are** enumerated somewhat as follows: high birth, the possession of numerous good friends, wealth, children, happy old age, bodily excellences of all kinds, good repute, honour, good fortune, virtue. All these are discussed separately, and Aristotle here shows himself possessed by a real mania for divisions and definitions. For example, bodily strength is explained as "the power to move other things at will;" and even the different modes of so moving them," pulling, pushing. lifting, pressing, binding together, do not go unmentioned. Or again: a good runner is he "who can throw his legs about in a particular way, moving them rapidly, and through a long range." In the middle of these truisms we find a warning which sounds like irony: "Yet for our purposes we have no need of pedantic minutiæ."

From the elements of happiness the investigation passes on to the main points of view which present themselves when we have to judge of the good and the useful, ends as well as means. We are surprised to meet once more with well-being, which is placed at the head of goods certainly, but yet as one among them, and side by side with virtue; though for Aristotle the moralist well-being is by definition "an acting according to virtue." There is perhaps some bearing on the technique of oratory in the review of the arguments which are available in this field on occasions of doubt. Thus among others: that is a good of which the opposite is an evil; or of which the opposite is advantageous, desirable, or welcome to an enemy. Or again: that is a good which has cost much labour and expense. And further: that which is striven after or competed for by many. Such a summary of the points of view from which it is possible to commend a thing or an action whose value is not evident at first sight might at times be of real use to an orator by leading him into the road most serviceable for his purpose.

In what follows it is presumed that opinions agree on the quality of a course of action, or on the predicate applicable to a fact, while disagreeing on the point of more or less. Here, again, there is much that is self-evident, but we yet note some features of interest, especially in the way in which opposed points of view are brought into prominence. It is possible to attribute greater guilt to the instigator than to the actual doer of a wrongful act, but so also is the reverse judgment. Sometimes we may rate more highly the rarity-value of an object, sometimes its utility-value ; so that at one time gold, at another iron, will be pronounced the more valuable. One and the same thing may be made to seem greater if we set out its parts in extended order, smaller if we lump them all together.

6. After a digression into the domain of the "Politics," and a reference to this work, praise and blame have their turn. The occasion is taken to discuss virtues and vices, moral beauty and ugliness. The purpose is twofold, partly that the orator may be able to praise and blame others in appropriate manner, partly that he may present himself to the audience in a favourable light, so as to win their confidence. In the treatment of the virtues, which are called the "capacities for well-doing," their social side is here placed in the forefront, just as everything else is viewed from the standpoint, not of the agent, but of the public. "The brave and the just are honoured chiefly because courage is useful to others in war and justice in peace." In the course of the discussion rhetoric slips gradually into a mere art of deception. We seem to be once more in the "Topics" (cf. pp. 53, 54). For the purpose both of praise and of blame it is recommended that things which are no more than closely allied should occasionally be treated as identical. It may be advisable to represent the cautious and reserved man as a dissembler, to praise as good those who are merely simple, as gentle those who are merely thick-skinned. Vicious extremes may be transformed into virtues. The foolhardy may be described as brave, the prodigal as generous, possibly with the help of such arguments as these : If that man hazards his life without need, how much more would he do so at the bidding of honour ! if this man is open-handed to all, how much more so to his friends ! Similarly, what is accidental may be represented as done with a purpose ; a characteristic

prized by a particular audience may be transfigured into some noble quality closely related to it. All this applies equally to the political speech and the display-oration. That which is recommended in the first, will, in the second, if this is of the eulogistic type, be represented as having been attained ; rules for invective may be obtained by inverting those for panegyric.

7. The forensic speech, in which both accusation and defence are included, gives an occasion for discussing the motives of unjust action, and indirectly brings under consideration the motives of all action. The doing of injustice which is called "a voluntary and unlawful injuring" (where the word "law" is to be understood in its widest sense), presupposes, in the first place, the voluntariness of the actions concerned. This notion is reduced to that of "action which is not constrained or unconscious," and which generally is also "purposeful." Three causes are named of involuntary action, and four of voluntary : chance, nature, and force on the one side ; habit, reflection, the active emotions, and the desires on the other. The aims pursued by voluntary actions are specified as the good or apparently good, and the pleasant or apparently pleasant ; herein is included also the removal or mitigation of real or apparent evils, and the really or apparently painful. But since the useful has already been treated in connexion with deliberative oratory, it is now time to speak of the pleasant, and that "in a manner neither obscure nor too precise." What actually follows is a treatise on pleasure, the essential content of which we have already considered in advance (cf. pp. 305, 306).

Actions may be pleasurable, not only when they are according to nature, but also when they are according to custom. Pleasure, too, belongs to mental images, which are "weakened sensations," whether they take the form of recollection or of expectation. And this is not really true in so far as what gives pleasure in the present produces the same effect by means of retrospect or prospect. Even past pain brings pleasure when it is thought of as overcome. Again, most desires are accompanied by a certain pleasure, that

which comes from the memory of past or the hope of future
satisfaction. Here, too, the pleasure of melancholy is mentioned. Grief for the present deprivation is coupled with
the remembrance of former possession. The pleasure of
victory is traced into the realms of the chase and of games.
Wherever competition rules, there is to be found the
pleasurable expectation of success or distinction. A remark on the joys of the dialectical combat "for those who
are trained and qualified for it," is drawn from the depths
of personal experience. Renown and honour infuse into us
the cheering belief that we actually possess the excellence
ascribed to us ; a similar effect is produced by the admiration and love which we receive, and the sham admiration
and friendship of the flatterer affect us by the same means.
The seeing again of highly valued persons and things
affords both the pleasure which comes from change and
that which is caused by the rareness of an experience.

There follow the pleasures of learning and of surprise.
When learning is called a " return to the normal state," the
reference is, no doubt, to the restoration of intellectual
tranquillity after the unrest of perplexity, investigation,
and doubt. The joys of beneficence are here regarded as
merely the pleasures of " possessing " (the means by which
the benefit is conferred) and of " excelling " (the person
benefited). The sympathetic feelings are here entirely
ignored ; moreover, the conception of benevolence, with
which we have already made acquaintance (pp. 291, 292),
goes to much greater depths. That Aristotle treats the
same problem, in one place with profundity, in another with
comparative shallowness, is a fact worth our notice. Distinguished as he is by fulness and abundance of thoughts,
he betrays occasionally lack of resisting power against
inadequate thoughts. Here, too, we encounter a touch of
perversity—the derivation of self-love from pleasure in the
similar and the cognate, which is represented as reaching
its culminating point in the relation of a man to himself !
Some artificiality, again, may be detected in the following
derivation. It is pleasurable to be regarded as wise ; for
wisdom is a means of rule, and nothing affords greater

satisfaction than to rule over others. What need, we may ask, was there of this circuit, since not all wisdom has that effect; and it would have been enough to appeal to the pleasure of "excelling," which had already been discussed?

8. After the motives of injustice, the subjects and objects of unjust action have their turn. The persons who are inclined to injustice are those who think themselves strong enough for it, or who have a prospect of remaining undiscovered, or who can foresee that their punishment, if it comes, will be light relatively to the pleasure or utility to be gained. In the elaboration of these thoughts we meet with not a little that is subtle, but at the same time, it must be admitted, with several examples of perverse ingenuity. One safeguard against detection, it is said, is a quality in the agent out of keeping with the punishable action; such would be bodily weakness in one guilty of violent assault, or poverty and ugliness in a seducer. Protection of the same kind is given not only by the secrecy of an action, but also by the exact opposite, its publicity; for people are not prepared for this, and so may easily omit the proper precautions. To have no enemy and to have many enemies may be considered equally advantageous. Those who are not hated count on the circumstance that no one is on his guard against them; those who are much-hated will hardly be credited with running any risks in face of the caution observed towards them, and they plead this improbability when on their defence. Wrong-doing is prompted both by frequent success and by repeated failure. The first encourages, the second spurs on to renewed endeavours in the hope of mending the record. A parallel is drawn between those to whom injustice brings gain, punishment merely dishonour, and those who, on the contrary, win some honour from the wrongful act (as in the case of avenging one's parents), while the punishment is not dishonouring, but amounts to a fine, banishment, or the like. In both ways an incentive is created to wrong-doing; not for the same persons, but for persons of opposite characters. The weak and the

strong of will are led into evil by motives of opposite
kinds—the first by a prospect of pleasure or profit in the
near future, the second by a prospect of gain or advantage,
which, though deferred, will be permanent. Good repute
and its opposite may produce the same effect. If a man
is highly esteemed, he will not readily be believed guilty ;
if he is already despised, an increase of infamy means little
for him.

This same fondness for making play with antitheses
appears again in the section on the objects of aggression.
Men are ready to attack both the very far and the very
near. They are beckoned on in the one case by an early
gain, in the other by a late punishment. Suitable objects
of attack are found in the confiding, the light-minded, the
timid, who willingly shirk a conflict. Those who have
never yet been attacked, and those who have been attacked
many times, are equally removed from caution : the first
because as yet such dangers lie outside their experience,
the second because they do not expect an immediate
repetition of what they have experienced. (One may with
some justice refer this last remark to a mania for paradox.
For one victim of theft who says, " I shall surely not be
robbed again just yet awhile," there are ten others who
learn wisdom from misfortune.) Next are mentioned
slandered persons and persons open to slander, who go to
law unwillingly, and for the most part without success.
Friends and enemies appear in strange conjunction. One
injures the first with pleasure and the second with ease.
It is next the turn of the friendless, the incompetent, the
over-busy, who shun lawsuits and may therefore without
difficulty be induced to compromise. Men are disposed
to commit wrongful acts which ingratiate them with those
on whom they depend. Again, wrong-doing hardly appears
as such when it has been preceded by strife and violent
disputation. Much the same is the case when the same
injury is threatened us by others, and we merely strike
the first blow. Or again, when, in the words of Jason, the
tyrant of Pheræ, "a little wrong gives us the means of
doing great good." In conclusion, cases of a more trivial

kind are mentioned, such as wrong which is universal, or at least of great frequency (we may instance smuggling on the small scale), the appropriation of objects hard to identify, and injuries which the victims will not willingly make public.

9. Some chapters of criminal jurisprudence are now inserted in the " Rhetoric," just as the " Poetics " contained a section on language. Here, as before, the author seizes an occasion to touch, even if summarily, on a subject as yet little developed. We pass over the distinctions, not new to us between the " written " and the " unwritten law " (cf. p. 328), to which latter is added the more comprehensive idea of universal or natural law, and again between voluntary and involuntary action (cf. pp. 249 and 263). Aristotle insists on the question of fact and the question of culpability being kept strictly separate ; he also urges the need of more exact definitions in this field, as, for example, mere removal of an object is not theft ; there must also be a suffering of loss on the one side and an appropriation on the other. He further enforces the difference between services which give proof of "superfluous merit" and bare fulfilment of legal duty. Equity, which fills up the gaps left intentionally and unintentionally by the laws, is treated at some length (cf. pp. 263, 264). The conclusion is as follows : " It is the part of equity to look not to the law but to the legislator, not to his words but to his thoughts, not to the deed but to the intention, not to the part but to the whole, not to the present but to the permanent qualities of the doer." We note, in passing, that the vigorous juristic sense which we have learnt in the school of Rome obviously remained as foreign to the Stagirite as to his contemporaries. There is nothing to support and much to rebut the supposition that he condemned the habit, so prominent in Attic forensic orations, of seeking to influence unduly the decision on a particular case by bringing under consideration the whole life of the accused, and especially his political conduct.

Another subject discussed in this section is the magnitude of guilt, and the different modes of measuring it. One point of view is the following. An injury is greater or less in proportion to the injustice from which it springs. According to this it may happen that the smallest possible injury becomes in special circumstances (as in sacrilege) the greatest of all. Other standards are supplied by the extent of the loss inflicted, the impossibility of complete reparation, the magnitude of the consequences (as when, for example, the injured person commits suicide in despair), also the unprecedented nature of the offence, though with this is coupled the precisely opposite quality of commonness. Other factors which come into consideration are the brutality of the misdeed ; its long premeditation ; its scene—for example, the court of justice in which perjury is committed—lastly, the disgracefulness of the act and the personality of the victim, who may, as an instance, be a benefactor of the delinquent. A violator of the unwritten law may be represented—by the help of a fallacy, we may add—as the more responsible : "For it is a greater merit to honour a law which lacks penal sanction ; hence its violation brings the heavier guilt." But the contrary inference is also legitimate : "How should a man who is not restrained even by the fear of punishment forbear a wrongful act for which no punishment awaits him ?" We note how quickly the teacher has given place to the dialectician. The latter continues to hold the field, and gives suggestions on the use of the "artless means of proof." These are specified as citations from the text of the law, depositions of witnesses, contracts, confessions made under torture, and the oaths of the parties.

10. We confine ourselves almost exclusively to the modes of interpreting the laws which Aristotle suggests for the deliberative assembly and the law court. The primary object is to resist the application of laws which run counter to the çause defended by the orator. A really sound piece of advice deserves to be quoted first : we are counselled to ask whether the law is not obsolete, whether it has not survived the conditions which led to its enactment? When we are bidden to examine the law cited against us for possible internal contradictions

and for a possible conflict with some law esteemed of higher importance, the recommendation sounds harmless enough. Much more questionable is the obviously arbitrary interpretation which, it is suggested, may be put upon the promise contained in the juror's oath to judge "according to one's best knowledge and conscience." This formula, it is suggested, may be made out to mean that we need not trouble ourselves about the written laws at all. We are to arrive at this result by contrasting the immutable permanence of equity and of universal or natural law with the variability of written law. Indeed, we may go so far as to maintain that the latter is really no law at all, since it does not fulfil the task required of law ; the judge resembles an assayer of coin ; it is for him to distinguish the genuine from the spurious in this department. It is also the part of the better man to honour the unwritten law.

The case is very different when the written law speaks in our favour. The above-mentioned formula must then receive only a very limited interpretation. It is not meant to justify us in judging contrary to the law, but only to relieve us from the charge of perjury if our knowledge of law happens to be defective. Contracts are treated in a particularly audacious manner. If they are in our favour, we are to play out our trump as follows : "The law itself is a contract ; he, therefore, who weakens fidelity to contracts weakens fidelity to the law." In the contrary case, it is open to us to exclaim : "How strange, if we hold ourselves free to refuse obedience to the laws when they are ill-made and their authors have erred, while we owe inviolable obedience to contracts !"

CHAPTER XXXVII.

ARISTOTLE AND RHETORIC.

(CONTINUATION: THE EMOTIONS AND TYPES OF CHARACTER.)

1. THE mixed feelings with which we take our leave of these ingenious hints on deception soon make way for much more uniform and agreeable impressions. We allude to the theory of the emotions and the descriptions of types of character, two brilliant sections, which occupy the first half of the second book. The transition is effected by the remark that men's judgment is not determined by proofs alone, but just as much by the personal impression which the speaker makes, and by the dispositions and moods of those to whom the speech is addressed. The second factor is of decisive significance in the forensic speech, the first in the political or deliberative speech.

The convincing power of a speech depends partly on three qualities of the orator: his wisdom, his rectitude, and his good will. For the first two points we are referred to the "Ethics;" for the third, and for modes of influencing the mood and disposition of the audiences, to the doctrine of the emotions which now follows. The emotions in question are specified as those "by the change of which the judgment itself becomes changed." The more accurate treatment of them comprises three heads: the disposition of mind from which the emotion springs; the persons towards which it is directed; the occasions which commonly give rise to it. This triple knowledge is the preliminary condition for the rousing of emotions by oratory. It is surprising to find this subject, which seems to belong much more properly to psychology or descriptive ethics, imported into a work on rhetoric, and there treated with an exhaustiveness that goes far beyond the end in view. That which moved Aristotle to this procedure was probably in the first place, the Platonic ideal of that art as set forth in the " Phædrus ; " and secondly the wish, cherished no less warmly by him than by his master, to separate the new exposition of rhetoric as widely as possible from the old empirical methods and routine wisdom. It so comes about that we have before us foundations of much greater depth and strength than is justified by the superstructure which rests upon them. We shall, perhaps, not be far wrong in conjecturing that Aristotle was glad of the opportunity to raise the tone of that initiation into rhetorical fencing tricks which practical considerations had forced upon him. Another cause operating in the same direction may have been a recollection of the fact that at the beginning of the work he had been unwilling to allow emotional effects any place at all in oratory (cf. pp. 421, 422). Now that he found himself constrained to descend from that ideal height, he preferred to do so in such a manner that the subject proscribed at first might appear in strictly scientific garb, not as merely auxiliary to rhetorical success.

2. At the head of the emotions stands anger, which is described as " a passionate longing for the real or apparent avenging of a real or apparent injury, inflicted on us by one who has no right to treat us or ours in such a manner." Mention has already been made of the pleasure which the hope of revenge mingles with the painful feeling (cf. p. 429). But apart from this hope, an element of pleasure is recognized as present in the mere dwelling on the thought of revenge. We are predisposed to anger by whatever emotion predominates in us for the moment. This is so because our anger is generally directed against those who oppose our present desires or needs, especially when we have thought ourselves entitled to expect the contrary. We are angry, too, with those who despise us in respect of matters on which we lay the greatest importance,

and more particularly when our self-confidence is not secure. An enumeration is given of the circumstances in which such contempt is felt as especially painful. Even the forgetting of our name may hurt our feelings as a sign of neglect or low esteem. Anger is diminished by diversion to another object ; it becomes extinguished when those with whom we are angry suffer worse harm than we were willing to inflict upon them.

The unusually exhaustive discussion of friendship surprises us, as already a whole quarter of the " Ethics " has been devoted to this subject. And yet we cannot say that there is real repetition. Friendship is defined as " unselfish benevolence practically manifested within the limits of possibility." There follows a review of the conditions or causes of friendship and its opposite. This section treats only of private friendship, and does not, like those two books of the " Ethics," include within its scope benevolent sentiments extended over whole groups.

Fear has the next turn. It is explained as an " unpleasant feeling or unrest which is caused by the idea of an imminent evil bringing injury or annoyance." The " imminence " is limited to the near future, for all men know that they must die some day, and yet are not constantly filled with the dread of death. We are given a long review of the different objects of fear, after which follows an account of the qualities of the fearing subject. Fear always implies an admixture of hope ; the absence of this produces dull despair, a cold indifference to the future.

Courage, the opposite of fear, next receives attention, and then shame, here described as a " disgust or uneasiness in respect of past, present, or future misdoings which seem of a kind to give one a bad reputation." Shamelessness, on the other hand, is a negligence or indifference shown in this direction. The next place is taken by "favour" or good will, the manifestations of which " are accorded to one who needs them neither out of gratitude nor in the interests of the person who accords them, but in the interests of the recipient." Here, as in some of the earlier sections, short practical applications to rhetoric are interspersed. Thus it is sometimes requisite in a speech to magnify the extent of favour entertained and the greatness of the consequent service ; at another time it may be desired to minimize the favour and the gratitude due for it—a purpose which is served by proving a selfish motive, a chance coincidence, external compulsion, or the absence of initiative (the service rendered being the repayment for one received).

Pity is defined as an unpleasant feeling excited by the contemplation of a real or supposed evil which is destructive or painful and at the same time undeserved. It is implied here, as we learn from an added remark, that the contemplator, or at least persons in close relation to him, must not be absolutely protected against the same or cognate evils. Neither the utterly miserable nor those who think themselves in the assured possession of good fortune are accessible to this emotion. Some consideration is now given to the qualities of those who are inclined to pity. They include those who have often been afflicted or threatened by fate ; the advanced in age, because of their richer reflexion and riper experience ; the educated, too, for the first of these reasons ; then come the weakly ; and, last of all, those who are exposed to ill fortuue at a multitude of points, as by the possession of parents, children, wives. Those are excluded who for the moment are dominated by the active emotions, as well as those who are absolutely filled with fear. In the first case, we may add, it is the quality of the prevailing emotion which bars the way to pity ; in the second, to a certain extent, its quantity. "Their own emotion holds them captive," so that they cannot share in the emotions of others, even when of similar kind. Those, too, are void of pity who think meanly of the worth of men, and who are, therefore, inclined to judge every misfortune well deserved.

From the discussion upon the objects of pity, we pick out the observation that these objects should not be too closely connected with ourselves. Otherwise the same thing may happen as in the tale of the Egyptian king who was dethroned by the Persian conqueror : he wept on seeing a friend begging who had been thrown into destitution by this catastrophe, but remained tearless when he saw his own son led to death.

3. We now reach the most instructive, if not the most interesting, parts of this section. The good will manifested in " pity " is contrasted with that element of feeling which may be called ill will or malice, though hardly without expressing in these words a judgment of condemnation which did not in ancient times command the same general assent that it does now. This is a point at which we encounter significant distinctions, on which it will repay us to dwell for a moment. Aristotle places at the head of this group of emotions a feeling for which we have no separate name—" a being pained by undeserved good fortune." This he sets by the side of pity, which is " a being pained by undeserved bad fortune ; " he represents both alike as the outflowing of a " well-formed character," and even appeals to the fact that " we attribute this feeling to the gods " no less than the other. The untranslatable Greek verb ($\nu\epsilon\mu\epsilon\sigma\hat{a}\nu$) is connected with Nemesis, the name of the goddess whose task is to watch over right " distribution " ($\nu\acute{\epsilon}\mu\epsilon\iota\nu$), and who is always ready to check and to punish every disturbance of the due order.

The modern namelessness of this emotion, which we might call with Nietzsche " the nobler brother of envy," is not accidental. It rests on the fact that the universal and therefore indiscriminating love of humanity which is constantly preached to us revolts against all ill will, even when of a kind that both springs from pure sources and is well fitted to produce salutary effects. Aristotle tells us that slavish natures are inaccessible to this emotion as well as evil persons and those destitute of the love of honour ; unusual susceptibility to it is possessed by those who thirst for action, especially when they see the goals to which they strive reached by the unworthy. Nor are there wanting external circumstances by which the strength of this emotion is increased or diminished. Goods bestowed by nature, such as noble birth or personal beauty, seem to give a kind of claim to the possession of other goods as well. And "since the familiar comes near to the natural," this feeling is aroused less by hereditary power and wealth than by the new acquisitions of the *parvenu.*

Envy, too, is directed against the prosperity of others, but not because it is undeserved. It strikes most readily at our equals and our like, those with whose lot we are accustomed to compare our own. (Let it be remarked, in passing, that we do not confute Aristotle by pointing out that the proletarian may envy the millionaire. This may happen in critical epochs, but not in ages when the inequality of life-conditions is secure against all critical attack.) At this point the "bad" emotion just named comes into close contact with another—again nameless for us moderns— which arises in the same circumstances, but differs in the ground of displeasure. We do not, in virtue of it, resent the fact that others possess "highly prized goods from which we are not excluded as a matter of course," but rather the fact that we do not ourselves possess them. This feeling, which stimulates energy and is therefore deemed "noble," might be named by us "emulation," but this term would not exhaust its content. The derivatives of the Greek word, ζῆλος, which was taken over by the Romans, form two series in the Romance languages—on the one hand, *zelo, zèle,* etc., on the other, *gelosia, jalousie,* etc. ; in English there are "zeal" and "jealousy." The words of the second series thus denote the unpleasant feeling which is the root of the emotions, while those of the first denote the active element, the eager striving and working, which results from it. In order to gauge the importance which this emotion had for the Greek, we must remember the wide space occupied in the life of the Hellenic nation by various forms of contest (gymnastic, musical, poetical, and particularly dramatic, prize competitions). So much for the distinctions and agreements within this group of emotions. Displeasure provoked by others' prosperity is common to them all, but they are differentiated in a remarkable manner. In the one first spoken of, A, the displeasure is due to the unworthiness of the favoured person, in B and C to their (real or supposed) equality with us ; B is an ignoble state of mind, while A and C are noble, A because of the moral appraisement contained in it, C because of the spur which it supplies to increased activity and self-perfecting.

4. This refined subtlety in the characterizations of emotions and in the exposition of their manifold ramifications does great honour to the Stagirite. Even the founder of modern philosophy yields place to him in this respect. We may recall, for example, how casually Descartes describes jealousy as a species of fear, or emulation as a form of courage, without bringing out the features of agreement and difference between these emotions and others akin to them. There is, moreover, a second point at which the comparison turns out in favour of Aristotle. He is well acquainted with, and he gives emphatic prominence to, the twofold nature of the emotions, which have their somatic as well as their psychic side. From the occasional occurrence of strong emotion without any sufficient cause that can be perceived, he infers that in these cases a physical predisposition plays a considerable part ; and he puts himself far in advance of his epoch by recognizing that "the investigation of psychic processes in general, or at least of this element in them, is the business of the nature-student." But in this case he observes a most wise self-restraint ; it is only by way of illustrating his general thought that he mentions the "surging of the blood in the region of the heart," which he supposed was the physiological accompaniment of a fit of anger. On the other hand, the early Stoics incorporated a physical counterpart, a "swelling" or "contraction," etc., in all their definitions relating to this subject. And Descartes hardly rendered a service to the progress of psychology by invoking the fantastic physiological creations of his day,—the "vital spirits," the affections of the pineal gland, and so forth.

But it should not be passed over in silence that in this field Descartes proved himself superior to Aristotle as an analyst. The latter described pleasure and its opposite, which he made the sources of desire, as ingredients in all emotions without exception, by defining the latter, taken collectively, as states of the soul which cloud the judgment, being charged with pleasure and pain. Not so Descartes, who expressly set a kind of surprise (*admiration*), in itself free from pleasure and pain, at the head of his six " fundamental emotions" (*passions primitives*), and explained all the emotions partly as combinations of those six (surprise, love, hate, desire, joy, and sorrow), partly as subordinate varieties of them.

5. No reservation of this nature qualifies the admiration aroused by the descriptive part of the theory of the emotions, or by the delineations which follow of different stages, and particularly different conditions of life. In youth the will is said to be rather violent than deep, much like the hunger and thirst of the sick. Youth is full of confidence, because it has not yet suffered many deceptions ; full of hope, because it has not yet experienced many failures. But the chief reason is that the young have hot blood by nature, as the drunken have it from wine. For them, too, the realm of hope, that is, the future, is immeasurably large, while the past, the realm of memory, is exceedingly small. They are lofty-minded, for life has not yet crushed them down ; they do not yet know the double standard of the noble and the useful. And since as yet they judge nothing according to its utility, not even friendships, youth has more feeling for friendship and companionship than any other stage of life. Their faults spring from neglect of the maxim : " Keep measure." The young love in excess and hate in excess ; they are full of assurance, and believe they know everything. The wrong which they do has its source in high spirits, not malice. They are full of pity because they think well of all the world, measuring their neighbours by the standard of their own inoffensiveness. They are fond of laughter, and therefore pleasant company ; they are prone to "cultured wantonness."

To all this age supplies the exact antithesis. The old have lived through many disappointments and failures, in consequence of which all confidence and assurance have departed from them. They "know" nothing, but only "think." They are suspicious from mistrust, mistrustful from experience. They love as if in the future they were destined to hate, and they hate as if they might some day love. They are narrow-hearted, because life has crushed them down. They know, too, by experience, how hard it is to gain anything, how easy to lose. They are as timid as the young are brave, since the coldness of age seconds the chill of fear. They cling to life, and the more so at the end, because desire is directed towards what is absent. They are selfish beyond due bounds, for this, too, is little-ness of mind. In consequence of their egoism they live more by the rule of the useful than by that of the beautiful. The loquacity of age is in great measure caused by the wide space which the past occupies in an old man's life. They also are full of pity, not as the young from love of humanity, but from weakness ; for no evil seems to them remote.

In all these points middle age holds an intermediate position. Here moderation and courage are found com-bined, while in the extreme stages of life they are only found separately. The young are both brave and dissolute, the old at the same time moderate and cowardly. There are other ways, too, in which the advantages which are divided between youth and age appear combined in middle life. It is here that excess and defect are replaced by the right measure and the befitting. The remark occurs that the body attains its full development between thirty and thirty-five, the soul at forty-nine. The remarkable precision of this last statement is probably to be ascribed to the influence which the significance of the number seven (7×7) had gained over the biological views of even an Aristotle.

6. Further sketches describe the types of the noble, the rich, the possessor of political power. The man of noble descent is inclined to look down even upon those who are as important in the present day as his own ancestors were in the old days. The former lack the transfiguring lustre of past time and many a decorative addition. Emphasis is laid on the distinction between noble birth and noble character. The latter is found in

those who have not degenerated from the family type. It is not possessed by the majority of the nobles, who are not raised above mediocrity (a different view is noted on p. 345). For generations vary, just like the harvests of good and bad years. Genius often sinks in posterity to wild passionateness, steadfastness to dull insensibility. For the rich, money becomes the standard of all value, and they hold everything purchasable. They are also inclined to self-importance, and do not care to put any constraint upon themselves, because they see that in any case their taste and their behaviour receive applause and set the fashion. "Beatific unintelligence" is the short phrase in which the character of the rich man is summarized. At the same time, it is admitted that these unlovely features belong less to old and hereditary wealth than to the *parvenu*, who may be described as " not brought up to riches." The possessor of political power shares many characteristics with the wealthy man ; in other respects, he is superior. He is more a lover of honour, manlier, more steadfast and serious,—for this reason if for no other, that he stands continually in the light of publicity. Recognition is given to the fact that success of all kinds predisposes to pride and self-conceit ; but to this remark another is added which somewhat surprises us moderns : the fortunate love the gods and trust in them because of the benefits they have received from fate.

CHAPTER XXXVIII.

ARISTOTLE AND RHETORIC.

(CONTINUATION AND CONCLUSION.)

1. AFTER this interlude, borrowed from descriptive ethics, the author returns to the main ingredient in rhetoric, the dialectical element. The two chief means of proof, the example and the enthymeme, are divided into their separate species. The simile and the animal-fable are distinguished from the " example " in the narrower sense, which consists of an appeal to real occurrences. The sentence or maxim appears as a particular variety of enthymeme ; it is most effective when it carries its justification in itself. Sententious speech is most becoming in the elderly, who draw from the stock of their own experience. Nor need the orator be afraid of commonplaces which express convictions held by all. But, on the other hand, it is also legitimate to contradict widespread opinions, even those embodied in proverbs and maxims, if by this means the orator can gain sharpness in characterizations or produce an effect of pathos. Thus a speaker may exclaim : " Even the saying, ' Nothing in excess,' is unprofitable, for one cannot hate the bad too much." But the chief use of the maxim is the favourable light in which it displays the speaker ; utterances of a noble kind cause him to appear noble.

Enthymemes should not be far-fetched or of too great generality. This is the reason why the less well-educated —for whom this limitation is not a matter of troublesome observance—often speak before the people more convincingly than their superiors in education. One of the modes of proof is the evidence from contraries. For example : " If the war is responsible for the present evils, peace must be well fitted to repair them." A second argument rests on the more or less, *e.g.* : " If a man beat his own father, how should he refrain from beating his fellow-man ? " Another method rests on division and consequent eliminations. Thus: " There are three motives for wrong-doing ; two of these are excluded by the circumstances of the case ; the third is not even asserted by the accuser." At another time again the pleader will appeal to a judgment pre- viously delivered on the same or a similar matter, or one of contrary character. This judgment, if possible, should be one which was arrived at unanimously, by a large majority, by persons of acknowledged authority, or even by the gods themselves. An illustrative example is taken from a poem of Sappho : " Death is an evil ; if it had not been, why should the gods have reserved immortality for themselves ? " Sometimes two inductions bearing on the same subject lead to opposite conclusions. Thus, one may sometimes warn men against education because of the disfavour which it brings ; at another time recommend it because wisdom is its fruit. To this place belongs the general advice, out of all possible suppositions to choose always that which best serves our ends. There is some- thing disconcerting in a piece of dialectical audacity like the following. From the very incredibility of a statement we may deduce its actual truth, by asking : " How, if it were not true, could any one have come to make so im- probable a statement ? " We may quote one observation which shows great psychological refinement. The processes of proof, it is said, which win the loudest applause are those of which the purpose is surmised from the beginning, and the conclusion approached step by step, so that before it is explicitly stated it has won the full assent of the audience. The effect of such a method, we may add, is that the tension is kept up to the end, and the well-prepared solu- tion is reached at the last without difficulty. At the same time, as Aristotle himself remarks, the self-esteem of the hearer is flattered by the pleasant consciousness of his perspicacity in anticipating the conclusion.

2. After the separate discussion of all these sham proofs, there comes a thorough treatment of fallacious enthymemes, which, it is said, must exist by the same necessity as the corresponding syllogistic fallacies. As the nature of the case exacts, there are here numerous reminiscences of the book "On Sophistic Refutations" (cf. p. 45). A lengthy exposition is devoted to the misuse of linguistic forms, as well as to that of forms of inference, homonymy and the like. A particularly copious source of deception is said to be the joining of what is separate and the separation of what is joined. Each of these aids to deception is illustrated by an interesting example. The rhetorician Polycrates—perhaps in his pamphlet against Socrates (cf. Vol. II. p. 114)— exalted the democratic leader Thrasybulus at the expense of other heroes of liberty by reasoning (as we may expand Aristotle's hint) somewhat as follows : " A overthrew this tyrant, B that, C a third ; each of these, therefore, has been held in the highest honour by his fellow-citizens. What honour, then, is due to him who wrested the supreme power from no fewer than thirty tyrants ? " Thus it was made to seem as if not one act of liberation only, as was really the case, but a great number of them, had here to be considered. Aristotle's friend and favourite pupil, Theodectes (cf. p. 415), pursued the opposite course in his tragedy " Orestes ; " for he justified the act of Orestes in killing his mother by combining two propositions, each unassailable in itself. " The murderess of a husband deserves death," and " It is the son's part to avenge his father." By setting the two propositions side by side, the illusion was created that the right of Orestes to kill his mother Clytæmnestra was hereby placed beyond doubt. There follow instances of false generalizations and illicit conversion, as well as of temporal succession represented as causal connexion (*post hoc, ergo propter hoc*). The example adduced in illustration is significant of our philosopher's political attitude. He tells us that Demades, a politician friendly to the Macedonian cause, had laid on the policy of Demosthenes the responsibility for all the ensuing evils, and so had confused the " after " with the " because." **If.**

as has been recently maintained, Aristotle had been a partisan of Philip, he would certainly not have undertaken to invalidate the charge brought against this king's chief opponent, Demosthenes. Another error mentioned is the confusion of the absolute with the relative. Among the examples of this appears the misuse of the notion of probability, which is apprehended sometimes in a narrower and sometimes in a wider sense, the more so as the corresponding Greek word is frequently used to mean what having regard to a restricted circle of causes is natural or normal. By taking the two meanings as one, it would be possible to prove even the identity of the probable with the improbable. Aristotle quotes a pleasing couple of lines from the tragic poet Agathon (cf. Vol. II. p. 383, *seq.*)—

> " This is the most improbable of all,
> That naught improbable should never hap."

Here, as Aristotle rightly thinks, there is no contradiction. The word " improbable " is used in a double meaning ; and the import of the lines, as we may add, is simply this : " It is matter of daily experience that many things happen which we are not led to expect, owing to our imperfect knowledge of causes and particularly of their co-operation."

We pass over a section of no great importance relating to " solutions and confutations," as also the remarks on " exaggerating and extenuating." These chapters amount to no more than this, that the modes of proof in question (which clearly had filled much space in the older handbooks) have in common not so much a particular nature as a particular purpose.

3. The third book of the " Rhetoric " is principally devoted to the more external elements of this art—diction and arrangement. In dealing but briefly with these we do not offend against the author's intentions ; for he placed the matter of speeches far above their form, and described the care which is expended on the latter as almost a necessary evil.

The art of delivery, as being the most external element, is assigned to the lowest place in words like those applied in the "Poetics" to the scenic apparatus of the drama. "Diction," too, ought, in strictness, to aim merely at preserving complete neutrality, "equally remote from pleasurable and painful impressions," in an exposition based on reasonings. We note, by the way, that a growing preponderance of substance over form passes with our philosopher almost for a law of literary development. The metre of tragedy had advanced from the stately and pretentious trochee to the iambus with its nearer approach to the language of conversation ; its style of expression similarly showed a constantly increasing preference for the ordinary ; and prose diverged more and more from poetry. The chief merits of diction, Aristotle continues, are clearness and appropriateness. Great caution is needed in attempts to ennoble the expression ; the speaker must not allow his purpose to become manifest, he must avoid every trace of affectation, and he must be on his guard whenever he rises above the every-day level. Metaphor alone among the adornments of speech is tolerated in prose. There are continual references to the "Poetics," to which supplementary additions are now made, one, for example, on beauty of sound, a subject passed over in the earlier work. The treatment of the frigid brings before us in striking manner the difference between ancient and modern taste. As an instance of a far-fetched and therefore frigid metaphor, Aristotle quotes an expression of Alcidamas which is quite consonant with modern feeling. This orator had called the "Odyssey" "a fair mirror of human life." We are not entitled on this account to charge Aristotle or his contemporaries with weakness or dulness of imagination. Quite the contrary. If they found an audacity ill befitting prose in words which produce no such impression on us, it was precisely because they took figurative language more seriously, because they had a keener feeling for metaphors, these not yet having reached that condition of a use-worn currency which is so common among metaphors now.

After the section on clearness and a few remarks relating to punctuation and syntax, there follows a

discussion on the weight or effectiveness of language.
Some subtle observations may here be found concerning
the cases where the name of a thing is to be preferred to a
description of it, or *vice versâ,* and those in which either the
negative or the positive mode of expression is the better.
The significant hint is here dropped that the mere negative
opens wider perspectives to the imagination and stimulates
it to heightened activity.

4. The section on appropriateness of language contains
much that for us is self-evident, but also not a few remarks
which reach greater depths. Thus we receive the counsel,
not a little surprising at first, " not to employ all the
consistent means of expression simultaneously." We should
rather have expected the opposite. But in reality the
problem is to hit the medium between two equally dangerous
extremes. If a man utters severe words with a soft voice
and gentle mien, this want of harmony raises doubts as to
the genuineness of the emotion. Aristotle by no means fails
to recognize this. He points out the danger ; but he warns
us much more emphatically against the opposite fault,
against the too exact agreement of word, voice, and gesture.
The purpose becomes too manifest, and all belief in the
speaker's artlessness disappears. The orator, truly, should
not be a bad actor, but on no account must he be too
good a one. The precepts regarding rhythm are conceived in a similar spirit. If the speech were actually in
metre, the obvious artifice would injure its credibility ; at
the same time, the attention of the hearer would be too
much diverted from the matter in hand. Want of rhythm
at the other extreme does not allow the structure of the
speech to appear in sufficient prominence, and makes it
unpleasing as well as obscure. Rhythm, therefore, should
not be rigorously uniform, and should only be employed
partially.

5. The points of view now touched upon and the
examples adduced in illustration present an abundance
and variety which defy summarization. Besides orators
properly so called, among whom Isocrates is referred to
with special frequency, in spite of the old antagonism

(cf. pp. 20, 24, and 303), prose writers and poets of every kind receive attention. For Aristotle has now enlarged his survey, and made literary expression in the widest sense the object of his study. He distinguishes the old co-ordinating or paratactic style (used by Herodotus) from the more advanced periodic form of composition. He touches on the economy of breath and warns against too long and too short periods, accompanying the second warning with a striking comparison (the unexpectedly early close acts like the sudden arrest of a movement which jerks one forward). Reference is made to *enjambement*, the carrying on of a sentence from one line of verse into the next ; and the practice is condemned in cases where the first line, taken alone, gives a complete sense, especially when this is misleading. Antithesis is praised because when two contraries are placed in immediate neighbourhood, they stand out against each other in the clearest and strongest relief. Attention is also given to the figures named after the rhetorician Gorgias, such as the connecting of the members of a sentence by the use of identical syllables or similar sounds, together with other artifices of like nature.

"Witty and popular sayings" give occasion for a closer consideration of images and comparisons. A starting-point is supplied by the principle that "easy learning is by nature pleasant to all." This result is often obtained by the use of an expression not literally applicable to its object. Thus a line of the "Odyssey" speaks of old age as "stubble ;" the comparison leads the mind to the common element in the two cases ; in both there is something past its flowering-time. Vividness, that most desirable quality in language, is obtained chiefly by speaking of lifeless things as though they had soul ; here again Homer is the unattainable model. At this point we are surprised by an omission. A line, perhaps the most picturesque in all Homer—

> "Back with a thunderous clatter leapt plainward the treacherous
> boulder,"

is quoted without a word of reference to the sound-painting.

There is much aptness (and some unconscious self-praise) in a passing remark to the effect that acuteness of perception nowhere reveals itself more clearly than in the discovery of hidden resemblances. This great gift, he tells us, operates "as in science" (we recall the feats of a Newton or a Franklin), so also in style "by the formation of happy metaphors." Mention is made and explanations given of the pleasure derived from well-constructed riddles, from successful parodies, from the witty employment of the different meanings borne by a single word, and from felicitous exaggerations.

6. From the general, Aristotle turns to the particular—that is, to the different modes of employing language, and the demands which may be made on each. The written communication of thought is described as the "most accurate" of all,—a judgment which calls to the mind Bacon's saying that "writing makes a precise man." But the same kind of matter, delivered orally, often seems curt and thin ; while the productions of the orator, when read, easily create an impression of amateurishness and banality. Some excellent remarks follow on the inner connexion between figures of speech and declamatory delivery. One amusing example may be quoted. Repetitions are rightly avoided in prose ; but in poetry, especially in comedy, they have their place. We know the fondness of the ancients for searching out inventors (cf. Vol. I. pp. 389 *seq*.). This practice, or the abuse of it, was very amusingly satirized in a comedy by Anaxandrides, entitled, "Old Man's Folly." That hero of civilization, Palamedes, the supposed "inventor" of the alphabet, of the game of draughts, of arithmetic, and so forth, was here coupled with Rhadamanthys, the son of Zeus, and all imaginable trifles ascribed to them as *inventions*. One line, for example, ran thus—

" Parasite's antics, invented by Palamede and Rhadamanthys."

The last words clearly formed the refrain of a long series of lines, in which the contrast between the trivial content and the solemn ending produced the most

ludicrous effect, especially in the mouth of the actor Philemon. There is a noteworthy comparison between speeches
addressed to the people and decorative painting. In both
cases—this is Aristotle's thought—crude effects are sought ;
refinement is not only a superfluity, but a disadvantage.
On the other hand, the language of the display-oration,
which is intended to be read aloud, makes the nearest
approach to written style ; next after it comes the forensic
speech.

7. The close of the work deals with the component
parts of a speech, in multiplying which, it is said, earlier
writers have gone too far. In reality, a speech has only
two main parts—one in which the orator states his case,
the other in which he makes it good ; just as in mathematics we have first the enunciation, then the proof. Still,
Aristotle so far follows the traditional practice as to distinguish, in some cases but not all, four main parts of a
speech, namely, "prelude, statement, argument, epilogue ;"
all these receive exhaustive treatment. Here again there
are several excursions from the field of rhetoric proper
into that of exposition in general, including even its
poetical forms.

The chief task to be fulfilled by the prelude or
introduction is that of disclosing the purpose of the speech.
The man who is defending himself must be at pains to
clear away suspicions right at the beginning of his speech,
in order to obtain a free course for the remainder of it ;
the accuser, on the contrary, makes the corresponding effort
at the end, in order that he may leave his hearers with the
desired impression fresh in their minds. The speaker's
task is sometimes to bring his hearers into a benevolent
mood, sometimes to arouse their indignation ; often, too,
he will seek to capture their attention—or to divert it.
This last will be his endeavour in those cases where the
speaker necessarily desires that his public should "attend
to anything in the world rather than the matter in hand."
According to the purpose of the moment, the orator will
represent the theme of his discourse as important, as
affecting the interests of his audience, as astonishing, as

agreeable (for all this attracts attention), or, on the other hand as trivial, as foreign to their interests, as of no importance, or as painful. This procedure, doubtless, is wanting in objectivity and only suited to inferior hearers. But—we must add mentally—such are the majority of hearers, and the author of this guide to rhetoric is bound to accommodate himself to the demands of actual life.

Fundamental importance belongs to an excursus on the arousing and the rebutting of suspicion. The chief points of view connected with the second of these tasks are the following. The defender may contest the alleged facts,—he may admit the action but deny its injuriousness absolute or relative, its magnitude, its illegality, or its dishonourableness ; or, again, admitting either of these last qualities, he may deny the degree assigned to it by the accusation. Then, too, while allowing that an action was injurious, one may maintain that it was morally excellent. The action may also be excused as an oversight, or as having been unavoidable. One may disclaim a malicious purpose, or explain the evil consequence as due to chance (this reminds us of the precisely contrary recommendation in the case of panegyric ; cf. p. 427). Yet another kind of situation is presented when the accuser himself, or persons in close relation to him, are now or have been formerly involved in a similar action, or if a similar entanglement affects others whose innocence is questioned by none. Or, again, cases may be turned to account in which accusations brought by the same person have proved groundless, or in which, without any charge being raised, similar suspicion has lighted on some one whose guiltlessness afterwards became manifest. Appeal may be made to a verdict already given (cf. p. 446), somewhat as was done by Euripides, who recalled the prize awarded to his drama " Hippolytus " when taken to task for the line contained in it : " My tongue hath sworn it, yet my mind is free." Among the artifices supplied for the use of accusers there is one which reminds us of Pope's " to damn by faint praise." One may begin by a long eulogy and then add an expression of censure which, though short, is decisive on the matter in hand ; or one may praise something trivial at great length, but at the same time condemn in a few words an action of much importance. With such refinements of insidiousness the limits of Aristotle's indulgence are reached, and these, at any rate, are not described without a word of severe reprobation.

8. We pass over the less characteristic remarks on the narrative portion of a speech, and from the following section, which deals with demonstration or argument, we single out the treatment of one particular rhetorical artifice, the question. This, it is said, may be employed most successfully in cases where the opponent has already conceded so much that it needs but the additional thrust of a question to destroy the tenability of his position. One of the chief uses of a question is to entangle the opponent in contradictions or to force him into paradox. Another case is that in which the only answer that can be given is of the form "yes and no"—"in one sense, yes ; in another, no." The audience then begins to murmur, for they take the answer to be an evasion due to perplexity. Now, cautiously limited judgments of the kind referred to are unusually frequent in the writings of Aristotle himself, and are not a little characteristic of his qualities as a thinker (cf. p. 58). It is thus well worthy of note how confidently he distinguishes the strength of himself and the *élite* who form his public from the "weakness of the (average) hearer." It is his own favourite mode of expression, which he advises the litigant to suggest to his opponent, in order that the latter may be tripped up by its use.

In answering questions put by the other side, it is necessary to point out at once the double meaning of ambiguous expressions, and to resolve, in the answer itself, the contradiction in which the antagonist is seeking to entangle us. If the opponent puts an inference adverse to our case into the form of a question which we cannot avoid answering affirmatively, we should insert in our reply words serving for our justification. Suppose a series of hostile questions has forced us to answer "yes" to the final query : "Have you, then, done what was evil ?" Our assent will be given with the immediate addition of a qualification :

"for it was the lesser evil of the two." Passing from this dialectic of question and answer, the author goes on to the use which may be made of the ludicrous. He quotes with approval the advice of Gorgias, to counter the opponent's earnest with jest and his jest with earnest.

The epilogue, the discussion of which forms the conclusion of the work itself, is divided into four parts. Its purpose is, firstly, to dispose the audience favourably towards the speaker, unfavourably towards his opponent (the author once more sets a part, the forensic speech, in the place of the whole) ; secondly, to raise or lower the importance of the subject-matter; thirdly, to inspire the audience with the desired emotions ; fourthly, to recapitulate the contents of the whole speech. By an ingenious device Aristotle contrives to end the whole lecture-course with a sentence quoted as an example of a good conclusion to a speech : "I have spoken ; you have heard ; you have the matter—judge !" This veiled challenge, like the unconcealed one at the end of the logical course (cf. p. 31), was doubtless answered with a salvo of applause.

9. We have treated the " Rhetoric" with greater fulness than has hitherto been customary. This is in accord with the main point of view which has governed our presentment of Aristotle's teachings in general. We regard the Stagirite as pre-eminently a classifier and encyclopædist, as a thinker who surveyed and divided the world of phenomena in all its breadth, the physical province as well as the psychical. We have followed him through his wide journeyings with steps now swifter, now slower, as the subject invited to a longer or shorter stay. There are departments in which Aristotle's work is now wholly obsolete, his results long ago superseded, his difficulties finally settled. We have necessarily given less space to these than to other fields of research in which as yet there is no similar record of incontestable progress. Who would care to assert that Aristotle's treatment of ethical and political questions has been eclipsed and supplanted by modern investigations in the same way as, say, his physics or his physiology ? For assigning the " Rhetoric " to the

second of these groups rather than to the first, we have sufficient warrant in the one fact that the art of oratory has practically disappeared from the list of subjects treated by modern writers.

It is true that a first glance at the three books of the "Rhetoric" may easily provoke an unfavourable judgment. The reader is not unlikely to find the work an agglomerate of inwardly unconnected parts rather than an organic structure. A great deal of dialectic, some politics, a little grammar and jurisprudence, a section on style, and considerable borrowings from descriptive ethics and psychology—one asks vainly at first what inner bond unites all these disparate elements into a whole? The thought readily suggests itself that considerations of an external order were mainly responsible for this so surprising conjunction of the dissimilar. Aristotle—the reader may say—wished to realize that unattainable ideal of a new rhetoric which was set forth in Plato's "Phædrus" (cf. p. 421); he also wished to outbid those predecessors of his for whom he felt so little esteem. He believed that this double purpose would be achieved if, without omitting an account of the old tricks and artifices, he took pains to ennoble his collection of them by incorporating in it considerable sections taken from other and more highly esteemed provinces of knowledge. This judgment, however, would be far from just, though there is certainly a grain of truth in it. The author of the "Rhetoric" found himself in a peculiarly difficult position. Between his ideal and the reality which he could not ignore there yawned a wide gulf. We have noted his old complaint that the labour bestowed on diction is little more than a necessary evil; we remember his contention that in the council-chamber, as in the law-court, the only justifiable form of exposition is that which is strictly objective, which relies entirely on argument, and not at all on the rousing of emotion. And yet he investigates thoroughly, and treats exhaustively, all these aids to rhetoric, and many others which he himself despises. We may see here the co-operation of two powerful factors. For the orator in

the popular assembly and before the tribunal, all those
resources were necessary which the philosopher, as such,
contemned or even repudiated.   If his lecture-hall was
not to remain empty, his text-book unread, he was compelled to have regard to what men are, not to what they
ought to be.

But the really decisive factor was the second : the
nature of Aristotle's mind. To one of his mental constitution it was an imperative necessity to sift and co-
ordinate the whole body of knowledge accessible to him.
Before this irresistible impulse all scruples were silent, or,
to speak more accurately, disappeared temporarily from
his range of vision.   It is thus that we are to understand
those instructions in deceit on which, so far as I can see,
the historians have greatly neglected to comment (cf. p. 54).
And yet there are numerous passages in the " Rhetoric "
where we are advised to employ on every occasion the mode
of exposition suited to our particular case, where we are
bidden to " use " this artifice, to " choose " that advocate's
trick.   It is only in one quite isolated case (really an
exception of the kind which proves the rule) that the
description of a particularly treacherous method of attack
is followed by a word of censure : " These are at once the
cleverest and the most unjust " practices (cf. p. 455).   In
by far the greater proportion of cases Aristotle's procedure
is neither moral nor immoral, but unmoral.   As long as
he is busy with these matters, his conscience does not
come into play ; he is submerged in the stream of dialectic ;
he sets himself without reservation in the place of the
accuser or defendant, the attorney or the party-man, and
inquires only into the greater or less effectiveness of
rhetorical expedients, not at all into their greater or less
moral justifiability.   He marshals and classifies this material
just like that of any other department of knowledge.

Yet another consequence followed from the excessive
strength of the dialectical impulse.   The framer of logical
divisions strives first and foremost to make his divisions
complete, without regard to the degree of interest or
importance which attaches to this or that term of the

classification. The "Rhetoric," as a result, is not free from sections poor in content, from lengthily developed truisms. As a counterpoise to these, and as a refreshing interlude between the chapters of dialectic and eristic, we have the brilliant portions taken from descriptive psychology and ethics, which found in the "Rhetoric" not, indeed, the only possible place, but still one by no means unsuited to them. If politics, the principal field for the employment of rhetoric, is not left wholly untouched, this need surprise us as little as the fact that the author was at no pains to observe strictly the boundary between the rhetorical form of exposition and others, namely, prose, and sometimes even poetical, writing. When we finally call attention once more to the very intelligible desire of the great encyclopædist to make provision for subjects as yet little developed and therefore unfitted for independent expositions—such subjects as the theory of language or of criminal law—by giving them harbourage within the domain of a more advanced branch of knowledge (cf. pp. 417 and 432), we have said enough to defend the "Rhetoric" against the charges to which a superficial consideration of it may easily give rise.

10. Thus once again we recognize the man who, in spite of his leaning to eristic over-subtlety, and in spite of many a relapse into primitive apriorism, is yet entitled to the highest honour, not only as the lavisher of untold treasures of knowledge, but still more as the marshal before whose baton the myriad facts in all provinces of nature and mental life range themselves of their own accord, into orderly ranks and compact battalions. That vast mass of knowledge, it is true, was on the verge of bursting the bonds which hitherto had held it together. From the parent stock of general knowledge one branch after another is shortly to become severed. Philosophy, in the sense which we have been accustomed to attach to this word, is on the point of extinction. Instead of one universal science, we shall now find, on the one hand the body of special sciences, on the other "philosophy" in the modern sense, which has now become a religion for the educated. Even the successors

of Aristotle were soon to set about the partition of his kingdom, just as the empire of his pupil, Alexander, was shared among the Diadochi.   But the figure of the universal researcher and thinker meets us yet once more in the person of Theophrastus, the man who was nominated director of the Peripatos by its founder and chosen by him for his heir.

CHAPTER XXXIX.

THEOPHRASTUS OF ERESUS.

1. THE life of Theophrastus is soon told. Born between 372 and 370, the son of a well-to-do fuller, he early left his native island of Lesbos for Athens, where he was not too late to hear the aged Plato, and where in Plato's school he made the acquaintance of Aristotle. He seems to have followed the latter to Macedonia; at any rate, after the Stagirite's return to Athens, he was bound to him by the closest ties of common life and work. The reader has already learnt (pp. 25 and 32) that he was chosen by Aristotle to succeed him in the headship of his school, and made the heir to his collection of books. As a further legacy, the master also offered him his daughter's hand, and entrusted him with the education of his son. There were certain works in the attribution of which tradition fluctuated between the teacher and the pupil. The latter, indeed, might well have published one or another item in the collection left behind by Aristotle; he might also have elaborated and continued what the teacher had merely sketched out. He is said to have called himself a "man of the school." His whole existence was, in fact, absorbed in study, in the giving of oral and written instruction. He was not without honour in his day. When he died at the age of eighty-five, the whole of the Athenian people followed his bier; and foreign potentates, the first Ptolemies and Antipater's son Cassandrus, also showed their high regard for him. It is possible that, indirectly, he exerted some influence on public affairs, especially in the ten years (317–307) during which his friend and pupil, Demetrius of Phalerum, guided the helm of the State, having been

chosen by the Athenians as their regent and confirmed by Cassandrus. For in the government of Demetrius—who was author as well as statesman, and who had raised himself from the status of a freed man by his ability and adroitness—there are several traces of Peripatetic influence. His legislation relating to luxury, the control which he sought to exercise over the private lives of the rich, the assumption by the State of burdensome services, such as the Choregia—all these remind us of proposals and hints put forward by Aristotle (cf. pp. 365, 366, and 376). The same remark applies to the fundamental tendency of his policy, which was directed towards the reconciliation of party and class antagonisms, and towards the upraising of the general condition of the people.

2. Little as Theophrastus took part in public life, he was yet on one occasion required to face a jury. It was probably his friendly relations with foreign princes that moved the fiery patriot, Hagnonides, to assail him with the weapon so much in favour against philosophers—a charge of impiety. This was almost certainly in the year 319 or 318, during the short authority of the newly-restored democracy. But the accuser met with an ignominious fiasco. Theophrastus was acquitted, and by so over-whelming a majority that Hagnonides barely escaped the fine of a thousand drachmæ. For the Attic law imposed this penalty on the frivolous accuser—that is, on one who failed to win to his side a fifth of the votes. More importance attached to a second conflict with the civil power in which Theophrastus was involved, but this time not alone. Sophocles, the son of Amphiclides, had proposed and carried a law by which the heads of the philosophers' schools were required to seek authorization of their position from the council and the people. This measure, in our opinion, was not inspired by party feeling. It applied to all schools without distinction—to the Academy, whose sympathies were then entirely democratic, as well as to the Peripatos, which was suspected of Macedonian leanings. But the leaders of the philosophic schools had no mind to consent to any such diminution of their independence.

With one accord they raised an emphatic protest against the demand made upon them by leaving the city—no doubt at the head of their pupils. A few months passed, and then, as so often at Athens, public feeling turned completely round. In this case it is possible that injury to the material interests of the citizens co-operated with more ideal considerations. The charge of illegality, the consequences of which were very severe (cf. Vol. II. p. 53), was brought against Sophocles. Intelligibly enough the accuser, Philo, belonged to one of the philosophers' schools, and indeed to that which stood highest among them in point of numbers and reputation—the school founded by Aristotle. But now party-politics came into play. The accusation had given the cue to the defence, which now became a counter-attack. Among the helpers of the accused, the first place was held by Demochares, the son of a cousin of Demosthenes, and heir to the orator's traditions. This hot-blooded and indefatigable champion of the radical-national party poured out the vials of his wrath, mingling together truth and falsehood after the manner so common in the fierce conflict of factions, both on Aristotle and on certain other pupils of Plato, such as Chæron, the tyrant of Pellene. But violent as was his invective, it failed of its effect. Sophocles—we know not on what technical ground—was condemned to a fine of five talents, the law enacting State-control was declared invalid, and the heads of the schools were invited to return from the exile into which they had retired.

3. Theophrastus was the incarnate ideal of the philosophic disciple. Dutiful, patient, unwearied, gifted with a power of work bordering on the fabulous, he accompanied the Stagirite through the whole range of his universal research. He helped him to collect his vast and varied stock of materials ; he continued and brought to a conclusion what the master had begun or outlined, he filled the gaps which he had left. But with all this faithful devotion, he was anything but a blind follower. How highly the critical faculty was developed in Theophrastus may be learnt merely from the fragments of that

work by which he made himself the forerunner of all historians of philosophy. The doctrines of the older sages were treated by him, partly in monographs, but chiefly in a comprehensive work of eighteen books. Beginning with Thales, and extending to Plato and Xenocrates, this work passed in review the "Opinions on Physics" (in the wide sense, including even psychology) which had been held by former thinkers. Numerous small fragments of this history remain to us, and one of greater extent "On Sense-Perception." We learn from this last that the work was doxographic in its arrangement (cf. Vol. I. p. 530). At the same time, the whole of the fragments show us that the work was permeated with criticism from beginning to end—a point on which we feel constrained to dwell for a moment.

To write the history of science without regard to the personal convictions of the writer seems to us an impossibility. In this as in other provinces we hold the so-called objective writing of history to be both an illusion, and a perverted ideal. Freedom from partiality and prejudice, the most sincere and the most earnest endeavour to do full justice to views even the most divergent from our own— these, it is true, are indispensable requisites for every historical performance of real value. But it is also necessary to have and to express an opinion of one's own on the subject concerned—necessary in the double sense of inevitability and of needfulness. Without intensity of interest there can be no sustained study ; and if this does not lead to the formation of an independent judgment, all cannot be well with the intellectual capacity of the historian. On the other hand—and here we have more particularly in view the investigator into the history of philosophy—how can he who brings no opinion of his own to bear on the historical processes described by him do as much as separate with any certainty the trivial from the important, the transient from the abiding ? And yet this discrimination is the fundamental condition for anything like adequate historical perspective. But, it may be replied, a narrative thus subjectively conditioned, and, therefore, also subjectively coloured, divests itself of all claim to permanence. No doubt it does, we answer ; this form of human activity can no more than any other escape the universal human destiny. But it escapes it least of all when the narrator aims at being a mere registering machine, in which he can never entirely succeed, or when he chooses one of the two alternatives which are alone open to him who renounces all critical treatment of his subject—when, that is to say, he either assumes the attitude of uncritical hero-worship, taking his author's position for his own without attempt at originality, or else, regarding his personal opinion as the only one tenable or possible, violently reads it into the works with which he deals. In the first case, the subject has not found its master ; in the second, it has found a tyrant.

This digression has been somewhat lengthy ; but we felt constrained to pay tribute to the ancestor of all historians of philosophy by an attempt to put before our reader a just view of the dignity and value of the historico-critical method which he followed. We have paid him the still more emphatic tribute of taking this method for our model.

4. Our attention has already been engaged by samples of the criticism which Theophrastus applied to the doctrines of the nature-philosophers (cf. Vol. I. pp. 376, 356). This criticism appears to possess the greatest significance in those cases where he tests the opinions of others by the standard not so much of what he deems their objective truth as of their inner consistency. Thus he believes himself in a position to point out discrepancies inherent in the teaching both of Democritus and of Plato on the senses : "Each of them arrives at results which contradict his fundamental principles." In the case of Democritus this contradiction is said to consist in this, that having declared the sensible qualities (which we call secondary) to be merely subjective "affections," he yet refers them to primary or objective properties of the atoms (their size, form, and arrangement). This contradiction, it must be admitted, is more a matter of words than of substance (cf. Vol. I. p. 320).

In our opinion one of the most baseless of Plato's

hypotheses is his false or "untrue pleasure" (cf. Vol. III. p. 190). Theophrastus clearly saw the perversity of this assumption ; but at the same time he pointed out the kernel of truth contained in it, namely, the distinction between normal and abnormal modes of feeling. In face of this boldness, this independent and penetrating judgment, we become interested to know how they were brought to bear upon the master's doctrines, and how the discipleship of Theophrastus was reconciled with them. At this point a truly remarkable spectacle is presented to us.

The most faithful allegiance and sober, ever-watchful doubt meet us in a combination which at first strikes us as wholly enigmatical. We can hardly read a dozen lines of Theophrastus' philosophical writings without lighting upon Aristotelian thoughts, indeed upon whole phrases and sentences borrowed from the Stagirite. And yet on almost every occasion when he confronts a main doctrine of his teacher, he gives expression to doubts and difficulties in great abundance. The reader has already (p. 201) made acquaintance with his searching objections against the theory of Nous, which was represented as entering the human embryo from without. Yet these difficulties did not prevent Theophrastus from recognizing Nous as a psychic element not depending on the body. The central point of Aristotle's cosmology is his doctrine concerning the origin of the movements of the universe (cf. p. 218). Here, too, Theophrastus finds difficulties in plenty. Why, he asks, should the striving of the heavenly spheres be directed towards motion and not towards rest ? And, conceding this point, why is this striving peculiar to the spheres and not shared by the centre of the universe, the earth ? (There was here an obvious inducement to call in question the earth's condition of rest and with it the geocentric theory in general ; our philosopher, however, remained unaffected by this temptation.) Again, a number of objections are raised by the disciple against the teleological principles of the master. In the first place, he dwells on the province, already touched on by Aristotle, of what we now call dysteleology. Thus he mentions rudimentary organs (such as the male nipple), ephemeral insects, whose structure—so we mentally add—seems adapted for a lengthened and yet fulfils its functions for so brief a span ; the stag's antlers which furnish an effective weapon, but yet by their gigantic development hinder the animal's vision and impede his movements. Instances like these are adduced and explained in genuinely Aristotelian fashion by a reference to the opposition which matter offers to the purposeful activity of nature (cf. p. 115). But this is not all. How, we vainly ask, can any expedient of this kind stand against the subversive objections formulated in the following sentences : " The things which do not obey that law of purpose are exceedingly numerous ; in fact, they outweigh the others in number. *For there are few things that have life, but things without number that have it not ; while even among living beings the better is but an imperceptible fraction"* ? And yet Theophrastus by no means abandoned Aristotle's teleology.

5. This endless accumulation of doubts and difficulties, which lead into blind alleys or are brought forward only to be discarded—how are we to understand them ? The key to the riddle is to be found, we think, in the word " system." A complete and rounded-off fabric of thought, even when these qualities belong to it only in broad outline, exercises a fascination which it would be hard to over-estimate. No serious attempt can be made to break through the system at any one point without involving other parts as well, and so threatening the stability of the edifice in which the mind has found a home. Now, the strength of Theophrastus was clearly inadequate for a work of reconstruction. He shrank therefore from any step likely to shake the foundations of a system which he admired, which was familiar to him, and which in large measure satisfied his intellect. Modifications of his master's theories were the utmost that he ventured on.

To dwell on these modifications would carry us outside our purpose. Logic, a branch of knowledge which had been almost entirely created by Aristotle, offered, just because of its newness, ample room for improvements and detailed developments. Theophrastus treated this

subject in nearly two dozen works ; and his fellow-pupil
Eudemus worked at the same time and in the same spirit.
The general verdict of a modern authority is that the
doctrines of Aristotle suffered no deteriorations in the
hands of Theophrastus, that the criticism of the latter
touches all the points which were open to objection, and
that his corrections may be regarded as real improvements.
The chief objects of this criticism were the theories of
hypothetical and of disjunctive inference together with that
of the conversion of judgments.   We are surprised to find
anticipated here Sir William Hamilton's quite modern
doctrine of the quantification of the predicate (" All negroes
are some black " instead of " All negroes are black ").   He
shewed himself a precursor of the scholastics by making
considerable additions to the forms of proof, that is, the
syllogistic moods (cf. pp. 44, 45).   The subtlety of his investigations seem here to betray a pronounced tendency
towards over-subtlety.

6. Theophrastus devoted to physics, in the widest sense
of the word, both a single work of eight books and also a
series of monographs, some of which have come down to
us.   The most important deviation from Aristotle's
teaching seems to us to be the removal of fire from the list
of the elements, an innovation which the Stagirite himself
accepted in a work written in maturer life (cf. p. 165).

The Aristotelian doctrine upon the eternity of the
universe, that is to say, which denied that it had had a
beginning or could ever come to an end (cf. pp. 123, 124), was
defended by Theophrastus against arguments of which we
have no fully authentic details, but which there is practically
no doubt were in substance as follows. Four main
arguments, and probably also one subsidiary argument
were brought forward against the eternity of the earth
which here took the place of the universe as being the only
portion of it accessible to our close observation.   If the
earth had existed from all eternity, its surface would
necessarily have been already completely levelled by the
incessant influence of precipitation.   Secondly, that receding
of the sea which is to be observed in many places would

similarly have reached by now its final limit. Thirdly, all the elements are transformed into each other ; from this perishability of the parts that of the whole may be inferred. If Aristotle attributed eternal duration not only to the earth itself but also to its inhabitants (plants, animals, and men), his opponents replied by referring to extinct species of animals and their fossil remains. They appear lastly, to have pleaded the low stage of development as yet reached by many arts and branches of knowledge ; here again there seemed to be an indication that the human race and its civilization had had a beginning in time, were indeed of comparatively late origin.

In answer to the first of these arguments Theophrastus invoked the principle which we may shortly describe as Plutonism. The levelling tendency of the atmospheric precipitations, so he contended, was counteracted by a tendency towards upheaval due to the fire enclosed in the earth's interior. Further, the decrease of the sea was not a universal but a local phenomenon, balanced in other regions by its opposite, the decrease of the land (cf. p. 127). The third argument entirely lacked probative force. The inference from the parts to the whole was not justified in this instance. The destruction of one form of matter was the genesis of some other form, so that in reality there was a perpetual circulation (cf. p. 66). To the fifth argument he opposed Aristotle's catastrophic theory, which assumed a periodically recurring extinction of the human race down to a small remnant (cf. pp. 125, 126). Particular species of animals might possibly have been wiped out altogether by these catastrophes ; the hypothesis seemed probable, and it was no great concession to admit it. The fact of one answer serving for both the fourth and the fifth of the hostile arguments (the last of which was not mentioned at the outset) seems in a manner to fuse the two into one.

In this polemic Theophrastus showed himself a strict adherent of Aristotle's system. On the other hand, the peculiar qualities of his own inquiring mind were manifested in an endless stream of special investigations. By collecting facts, by developing the results of observations made both by himself and by others, he gave employment in a great variety of fields to the predominantly inductive spirit which animated his studies. In the realm of inorganic nature he left monographs on *signs of the weather,** on *winds,* on water (three books), on *fire,* on heat and cold, on the sea, on *stones,* on petrifactions (two books), on salts, salt-petre, and alum, on minerals, on the Sicilian lava, on fusion and congelation. To the field of physiology and medicine we may assign the essays whose subjects were *dizziness, perspiration,* states of fatigue, *fainting, paralysis,* melancholy, epilepsy, intoxication, insanity, and plagues. The writings on sleep and dreams, on sight (three books), on tastes, and on *smells,* must have been half pyschological in character. Among his zoological works we find mentioned not only an excerpt from Aristotle's writings on the subject, and seven books "On Animals," but also "special" (?) treatises on changes of colour in animals, on hibernation, on the difference between the voices of closely related animals, on the belief in the disfavour of animals, on spontaneous generation, on aquatic animals which retain life in the dry state, on local differences of animals (or their distribution ?), on biting and poisonous animals; we may add here the special writings on the colour and taste of different kinds of meat and on varieties of honey. The subject most meagrely represented in the series of monographs is botany, to which only one essay was devoted, "On Wine and Oil." This science was, however, treated comprehensively by Theophrastus in two large works which have come down to us.

* The italics indicate treatises which have come down to us whole or in part.

CHAPTER XL.

THEOPHRASTUS OF ERESUS.

(CONTINUATION: THEOPHRASTUS AS BOTANIST.)

1. ONE of these works, entitled "Plant-lore," treats of what we now call systematic botany, together with the geography of plants; the other, the title of which may be rendered "Causes of Vegetable Processes" corresponds to our physiological botany. The pupil did not gain much assistance from the work already done by his master, whose progress had been still less in the first of these departments than in the second. Aristotle had indeed written a work in two books (now lost) "On Plants;" but his teaching here was confined to the soul or vital force ascribed to plants, the functions of which was not supposed to go beyond nutrition and reproduction. Plants were distinguished from animals by their lack of sensation and locomotion—two theses of which the unqualified validity has of late been contested with much expenditure of research. He held, further, that their life lacked strict unity. This was shown by the survival of parts separated from the whole, and consequently the individual plant was comparable with a colony of animals. We have already (p. 157) mentioned the remarkable deficiency in Aristotle's knowledge shown by his flatly rejecting the distinction between the sexes in plants. We have also adverted to his ingenious comparison between the root of a plant and the head of an animal (p. 161). The importance of a general principle belongs to Aristotle's assertion that the indications of purpose in nature are less clearly marked in the vegetable than in the animal

world. We know, too, that Aristotle expressed views
on the nutrition of plants, on the formation of seeds and
fruits from their surplus nutriment, on their propagation
by layers, and on the phenomenon, which he held real,
of spontaneous generation.

Theophrastus was advanced in age, at least in the
middle of the sixties, when he consolidated the results
of his own and others' researches in the two works we
have named. Of these, the work on systematic botany,
the earlier in composition, is much the more valuable ;
the other is notable rather for the statement than for the
solution of problems. His chief predecessors were the
Nature-philosophers, among whom he mentions Democritus,
the most frequently, though for the most part with reference to questions but loosely connected with botany ;
besides these there were writers on agriculture, on dietetics,
on medicaments, and on poisons. Very numerous, too,
are the occasions on which he appeals to the statements
of peasants, of woodcutters, bee-keepers, divers, torch-
makers, and so on. But among his predecessors there
must also have been botanists in the true sense. For he
quotes principles and opinions of the most general scope
e.g. in regard to the arrangement of buds, such as could
not have proceeded from any but real students of this
branch of knowledge. We naturally think of Speusippus
(cf. p. 2) to whom in one important respect Theophrastus
offered a close parallel ; the Menestor, too, whom he
names is, we think, wrongly enumerated among the authors
on agriculture. Theophrastus did not undertake extensive
travels. He derived, however, a large measure of compensation from the work of the scientific staff which
accompanied Alexander in his Oriental campaigns, and
members of which were sometimes dispatched on special
expeditions. Their reports were preserved in the central
archives of the Empire at Babylon. The conqueror of the
world himself, it is said, did not disdain to take considerable personal interest in them. It might almost be conjectured that he thought of having the scientific results of
his expedition immortalized by a monumental work, much

as was done in the case of Napoleon's Egyptian expedition. Modern specialists cannot find adequate words in which to praise the botanical work done by that staff, and they are transported by admiration for the " morphological genius and acumen," which distinguishes, for example, the description of the gigantic Indian fig-tree. It need not, they say, fear comparison with the descriptions of a Schimper or a Van Tieghem. The first place, however, belongs to the achievement of Androsthenes of Thasos, the admiral entrusted by Alexander with the task (performed with only half success) of transporting his troops from Arabia. His description of the flora of the Bahrein island Tylos has aroused the enthusiastic admiration of a modern critic possessing uncommon special knowledge.

By incorporating these valuable communications in his systematic treatise, Theophrastus notably advanced the science of geographical botany. Indeed, he did more ; this branch of knowledge, to which he devoted the fourth book of his " Plant-Lore," was actually created by him. He was both the first and the last writer of antiquity to treat of it. When he "fused together into so wonderful a picture " the reports of his authorities, his thoughts were guided pre-eminently by a desire to give an account of the " botanico-geographical formations " which are defined and bound together by " physiological factors." For this reason he divides " the special plant-geography of woody plants into the two great physiological main groups of land and water vegetation." (The " division of aquatic flora," for its part, begins " with the distinction between salt and fresh waters.") It is not till afterwards that the geographical principle comes into prominence, being applied, so far as it is appropriate, within these two main natural groups. " The formations . . . the product of soil and climate," are described, just as in modern works, " in their typical plants with geographical subdivision."

The expert whom we have here followed felt himself justified, and that quite recently, in speaking of this and other parts of Theophrastus' botanical works as still needing to be " unlocked." His use of this expression was due to the difficulties of identifying many species of plants and many localities. But the greater the amount of study devoted to this problem by modern scholars equipped with the rare union of botanical and philological qualifications, the greater has been their admiration for the unique achievement of Theophrastus. This, indeed, is not to be found where we should naturally first look for it in the case of a pupil of Aristotle. It is true that both are morphologists of the first order. But to an attentive reader a great difference is soon revealed. Aristotle is the classifier *par excellence;* for Theophrastus, classification is a makeshift not to be dispensed with, but one yielding definitions which ought not to be "taken too seriously." If we are not greatly mistaken, it was rather the standpoint of Speusippus that he adopted in questions of class-division than that of his own teacher. Once more we meet the antithesis of definition and types; indeed, in an important passage of his "General Morphology," we seem to catch the true accents of a modern defender of the natural system (cf. p. 3). That he did not himself venture on the founding of such a system may be ascribed to the abundance, bewildering in its first effects, of the details which he saw so clearly and so exactly. Moreover, the extension of the geographical horizon considerably weakened the rigidity of the old divisions. Theophrastus knew how climatic influences modify organisms; more particularly, the newly-gained acquaintance with the products of the tropics supplied him with instances of the most marvellous transformations. He mentions plants which in his own country lose their leaves every year, while under the Tropic of Cancer they retain their foliage throughout the winter; he knows, too, a herb, a species of mallow, which under certain circumstances becomes an arborescent plant. It thus comes about that even the great division of the vegetable kingdom into trees, shrubs, bushes, and herbs, to which he holds fast in the main, loses for him something of its stringency, and claims no more than a secondary importance.

2. Theophrastus' masterly skill in the morphological

part of natural science is based on the extraordinary fineness of his senses, on the most conscientious utilization
of their testimony, and not least on what may be called
an intuitive feeling for the functional significance of structural elements and of all their variations, however slight.
He himself lays the greatest stress on " sense-perception,"
and the exact knowledge of detail thence derived, in antithesis to "reflexion." This is in a passage where he is
speaking of differences of situation and their influence on
the growth of plants.

For the Eresian, as for every worker in descriptive
natural science, the sense of similarity, the power of tracing
out even concealed analogies, is very fittingly the principal
instrument of research. It is thus no small testimony to
the mental equipoise of the man, to his dread of all onesidedness, that he anxiously guards against any possible
abuse of this in itself so wholesome tendency. Similarities
or analogies—it is thus, roughly, that he expresses himself
—should not be dragged in by force. Every attempt of
the kind has a doubly mischievous effect. It is not only
useless and unfruitful ; it has the further tendency to veil
or obscure the specific quality of the object. Such is the
fully expanded meaning of a pregnant sentence in which
Theophrastus warns against an exaggeration of the parallel
which he himself drew between vegetable and animal organs.
We are, perhaps, not mistaken when we conjecture that
this warning conceals a polemical point, directed against
no less a person than the Stagirite himself, and relating to
his comparison, an ingenious one, but not here accepted as
satisfactory, between the roots of plants and the heads of
animals (cf. p. 161). We are supported in this conjecture
by the fact that this parallel is absent from what would
have been its place in Theophrastus' work, and is superseded
in another context by a quite different comparison by which
a root is likened to the digestive canal.

The field in which Theophrastus plucked his richest
laurels is that of detail-research, of affectionate devotion to
the particular. In praise of one of his descriptions Kurt
Sprengel has said that one will " hardly find a more exact

description than this in the works of ancient writers." The specialist whom we have already quoted several times pronounces his description of the banana-leaf, "surprising in its truth and vividness, unique in its kind." Referring to a passage which alludes to an important distinction between two closely allied species of plants, the historian of botany Ernst Meyer expresses a doubt whether this distinction was "ever heeded by any botanist before Link and Robert Brown." With regard to roots—so another specialist ex presses himself—"he developed with astonishing strictness the ideas of rhizome, bulb, tuber, and distinguished them morphologically from true roots." The unremitting rigour of his distinctions seems to us no less well attested by his short account of the results obtained by the experiments in acclimatization conducted by the Persian satrap Harpalus in the parks of Babylon. He is not content with saying that some of the species transplanted from Greece throve and others succumbed. He distinguishes from both these categories those other plants which barely "pulled through," and owed their preservation solely to laborious "nursing."

The chorus of laudatory voices is now and again disturbed by a harsh discord. Scholars are not altogether wanting who give a onesided prominence to the erroneous pronouncements of this and other ancient teachers, possibly in order to show us what glorious progress we have made since. But this is a quite unjustifiable procedure. The value and significance of particular researches is decided not by the point reached but by the direction followed. It is in this spirit that we take leave to notice two problems in the treatment of which Aristotle's pupil far outstripped his master.

3. Theophrastus did not reject the theory of spontaneous generation. Still, he opened up paths of research which might well have led to the extinction of this error. It is true that he borrows from the old Nature-philosophers that doctrine which ascribes to the putrefaction of earth and water an influence on the origin of plants. But he opposes this hypothesis, as one "remote from sense-perception," to the "manifest and visible" modes of generation.

Accordingly, in particular cases he admits spontaneous generation as a mere possibility in addition to the other kinds of origin. And if in one passage he ascribes such spontaneous origin to many of the smaller and even some of the larger plants, in another passage, where he goes more deeply into the subject, he expresses a doubt as to whether this explanation applies to any of the larger plants at all. He lays emphasis, in this connexion, on the fact that the germs are often "small and scarcely visible." Lastly—and this is the main point—he knows that plant-germs reach the soil by the agency of winds, of rain-bursts, of inundations and the formation of new river-beds. Thus Theophrastus, by supplying the opponents of spontaneous generation with their most effective weapons, stands really, in spite of all appearances to the contrary, at the head of those who finally overthrew this doctrine of Aristotle and his predecessors (cf. p. 171).

The position is much the same with regard to the movements of plants. Not the slightest blame attaches to Aristotle for having drawn the line between plants and animals by denying motion and sensation to the former. For he readily acknowledged the existence of transition-stages in respect of both these distinctions (cf. pp. 155, 156). But in erecting this boundary-post he ran the risk of bringing about an unintended consequence, namely, the neglect or overlooking of those movements of plants which are not displacements of the whole organism. It is thus no slight merit of Theophrastus that he devoted minute attention to the facts bearing on the subject, even those of rare occurrence. He knows and describes with the greatest exactness "the high degree of sensitiveness possessed by the leaves of *Mimosa aspera*," a plant which then grew at Memphis, but which has since, according to Schweinfurth, receded further to the South. Another phenomenon which he knows and which he describes "with inimitable vividness" (here, certainly, following in the footsteps of Alexander's botanists) is the plant-sleep of *Tamarindus Indica*, the delicate plumes of which "open at sunrise, are fully unfolded at noon, bend together in pairs during the

evening, and are closed throughout the night." His full
attention was given, not only to these nyctitropic movements,
as they are now called, but also to the heliotropic movements. He knows as well as a modern botanist that many
flowers and the leaves of not a few species "continually
rotate with the sun, bend and turn towards it." He even
attempted an explanation of the fact that the highest
degree of this kind of sensitiveness is exhibited by those
aquatic plants of the hot South which dip under water
during the night ; and he finds the cause in the heightened
contrast between water and air temperatures observed in
those "warm and sun-baked regions." While dealing with
this subject he once even lets slip the word "sensation,"
and so unconsciously connects himself with those researches
of the most recent times who treat or have treated "the
irritability and sensitivity of plants." There is yet another
passage in which the Eresian has helped towards breaking
down the wall which separates the two organic kingdoms.
Unlike his master, he is not unacquainted with the duality
of sex presented by many species of plants (cf. p. 157) ; thus
he describes in a manner perfectly true to the facts the
process of fertilization which occurs in the date-palm ;
indeed he explicitly compares this process as observed in
plants with the union of the sexes in animals.

4. While Theophrastus thus appears as a pioneer in the
realm of botany, we observe, not without some astonishment,
that the path opened by him remained untrodden for nigh
two thousand years. His successors of the ancient age
one and all returned to the standpoint of most of his
predecessors, the rhizotomes or authors of herb-books.
Even the most important among them, a Crateuas (first
century B.C.), a Sextius Niger and Dioscorides (first century
A.D.), cultivated botany merely as a branch of pharmacology ;
they gave verbal descriptions, or merely pictorial representations, of medical plants, and ranked them according to their
healing powers. The achievement of Theophrastus was
regarded as final ; it was perpetually used, but not carried
forward. Its very perfection, leaving as it did scarcely any
room for supplementary additions or corrections, was

perhaps the chief reason why this whole domain was left untouched by the special researches, so active in other fields, of the Alexandrine age. With this no doubt co-operated the circumstance that the decisive extension of the botanico-geographical horizon, the opening to view of the tropical flora, had already been accomplished by Alexander's expedition and fully turned to account by the Eresian.

The one important mediæval writer on plants, a man who in the judgment of experts lacked originality in this as in other fields—we refer to Albertus Magnus, who died in 1280—possessed only a second-hand knowledge of Theophrastus. On the other hand, Andrea Cesalpini (1519–1603), who is regarded as the true renovator of this branch of science in the Renaissance age, exhibits a most accurate acquaintance with his great predecessor. One need scarcely do more than turn the leaves of his sixteen books " On Plants " in order to meet at every turn not only the name of Theophrastus but also serious and in part successful attempts to make original contributions to the textual criticism and the interpretation of the " Plant-Lore." In the succeeding centuries great botanists did not cease to study and to utilize the works of Theophrastus. The name of the eminent botanist Heinrich Friedrich Link (1767–1850) is continually met with in the list of those who have thought it worth while to treat critically the text of those works. And only a few years ago an accurate student of the subject, one whom we have quoted several times already, was in a position to write these sentences: " Beluchistan is still shrouded in thick darkness. Botanically, we have almost nothing beyond short notices . . . Then the botanical geography of Theophrastus provided us with a picture of the plant-life on the coast such as we should never have dreamt of." Thus the " Plant-Lore," especially its geographical portion, has even at the present hour not ceased to possess a more than historical interest. Theophrastus is even to-day a living and not a dead botanist.

CHAPTER XLI.

THEOPHRASTUS OF ERESUS.

(CONTINUATION : THE DELINEATOR OF CHARACTERS.)

1. IT was not only in the field of descriptive natural
science that Theophrastus proved himself a pre-eminent
morphologist. His keen eye for the peculiarities of things,
for their agreements and differences, was also exercised
in a quite other and far distant sphere. He became
the creator of a new literary genus—the description of
types of human character. Here again it is true that
he did not absolutely lack precedents. Brilliant descriptions of character-types have already presented themselves when we took our survey of the "Ethics" and the
"Rhetoric" of Aristotle (cf. pp. 251 and 436). But that
which for the master was a casual addition, became for the
pupil a theme for independent development. The relation
of Theophrastus to his teacher was here essentially the same
as it was with regard to the history of philosophy. In his
"Metaphysics," particularly in the opening chapters, and
again in the first of his three books "On the Soul," Aristotle had treated of his predecessors in these subjects ;
Plato also had done the same in some of his dialogues (cf.
Vol. III. p. 144). But with Aristotle this historical matter
had been merely accessory. He kept constantly in view
doctrines of his own which he found prefigured or anticipated
in this or that quarter ; he proposed, above all, to use the
real or supposed errors of his predecessors as a foil to his
own teaching. It may be added that ancient thinkers so
treated often lose a great part of their individual quality :
thus the subtle and profound Heraclitus shrinks, in Aristotle's hands, into the mere standard-bearer of an absurd

thesis—the denial of the principle of contradiction. In both cases alike Theophrastus carried to full development scientific and literary species before present only in germ, and incorporated them in the stock of acknowledged subjects and departments of letters. As a describer of characters, moreover, Theophrastus was influenced less by the example of Aristotle than by contemporary comedy with its subtle elaboration of typical figures, and by the note of realism as we may call it, which pervaded the age. Menander, the leading light of the newer comedy, was a younger contemporary (342–291) and a pupil of Theophrastus. In poetry, the *genre*-style was soon victorious; we call to mind the "Syracusan Women" of Theocritus (from about 310 to about 245), or the affectionate delineation of commonplace city-life which we find in the "Hecale" of Callimachus (about 310 to about 240). Even in the plastic arts portrait and *genre* were gaining the upper hand over the idealistic creations of an earlier generation.

2. A book entitled "Ethical Characters" occurs in ancient lists among the writings of the Eresian. The true nature of the "golden" booklet (so named by Casaubon, the celebrated scholar of the Renaissance age), which is still in our hands, has been often and obstinately misunderstood. At one time its authenticity was doubted, in spite of the testimony of those ancient lists; and, up to a few decades ago, almost universal acceptance was given to the hypothesis that the "characters" are at the best excerpts from Theophrastus' ethical or rhetorical works. The matter was supposed to be due to him, but not the form. A certain plausibility was indeed lent to this sceptical view by the circumstance that the book is, as a matter of fact, by no means free from foreign additions. The moment we open it, the first thing that meets the eye is a dedicatory epistle bearing on its front the plain stamp of spuriousness. In this the "ninety-nine years old" (!) author propounds the truly stupid question: Why do the Greeks display divergences of character, seeing they all live under the same climate and receive the same education? Hardly less perverse is the expectation, to which expression is given

in this preface, that by becoming acquainted with the character-descriptions to follow, posterity will become " better " than their ancestors. This pretentious introduction is incompatible alike with the known circumstances of Theophrastus' life and with the contents of the " Characters " itself; that it is the clumsy addition of a later age, is a conclusion placed beyond doubt more than a century ago, when the investigations of Karl Gottlieb Sonntag (1787) ended all controversy on the subject. Moreover, the mistrust thus aroused at the threshold has cast its shadow over the book itself, although there is not the slightest community of spirit or language between it and the introduction. Nor is that all. Each of the character-sketches is headed by a definition of the quality hereinafter depicted, and in more than one case a violent contradiction may be noted between the definition and the portrait. A discrepancy of this nature meets us in the very first section. The subject is " irony," the double meaning of which word we have already had occasion to consider (Vol. II. p. 49; Vol. III. p. 177) when dealing with the irony of Socrates. The fundamental meaning of the word is "love of hoaxing." Out of this original and wider meaning there arose, in a manner which we have already explained, a narrower use of the term, in which it denoted " self-depreciation," or "inverted hypocrisy." Now, it is the second kind of irony to which the definition applies, while the character-sketch depicts the first. It follows with irresistible cogency that the two are not the work / of the same hand. We cannot, to be sure, attribute this wrongly placed definition to the same forger who composed the absurd preface. It is, on the contrary, the genuine property of Aristotle, perhaps of Theophrastus as well; only, it was not meant for this context. In some cases supplementary expansions are found at the close of the descriptions, the genuineness of which has been disproved ; several other audacious additions betray their Byzantine origin by their linguistic forms. It was precisely the simple and unadorned character of the little work that invited these interpolations.

3. The collection before us may perhaps be best described as the loose leaves of a sketch-book. The ancients distinguished the writings which they named "hypomnematic" (collections of materials, preliminary studies, notes for personal use) from works essentially and originally intended for publication. Literary productions, however, existed which occupied a middle position between the two classes. With one example of this type the reader has already made acquaintance, Aristotle's work " On the Constitution of Athens." In it we recognized both a preliminary study for the " Politics " and a " collection of materials worked up into a readable book " (p. 378). The case may be the same with the "characters." The material there stored up may have been intended by Theophrastus for use in his systematic works. We have no means of knowing whether he seriously entertained such a purpose or whether he actually carried it out. In any case, the means became for him at the same time an end. The sketch lightly thrown off by a master hand retains its own value apart from the picture founded upon it, and that, too, even if the ampler design has never been executed. Indeed, it may happen that with its more immediate appeal, its more arresting truth and vividness, the sketch possesses the advantage over the finished painting. The character-descriptions of Theophrastus have often been adversely criticized for a simplicity which often amounts to monotony. Concerning each of the numerous figures which are brought before us we are told : he is the man to do so-and-so, he is capable, he is able to do this or that ; or again, he is strong in this or that ; or, lastly, one may see him acting thus or thus. Such is the simple mechanism, a bare half-dozen of phrases like those we have quoted, which the auther of the " Characters " finds sufficient for his task. Philological critics have drawn the strangest conclusions from this poverty of stylistic resources. It has, indeed, by what we are inclined to term an almost incomprehensible inversion of the true bearings of the case, been held by some to support the excerpt-theory. Surely the unity discernible in the form of a work proves anything

else rather than the diverse origin of its parts. By
what miracle could it have been brought about that
Theophrastus should have given precisely the same form
to a large number of quite unconnected passages in his
ethical and rhetorical works, so that by the mere act of
bringing together the scattered fragments a whole could be
produced possessing a high and even excessive degree of
unity? But this latest and absurdest form of the theory
was forced upon its defenders. They could no longer
blind themselves to a manifest fact which was compatible
with no other form of their hypothesis. The character-
sketches of another and much later Aristotelian, Ariston of
Ceos, have become known to us through copious quotations contained in a work by Philodemus the Epicurean,
which had lain buried in the ashes of Herculaneum. Well,
the form in which they were presented turned out to
be identical with that employed by Theophrastus. There
is just the same constant repetition of a few modes of
expression. Obviously Ariston came after Theophrastus
and imitated him. With this discovery the last possibility
vanished of separating the form of the "Characters" from
its matter and attributing the work to an excerptor. That
is to say, the collapse of the excerpt-theory was inevitable.
The writer of these lines is perhaps entitled to claim some
credit for having drawn this inference in an investigation
published more than twenty years ago.

The refined taste of antiquity found nothing to offend
it in the stylistic form of the "Characters." Are we called
upon to pass another and a severer verdict? The answer
may be given by a simile. No one has ever found fault
with a rope of pearls because the thread on which they are
strung exhibits no variety of colouring. Possibly it may
be objected that this thread is only visible accidentally and
at isolated points. But then, almost exactly the same may
be said of our case. The reader hastens from trait to
trait along the closely packed series, and scarcely notes the
stock phrases by which they are joined together. Indeed,
we may go further. The reason, we think, why each
character as presented to us stands out with so much life

and actuality is simply this, that we nowhere see the
showman's hand pulling the wires, that the decorative arts
of expression never divert our attention from the portrait
to the painter. There is a single exception, and it confirms
the rule. In one of the sketches (the sixth) one observes
a heightened striving after variety, a deliberate "accumulation of introductory formulæ ;" half a dozen such are
employed in the course of little more than twenty-five
lines. Immediately an impression of artificiality is created ;
the effect is weakened and lags behind that produced by
other and more artless descriptions.

4. We turn from the form to the matter. In suggesting the possibility that the thirty character-sketches were
intended as a preliminary study for the ethical works of
Theophrastus, we had in mind not normative but descriptive
ethics, the science which, beginning with Aristotle, received
such intensive culture in the peripatetic school. It is true
that we must here exclude one branch, and that not the
least important, of this study, the description of national
characters. And yet the descriptive part of individual
ethics did not by itself furnish the whole motive for the
"Characters." For among the types portrayed are some,
such as that of the "Late Learner" or the "Novelty-
monger," which, ethically speaking, are of a neutral order,
and which accordingly, it may be added, have aroused
the displeasure of several critics. With this goes another
circumstance which also has caused much sceptical amazement. Even where our author is depicting truly ethical
defects and perversities, he works less with the severe lines
of the moral philosopher than with the gentle touch of the
humorist. Humour, indeed, is the fundamental background
which lends unity of colouring to all these delineations
of manners. Nor is it the "Characters" alone that prove
Theophrastus to have been a humorist. The same quality
appears also in a droll description of the woes of marriage
preserved for us by St. Jerome. (We may instance the
curtain-lecture : " This woman appears in finer dress, that
one is esteemed highly by all ; I play the sorriest part in
the company of woman. Why did you look at the lady

next door? What were you saying to the little maid-
servant? You have been to market; what have you
brought for me?" and so on.) Much the same may be
said of the persiflage of the "Dionysius-Flatterers," for our
knowledge of which we are indebted to Athenæus. It is
recorded that he sometimes went so far as to employ his
histrionic powers in aid of his descriptions of manners, that
when in his lecture-hall he sketched the likeness of the
epicure, he reinforced his verbal account by illustrative
gestures. We have here not the weakest testimony to
the strength of the impulse by which he was moved to
reproduce ordinary reality both with mimetic truth and
with humour. The Theophrastus who looks forth upon us
from the pages of this book possesses no single feature
which our other sources of information do not ascribe to
the real Theophrastus, either explicitly or by giving us
reasonable grounds for inferring them. The most eminent
botanist of antiquity observes the doings of men with the
keen and unerring vision of a natural historian. The
peripatetic, for whom good and evil are chiefly a question
of measure, for whom the two are divided by a constantly
fluctuating boundary-line, reviews a host of varied formations and malformations with the cool indifference of an
anatomist, not greeting every deviation from the law of
normal growth with a shriek of indignation. The philosopher, lastly, whose heart throbbed with sympathy for all
that has life, who was a full and complete man, but lacked
both the desire and the power to be a superman, found in
humour what his rivals with weaker feelings or stronger
wills had found in "freedom from emotion" or "imperturba-
bility"—a liberating force which transfigured existence for
him and raised him victorious over its meannesses.

5. Finally, we propose to extract from a few of the
character-sketches such traits as may be understood without prolix explanations and reproduced without cumbrous
periphrases. Thus the "tactless" (or, more accurately, the
"unseasonable") man is described in the following manner:
He approaches a man overwhelmed with business in order
to enter into consultation with him. He treats his beloved

to a serenade while she lies sick of a fever.   Needing a
surety, he applies to some one who has just lost money
through standing surety for another person.   Summoned
as a witness, he appears after the verdict.   At a wedding
feast he indulges in invectives against the female sex.   He
invites one who has just returned home tired to be his
companion in a walk.   To a man who has just concluded
a sale, he introduces a new buyer with a better offer.
In a company which has heard a subject exhaustively
discussed, he puts himself forward to give fresh instruction
on it.   He appears at a sacrificial feast in order to claim
interest due to him.   If he sees a slave flogged, he tells
the master a story of one of his own slaves who was
similarly punished and thereupon hanged himself.   As
arbitrator, he eggs the parties on to renewed strife when
they are on the brink of a compromise.   In a (wanton)
dance he seizes (for his partner) another man who is not
yet heated with wine.

The vain man (or man of petty ambitions) is portrayed
more or less after this style.   When invited to a meal, he
makes a point of having the place next to his host.   The
slave who accompanies him in his walks must, if possible,
be a negro.   If he has to pay a hundred drachmæ, the
coins must be new.   Suppose he keeps a jackdaw; he
buys it a little ladder, and has a little brazen breastplate
made for it to wear as it hops up and down the rungs.
Having sacrificed a steer, he takes the skin of the forehead
(horns and all), winds it round with a huge garland, and
nails it up on his house-door, in order that his sacrifice may
be known to all.   After taking part in a procession of the
"Knights," he sends his servant home with the other
things, while he himself throws back his mantle and walks
up and down the market-place in his spurs.   If his Melitean
dog dies, he sets up a tombstone inscribed "A Scion of
Melite."   If he has placed a brazen finger as a votive
offering in a shrine of Æsculapius, he comes every day to
polish and anoint it.   When he is one of the officials who
preside over the assembly of the people, he prevails on
his colleagues to let him announce the result of the

sacrifice; he stands before the people, splendidly robed and garlanded, speaks (the customary ritual formula), and hastens home to tell his wife of his magnificent success.

The fate-reviler (or person always discontented with his lot) is characterized in the following sentences. If a friend has sent him a portion from a banquet, he says to the bearer: "He grudges me the soup and the drop of wine; that is why I was not invited to the table." If his lady-love embraces him "he would be surprised if her kisses came from the heart." He is wroth with Zeus, not for sending rain, but for sending it too late. If he finds a purse in the street, he exclaims: "All the same I have never yet found a buried treasure." Having by dint of much importunity bought a slave cheap, he grumbles: "I doubt if I've got such a wonderful bargain after all." When a messenger brings him the good news, "You have a son born to you," he answers, "Go on and say, 'You have lost half your possessions;' then you will have told the truth." If he wins a lawsuit by the unanimous verdict of the judges, he reproaches his advocate for leaving out quite a number of legal arguments in his favour. Suppose his friends have raised a subscription for him, and some one says to him, "Take heart," he answers, "Why should I? I shall have to repay each man his contribution and show him gratitude as a benefactor as well."

We proceed to extract the main features from the character of the boastful man. Standing on the quay, he tells strangers how great a part of his property is afloat on the sea; he launches into a discourse on bottomry; how extensive a business it is, how much he has himself saved, and also lost, in it. In the course of his speech he sends his servant (by way of corroboration, we must add in thought) to the bank, where in point of fact a single drachma stands to his account. On making a chance acquaintance by the wayside, he relates how he took part in Alexander's campaigns, tells what was the footing on which he stood with the great general, also how many jewelled goblets he brought home with him : he takes occasion to praise (with the air of a connoisseur) the superiority of Oriental handiwork. And all this without his having ever left his home. Antipater—he continues— has already written to him thrice to invite him to Macedonia; he has been offered the privilege of exporting timber from that country free of toll ; he has, however, declined, lest he should fall under suspicion and be accused of too intimate relations with the Macedonians. In time of famine, he says he has expended more than five talents in the relief of his fellow-citizens, he is quite incapable of saying "No." . . . When he enters the horse-fair he manifests a desire to buy the best foals. At the clothing-mart he chooses goods to the value of two talents, and scolds his man for having left his purse at home. To those who do not know the facts he represents the house rented by him as the home of his ancestors, and declares that he will soon have to sell it because it is no longer large enough for his guests.

The endeavour to reproduce these extracts has made me more conscious than ever of the unattainable excellences possessed by the original. How unerring is the selection of the most expressive words ! How anxious is the avoidance of every superfluity, and, in particular, of even the slightest subjective addition ! This astonishing parsimony heightens the effect of the sketches in a twofold manner. It increases both the compact force of the description and the plastic objectivity of the figures. Yet, in spite of this, many critics—Edward Zeller at their head, though he was at last converted—have confidently asserted that "the authenticity of this little work" is "not to be thought of," that, indeed we can hardly even believe it "based on a genuine work of Theophrastus." Posterity will surely prefer to acquiesce in the judgment of La Bruyère (1645-1696), for whom this book was a "masterpiece" and model a perfect embodiment of "Greek elegance" and of "Attic taste."

CHAPTER XLII.

THEOPHRASTUS OF ERESUS.

(CONTINUATION AND CONCLUSION.)

1. THE "Characters" founded a school. We have already spoken of the imitation produced by Ariston of Ceos. Those characterisms of his which are known to us come from a work, "On Empty Illusion." The second successor of Theophrastus in the headship of the Peripatetic School, Lycon, wrote a book from which the description of the "drunkard" has been preserved to us in a Latin translation. We also possess a portrait of the "dissolute" man taken from a work, "On Characters," by another Peripatetic, Satyrus.

Besides the description of individual characters, there is another and closely related branch of literature to be mentioned, which was founded mainly by Theophrastus. We allude to works "On Manners," and "On Modes or Conditions of Life"—two themes which were treated separately by Theophrastus and some of his followers, conjointly by Zeno the Epicurean, who certainly added considerations on individual types. Works with the titles just quoted were in existence, written not only by the Eresian himself, but also by Clearchus of Soli (in Cyprus), his contemporary and fellow-student; by Heraclides (cf. pp. 13 *seqq.*) ; and, lastly, by Straton, his successor in the headship of the school. The work of Theophrastus, "On Manners," by the wealth of its historical contents, supplied abundant material for the labours of commentators. This one fact is nearly all that we know about it. This little knowledge, however, is enough, taken in connexion with the existing remains of similar works, to teach us that in the circle of Theophrastus' studies an important space was allotted, both to political history and the history of civilization. The work of Clearchus, "On Modes of Life," as we learn from the comparatively numerous fragments, dealt with descriptive national psychology and ethics. Dicæarchus, another pupil of Aristotle, undertook to describe, or rather to reconstruct, the beginnings of civilization, with especial reference to Greece, in a work entitled "Life in Hellas."

2. The great extent to which interest in the whole breadth of empirical and historical reality had increased in that generation of the Peripatetics appears from each glance we take at the products of their researches. Probably no one had so close relations with our philosopher as Phainias, his fellow-citizen, fellow-student, and fellow-botanist. From the list of his works, which are for the greater part known to us by name alone, we select for mention three treatises on special historical subjects: a chronicle of his native city (more accurately, "On the Prytanes or Chief Magistrates of Eresus"), a book "On the Sicilian Tyrants," and another, "On the Murder of Tyrants out of Private Vengeance," a theme which the Stagirite himself had treated in a few sentences (cf. p. 378). While we cannot help noting with some uneasiness the danger of small-minded specialization choking the great conceptions of science, it is, on the other hand, hardly possible to over-estimate the value of this strengthening of the historical sense as a counterpoise to all unsubstantial speculation. No one, for example, will expect from Theophrastus a fantastic political or social Utopia, written in entire disregard of existing facts, when he learns that he compiled a comprehensive "collection of historical materials," that he composed a work in four books, full of historical examples, "On Statecraft or Applied Politics," and that in addition he compiled a genuine "Lexicon of Politics or Law," in twenty-four books, parts of which have been preserved to us, particularly a solid and comprehensive chapter "On Contracts of Sale."

Little as we know of his normative writings on these

subjects—there were two books of "Politics," two "On Monarchy," two "On Laws" and "On Illegalities," two "On the Best Constitution" and "On the Best Administration"—we shall hardly go wrong in assuming that in them he took up a position much further removed from all Platonic audacity of revolutionary innovation than Aristotle had done in his incomplete theory of the "best state" (cf. pp. 393 *seqq*). We know little more than the names of his Supplements to the "Poetics" ("On Comedy," "Against Æschylus," a book "On the Art of Poetry"). Greater importance and influence attached to his works in the department of rhetoric, of which there were counted no fewer than seventeen ; it is only quite recently that the extent to which these works affected later writers on the subject has been recognized and described. He made valuable contributions to the history of astronomy and the purely mathematical subjects, thus taking a place beside his fellow-student Eudemus, who founded this branch of the history of science (cf. Vol. I. p. 140). He similarly deserves mention along with Aristoxenus, the great musical classic, as a contributor both to the theory and the history of that art. It is noteworthy that in the first of these capacities he judged musical expression limited to "joy, mourning, and enthusiasm." There is, however, one department in which he would seem to have been the first to labour, and that with very considerable success —we mean the history of religion, his first work on which contained an objective exposition in six books, a kind of general survey. This was followed by three books of argumentative theology, "On Gods," and, lastly by his chief work, "On Piety," in which he set forth his own opinions on religious faith and observance ; these opinions he endeavoured to support by historical and ethnological parallels.

3. While perhaps still more alienated from all mythology than even Aristotle, and inclined to allegorical interpretations of popular legends, Theophrastus was filled with earnest faith in God. He went so far in his devout-mindedness as to ascribe the destruction of a whole popula-

tion, the inhabitants of Mount Athos, to their ungodliness. His theology was often criticized by the ancients as being inconsistent and indefinite. "For him"—so exclaims St. Clement—"God is now the heaven, now the breath (of life)." A similar complaint is made by Cicero. In his dialogue "On the Nature of the Gods," he makes Velleius the Epicurean say that Theophrastus attributes "the divine rule now to the spirit, now to the heaven, and then again to the stars." If we remember the Nous of Aristotle, its garment of ether, the divine nature of the upper celestial space, and the sphere-spirits, we shall hardly be able to detect any fundamental distinction between the teaching of the disciple and that of his master. Possibly the cosmic theory of Theophrastus ignored or laid small stress on the operation of the "First Mover;" so, at least, we are led to conjecture by the difficulties which he found in Aristotle's doctrine on the origin of the cosmic movements.

In his teaching on worship there is one point about which we have much more exact information than we have about his theology. The subject of sacrifice was treated by him at considerable length in the work "On Piety," in which he came forward as a determined opponent of animal-sacrifices. It was this antagonism which led the Neo-Platonist Porphyrius, an early champion of vegetarianism (cf. p. 38), to borrow considerable portions from that work and to incorporate them in his treatise "On Abstinence from Flesh Food"—a proceeding which was detected and convincingly demonstrated by the critical acumen of Jakob Bernays. This campaign against the sacrificing of animals was conducted by Theophrastus with an emphasis and a thoroughness which enable us to see a long way into his method, his habits of thought and even of feeling, an insight which extends far beyond his treatment of this one question.

4. The shedding of blood in sacrifice, so runs the first of his arguments, is a comparatively late innovation. The custom was foreign to the primeval age of mankind, which was content to offer the fruits of the field. In support of this thesis Theophrastus draws inferences both from the

worship paid to animals by the oldest civilized people, the
Egyptians, and from Greek customs and appellations. The
method here employed is that of inverse deduction,
such as we have already met with in Thucydides and afterwards in Aristotle, so far as the latter was a student of
antiquity (cf. Vol. I. p. 506). This historico-ethnological
section contains a great deal of pleasing and instructive
reading, from which we propose now to offer a few
selections. One weapon employed against the sacrificing
of animals is a parallel with the abominable custom of
human sacrifice ; both, he says, are symptoms of degeneracy,
and the two are found together not only among foreign
peoples but even among the Hellenes. Human sacrifices
are offered to the Carthaginian Baal (here named Cronos)
and even to Zeus at the Lycæan festival in Arcadia " up
to the present day." (It may be added that the horrible
custom continued till the time of the Roman Empire.)
Elsewhere " the altars are sprinkled with the blood of
fellow-tribesmen in memory of the former practice." In
the course of this polemic the Jewish people is mentioned,
among others, and its sacrificial ritual described. We should
say that this was the earliest unequivocal reference to this
people in Greek literature, were it not that Clearchus, the
fellow-pupil of Theophrastus, whom we have mentioned
already (cf. p. 490), had composed a dialogue in which he
brought forward Aristotle as conversing with a Jew and
warmly acknowledging the strictness of Jewish morals and
their habits of abstinence. Our philosopher distinguished
the Jews from the mass of the Syrians, with whom they
had previously been lumped, and, probably on account
of their monotheism, named them a " philosophic " race.
His account contains falsehood mixed with the truth ; like
Clearchus, he seems to have confused the whole Jewish
people with their priestly caste, and to have regarded them
as a Syrian analogue to the Indian Brahmins. The following are for him the most important points : the Jews
celebrate no sacrificial banquets ; they do not feed upon the
flesh of the victims, and therefore must not be counted
with those who hold to the rite " for the sake of pleasure,"

who "slaughter and skin edible animals under the patron-age of the Deity."

Still more important and still more characteristic of Theophrastus' mind is the argument drawn from the kinship or solidarity of man and beast. He takes his stand here on the similarity in composition of the human and the animal body, specially emphasizing the identity of their tissues (skin, flesh, and so on), as also of their blood and other humours. But he lays equal stress on their mental kinship. This, he claims, exists and provides a foundation for a universality of friendly relations, not only "of all men among each other," but also between them and the animals. Differences of degree no doubt occur on the most extensive scale ; but there are no really qualitative distinctions with regard either to the intellect or the emotions, and still less with regard to sense-perception. In the mental as in the physical sphere the "fundamental ingredients" or elementary facts are the same. Theophrastus hastens to meet the objection which might be derived from the savageness of many animal species. He compares these with criminals, whom we are likewise compelled to render harmless ; the bond of kin-ship subsists notwithstanding. That germ of cosmopolitan, of truly humanitarian feeling which we met with now and again in Aristotle (cf. pp. 287 and 332) now appears fully developed. With this child of the Hellenistic age the belief in the privileged position of his people is as com-pletely eradicated as it was with the Cynics. But the spirit in which he regarded the animal world found no second expression till the present age, with its associations for the protection of animals and its beginnings of a legislation in their interests. It is unfortunate that we know no more than the title of a work by Theophrastus, which was without doubt intended to expand and justify the thoughts on this subject adumbrated in the book "On Piety." This title, however, is significant enough—"On the Intelligence and Disposition of Animals." It is a work which Plutarch seems to have laid under large contribution in a similarly entitled treatise.

5. We have entered, without perceiving it, on the field
of Theophrastus' ethics. From the theory of religion
and sacrifices he passes on to maxims which forbid all
unnecessary killing of animals and lay the chief stress on
the sacrificer's purity of heart. But before we proceed, a
word or two may still be said in supplement of what we
have just noted with respect to our philosopher's appreciation of the animals and their capacities, and the close bond
which unites them with mankind. All this, it may be said,
calls aloud for the theory of descent. How does it come
about that the Eresian fails to pick up the threads which
Anaximander had first spun, and which Plato had carried
further in his " inverted theory of descent" (cf. Vol. I. p. 54 ;
and Vol. III. p. 208) ? Hardly any other answer remains
except this : he was held in thrall by the master's authority
and by his doctrine on the eternity of the earth and
its inhabitants ; thus he was prevented from drawing the
conclusions towards which both his premises and his
inclinations seemed so fitted to impel him.

The ethics of the successor were not essentially different
from those of the predecessor. Theophrastus held firmly
to the doctrine of the " mean," even at that point which
seemed to offer largest opening to our criticism, namely,
the treatment of justice (cf. p. 260). The same moderate
temper, the same avoidance of exaggerations, meets us
now in the pupil as formerly in the master. There is just
this difference—that, with exaggeration in fashion all
around him, among Stoics as well as Epicureans, the pupil
incurred more emphatic condemnation for his opposition
to it, for the regard which he paid in estimating the happiness of life to the power of fate and to external goods
(cf. p. 244). He was reproached for having lowered the
worth of virtue because he did not regard it as alone
sufficient for happiness. Since he was unwilling to admit
that the wise man may be happy amid torments, laxity in
moral things was charged against him. That which gave
the greatest offence was his quoting a line of poetry :
" Good luck is all, and not the prudent mind." It is not
out of place to recall that this quotation occurred in his

dialogue " Callisthenes, or on Mourning," and was almost certainly occasioned by the astounding changes in the fortunes of this friend of his youth, for, from its original wording, the line bears exclusive reference to the external circumstances of human life. Dedicated to the memory of Aristotle's kinsman and of Alexander's victim, this dialogue is the only one among those composed by its author of which we know more than the bare title. And yet it was these " Dialogues," intended as they were for a wide circle of readers and therefore carefully elaborated in point of style, which supplied the base for the criticism of Theophrastus as an author, just as had been the case with Aristotle (cf. p. 30). It was for these that the praise was awarded him of being the " most graceful " of authors and of surpassing all the other philosophers in " elegance " of expression. The most celebrated among his works were —the book " On Happiness," the three books " On Friendship," a work " On (more properly, against) Marriage," a condition which he found in no case suitable for a philosopher (cf. p. 485) ; besides these, there were monographs " On Divine Happiness," " On Pleasure," " On Virtue ; " two works " On Love," one of which was composed in dialogue form, together with books " On Education," " On Fortune," " On Revenge," " On Ambition."

We part with reluctance from the amiable and venerable man—one of the most attractive in the long series of figures which have passed before us. A free and fine intellect, a mild temper ; an observer with keen and searching vision, whether forms of plant-life or types of human character are his theme ; animated by a hardly conceivable love of work ; moderate in his view of life, averse from all violence and exaggeration ; shrewdly surveying men and their doings, and transfiguring even the less commendable features with smiling humour ; a stranger to all contentiousness and the wrangling of the schools ; entirely free from pride of race and national self-conceit, filled with the strongest sympathy with all that has life—such was the extraordinary man who has been engaging our attention. We count him not unworthy to number a Socrates, a Plato, and an Aristotle among his intellectual ancestors; and though he lacked the highest originality as a universal thinker, within his limitations he won for himself a position of very great significance, and he never desired to be more than what he was.

CHAPTER XLIII.

STRATON OF LAMPSACUS.

1. OF Straton's life (he died between 270 and 268) we know but little. On the recommendation either of Theophrastus or of Demetrius Phalereus, he was received at the Egyptian Court, and, in conjunction with the poet Philetas of Cos, entrusted with the education of the second Ptolemy. About the time (285) when the latter ascended the throne as co-regent, the aged Theophrastus departed this life. Straton was named in his teacher's will as one of ten men entrusted with the management of the Peripatetic school at Athens ; he at once took the leading position among his colleagues, and retained it till his death eighteen years later. It would seem that he, too, reached an advanced age, for his end came without disease, simply from emaciation and weakness. His will, like that of his predecessor, appointed ten of his intimate friends as curators ; and one of these, Lycon, was nominated head of the school. We should know more about his personal relations were it not that the collection of his letters has been lost. First among these stood a missive addressed to Arsinoë, the sister and consort of Ptolemy Philadelphus, of which we know only the introductory formula. We are thus unable to say whether he initiated the royal lady into the elements of science ; whether he became, in a manner, a predecessor of Leibniz and Euler. As a teacher, he drew a smaller attendance than his contemporary, Menedemus the Eretrian (cf. Vol. II. p. 206). This inferiority inspired him with a witty remark : " What wonder if the number of those who desire to bathe is greater than that of those who wish to be anointed as well ? " He himself thus represented his own teaching as too refined for the great mass, and as intended only for a

comparatively narrow circle. As an author he is said to have acquitted himself most brilliantly in polemics, and to have been much weaker in the exposition of his own doctrines. The extant fragments are too trivial in extent to enable us to check this verdict, which was that of the historian Polybius.

2. Though not so voluminous an author as Theophrastus, he yet devoted assiduous attention to the most diverse regions of science, from logic and metaphysics to ethics and politics. So much, though certainly not much more, is to be learnt from the list of the works composed by him. When we are told that he wrote "On Chance" and "On Definition," we at least gather that he did not rest content with the current Peripatetic opinions on these problems. He only touched on the descriptive natural sciences. Three works of his are entitled, "On Disputed or Doubtful Animals," "On Mythological Animals," and "On the Origin of Animals;" botany he passed over altogether, being obviously satisfied with his teacher's thorough treatment of that subject. He did not fail to produce monographs, after the manner of Theophrastus, on questions of physiology and psychology. Thus he wrote, "On Sleep," "On Dreams," "On Sensation," "On Pleasure," "On Sight," "On Colours," "On Dizziness (?) and Numbness," "On Nutrition and Growth." A book "On Diseases," and perhaps the one "On Crises" show him to have been at home in the province of medicine. A great number of his works were devoted to ethical questions; thus there were three books "On the Good," as many "On Justice," one "On Injustice," another "On Courage," one each "On Enthusiasm" and "On Happiness." With respect to politics, the changed times manifest themselves in the fact that Straton discussed monarchy in at least three books, perhaps also in a special work "On the Philosophic King," while the old Greek city-state, the πόλις, is left out of the reckoning. We have already mentioned the work "On Modes of Life" (p. 490): here, if anywhere, historical and ethnographical learning were bound to come into play.

3. But the centre of gravity of Straton's teaching and investigation lay elsewhere—in physics and in the closely allied departments of psychology. We have already referred to his resumption of the atomistic theory. The case may be stated more accurately as follows. From the doctrine of Leucippus and Democritus he borrowed two fundamental suppositions, the existence of indestructible and undecomposable primary particles, and the existence of empty space. Both hypotheses were affected by a single modification of the main doctrine. The primary particles were supposed to be completely separated from each other by the intervening void. Thus the whole apparatus which had served the purpose of binding, interlocking, hooking the atoms together was abandoned ; possibly it was with main reference to this mechanism and the infinite variety of forms which it supposed in the atoms, that Straton expressed the disparaging verdict in which he termed the atomic theory of Democritus a "dream" or phantasy. The void, too, he supposed, merely occupied the interstices between the particles, and nowhere existed as a connected or continuous whole. On the use which our physicist made of his corpuscular theory we are not informed with sufficient exactness. One point, however, is in a high degree worthy of notice. The void, on which Straton wrote an entire book, played for him, in more than one respect, the part which modern physicists assign to the ether (cf. Vol. I. p. 330). But, in our opinion, there can be no suggestion of an approach to the undulatory theory. For how should the "void" undulate ? We are much more forcibly reminded of Newton's emission theory. The object in view was to make intelligible the propagation of light, of electricity, and of magnetism—a noteworthy triad. The penetration of water by light rays, as seen in reflexion ; the passage of a magnet's attractive force through a chain of iron rings touching each other ; the electric shock which leaves the torpedo-fish and strikes the hand of the fisherman through his trident ;—these are some of the phenomena which Straton believed could be explained only on his hypothesis ; while uninterrupted matter, completely filling space, would have

obstructed the free motion of the factors in question, which
he clearly regarded as material.   The existence of empty
interspaces seemed to him a necessary condition for elas-
ticity (εὐτονία).   Without them, cases of complete mixture
—as of water and wine—the diffusion of light, and the propagation of heat through solid bodies like the metals, would
be inexplicable.   On the other hand, extensive empty
spaces could only be produced artificially, or " by violence."
The belief that such spaces existed in nature was engendered, so he said, by a confusion between empty space and
space filled with air.   At this point he repeats, in slightly
altered form, an experiment which, as we know, dates from
Empedocles (cf. Vol. I. p. 238). We refer to the dipping of an
apparently empty tube or beaker into a basin of water in
such a way that the air present in the former prevents the
water from entering it. He maintained, on the other hand,
that a continuous vacuum can be artificially produced ; and
he supported this view by another little experiment, in
which a light vessel was applied to the lips and remained
attached to them after the air within had been sucked out.
The experiments employed in these reasonings are of an
extremely simple character.   What makes them worthy of
notice is the accumulation of them, and the stress which
Straton laid both on them and on the mode of "ocular
demonstration " which they represent.

   4. Scarcely less significant than the resumption, real, if
limited, of atomism is the return to another and closely related fundamental principle of the Abderite, the doctrine of
displacement (cf. p. 64).   Straton abandoned the Platonic
and Aristotelian theory of " natural places."   Fire and air
ascend, not because they press aloft of themselves as
towards their home, but because they are thrust upwards
by heavier matter.   The tendency to downward motion is
thus represented as common to matter in every form.   A
breach was made with the puerile conceptions which treated
superficial appearance as ultimate fact.   An end was made
of a parting wall which had held the diverse kinds of matter
asunder.   Additional unity, too, was given to the picture
of the universe. For the ascent of fire, regarded as a

struggle of the element to regain its "natural place," was intimately bound up with Aristotle's division of the universe into fundamentally different regions.

It is true that Straton did not advance along the path thus opened up so far as Leucippus and Democritus had done. The latter, by denying all original distinctions of quality in matter, by allowing no differences but those involved in the varying size, form, and position of the atoms, had at once retained the old doctrine of the *one* primary matter, and pointed out to future research means by which the multiplicity of material qualities might in time come to be explained. Let this bold venture have its due meed of praise and wonder ; the fact remains that those who made it were anticipating a future which even to-day is still remote. The chemistry of our own time has not yet reached the goal then pointed out. That the different elements are merely modifications of a single primary substance—this is still a surmise rather than an established result of scientific research. The chemists of our day, without renouncing the hope of that future simplification, content themselves provisionally with the seventy odd elements, the resolution of which into simpler components has not yet been effected. Straton, then, was certainly well advised to work with primary corpuscles differing among each other qualitatively, and with their qualities, instead of launching, like the older Atomists, into venturesome speculations on the origin of qualitative differences in general.

5. It might have been conjectured in advance that this return to the fundamental doctrines of the Atomists would prove to have been associated with a departure from the theology of Plato and Aristotle. In point of fact, our "physicist" is often reproached for having set Nature in the place of the Deity. We should much like to know how far this naturalism extended, and what were the contents of his three books " On the Gods." His declaration that " he does not make use of the gods in explaining the origin of the world," reminds us at first of the saying ascribed to Laplace : " Je n'avais pas besoin de cette hypothèse." But there are here two possibilities, between which we

cannot choose with any certainty. Did Straton propound a cosmogony in which he left no space for supernatural intervention ? Or did he deem the whole subject outside the province of human understanding, and content himself with describing observed phenomena and referring them to natural regularities ? The wording of the above declaration, as reported by Cicero, speaks for the former view ; the second is supported by the heightened feeling for reality which we find in Straton, and by his shrinking from intellectual adventures like the " dreams " of Democritus.

We have insufficient information on the details of his teaching in natural science. The most significant fact is the high esteem which the whole of antiquity paid to the " physicist," in spite of his open estrangement from the faith of the people. Still more instructive is the powerful influence which he exercised on ancient natural science. Aristarchus of Samos, the Copernicus of antiquity (cf. p. 226, and Vol. I. pp. 121, 122), was among his hearers, and at least the theory of colours held by the disciple was identical with that of the master. Aristarchus is liberally quoted by Archimedes in his work " On the Number of the Sand ; " and he thus forms a bridge between Straton and the greatest mathematical and physical genius of antiquity. A second such bridge was supplied in the person of the great Alexandrine *savant* Eratosthenes. This writer was not above compiling a selection from a geological work by our philosopher ; while he was on a footing of intimate friendship and active scientific intercourse with Archimedes, as we learn from a book by the latter, dedicated to him, which has recently been discovered. Again, the eminent mechanician Ctesibius (the inventor of the air-gun), and Erasistratus the founder of an important medical school, were directly and permanently influenced by Straton in their fundamental conceptions of physics.

6. Straton may be termed a Monist. For him, as it seems, God and Nature were fused into one ; nor was he willing to acknowledge a boundary separating soul and body. Here there was, in truth, not very much left for him to do. The soul, as we have already been told by Aristotle,

is " something of the body " (cf. p. 176). To this principle
the Stagirite allowed only one exception. Nous, or pure
intellect, according to his view entered the human body
from without, and was accordingly exempt from the doom
of mortality. With the difficulties of this doctrine Theophrastus had vainly wrestled (cf. p. 199). He finally
surrendered to the master's authority (cf. p. 466), but broke
away from it once more, indirectly, by allowing only differences of degree between the human and the animal
intellect (cf. p. 495). His successor followed the same path
still further. He defended the unity of all psychic life by
a twofold argument. Just as thought has all its material
supplied to it by perception, so, too, he contended, perception itself never consists in a merely passive acceptance.
The activity of the soul, which some had thought reserved
to the highest intellectual operations, is indispensable to
the simplest perceptions. " Without thought, there can be
no sensation at all." Our eye may range over a written
sheet, the sound of words may enter into our ears : neither
the one nor the other reaches our consciousness if, and so
long as, our attention is otherwise engaged. With the
removal of the obstacle, perception supervenes ; thus (to
add an illustration) we may perceive and count the strokes
of a clock after it has ceased to strike.

The seat of the psychic functions was placed by Straton
in the region between the eyebrows—an assumption which
has found renewed support in quite recent times (S. Stricker).
He was perhaps led to this view by the contraction of the
brows which occurs at moments of intense thought. But
in this doctrine there was no room for the immortality of
the soul or of a particular, rational, part of it. Thus when
Straton pulled Plato's proofs of immortality to pieces easily
and ruthlessly, he was only drawing the conclusions which
necessarily flowed from his premisses. Nor was our
" physicist " without predecessors in his denial of a special,
psychic principle which survives the body ; we may refer
to what we have said in anticipation when dealing with
the Peripatetics Aristoxenus and Dicæarchus (Vol. III.
pp. 43, 33).

7. The conclusion of this work has returned to its starting-point. Our exposition opened with the nature-philosophers of Ionia. It closes with a thinker whose home was Lampsacus—an Ionian city, though situated on the Hellespont—and who likewise, as his appellation "the physicist" shows, made Nature the chief object of his study. His influence was felt in especial degree by great investigators of Nature, while his numerous writings on other subjects produced no important effects that we can trace. Philosophy, in its original sense of universal science, has now been thrust into the background by the rich development of the special sciences, and had been robbed of its old leadership in the field of general research (cf. p. 459).

There is, however, one characteristic feature which unites the pupil and successor of Theophrastus with the founders of philosophic schools who lived in his own age. Zeno, the head of the Stoa (who died in 264), combined the physics of Heraclitus with the ethical systems of the Cynics, a branch of the Socratic school; Epicurus (341–270) joined to the natural philosophy of Democritus the ethics of another Socratic school, the Cyrenaic. Straton similarly incorporated portions of the physical doctrines of Democritus in the system of his intellectual ancestor Aristotle, who likewise was of the race of Socrates. But with him the fusion of the heterogeneous doctrines was by no means so intimate as in the two parallel cases which we have just named (cf. Vol. II. pp. 244, 245). The crossing of strains, if we may use the metaphor, thoroughly renovated the other two varieties of Socratism and infused into them vigorous life. Here we meet with a notable contrast. The systems created by Zeno and Epicurus did little to promote the advance of the positive sciences; but they became a force enveloping the whole life of the educated classes in Greece and Rome, a religion of the enlightened. The teachings of the Peripatetics, on the other hand, made scarcely any impression on the world outside the school. They exercised but little influence on the general mass of the educated; but the progress of positive science gained from them a powerful stimulus.

NOTES AND ADDITIONS.

—◆◆—

VOL. IV.

The motto is taken from Bonitz' *Commentary* on the
Metaphysics, p. 29.

BOOK VI.—CHAPTER I.

Sect. 1. Speusippus is dealt with briefly in the *Index Academicorum*, col. vi. p. 37/8, ed. Mekler ; with greater fulness by Diogenes Laertius, iv. c. 1. We have mentioned him in Vol. II. pp. 271, 273, 277 ; Vol. III. p. 137. Krische is excellent, as always, in *Die Theologischen Lehrer der Griechischen Denker*, pp. 247–258.

Page 2 (Bottom). "Development :" cf. Krische, *op. cit.*, p. 257. "What we are told by Aristotle :" *Metaph.*, xiii. 7, 1072 b, 31, compared with xiv. 5, 1092 a, 9. "Taunt of atheism :" Cicero, *De Natura Deorum*, i. 13, 32.

Page 3 (Top). "Rejection of the doctrine of Ideas :" the chief authority is Aristotle, *Metaph.*, xiii. 8, 1083 a, 21, with Zeller's discussion of the passage, vol. ii. part 1 (ed. 4), p. 1004. On what follows compare (on the subject of Antisthenes) *Greek Thinkers*, Vol. II. pp. 183, 184 ; Aristotle, *Anal. Post.*, ii. 13, 97 a, 46 *seqq.*, with the Commentary of Themistius, p. 58, 4 *seqq.*, ed. Wallies ; and *Eudemi Fragmenta*, 164, 21, ed. Spengel ; lastly, Joannes Philoponus in *Anal. Post.* (ed. Wallies, p. 405, 27 *seqq.*). (Bottom) Whewell, *History of Scientific Ideas*, ii. 120 *seqq.*

Page 4 (Top). "Fragments of Speusippus' work." These are contained in many passages of Athenæus. "On the Patterns . . ." The title, Περὶ γενῶν καὶ εἰδῶν παραδειγμάτων, is given by Diog. Laert., iv. 5, but incorrectly reproduced in the Latin translation. Plato's self-correction is recorded in the *Statesman*, 287 C. : κατὰ μέλη . . . διαιρώμεθα, δίχα ἀδυνατοῦμεν. "Duality" not "the principle of evil :" cf. *Metaph.*, xiv. 4, 1091 b, 30, *seq.*, with the remarks of Krische, *op. cit.*, p. 254. "Numbers" as the "prime causes of things :" cf. the passages of the *Metaphysics* discussed by Zeller, vol. ii. pt. 1 (ed. 4), p. 1003 *seq.* On what follows cf. the *Theolog. Arithm.*, p. 62.

Page 5 (Top). "The point not identical with unity : " reason not identical with unity and the Good, but ἰδιοφυής : according to Aristotle, *Metaph.*, xiii. 9, 1085 a, 22, and Stobæus, *Ecl.*, i. 58 = p. 35, 3, *ed.* Wachsmuth. On his ethics compare Clemens, *Strom.*, ii. 133, 500 P ; Plutarch, *De Comm. Not.*, 13, 1 (*Moralia*, 1302, 49, G. Dübner) ; Seneca, *Epist.*, 85, 18.

Sect. 2. Xenocrates is treated of by Diog. Laert., iv. 2 ; the *Index Acad.*, col. vi. *seq.*, pp. 38 *seqq.*, Mekler ; Cicero, *Tusc.*, v. 32. Compare the author's essay, *Die Akademie und ihr vermeintlicher Philo-Macedonismus*, Wiener Studien, iv. 102 *seqq.* The fragments have been collected and excellently elucidated by Richard Heinze, *Xenocrates* (Leipzig, 1892).

Page 6 (Bottom). "Whose founder was one of his pupils." This pupilship of Zeno, the head of the Stoa, is attested by Diog. Laert., vii. 2, and by Numenius, quoted in Eusebius, *Præp. Ev.*, xiv. 5, 11. It has been disputed on chronological grounds, the untenability of which the present author has endeavoured to show in *Zur Chronologie des Stoikers Zenon*, Wiener Sitzungsberichte, Band 146, Abhandlung 6. The connexion between the two men has been already noticed by Krische, *op. cit.*, p. 323, apropos of their religious teaching.—Examples of his συνοικείωσις are given by Krische, *op. cit.*, p. 324, and by Heinze, p. 143.—On the μόνας and δύας as deities, cf. Stobæus, *Ecl.*, i. 62 (p. 36, 6 *seqq.*, ed. Wachsmuth).—On his dæmonology, see the exposition of Krische, pp. 320 *seqq.*, which Heinze (pp. 81, note 2) rightly regards as of fundamental value.

Page 7 (Middle). Definition of the soul : see chiefly Aristotle, *De Anima*, i. 2, 404 b, 29 *seq.*, and his criticism in 408 b, 32.

Page 8 (Middle). Plato's doctrine of ideal numbers : the chief passages are Aristotle, *Metaphysica*, i. 6, xiii. 6 *seqq.* ; *De Anima*, i. 2. The author has entirely failed to be convinced by the most recent treatment of the subject by Natorp (*Plato's Ideenlehre*, p. 413 *seqq.*), in which he scents everywhere misunderstandings of Plato on the part of Aristotle.—"A well-informed commentator : " Simplicius on *Physica*, iii. 4 (453, 30, Diels).

Page 9 (Top). "Parallelism dealing with the region of knowledge : " cf. Aristotle, *De Anima*, i. 2, 404 b, 21 *seqq.*

Page 11 (Middle). Threefold subdivision of philosophy : according to Sextus, *Adv. Math.*, vii. 16 (but also presupposed by Aristotle, *Top.*, i. 13, 105 b, 20, 21). Other triads, *ibid.*, vii. 147 (193, 194 and 223, 16 *seqq.*, Bekker).—The physics of Xenocrates : cf. Heinze, pp. 67 *seqq.* His teaching on goods : *ibid.*, p. 147 *seqq.*—"Refinement of feeling : " the utterance referred to is found in Ælian, *V. H.*, xiv. 42, and was long ago compared with Matt. v. 28.

Sect. 3. Page 12. The circumstances of Polemon's life are treated fully in the *Index Hercul.*, chiefly on the authority of Antigonus of Carystus. Compare *Die herkulanische Biographie des Polemon*, by the present author, in *Philosophische Aufsätze, Ed. Zeller gewidmet* (Leipzig, 1887), pp. 141 *seqq.* Diogenes Laertius (iv. ch. 3) gives little more than a short extract. (Middle) Nature as guide : in a work, Περὶ τοῦ κατὰ φύσιν βίου, quoted by Clemens, *Strom.*, vii. 32 (= 849, Potter). According to this, Polemon was also an opponent of flesh-eating, by which, as he contended, men become participators in the irrationality of animals. (Bottom) On Crantor, see *Index Acad.*, col. xv. pp. 59 *seqq.*, ed. Mekler, and the excerpts given by Diogenes Laertius, iv. 5.—For his commentary on the *Timæus*, see vol. iii. pp. 201, 362. Short fragments from it are given by Fr. Kaiser, *De Crantore Academico*, pp. 12 *seqq.* Fragments of the book, "On Mourning :" see the same work, pp. 34 *seqq.* The pros and cons of immortality : Hirzel, *Der Dialog.*, i. 340. The most important fragment is preserved by Plutarch, *Consol. ad Apoll.*, ch. 3 (*Mor.*, 122, 20, ed. Dübner).

Page 13 (Top). The contest of the "goods" is described by Sextus, *Adv. Math.*, xi. 51 *seqq.* (556, 24 *seqq.*, ed. Bekker). For Crates, Antigonus is again the chief source ; this time, however, his account is better preserved by Diogenes Laertius (iv. 4) than in the *Index Acad.* The political activity of Crates and his ambassadorial journeys are inferred from the Λόγοι δημηγορικοί καὶ πρεσβευτικοί mentioned by Diog. Laert., *loc. cit.* The same passage refers to his book "On Comedy," and to his Φιλοσοφούμενα, without adding any further information on their contents.

Sect. 4. Page 13 (Bottom). On Heraclides, cf. Otto Voss, *De Heraclidis Pontici Vita et Scriptis*, Rostock, 1896. The chief source is Diog. Laert., v. 6, in addition, *Index Acad.*, col. ix. pp. 24 *seqq.*, Mekler ; also col. vii., p. 39.

Page 14. The instructions which he received from Aristotle must have been given during the lifetime of Plato, at a time when Aristotle taught rhetoric only (cf. Grote, *Aristotle*, i. 32). For after the death of Plato, Aristotle left Athens, and Heraclides did the same after the death of Speusippus. The statement of Diogenes or Sotion, παρέβαλεν πρῶτον μὲν Σπευσίππῳ, no doubt refers merely to close personal relations. The circumstance of his having taken the place of Plato during a journey, probably the third, of the latter to Sicily, is reported by Suidas, *s.v.* 'Ηρακλείδης.—I can see no reason for supposing the story of his death to be fabulous. I might have mentioned not *one* Olympic victor only, but several, and also the father of one such victor. See Pausanius, iii. 18, 5 ; Ælian, *V. H.*, ix. 31 ; and Diogenes Laertius, i. 72, with the emendation of Jahn, *Philologus*, 26, p. 3.—The charge of plagiarism was brought against him by Chamæleon, Diogenes Laertius, i. 92.—The wooden criticism which was applied to him in ancient days by the malevolent Timæus, and the character of his diologues in general, have been excellently treated by Hirzel, in *Der Dialog.*, pp. 321 *seqq.*

Page 16. On the atomic theory of Heraclides, cf. the testimonies cited by Voss, p. 66 *seq.*—" Unarticulated particles :" my interpretation of the ἄναρμοι ὄγκοι is new, but, as I think, the only tenable one. It is usual to refer ἄναρμοι to the lack of connecting bonds between the primary particles, but this is in sheer contradiction with the minute description given by Cælius Aurelianus, *De Morbis Acutis*, i. 14, that is, in the Latin translation of the thoroughly expert Soranus.

BOOK VI.—CHAPTER II.

Sect. 1. Page 18. "Master of those who know:" Dante, *Inferno*, iv. 131.

On Aristotle's influence in the Middle Ages, see, for the general aspects of the subject, Sir Alexander Grant, *Aristotle*. More detailed information is given by Renan, *De Philosophia Peripatetica apud Syros*, Paris, 1852, especially in ch. 8, "Syri magistri Arabum fiunt in philosophia Græca." (The Syrians were acquainted with Aristotle as early as the middle of the fifth century. Edessa was the chief seat of their labours in translation. The translators were the Nestorians, who, expelled from that city, spread the knowledge of Peripatetic philosophy among the Persians and Arabians.) Renan's work, *Averroës et l'Averroisme*, Paris, 1852, may also be referred to, and those of F. H. Dieterici's writings, which bear on the subject ; the most recent of these last is the book *Die sogenannte Theologie des Aristoteles*, Leipzig, 1883.

Page 19. The life of Aristotle is treated by Diogenes Laertius, book v. ch. 1. Besides this, we have the two lives in Westermann's Βιογράφοι, pp. 398 *seqq.*, together with the variant of the second Βίος edited by Robbe, Leyden, 1861 ; and a few, but valuable, notices in the letter of Dionysius to Ammæus, ch. 5 (*Dionysii Halicarnassei Opuscula*, ed. Usener et Radermacher, i. 262 *seq.*). The chronological data are taken from Apollodorus, quoted by Diogenes Laertius, v. 1, 9. As against this authority, little weight attaches to the narratives of Epicurus and Timæus respecting a stormy youth of Aristotle (cited by Eusebius, *Præp. Ev.*, xv. 2), although Grote does not altogether refuse it credit in the otherwise excellent biographical section of his *Aristotle*, i. p. 4. Portraits : F. Studniczka, *Das Bildnis des Aristoteles*, Leipzig, 1908. (Middle) Reported quarrel with Plato : Diog. Laert., § 2. The saying from the " Nicomachean Ethics : " i. 4, 1096 a, 16.—" He struck at Plato," etc. : on the authority of Eusebius, *Præp. Ev.*, xiv. 6.

Page 20 (Top). On the rivalry with Isocrates, cf. Cicero, *De Oratore*, iii. 35, 141, and the other quotations in Grote, *op. cit.*, p. 35. This author, however, misjudges the polemical application of the Euripidean line (fragm. 796 N., ed. 2, αἰσχρὸν σιωπᾶν, βαρβάρους δ' ἐᾶν λέγειν). (Bottom) Aristotle and Xenocrates at the Court of Hermias : see especially *Index Acad.*, col. v. p. 22 *seq.*, Mekler. On Hermias, cf. Böckh's treatise in *Kleine Schriften*, Band vi. pp. 185 *seqq.* ; also

Didymus, in the commentary on Demosthenes edited by Diels and Schubart, pp. 17 *seqq.* and 21 *seqq.*

Page 21 (Bottom). Mieza : the site does not appear to be as yet determined with complete certainty. Even the stalactite cave, mentioned by Pliny, *Nat. Hist.*, 31, 2, 20, affords no trustworthy indication ; for such caves, as my colleague Jireček kindly informs me, are anything but rare in the district. The locality is also dealt with by Plutarch, *Vita Alexandri*, ch. 7, 2 (*Vitæ*, 797, 1, Döhner).

Page 22 (Bottom). The later relations between Aristotle and Alexander are perhaps best treated by Plutarch, *op. cit.*, ch. 8, § 3 (797, 39 D). The moderation of this account contrasts very strongly with the vituperation put in the mouth of Alexander in ch. 74, § 2, and 55, 3 of the same work (842, 8 and 830-1, Döhner). In the first case the letters supplied the foundation, in the second unverifiable hearsay. On the political counsel given to Alexander by Aristotle, cf. Eratosthenes, quoted in Strabo, i. p. 66, Cas, and the remarks of Bernays in *Diologe des Aristoteles*, p. 155.—" Financial support : " this is attested, with evident exaggeration in detail, by Athenæus, ix. 398 e, and Pliny, *N. H.*, viii. 17, 44.—" Rebuilding of Stagira : " cf. Dion, *Oration* 47 (ii. 224 Reiske = ii. 82, 83 Arnim).

Page 23 (Top). " Never a practical politician : " see the author's essay in controversion of Bernays' *Phokion, Die Akademie*, etc. (Wiener Studien iv.). (Middle) " Allies, not subjects : " τοῖς μὲν Ἕλλησιν ὡς φίλοις χρῆσθαι, τοῖς δὲ βαρβάροις ὡς πολεμίοις, according to Strabo, *loc. cit.*, probably in the work Περὶ Βασιλείας (cf. Bernays, *loc. cit.*). (Bottom) On the mission of Nicanor, cf. Diodorus, xviii. 8, 3, and Dinarchus against Demosthenes, § 81 (p. 33, Blass). Grote deals excellently with the subject, *History of Greece*, ch. 95 (xii. 416 *seqq.*, ed. 1), and *Aristotle*, i. 14 *seqq.* On Nicanor, cf. R. Heberdey in the *Festschrift*, dedicated to the present author, pp. 414 *seqq.*

Page 24 (Middle). On the accusation, see chiefly Diogenes Laertius, v. 5, and Athenæus, xv. 696 a. One point objected against him is said to have been his teaching, contained probably in the dialogue Περὶ εὐχῆς, on the inefficacy of prayer ; on this, and on the trial in general, see Grote, *Aristotle*, p. 18. According to a plausible conjecture of Lenormant (*Dictionnaire des Antiquités*, ii. 555), another point in the accusation was the sacrifice offered to the dead Pythias ; cf. Diogenes Laertius, v. 1, 4. (Bottom) The poem on Hermias, see Diog. Laert., v. 7.—The statue erected at Delphi, *ibid.*, 6. " Athens must not sin again . . . : " cf. the second *Vita* in Westermann, p. 400, and Ælian, *V. H.*, iii. 36.

Page 25. Testamentary dispositions : Diog. Laert., v. 11 *seqq.* (Bottom) Herpyllis : on the name, cf. v. Willomowitz, *Aristoteles und Athen*, ii. 90. That the situation of the παλλακή enjoyed some measure of legal protection appears from the law cited in Demosthenes, *Oration* 23, § 55, where the concubine is mentioned along with the wife and other female connexions ; cf. also Lysias, *Oration* 1, 30-1. She is here spoken of as "inferior," just as in the pseudo-Demosthenic *Oration* 59, § 122, she takes an intermediate position between the *hetæra* and the legitimate wife.

BOOK VI.—CHAPTER III.

The works of Aristotle have been published in recent times by the Berlin Academy—five volumes, including Latin translations (iii.), Scholia (iv.), Fragments and a special lexicon (v.). Besides these there are several supplementary volumes and a series, recently completed, of commentators, mostly Greek ones. Another collected edition is that published by Firmin-Didot in five volumes.

Admittedly spurious writings are the Περὶ κόσμου, which is the work of a Stoic, and also the Περὶ φυτῶν, the Περὶ χρωμάτων, the Φυσιογνωμονικά, the Περὶ Ξενοφάνους, κ.τ.λ., the Περὶ ἀτόμων γραμμῶν, and the Θαυμάσια ἀκούσματα. Works of doubtful authenticity are dealt with incidentally in the separate sections. I make no use of the *Problems*, nor of the Μηχανικά, which also are composed in problem-form (always beginning with a διὰ τί ;), not because they must be held spurious as wholes, but because they undoubtedly contain spurious parts—the very form of these investigatory queries was a continual invitation to new additions —and because there are no means of distinguishing the genuine from the spurious with any certainty.

Page 27 (Top). "Moderate to excess:" μέτριος . . . τοῖς ἤθεσιν εἰς ὑπερβολήν, *Vita* No. 2 in Westermann, p. 401.—Cancellation of Delphic honours : cf. Ælian, *V. H.*, xiv. 1. On the cancellation and subsequent restoration of honours in Athens, see *Ath. Mitteil.*, xiii. 369. (Bottom) "Praise of justice:" *Eth. Nic.*, v. 3, 1129 b, 26. Here, too, we may perhaps also cite the words in which Aristotle affirms the superiority of "first philosophy" to all other sciences : "They are all more necessary than it, but none of them better" (*Metaph.*, i. 3, 983 a, 10).

Page 28 (Top). The "Constitution of the Athenians:" first published by F. G. Kenyon, *Aristotle on the Constitution of Athens*, London, 1891. In what follows details are repeated from the present author's lecture on "Aristotle and his newly discovered Work, etc.," in the *Deutsche Rundschau*, May, 1891 (*Essays und Erinnerungen*, pp. 154 *seqq.*). (Bottom) The charge here discussed has been urged against Aristotle most emphatically by Lutoslawski, in *Erhaltung und Untergang der Staatsverfassungen nach Plato, Aristoteles, und Macchiavelli*, Breslau, 1888, pp. 81 *seqq.* Here he does indeed demonstrate an uncommonly close relation of dependence, reaching into minute detail, between Aristotle's theory of the State and Plato's ; but it is a sheer impossibility for us to believe in a "malicious criticism " (p. 90) on Aristotle's part, or in deliberate misunderstandings such as are attributed to him by Lutoslawsky, partly with the concurrence of Teichmüller (*Literarische Fehden*, i. 165). It may be added that, had Aristotle desired to conceal his dependence upon Plato, the frequent verbal agreements which he presents might very easily have been avoided. Severe self-criticism is practised by him in, *e.g., Topics*, vi. 11, 149 a, 20.

Page 29 (Top). "The house of the reader:" in the second *Vita* of Westermann's *Biographi*, p. 399.—"The lonelier . . . :" Fragment, 618 (1582 b, 10).—The sarcasm against the Athenians: in Diog. Laert., v. 1, 17.—The epithet μικρόμματος is applied to Aristotle by the same writer, v. 1, 1.

Sect. 2. Page 29. "Artistic qualities of his style." Dionysius of Halicarnassus ranks Aristotle among pattern writers in *De Compositione Verborum*, ch. 24, *fin.* (p. 189, 14 *seq.*, Usener-Radermacher), and elsewhere. Other eulogies are : Cicero, *Acad. Priora*, ii. 38 ; *Top.*, i. 3 ; *De Oratore*, iii. 19, 71 ; *Ad Atticum*, ii. 1, 1. In what follows the author has borrowed to a certain extent from his necrologue on Jakob Bernays, *Beilage zur Allg. Zeitung*, 1881, Nos. 308 and 309 (*Essays und Erinnerungen*, p. 106 *seqq.*). Aristotle himself as a character in the dialogue : Cicero (*Ad Att.*, xiii. 9, 4) calls this "'Αριστοτέλειον morem."

Page 30 (Bottom). "List of Aristotle's works : " the chief of these is to be found in Diogenes Laertius, v. 1, 22 *seqq.* ; others occur in the third *Vita*, p. 402 *seqq.*, of Westermann's edition, and in two Arabic documents, based on Ptolemæus Chennus, which are dealt with by M. Steinschneider in the Berlin Academy edition (1469 *seqq.*). E. Heitz, in *Die Verlorenen Schriften des Aristoteles*, pp. 7 *seqq.*, has conclusively shown that the main list is to be traced back, not to Andronicus, but to Hermippus, and so to the πίνακες of the Alexandrian library. The contrary had been maintained by Bernays, *Dialoge der Aristoteles*, p. 133, and v. Rose, *Aristoteles Pseudepigraphus*, p. 8.

Page 31 (Top). The "hearer" is mentioned instead of the reader in *Eth. Nic.*, i. 1, 1095 a, 2 ; *Metaph.*, iv. 3, 1005 b, 4. An "address to the audience" is found at the close of the course on logic : *Soph. El.*, c. 33 *fin.*, 184 b, 3 *seqq.*

Page 32 (Bottom). Fate of Aristotle's works : the chief sources are the will of Theophrastus, given by Diogenes Laertius, v. 2, 52 ; Strabo, xiii. 608-9, Cas. ; Plutarch, *Sulla*, c. 26 ; Plotinus, *Life of Porphyrius*, c. 24 (*Plotini Enneades*, Volkmann, i. 33).—On Andronicus of Rhodes (head of Aristotle's school between 78 and 47 B.C.), cf. the Gymnasium. Programm of Fr. Littig, which bears his name as title (Münich, 1890). Usener (in *Göttinger gelehrte Nachrichtungen*, 1892, p. 204) comes to the same conclusion as we have done on the events here in question. Zeller (ii. 2, 138 *seqq.*, ed. 3), who discusses this subject on the whole with extreme thoroughness, seems to minimize their significance unduly.

Sect. 3. Page 34. "On the Territorial Claims of States:" this complete title, τὰ περὶ τῶν (τό)πων δικαιώματα πόλεων, was obtained by myself from Philodemus, *Zeitschrift für österreichische Gymnasia*, 1865, p. 816. In the same passage, *Papyrus Hereul.*, 1015, fol. 70, we also read : καὶ διὰ ταῦτ' ἐφωρᾶ(το) τούς τε νόμου(s) συνάγωνᾶμα τῷ μαθητ(ῇ), where the reference is to Theophrastus. (Middle) "The Delphic inscription:" best treated by Homolle, *Bulletin de Corresp. hellén.*, xxii. 260 *seqq.*; this writer has also drawn the inference relative to the edition of the *Iliad*. (Bottom) "Details of costume :" cf. Bernays, *Die Dialoge des Aristoteles*, p. 12.

Page 35. "History of medicine :" on the Μενώνεια or Ἰατρικὴ συναγωγή, cf. Diels, in his edition of the *Anonymus Londinensis*, p. xvi.

BOOK VI.—CHAPTER IV.

The spuriousness of the *Categories* has been maintained chiefly by Prantl, *Geschichte der Logik*, i. 91, and finally disproved more particularly by Zeller, ii. 2, 67–69 (ed. 3). The δεύτεραι οὐσίαι, which occur in this work alone, are often implied in other writings as intermediate between the πρῶται and the τρίται οὐσίαι. The πρός τί πως ἔχειν, which was supposed to indicate Stoic influences, has been pointed out by Zeller in many other passages. The appendix on the so-called post-predicaments (c. 10 *seqq.*) did not, as we must believe on the authority of Andronicus, form part of the work originally. The lectures on which the work is based must be supposed to have been delivered already at Athens, for the Lyceum is several times used as an illustration (p. 2 a 1, and 11 b 14). For this reason I cannot, with Zeller (*loc. cit.*), set down "many clumsinesses of expression" to the account of a particularly early date of composition. I should prefer to suppose that the lecture-notes were not revised and edited with sufficient care.

Sect. 2. Page 38. "Endless annotations : " cf. Dexippus, *In Categorias*, 5, 7 *seqq.*, ed. Busse ; and Simplicius, *In Categorias*, 1, 1 *seqq.*, ed. Kalbfleisch.—"The only text-book of logic:" cf. Zenker, *Aristotelis Categoriæ Græce cum versione Arabica . . . p.* 13. Athenodorus : cf. Simplicius, i. 1, p. 62, 24 *seqq.*, and Porphyrius, *In Categorias*, p. 59, 6 *seqq.*, ed. Busse. Plotinus : *Enneades*, vi. 1, 23 *seq.* (p. 255, Müller); an incisive criticism is here applied to κεῖσθαι and ἔχειν. Kant : *Werke*, ii. p. 111, ed. Hartenstein. Hegel : *Werke*, xiv. 361. J. S. Mill : *System of Logic*, book i. ch. 3, § 1.

Page 39 (Bottom). There are only two passages in which the number of the categories is given as ten, namely, *Categoriæ*, 4, 1 b, 25 *seqq.*, and *Topica*, i. 9, 103 b, 22 *seqq.* On the "gradations in the completeness of the enumeration" (Bonitz, *Ueber die Kategorien des Aristoteles*, Wiener Sitzungsberichte, 1853, p. 610, A, 3), cf. Brandis, *Griechisch-römische Philosophie*, ii. 2, 1, p. 397, A, 558.—"Lumped together as affections " (πάθη): see the very useful quotations collected by Prantl, *op. cit.*, p. 207, and Apelt, *Beiträge zur Geschichte der Griechischen Philosophie*, p. 140 *seq.*

Page 40 (Top). "Many contradictory answers :" see especially Trendelenburg, *Geschichte der Kategorienlehre* (Historische Beiträge zur Philosophie, Band i.), Bonitz, *loc. cit.*; and Apelt, *Die Kategorienlehre des Aristoteles*, p. 103 *seqq.* Our exposition has most affinity with the views of Bonitz.

Sect. 3. Page 41. "Here too much, there too little :" this was recognized by the Stoics, who, according to Porphyrius (*In Categorias Proœmium*, p. 59, 6 *seqq.*, ed. Busse), condemned the classification, ὡς πολλὰ παριεῖσαν καὶ μὴ περιλαμβάνουσαν ἢ καὶ πάλιν πλεονάζουσαν.

Page 42 (Top). "As a contemporary expresses it :" Apelt, *op. cit.*, p. 160. The confident assertion that "the categories cannot be increased or diminished in number at will" is hardly in accord with the apology on p. 152 : "But we really ought not to lay too much stress on the categories κεῖσθαι and ἔχειν."

BOOK VI.—CHAPTER V.

Sect. 1. Page 44. "The work *On Interpretation :*" Andronicus (as reported by Ammonius, *In Aristotelis de Interpret.*, p. 6, 14 *seqq.*, Busse) marked the Περὶ ἑρμηνείας as spurious. His verdict is impugned (on good grounds, in my opinion) by H. Maier, in *Archiv für die Geschichte der Philosophie*, xiii. 37. The arguments there adduced (p. 51) in support of the genuineness of the work are worth consideration. The objections to which the little book gives an opening may be disposed of by the assumption that what we have before us is only the memoranda of a pupil. (Bottom) Cf. Grote, *Aristotle*, i. 288 : "In his numerous treatises . . . scarcely any allusion is made to the Syllogism ; nor is appeal made to the rules laid down for it in the *Analytica*."

Page 46 (Top). "One of Euclid's axioms :" cf. *Anal. Post.*, i. 10, 76 a, 41 (compared with Euclid's *Opera*, i. 10, ed. Heiberg); it also appears in *Metaph.*, xi. 4, 1061 b, 19. On what follows, cf. *Metaph.*, iv. 3, *in.*, also the remainder of this and the whole of the following chapter. On mathematical definitions, cf. among other passages *Topica*, vi. c. 11, *in.*, and viii. c. 3, 154 b, 24 *seqq.*

Sect. 2. The Sceptics : cf. Sextus Empiricus, *Pyrrhon. Hypotyp.*, ii. 154 *seqq.* = pp. 92, 93, Bekker.

Page 47 (Middle). J. S. Mill : *Logic*, Book ii. ch. 3. In point of fact, Aristotle himself anticipated the objection that the syllogism involves a *petitio principii*. The passages concerned, *Anal. Prior.*, ii. 21, 67 a, 22, and *Anal. Post.*, i. 1, 71 a, 31, were recently pointed out, apparently for the first time, by H. Maier, *Syllogistik des Aristoteles*, ii. 2, pp. 173 *seq.*

Page 49 (Bottom). "Aristotle frankly admits as much :" cf. especially the final chapter of the *Analytica Posteriora*, in particular p. 100 b, 3 : δῆλον δὴ ὅτι ἡμῖν τὰ πρῶτα ἐπαγωγῇ γνωρίζειν ἀναγκαῖον.

Page 50 (Top). "Astronomy, optics . . .": cf. *Anal. Post.*, i. 9, 76 a, 23-25, also 75 b, 16, and 79 a, 18-20. A more exact account of the relation between these subjects and mathematics is given in *Physica*, ii. 2, 194 a, 7 *seqq.* Our "mathematical physics" is there called τὰ φυσικώτερα τῶν μαθημάτων. The complaint mentioned just previously occurs in *Metaph.*, i. 9, 992 a, 32 : ἀλλὰ γέγονε τὰ μαθήματα τοῖς νῦν ἡ φιλοσοφία.

Page 51 (Bottom). "Ill-founded theories of nature . . .:" *Anal. Post.*, ii. 10 (94 a, 3 *seqq.*) and 16, *in.*

Page 52 (Top). "In agreement with Aristotle himself": *Topica*, 11. (Middle) "*Emboîtement* of ideas:" see Dühring, *Kritische Geschichte der Philosophie*, 119, 120.

Page 53 (Middle). "Instructions on the means of deceiving the adversary:" cf. *Topica*, i. 18, 108 a, 26: χρήσιμον δὲ καὶ πρὸς τὸ μὴ παραλογισθῆναι καὶ πρὸς τὸ παραλογίσασθαι. Special artifices of deception are mentioned in vi. 148 a, b: ἐρωτῶντι μὲν ὡς συνωνύμοις χρηστέον . . . αὐτῷ δ' ἀποκρινομένῳ διαιρετέον. The opponent is enticed into a snare by means of agreements previously made: μᾶλλον γὰρ συγχωροῦσιν οὐ προορῶντες τὸ συμβησόμενον, 148 b, 9 ; viii. I, 155 b, 23 : ἢ πρὸς κρύψιν τοῦ συμπεράσματος; also l. 30 : ἀλλ' ἀποστατέον ὅτι ἀνωτάτω, *i.e.* one should begin with the most general possible propositions, as remote as possible from the goal for which one is making, in order to inveigle him into admissions which he would otherwise avoid : διὰ τὸ . . . προορᾶν τὸ συμβησόμενον (ll. 13, 14). The strongest instance is perhaps the recommendation to put forward objections against one's own case because the appearance of fairness wins the opponent's confidence (156 b, 18-20). Here, too, we may place the warning against undue zeal (156 b, 23 *seqq.*), the advice to disturb the natural sequence of the propositions in order to lead the opponent off the track by the distortion (156 a, 23 *seqq.*), the sly *captatio benevolentiæ* in 160 a, 3, and the advice to protract the discussion of 161 a, 9-12. This last device is certainly described as the χειρίστη τῶν ἐνστάσεων; but it is recommended without any reservation in 157 a, 1 : ἔτι τὸ μηκύνειν καὶ παρεμβάλλειν, κ.τ.λ., with the final remark : εἰς μέν οὖν κρύψιν τοῖς εἰρημένοις χρηστέον.—Definition of Surprise: *Topica*, iv. 5, 126 b, 13 *seqq.*

Page 54 (Top). Zest in Self-criticism: vi. 11, 149 a 20: ἢ τοῦτο μὲν γελοῖον τὸ ἐπιτίμημα. On what follows, cf. the warning given at the close of the *Topica* not to enter recklessly into discussion with every chance opponent : καὶ γὰρ οἱ γυμναζόμενοι ἀδυνατοῦσιν ἀπέχεσθαι τοῦ διαλέγεσθαι μὴ ἀγωνιστικῶς. (Middle) "In one place . . . elsewhere:" the two passages are found in v. 5, *fin.*, and viii. 14, *fin.* In this closing section the point of view of training and practice receives preponderant emphasis (ch. 14, *in.*: πρός τε γυμνασίαν καὶ μελέτην, κ.τ.λ.). One might almost say that Aristotle is here a little ashamed of having taught the art of mere contention. The words ἀγωνίζεσθαι, ἀγωνιστικός, etc., are used as terms of censure. It is so several times

In viii. 11, where, too, we find the combination διαλεκτικῶς καὶ μὴ ἐριστικῶς (161 a, 33).

Page 55. "Near the close of the main work on logic : " *Anal. Post.*, ii. 19, 99, 100.

BOOK VI.—CHAPTER VI.

Sect. 1. Page 56. "Thirst for knowledge : " φιλοσοφίας διψῆν, *De Cœlo*, ii. 12, *in.*—"The spectator's pleasures : " *Metaph.*, i. 1.—"Lunar rainbow : " *Meteorol.*, iii. 2, 372 a, 28 ; cf. also i. 6, 343 b, 11, and 30 ; and *De Cœlo*, ii. 12, 292 a, 3 *seqq.*—Operations of the embroiderer : *Meteorol.*, iii. 4, 375 a, 26 *seqq.* ; of the gardener : *De Gen. et Corr.*, ii. 8, 535 a, 13 *seq.*—"Stroke of the oar : " *Meteorol.*, ii. 8, 369 b, 10 *seq.* (Bottom) Cuvier : *Histoire des Sciences Naturelles* (1841, i. 132) ; Darwin : *Life and Letters*, iii. 252.

Page 57. "Yolk-sac of the smooth pike : " the chief passage is *Hist. An.*, vi. 10, 565 b ; it is discussed by Joh. Müller in *Über den glatten Hai des Aristoteles*, Berliner Akad. Abh., 1840, p. 187.—"The cold brain : " cf. Bonitz, *Index Aristot.*, *s.v.* ἐγκέφαλος, No. 5.— "Number of the teeth : " *Hist. An.*, ii. 3, 501 b, 19 *seqq.*—Reference to Herodotus as a "teller of tales " (μυθολόγος) : *Hist. An.*, vi. 31, 569 b, 2 ; and *De Gen. An.*, iii. 5, 756 a, 6.—"Impregnation of the hen-partridge : " *Hist. An.*, v. 5, 541 a, 26 *seqq.* ; cf. 560 a, 6 *seqq.* and b 11 *seqq.;* also *De Gen. An.*, iii. 1, 751 a, 13 *seqq.*—"Ravens turned white," etc. : *Hist. An.*, iii. 12, 519 a, 3 *seqq.* According to the conjecture of Aubert and Wimmer (Translation of the *Historia Animalium*, i. 347, note 77), what misled Aristotle was the occurrence of albino varieties. —"Reddening of a mirror : " *De Insomniis*, 2, 459 b, 27 *seqq.*

Page 58 (Top). "Popular belief, purged of inner contradictions : " this is practically identified with truth in *Eth. Nic.*, vii. 1, 1145 b, 6 *seq.* : ἐὰν γὰρ λύηται τε τὰ δυσχερῆ καὶ καταλείπηται τὰ ἔνδοξα, δεδειγμένον ἂν εἴη ἱκανῶς.

Page 59 (Top). "Process of generation among bees : " *De Gen. An.*, iii. 10, 760 b, 27 *seqq.*—"The eye of experience : " *Eth. Nic.*, vi. 2, 1143 b, 13 *seq.*—"The Eleatic doctrine . . . borders on insanity : " *De Gen. et Corr.*, i. 8, 325 a, 17 *seqq.* On what follows, cf. again *De Gen. et Corr.*, i. 8, 324, 325.

Page 60 (Top). "Expressions of humility : " *De Cœlo*, ii. 12, 292 a, 15 *seq.* ; ii. 5, 287, 288, where the concluding words, νῦν δὲ τὸ φαινόμενον ῥητέον, may be compared with : πειρατέον λέγειν τὸ φαινόμενον, *ib.*, 12, 291 b, 25 *seqq.*—"Stricter methods and more cogent proofs : " this seems a fair translation of ἀκριβεστέραις ἀνάγκαις, 287 b, 34. (Bottom) "Hypothesis of empty space : " *Phys.*, iv. 8, 216 a, 13 *seqq.*, particularly l. 20 *seq.* : ἰσοταχῆ ἄρα πάντ' ἔσται· ἀλλ' ἀδύνατον, and l. 27 : φανείη ἂν τὸ λεγόμενον κενὸν ὡς ἀληθῶς κενόν.

Page 61 (Top). Against the breathing of aquatic animals : *De Respir.*, 2, 470.

BOOK VI.—CHAPTER VII.

Page 63 (Top).   " Random hypotheses : " *Metaph.*, xiv. 3, 1090 b, 29.

Sect 2.   "Trinity of elements : " *De Cœlo*, i. 2; air and water are admitted in addition, ii. 3.   (Bottom) Construction of the four fundamental substances : *De Gen. et Corr.*, ii. 1, *fin.*—ii. 3, *in.*

Page 64 (Top).   The Empedoclean doctrine of chemical proportions is casually referred to in *De Anima*, i. 4, 408 a, 14 *seqq.*, and 410 a, 1 *seqq.*   Page 64 (Middle).   The doctrine of "displacement" is attacked in *De Cœlo*, i. 8, 277 b *seqq.*   (Bottom) Schopenhauer : *Werke*, iii. 334.

Page 64 (Bottom).   The contradiction here emphasized appears most clearly in *Physica*, viii. 4—a discussion, the close of which (256 a, 1) leaves us free to choose between two causes of the natural motions.   We have either to assume an entity which has endowed the substances with these tendencies to movement, or to find the cause in the agent which, let us say, has removed the support from beneath the downward-tending stone.   A singular choice, assuredly !   In another passage, it is true, not only are these tendencies of the elements reckoned, as here (254, 255), among natural forces, but it is also said of natural objects that they carry in themselves the origin of rest and motion : *Physica*, ii. 1, 192 b, 13.   But this is clearly only a mode of laying stress on their difference from the products of art, and does not rule out the possibility of tracing back still further the origin of motion (ἀρχὴ κινήσεως καὶ στάσεως).   The exclusively passive character of inanimate matter is expressly emphasized in the passage first quoted (255 b, 31 : οὐ τοῦ κινεῖν . . . ἀλλὰ τοῦ πάσχειν).

Page 65 (Bottom).   "Circulation of matter : " *De Gen. et Corr.*, ii. 10, 336 a, 1.—Reference to motion in the circle of the ecliptic : 337 a, 32 *seqq.*

Sect. 4.   Page 66.   Repudiation of the earlier attempts : *De Gen. et Corr.*, i. 2, especially 317 a, 20 *seqq.*

BOOK VI.—CHAPTER VIII.

Page 69.   Title : these principles are called συλλογιστικαὶ ἀρχαί in *Metaph.*, iv. 3, 1005 b, 7 ; ἀποδεικτικαὶ ἀρχαί in iii. 2, 996 b, 26.   Axioms of the mathematicians : *Metaph.*, iv. 3, *in.*—"Some of the nature-philosophers : " *ibid.*, 1005 a, 31.—Formulation of the principle of contradiction : *ibid.*, 1005 b, 19 *seqq.* ; the same more narrowly conceived in *Metaph.*, iii. 2, 996 b, 29 (καὶ ἀδύνατον ἅμα εἶναι καὶ μὴ εἶναι).   See also iv. 7, 1011 b, 13 : βεβαιοτάτη δόξα πασῶν τὸ μὴ εἶναι ἀληθεῖς ἅμα τὰς ἀντικειμένας φάσεις.—Against and concerning Heraclitus : *Metaph.*, iv. 3, 1005 b, 24 *seqq.*   On what follows : *Metaph.*, i. 6, 987 a, 33 ; also iv. 5, 1009 a, 22.

Page 70 (end of 1st par.). Comparison with the boy : *ibid.*, 1009 b-
1010 a.—Principle of the " Excluded Middle : " *Metaph.*, iii. 2, 996 b, 29 :
πᾶν ἀναγκαῖον ἢ φάναι ἢ ἀποφάναι. So again iv. 7, *in.* Cf. also *Greek
Thinkers*, Vol. II. p. 195.

Page 71 (Middle). " It has been objected : " my allusion is to
Mill, *Logic*, Book ii. § 5 of the last chapter.

Page 72 (Top). " Sharply distinguishing the different kinds of
opposition : " cf. Bonitz in his *Index*, *s.vv.* Ἀντικεῖσθαι and Ἐναντίος.
(Below) Sir William Hamilton : see Mill, *loc. cit.* (Bottom) Aristotle
on rest and motion : in the important passage, *Physica*, iv. 12, 221 b,
12 *seqq.* : οὐ γὰρ πᾶν τὸ ἀκίνητον ἠρεμεῖ, ἀλλὰ τὸ ἐστερημένον κινήσεως πέφυκὸς
δὲ κινεῖσθαι. Thus the disjunction, " A is either at rest or in motion,"
is not applicable where rest and motion are not states accessible to
the subject of discourse. Cf. also *Physica*, iii. 4, *in.*, and Prantl's
apposite comment, *Aristoteles acht Bücher Physik, griechisch una
deutsch*, p. 489.—In sharpness of distinction between contradictory and
contrary opposition, Mill (*loc. cit.*) is surpassed by Aristotle. Cf. also
De Part. An., ii. 2, 649 a, 18 : τό ψυχρὸν φύσις τις ἀλλ' οὐ στέρησίς ἐστιν.

Sect. 2. On what follows, cf. *Metaph.*, iv. 4. I have made Aristotle
speak of a " block " instead of a plant (ὅμοιος γὰρ φυτῷ ὁ τοιοῦτος, *ibid.*,
1006 a, 14). On what follows next, cf. *ibid.*, 1006 a, 5 : ἀξιοῦσι δὴ καὶ
τοῦτο ἀποδεικνύναι τινὲς δι' ἀπαιδευσίαν.

Page 74 (Bottom). Presence and absence of phenomena : cf.
Greek Thinkers, Vol. III. pp. 170, 171.

Sect. 3. Page 75. Aristotle on induction as the source of our
knowledge of axioms : *Anal. Post.*, ii. 19, 100 b, 3 : δῆλον δὴ ὅτι ἡμῖν τὰ
πρῶτα ἐπαγωγῇ γνωρίζειν ἀναγκαῖον. The part played by νοῦς is explained
in the same context. On Aristotelian induction compare the collection
of passages in Zeller, ii. 2 (ed. 3), p. 241, note 3. Here we find repelled with full justice the critical assault of Trendelenburg and
Brandis, who would not allow Aristotle to say that " all undemon-
strated knowledge rests on induction."—George Grote : *Aristotle*,
ii. 288 *seqq.*—" Universally accepted beliefs : " τὰ ἔνδοξα ; cf. *Topica*,
i. 1. On this see Zeller, ii. 2 (ed. 3), p. 242 *seqq.*

Page 76 (Top). The chief passage on the Principle of Identity :
Metaph., iv. 7, *in.* Cf. also ix. 10, 1051 b, 3 : ὁ τὸ διῃρημένον οἰόμενος
διῃρῆσθαι καὶ συγκείμενον συγκεῖσθαι.—On the Principle of Identity, cf.
Ueberweg, *System der Logik*, p. 185 (ed. 3), and Grote, *Minor Works*,
p. 359 *seq.*

BOOK VI.—CHAPTER IX.

Page 77. The contradictions in the treatment of the problem
of substance are fully treated by W. Freytag, *Die Entwicklung der
griechischen Erkenntnistheorie bis Aristoteles*, Halle, 1905, pp. 82 *seqq.*
—The quotation, " As by an irresistible fate," etc., is from p. 96 of that
work.

Page 79 (par. 2). Four main arguments against the doctrine of Ideas : *Metaph.*, i. 9.

Page 81 (Bottom). " A highly noteworthy passage : " *Metaph.*, xiii. 3, 1077 b, 25 *seqq.*

Page 83 (par. 2). " Hierarchy of the sciences : " cf. *Greek Thinkers*, Vol. III. p. 334. To the passages there mentioned should be added *Metaph.*, xiii. 3, 1078 a, 9.—D'Alembert : in the *Discours préliminaire de l'Encyclopédie*, Œuvres de d'Alembert, Paris, 1853, p. 88 ; cf. also p. 81.

Page 84 (Top). " Such passages as that which follows : " *Metaph.*, vii. 1, 1028 b, 2 *seqq.* The quotation a little further on is from Freytag, *op. cit.*, p. 83. The conjecture referred to was put forward by Freytag, *loc. cit.*, p. 85.

Page 85 (Top). The concept . . . the form-giving principle : according to *Metaph.*, vii. 2, *fin.* On ·the relativity of the ideas form and matter, cf. the passages quoted by Zeller, ii. 2 (ed. 3), p. 210, note 1 ; and p. 325, notes 2, 3, 4.

Page 86 (Middle). " Aristotle himself informs us : " *Metaph.*, ix. 6, 1048 a, b. " A rising scale is thus constituted : " cf. *De Gen. An.*, ii. 1, 735 a, 9. On the first entelechy, cf. *De An.*, ii. 1, 412 a, 27. On what follows see Bonitz' *Index*, *s.v.* 'Εντελέχεια.

Page 87 (Bottom). Bonitz complains of Aristotle's " mira levitas " and " nimia levitas " in his commentary on the *Metaphysica*, p. 395, note 1, and p. 569, note 1.

Page 89 (Middle). " Form and active force " (μορφὴ καὶ ἐνέργεια) *Metaph.*, viii. 2, *fin.* (Bottom) " In one passage of the *Metaphysics* : " i. 3, 983 a, 28.

Page 90 (par. 2). " Why is fire hot ? " *Metaph.*, i. 1, 981 b, 11.

Page 91 (Middle). " Contributions of Plato and Heraclitus : " cf. *Greek Thinkers*, Vol. I. p. 71 and *Republic*, viii. 563 E. To this connexion also belongs the saying : αἱ ἐπ' ἄκρον εὐεξίαι σφαλεραί in Hippocrates' *Aphorisms*, i. 3 (iv. 458, Littré). (Bottom) " Chief passage of the *Physics* : " i. 5, 188, 189, also 6 and 7.

Sect. 6. Page 92. " Other expositors : " these include Zeller, ii. 2 (ed. 3), 315 *seq.*, and 348 *seq.*

Page 93 (Top). " The typical Aristotelian instance : " see *De Gen. et Corr.*, i. 4, 319 b, 25.

BOOK VI.—CHAPTER X.

Page 95 (Middle). " A drop of luck," etc. (θέλω τύχης σταλαγμὸν ἢ φρένῶν πίθον) : Meineke, *Com. Græc. Fragm.*, iv. 347. The other line mentioned : *ibid.*, 340.

Sect. 2. Page 96. The chief passage on Accident is *Metaph.*, v. 2, 1014 a, 4 *seqq.* See, in addition, *Physica*, ii. 1, 192 b, 25. Reference may also be made to 196 b, 28, and *Poetica*, 1451 a, 18 (the second relating to events, the first to qualities).

Sect. 3. Page 97. Cf. *Physica*, ii. 4-6, with Torstrik's Commentary in Hermes, ix. 425 *seqq.*—Denial of absolute chance: *loc. cit.*, 197 a, 13 : καὶ ἔστιν αἴτιον ὡς συμβεβηκὸς ἡ τύχη, ὡς δ' ἁπλῶς οὐδενός. By the side of this, even such a passage as *Rhet.*, i. 10, 1369 a, b, proves nothing to the contrary. I might, indeed, have expressed myself much more decidedly, as is clear from *Metaph.*, v. 30. There is, in truth, no shadow of a reason for the common assumption that Aristotle reserved a separate sphere for the reign of chance. See *De Interpret.*, c. 9 ; and *Metaph.*, vi. 2, 1026, 1027. Even Wundt, *Logik*, i. (ed. 3), p. 575 *seq.*, fails here to take a sufficiently comprehensive view. The two passages of the *Metaphysics* just quoted do not prove what he supposes them to prove.

Page 98. " Work *On the Art :*" cf. the author's book, *Apologie der Heilkunst*, ed. 2, p. 49, § 6, *fin.*

Page 99 (Middle). Winter cold in midsummer: *Metaph.*, xi. 8, 1064, 1065.

Pages 99, 100. The universe the product of chance ? See *Metaph.*, i. 3, 984 b, 14.

Page 101 (Middle). J. S. Mill : *Logic*, book iii. ch. 5, supplementary note ; also *Dissertations and Discussions*, iv. 197. Grote writes similarly : *Aristotle*, i. 296. (Below) The passage of the *Nicomachean Ethics*, i. 10, 1099 b, 24.

Page 101 (Middle). The " decision to be extracted from concepts :" *Physica*, ii. 6, *fin.*

Page 102 (Middle). " Notion of tendency : " cf. Bonitz, *Index*, *s.v.* βούλεσθαι, 140 b, 38 *seqq.* Also the author's *Beiträge zur Kritik* . . ., viii. 16.—" Conflict of movement impulses," and of volitions as well : *De Cælo*, ii. 13, 295 b, 30 ; *Topica*, vi. 6, 145 b, 16.

Page 103 (Top). " Paleness of a woman :" *Anal. Prior.*, ii. 27, 70 a, 36.

Page 104 (Top). "Habit a second nature:" this is what he practically says in *Rhet.*, i. 11, 1370 a, 7 : ὅμοιον γάρ τι τὸ ἔθος τῇ φύσει.— Probability in the *Poetics :* ch. 8, 1451 a, 27 ; ch. 9, *in.*, 1451 b, 9 and 12 ; ch. 10, 1452 a, 18 *seqq.* ; ch. 15, 1454 a, 33 *seqq.*

Page 105 (Top). The view which reduces chance to the limitations of our knowledge is certainly not upheld in the *Eudemian Ethics*, vii. 14, 1247 b, 4 *seqq.* But it is permissible to lay the responsibility for this on Eudemus rather than on Aristotle, the more so as the preceding chapter clearly betrays the hand of the historian of geometry ; cf. the remarks on the character and life of the geometer Hippocrates : *ibid.*, 1247 a, 17.

Sect. 6. Page 106. Cf. *De Interpret.*, c. 9. Sentences such as ἀλλὰ πάντα εἶναι καὶ γίγνεσθαι ἐξ ἀνάγκης (18 b, 30) and οὐδὲν ἄρα . . . ἀπὸ τύχης ἔσται (18 b, 14-16) should not be interpreted—which would be a *reductio ad absurdum*—as attacks by Aristotle on universal causality. To avoid such misunderstandings, cf. *Metaph.*, xi. 8, 1065 a,

8 : ἔσται γὰρ ἅπαντ' ἐξ ἀνάγκης, on the supposition, that is, that there exist causes and principles for the accidental (τοῦ κατὰ συμβεβηκὸς ὄντος) of the same nature as for the self-existent (τοῦ καθ' αὑτὸ ὄντος). There is here no denial of causality and no limitation of the sphere within which it works. These sentences throw a good light on the often misunderstood passage of the *De Interpretatione.* In both cases the chance which is spoken of is chance in the strictly correct and admissible sense, the overlapping of distinct fields of causation, or, as Aristotle would have preferred to say, of concepts. To take an example : General N. has a mole. For the individual N. this may be an inheritance from parents or remoter ancestors. For the general, *as such,* it is a mere accident, a συμβεβηκός. He who fails to see this assumes causal connexion where it does not exist ; he wrongly denies chance and explains everything as the result of necessity.

BOOK VI.—CHAPTER XI.

Page 110 (Top). Cf. *Metaph.*, xi. 10, 1075 b, 13 : καὶ διὰ τί τὰ μὲν φθαρτὰ τὰ δ' ἄφθαρτα, οὐθεὶς λέγει· πάντα γὰρ τὰ ὄντα ποιοῦσιν ἐκ τῶν αὐτῶν ἀρχῶν. Cf. also *Metaph.*, iii. 4, 1000 a, 6 *seqq.*—" Ether in the highest heavenly regions :" *De Cœlo*, i. 3, 270 b, 7. (Middle) "The Milky Way :" *Meteorol.*, i. 8. " Comets :" *ibid.*, i. 6 and 7. Seneca : *Natural. Quæst.*, vii. c. 22 *seqq.* (ii. 310 *seqq.* ; Haase). The most noteworthy passage is c. 25, § 3 : "Quid ergo miramur cometas, tam rarum mundi spectaculum, nondum teneri legibus certis . . . *veniet tempus quo posteri nostri tam aperta nos nescisse mirentur.*"

Page 111 (Middle). Objection against the main principle of the Atomists : *De Gen. et Corr.*, i. 8, 326 a, 28 *seq.* On what follows, cf. *ibid.*, 327 a, 21 *seqq.*

Page 112 (Middle). " Mingling and mixture :" *De Gen. et Corr.*, i. 10. (Bottom) Lynceus : *ibid.*, 328 a, 14.

Page 113 (Top). "A drop of wine in 20,000 quarts of water :" *ibid.*, 328 a, 27. (Bottom) "An animal 10,000 stadia long :" *Poetica*, c. 18, 1451 a, 2.

Page 114 (Top). "A ship a span long :" *Politica*, vii. 4, 1326 a, 40. The calculation depends on the assumption that the χοῦς of 12 κοτύλαι contains 90 ounces. A drop is taken as 0·05 of a cubic centimetre. The statements on the detectability of small quantities of sodium vapour and silver iodide are made on the authority of my brother-in-law, the late Professor Hans Jahn.

Sect. 4. Page 115. The four causes : *Physica*, ii. 3 ; *Metaph.*, i. 3, *in.* Their grouping : *Physica*, ii. 7 ; *De Anima*, ii. 4 ; *De Gen. An.*, i. 1 ; *Metaph.*, xii. 4.—The example of bodily exercise : *Physica*, ii. 3, 195 a, 8.—" Pure passivity of matter :" *De Gen. et Corr.*, i. 7, 324 b, 5 : ὅσα δ' ἐν ὕλῃ, παθητικά. Also *ibid.*, 18 : ἡ δ' ὕλη ᾗ ὕλη παθητικόν. Again,

ii. 9, 335 b, 29 : τῆς . . . ὕλης τὸ πάσχειν ἐστὶ καὶ τὸ κινεῖσθαι.—" Dysteleology : " the main passage is *De Gen. An.*, iv. 10, 778 a, 4 : βούλεται μὲν οὖν ἡ φύσις . . . οὐκ ἀκριβοῖ δὲ διά τε τὴν τῆς ὕλης ἀοριστίαν, κ.τ.λ.—" Sexual characters : " treated with almost grotesque inconsistency in *Metaph.*, vii. 5 and x. 9, *in.*—Manifestations of "the old Hellenic spirit : " in combinations like ὁ θεὸς καὶ ἡ φύσις, or *Eth. Nic.*, vii. 14 : πάντα γὰρ φύσει ἔχει τι θεῖον. *Physica*, i. 9, 192 a, 16 : ὄντος γάρ τινος θείου καὶ ἀγαθοῦ καὶ ἐφετοῦ . . . τὸ δὲ (φαμὲν εἶναι) ὃ πέφυκεν ἐφίεσθαι καὶ ὀρέγεσθαι αὐτοῦ κατὰ τὴν ἑαυτοῦ φύσιν. *De Gen. An.*, iii. 11, 772 a, 21 : ὥστε τρόπον τινὰ πάντα ψυχῆς εἶναι πλήρη. Again, iv. 10, 778 a, 2 ; βίος γάρ τις καὶ πνεύματός ἐστι, κ.τ.λ. (Middle) "The Unmoved Mover : " see later, pp. 233 *seqq.*

Page 116 (Bottom). Change of place a condition of other changes : cf. *De Gen. et Corr.*, ii. 10, 336 a, 16 *seqq.*, and i. 6, 322 b, 22 *seqq.*

Page 117 (Top). "Actuality of the potential : " cf. *Physica*, iii. 1, 201 b, 4 *seq.*—"Incomplete reality : " *Physica*, iii. 2, 201 b, 31 *seq.* —" An eminent contemporary : " Dühring, *Kritische Geschichte der Philosophie*, p. 126. (Bottom) "Definition of time : " *Physica*, iv. 11, 219 b, 1 *seq.*, supplemented by 220 a, 25 *seq.*—" Misunderstandings : " *e.g.* on the part of Dühring, p. 128, who makes Aristotle confuse " the accidental means of measurement with the properties of the measured object,"—a confusion against which Aristotle, *loc. cit.*, 219 b, 6-9, expressly guarded. Prantl's translation is open to objection, nor does Zeller's version, ii. 2 (ed. 3), p. 399, give me complete satisfaction.

Page 118 (Top). "For even when it is dark . . . : " *Physica*, iv. 11, 219 a, 4 *seqq.*—" Earlier and later : " used in the spatial sense, *ibid.*, 219 a, 14 *seqq.* (Bottom) "Fore-gleam of the Critical philosophy : " *Physica*, iv. 14, 223 a, 21 *seqq.* ; and *De Anima*, iii. 8, 431 b, 28.

Page 119 (Top). The argument for the infinity of time : *Physica*, viii. 1, 251 b, 20 ; and *Metaph.*, xii. 6, 1071 b, 7 *seqq.* (Bottom) " The three dimensions : " *De Cælo*, i. 1. Arguments against empty space : *Physica*, iv. 6 *seqq.*, especially 8, 214 b, 13 *seqq.*

Page 120 (Top). Possibility of making way : *ibid.*, 7, 204 a, 29 *seqq.* (Middle) " A wonderfully pregnant little sentence : " *Physica*, iii. 7, 207 b, 14 : οὐδὲ μένει ἡ ἀπειρία ἀλλὰ γίνεται. The discussion of infinity : *Physica*, iii. 6 *seqq.*

Page 121 (Top). Cf. *De Gen. et Corr.*, i. 2, 316 b, 30 : εἴη ἂν ἄπειρος ἡ θρύψις (similarly Plato, *Parmen.*, 165 B : θρύπτεσθαι . . . κερματιζόμενον ἀνάγκη πᾶν τὸ ὅλον), and above, 25 : καὶ εἰς ἀσώματον ἐφθαρμένον τὸ σῶμα. (Bottom) Opposition of thought and fact : *ibid.*, 208 a, 16-19. Before this comes an excellent reply to Anaximander's argument (given by pseudo-Plutarch, *Placita*, i. 3). This argument was to the effect that infinity is necessary in order that material may not fail for new formations (ἵνα ἡ γένεσις μὴ ἐπιλείπῃ). To this Aristotle answers : ἐνδέχεται γὰρ τὴν θατέρου φθορὰν θατέρου εἶναι γένεσιν. This is the third of the five arguments for the hypothesis of an actual infinite. Cf. on these, *Physica*, iii. 4, 203 b, 15 *seqq.* (1) From the infinity of time. (2) From the infinite divisibility of spatial magnitudes. (4) Every boundary meets yet another. (5, and chief) From the absence of a halting-place for thought, we may conclude a similar absence in the world of realities. Now, Aristotle admits the infinity of time, but only as a growing, not a completed magnitude. He deals similarly with the infinite divisibility of the corporal. The fourth and most difficult argument is treated—shall we say, just because of its difficulty?—at the shortest length, by the distinction between touching (ἅπτεσθαι), and being bounded (πεπεράνθαι). The first, he says, is a relative, the second an absolute notion. The unimaginability of a spatially bounded universe does not prevent Aristotle from accepting the hypothesis of such a universe. Objection 5 is answered in the passage first quoted in this note.

Page 122 (Top). "Eminent thinkers of our own time:" I allude to Wilhelm Wundt and his essay, *Das Kosmologische Problem* (Vierteljahrschrift f. wiss. Philos., i. pp. 80 *seqq.*). He says (p. 104, quoted by Remigius Stölzle, *Die Lehre vom Unendlichen bei Aristoteles*, p. 54) that "the hypothesis of a universe infinite in space and matter leads to insoluble contradictions."—" The great majority of the old nature-philosophers:" οἱ πλεῖστοι τῶν ἀρχαίων φιλοσόφων, *De Cœlo*, i. 5, *in.* (Bottom) "The visible sphere of the heavens ...:" cf. *De Cœlo*, i. 5 *seqq.*

Sect. 9. Page 123. "The one, only, and perfect heaven :" *De Cœlo*, i. 9, *in.*, and 279 a, 10 *seq.* (Middle) This objection and its answer in *De Cœlo*, i. 9. (Bottom) On the eternity of the heavens : *ibid.*, ch. 3, especially 270 b, 13 *seqq.*, and ch. 10.

Page 124 (Bottom). "Egyptians and Babylonians :" cf. *De Cœlo*, ii. 12, 292 a, 7–9.

Sect. 10. Page 125. See Zeller's fine treatise *Die Lehre des Aristoteles von der Ewigkeit der Welt* (Vorträge und Abhandlungen, iii. Sammlung), pp. 10 *seqq.* On the cyclic theories : *De Cœlo*, i. 10, 28 a, 11 *seqq.*; also *Physica*, viii. 1, 252 a, 5 *seqq.*

Page 126 (Top). The eternity of the human race is tacitly assumed ; the possibility of men having been produced by the earth (γηγενεῖς) is only assumed as an hypothesis or as the teaching of others : *De Gen. An.*, iii. 11, 762 b, 29 ; and *Politica*, ii. 8, 1269 a, 5 : τοὺς πρώτους εἴτε γηγενεῖς ἦσαν εἴτ' ἐκ φθορᾶς τινὸς ἐσώθησαν. To such φθοραί Aristotle alludes in *De Cœlo*, i. 3, 270 b, 19 ; *Meteorol.*, i. 3, 389 b, 27 ; *Metaph.*, xii. 8, 1074 a, 38 *seqq.*, and *Fragm.*, 2.

Sect. 11. Page 127. The Aristotelian geology is found chiefly in *Meteorol.*, i. 13 and 14. We gather, by the way, from ch. 13 that the geography of Europe was still very imperfectly known to Aristotle. The Black Forest, the Alps, and the Pyrenees are for him a single mountain range, from which both the Danube and the Guadalquivir take their rise.—Argument for the changelessness of the Kosmos : *De Gen. et Corr.*, ii. 10, 336 a, 27.

Page 128 (Top). "An astonishingly pretentious opening remark :" *Meteorol., loc. cit.*, 349 a, 15 *seq.*: οὐθὲν . . . ὃ μὴ κἂν ὁ τυχὼν εἴπειεν. He is scornful in what follows : τῶν σοφῶς βουλομένων λέγειν τινὲς καὶ τὸ κόμψευμα ἂν εἴη τοῦτο ψεῦδος. Cf. *ibid.*, ii. 4, especially 360 a, 19 *seqq.*; and for Aristotle's own theory of the winds, 361 a, 30 *seqq.* (Bottom) "Dry exhalation :" cf. *Meteorol.*, ii. 4, 360 a, 8 *seqq.* ; also iii. 6, 378 a, 21 *seqq.*—Against atmospheric precipitation as the origin of springs : *Meteorol.*, i. 13, 340 a, b.—On the saltness of the sea : *Meteorol.*, ii. 3. On this cf. the fragment, probably of Theophrastus in the *Hibeh Papyri* (ed. Grenfell), p. 62, in which there lies embedded a fragment of Democritus, vol. i. p. 368 in Diels' *Fragmente der Vorsokratiker* (ed. 2).

BOOK VI.—CHAPTER XII.

Page 130 *seqq.* In the writing of this section two books have rendered me most important service : G. Pouchet, *La Biologie Aristo-télique*, Paris, 1885 ; and J. B. Meyer, *Aristoteles' Tierkunde*, Berlin, 1855. Very useful also were the introductions and annotations in Aubert and Wimmer's editions, with German translations, of Aristotle's Περὶ ζῴων γενέσεως (Liepzig, 1860) and Περὶ ζῴων ἱστορίαι (2 vols., Leipzig, 1868). I may say the same of the similar edition of Aristotle's Περὶ ζῴων μορίων by Frantzius (Leipzig, 1853). Nor should G. H. Lewes' *Aristotle, a Chapter from the History of Science*, go unmentioned, though this brilliantly written book of the many-sided *littérateur*, with its alternations between eulogy and pasquinade, rather presents us with a dazzling show-piece than affords trustworthy guidance. Lastly, I owe specially grateful acknowledgments to a contemporary, the late Professor Rudolf Burckhardt of Basle, who greatly added to my familiarity with this branch of research, not only by the important works which he and his pupil Bloch produced, but also by many private communications. The Περὶ ζῴων κινήσεως is not of assured genuineness ; the Περὶ πνεύματος is certainly spurious.

A genuine writing *On Plants* was displaced by the great work of Theophrastus, and was thus early lost. See the discussion in Zeller, ii. 2 (ed. 3), p. 98.

Page 131 (par. 2). Aristotle on the grounds of his preference for the organic world : *De Part. An.*, i. 5, *in.*

Page 132 (Top). The colours of eyes : *De Gen. An.*, v. 1, 778 a, 30 *seqq.*—"A noteworthy passage of the *Physica*," ii. 8, 199 a, 12. This chapter is also freely utilized in what follows. (Middle) "Nature does nothing in vain :" ἡ φύσις οὐθὲν ποιεῖ μάτην, *De Incessu Animal*, 2, 704 b, 15.—"His mind travels in the grooves cut by Plato :" cf. *e.g.* *Tim.*, 42 E : κατὰ δύναμιν ὅτι κάλλιστα καὶ ἄριστα with *De Incessu Animal.* (*loc. cit.*): ἀεὶ ἐκ τῶν ἐνδεχομένων . . . τὸ ἄριστον.

Page 133 (Top). "A passage on this subject in the *Phyisca* :" in book ii. ch. 8, quoted above. On what follows, cf. Aristotle, *Fragm.*, 12–14 (from the dialogue Περὶ φιλοσοφίας), 1475, 1476. The following matter again rests on *Physica*, ii. 8.

Page 134 (Middle). "Zeus does not send rain," etc. : *Physica*, ii. 8, 198 b, 18 *seqq.* (Below) "A passage full of meaning:" *De Gen. An.*, v. 8, 789 b, 2 *seqq.* The same passage is also the basis of what follows. In addition, see *Physica*, ii. 8, *in.*, once more, and ii. 7, *fin.* Other passages are : *De Part. An.*, iv. 2, 677 a, 17–19 : οὐ μὴν διὰ τοῦτο δεῖ ζητεῖν πάντα ἕνεκα τίνος, ἀλλὰ τινῶν ὄντων τοιούτων, ἕτερα ἐξ ἀνάγκης συμβαίνει διὰ ταῦτα πολλά.

Page 135 (Middle). The number of the sutures : this is treated of in *De Part. An.*, ii. 7, 653 a, 27, b, 8 ; cf. Frantzius, note 37, p. 276 : "With regard to the sutures of the skull, there is no such diversity in mammalia as Aristotle assumes. . . . On the other hand, in the lower vertebrates, the number of skull-bones, and therefore . . . of sutures, is considerably greater. . . . Just as little is there any difference in this respect between men and women." See also Lewes, p. 306.

Sect. 3. Phenomena, causes, development : *De Part. An.*, i. 3, 640 a, 14 *seq.*—"A chorus of enthusiastic voices :" see the collection given by Lewes, pp. 154, 155 ; also Charles Darwin, *Life and Letters*, iii. 252. On what follows, cf. Lewes, pp. 156, 323 *seqq.*, 325, 326 ; the quotation is from p. 158.

Page 136 (Bottom). On brain, heart, and lungs, see the passages referred to in the *Index Aristot.*, *s.vv.* ἐγκέφαλος, 213 b, 40, καρδία, 365 b, 34, and ἀναπνοή, 52 a, 10.—"The hypothesis of spontaneous generation :" on this see Aubert and Wimmer, p. 40, note 5 ; "Aristotle ascribes spontaneous generation to a part of the insects and to all testaceous animals." The main passage is *De Gen. An.*, iii. 11, 762 a, 8 *seqq.*

Sect. 4. Page 137. "An opinion formerly widespread :" cf. Zeller, ii. 2 (ed. 3, 1879), p. 513. (Bottom) Syennesis, Polybus, Diogenes : *Hist. An.*, ii. 2, 511 b, 23, and 3, 512 b, 12. Leophanes (called Cleophanes by the pseudo-Plutarch, *Placita*, v. 7) : *De Gen. An.*, iv. 1, 765 a, 25. That the last-named is the author of the pseudo-Hippocratic treatise on superfetation was conjectured, with high probability, by Littré (*Œuvres d Hippocrate*, i. 380, 381).

Page 138 (Top). "Practical specialists :" the relevant passages have been collected and illustrated by Brandis, ii. 2, 1303. The biological teachings of Democritus are discussed in numerous passages, to which references are given in the *Index Aristot.*, *s.v.* Δημόκριτος, 176 a, 21 *seqq.* The monograph on the chameleon, ascribed to him by Pliny (*Hist. Nat.*, 28, p. 112), is rejected, probably with justice, by A. Gellius (*Noctes Atticæ*, x. 12), on the ground of the marvels in it. (Middle) "Herodorus of Heraclea :" probably identical with the Herodorus mentioned in two passages of the *Hist. An.*, as father of the sophist Bryson, *De Gen. An.*, iii. 6, 757 a, 4. (Below) "The time of Herodotus:" cf. Herodotus, iii. 106. On zoological gardens in Egypt, see the notices in Beloch, *Gr. Gesch.*, iii. 1, 484; and also an inscription from Panopolis, *Revue des Études Grecques*, iv. 53. On the exhibition of rare beasts at Athens, cf. Antiphon (*Fragm.*, 57–59, Blass) quoted by Athenæus, ix. 397 c, d. " Menageries:" cf. Isocrates, *Orat.*, xv. (Περὶ ἀντιδόσεως), § 213. On Alexander's reported subsidies, cf. Zeller, ii. 2 (ed. 3), p. 32. The chronological objection is not raised there.

Page 139 (Top). On the number of animal species, cf. J. B. Meyer, p. 144 (on the authority of Bronn) ; Pouchet (p. 121) admits only about 400 species.—" A middle thing between plant and animal :" it is thus that Aristotle speaks of the ὀστρακόδερμα in *De Gen. An.*, i., *fin.* 731 b, 8 *seq.*

Sect. 5. Aristotle's slight knowledge of the human inward parts is confessed by himself in *Hist. An.*, i. 16, 494 b, 21 *seqq.* Cf. Aubert and Wimmer, Introduction to Περὶ ζῴων γενέσεως, p. 4, and Frantzius on *De Part. An.*, p. 276, note 37, and 297 *seq.*, notes 57 and 62.—" Anatomical diagrams :" the seven books of the Ἀνατομαί were furnished with illustrations, probably schematic. Cf. *De Respir.*, 16, 478 a, b : πρὸς μὲν τὴν ὄψιν ἐκ τῶν ἀνατομῶν δεῖ θεωρεῖν, πρὸς δ' ἀκρίβειαν ἐκ τῶν ἱστοριῶν. (Bottom) The arm of the cuttle-fish : *De Gen. An.*, i. 15, 720 b, 32 *seqq.* ; cf. Pouchet, p. 129.

Page 140 (Top). Frequent dissection of the human fœtus : *De Gen. An.*, iv. 1, 764 a, 34 and 765 a, 17. In the former passage note the express declaration: καὶ τοῦθ' ἱκανῶς τεθεωρήκαμεν, κ.τ.λ. (Middle) Artificial emaciation and strangling of animals : these practices are attested by *Hist. An.*, iii. 3, 513 a, 12 *seqq.* The word προλεπτύνω also occurs in *De Gen. An.*, i. 18, 726 a, 1 : the herdsmen are said to make the he-goats thin before the mating season, because the fat ones are less inclined to do their part. See also *De Part. An.*, iii. 5, 668 a, 21 : γίνεται κατάδηλον ἐν τοῖς μάλιστα καταλελεπτυσμένοις, where there is no reference to the intentional production of thinness for the purpose of investigation. (Bottom) " Childish reluctance:" διὸ δεῖ μὴ δυσχεραίνειν παιδικῶς τὴν περὶ τὴν ἀτιμοτέρων ζῴων ἐπίσκεψιν (*De Part. An.*, i. 5, 645 a, 15).

Page 141 (Top). John Hunter: cf. Lewes, p. 323, whence also we borrow the quotation from Tiedemann's *Physiologie des Menschen.* (Below) " Specific principles:" *De Gen. An.*, ii. 7, at the end of the discussion on the sterility of mules, 748 a, 7 : οὗτος μὲν οὖν ὁ λόγος καθόλου λίαν καὶ κενός, οἱ γὰρ μὴ ἐκ τῶν οἰκείων ἀρχῶν λόγοι κενοί, κ.τ.λ. " Too far-fetched:" *De Gen. An.*, iv. 1, 765 b, 4, ἀλλὰ λίαν τὸ λέγειν οὕτω πόρρωθέν ἐστιν ἅπτεσθαι τῆς αἰτίας, κ.τ.λ.

Page 143 (Top). " Palpitation:" cf. *De Respir.*, 20, 479 b, 22–26 : ὥσ-' ἐνίοτ' ἀποσβέννυσθαι (sc. τὸ θερμὸν) τὰ ζῷα καὶ (read καὶ τὰ ζῷα) ἀποθνήσκειν διὰ φόβον. (Below) Size of the heart: *De Part. An.*, iii. 4, where, in

addition, the hardness and softness of the heart are made responsible
for the degree of psychic sensitiveness (667 a, 11 *seq.*).   For the
mistaken explanations which follow, see *De Gen. An.*, v. 3, 783 a, 12
seqq. ; 7, 787, 788 ; 3, 783 b, 28 *seq.*   Cf. Georges Pouchet, *op. cit.*,
p. 37.

Page 144 (Top).   " Different phases of his activity : " for the purpose
of adjudicating the chronological sequence of the works, we have,
besides general considerations, two resources at command :   the
forward and backward references of the author himself (though these
are not seldom confusing), and casual allusions to events of ascertain-
able date.   The first of these has been exhausted by Bonitz, with his
customary exactitude and thoroughness, in his *Index, s.v.* Ἀριστοτέλης;
the discussion of those allusions which for some of the writings supply
absolute chronological landmarks (instead of the relative ones obtained
by the first method) may be found in Zeller, ii. 2 (ed. 3), p. 154 *seq.*
The order of succession which is thus deduced with a high degree of
probability runs as follows :   The *Organon,* the four chief physical
works (*Physica, De Cœlo, De Gen. et Corr., Meteorologia* ; cf. *Meteorol.,*
i. *in.,* and iv. *fin.*) ;   then *De Anima* with *Parva Naturalia,* and the
biological works, *Hist. An., De Part. An., De Gen. An.* (three crucial
passages are *De Part. An.,* i. 1, 639 b, 8-10, and 640 a, 14 *seq.*, 689 a,
18 *seqq.* ; again *De Gen. An.* v. 1, 779 b, 21 *seqq.*, where it is well to note
the unusually exact indications πρότερον and ἔτι πρότερον) ;   lastly come
the works which may be called anthropological in the widest sense of
the word :   *Ethica, Politica, Poetica, Rhetorica.*   I say nothing of the
Metaphysica ;   it was never published as a whole by Aristotle himself.

BOOK VI.—CHAPTER XIII.

Page 147 (end of sect. 1).   "Dietary prohibitions of the Old Testament : "   Leviticus, ch. xi.   (Bottom) Diocles (of Carystus) belongs to
the first third of the fourth century ;   he wrote, among other things, an
Ἀνατομή.   He is treated of by Wellmann in Pauly-Wissowa, v. 802
seqq. ; cf. the same scholar's *Fragment-Sammlung der griechischen
Arzte,* i.   In Fragm. 132 (= Athenæus, vii. 316 c) we find the
comprehensive term μαλάκια (soft animals).   In Athenæus, iii. 105 b
Speusippus is made to speak of "soft shell-fish" (μαλακόστρακα);
Aristotle himself (*De Part. An.,* iii. 4, 665 a, 31) credits Democritus
with the expression "bloodless" (ἄναιμα).   The possibility that
Athenæus in the one case or Aristotle in the other may have
substituted the comprehensive designations for narrower terms used
by the older writers cannot be absolutely rejected.   The same holds
of the class-name of the "single-hoofed" animals: Aristotle, *De Part.
An.,* iv. 2, 677 a, 32.   The "old" writers there referred to may have
treated simply of the horse, the ass, etc.   But who will fail to see that
the probability of this hypothesis becomes smaller the more often we

have to make use of it?—"A contemporary:" unfortunately, one no longer. I refer to Rudolf Burckhardt, *Das koische Tiersystem, eine Vorstufe der zoologischen Systematik des Aristoteles* (off-printed from the *Verhandl. d. naturforsch. Gesellsch.* in Basel, xv. 3). This uncommonly valuable investigation is the source of the quotation overleaf.

Page 148 (Middle). Linnæus on the whale: I take these details from Louis Agassiz' *Essay on Classification,* p. 304.

Sect. 3. "Rejection of dichotomy:" this subject, as well as "the principles of division" in general, is treated with great thoroughness by J. B. Meyer in *Aristoteles' Tierkunde,* 70-100. It is of little importance that on p. 76 he overlooks the limitation of the dichotomic principle in Plato's *Statesman* and *Philebus.* Cf. *Greek Thinkers,* Vol. III. p. 359, note to p. 187, and note to p. 4 of the present volume. Aristotle treats of these questions in *Topica,* vi. 6, 144, 145, and *De Part. An.,* i. 2-4, with the final result: τὸ διχοτομεῖν τῇ μὲν ἀδύνατον τῇ δὲ κενόν, 644 b, 19.

Page 149 (Bottom). Lewes: *op. cit.,* p. 296. On the other hand, Pouchet writes (*op. cit.,* p. 122 *seq.*): "La classification d'Aristote est *naturelle* . . . La zoologie contemporaine ne procède pas autrement pour établir ses classifications." Jürgen Bona Meyer : *op. cit.,* p. 76 *seqq.* Cf. his collection of passages, p. 102 *seqq.* Among these particular attention is due to *De Part. An.,* i. 3, 643 b, 9 *seqq.* and 23.— "Functions and performances" (ἔργα and πράξεις) : see J. B. Meyer, p. 88 *seqq.* The chief passage is *De Part. An.,* i. 3, 643 a, 35 *seqq.* Specially important is Meyer's demonstration that, in spite of the appearance to the contrary, Aristotle did not make the mode of reproduction a main ground of division, nor yet the special character of the feeding habits or locomotion (pp. 99–102).

Page 150 (Top). "Animals differing in species . . . :" *Hist. An.,* i. 6, 491 a, 14 *seqq.,* and *De Part. An.,* i. 4, 644 a, 16, also 644 b, 1 *seqq.* To these add *Hist. An.,* ii. 1, 497 b, 9. (Below) Louis Agassiz : *op. cit.,* p. 306 *seqq.,* compared with Rudolf Burckhardt, *Das koische Tiersystem,* p. 410. The latter author also offers, on p. 379, a general view of Aristotle's principles of systematization. Cf. the enumeration of the γένη μέγιστα and the main distinctions between them in *Hist. An.* i. 6, iv. 1., and *De Part. An.,* iv. 5. (Bottom) "Man : " see especially *Hist. An.,* i. 6, 490 b, 15 *seqq.* ; ii. 8, 502 a, 16 *seq.* ; and *De Gen. An.,* ii. 4, 737 b, 26. This question is excellently treated by Zeller, ii. 2 (ed. 3), 563, 564.—"Genus" and "species :" on the varying use of γένος and εἶδος, cf. Meyer, *op. cit.,* 345 *seqq.* It is astonishing that γένος is occasionally "employed even of varieties" (347).

Page 151 (Top). "Metres," as distinguished from μέλος and μελοποιία: *Poetica,* 1, 1447 b, 25 ; 6, 1449 b, 30 and 35.

Sect. 4. "Namelessness:" the chief passage is *Hist. An.,* i. 5, 490 a, 12 *seqq.,* also 31.—"Relationship of form:" *Hist. An.,* ix.

40, 623 b, 5. All the members of a certain group of insects without a name are said to possess τὴν μορφὴν συγγενικήν. On what follows, cf. E. Dennert, *Das Princip der Korrelation bei Aristoteles* (Naturwiss. Wochenschr. N. F. iv. Nr. 43).—On functional unity, cf. Pouchet, *op. cit.*, pp. 138, 139. (Bottom) "A variation . . . :" *Hist. An.*, viii. 2, 589, 590.

Page 152 (Top). "Ruminants :" cf. *De Part. An.*, iii. 14; Pouchet, *op. cit.*, pp. 105, 106, also 112, 113.—"Nature of eggs :" *De Gen. An.*, ii. 1, 733 a, 6 *seqq.* Again, in *Hist. An.*, ii. 12, *in.*, birds and reptiles, which Huxley joined together as "Sauropsidæ," are regarded as closely related to each other.—Cuvier : cited by J. B. Meyer, p. 468. Sect. 5. Geoffroy St. Hilaire : cf. the quotation in Finot, *Le préjugé des races*, p. 274.—Goethe : 36, 380 in the 40-vol. edition. For the following matter, cf. *De Gen. An.*, iii. 1, 749 b, 8 and 750 a, 3, also *De Part. An.*, ii. 9, 655 a, 27 ; ii. 14, 658 a, 35 ; iii. 1, 662 a, 18, and iv. 8, 684 a, 17.

Page 153 (Middle). On the spit-candlestick, see *De Part. An.*, iv. 6, 683 a, 25, where I was obliged to translate εὐτέλεια by "cheapness." The word, however, has an accessory implication of meanness or triviality, as when the εὐτέλεια of thoughts is spoken of. This has been overlooked by those who (like J. B. Meyer, *op. cit.*, p. 489) have sought to establish a contradiction between this avoidance of εὐτέλεια and the housekeeper-like frugality of nature. On this and on the Delphic knife, cf. *Politica*, i. 2, 1252 b, 2 and iv. 15, 1299 b, 10.

Page 154. A passage of the first importance on the poorer and richer endowment of organisms is to be found in *De Part. An.*, ii. 10, 655, 656. Plants, with their smaller number of functions and organs, are contrasted with animal nature, which πολυμορφοτέραν ἔχει τὴν ἰδέαν καὶ τούτων ἕτερα πρὸ ἑτέρων μᾶλλον, καὶ πολυχουστέραν. Below the blood animals stand the bloodless, and below these again the ὀστρακόδερμα καὶ μαλακόστρακα τὰ ἔσχατα, *De Gen. An.*, iii. 6, 743 b, 10. On what follows, cf. *Parva Nat.*, 467 a, 18 *seqq.*, and 468 a, 13-b, 15. Note, for instance, the assertion about plants in 467 a, 21 : οὐ γὰρ ἔχει ὄργανα, and 468 a, 17 : διήρθρωται δὲ μᾶλλον (*sc.* τὸ στῆθος) ἑτέροις ἑτέρων. (Middle) "Gradation of all living beings :" cf. Burckhardt, *Zur Geschichte der biologischen Systematik*, Basel, 1903, p. 409 (from the 16th vol. of the Verhandl. d. naturforsch. Gesellsch. in Basel). Our difficulty in clearly separating the genetic from the merely systematic point of view is not entirely due to Aristotle's interpreters, who wrongly credit him with a development theory of his own, but also, here and there, to Aristotle himself. Take, for example, *Hist. An.*, i. 2, 590 a, 1 and 6. The first passage deals with castration and its effects : μικροῦ γὰρ μορίου πηρωθέντος εἰς τὸ θῆλυ μεταβάλλει τὸ ζῷον. The second passage, following almost immediately on the first, treats of the distinction between closely related land- and sea-animals : ἐν μικροῖς μορίοις γινομένης τῆς μεταβολῆς συμβαίνει γίνεσθαι τὰ μὲν πεζὰ τὰ δ ἔνυδρα τῶν ζῴων. Yet even here it would be following a deceptive appearance to suppose that the author had in view a real metamorphosis or genetic process. That would be in contradiction to the principles, held by him with the fullest consistency, of the eternity of the earth and its inhabitants, including man at the head of them. There is here in play that same misleading fashion of speech which prompts us to say, for example : "at this point of the journey a mountain *rises* before us." Aristotle's words in the second passage suggest to us a transformation actually undergone at some definite time, whereas he only desires to say that one particular difference is accompanied by a second, or, possibly, that diversity in habitat conditions the structure of a few unimportant organs, and through these numerous and far-reaching diversities in the whole frame of the animals considered.

Page 155 (Bottom). "Beginning with the inanimate world :" *Hist. An.*, viii. 1, 558–589. Another passage is iv. 5, 681 a, 12. Notice the constant recurrence here of such words as συνεχής, συνεχῶς, συνέχεια or μᾶλλον καὶ ἧττον, κατὰ μικρόν ; also ἴχνη and σπέρματα, as well as μεταβαίνειν and μετάβασις ; and observe how the whole discussion is governed by the ideas of the continuous and gradual as opposed to the discontinuous and abrupt.

Page 156 (Middle). "Socialization : " πολιτικώτερον χρῶνται, *op. cit.*, 589 a, 2.

Sect. 8. For this section in general, cf. J. B. Meyer, p. 485 *seqq.* On, bees and ants, see *De Part. An.*, ii. 2, 648 a, 5 : διὸ καὶ μέλιτται καὶ ἄλλα, τοιαῦτα ζῷα φρονιμώτερα τὴν φύσιν ἐστὶν ἐναίμων πολλῶν, and 4, 650 b, 18.

Page 157 (Middle). "Division into two sexes : " *De Gen. An.*, ii. 1, 732 a, 3, iii. 8, 757, 758. Denial of sexual differentiation in plants: *De Gen. An.*, i. 23, 731 a, 1, 2. "Male palm :" Herodotus, i. 193 ; this passage also shows that the Babylonians were well acquainted with the diœcious character of the date-palm. What I say of "every Arabian child" rests on a communication kindly made to me by my colleague, Julius Wiesner. Theophrastus shows correct knowledge of the process of fertilization in treating of this same tree, *Caus. Plant.*, iii. 18, 1 : τὸ δὲ μὴ ἐπιμένειν ἐπὶ τῷ θήλει φοίνικι τὸν καρπόν, ἂν μὴ τὸ τοῦ ἄρρενος ἄνθος κατασείωσι ἅμα τῷ κονιορτῷ κατ' αὐτοῦ, κ.τ.λ.

Page 158 (Middle). "Work *On Respiration* :" *De Respir.*, 6, 743 a, 3 *seqq.*

Sect. 10. Page 159. "The word 'organic' : " cf. *De An.*, ii. 2, 412 a, b ; also *De Part. An.*, i. 5, 645 b, 14 *seqq.* On "entelechy," cf. the sound and full exposition in Trendelenburg's edition of the *De Anima*, p. 242 *seqq.*, ed. 2. "Unlike" and "like" parts : cf. Bonitz, *Index*, 62 a and 510 b. (Bottom) "A line of Empedocles : " cf. *Greek Thinkers*, Vol. I. p. 244. The line is fragm. 82 in Diels' *Fragmente der Vorsokratiker*, p. 195, and is quoted by Aristotle, *Meteorol.* iv. 9, 387 b, *in.*— "The human arm, the fore legs :" *De Part. An.*, iv. 12, 693 a, b.

Page 160 (Top). " The human hand : " cf. *ibid.*, 692 b, 16 and 8, 683 b, 33 ; also 10, 687 a, 7 *seqq.*—On the elephant's trunk, cf. ii. 16 *in.* (Middle) " Functional unity : " cf. Pouchet, *op. cit.*, p. 79. The chief passage on analogy is *Hist. An.*, i. 1, 486 b, 19 *seqq.* " Framework of bones : " *De Part. An.*, ii. 8, 653, 654 ; "nutritive fluid : " *Hist. An.*, i. 3, 419 a, 22. "Analogous structures : " see J. B. Meyer, p. 429, *seq.*—" Urine-like excretions : " *De Part. An.*, iv. 3, 969 a, 17 ; cf. Pouchet, p. 78.—" Gills and lungs : " the most important passage is *De Part. An.*, iii. 6 *in.*, 668 a, b.

Page 161 (Top). " Mouth " and "roots : " *De Part. An.*, iv. 10, 686, 687.—Warmth as a guiding principle : see J. B. Meyer, pp. 485, 486. (Middle) " All but quite a few : " *Hist. An.*, i. 5, 490 a, 20 *seq.* (Bottom) " Rudimentary organs : " the chief passages are *De Part. An.*, iii. 7, 669 b, 29 *seq.*, and *Hist. An.*, ii. 8, 502 b, 22 *seq.* Schopenhauer's very similar exposition of the subject was almost certainly influenced by Aristotle, whose work on the parts of animals is quoted by him immediately afterwards (*Werke*, iii. 376 *seq.*).

Page 162 (Top). " Food must be mixed : " *De Gen. et Corr.*, ii. 8, 335 a, 10. (Middle) Opitz : quoted in Grimm's Dictionary, *s.v.* " Kochen," v. 1556. Hegel's *Encyclopædia* : p. 688 (new Leyden edition). (Bottom) " Phlegm : " cf. the definition in *Topica*, vi. 3. Blood is called ἐσχάτη τροφή in *De Part. An.*, ii. 4, 651 a, 14 ; it is also called τελευταία τροφή in *De Juv. et Senect.*, 3, 469 a, 1.

Page 163 (Top). " Flesh and the substance of the other sense-organs : " *De Gen. An.*, ii. 6, 744 b, 22 *seqq.* Immediately before comes the comparison with a household.—" Source of warmth and sensation : " *De Part. An.*, iii. 5, 667 b, 29.—" Hearth " and " acropolis : " *ibid.*, 7, 670 a, 25 *seq.*—" Water-courses : " *ibid.*, 5, 668 a, 13 *seqq.* (Bottom) " Ignorance of the nerves : " there is a controversy as to whether the ἶνες, which in *Hist. An.*, iii. 6, 515 b, 27, are placed μεταξὺ νεύρου καὶ φλεβός, should be understood as nerves or not ; cf. J. B. Meyer, p. 434. Pages 441 and 428 of the same work may also be referred to for what follows.

Page 164. " Marionettes : " this comparison (*De Anim. Motione*, 7, 701 b, 2 *seqq.*) is treated by Pouchet, p. 41. The genuineness of this little work, much as it has been contested, seems to me perfectly well established. But the arguments which led to this result would exceed the limits of a note.

Book VI.—Chapter XIV.

Page 165 (Top). The chronological position of the *De Anima* is made plain by the forward and backward references which Bonitz has collected in his *Index Aristot.*, p. 100 a, b.—" Fire : " *De Gen. An.*, iii. 11, 761 b, 17 *seqq.* On the following matter, cf. *De Gen. An.*, iv. 4, 770 b, 9 *seqq.* ; also 767 b, 13 *seqq.* ; iv. 9, *fin.* ; ii. 6, 742 a, 16 ; iii. 5, 756 a, 4 ; to these add the passages already quoted in illustration of Bk. VI.

ch. xii.: ii. 7, 748 a, 7 ; iv. 1, 765 b, 4 ; iii. 10 ; 760 b, 30 *seqq.* ; lastly, iv. 1, 765 a, 25 *seqq.* Some of these pronouncements, among which it is not an easy matter to make a selection, run as follows: ἔστι γὰρ τὸ τέρας τῶν παρὰ φύσιν τι, παρὰ φύσιν δ' οὐ πᾶσαν, ἀλλὰ τὴν ὡς ἐπὶ τὸ πολύ . . . ἐπεὶ καὶ τούτων . . . ἧττον εἶναι δοκεῖ τέρας διὰ τὸ καὶ τὸ παρὰ φύσιν εἶναι τρόπον τινὰ κατὰ φύσιν, ὅταν μὴ κρατήσῃ τὴν κατὰ τὴν ὕλην ἢ κατὰ τὸ εἶδος φύσις. Or: βούλεται μὲν οὖν ἡ φύσις τοῖς τούτων ἀριθμοῖς ἀριθμεῖν τὰς γενέσεις καὶ τὰς τελευτάς, οὐκ ἀκριβοῖ δὲ . . . διὰ τὸ γίνεσθαι πολλὰς ἀρχάς, αἳ τὰς γενέσεις τὰς κατὰ φύσιν καὶ τὰς φθορὰς ἐμποδίζουσαι πολλάκις αἴτίαι τῶν παρὰ φύσιν συμπιπτόντων εἰσίν.— "Plausible conjecture:" οὐκ ἀληθῆ λέγοντες, ἀλλὰ μαντευόμενοι τὸ συμβησόμενον ἐκ τῶν εἰκότων, καὶ προλαμβάνοντες ὡς οὕτως ἔχον πρὶν γινόμενον οὕτως ἰδεῖν. Pages 165, 166. "Ocular evidence:" cf. *De Gen. An.*, iv. 1, 764 a, 34: καὶ τοῦθ' ἱκανῶς τεθεωρήκαμεν ἐκ τῶν ἀνατομῶν ἐν πᾶσι τοῖς ζῳοτοκοῦσι, καὶ ἐν τοῖς πεζοῖς καὶ ἐν τοῖς ἰχθύσιν.

Page 166 (Top). The modern work quoted is by Bruno Bloch, *Die Grundzüge der älteren Embryologie bis Harvey* (Zoologische Annalen, i. 51 *seqq.*, 1904). " In the Hippocratic collection :" vii. 530, Littré. (Bottom) "Cotyledons:" *De Gen. An.*, ii. 7, 745 b, 30 *seqq.*

Page 167 (Top). " Position of the pig :" *De Gen. An.*, iv. 6, 774 b, 17 *seqq.* (Middle) "Teratology:" see Pouchet, *op. cit.*, p. 97 *seqq.* (Bottom) "Two-headed snake :" *De Gen. An.*, iv. 4, 770 a, 23.—" Bees and wasps :" *ibid.*, 27. Pouchet: p. 98 *seq.* On the following matter, cf. Aristotle, *ibid.*, 770 a, b.

Page 168 (Top). "Crowding of eggs :" *ibid.*, 770 a, 26 *seqq.*— " Greater frequency of malformations in the male sex :" *ibid.*, iv. 6, 775 a, 5 *seqq.* "Our specialists :" see Pouchet, p. 97 ; Aubert and Wimmer, p. 338, note 1. According to these authors, the preponderance of female malformations is even remarkably high. (Par. 2) "Monstrosity" and " dissimilarity : " cf. *De Gen. An.*, iv. 4,770 b, 3 : ἀλλὰ προωδοποίηται τῇ φύσει πρὸς τὸ τερατοποιεῖν τὸ μὴ γεννᾶν ὅμοια . . . ἔστι δὲ καὶ τὸ τέρας τῶν ἀνομοίων. Similarly, *ibid.*, 3, 767 b, 5 : καὶ γὰρ ὁ μὴ ἐοικὼς τοῖς γονεῦσιν ἤδη τρόπον τινὰ τέρας ἐστίν.—" Resemble remote ancestors :" *De Gen. An.*, i. 18, 722 a, 7 : ἔτι τοῖς ἄνωθεν γονεῦσιν ἐοίκασιν. The explanation of this, *ibid.*, iv. 3, 767, 768. (Bottom) Charles Darwin: *Origin of Species*, pp. 189-196 (ed. 5). Cf. especially p. 189: "the tendency to *reversion* and *variability* on the other hand," and p. 190 on monstrosities.

Page 169 (Top). " The Hippocratics :" cf. *De Semine*, § 3 (vii. 474 L.): τὴν δὲ γονήν φημὶ ἀποκρίνεσθαι ἀπὸ παντὸς τοῦ σώματος. On the other hand, Aristotle writes : καὶ πότερον ἀπὸ παντὸς ἀπέρχεται τοῦ σώματος, κ.τ.λ., *De Gen. An.*, i. 17, 721 b, 9. On what follows, cf. *ibid.*, c. 18, *in.*

Sect. 4. Male and female births : treated of in *De Gen. An.*, iv. c. 1 and 2.

Page 170 (Top). "Practical measures and maxims: see the treatise "On Superfetation" (*Œuvres d'Hippocrate*, viii. 500 L.). Similarly in book vi. of the *Epidemics* (v. 312 L.). The practice recommended in the first passage is said to be much resorted to in India at the present day. —" Cases of amputation : " *op. cit.*, I 765 a, 25 *seqq.* : καὶ ἐπὶ τῶν ἐκτεμνομένων τὸν ἕτερον ὄρχιν, κ.τ.λ. (Bottom) "Age of the parent or parents : " the first version appears in *op. cit.*, iv. 2, 766 b, 29 *seqq.*, where note, in particular, the word γυναικικώτερα, which can hardly refer to a female body ; the second is represented by *Hist. An.*, vii. 6, 585 b, 14 ; νέοι μὲν ὄντες μετ᾽ ἀλλήλων θήλεα γεννῶσι, κ.τ.λ.—"As late as half a century ago : " cf. Aubert and Wimmer's edition of *De Gen. An.* (1890), p. 296, with the reference to Quetelet's *De l'Homme* (1835) and Rud. Wagner's *Handwörterbuch der Physiologie* (1842–53). Sect. 5. Page 171. "Spontaneous generation : " the main passages are *Hist. An.*, v. 11, 563 b, 17 *seq.*, 547 b, 18 *seqq.*, vi. 15, *in.* Add 569 a, 10 *seqq.*, and 26 *seqq.* The most comprehensive view in *De Gen. An.*, iii. 11, 762 a, 18 *seqq.*—"All shellfish . . .:" cf. *De Gen. An.*, iii. 11, 773 a, b.

Page 173 (Top). On the bay of Pyrrha and its marine fauna, cf. Smith, *Dictionary of Greek and Roman Geography*, *s.v.* "Lesbos." Also Bonitz' *Index*, *s.v.* "Pyrrha," 662, 663. (Bottom) Anaxagoras, Archelaus, and Democritus : cf. Diels, *Doxogr.*, 563, 567 ; 564, 2 ; and p. 16. See also the present author in "Wiener Studien," ii. 12, and Censorinus, *De Die Natali*, iv. 9.

BOOK VI.—CHAPTER XV.

Page 175 (Below). On the three souls : cf. Pouchet, ch. 2, p. 23 *seqq.* Distinction between conservation and growth : *De Juventute*, 3 *fin.*, 469 a, 25–27. The soul also appears as divided into two parts, the irrational part being opposed to the rational, *e.g.* *De Anima*, ii. 9, 432 a, 26. "Quadrilateral and triangles : " cf. *De An.*, ii. 3, 414 b, 29 *seqq.*

Page 176 (Top). Comparison with the power of sight : *ibid.*, ii. 1, 412 b, 18 *seqq.*—The soul neither corporeal nor incorporeal : *ibid.*, ii. 2, 414 a, 20.—"Something of the body : " *ibid.*, 21 : σώματος δέ τι.— The eye of stone or painted eye : *ibid.*, ii. 1, 412 b, 20 *seqq.* A hand of the same kind : *e.g. De Gen. An.*, i. 19, 726 b, 22 *seqq.*, or *De Part. An.*, i. 1, 640, 641. (Bottom) "The Pythagorean thesis : " *De An.*, i. 3. 407 b, 21 *seqq.*—The soul a harmony : against this *De An.*, i. 4, *in.*

Sect. 3. Page 177. "Necessity of a medium : " *De An.*, ii. 7, 419 a, 11 *seqq.* ; also *De Sensu*, 2, 438 b, 3–5 : ἡ διὰ τούτου κίνησίς ἐστιν ἡ ποιοῦσα τὸ ὁρᾶν.

Page 178 (par. 2). The sense of touch a collective name : *De An.*, ii. 11, *in.* See this chapter also for what follows.

Page 179. Parallelism between the senses and the elements : *De Sensu*, 2. For what follows, cf. 7 ; also *De An*., ii. 9, *in*. Lastly, *De An*., ii. 10, 422 a, 20 *seqq*. ; also iii. 13, 435 b, 15 ; and ii. 11, 424 b, 28 *seqq*.

Page 180 (Middle). Sense of touch : *De Sensu*, i. 436 b, 12 *seqq*. ; *De An*., ii. 2, 413 b, 4 *seq*. ; ii. 9, 421 a, 19 *seqq*.—" Blind from birth : " *De Sensu*, 1, *fin*.

Sect. 5. The following are the chief passages for Aristotle's theory of colour : *De An*., ii. c. 7, and *De Sensu*, 2, 3. C. Prantl treated the subject thoroughly, and proved the spuriousness of the extant treatise Περὶ χρωμάτων in *Aristoteles über die Farben* (Munich, 1849), p. 82 *seqq*. On tastes : *De Sensu*, c. 4, 442 a, 12 *seqq*.

Page 181 (end of par. 1). Schopenhauer : *Werke*, i. Bd. ii. pp. 30, 31.

Sect. 6. " After-images : " *De An*., iii. 1, 425 b, 24 : διὸ καὶ ἀπελθόντων τῶν αἰσθητῶν ἔνεισιν αἱ αἰσθήσεις καὶ φαντασίαι ἐν τοῖς αἰσθητηρίοις : also *De Insomn*., 2, 460 b. 2, 3.—" Complementary colours : " *ibid*., 1, 459 b, 13 *seqq*. : κἂν πρὸς τὸν ἥλιον βλέψαντες ἢ ἄλλο τι λαμπρὸν μυσῶμεν . . . φαίνεται . . . πρῶτον μὲν τοιοῦτον τὴν χρόαν, εἶτα μεταβάλλει εἰς φοινικοῦν, κ.τ.λ.

Page 182 (Top). " Continued operation of a mechanical impulse : " *ibid*., 459 a, 28-30.—" Permanent residues : " *ibid*., 3, 461 b, 21 : ὑπόλειμμα τοῦ ἐν τῇ ἐνεργείᾳ αἰσθήματος.— " Fundamental laws of association : " *De Memoria*, 2, 451 b, 18 *seqq*.—" Strength of emotion : " *De Insomn*., 2, 460 b, 2 *seqq*. (Middle) " Attempts at physiological explanation : " 453 a, b. Also for the following. (Bottom) " Memory and recollection : " Περὶ μνήμης καὶ ἀναμνήσεως ; this is the title of the section of the *Parva Naturalia* devoted to this subject. The distinction, which is a little strange to us, comes from Plato (Phædo, 73 B, and Philebus, 34 B, passages to which W. A. Hammond refers in his valuable translation and explanation of the books *De Anima* and the *Parva Naturalia*. *Aristotle's Psychology*, London, 1902, p. 195).

Page 183 (Top). The (supposed) distinction between men and animals : *ibid*., 2, 453 a, 7. (Par. 2) Image and seal-impression : *De Mem*., 1, 450 a, b.

Sect. 7. " Memory-pictures . . . phantasms : " *De Mem*., 1, 451 a, 15. For what follows, cf. *De Insomn*., 3, particularly 461 a, 1 : ὥσπερ παρὰ πολὺ πῦρ ἔλαττον, and 461 b, 15 (artificial frogs).

Page 184 (Top). Physiological explanation of sleep : *De Somno*, 3, 456 b, 2 *seqq*. On what follows, *ibid*., 2, 455 a, 31 *seqq*., and 455 b, 13 *seqq*. (Bottom) The two sets of instances : *De Insomn*., 3, 462 a, 19 *seqq*., and *De Divinatione in Somno*, 1, 463 a, 10 *seqq*.

Page 185 (par. 2). " Significance of dreams : " *ibid*., 463 a, b, and 463 a, 5 *seqq*.

Sect. 8. " Against god-sent dreams : " *De Divin*., 1, 462 b, 20 *seqq*.

Page 186 (Top). " Telepathy," etc. : *ibid*., 2, especially 464 a, 24 *seqq*. (Middle) " Somnambulism : " *De Somno*, 2, *fin*.

Sect. 9. "Phantasy" fundamentally distinct from "assertion:" *De An.*, iii. 8, 432 a, 10. "The majority of phantasies false:" *ibid.*, 3, 428 a, 12: αἱ δὲ φαντασίαι γίνονται αἱ πλείους ψευδεῖς. Page 187 (Top). The sun "a foot in breadth:" *ibid.*, 3, 428 b, *5 seq.*; *De Insomn.*, 1, 458 a, 28, and 2, 460 b, *18 seq.*—"Weakened sensation:" *Rhet.*, i. 11, 1370 a, 28: αἴσθησίς τις ἀσθενής.—"Reflexions in water:" *De Divin.*, 2, 464 b, 9.

Sect. 10. "Veracity of sensation:" *Metaph.*, iv. 5, 1010 b, 2, 3· The text has suffered, but has undoubtedly been restored with essential corrections by Bonitz, whose (μὴ) ψευδὴς I replace by (ἀ)ψευδής: πρῶτον μὲν ὅτι οὐδ' (εἰ) ἡ αἴσθησις (ἀ)ψευδὴς τοῦ ἰδίου ἐστίν, κ.τ.λ. On the expression, cf. Plato, *Theætetus*, 160 D, and 199 B. On τὸ ἴδιον, cf., in addition to 1010 b, 14 *seqq.*, *De An.*, ii. 6, *in.*, particularly περὶ ὃ μὴ ἐνδέχεται ἀπατηθῆναι, οἷον ὄψις χρώματος καὶ ἀκοὴ ψόφου καὶ γεῦσις χυμοῦ. Also *De An.*, iii. 3, 427 b, 11: ἡ μὲν γὰρ αἴσθησις τῶν ἰδίων ἀεὶ ἀληθής.—"I see white:" *De An.*, iii. 6, 430 b, 29. On the other hand, see *ibid.*, 428 b, 18: ἡ αἴσθησις τῶν μὲν ἰδίων ἀληθής ἐστιν ἢ ὅτι ὀλίγιστον ἔχουσα τὸ ψεῦδος. On illusions of the senses in general, cf. *Metaph.*, iv. 5, 1010 b, 3 *seqq.*

Page 188 (par. 2). Correction of one sense by another: *De Insomn.*, 2, 460 b, 20 *seqq.*—"General qualities:" *De An.*, ii. 6, 418 a, 17; iii. 1, 425 a, 14; *De Sensu*, 1, 437 a, 9; 4, 442 b, 5 *seqq.*—"An extreme case:" *De An.*, iii. 1, 425 b, 4 *seqq.*

Page 189 (par. 2). Berkeley: his theory of vision is tersely formulated by J. S. Mill in *Dissertations and Discussions*, ii. 89: "That the information obtained through the eye consists of two things—sensations and *inferences* from those sensations: that the sensations are merely *colours* variously arranged, and changes of colour; that all else is inference," etc. Aristotle's Ὀπτικόν α', mentioned by Diog. Laert., v. 26. Alexander of Aphrodisias: *De Anima Libri Mantissa*, especially p. 146 *seq.* (*Supplementum Aristotelicum*, ii. 1, ed. Ivo Bruns, 1887). Compare the excellent monograph, *Antike Lichttheorien*, by Arthur Erich Haas in the Archiv. f. Gesch. d. Philos., xx. 3 (1907). Co-operation (sometimes also productive of illusions): *De Sensu*, 4, 442 b, 8: καὶ περὶ μὲν τούτων ἀπατῶνται, περὶ δὲ τῶν ἰδίων οὐκ ἀπατῶνται, οἷον ἡ ὄψις περὶ χρώματος, κ.τ.λ.

Sect. 11. "Thinking in concepts . . . representations:" *De An.*, iii. 7, 431 a, 16 *seq.*: διὸ οὐδέποτε νοεῖ ἄνευ φαντάσματος ἡ ψυχή; iii. 8, 432 a, 8: ὅταν τε θεωρῇ, ἀνάγκη ἅμα φάντασμά τι θεωρεῖν. *De Mem.*, 1, 449 b, 31 *seq.*: καὶ νοεῖν οὐκ ἔστιν ἄνευ φαντάσματος.—"Without phantasy . . . desire is impossible:" *De An.*, iii. 11, 433 b, 28: ὀρεκτικὸν δὲ οὐκ ἄνευ φαντασίας.

Page 190 (Top). "Deliberative phantasy:" *ibid.*—"Desire appears:" *De Motione Animal.*, 7, 701 a, 32 *seqq.*—For what follows, cf. *ibid.*, 13 *seqq.*—"A living being is confronted with a choice:" *De An.*, ii. 11, 434 a, 6 *seq.*, particularly 10 *seq.*: καὶ αἴτιον τοῦτο τοῦ δόξαν μὴ δοκεῖν ἔχειν ὅτι τὴν ἐκ συλλογισμοῦ οὐκ ἔχει. This important passage has not, as far as I can see, received sufficient attention, nor has its great significance been appreciated. It is in contradiction with the doctrine elsewhere firmly maintained as to the proceeding of actions from syllogistic deliberation, *e.g. Eth. Nic.*, 5, 147 a, 25 *seqq.*

BOOK VI.—CHAPTER XVI.

Page 192. In regard to Aristotle's treatment of the problem of will there reigns a perfectly bewildering variety of opinions. For Zeller (ii. 2, p. 587, 588, ed. 3) Aristotle is an indeterminist, though he represents him as acknowledging that " man with his free will " is nevertheless dependent on his " moral states " in such a way " that the external action proceeds with necessity from the will, when once this has taken a determinate direction." The passages cited in support of these antagonistic theses stand in close juxtaposition : *Eth. Nic.*, iii. 7, 1113 b, 6 : ἐφ' ἡμῖν δὲ καὶ ἡ ἀρετή, ὁμοίως δὲ καὶ ἡ κακία κ.τ.λ. ; shortly afterwards, however, he describes the origin of states (ἕξεις), which, however they displease us, we can no more alter directly than the sick man his sickness (1114 a, 9). The solution of the contradiction, *ibid.* : ἡ γὰρ ἀρχὴ ἐπ' αὐτῷ ... γενομένοις δ' οὐκέτι ἔξεστι μὴ εἶναι. Purely deterministic passages, like *Metaph.*, ix. 5, 1048 a, 11 : ὁποτέρου γὰρ ἂν ὀρέγηται κυρίως, τοῦτο ποιήσει, are taken by Löning, in his valuable book, *Die Zurechnungslehre des Aristoteles* as a basis on which to rest a representation of him as a determinist of the purest water.—" Spontaneous actions : " cf. *Eth. Nic.*, 4, iii. 1111 b, 8 : τοῦ μὲν γὰρ ἑκουσίου καὶ παῖδες καὶ τἆλλα ζῷα κοινωνεῖ, προαιρέσεως δ' οὔ. This is well applied by Löning, *op. cit.*, pp. 137 and 283. This writer also aptly remarks *(ibid.)* : " It (τὸ ἐφ' ἡμῖν εἶναι) does not mean that the will depends on itself, but that action depends on the will." On the qualities (ἕξεις), cf. *Eth. Nic.*, iii. 7 and 8. In the same passage is the comparison of vice with illness, and the emphasization of the impossibility of shaking off either by a mere act of the will : οὐ μὴν ἐάν γεβούληται, ἄδικος ὢν παύσεται καὶ ἔσται δίκαιος· οὐδὲ γὰρ ὁ νοσῶν ὑγιής (1114 a, 13 *seqq.*). (Bottom) " A passage of the *Ethics* : " v. 13, 1137 a, 6, *seqq.*, συγγενέσθαι μὲν γὰρ τῇ τοῦ γείτονος καὶ πατάξαι τὸν πλησίον καὶ δοῦναι τῇ χειρὶ τὸ ἀργύρον ῥᾴδιον καὶ ἐπ' αὐτοῖς, ἀλλὰ τὸ ὡδὶ ἔχοντας ταῦτα ποιεῖν οὔτε ῥᾴδιον οὔτ' ἐπ' αὐτοῖς.

Page 193 (Top). " A modern determinist : " J. S. Mill, *Logic*, book vi. ch. 2, § 3.

Page 194 (Middle). " For the good as for the bad . . . : " ἀμφοῖν γὰρ ὁμοίως, τῷ ἀγαθῷ καὶ τῷ κακῷ, τὸ τέλος φύσει ἢ ὁπωσδήποτε φαίνεται καὶ κεῖται, *Eth. Nic.*, iii. 7, 1114 b, 13–15.

Sect. 2. Page 195. " Social utility : " *Politics*, ii. *fin.* 1274 b, 21 *seqq.* : οὐ πρὸς τὴν συγγνώμην ἀπέβλεψεν ἀλλὰ πρὸς τὸ συμφέρον. On this and what follows, *Eth. Nic.*, *loc. cit.*, 1113 b, 19 *seqq.*

Page 197 (Top). " As our philósopher elsewhere emphatically acknowledges:" *Rhet.*, ii. 1, 1378 a, 20.—The " automatic necessity " of Epicurus : In his polemic against fatalism he represents the substance of this doctrine as being the belief τὴν ἀνάγκην καὶ ταὐτόματον πάντα δύνασθαι. These words occur in a fragment of the Περὶ φύσεως which the present author communicated to the Wiener akademische Sitzungsberichte, p. 94, April, 1876. See also Wiener Studien, i. 31. (Bottom) Chrysippus : The chief passage is in Eusebius, *Præp. Evan.*, vi. 8, 29 : πολλὰ γὰρ μὴ δύνασθαι χωρὶs τοῦ καὶ ἡμᾶs βούλεσθαι καὶ ἐκτενεστάτην γε περὶ αὐτὰ προθυμίαν τε καὶ σπουδὴν εἰσφέρεσθαι. Here, perhaps, we may repair an omission in the text by considering the difference in meaning between certain Greek terms which have no precise modern equivalents. In general, βούλεσθαι may be rightly translated "to will," but there enters into the meaning of the ancient word an implication of wish which is absent from the modern one. Βούλησιs, unlike our " will " or "volition," may refer to what is in itself impossible, *e.g.* to immunity from death (βούλησιs δ' ἐστὶ (καὶ) τῶν ἀδυνάτων, οἷον ἀθανασίας, *Eth. Nic.*, iii.4, 1111 b, 22), as also to objects of which the attainment does not depend on ourselves alone. Thus βούλησιs is directed towards an end ; προαίρεσιs (intention) is distinct from it and relates to the means by which the end is attained. By definition, προαίρεσιs is a desire, based on deliberation, of such things as are in our power (βουλευτικὴ ὄρεξιs τῶν ἐφ' ἡμῖν, *ibid.*, 5, 1113 a, 10 *seq.*). In view of the assumption here made, that all desire which can rightly rank as will rests on choice guided by reflexion, it is surprising to find a doubt expressed (*ibid.*, c. 3, *in.*) as to whether actions performed under stress of emotion may be termed " involuntary " (ἴσωs γὰρ οὐ καλῶs λέγεται ἀκούσια εἶναι τὰ διὰ θυμὸν ἢ δι' ἐπιθυμίαν, 1111 a, 24 *seq.*) ; a doubt, by the way, which is supported on very insufficient grounds.

BOOK VI.—CHAPTER XVII.

Page 198. The passages quoted are partly from *Anal. Post.*, ii. *fin.*, partly from *Metaph.*, i. 1.

Page 199 (Top). On the influence of Alcmæon, cf. Vol. I. p 150, and the corresponding note on p. 549. Aristotle's words, ὃ δ' ἐλέχθη μὲν πάλαι, οὐ σαφῶs δ' ἐλέχθη (*Anal. Post.*, ii. *fin.*, 100 a, 14, *seq.*), cannot, as shown by Grote (*Aristotle*, i. 372), be referred, as is done by Waitz or B. St. Hilaire, to a passage of the same work. Unless I am entirely deceived, they are aimed at Alcmæon, and are meant to serve towards justifying the repetition of this thinker's utterances.

Sect. 2. Theophrastus : cited by Themistius, *In Libros de Anima Paraphrasis*, p. 102, 25 ed. R. Heinze.

Page 200 (Top). " The rational prıncıple ımplanted ın man ;" *De Gen. An.*, ii. 3, 736 b, 27 *seqq.*: λείπεται δὲ τὸν νοῦν μόνον θύραθεν ἐπεισιέναι καὶ θεῖον εἶναι μόνον. On the imperishability and immateriality of Nous and the ether, cf. Kampe, *Die Erkenntnistheorie des Aristoteles*, p. 3c *seqq.* In many passages of the *Metaphysica* Aristotle distinguishes the ὕλη τοπική or μόνον κατὰ τόπον κινητή, ἀλλ᾽ οὐ γεννητή, from ordinary materiality which is associated with change, passivity, and perishability. That which holds of the stars holds of the ether and of Nous which thence derives its origin. They do not possess the "common matter which is subject to the changes of genesis and destruction ;" but "only so far as change of place demands such matter." How closely related the substance of Nous is to that of the heavenly bodies may be seen from the similar turns of phrase : ἥ τε γὰρ τῶν ἄστρων φύσις ἀΐδιος οὐσία τις οὖσα, *Metaph.*, xi. 8, 1073 a, 34, and ὁ δὲ νοῦς ἔοικεν ἐγγίνεσθαι οὐσία τις οὖσα καὶ οὐ φθείρεσθαι, *De An.*, i. 4, 408 b, 18 *seq.* On the immortality of Nous, that is, of active Nous, cf. *De An.*, iii. 5, *fin.* (Bottom) On the return of Nous, which is alone "divine," to the remainder of the soul, which is described as "diviner" than the elements, and on its seat in the breath of life, cf. the passage quoted above, *De Gen. An.*, ii. 3, 736 b, 27 *seqq.* In this θεῖον μόνον side by side with θειότερον, Grote (*Aristotle*, ii. 222) found a contradiction which my view of the passage, as I think, removes. In Aristotle's opinion the soul as a whole is diviner than the so-called elements ; but it is only the Nous in the soul which is truly divine.

Page 201 (Middle). "Fire has most of the nature of form . . . :" *De Cœlo*, iv. 3, 310 b, 14 : ἀεὶ γὰρ τό ἀνώτερον πρὸς τὸ ὑφ᾽ αὐτό, ὡς εἶδος πρὸς ὕλην, οὕτως ἔχει πρὸς ἄλληλα. *De Gen. et Corr.*, ii. 8, 335 a, 18 : μόνον γὰρ ἐστι καὶ μάλιστα τοῦ εἴδους τὸ πῦρ. (Below) "Form of forms :" ὁ νοῦς εἶδος εἰδῶν, *De An.*, iii. 8, 432 b, 2.

Page 202 (Top). Comparison of Nous with the eyes of nocturnal animals : *Metaph.*, ii. 1, 993, b 7 *seqq.* That the thought is Aristotelian, or indeed Platonic (remember the cave-simile in the *Republic*), may well be believed, even if one supposes this book of the *Metaphysic:* (a) to have been written by the hand of a pupil. (Middle) "Or is it perhaps through mixture ?" I understand the clause ἤ διὰ τὴν μῖξιν as a question, differently from the editors. On what follows, cf. the principal passage, *De An.*, iii. 4, 5. The words in 5, *fin.*, οὐ μνημονεύομεν δέ, are probably best explained by Schlottman, *Das Vergängliche und Unvergängliche in der menschlichen Seele nach Aristoteles*, p. 50 *seqq.*

Sect. 5. Page 203. "The identity of Nous with its object :" τὸ δ᾽ αὐτό ἐστιν ἡ κατ᾽ ἐνέργειαν ἐπιστήμη τῷ πράγματι, *De An.*, iii. 5, 430 a, 19 *seq.* ; *Ibid.*, 4, 430 a, 3 : ἐπὶ μὲν γὰρ τῶν ἄνευ ὕλης τὸ αὐτό ἐστι τὸ νοοῦν καὶ τὸ νοούμενον. Also *Metaph.*, xii. 7, 1072 b, 21 : ὥστε ταὐτὸν νοῦς τε καὶ νοητόν. Again, *ibid.*, 10, 1075 a, 4 : καὶ ἡ νόησις τῷ νοουμένῳ μία,

Sect. 6. Page 205. Nous in the narrower and wider sense : we find the latter in *De An.*, iii. 4, 429 a, 22 : λέγω δὲ νοῦν ᾧ διανοεῖται καὶ ὑπολαμβάνει ἡ ψυχή. It is very different in *Eth. Nic.*, vi. 12, 1143 a, 35 : ὁ νοῦς τῶν ἐσχάτων ἐπ᾽ ἀμφότερα· καὶ γὰρ τῶν πρώτων ὅρων καὶ τῶν ἐσχάτων νοῦς ἐστὶ καὶ οὐ λόγος. *Ibid.*, 9, 1142 a, 25 : ὁ μὲν γὰρ νοῦς τῶν ὅρων ὧν οὐκ ἔστι λόγος. I am pleased to find this double sense recognized in John Burnet's excellent exegetical edition of the *Ethics* (*The Ethics of Aristotle*, p. 280 note) : " The chief point to remember is that *νοῦς in its restricted sense* . . . is a δύναμις which apprehends its object immediately (τῷ θιγεῖν) like αἴσθησις, not mediately like ἀπόδειξις or βούλευσις."—" A touching : " *Metaph.*, xii. 7, 1072 b, 20 *seq.* : νοητὸς γὰρ γίγνεται θιγγάνων καὶ νοῶν. Also ix. 10. 1052 a, 24 : τὸ μὲν θιγεῖν καὶ φάναι ἀληθές . . . τὸ δ' ἀγνοεῖν μὴ θιγγάνειν.

Page 206 (par. 2 end). "The limits of this discrepancy :" such limits are also recognized by Ueberweg–Heinze, *Grundriss*, i. 220 (ed. 8). Grote detects, not a genuine contradiction, but something very like one (*Aristotle*, i. 332 : " But in these chapters "—those which treat of the προτάσεις ἄμεσοι—" he hardly alludes to induction ").

Sect. 7. The comparison of vision with the faculty of thought occurs in *De An.*, i. 4, 408 b, 19 *seqq.*, ending with the words : καὶ τὸ νοεῖν δὴ καὶ τὸ θεωρεῖν μαραίνεται ἄλλου τινὸς ἔσω φθειρομένου, αὐτὸ δὲ ἀπαθές ἐστιν. On what follows, cf. *De An.*, ii. 6, 430 a, 26 : ἡ μὲν οὖν τῶν ἀδιαιρέτων (these are simple concepts of the highest order) νόησις ἐν τούτοις περὶ ἃ οὐκ ἔστι τὸ ψεῦδος· ἐν οἷς δὲ καὶ τὸ ψεῦδος καὶ τὸ ἀληθές, σύνθεσίς τις ἤδη νοημάτων ὥσπερ ἐν ὄντων. Similarly in *Metaph.*, ix. 10, a chapter in which the bounds of intuitive cognition are traced more clearly than anywhere else. In the place of concepts, νοήματα, we now find in several instances, facts, πράγματα, making their appearance.— " Immediate propositions :" cf. *Index Aristotelicus*, *s.v.* ἄμεσος, also *Anal. Post.*, ii. 3, 90 b, 24 *seqq.* : ἔτι αἱ ἀρχαὶ τῶν ἀποδείξεων ὁ ρ ι σ μ ο ί . . . ἢ τὰ πρῶτα ὁρισμοὶ ἔσονται ἀναπόδεικτοι. A survey of the relevant passages shows that by the ἄμεσοι ἀρχαί or προτάσεις we are to understand, preponderantly if not exclusively, ὁρισμοί, or definitions. Aristotle might have been thinking here of axioms or principles of proof, but apparently they were not actually in his mind.—The comparison with sense-perception : *De An.*, ii. 5, 417 b, 22. Although in this passage, as in those quoted just previously, Nous is not explicitly limited to its narrower sense, it is this alone that can be meant. For what follows, see also Zeller, ii. 2 (ed. 3), pp. 190, 191.

Page 207. "Nous a mere capacity :" cf. *De An.*, iii. 4, 429, 430. Predicates of Nous : *De An.*, iii. 5, 430 a, 17 : καὶ οὗτος ὁ νοῦς χωριστὸς καὶ ἀπαθὴς καὶ ἀμιγής, τῇ οὐσίᾳ ὢν ἐνέργεια. Cf. i. 4, 408 b, 18 : ὁ δὲ νοῦς ἔοικεν ἐγγίνεσθαι οὐσία τις οὖσα καὶ οὐ φθείρεσθαι. (Last par.) "We shall meet with Nous again :" namely, in the already quoted passage, *Eth. Nic.*, vi. 12, 1143 a, 35 *seqq.* On what follows, cf. *De An.*, i. 4, 408 b, 29 : ὁ δὲ νοῦς ἴσως θειότερόν τι καὶ ἀπαθές ἐστιν, *Eth. Nic.*, x. 7, 1177 a, 15 : (ὁ νοῦς) εἴτε θεῖον ὂν καὶ αὐτὸ εἴτε τῶν ἐν ἡμῖν θειότατον. Fragm. 46 (1483 a, 27): ὅτι ὁ θεὸς ἢ νοῦς ἐστιν ἢ ἐπέκεινά τι τοῦ νοῦ.

BOOK VI.—CHAPTER XVIII.

Page 209 (Top). The sublunary world an "evanescent part of the All :" οὐθὲν ὡς εἰπεῖν μόριον τοῦ παντός, *Metaph.*, iv. 1010 a, 30. Nature not "episodic :" *Metaph.*, xiv. 3, 1090 b, 19 ; also xii. *fin.* (Middle) "Praise of Anaxagoras :" νοῦν δή τις εἰπὼν, κ.τ.λ. ; *Metaph.*, i. 3, 984 b, 15 *seqq.*—"Bad is the lordship of many . . . :" *Iliad*, ii. 204, quoted *Metaph.*, xii. *fin.*

Page 210 (Middle). Aristotle on matter : see *De Gen. et Corr.*, i. 7, 324 b, 18 : ἡ δ' ὕλη ᾖ ὕλη παθητικόν ; also note to ch. 11, § 2. (Below) "This is what Nature wills :" see the note just referred to.—"Nature does nothing in vain :" *De Cœlo*, ii. 11, 291 b, 13 *seq.*—"God and Nature :" *De Cœlo*, i. 4, 271 a, 33 : ὁ δὲ θεὸς καὶ ἡ φύσις οὐδὲν μάτην ποιοῦσιν.

Page 211 (Top). Aristotle denies all work and action to the Deity : the chief passage is *Eth. Nic.*, x. 8, especially 1178 b, 20 *seq.* : τῷ δὴ ζῶντι τοῦ πράττειν ἀφαιρουμένου, ἔτι δὲ μᾶλλον τοῦ ποιεῖν, κ.τ.λ. The grounds of the denial are fully given in the same context. Other references in Zeller, ii. 2 (ed. 3), p. 368 *seqq.* There is a remarkable contradiction in this last-named work between note 1, p. 368, and note 2, p. 374. In the first we read, "he says quite generally that both ποιεῖν and πράττειν are to be denied to the Deity ;" in the second, "only a particular kind of ποίησις is denied to the Deity." Cf. also *De Cœlo*, ii. 12, especially 292 a, 22 and b 4, 5 : τῷ δ' ὡς ἄριστα ἔχοντι οὐδὲά δεῖ πράξεως.

Page 213 (Top). "Mythical accretion" and "mythical envelope :" cf. *Metaph.*, xii. 8, 1074 a, 1 *seq.*, ἐν μύθου σχήματι and 1074 b, 3 : τὰ δὲ λοιπὰ μυθικῶς ἤδη προσῆκται, κ.τ.λ.

Page 214 (Middle). "Almost icy coldness :" the phrase is from Elser, *Die Lehre des Aristoteles über das Wirken Gottes*, Münster, 1893, p. 75. (Bottom) "The most eminent historian :" Zeller, ii. 2 (ed. 3), p. 375.

Page 215 (Middle). Theophrastus : *Fragm.*, 12 (iii. 152, Wimmer). (Par. 2) Origin of the belief in gods : *Aristotelis Fragmenta*, 12–14.

Page 216 (end of sect. 4). The author referred to is Zeller, *op. cit.*, p. 360.

Page 217 (Top). "A sentence in the *Rhetoric* :" ii. 23, 1398 a, 15. The author critized here is Franz Brentano, *Psychologie des Aristoteles*, 239 : "Lastly, we also find the expression 'work of God' : τὸ δαιμόνιον οὐδέν ἐστιν, ἀλλ' ἢ θεὸς ἢ θεοῦ ἔργον." These and kindred fallacies are well dealt with by Elser, *op. cit.*, p. 103 *seq.* (Bottom) "Where there is a better . . . there must also be a best :" *Aristot. Fragm.*, 15.

Page 218 (Middle). "A probable, not to say necessary, assumption :" εὔλογον, ἵνα μὴ ἀναγκαῖον εἴπωμεν, καὶ τὸ τρίτον εἶναι ὃ κινεῖ ἀκίνητον ὄν, *Physica*, viii. 5, 256 b, 23. A similar argument is found in *De An.*, iii. 10, 433 b, 13 *seqq.*, and *Metaph.*, xii. 7 *in.*, where I read with

Bonitz: ἐπεὶ δὲ τὸ μὲν κινούμενον καὶ μὴ κινοῦν, τὸ δὲ κινούμενον καὶ κινοῦν, καὶ τρίτον τοίνυν ἔστι τι ὃ οὐ κινούμενον κινεῖ, 1072 a, 24 *seq.* Zeller's interpretation (*op. cit.*, p. 359) of the moved non-mover as *matter*, of the moved mover as *nature*, seems to me quite without foundation. It is not only that no word in the passages concerned points to this interpretation ; the moved mover is illustrated by examples which are actually forms of matter, such as air and water. Cf. *Physica*, viii. 10, 266 b, 31 *seq.*, and 267 a, 3 *seqq.*: οἷον τὸν ἀέρα, ὃς κινούμενος κινεῖ, and ἢ τὸν ἀέρα τοιοῦτον ἢ τὸ ὕδωρ ἤ τι ἄλλο τοιοῦτον ὃ πέφυκε κινεῖν καὶ κινεῖσθαι. Even if air and water could be counted as nature, in opposition, say, to unspecialized matter, we should still ask in vain why these particular cases are adduced instead of a reference being given to Nature as a whole.

Sect. 7.   Page 219.   Gottfried Keller: *Der Grüne Heinrich*, iii. ch. 1, p. 13 (22nd ed., 1901).   On what follows, cf. *Physica*, viii. 5.

Page 220 (Par. 2).   "The highest generality : " cf. *Metaph.*, iv. 8, 1049 b, 24 *seqq.* ; *De Gen. An.*, ii. 1, 734 b, 21 *seq.* ; and *Metaph.*, xii. 7, 1072 b, 3 *seqq.* The application to the supreme principle of the universe : *Metaph.*, xii. 6, 1071 b, 13 *seq.*: ἐνδέχεται γὰρ τὸ δύναμιν ἔχον μὴ ἐνεργεῖν . . . εἰ γὰρ μὴ ἐνεργήσει, οὐκ ἔσται κίνησις. The passages quoted : *ibid.*, 24 *seq.* and 13 *seq.* It is just this highly important chapter which supplies the most cogent proof that the Aristotelian philosophy was *not*, as is so often assumed, one of development. He makes a vigorous and determined attack on the representatives of such a theory, on " the Pythagoreans and Speusippus, who did not place the fairest and best at the beginning," but treated it as the perfection, we might say the consummation, of a process of development (1072 b, 30 *seqq.*). By recognizing a scale of living beings, Aristotle did work preliminary to the theory of development and greatly assisted its progress. But these grades of worth or dignity were emphatically not identified by him with a succession in time. The highest and the lowest, in his view, have existed side by side in the organic world from all eternity. If this is to be called a theory of development, it is difficult to see what can be the meaning of the name. But the ease with which the two ideas may be confused, or the one expressed so as to be hardly distinguishable from the other, may be illustrated by many an instructive quotation from Aristotle's modern interpreters. Thus, no less a writer than Zeller (*op. cit.*, p. 359) expresses himself as follows : " The scale of being, which starts from primary formless matter rises to its culmination in the Deity." This almost suggests that for Aristotle, as for Hartmann, God was a product of development, though no principle of his is so firmly held as that the fairest and best must have existed from the beginning, and not be reserved to the end. Zeller knew this better than any one. But by expressing himself as though he believed the contrary, he shows how easy it is to glide from the true view to the false. Many a reader, unaccustomed to go to the sources, might be misled by expressions of this kind when used by high authorities. These remarks may also serve to supplement what has been said in ch. xiii., § 6, pp. 154, 155.

BOOK VI.—CHAPTER XIX.

Pages 223, 224. Estimate of the earth's circumference : *De Cælo,* ii. 13, 298 a, 15 *seqq.* On what follows, cf. *ibid.,* 19 *seq.* : ὄγκον ... μὴ μέγαν πρὸς τὸ τῶν ἄλλων ἄστρων μέγεθος. Similarly, *Meteor.,* i. 3, 340 a, 6 : οὐθὲν γὰρ ὡς εἰπεῖν μόριον ὁ τῆς γῆς ἐστὶν ὄγκος, and 352 a, 26 : ὁ δὲ τῆς γῆς ὄγκος καὶ τὸ μέγεθος οὐθέν ἐστι δήπου πρὸς τὸν ὅλον οὐρανόν, *Meteorol.,* ii. 1, 353 a, b : οἱ μὲν οὖν ἀρχαῖοι . . . ὡς μέγα τι τοῦ πάντος τοῦτο μόριον ὄν· καὶ τὸν λοιπὸν οὐρανὸν ὅλον περὶ τοῦτον συστῆναι τὸν τόπον καὶ τούτου χάριν ὡς ὄντα τιμιώτατον καὶ ἀρχήν.

Page 224 (Middle). "A star among stars :" *De Cælo,* ii. 13, 293 a, 22 : τὴν δὲ γῆν ἐν τῶν ἄστρων οὖσαν, κύκλῳ φερομένην περὶ τὸ μέσον, νύκτα τε καὶ ἡμέραν ποιεῖν. (Par. 2) On the subject here treated, cf. Hultsch, in the *Real-Enzyklopædie d. klass. Altertumswiss* of Pauly-Wissowa, article "Astronomie," ii. 2, 1843 *seqq.* The passages quoted in the text are from *De Cælo,* ii. 13. In particular, compare 293 a, 30 : τῷ γὰρ τιμιωτάτῳ οἴονται προσήκειν τὴν τιμιωτάτην ὑπάρχειν χώραν with *De Cælo,* ii. 5, 288 a, 2 : εἰ γὰρ ἡ φύσις ἀεὶ ποιεῖ τῶν ἐνδεχομένων τὸ βέλτιστον, ἔστι δὲ ... ἡ πρὸς τὸν ἄνω τόπον τιμιωτέρα, κ.τ.λ.

Page 226 (par. 2). Paul Tannery : *Recherches sur l'histoire de l'astronomie ancienne,* p. 101. On what follows see S. Newcomb, *Popular Astronomy,* pp. 201, 202 (ed. 2) : "It is probable that no one thing tended more strongly to impress the minds of thoughtful men in former times with the belief that the earth is immovable than did the absence of stellar parallax." Tannery (*op. cit.,* p. 97) makes it highly probable that Aristarchus actually looked for the annual parallaxes of the fixed stars, and explained their absence by the great distances, which he regarded as practically, though not absolutely, infinite.

Page 228 (end of par. 1). Plato's question : on the authority of Eudemus, quoted by Simplicius in his Commentary on the *De Cælo,* ii. 12 (488, 37 *seqq.,* Heiberg) : τίνων ὑποτεθεισῶν ὁμαλῶν καὶ τεταγμένων κινήσεων διασωθῇ τὰ περὶ τὰς κινήσεις τῶν πλανωμένων φαινόμενα. (Par. 2) Aristotle's statement and justification of the sphere-theory is to be found in *Metaph.,* xii. 8, and *De Cælo,* ii. 7-12. To these should be added Simplicius in his Commentary on the *De Cælo* (p. 488, 20, ed. Heiberg), or, as the case may be, Sosigenes, whose Commentary is freely used by Simplicius. In modern literature the first place is taken by Schiaparelli's monograph *Le sfere omocentriche di Eudosso, di Callippo e di Aristotele,* Milan, 1875.

Page 229 (Middle). "Foresight :" *De Cælo,* ii. 9, 291 a, 24 *seq.* : προνοούσης τῆς φύσεως.

Page 230 (Middle). "Some of the most eminent specialists :"

particularly Schiaparelli, *op. cit.*, p. 48 *seq.* He is followed by Hultsch, *loc. cit.*

Page 231 (Top). "Mathematicians :" mentioned in many passages. The "stronger :" *Metaph.*, xii. 8, 1074 a, 16 *seq.* ; τὸ γὰρ ἀναγκαῖον ἀφείσθω τοῖς ἰσχυροτέροις λέγειν. Contemporaries bound to him by close personal ties : Eudoxus has already been mentioned several times in Vols. II. and III. as an at least temporary member of the Platonic circle. Simplicius (*op. cit.* p. 493, 5 *seqq.*, ed. Heiberg) speaks of Callippus as a friend and fellow-worker of Aristotle. He came to Athens, and τῷ Ἀριστοτέλει συγκατεβίω τὰ ὑπὸ τοῦ Εὐδόξου εὑρεθέντα σὺν τῷ Ἀριστοτέλει διορθούμενός τε καὶ προσαναπληρῶν. Aristotle himself, however, supplies (*Metaph.*, xii. 8, 1073 b, 32 *seqq.*) a distinction between the number of spheres which Calippus postulated and that accepted by Eudoxus. From this same passage it appears that Simplicius (*loc. cit.*, b, 4, 5) is wrong in tracing the theory of retrograde spheres as far back as to Eudoxus. (Middle) "A credible tradition :" the anecdote embodying it (Gellius, *Noctes Atticæ*, xiii. 5) may perhaps be refused belief ; but we may reasonably accept as true the statement that in choosing his successor Aristotle hesitated between his two most important pupils, Theophrastus and Eudemus. On the monograph of Sosigenes, cf. Schiaparelli, p. 50. His severe criticism of the sphere-theory of Aristotle, as well as of those taught by Eudoxus and Callippus, is reported in Simplicius, *loc. cit.*, p. 504, 16 *seqq.*

Page 232 (Top). Apollonius and Hipparchus : cf. Hultsch, *op. cit.*, ii. 2, 1647 *seq.*, and ii. 1, 160. On the survival of the planetary spheres in astrology and in the Oriental mysteries, cf. F. Cumont, *Les religions orientales dans le paganisme romain* (Paris, 1906), pp. 192, 199, 214, 300, 311, 328 ; p. 152 seems also relevant, as the ascent of souls on their journey of purification "de zone en zone" must be equivalent to "de sphère en sphère." The controversy on the origin of the belief in the traversing of the seven spheres need not be touched on here. The literature relating to it is given by Cumont, *ibid.*, pp. 292, 293. (Middle) Claudius Ptolemæus : Σύνταξις, ix. *in.*, 114 *seq.*, Halma, but more particularly in the second book of the Ὑποθέσεις, up to the present accessible only in the Arabic translations (I am indebted to Herr Heiberg for information given privately).

Sect. 6. Page 233. In treating these subjects Aristotle constantly presupposes the proximity of the stellar sphere to the First Mover ; yet at the same time the latter is conceived as external to space, which is bounded by the sphere of the fixed stars : *De Cælo*, i. 9, 279 a, 18 : διόπερ οὔτ' ἐν τόπῳ τἀκεῖ πέφυκεν, κ.τ.λ., and l. 11 above : ἅμα δὲ δῆλον ὅτι οὐδὲ τόπος οὐδὲ κενὸν οὐδὲ χρόνος ἐστὶν ἔξω τοῦ οὐρανοῦ.

Page 234 (Top). "Contact :" see *De Gen. et Corr.*, i. 16, 323 a, 28 ; *Physica*, iii. 2, 202 a, 7 *seq.*, and vii. 2, *in.*

Page 235 (Top). "The following consideration :" φορὰ γὰρ ἡ πρώτη τῶν μεταβολῶν, ταύτης δὲ ἡ κύκλῳ (*Metaph.*, xii. 7, 1072 b, 8).

Sect. 7. Zeller (*op. cit.*, p. 456, note 1) judges very aptly, as I think, on the nature of the star-gods and their identity with the sphere-spirits. It is only in regard to the fixed stars, which are all supposed attached to a single sphere, that the ground for this identification disappears.

Page 236 (Bottom). The two difficulties and the answers to them in *De Cœlo*, ii. 12.

Page 237 (par. 2). "Life" and "activity:" cf. *De Cœlo*, ii. 12, 292 a, 18, and b, 1 : ἀλλ' ἡμεῖς ὡς περὶ σωμάτων αὐτῶν μόνον . . . ἀψύχων δὲ πάμπαν, διανοούμεθα· δεῖ δ' ὡς μετεχόντων ὑπολαμβάνειν πράξεως καὶ ζωῆς. And again : διὸ δεῖ νομίζειν καὶ τὴν τῶν ἄστρων πρᾶξιν εἶναι τοιαύτην οἵα περ ἡ τῶν ζῴων καὶ φυτῶν. Once more, *ibid.*, ii. 8 289 b, 31 : λείπεται τοὺς μὲν κύκλους κινεῖσθαι, τὰ δὲ ἄστρα ἠρεμεῖν καὶ ἐνδεδεμένα τοῖς κύκλοις φέρεσθαι.

Sect. 8. Page 238. The chief passages on the self-thinking of the Godhead are *Metaph.*, xii. 7, 1072 b, 24 *seqq.* and *ibid.*, 9, 1074 b, 17 *seqq.* To these add *Eth. Nic.*, x. 8, 1178 b, 8 *seqq.* The quotation from Thomas Aquinas, the remark on Duns Scotus, as well as the references to Petrus Ramus and Jules Simon, are taken from Elser, *op. cit.*, pp. 38, 46. The supposed " dogma " of the " all-ignorance of Aristotle's God " is ridiculed in Brentano's *Die Psychologie des Aristoteles*, p. 195. To this writer, also, belong the words, "the most elevated doctrine . . ." at the beginning of par. 3.

BOOK VI.—CHAPTER XX.

Page 240. The relations between the three works on ethics were first cleared up by Leonhard Spengel, *Abhandl. d. k. bayer. Akad.*, iii. 439 *seqq.* Special mention must here be made of John Burnet's edition (*The Ethics of Aristotle*, London, 1900). Throughout we find below the text of the *Nicomachean Ethics* the passages of the *Eudemian Ethics* which exhibit important variations. The editor constantly keeps the whole Aristotle before him, and, indeed, the whole Plato. We do not hesitate to give this distinguished work the first place among all the writings in interpretation of Aristotle that are known to us. A single reservation must be made. Burnet distinguishes much more strictly than we think admissible between the arguments which the philosopher bases on his personal convictions and those which rest for him merely on current opinion (τὰ ἔνδοξα). In our view this sharp distinction was alien to Aristotle's mind. We have said something on this subject on p. 216; and to this may be added various remarks that we have made in the text, without entering into polemics against Burnet. In explaining the title we have followed Burnet, p. xii.—The " half-dozen quotations from himself:" references to these are given by Bonitz in the *Index*, 101 b, 19 *seqq.* With one exception (*Metaph.* i. 1, 981 b, 25), the quotations are found in the

Politics. This work is presented as a continuation of the *Ethics*, and its title sometimes includes the *Ethics*—the science of society, as we might put it. It is so, for example, in a passage which we have already mentioned, in the opening chapter of the *Nicomachean Ethics* : διὸ τῆς πολιτικῆς οὐκ ἔστιν οἰκεῖος ἀκροατὴς ὁ νέος.—On the "desultory remarks . . .," cf. Burnet, p. 319. This author makes no remark on the almost verbal agreement of 1148 a, 17 *seqq.* with 1150 a, 27 *seqq.* The section vii. 12–15 is sketchy in character. There, too, we find signs of a remarkable negligence in point of style. Thus a string of hostile arguments occurs, joined together by the mere repetition of ἔτι three times in two lines (1152 b, 15–17).

Page 247 (Middle). "The rustling of a mouse:" this touch is taken from a later book (vii. 6, 1149 a, 7).

Page 248 (Top). A reproach urged by the "logically rigorous Herbartians :" cf. Hartenstein, *Histor.-philos. Abhandlungen*, p. 280, note 91. Bonitz took a quite similar line in his lectures (unpublished).

Page 249 (Middle). The line from Homer is *Iliad*, iii. 156 : ἀλλὰ καὶ ὣς τοιήπερ ἐοῦσ' οἰκόνδε νεέσθω.

Page 252 (Bottom). It is an ancient conjecture that Aristotle took his pupil Alexander as the model of the magnanimous (μεγαλόψυχος) character.

Page 254 (Top). "In the Peripatetic school:" cf. Philodemus, *De Ira* (Index, *s.v.* "Peripatetici" in my edition). See also Seneca, *De Ira*, i. 9.

BOOK VI.—CHAPTER XXI.

Page 257 (Middle). "In the Homeric poems :" especially *Odyssey*, xix. 109 *seqq.*

Page 258 (Top). "Rejects Plato's attempt :" in the closing sentence of the fifth book, 1138 b, 5 *seqq.* The concealed allusion is excellently interpreted by Burnet, *op. cit.*, p. 246.

Sect. 2. Page 259. On corrective or directive justice, see Burnet, p. 213.

Page 260 (Top). "The only contrast to justice is injustice :" this was expressed quite correctly by Heliodorus in his paraphrase : ἡ δὲ δικαιοσύνη . . . μόνῃ τῇ ἀδικίᾳ ἀντίκειται (p. 99, 9, Heylbut). Herbert Spencer (*Principles of Ethics*, i. 556 *seq.*) wittily ridicules the application of the theory of the mean to the departments of justice and truth, while fully and gladly acknowledging its applicability to self-regarding morality.

Page 261 (Middle). "The best modern interpreter :" the reference is once more to Burnet, p. 218 : "but surely Aristotle is not to be credited with the childish doctrine that a court of law simply awards compensation."

Page 262 (Top). "In another passage of the same book:" v. 5, 1, 32 b, 21.

Page 263 (Bottom). "An ancient expositor:" Heliodorus, in his paraphrase of the *Nicomachean Ethics*; the passage corresponds to v. 16 (109, 23 *seqq.*, Heylbut).

Page 264 (Middle). John Austin : *Lectures on Jurisprudence*, ii. 274-277.

Page 265 (Top). "The Platonic and Pythagorean conception:" cf. *Phædo*, 61 D *seqq.*—The punishment of suicides at Athens : cf. Æschines, *In Ctes.*, p. 88, § 244.

BOOK VI.—CHAPTER XXII.

Aristotle's doctrine of the intellectual virtues has been treated by Karl Prantl in an excellent monograph entitled *Die dianoëtischen Tugenden in der Nikomacheischen Ethik* (Munich, 1852). On p. 5 *seqq.* of this work decisive grounds are given for rejecting the attempts which have been made to assign books vi. and vii. to the *Eudemian Ethics*. Prantl is here in agreement with L. Spengel (Münchener Akademie-Abhandlungen, iii. 2).

Page 270 (Top). "A minimum of experience is sufficient:" cf. Burnet, *op. cit.*, p. 273, and his reference to *Anal. Post.*, i. 13, 81 b, 2. The two sentences from Aristotle quoted below are : καὶ τὰ μὲν οὐ πιστεύουσιν οἱ νέοι, ἀλλὰ λέγουσιν (1142 a, 19), and : καὶ οἱ πρῶτον μαθόντες συνείρουσι μὲν τοὺς λόγους, ἴσασι δ' οὔπω· δεῖ γὰρ συμφῦναι. The astonishing precosity of some of the mathematicians named in the text has been lately noticed by Dr. H. G. Parker ; see the *Beilage zur Allgemeinen Zeitung* of February 8, 1908, p. 483. Aristotle's remark is found at 1142 a, 12.

Page 271 (Top). "If reason and sense-perception sometimes change places :" 1143 b, 5 : τούτων οὖν (τῶν καθ' ἕκαστα) ἔχειν δεῖ αἴσθησιν, αὕτη δ' ἐστὶ νοῦς. Cf. Burnet, *op. cit*, p. 281 : "So we say 'I see' when we mean an intellectual not a sensuous perception . . . We were told . . . that this αἴσθησις ἀντίκειται τῷ νῷ, here that it is νοῦς." (Bottom) "In the circle of the Platonists:" cf. Burnet, p. 3, and the reference there given to Plato, *Philebus*, 11 D : ἡμῶν ἑκάτερος ἕξιν ψυχῆς καὶ διάθεσιν ἀποφαίνειν τινὰ ἐπιχειρήσει τὴν δυναμένην ἀνθρώποις πᾶσι τὸν βίον εὐδαίμονα παρέχειν. This involves the supposition that not only εὐδαιμονία but also its cause, ἀρετή, is a ἕξις.

Page 272 (Middle). Xenocrates : see Clemens, *Strom.*, ii. 21 (p. 50, Potter), which Burnet also quotes. Speusippus and Xenocrates are both mentioned there ; and of the latter it is said that τὴν εὐδαιμονίαν ἀποδίδωσι κτῆσιν τῆς οἰκείας ἀρετῆς. It is particularly against this κτῆσιν that Aristotle's polemic is directed at the beginning of the *Eth. Nic.* (Bottom) "Connexion between character and intellect:" cf. the remarkable sentence (1144 a, 34), which even Burnet does not explain too accurately : διαστρέφει γὰρ ἡ μοχθηρία καὶ διαψεύδεσθαι ποιεῖ περὶ τὰς πρα τικὰς ἀρχάς.

Pages 273, 274. Prantl, *op. cit.*, pp. 18, 19, suggests, though in other words, the same connexion between books vi. and vii. His conclusion is stated as follows : " Thus the treatment of these qualities (ἐγκράτεια and καρτερία), which follows in the seventh book, forms the immediate and necessary continuation of the sixth."

Page 275 (Top). " The work, probably, of Academics : " so Burnet conjectures, p. 294, commenting on 1145, 1146.

Page 278 (Middle). This mistake in the choice between two syllogisms seems to us much more intelligible than the other explanation (1147 b, 9 *seqq*.), ignored by us in the text, according to which the minor premiss of the syllogism inviting to action, such a proposition as "this thing is sweet " (cf. Burnet, pp. 104, 105), must be regarded as the real seat of the error.

Page 282 (Bottom). " The striking negligence of the style : " see note to p. 240.

On the question as to the genuineness of the section 1152 b, 1-1154 a, 7, cf. Prantl, *Über die dianoëtischen Tugenden*, p. 6, and, more particularly, Burnet, p. 330 *seqq.*, where the polemic against Speusippus is made highly probable. See also Aspasius (*op. cit.*, p. 151, 24, Heylbut), who first draws from the silence of book x. the inference that this part does not belong to Aristotle, but to Eudemus (here he probably has in his mind the whole of the three books common to the *Nicomachean* and the *Eudemian Ethics*), while immediately afterwards he cuts away the chief support of this expropriation by adding : πλὴν εἴτε Εὐδήμου ταῦτά ἐστιν εἴτε ᾽Αριστοτέλους, ἐνδόξως εἴρηται. For if the exposition was intended dialectically and not dogmatically, the chief ground for contesting its Aristotelian authorship disappears.

BOOK VI.—CHAPTER XXIII.

Page 284 (Middle). "The love of boys . . . unnatural : " cf. *Eth. Nic.*, vii. 6, 1148 b, 28 : πρὸς δὲ τούτοις ἡ τῶν ἀφροδισίων τοῖς ἄρρεσιν. The chief passage on wedded union is viii. 14, 1162 a, 20 *seqq.*

Page 286 (Top). " Community of studies and thoughts : " cf. ix. 9, 1170 b, 10 *seqq.*: συναισθάνεσθαι ἄρα δεῖ καὶ τοῦ φίλου ὅτι ἔστιν, τοῦτο δὲ γίνοιτ᾽ ἂν ἐν τῷ συζῆν καὶ κοινωνεῖν λόγων καὶ διανοίας. My translation of the difficult λόγων as "studies " may not seem absolutely necessary ; it seems, however, beyond doubt that Aristotle has here in mind community of contemplative, not of practical life ; the association of two politicians, for example, would be characterized by him differently.

Sect. 2. On the question as to the order of the books, see Burnet, *op. cit.*, p. 344. Here, too, the traditional order is justified, but on grounds, suggested by a hint of Teichmüller, which we do not acknowledge as sound.

Sect. 3. " A remarkable saying : " ἴδοι δ᾽ ἄν τις καὶ ἐν ταῖς πλάναις ὡς οἰκεῖον ἅπας ἄνθρωπος ἀνθρώπῳ καὶ φίλον (viii. 1, 1155 a, 21). Burnet calls the passage "one of the few places in Aristotle where we see a sign of the coming cosmopolitanism."

Page 292 (Middle). George Eliot : cf. Spencer's *Autobiography,* ii. 305. Dickens : see *The Letters of Charles Dickens,* i. 36, also 37 and 42.

Page 293 (Bottom). J. S. Mill : *System of Logic,* book vi. ch. 12, § 7. Page 294 (Middle). Theodore Meynert : *Populärwissenschaftliche Vorträge* (Vienna, 1892), p. 169 *seqq.,* especially p. 171 : "The expansion of the secondary ego, in which it becomes fused with the whole as a subservient member, is associated with the idea of mutualism, of reciprocity, of brotherhood."

BOOK VI.—CHAPTER XXIV.

Page 298 (Top). "In an earlier section : " ix. 4, 1166 a, 4 *seqq.* : οὗτος γὰρ ὁμογνωμονεῖ ἑαυτῷ καὶ τῶν αὐτῶν ὀρέγεται κατὰ πᾶσαν τὴν ψυχήν. The passage reproduced in the text is x. 5, 1176 a, 15 *seqq.*

Page 303 (par. 2). "The inactivity of God." This doctrine, though enounced with the greatest emphasis (cf. note to p. 238), is yet completely ignored in one passage (*Eth. Nic.,* x. 10, 1179 a, 22 *seqq.*). The provident care of the gods for human affairs is here assumed, and the consequence drawn that on this ground too the wise man must be the happiest ; for the gods love him who most cultivates that which is the best and the most closely related to themselves—that is to say, reason. The glaring contradiction, as also the inappropriateness of the passage to the context, where it breaks the thread, have roused in at least one editor (Ramsauer) doubts as to its genuineness. We hold, with Burnet, that the passage is genuine, even if not meant for the place where it is found, and that the view expressed in it is merely an ἔνδοξον, as is shown in addition by the accumulated limitations (εἰ γάρ τις ἐπιμέλεια . . . ὥσπερ δοκεῖ, καὶ εἴη ἂν εὔλογον). Here, as so often elsewhere, the never-wearied dialectician cannot bring himself to omit an argument favourable to his thesis, even though its ground is entirely foreign to his mind.

Sect. 6. Isocrates : *Or.* 15 (Περὶ ἀντιδόσεως), § 82 *seq.* As was recognized by Spengel, the polemic of Aristotle contains verbal echoes from the writer whom he is attacking. On his emphatic condemnation of the eclectic method, cf. 1181 a, 21 : καὶ ποῖα ποίοις συνᾴδει, and 1181 b, 9 : καὶ ποῖα ποίοις ἁρμόττει, or, again, *Rhet.,* i. 4, 1360 a, 33 : αἱ ποῖαι τοῖς ποίοις ἁρμόττουσιν, where, too, all these questions are removed from the domain of rhetoric and assigned exclusively to politics.

BOOK VI.—CHAPTER XXV.

Sect. 1. Page 305. This statement of Aristotle's views on pleasure is based chiefly on *Eth. Nic.,* i. 1-4 ; vii. 12-15 ; x. 1-3 ; *Rhetoric,* i. 11.

Page 307 (Bottom). "The thesis of Eudoxus :" *Eth. Nic.*, x. 2, *in*. Sir Alexander Grant and Burnet have shown that in all probability the passage 1172 b, 9 *seqq*., is a verbal quotation, by arguing from the two words ἔλλογα and φέρεσθαι. The first is otherwise unknown in Aristotle, and is entered by Bonitz in his *Index* with the comment, "fortasse ex Eudoxo." The second, though here used of volitions, is elsewhere applied only to motion in space ; and Burnet (p. 442) aptly describes it as " an unusual word in this connexion, but natural in the mouth of an astronomer." From this passage and its agreement with the opening words of the *Ethics* it has been rightly inferred that in the sentence : διὸ καλῶς ἀπεφήναντο τἀγαθόν, οὗ πάντ' ἐφίεται, the reference is to Eudoxus.

Page 308 (Middle). "Of that which appears to all . . . :" *Eth. Nic.*, x. 2, 1172, 173 : ὃ γὰρ πᾶσι δοκεῖ, τοῦτ' εἶναί φάμεν· ὁ δ' ἀναιρῶν ταύτην τὴν πίστιν, οὐ πάνυ πιστότερα ἐρεῖ.

Page 310 (Middle). Man a "social being :" ἄνθρωπος φύσει πολιτικὸν ζῷον, *Politica*, i. 2, 1253 a, 2 ; iii. 6, 1278 b, 19, where the craving after life in common is not based on economic necessity alone. See also *Eth. Nic.*, i. 5, 1097 b, 11 (φύσει πολιτικὸς ἄνθρωπος); ix. 9, 1169 b, 18 (πολιτικὸν γὰρ ὁ ἄνθρωπος καὶ συζῆν πεφυκός), etc.

BOOK VI.—CHAPTER XXVI.

Page 311 (Middle). The chief passages relating to communities of animals are : *Hist. An.*, viii. 1, 589 a, 1 : τὰ δὲ συνετώτερα καὶ κοινωνοῦντα μνήμης ἐπὶ πλέον καὶ πολιτικώτερον χρῶνται τοῖς ἀπογόνοις, and i. 1, 488 a, 7 *seqq.* : πολιτικὰ δ' ἐστὶν ὧν ἕν τι καὶ κοινὸν γίνεται πάντων τὸ ἔργον, κ.τ.λ.

Page 312 (Bottom). "Rome and Carthage :" cf. Fragment 568 (1571 b, 15 *seqq.*) relating to the Gallic invasion—an event then of recent date (six years before Aristotle's birth). Fragment 567 also deals with Roman history. Carthaginian institutions are treated of in several passages of the *Politics* and *Rhetoric*. On the popular works mentioned a little further on, most of them composed in dialogue form, cf. Bernays, *Dialoge des Aristoteles*, pp. 49, 53–57, 151–157.

Page 313 (Middle). The entry Οἰκονομικός α' in the ancient indices (Diog. Laert., v. 1, 22) bears witness at once for the genuineness of the first book of the *Economics* and against that of the second. The fact that Philodemus the Epicurean (*De Œconomia*, col. vii. 38 and 44 = p. 26, Chr. Jensen) cites this little book as the work of Theophrastus is in comparison evidence of little weight, and need hardly be taken into consideration. We shall show elsewhere that the grounds which have been urged against the authenticity of this first book amount to nothing. The spuriousness of the second book—to which, it may be remarked, we owe the expression " political economy"—is at once revealed by the division of the subject into four main varieties : royal, *satrapic*, political (that is, municipal), and private economy. A more detailed examination of the date and the disparate components of the book is given by U. Wilcken, Hermes, xxxvi. 187 *seqq.* Pages 313, 314. The " first investigation : " iv. 2, *in.* : ἐπεὶ δ᾽ ἐν τῇ πρώτῃ μεθόδῳ, κ.τ.λ. The "first sections : " vii. 2, 1325 a, 30 : διώρισται δὲ περὶ αὐτῶν ἱκανῶς ἐν τοῖς πρώτοις λόγοις. The passages in books iii. and iv. most nearly concerned are : διωρισμένων δὲ τούτων περὶ τῆς πολιτείας ἤδη πειρατέον λέγειν τῆς ἀρίστης, κ.τ.λ. (iii. *fin.*), compared with 1 *fin.* : ἄλλην ἀρχὴν ποιησάμενοι λέγωμεν, καὶ πρῶτον ἐπισκεψώμεθα περὶ τῶν ἀποφηναμένων περὶ τῆς πολιτείας τῆς ἀρίστης, and iv. 2, 1289 a, 30 : καὶ περὶ μὲν ἀριστοκρατίας καὶ βασιλείας εἴρηται.

Page 314 (Middle). " Monarchy : " this form of constitution is sometimes placed by Aristotle above all others. It is so in *Eth. Nic.*, viii. 10, 1160 a, 35 : τούτων δὲ βελτίστη μὲν ἡ βασιλεία (which two lines earlier is joined with ἀριστοκρατία). Burnet, in commenting on the passage (p. 384), has aptly remarked that we are here to think only of the ideal ruler, the man of divine or heroic virtue.

I have already in the text indicated my opinion that the transference of books vii. and viii., which has been proposed and adopted by several eminent scholars, is wholly unjustifiable. The tendency of textual criticism in our day is towards increased conservatism, and it grows more and more averse from violences of this kind. For me, two considerations are decisive. An incomplete section, like the last book, naturally belongs to the end of a work. To take it from that place and set it in the middle is to exchange an easily intelligible and not rare state, of things for one which, though not in itself impossible, is quite exceptional and improbable in the highest degree. Nor can sober thought commend a procedure which thrusts so extensive a section as that formed by the last two books like a sundering wedge into the heart of a closely connected whole, the description of the main constitutional forms. This rearrangement was first proposed by the Jesuit Scaino da Salo (1577), and afterwards by many others ; the transposition of books v. and vi. was adopted by Barthélemy St. Hilaire in his translation of the *Politics* (1837).

Page 316 (Bottom). The reference to Plato's *Statesman* is 258 A : πότερον οὖν τὸν πολιτικὸν καὶ βασιλέα καὶ δεσπότην καὶ ἔτ᾽ οἰκονόμον θήσομεν ὡς ἐν πάντα ταῦτα προσαγορεύοντες. Aristotle is clearly controverting this in *Politica*, i. 1, 1252 a, 7 *seqq.* : ὅσοι μὲν οὖν οἴονται πολιτικὸν καὶ βασιλικὸν καὶ οἰκονομικὸν καὶ δεσποτικὸν εἶναι τὸν αὐτόν, οὐ καλῶς λέγουσιν : and again, after elaborating this thought, in l. 16 : ταῦτα δ᾽ οὐκ ἔστιν ἀληθῆ. It will hardly be denied that the criticism is too severe when regard is had to the fact that a little further on Aristotle points out the close relationship between royal and patriarchal power.

Page 319 (Top). Emil Steinbach : in his work *Erwerb und Beruf*,

Vienna, 1896 ; and again in *Die Rechtsgeschäfte der wirthschaftlichen Organisation*, Vienna, 1897. (Below) Bentham : in his *Defence of Usury* (Letter x.), iii. 16 b, ed. Bowring. If money is barren by nature, then, in Bentham's opinion, what Aristotle prohibits would be not merely illegitimate but impossible (" that it would be to no purpose for a man to try to get five per cent. out of money—not that, if he could contrive to get so much, there would be any harm in it ").

Page 321. " A woman, for example . . .:" *Politica*, iii. 4, 1277 b, 20 *seqq.*

BOOK VI.—CHAPTER XXVII.

The question of slavery is principally treated in chapters iv.-vii. of the first book of the *Politics*.

Page 322 (Bottom). "Typical slave-names :" cf. Lambertz, *Die griechischen Sklavennamen* (Wiener Gymn. Prog., 1907, p. 12, n. 17, and p. 71).

Page 323 (Middle). " Superior and subordinate elements in nature as in the human soul : " *Pol.*, i. 12, 1260 a, 9 *seqq.*

Page 324. " Frustrated hereditary tendencies : " *Pol.*, i. 6, 1255 b, 2 ; 5. 1254 b, 27.

Page 325 (Top). " Line of poetry :" Euripides, *Iph. in Aul.*, 1400 *seq.* See also Aristotle, *Pol.*, i. 2, 1252 b, 8 : ὡς ταὐτὸ φύσει βάρβαρον καὶ δοῦλον ὄν. (Middle) "The peoples of the cold North . . . . :" vii. 7.

Page 326 (Top). " The rise of a monarchy seemed excluded : " cf. v. 10, 1313 a, 3 : οὐ γίγνονται δ' ἔτι βασιλεῖαι νῦν . . . διὰ τὸ τὴν βασιλείαν ἑκούσιον μὲν ἀρχὴν εἶναι . . . πολλοὺς δ' εἶναι τοὺς ὁμοίους, καὶ μηδένα διαφέροντα τοσοῦτον ὥστε, κ.τ.λ. (End of par. 1) " The federal state hardly receives even the most casual mention : " this is really an understatement of the case ; for the passage referred to (vii. 14, 1333-4) contemplates merely an hegemony which respects the interests of its subjects. (Bottom) " The Carthaginian constitution :" ii. 11.

Page 327 (Top). " Capacity for reflexion : " it is thus that τὸ βουλευτικόν is translated by Bernays (whom I follow here in several instances) in *Aristoteles Politik*, i., ii. *und* iii. *Buch*, p. 46.—" An altogether contemptible being :" *Poetica*, 15, 1454 a, 20 *seqq.* : καὶ γὰρ γυνή ἐστι χρηστὴ καὶ δοῦλος· καίτοι γε ἴσως τούτων τὸ μὲν χεῖρον, τὸ δὲ ὅλως φαῦλόν ἐστιν. (Par. 2) " Emancipation :" *Pol.*, vii. 10 *fin.* See also Hildebrand, *Geschichte und System der Rechts- und Staatsphilosophie*, i. 400.

Page 328 (Top). " Unwritten law :" ἄγραφος νόμος, cf. Bonitz in the *Index*, *s.v.* ἄγραφος.—" Too simple and barbaric : " *Politica*, ii. 8, 1268 b, 39 *seq.* (Bottom) Eratosthenes : quoted in Strabo, i. *fin.* = i. 87, 17 Meineke.

Page 329 (Middle). Plato's *Statesman*, pp. 262, 263.

Page 330 (Middle). " The statues of Dædalus," etc. : *Politica*, i. 4, 1253 b, 33 *seqq.*

Page 331 (Top). " Domestic slavery among the Islamic peoples : " see the particularly instructive article " ' Abd " (by Juynboll) in the *Enzyklopædie des Islam,* i. 16 *seqq.* (1908). For my knowledge of Hammond's *Two Letters on Slavery in the United States, addressed to Thomas Clarkson, Esq.,* I am indebted to the London monthly, *The Secular World* (Feb., 1863). The manifesto is entitled " Address to Christians throughout the World, by the Clergy of the Confederate States of America." The passages utilized or quoted are found on pp. 7, 11 *seq.,* and 16. (Bottom) For the quotations the following references may be given : ὄργανον πρὸ ὀργάνων, *Pol.,* i. 4, 1253 b, 19 ; κτῆμά τι ἔμψυχον, *ibid.* ; ἔμψυχον ὄργανον, *Eth. Nic.,* viii. 13, 1161 b, 4 ; οὐδὲ πρὸς ἵππον ἢ βοῦν (*sc.* δίκαιόν ἐστιν), *ibid.,* 1161 b, 2.—" His master's advantage is his highest law :" *ibid.,* 1160 b, 20 *seq.* : τὸ γὰρ τοῦ δεσπότου συμφέρον ἐν αὐτῇ πράττεται. Also : ἀρετῆς δεῖται μικρᾶς, *Pol.,* i. 13, 1260 a, 35. No " friendship between bond and free : " *Eth. Nic.,* viii. 13, 1161 a, 35. A little above, 1161 b, 6, is a passage which is translated somewhat freely in the text : δοκεῖ γὰρ εἶναί τι δίκαιον παντὶ ἀνθρώπῳ πρὸς πάντα τὸν δυνάμενον κοινωνῆσαι νόμου καὶ συνθήκης· καὶ φιλίας δή, καθ' ὅσον ἄνθρωπος.

Sect. 7. Page 333. " A limited slavery : " ἀφωρισμένην . . . δουλείαν, *Pol.* i. *fin.,* 1260 a, b. The " banausic condition : " under this heading is included manual work, trade (wholesale as well as retail), and the class of day-labourers, while agriculture is specially singled out for mention in iv. 4, 1290, 1291. In many other passages all these occupations are termed banausic. Those of them ἐν οἷς τὰ σώματα λωβῶνται μάλιστα are called βαναυσόταται (i. 11, 1158 b, 37). (Bottom) Plutarch : *Vita Periclis,* c. 1, 2 ; the first passage has already been quoted in Vol. I. p. 581.

Page 334 (Top). " A learned observation : " *Pol.,* viii. 5, 1339 b, 7 *seqq.* The next quotation is from *Pol.,* viii. 5, 1339 b, 7 *seqq.* Callicles in the *Gorgias* : see especially 484 C, where the pursuit of philosophy is praised : ἄν τις αὐτοῦ μετρίως ἅψηται, κ.τ.λ., and 485 A, with its antithesis between ἐλευθέριον and ἀνελεύθερον, based on the same standard. We may add Aristotle, *Pol.,* viii. 2, 1337 b, 15 : ἔστι δὲ καὶ τῶν ἐλευθερίων ἐπιστημῶν μέχρι μέν τινος ἐνίων μετέχειν οὐκ ἀνελεύθερον. (End of section) Cf. again *Pol.* viii. 2, 1337 b, 5 *seqq.,* and also 15 *seq.* : ἄσχολον γὰρ ποιοῦσι τὴν διάνοιαν καὶ ταπεινήν.

Sect. 8. Cf. *Pol.,* iii. 5, 1278 a, *seqq.*; iv. 4. 1291 a, 1 *seqq.*; vi. 4, 1319 a, 26 *seqq.*

BOOK VI.—CHAPTER XXVIII.

Page 337 (Top). Humboldt : *Ideen zu einem Versuch, die Grenzen der Wirksamkeit des Staates zu bestimmen* (Ges. Werke, vii., Berlin, 1852). The quotation is from pp. 186 *seq.*

Page 338. (Bottom) Lycophron on nobility : quoted by Aristotle,

Περὶ εὐγενείας, Fragm. 82 (1490 a, 10 *seqq*.) ; also by the pseudo-Plutarch, *Pro Nobilitate*, xvii. 2 (p. 75, 48 Dübner). Aristotle's praise of εὐγένεια in *Pol.*, iii. 13, 1283 a, 33 *seqq.*—" Mutual guarantor of rights : " *Pol.*, iii. 9, 1280 b, 11 : ἐγγυητὴς ἀλλήλοις τῶν δικαίων, ἀλλ' οὐχ οἷος ποιεῖν ἀγαθοὺς καὶ δικαίους τοὺς πολίτας. It is not absolutely certain that the preceding words, καὶ ὁ νόμος συνθήκη, are also a quotation from Lycophron, but the context is in favour of the supposition. The attempt has been made (as by Susemihl, *Aristoteles' Politik*, ii. 67 *seq*.) to show that Hippodamus, too, was an advocate of the policeman-state ; but in our opinion this view is untenable. See Vol. I. p. 578, bottom.

Sects. 2 and 3. Pages 339, 340. These sections are based on *Pol.*, iii. 6–13.

Sect. 4. Page 341. The various forms of government are also treated in *Rhet.*, i. 8 and *Eth. Nic.*, ix. 12. The word "monarchy" is used by Aristotle predominantly in the wider generic sense, under which kingship (κατὰ τάξιν τινά) and despotic tyranny are comprehended as subordinate species; it is so in *Rhet.*, *cap. cit.*, 1366 a, 1 *seqq.*, or in *Pol.*, iii. 7, 1279 a, 32, and b, 16 ; occasionally, however, it is used in the narrower sense of absolute rule, as in *Pol.*, v. 10, 1313 a, 3, *seqq.*: οὐ γίγνονται δ' ἔτι βασιλεῖαι νῦν, ἀλλ' ἄνπερ γίγνωνται, μοναρχίαι καὶ τυραννίδες μᾶλλον.

Page 343 (Top). The comparison with a picnic occurs in iii. 10, 1281 b, 2, and again in iii. 15, 1286 a, 29. (Bottom) Censure of "musical fashions :" *Pol.*, viii. 7, 1342 a, 18 *seqq*.

Sect. 6. Page 345. The conjecture of Bernays (p. 172), that "chapters xii. and xiii. follow a separate plan," does not seem to me well-founded. What we have here is a number of repetitions ; there is no systematic advance. But other professors also, including some less negligent than Aristotle in the matter of systematic arrangement, sometimes resume thoughts touched upon, but not exhausted, in a previous lecture, in order to follow them out into developments which have only gradually become known to them. Besides it would be very strange if the close connexion between *cap*. xiii. *fin*. and xiv. *in*. (ὥστε βασιλέας εἶναι τοὺς τοιούτους ἀιδίους ἐν ταῖς πόλεσιν and ἴσως τε καλῶς ἔχειν σκέψασθαι περὶ βασιλέας) were a mere coincidence.

Page 346 (Middle). Antisthenes : perhaps, according to the conjecture of Ad. Müller (Vitzthumsches Gym. Progr., 1860, p. 46), in his work Περὶ νόμου ἢ περὶ πολιτείας. A bold guess was hazarded by Karl Joël in *Der echte und der xenophontische Sokrates*, ii. 801.

Page 348 (Middle). The picnic comparison : see the apt remarks of Trendelenburg, *Naturrecht auf dem Grunde der Ethik*, p. 525, ed. 2, especially the following sentence : " That collective fund of knowledge which Aristotle compares with a feast made up of individual contributions is fundamentally warped and deranged by the falsehood which is also contributed ; while the integration of the truth ... is obstructed or even frustrated by the resistance of error and selfishness."

Book VI.—Chapter XXIX.

Page 351. The opening paragraph is based on *Pol.*, iii. 14–17, supplemented by v. 10, 1310 a, 39–1311 a, 5. " Monarchy the best of all forms of government : " *Eth. Nic.*, viii. 12, 1160 a, 35. For what follows see 1160 a, b. (Bottom) " An anthology . . . : " *Eth. Nic.*, viii. 7, 1158 a, 27 *seqq.* : οἱ δ' ἐν ταῖς ἐξουσίαις, κ.τ.λ.; x. 6, 1176 b, 18 *seqq.* : οὐ γὰρ ἐν τῷ δυναστεύειν ἡ ἀρετὴ οὐδ' ὁ νοῦς : x. 10, 1179 a, 6 *seqq.* : οἱ γὰρ ἰδιῶται τῶν δυναστῶν οὐχ ἧττον δοκοῦσι τὰ ἐπιεικῆ πράττειν ἀλλὰ καὶ μᾶλλον. Sect. 2. Page 352. " Heaven-favoured exceptional natures : " cf. *Pol.*, iii. 13, 1284 a, 3 and b, 25, 1288 a, 19 *seqq.* Page 353 (Middle). Re-employment of it in the " Constitution of the Athenians : " 'Αθηναίων πολιτεία, 41, 2 *fin.* (p. 131, Kenyon, ed. 3), compared with *Pol.*, ii. 15, 1286 a, 31 *seqq.* Page 356 (end of sect. 4). Aristotle's censure of the Spartan double monarchy : this is to be found in the words : καὶ σωτηρίαν ἐνόμιζον τῇ πόλει εἶναι τὸ στασιάζειν τοὺς βασιλεῖς, *Pol.*, ii. 9, 1271 a, 25. This "disunion of the kings" may have prevented much harm, but it must necessarily have produced as great or greater. (Middle) The barbarians who are "by nature more inclined to serve : " iii. 14, 1285 a, 19 : διὰ γὰρ τὸ δουλικώτεροι εἶναι τὰ ἤθη φύσει οἱ μὲν βάρβαροι τῶν Ἑλλήνων. (Bottom) Only democratic constitutions possible in the future : *Pol.*, iii. 15, 1286 b, 20 *seqq.* The counsel addressed to Alexander : Strabo, i. p. 66 = i. 87 Meineke ; Plutarch, *De Fortuna Alexandri*, i. 6 (404, 8 *seqq.*, Dübner). Cf. Bernays, *Dialoge des Aristoteles*, pp. 154 *seq.*, (*Aristotelis Fragm.* 81, 1489 b, 26 *seqq.*).

Page 357 (end of chapter). Alexis de Tocqueville : *La démocratie en Amérique* (ed. 14), i. ch. 3, especially pp. 82–85, and many other passages. In my essay *Die Akademie und ihr vermeintlicher Philomazedonismus*, Wiener Studien, iv. (1882), p. 102 *seqq.*, I believe I have said all that is necessary against the groundless suggestion that Aristotle worked towards the absorption of Greece by Macedon. I may not, however, have sufficiently emphasized the fact that the Stagirite's personal relations with Alexander, with Antipater, and with Nicanor influenced his political thought in a surprisingly small degree. The Macedonians were and remained for him barbarians (cf. *ibid.*, p. 117, 118). The manner, too, in which King Philip's murder is mentioned by him as one among many instances of the assassination of potentates from private revenge (*Pol.*, v. 10, 1311 b, 2), does not in the least suggest that he had been bound to his former master by any intimate tie. The unfavourable impressions of court life which he had received are probably to be traced back, preponderantly if not exclusively, to his Macedonian experience.

BOOK VI.—CHAPTER XXX.

Page 358 (Top). "The chief thoughts in this description:" cf. iv. 12 *in.*: τίς δὲ πολιτεία τίσιν καὶ ποία συμφέρει ποίοις, or 15, 1299 a, 14 : ποίαις ποῖαι πολιτεῖαι συμφέρουσιν, or *ibid.*, 1300 b, 7 : τίνα δὲ τίσιν συμφέρει. "Not merely *one* democracy and *one* oligarchy:" 1289 a, 8: νῦν δὲ μίαν δημοκρατίαν οἴονταί τινες εἶναι καὶ μίαν ὀλιγαρχίαν. Immediately after : καὶ νόμους τοὺς ἀρίστους ἰδεῖν (*sc.* δεῖ) καὶ τοὺς ἑκάστῃ τῶν πολιτειῶν ἁρμόττοντας. There is an echo of mathematical language in 1288 b, 27 : ἔτι δὲ τρίτην (namely, the "best constitution" in the third sense of the expression) τὴν ἐξ ὑποθέσεως· δεῖ γὰρ καὶ τὴν δοθεῖσαν δύνασθαι θεωρεῖν. See, for example, Heyberg's Index to Archimedes, *s.v.* δίδωμι; or Autolycus, *De Sphæra*, etc., p. 96, 19, Hultsch : τῆς δοθείσης περιφερείας. The chief passage on the varying types of constitution and their dependence on the state of society is *Pol.*, iv. 4, 1291 b, 17 : εἴδη γὰρ πλείω . . . οἷον δήμου μὲν εἴδη ἓν μὲν οἱ γεωργοί, ἕτερον δὲ τὸ περὶ τὰς τέχνας, κ.τ.λ.

Page 360 (Middle). "Education and custom :" τῇ δ' ἀγωγῇ καὶ τοῖς ἔθεσιν, *Pol.*, iv. 5, 1292 b, 16.

Page 362 (Bottom). The work "On the Constitution of the Athenians:" on the remarks there made in favour of the Athenian democracy, cf. Szanto, *Ausgewählte Abhandlungen*, pp. 331 *seqq.*, particularly 334 *seq.*; also pp. 301 *seqq.* See also the present author's *Essays und Erinnerungen*, p. 172 *seq.*

BOOK VI.—CHAPTER XXXI.

Page 370 (par. 2). "Sources of sedition :" ἀρχαὶ . . . καὶ πηγαὶ τῶν στάσεων, *Pol.*, v. 1301 b, 5.

Page 371 (Bottom). The saying on the causes of civil conflicts: *ibid.*, 1303 b, 17 *seq.*: γίγνονται μὲν οὖν αἱ στάσεις οὐ περὶ μικρῶν ἀλλ' ἐκ μικρῶν.

Page 372 (end of par. 2). "They are a very small company in comparison with the whole :" *ibid.*, 1301 a, b, and 1304 b, 4–5.

Page 373 (Bottom). "Property-qualification and assessment :" *Pol.*, v. 8, 1308, 1309.

Sects 3 and 4. Pages 374–377. *Pol.*, v. 8 and 9.

Page 377 (Top). "Education in the spirit of the constitution :" τὸ παιδεύεσθαι πρὸς τὰς πολιτείας, *ibid.*, 1310 a, 14.

Sects. 5 and 6. "The turn now comes of monarchy . . . :" *Pol.*, v. 10–12.

Page 378 (Middle). Philip of Macedon : a glorification of this monarch was read out of *Pol.*, iv. 11, 1296 a, b, by Oncken, in *Staatslehre des Aristoteles*. The expression "a single man" (εἷς γὰρ ἀνήρ, κ.τ.λ.) cannot, however, because of the addition τῶν πρότερον, have referred to a contemporary ; most probably Solon was meant. I have already said, ın the essay referred to in the note to p. 357, what seemed to be required in refutation of Bernays' unsuccessful attempt to represent Aristotle and even Plato as partizans of the Macedonian policy (*Phokion und seine neueren Beurteiler*, pp. 35 *seqq.*, especially p. 41).

Page 383 (Top). " Electoral divisions : " *Pol.*, vi. 3, 1318 a, b. Sect. 9. Page 384. "The concluding portion of the book : " *Pol.*, vi. 4 *seqq.*

BOOK VI.—CHAPTER XXXII.

Page 387 (Top). Aristotle's criticism of political ideals : *Pol.*, ii. 1 *seqq.* ; criticism of Plato's *Laws*, etc., c. 6–8.

Page 389 (Bottom). " Great caution" recommended : *Pol.*, v. 8, 1269 a, 14 *seqq.*

Sect 4. Page 390. " Criticism of the works of legislators : " *Pol.*, ii. 12. (Bottom) Criticisms of the Lycurgean legislation : ii. 9.

Page 391 (Bottom). The remark on the " mechanical drill " of the Spartans occurs in *Pol.*, viii. 4, 1338 b, 32 *seqq.*

BOOK VI.—CHAPTER XXXIII.

Page 393 (Bottom). The chronological relations of the *Politics*, the *Poetics*, and the *Rhetoric* are clear from *Pol.*, viii. 7, 1341 b, 37 *seqq.* : τί δὲ λέγομεν τὴν κάθαρσιν, νῦν μὲν ἁπλῶς, πάλιν δ' ἐν τοῖς περὶ ποιητικῆς ἐροῦμεν σαφέστερον, and *Poetica*, 19, 1456 a, 34 *seq.* : τὰ μὲν οὖν περὶ τὴν διάνοιαν ἐν τοῖς περὶ ῥητορικῆς κείσθω. See also the retrospective references in *Rhet.*, i. 11, 1372 a, 1, and iii. 18, 1419 b, 5.

Pages 394, 395. "Aristotle's love of compromise :" the examples are from *Pol.*, vii. 11, 1330 b, 27 *seqq.* ; *ibid.*, 1330 a, 9 *seqq.* ; *ibid.*, 30 *seq.*

Page 399 (Top). " The Egyptian caste-system : " *Pol.*, vii. 10 *in.*, and 1329 b, 23 *seqq.*—On " common meals of men : " *ibid.* On watersupply : vii. 11, 1330 b, 4 *seqq.*

BOOK VI.—CHAPTER XXXIV.

The opening quotation is from G. Lowes Dickinson, *A Modern Symposium* (London, 1907), p. 86. In what follows exclusive use is made of books vii. and viii. of the *Politics*, almost entirely in the order of the original, so that special references seem unnecessary here.

BOOK VI.—CHAPTER XXXV.

The chief source of this section, the extant first book of the *Poetics* —of the second and last only a few meagre relics are known—has in recent times been most exhaustively treated by Johannes Vahlen, especially in his critical edition (Leipzig, 1885, ed. 3), and in his *Beiträge zu Aristoteles' Poetik* (Wiener Sitzungsberichte, 1865–7). The present author has several times found himself impelled to protest against Vahlen's ever-growing hyper-conservatism in matters of textual criticism. See my *Aufsätze zu Aristoteles' Poetik*, i.–iii., Wiener Sitzungsberichte, 1888–1896, and my essay on the last chapter of the *Poetics* in *Eranos Vindobonensis*, 1893. To these may be added my translation of Aristotle's *Poetics*, Leipzig, 1897, the preface of which treats many questions of principle. Out of the remaining literature, which is very abundant, we may select for special notice the critical editions of Wilhelm Christ (1878) and Ingram Bywater (1898). The last-named author has also recently published a masterly work, *Aristotle on the Art of Poetry*—containing text, history of the text, translation, and commentary—Oxford, 1909. But more particularly we must mention the truly pioneer work of Jakob Bernays, *Grundzüge der verlorenen Abhandlung des Aristoteles über die Wirkung der Tragödie*, Berlin, 1857 (with the expanded reprint *Zwei Abhandlungen über die Aristotelische Theorie des Dramas*, Berlin, 1880). This exceptionally fine performance, which in its turn has called forth an extensive literature, does not bear a perfectly appropriate title ; for Aristotle certainly did not express his views on the subject in question, the tragic catharsis, in a separate treatise, but in a passage of the lost second book which Vahlen's perspicuity has enabled him to reconstruct. Cf. the present author's essay, *Jakob Bernays* in *Essays und Erinnerungen*, pp. 118–122. In addition to Bernays, and earlier in date, we may name Henri Weil, that *doyen* among scholars, who arrived at the same conclusion and supported it by detailed proofs (cf. the Verhandlungen der x. Versammlung deutscher Philologen, Bâle, 1848, pp. 131 *seqq.*). Bernays himself devotes some space to this predecessor of his in *Zwei Abhandlungen*, pp. 119–121.

Page 404 (Top). Pauson and Polygnotus : *Pol.*, viii. 5, 1340 a, 35 *seqq.* ; compare *Poet.*, 2, 1448 a, 5 *seq.*, and 6, 1450 a, 27 *seq.* See also the index to my translation of the *Poetics*, pp. 120, 121. (Middle) " The classification of poetry : " *Poet.*, 4, 1448 b, 24 : διεσπάσθη δὲ κατὰ τὰ οἰκεῖα ἤθη ἡ ποίησις. (Bottom) " Dancing : " *Poet.*, i. 1447 a, 26 *seqq.* Cf. the author's first essay on the *Poetics*, p. 5. For what follows see again *Pol.*, viii. 5, especially the sentences : ἐν δὲ τοῖς μέλεσιν αὐτοῖς ἐστὶ μιμήματα τῶν ἠθῶν, and, φανερὸν ὅτι δύναται ποιόν τι τὸ τῆς ψυχῆς ἦθος ἡ μουσικὴ παρασκευάζειν (1340 a, 38 and 1340 b, 11).

Sect. 2. Page 405. The chief passage on the subdivision of music, and more particularly on catharsis, in *Pol.*, viii. 7, 1341 b, 19–1342 a, 31, on which see Bernays, *Grundzüge*, pp. 139 *seqq.* = *Zwei Abhandlungen*, p. 7 *seqq.*—On "flourishes and embellishments," see *ibid.*, 1342 a, 24, compared with Plutarch, *Quœst. Conviv.*, iii. 1, 1–ii. 783, 10 Dübner, and *De Musica*, § 187, with Th. Reinach's commentary in the separate edition by himself and H. Weil, pp. lviii. and 79 (Paris, 1900).

Page 406 (Top). "Definition of tragedy : " *Poet.* c. 6 *in.* The closing words run thus : δι' ἐλέου καὶ φόβου περαίνουσα τὴν τῶν τοιούτων παθημάτων κάθαρσιν (1449 b, 26 *seq.*).—Sympathetic fear is explained in *De Anima*, iii. 3, 427 b, 21 : ὅταν μὲν δοξάσωμεν δεινόν τι ἢ φοβερόν, εὐθὺς συμπάσχομεν. More detailed references to the literature mentioned in the text may be found in the treatise of Bernays.—"Truth and error" in Aristotle's theory of catharsis : see the treatise on this subject by Alfred Freiherr von Berger ; it is incorporated in my translation of the *Poetics*, pp. 71–98. (Middle) Plato : *Republic*, x. 606 A : εἰ ἐνθυμοῖο ὅτι τὸ βίᾳ κατεχόμενον τότε ἐν ταῖς οἰκείαις ξυμφοραῖς καὶ πεπεινηκὸς τοῦ δακρῦσαί τε καὶ ἀποδύρασθαι ἱκανῶς καὶ ἀποπλησθῆναι . . . τότ' ἐστὶ τοῦτο τὸ ὑπό τῶν ποιητῶν πιμπλάμενον καὶ χαῖρον. This, to be sure, is in Plato's mouth not praise, but blame. On this and kindred passages cf. the very instructive treatise by Christian Belger, *De Aristotele etiam in Arte Poetica Componenda Platonis Discipulo*, p. 62 *seqq.* (Berlin, 1872). (Bottom) Dubos and Sulzer : on their views, see Oskar Walzel's study *Lessings Begriff des Tragischen.* Lessing ; his attempt to explain the pleasure given by tragedy, and to illustrate it by the ingenious comparison with the sympathetic vibrations of a violin, may be found in his letter to Mendelssohn (xii. p. 86, ed. Lachmann and Maltzahn). There follows (p. 87) the brilliant and profound "example from the corporeal world."

Page 407 (Top). "The language of a contemporary : " Alfred von Berger, *op. cit.*, p. 88. (Bottom) " Divisions of poetic art : " cf. *Poet.*, c. 1–3.

Page 408 (Top). " The historical part of his exposition : " *Poet.*, c. 4, 1448 b, 27. (Middle) " Embellishments of·language : " *Poet.*, c. 22 *fin.*—" A line of Pindar : " *Olymp.*, 3, 32, seems to be alluded to in *Poet.*, 25, 1460 b, 31 ; cf. Vahlen's Commentary. On the " procemium" in the *Rhetoric* : iii. 14, 1415 a, 9–11, where dramatic, epic, and dithy-rambic poetry are mentioned, but no notice is taken of the triumphal odes of a Pindar or Bacchylides, though they, too, by no means lack procemia. (Bottom) " Plot-construction : " mentioned as early as the second line of the *Poetics* : καὶ πῶς δεῖ συνίστασθαι τοὺς μύθους. Among the component parts of drama the plot takes the highest place ; cf. *Poet.*, c. 6, 1450 a, 15 : μέγιστον δὲ τούτων ἐστὶν ἡ τῶν πραγμάτων σύστασις, and 38 : ἀρχὴ μὲν οὖν καὶ οἷον ψυχὴ ὁ μῦθος τῆς τραγῳδίας. Let it not be objected that these passages are in the part devoted specially to drama ; I have quoted them to illustrate the predominant importance which Aristotle assigns to action. Moreover, speaking of the musical arts in general, and without any limitation to drama, he says (c. 2, *in.*) : ἐπεὶ δὲ μιμοῦνται οἱ μιμούμενοι πράττοντας.

Page 409 (Top). Main types of poetic endowment : *Poet.*, c. 17, 1455 a, 32–34. I have adopted Tyrrwhitt's emendation ἐκστατικοὶ for ἐξεταστικοὶ, and defended it at length against Vahlen in *Zu Aristoteles' Poetik.*, iii. 8 *seq.* On the whole passage cf. also Aristotle. *Problemata*, 954 a, 32, to which reference was also made by Tyrrwhitt. (Par. 2)

Chamæleon and Dicæarchus : see the articles in Pauly and Wissowa's *Real-Enzykl. d. Klass. Altert.-Wiss.* It has not been determined with certainty whether Chamæleon was an immediate pupil of Aristotle or only a pupil's pupil. " Dionysius of Halicarnassus : " *De Compos. Verb.*, ii. 1, 114 *seqq.*, ed. Usener and Radermacher.

Page 410 (Top). " Imitations are contemplated with satisfaction : " *Poet.*, c. 4, 1458 b, 15 *seqq.* Also *Rhet.*, i. 11, 1371 b, 4 *seqq.* (End of sect. 4) Relative rank of the elements of tragedy : *Poet.*, c. 6, 1450 a, 15. (Sect. 5) Compare Külpe's valuable essay, *Anfäge psychologischer Æsthetik bei den Griechen* in *Philosophische Abhandlungen, Max Heinze gewidmet*, Berlin, 1906, p. 102 *seqq.*

I cannot, however, share Külpe's view of Plato's theory of art as developed in *Laws*, ii. 667 *seqq.* Plato there entirely ignores artistic pleasure, the enjoyment of works of art. Such works are regarded by him as valuable only when and because they impart instruction, or if (and this seems to have been Plato's chief concern) they do not falsify our picture of the universe. Æsthetic pleasure is for him merely a " harmless " accessory, an " innocent sport." All this is fully acknowledged by Külpe on p. 113 ; but he ought not, I think, to have added, on p. 114, that " Plato here recognized an æsthetic law of the widest applicability." It is worthy of notice that some quite recent writers on æsthetics have expressed very similar views. Fr. Jodl summarizes them thus : " The feelings of pleasure which arise on the contemplation of the beautiful are not the source of the value assigned to it, but only an accompanying phenomenon, an immediate consequence of the act of intuitive cognition in which man directly apprehends the relation between form and essence " (*Öster. Rundschau*, xvii. 3, 223 a). Kindred notions have, in fact, dominated German æsthetics from the time of its founder, Baumgarten, onwards, and, as remarked by its historian, have long continued to injure it (H. Lotze, *Geschichte der Ästhetik in Deutschland*, p. 11).

Compare, too, the following passage from Aristotle, which is also made use of in Kulpe's work : καλὸν μὲν οὖν ἐστίν, ὃ ἂν δι' αὑτὸ αἱρετὸν ὂν ἐπαινετὸν ᾖ, ἢ ὃ ἂν ἀγαθὸν ὂν ἡδὺ ᾖ (*Rhet.*, i. 9, 1366 a, 33 *seqq.*). The beautiful is thus regarded either as a " praiseworthy end-in-itself " or as a " pleasure-yielding good." The first alternative does not distinguish the beautiful from the morally good, nor the second from such a good as health. (Bottom) " The elements of beauty : " *Metaph.*, xii. 3, 1078 a, b : τοῦ δὲ καλοῦ μέγιστα εἴδη τάξις καὶ συμμετρία καὶ τὸ ὡρισμένον. Also, earlier, 1078 a, 31 *seqq.* : τὸ (*sc.* τὸ ἀγαθὸν) μὲν γὰρ ἀεὶ ἐν πράξει, τὸ δὲ καλὸν καὶ ἐν τοῖς ἀκινήτοις.—" In the *Poetics* : " c. 7, 1451 a, 4 *seqq.*, and c. 4, 1448 b, 20 *seq.*

Page 411 (Top). Comparison of poets with portrait-painters : *Poet.*. c. 15, 1454 b, 9 *seqq.*—" A saying of Sophocles : " c. 25, 1460 b, 33 *seq.*—Zeuxis : *ibid.*, 1461 b, 12 *seq.*

Page 412 (Top). " Dialogues like those of Plato : " *Poet.*, i. 1447

b, 2-4. (Middle) Homer and Empedocles : *ibid.*, 1447 b, 17 *seq*.
(Below) Design and execution : cf. *Rhet.*, i. 13, 1374 b, 13 *seq*. ; it is
just μὴ πρὸς τὴν πρᾶξιν, ἀλλὰ πρὸς τὴν προαίρεσιν (σκοπεῖν). Again, *Eth.*
Eudem., ii. *fin.*, 1228 a, 11 *seqq*. : ἔτι πάντας ἐπαινοῦμεν καὶ ψέγομεν εἰς τὴν
προαίρεσιν βλέποντες μᾶλλον ἢ εἰς τὰ ἔργα. On the other hand, we have
Poet., 25, 1460 b, 16 *seq*. : εἰ μὲν γὰρ προείλετο μιμήσασθαι (ὀρθῶς, ἀπέτυχε
δὲ δι') ἀδυναμίαν, αὐτῆς ἡ ἁμαρτία· εἰ δὲ τὸ προελέσθαι μὴ ὀρθῶς . . . καθ' ἑκάστην
τέχνην (τὸ) ἁμάρτημα, κ.τ.λ. I have treated the passage fully, both on the
critical and the exegetical side, in my study *Zu Philodems Büchern*
von der Musik (Vienna, 1885, p. 26). (Bottom) " A saying of Schopenhauer : " *Werke*, iii. 439.
    Page 413 (Top). " An error has been committed . . . : " *Poet.*,
c. 25, 1460 b, 23 *seqq*.—" Unity of the action : " *Poet.*, c. 7 and 8.—
" Unity of time : " touched on incidentally and indirectly in *Poet.*, c.
5, 1449 b, 11 *seq*. : ἡ μὲν (*sc.* ἡ τραγῳδία) ὅτι μάλιστα πειρᾶται ὑπὸ μίαν περίοδον
ἡλίου εἶναι ἢ μικρὸν ἐξαλλάττειν.
    Page 414 (Bottom). See *Poet.*, c. 17, 1455 a, b ; c. 9, 1451 b, 25 ;
c. 4, 1449 a, 7 *seqq*. ; c. 9, 1451 b, 5 *seqq*. : διὸ καὶ φιλοσοφώτερον καὶ
σπουδαιότερον ποίησις ἱστορίας ἐστίν, κ.τ.λ.
    Sect. 8. In this section I have made more use than hitherto of
the Preface to my translation of the *Poetics*. For my conjecture
relative to Theodectes, see the index to that translation.
    Page 416 (Bottom). On " scenic apparatus " and " song-com-
position," cf. *Poet.*, c. 6, 1460 b, 16 *seq*., where the latter is called
μέγιστον τῶν ἡδυσμάτων, and the former ψυχαγωγικὸν μὲν, ἀτεχνότατον δὲ καὶ
ἥκιστα οἰκεῖον τῆς ποιητικῆς. Similarly, in c. 26, 1462 a, 15, where it is
said of music in the drama that by it αἱ ἡδοναὶ συνίστανται ἐναργέστατα.
    Sect. 9. Page 418. Homer : *Poet.*, c. 24, 1460 a, 5 *seqq*., and
Plato's *Republic*, iii. 392 D *seqq*. If it be asked how the narrating
poet can be an " imitative portrayer," even apart from the dramatic
episodes which may be interwoven with his story, it may be answered
that the artistic medium of language, consisting as it does in a
succession of symbols, is adapted for the representation of actions as
forming a series in time (cf. Lessing, *Laokoon*, ch. xvi.). To this may
be added the decisive consideration that the movements of the speech-
organs in producing articulate sounds are well fitted to bring
vividly before us other movements, those of psychic nature by their
rhythm, and movements of matter both by their rhythm and by other
points of agreement. Some approach was made to this view, not so
much by Lessing in the *Laokoon* as by Herder (*Kritische Wälder*, Bd.
13, pp. 180 *seqq*., ed. of 1829).
    Page 419 (Top). " Tragedy has everything which belongs to
epic . . . : " *Poet.*, c. 26, 1462 a, 14 *seqq*. Agents (πράττοντες) as
subjects of poetic portrayal in general, with the distinctions belonging
to the subject: *Poet.*, c. 2 *in*. Philodemus (of Gadara in Syria, an
Epicurean author, contemporary with Cicero): in an extremely

noteworthy fragment of his work " On Poems " = *Volum. Hercul. Coll. Alt.*, ii. fol. 154) treated by the present author in the Zeitschr. f. Österr. Gymn., 1865, 719, and more fully in the *Festschrift* contributed by the Vienna Eranos to the meeting of philologists at Graz, September, 1909.

BOOK VI.—CHAPTER XXXVI.

Besides the three books *On Rhetoric* (we hold the third to be genuine, agreeing with Diels in *Über das dritte Buch der aristotelischen Rhetorik*, Berl. Akad. Abh., 1886, and in spite of the objections argued by Marx in *Aristoteles' Rhetorik*, Berichte d. Sächs. Gessellsch. d. Wiss. 1900), Aristotle published a dialogue, *Gryllus*, devoted to this subject, further, a handbook consisting of materials left behind by his favourite pupil Theodectes, and possibly based on his own lectures, and lastly, a comprehensive review of the older treatises on rhetoric, entitled Τεχνῶν συναγωγή; cf. the few but valuable fragments in the Berlin Academy edition, pp. 1500 *seq.* The best annotated edition of the *Rhetoric* is that of Leonhard Spengel, Leipzig, Teubner, 1867, 2 vols. The 'Ρητορικὴ πρὸς 'Αλέξανδρον has long been recognized as spurious ; and in quite recent times it has been assigned with the highest degree of probability to the rhetorician Anaximenes (cf. Wendland, Hermes, xxxix. 499 and *Anaximenes von Lampsakos*, Berlin, 1905).

Page 420 (Top). " To be a speaker of words . . . :" *Iliad*, ix. 443. —" Corax and Tisias : " Cicero (*Brutus*, 12), where he appeals to the authority of Aristotle (1500 a–1501 a). Cf. *Greek Thinkers*, Vol. I. p. 229, and Christ, *Gesch. d. griech. Lit.*, 3rd (1908) ed. revised by W. Schmid, p. 512.

Page 421 (Middle). Grote : *Plato*, ii. 234 *seqq.*, particularly 248 and 253.

Page 423 (Top). "A long series of writers : " cf. Chrysippus, quoted by Plutarch, *De Repugnantiis Stoicis*, x. 15 = *Moralia*, ii. 1268, 37, Dübner. Also Philodemus, *De Rhetorica, Hercul. Volum. Coll. Alt.*, iii. col. 57 (i. 351, Sudhaus), treated by the present author in Zeitschr. f. Österr. Gymn., 1866, p. 698, where reference is given to the use of the same comparison (of rhetoric with a weapon) in Horace, *Sat.*, ii. 1, 39, and also to Sextus Empiricus, *Adv. Math.*, ii. 44 *seqq.* = 683 *seq.*, Bekker. The previously mentioned possibility of misusing all goods except virtue is touched on by Aristotle in *Rhet.*, i. 1, 1355 b. 2 *seqq.* and in *Pol.*, i. 2, 1253 a, 31 *seqq.*

BOOK VI.—CHAPTER XXXVII.

In the preceding chapter my account follows the order of the sections in *Rhet.*, i. The theory of emotions and types of character is contained in book ii. 1–17.

Page 438 (Bottom). The " Egyptian king " referred to here

(*Rhet.*, ii. 8, 1386 a, 19) by the name of Amasis is called Psammenites by Herodotus (iii. 14).

Page 439 (par. 3). Nietzsche : *Menschliches-Allzumenschliches*, ii. 2, Abt. 29.

Page 441 (Top). Descartes : *Traité des Passions*, 2ᵐᵉ partie, article 51 *seqq.* Subtler remarks on the distinction between *jalousie* and *émulation* are found in Labruyère, *Les Caractères*, ii. 104 *seq.* (Paris, 1823). (Middle) " The twofold nature of the emotions : " cf. *De Anima*, i. 1, 403 a, 5 *seqq.*: φαίνεται δὲ τῶν πλείστων οὐθὲν ἄνευ σώματος πάσχειν οὐδὲ ποιεῖν. Again, l. 22 *seqq.*, especially 27 : καὶ διὰ ταῦτα ἤδη φυσικοῦ τὸ θεωρῆσαι περὶ ψυχῆς ἢ πάσης ἢ τῆς τοιαύτης, κ.τ.λ.; cf. also the important utterance in *De Memoria*, 2, 453 a, 26, which in my opinion has been so often misunderstood ; the bodily processes set up by anger or fear survive their psychic origin and sometimes even thwart the endeavour to calm the emotion. (Bottom) " Pleasure and its opposite . . .:" *De Anima*, iii. 11, 434 a, 2 *seqq.*: φαίνεται γὰρ λύπη καὶ ἡδονὴ ἐνοῦσα· εἰ δὲ ταῦτα καὶ ἐπιθυμίαν ἀνάγκη. Again, *Eth. Nic.*, iii. 14, 1119 a, 4 : μετὰ λύπης ἡ ἐπιθυμία, or *Top.*, vi. 3, 140 b, 27 : πᾶσα γὰρ ἐπιθυμία ἡδέος ἐστίν. The emotions are defined in *Rhet.*, ii. 1, 1378 a, 20 *seqq.*: ἔστι δὲ τὰ πάθη, δι' ὅσα μεταβάλλοντες διαφέρουσι τὰς κρίσεις, οἷς ἕπεται λύπη καὶ ἡδονή, οἷον ὀργὴ, κ.τ.λ. Similarly, *Eth. Nic.*, ii. 4, 1105 b, 21 : λέγω δὴ πάθη μὲν ἐπιθυμίαν, ὀργήν . . . ὅλως οἷς ἕπεται ἡδονὴ ἢ λύπη. If Aristotle had not in the first passage been so true to his character of cool reasoner as to set the judgment-disturbing effect of emotion in the foreground, he might perhaps have succeeded in giving the definition a stricter form, in which it would have excluded perceptive sensations uncoloured by pleasure or pain. We might suggest the following : Emotions are *among* states of the soul involving pleasure or pain *those which* exert a clouding influence on the judgment. He does, in fact, make an approach to this subsumption ; for at least he does not connect the two defining attributes by a καί which would have made them strictly co-ordinate.

Page 442 (Bottom). In the character here given of old age we note the omission of that crabbed obstinacy which is sometimes observed at this period of life, and which forms the counterpart of the diffidence mentioned by Aristotle.

(End of sect. 5) This passage, *Rhet.*, ii. 14, 1390 b, 11, is over-looked in W. H. Roscher's treatise *Die Hebdomadenlehren der griechischen Philosophen und Ärzte*, Leipzig, 1906. This work, however, makes it clear that Aristotle attached to the number seven a very great importance in biological processes, although in *Pol.*, vii. 17, 1336, 1337, he insists on precedence being given to the facts of nature over *à priori* presumptions of this kind—an expression of opinion to which Roscher (p. 97, note 152) does not, I think, do full justice. Not even Theophrastus, who was much freer from *à priori* prejudices, could entirely emancipate himself from the spell of the number seven ; cf. *Caus. Plant.*, vi. 4, 2 : ὁ δὲ ἀριθμὸς ὁ τῶν ἑπτὰ καιριώτατος καὶ φυσικώτατος. Cf. also vi. 4, 1.

BOOK VI.—CHAPTER XXXVIII.

Sect. 1. Several of the passages from the second and third books of the *Rhetoric*, which are here made use of, have been treated critically and exegetically in my *Beiträge zur Kritik und Erklarung griech. Schrifsteller*, viii. 1–14.

Page 448 (Middle). Quotation from Agathon : *Rhet.*, ii. 24, 1402 a, 10 ; also alluded to in *Poet.*, 18, 1456 a, 24 *seqq.*, 1461 b, 15 ; p. 765 in Nauck's *Tragicor. Græc. Fragmenta*, ed. 2.

Pages 448, 449. The art of delivery and scenic apparatus : the latter is called ἀτεχνότερον in *Rhet.*, iii. 1, 1404 a, 16 ; the former, as already mentioned, is termed ἀτεχνότατον in *Poet.*, 6, 1450 b, 17.

Page 449 (Bottom). "An expression of Alcidamas :" *Rhet.*, iii. 3, 1406 b, 12 = *Oratores Attici*, ii. 156 a, b.

Page 451 (Bottom). " A line of the *Odyssey* : " xiv. 214. " Down with a thunderous clatter . . . : " *Od.*, xi. 598.

Page 452 (Top). " The discovery of hidden resemblances : " *Rhet.*, ii. 11, 1412 a, 11 : δεῖ δὲ μεταφέρειν . . . ἀπ᾽ οἰκείων καὶ μὴ φανερῶν οἷον καὶ ἐν φιλοσοφίᾳ τὸ ὅμοιον καὶ ἐν πολὺ διέχουσι θεωρεῖν εὐστόχου. Similarly, *Poet.*, 22, 1459 a, 6 : μόνον γὰρ τοῦτο οὔτε παρ᾽ ἄλλου ἔστι λαβεῖν εὐφυΐας τε σημεῖόν ἐστιν· τὸ γὰρ εὖ μεταφέρειν τὸ τὸ ὅμοιον θεωρεῖν ἐστίν.

Franklin's identification of the electricity in lightning and in an electric machine, Newton's great intellectual feat, are two apt instances of the identification of similars ἐν πολὺ διέχουσι. Alexander Bain rightly says (*The Senses and the Intellect*, p. 490, ed. 3) : " The operation of similarity sets forth the workings of genius." On Franklin's achievement he remarks (p. 521) : " Next to the discovery of gravitation, this is perhaps the most remarkable fetch of remote identification in the history of science." In this connexion Bain presently (pp. 531, *seqq.*) treats of similes in poets and orators, particularly in Shakespeare, of whom he remarks : " He had perhaps the greatest intellectual reach of similarity . . . that the mind of man ever attained to " (p. 533). (Bottom) The allusion to the comedy of Anaxandrides, *Rhet.*, iii. 12, 1413 b, 25 *seq.*, would have been hardly intelligible to us without the supplementary information given by *Athenæus*, xiv. 614 c. The line runs : τὸ δ᾽ ἀσύμβολον εὗρε γελοῖα λέγειν Ῥαδάμανθυς καὶ Παλαμήδης = *Comici Græci*, ii. 139, Kock. On Palamedes as an inventor, cf. Æschylus, *Fragm.*, 180 and 182 ; Sophocles, *Fragm.*, 438 ; and Euripides, *Fragm.*, 578, Nauck (ed. 2).

Page 453 (Top). " Comparison between speeches addressed to the people and decorative painting : " the passage *Rhet.*, iii. 13, 1414 a, 7 *seq.* : ἡ μὲν οὖν δημηγορικὴ λέξις καὶ παντελῶς ἔοικε τῇ σκιαγραφίᾳ has been almost grotesquely misunderstood in K. L. Roth's translation.

Spengel's commentary, too, fails to bring out the common element in the two subjects of comparison. To my remark on this (*Beiträge*, viii. 7) I may now add a parallel from the most recent times. In a German parliamentary speech we read : " Nowadays, if one desires to be chosen by the mass, one must work with broad effects, much as the secessionist painters aim at impressing the distant spectator " (*Neue Freie Presse*, Feb. 8, 1906, p. 5). (Par. 3) " Prelude : " *Rhet.*, iii. 14.

Page 454 (Bottom). The line in the *Hippolytus* of Euripides (612) : ἡ γλῶσσ' ὀμώμοχ', ἡ δὲ φρὴν ἀνώμοτος.

Sect. 8. Page 455. " Treatment of . . . the question : " *Rhet.*, iii. 18, 1418, 1419.

Page 456 (Top). " The advice of Gorgias : " *ibid.*, 1419 b, 3 = *Oratores Attici*, p. 131 a, 3 *seqq.* (End of par. 2) " I have spoken ; you have heard . . ." *Rhet.*, iii. *fin.* : εἴρηκα, ἀκηκόατε, ἔχετε, κρίνατε. Spengel, too, in the conclusion of his commentary, recognized the operation here of well-calculating design : " Incerti oratoris verba, acute ab Aristotele sic fine operis posita ut de sua arte rhetorica cum cæteris comparanda valerent." He might also have mentioned the effect which these words were intended to produce in the lecture-room and the parallel with the closing sentences of the logic course (*De Soph. El., fin.*, p. 184 b, 3 *seqq.*). The design is the more unmistakable, as it follows, at no great distance, the treatment of asyndeton and its applications, *Rhet.*, iii. 12, 1413 b, 19 *seqq.* How natural it would have been to mention in that place the employment of this figure in perorations, had not the author desired to reserve the point for the close of the work itself for the sake of the illustrative example ! Even if our present third book once had an independent existence, this appeal to the audience (like its parallel in the logic course) could only have applied to a larger whole, such as the *Rhetoric* in its complete form. Cf. Diels, who defends that original independence of the book Περὶ λέξεως (= *Über das dritte Buch der Rhetorik*, p. 17, note 5) : " None the less Aristotle certainly combined the different parts of his rhetorical teaching into an ideal whole, just as he joined together the works on politics and ethics, the *De Anima* and the *Parva Naturalia*, the complex of the physical [as also of the logical and biological] works to form comprehensive manuals."

Page 457 (Bottom). " We have noted his old complaint : " *Rhet.*, iii. 1, 1404 2, *seq.* : οὐκ ὀρθῶς ἔχοντος, ἀλλ' ὡς ἀναγκαίου τὴν ἐπιμέλειαν ποιητέον, κ.τ.λ.

Page 458 (Middle) " We are bidden to ' use ' this artifice, to ' choose ' that advocate's trick : " *Rhet.*, i. 9, 1367 a, 32 *seqq.* : ληπτέον δὲ καὶ τὰ σύνεγγυς τοῖς ὑπάρχουσιν ὡς ταὐτὰ ὄντα, κ.τ.λ. ; or 1367 b, 24 *seq.* : διὸ καὶ τὰ συμπτώματα καὶ τὰ ἀπὸ τύχης ὡς ἐν προαιρέσει ληπτέον, or ii. 23, 1399 b, 13 : ληπτέον δ' ὁπότερον ἂν ᾖ χρήσιμον, and many similar sentences. Any one who, in face of these passages, seriously maintains that Aristotle's sole object was to *warn* against the deceptive arts described must himself have developed the art of self-deception to an astonishing degree.—" These are at once the cleverest and the most unjust practices : " *Rhet.*, iii. 15, 1416 b, 6 *seq.* : τοιοῦτοι δὲ οἱ τεχνικώτατοι καὶ ἀδικώτατοι.

Sect. 10. Page 459. The first sentences are partly borrowed from my lecture on *Aristotle and his newly discovered Work on the Constitution of the Athenians* (*Essays und Erinnerungen*, p. 175).

BOOK VI.—CHAPTER XXXIX.

The works of Theophrastus have been edited by J. G. Schneider (5 vols., Leipzig, 1818–1821), and later by Fr. Wimmer (3 vols., Leipzig, Teubner, 1854–1862). H. Usener had made extensive preparations for a revision of the third volume of Wimmer's edition, containing the fragments. Diogenes Laertius treats of Theophrastus in book v., ch. 2. The dates of his birth and death have been approximately determined by Beloch, *Griechische Geschichte*, iii. 2, p. 469. According to the investigations of this writer, the death took place in 288-7 or 287-6, the birth in 372-1 or 371-0 B.C. That he followed Aristotle into Macedonia appears with great probability from his possession of an estate in Stagira (cf. his will in Diog. Laert., v. 2, 52), and from his friendship with Callisthenes (Cicero, *Tusc.*, iii. 10, 21).

Page 461 (Bottom). " Demetrius of Phalerum : " treated of by Diog. Laert., v. 5. Cf. especially Beloch, *Gr. Gesch.*, iii. 1, 151 *seqq.* ; also the article in Pauly-Wissowa, *s.v.* Some critical remarks may find a place here. The Ὑπὲρ τῆς πολιτείας α′, which is enumerated among his works, was certainly not a " recommendation of the Aristotelian Politeia κατ' ἐξοχήν." I take it to be identical with the adjacent item, Περὶ τῆς δεκαετίας α′, and to have been a defence, as indicated by the ὑπέρ, of his ten years' regency. The doubts which the writer of the encyclopædia article expresses as to Demetrius's activity as " historian of the Orient," seem to me to lack foundation. Why should we be so ready to assume an " error of the learned Father of the Church," Tertullian ? For Demetrius certainly spent many years in Egypt ; and the interest of his contemporaries and fellow-students, Theophrastus and Eudemus, was very warmly engaged by the history of religion and civilization abroad as well as at home. Immediately afterwards (Pauly-Wissowa, iv. 2, 2838) we find a statement of Josephus (*Contra Apionem*, 218 ; i. 23 = vi. 207, 19, ed. Becker), in which this Demetrius is named as an authority on Jewish things, described as a " confusion." But I may here point out that according to the testimony of Diogenes Laertius, Demetrius was one of the most prolific writers of his day. His " historical " works are there given the first place ; and the enumeration of them is manifestly very incomplete.

Page 462 (Middle). Hagnonides : friend of Demosthenes and

his defender in the matter of Harpalus (Grote, xii. 437). At the close of the Lamian War he was banished by Antipater to the Peloponnese, but afterwards returned to Athens. He accused Phocion, as well as Theophrastus, and in both cases alike he was no doubt impelled by political motives. (Bottom) The law of Sophocles: Diog. Laert., v. 2 (38), Athenæus, xiii. 610 e, f, and *Oratores Attici*, ii. 341 *seq.*, but Athenæus, xi. 509 b, must be added to the fragments of the speech of Demochares. My view of the effect of the law agrees with that of Grote (xii. 512). The exaggeration of Athenæus, *loc. cit.* (Σοφοκλῆs . . . ἐξήλασε πάντας φιλοσόφους) is in contradiction with the wording of the law. The departure from Athens was "a spirited protest against authoritative restriction on the liberty of philosophy and teaching" (Grote, *loc. cit.*). A different conclusion, it is true, has been arrived at in recent times by Beloch (*op. cit.*, p. 432): "Theophrastus thus found himself compelled to leave the city." It was not Theophrastus alone who left the city, but he καὶ πάντες οἱ λοιποὶ φιλόσοφοι (Diog. Laert., *loc. cit.*) ; and it is quite beside the mark to speak of compulsion. As I am now occupied in criticizing Beloch's excellent work, I may as well here renew my protest against the now common assumption (repeated by Beloch on p. 433) that the Peripatetic school was raised by Theophrastus to the status of a "juristic personality." Cf. my argument to the contrary in *Platonische Aufsätze*, ii. pp. 9, 10. Nor can I find any point of support for the closely related opinion that the philosophic schools were religious associations (θίασοι), "organized for the cult of the Muses." Sacrifices and festivals in honour of the Muses were common to the philosophic schools with the schools attended by children (cf. Theophrastus, *Characters*, xxii.) ; in both alike they played the same part as the cult of Hermes in the gymnasia (cf. Plato's *Lysis*). The identification in question is decisively contradicted by the circumstance that the religious associations "étaient considérées comme des personnes civiles, pouvant posséder, vendre, acheter en leur propre nom" (P. Foucart, *Des associations religieuses chez les Grecs*, p. 48), while in the philosophers' wills of that period there is no question of any but *personal* inheritance and the *moral* obligation attached to it of allowing the "fellow-philosophers" to share in the enjoyment of it. Cf. my essay referred to above, p. 3. Again, such phrases as καταλείπω δὲ τὴν μὲν διατριβὴν Λύκωνι (in Straton's will, Diog. Laert., v. 3, 62) prove anything else rather than the existence of a philosophic association as a juristic personality. It may be added that jurists who have given their attention to the subject, like Bruns and Dareste, have fully recognized and clearly expressed this fact (cf. my essay, p. 10).

Sect. 3. Pages 463, 465. On Theophrastus' literary activity in general, cf. Usener's well-executed work *Analecta Theophrastea*, Leipzig, 1850. The remains of the Φυσικαὶ δόξαι are treated by him, *ibid.*, p. 25 *seqq.* These were utilized with great thoroughness and exactness by Diels in his *Doxographi*. Brandis discusses the relations of the separate monographs to the main work without reaching any firmly established conclusion (*Handbuch d. Gesch. d. Griech.-Röm. Philosophie*, iii. 1, 291, 292). The same author, by the way, has given a very careful account of Theophrastus' doctrines.

Page 465 (Bottom). "Each of them arrives at results:" ὥστε δόξειεν ἂν ἑκάτερος ἐναντίως τῇ ὑποθέσει λέγειν, in Περὶ αἰσθήσεως, Diels, *Doxographi*, 516, 21. In the next line I should prefer to insert the article and read: ὁ μὲν γὰρ πάθη ποιῶν (τὰ) τῆς αἰσθήσεως καθ' αὑτὰ διορίζει τὴν φύσιν.

Page 466 (Top). Against Plato's "untrue pleasures :" cf. fragment 85 in Wimmer, iii. 184. This polemic must no doubt have formed the content of the monograph Περὶ ψευδοῦς ἡδονῆς (Usener, p. 8). (Par. 2) Aristotelian thoughts, phrases, and sentences. For instance, in the introduction of the *De Causis Plantarum*, i. 1 : ἡ γὰρ φύσις οὐδὲν ποιεῖ μάτην, compared with Aristotle, *De Cælo*, i. 4, 271 a, 33, or ii. 11, 291 b, 13. Or again, in the metaphysical fragment, p. 308 Brandis = Usener, p. iv. 13 (Bonner Winterprogramm, 1890, 1891) : εὐλογώτερον δ' οὖν εἶναί τινα συναφὴν καὶ μὴ ἐπεισοδιῶδες τὸ πᾶν, compared with *Metaph.*, xiv. 3, 1090 b, 19, or xii. *fin.* 1076 a, 1. Who, without close familiarity with Aristotle, could understand an allusion that occurs a little further on (Usener, pp. v., 2) : τοιαύτη δ' ἡ τοῦ ὀρεκτοῦ φύσις ? This has reference to the First Mover, and must be read in the light of *Metaph.*, xii. 7, 1072 a, 26 : τὸ ὀρεκτὸν κινεῖ τὸ κινούμενον, and *ibid.*, 1072 b, 3 : κινεῖ ὡς ἐρώμενον. (Middle) Doctrine of Nous : I cannot agree with Brandis (p. 283, note 150), who, in quoting a passage from Simplicius (*Commentary on the "Physics,"* p. 964, 30 *seqq.*, Diels), finds there an "expression of doubt as to an activity of the mind wholly independent of the body." In that passage Theophrastus (Fragm. 53 W.) distinguishes the emotions and desires, as bodily movements, from the κρίσεις and θεωρίαι which cannot be traced to an external origin, the beginning, progress, and end of which is wholly psychic. He continues : εἰ δὲ δὴ καὶ ὁ νοῦς κρεῖττόν τι μέρος καὶ θειότερον, ἅ τε δὴ ἔξωθεν ἐπεισιὼν καὶ παντέλειος. The adversative δέ is so little in place here that we must either erase it or, with Diels, substitute γε. The ἔξωθεν, on the other hand, is made more precise in meaning by the fragment contained in Themistius, *De Anima*, 91 (p. 107, 35 *seqq.*, Heinze) : ἀλλὰ τὰ ἔξωθεν ἆρα οὐχ ὡς ἐπίθετον, ἀλλ' ὡς ἐν τῇ πρώτῃ γενέσει συμπαραλαμβανόμενον θετέον, κ.τ.λ. The traditional reading is here συμπεριλαμβάνον, out of which Brandis (p. 289) makes συμπεριλαμβανόμενον. In my opinion only συμπαραλαμβανόμενον fits the sense. Conception is expressed by σύλληψις ; as, however, there is here an idea of double transmission, the compound is quite appropriate. Aristotle, we know not on what ground, represented Nous as entering into the embryo ; Theophrastus finds it more credible that this element too is received along with the paternal γονή. In Themistius (*loc. cit.*, 108, 17) we read : καὶ προϊών, φησι, τὰς μὲν αἰσθήσεις οὐκ ἄνευ σώματος, τὸν δὲ νοῦν χωριστόν. Theophrastus thus did not doubt the independence of Nous ; he did, however, protest against regarding it as an external addition ; he wished to substitute an organic for the mechanical conception of its relation to the body, as is borne out by the word συμφυής, which occurs in the neighbourhood of the passage under consideration. The chief sources for Theophrastus' psychology are the extensive fragment, Περὶ αἰσθήσεως —a well-preserved portion of the Φυσικαὶ δόξαι—in Diels, *Doxog. Græc.*. 497-527, and Priscian's Μετάφρασις τῶν Θεοφράστου περὶ αἰσθήσεως καὶ φαντασίας, iii. 232 *seqq.*, and 261 *seqq.*, Wimmer.—Difficulties concerning the movement of the universe : cf. the metaphysical fragment, p. v. a, b, Usener. (Bottom) Objections against teleological principles : *ibid.*, p. x. *seq.* On this passage, cf. also Usener in Rhein. Mus., xvi. 259 *seqq.*, *Zu Theophrasts Metaphysischem Bruchstück.* It may be observed that when Usener wrote this essay at the age of twenty-six he was not so familiar as he afterwards became with the language of the Peripatetic school. Otherwise he would not have translated ἐν ὕλης εἴδει by " kinds of matter " (p. 280, l. 4), since in Aristotle this combination of words means simply " material." Cf. *Metaph.*, i. 3, 983 b, 7 ; the majority of the earliest philosophers have only sought material causes (τὰς ἐν ὕλης εἴδει μόνας ᾠήθησαν ἀρχὰς εἶναι πάντων).

Page 467 (Bottom). On Theophrastus' innovations in logic, cf. Prantl, *Geschichte der Logik,* i. 347-400 (" Die älteren Peripatetiker "). Prantl enumerates twenty-four logical works, including some which were " probably logical as well as historical in content " (p. 350, note 6). No doubt some pruning is required. The work Περὶ προθέσεως καὶ διηγήματος was certainly devoted to rhetoric alone : cf. Aristotle, *Rhet.*, iii. 13, 1414 b, 7-9 and 16, 1416 b, 16 *seqq.* The " modern authority " whose judgment I quote is H. Maier, *Die Syllogistik des Aristoteles,* ii. 1, p. 213.

Page 468 (Bottom). " Aristotle's doctrine of the eternity of the universe : " the source is the Philonic work Περὶ ἀφθαρσίας κόσμου (pp. 510-516, Mangey), treated by Diels, *Doxogr. Græc.,* pp. 486 *seqq.* ; in Wimmer, iii. 168 *seqq.* Zeller (Hermes, xi. 422 *seqq.*, later, with less confidence, in xv. 137 *seqq.*) has maintained that the string of proofs is directed against Zeno. The version of them which we possess seems to me to have been retouched, chiefly because the ornate and artificial mode of expression deviates considerably from the usual simplicity of Theophrastus (cf. Diels, *Doxogr.,* Prolegomena, p. 106 *seqq.*). This question of authenticity has been repeatedly discussed by Arnim, last of all in the Neue Jahrbücher f. d. Klass. Philologie, 1893, pp. 449 *seqq.* I cannot entirely agree with him. He attaches what I think an excessive importance to isolated expressions like ἀπάτη and ἀπατηθῆναι. The " thought embodied in the first argument, that the continued existence of the earth, despite the visible and incessant operation of the forces tending to destroy it, would not be explicable if it had existed from eternity " (p. 451), seems to me a very obvious one, and anything but "artificial" or far-fetched. If we perceive the action of a force which is opposed by no other force, and which nevertheless has not yet reached its goal, every physicist or philosopher must at once be driven to the inference that the force in question must have begun to act at some point in time; for if it had acted from all eternity its goal would have been reached long ago. Besides, Arnim's admission that the propositions directly associated with the name of Theophrastus do in truth proceed from him is enough to justify my account of the matter. There is still one point which claims the reader's attention. The opponents of the theory which makes the universe without beginning and incapable of destruction are by no means the champions of a theory of creation. What they really dispute is not the eternity of the *matter* composing the universe, but that of its present *form*. They have in mind the periodical destruction of the universe by *fire*, the Heraclitean ἐκπύρωσις, which was revived by the Stoics.

Page 470 (Top). "On the sea:" the probably unique fragment (xxxix., Wimmer) relates to the origin of the sea. Cf. Hugo Berger, *Geschichte der Wissenschaftliche Erdkunde*, p. 383, ed. 2.

BOOK VI.—CHAPTER XL.

Page 471. The two botanical works of Theophrastus, the Περὶ φυτῶν ἱστορία and the Περὶ φυτῶν αἰτίαι, occupy the first two volumes of Wimmer's edition. In speaking of the descriptive or systematic work as prior in date to the explanatory or physiological treatise, we are in agreement both with the nature of the case and with the express testimony of Theophrastus himself in the first sentence of the second work: ἐν ταῖς ἱστορίαις εἴρηται πρότερον.

On the (predominantly physiological) contents of the lost genuine work of Aristotle on plants (Περὶ φυτῶν β'), we are enabled to form some general idea by the forward and backward references of the Stagirite himself. These are collected by Bonitz in the *Index Aristotelicus*, 104 b, 38 seqq. It may be noted, by the way, that in the quotation at l. 40, 41 (τὰ πάθη . . . περὶ φυτῶν), the reference, 442 b, 25, has been accidentally omitted. These passages have been treated by Ernst Meyer (*Geschichte der Botanik*, i. 88 seqq.), and also by Zeller (ii. 2, 509 seqq., ed. 3). A new edition of the two botanical works, with commentary and translation, is a pressing desideratum. So far as the *Historia Plantarum* is concerned, such a work was published in 1822 by Carl Sprengel. The *De Causis Plantarum* has not, to my knowledge, been translated.

Page 472 (par. 2). Date of composition of the two botanical works: this question has been treated in a scholarly manner by Oskar Kirchner in his valuable essay, *Die botanischen Schriften des*

Thèophrast (Jahrb. f. Klass. Philologie, Suppl. Bd. vii. 451-539).
He refers (p. 475) to *Hist. Plant.*, v. 8, 1, and iv. 3, 2. The Demetrius
who had ships built in Cyprus was certainly not "Demetrius of
Phalerum," but Demetrius Poliorcetes. But in spite of this slip the
chronological argument is sound. After the battle near Salamis in
Cyprus, the island was taken possession of by Demetrius. This battle
took place in the year 306. The expedition of Ophelas to Carthage,
which is mentioned in a second passage, falls in the autumn of
309 (cf. Beloch, *Gr. Gesch.*, iii. 1, 200). The *De Causis Plantarum*,
"notable rather for the statement than for the solution of problems : "
this is the judgment of Ernst Meyer, *op. cit.*, i. 167 : "I may therefore
be allowed to dwell principally on the *phenomena* which are explained
and to pass over the explanations."—"Predecessors : " on these see
again the information collected by Kirchner, pp. 499 *seqq.* (Middle)
"Botanists in the true sense : " this is decisively attested by *Hist.
Plant.*, i. 8, 3, on the arrangement of buds, where the words, δι' ὃ καὶ
ταξιόζωτα ταῦτα καλοῦσιν can only refer to writers on plants who both
described and generalized. That Menestor also belonged to this
class seems to me plain from *Hist. Plant.*, i. 2, 3 : ὃ δὴ καλοῦσί τινες
ἁπλῶς ἐν ἅπασιν ὁπόν, ὥσπερ καὶ Μενέστωρ; while the passages quoted by
Kirchner on pp. 505-507 are all in agreement with this supposition.
Kirchner contradicts himself when he writes (p. 507) : "If we assume
that he was a writer on agriculture, we are entitled to infer from the
quotations of Theophrastus that he gave more attention to the life
and nature of plants in general." Thus Ferdinand Cohn (*Die Pflanze*,
i. 4, 5, ed. 2) certainly goes too far in denying that Theophrastus
had any really scientific predecessors. One such predecessor, not
mentioned by Kirchner, must without doubt be recognized in the
person of the celebrated physician Diocles of Carystus (first third of
the fourth century). It is true that Theophrastus names him only
once, namely, in the fragment of the work "On Stones" (iii. 40,
Wimmer). But he makes copious use of him, as has been shown
in detail by Wellmann in his essay, *Das älteste Kräuterbuch der
Griechen* ("Festgabe für Franz Susemihl").—Alexander's "scientific
staff : " on this and on the matters which form the subject of what
follows, cf. Hugo Bretzl's *Botanische Forschungen des Alexanderzuges*
(Leipzig, 1903), a work of distinguished merit, based on a rare
combination of botanical and historico-philological knowledge. The
chief passages bearing on the subject are Strabo, ii. 69 ; xv. 685,
692, 694. The references on p. 473 (top) are to Bretzl's book (see
pp. 158, 115, 192, 193, 88, 518).

Page 474. On Theophrastus as a classifier, see *Hist. Pl.*, i. 3. The
chief passage is *ibid.*, i. 3, 5 : διὰ δὴ ταῦτα ὥσπερ λέγομεν οὐκ ἀκριβολογητέον
ὄρῳ, ἀλλὰ τῷ τύπῳ ληπτέον τοὺς ἀφορισμούς. Also, earlier, i. 3, 2 : δεῖ δὲ
τοὺς ὅρους οὕτως ἀποδέχεσθαι καὶ λαμβάνειν ὡς τύπῳ καὶ ἐπὶ τὸ πᾶν λεγομένους.
(Middle) "How climatic influences modify organisms," and the

examples: *ibid.*, i. 3, 5, 6. For the example of the mallow which sometimes becomes an arborescent plant (οἷον μαλάχη τε εἰς ὕψος ἀναγομένη καὶ ἀποδενδρουμένη, i. 3, 2), cf. F. Cohn, *Die Pflanze*, i. 403 (ed. 2): "The family of the mallows, represented in our regions by humble weeds, develops in the torrid zone into gigantic trees, and even on the shores of the Mediterranean appears in the form of a well-sized bush."

Page 475 (Top). The passage on sense-perception is *De Causis Plant.*, ii. 4, 8: ἐν τοῖς καθ' ἕκαστα τὸ ἀκριβὲς μᾶλλον αἰσθητικῆς δεῖται συνέσεως, λόγῳ δ' οὐκ εὐμαρὲς ἀφορίσαι. (Middle) "Similarities should not be dragged in by force:" *Hist. Plant.*, i. 1, 4: ὅσα γὰρ μὴ οἷόν τε ἀφομοιοῦν, περίεργον τὸ γλίχεσθαι πάντως, ἵνα μὴ καὶ τὴν οἰκείαν ἀποβάλλωμεν θεωρίαν.— Comparison between the roots of plants and the digestive tract: *De Causis Pl.*, vi. 11, 5. (Bottom) Kurt Sprengel: quoted by Ernst Meyer, *op. cit.*, i. p. 165.—Description of the banana-leaf: Bretzl, *op. cit.*, p. 196. —Link and Robert Brown: Ernst Meyer, *op. cit.*, 166.—"Rhizome, bulb, tuber," etc.: Bretzl., p. 163.

Page 476 (Middle). The experiments of Harpalus in acclimatization: *Hist. Pl.*, iv. 4, 1. See, on these, Bretzl, 234 *seqq.* An interesting parallel, which shows the fondness of the Persians for experiments of this kind, is afforded by the missive of Darius I. to the satrap Gadatas (Bulletin de Corresp. Hellénique, xiii. 529 *seqq.*, with critical postscript, xiv. 646 *seqq.*; Dittenberger, *Sylloge Inscr. Gr.*, 2, ed. 2). (Bottom) "Spontaneous generation:" cf. *Hist. Pl.*, ii. 1, 1; ii. 1, 4; iii. 1, 4–6; *De Causis Pl.*, iv. 4, 11; *Hist. Pl.*, vii. 7, 3; i. 5, 1–3; v. 4, 6.

Page 477 (Middle). "Movements of plants:" leaves of *Mimosa aspera*: cf. Bretzl., p. 127, *seq.*—*Tamarindus Indica: ibid.*, 153 *seqq.*, based on *Hist. Pl.*, iv. 2, 11; iv. 7, 8; *De Causis Pl.*, ii. 19, 1 (the steep of plants). F. Cohn writes quite similarly on this, *Die Pflanze*, i. 257, ed. 2.

Page 478 (Top). "Heliotropic movements:" cf. *ibid.*, 261 *seqq.*, and *De Causis Pl.*, ii. 19, 3. On what follows see ii. 19, 4. It is there, too, that we meet with the word "sensation:" ἡ δὲ αἴσθησις οὕτως ὀξεῖα γινομένη, κ.τ.λ.—"The irritability and sensitivity of plants:" this was the title of a lecture delivered by G. Haberlandt at the festival session of the Kais. Akademie der Wissenschaften, May 30, 1908. Cf. the same author's essay "*Über Bewegung und Empfindung im Pflanzenreich*," in the Rivista di Scienza, iii. 290–300. (Middle) "Duality of sex in plants:" *Hist. Pl.*, ii. 6, 5; comparison with the mating of animals: ii. 8, 4: ἀλλ' ἢ μὲν οἷον μῖξις; also *De Causis Pl.*, iii. 18, 1.

Page 479 (par. 2). Albertus Magnus possessed only a second-hand knowledge of Theophrastus: cf. *De Vegetabilibus, libri* vii., ed C. Jessen, p. 109 (ii. 15): "*Dicunt* autem, Plinium apud Latinos et Theophrastum apud Græcos hanc tenuisse sententiam."—Andrea Cesalpini: *De Plantis, libri* xvi., Florence, 1583. The work begins with a sentence on the θρεπτικὴ ψυχή ("illud solum genus animæ quo alantur, crescant et gignant sibi similia ") which is appropriate only to plants. Here, therefore, he speaks exactly like an Aristotelian. Some samples of his critical and exegetical labours may well find a place here. In x. 46, p. 429, he says of a Theophrastean sentence (the allusion is to *Hist. Pl.*, ix. 18, 3): "Multis mendis scatet et corrigendus est hoc modo." Schneider (*Theophrasti Opera*, iii. 817) calls the passage in question " scripturam vexatissimam et aperte mendosam." He quotes Cesalpini's restoration among others, hopes for help from manuscripts, and finally contents himself with a conjecture of the botanist H. F. Link. In a second instance (ii. 3, p. 36) Cesalpini at least comes nearer the truth than his predecessors. In *Hist. Pl.*, iii. 10, φύλλον διοχιδές had been previously read, and the last word translated "bifidum." Cesalpini's version is "folium difficile ad findendum." Thus he makes, at any rate, some approach to the obviously correct reading, φύλλον δ' ἀσχιδές, which is now accepted. Strictly speaking, his rendering requires δυσσχιδές ; and he may have had this word in his mind. But the context makes the adversative particle necessary. (Bottom) "Beluchistan . . .:" Bretzl, p. 250.

BOOK VI.—CHAPTER XLI.

Page 482 (Top). Karl Gottlieb Sonntag: *Dissertatio in Prooemium Characterum Theophrasti*, Leipzig, 1787. (Bottom) "The genuine property of Aristotle :" *Eth. Nic.*, ii. 7, 1108 a, 20 ; iv. 13, 1127 a, 20; also *Eth. Eudem.*, iii. 7, 1233 b, 39, and *Magna Moralia*, i. 33, 1193 a, 29. "Supplementary expansions :" these *clausulæ* are found in chapters i., iii., vi., viii., xxviii., and xxix. (cf. my treatise referred to below) ; on the additions of a Byzantine writer, see Hermann Diels, *Theophrastea*, Berlin, 1883. This scholar has lately (1909) published a standard edition of the *Characters* in the Clarendon Press Series.

Page 484 (Top). "Character-sketches of Ariston of Chios : " cf. H. Sauppe, *Philodemi de Vitiis liber decimus*, Leipzig, 1853 (on the basis of *Voll. Hercul. Coll. prior.* iii.). Also J. L. Ussing, *Theophrasti Characteres et Philodemi de Vitiis liber* x., Copenhagen, 1868. (End of par.) "The writer of these lines . . .:" my treatise, *Über die Charactere Theophrasts*, was published in the Transactions of the Vienna Academy, Philos. histor. Klasse, as No. x. of vol. 117, Vienna, 1888. The excerpt-theory had previously been warmly attacked by Friedrich Ast, *Theophrasti Characteres*, Leipzig, 1816, and by R. C. Jebb, *The Characters of Theophrastus*, London and Cambridge, 1870. Its last champion was Eugen Petersen, *Theophrasti Characteres*, Leipzig, 1856, pp. 87, 88. The first to draw attention to the formal agreement between the character-sketches of Ariston and those of Theophrastus were Sauppe (*op. cit.*, p. 6) and Petersen (*op. cit.*, p. 89).

Page 485 (Top). "A single exception, and it confirms the rule :"

cf. the very erudite Leipzig edition of Theophrastus' *Characters* (1897), p. 51 : "Note here (in chapter vi.) the accumulation of introductory formulæ : τοιοῦτος οἷος, ἀμέλει δυνατός, δεινός, καὶ τούτων ἂν εἶναι δόξειε, ἱκανός, οὐκ ἀποδοκιμάζειν δέ." (Bottom) St. Jerome : *Adversus Jovianum*, i. 47, vol. ii. p. 313, Vallarsi.

Page 486 (Top). Athenæus : vi. 249 f and x. 439 e. Cf. G. Heylbut's dissertation, *De Theophrast Libris* Περὶ φιλίας, Bonn, 1876. These records relate to Theophrastus' book, Περὶ κολακείας, which is also mentioned in the ancient list of his writings. It is quoted by Athenæus in vi. 254 d. It must have been, at least in part, historical or anecdotal in character.—"The likeness of the epicure : " on the authority of Hermippus, quoted by Athenæus, i. 21 a, where there is also mention of Theophrastus' well-groomed appearance, of his elegant *tenue* in the lecture-room. (Bottom) "Not a superman : " there is much significance in the impression which Arcesilaus received when he migrated from the school of Theophrastus to that of Polemon (cf. pp. 12, 13) : ἔφη δὲ ᾿Αρκεσίλαος ὅτι αὐτῷ παρὰ Θεοφράστου μετελθόντι φανείησαν οἱ περὶ τὸν Πολέμωνα θεοί τινες ἢ λείψανα τῶν ἀρχαίων ἐκείνων καὶ ἐκ τοῦ χρυσοῦ γένους διαπεπλασμένων ἀνθρώπων (*Index Academicorum*, col. xv. 3 *seqq.*, pp. 55, 56, Mekler ; an abbreviated version in Diog. Laert., iv. 4, 22).

Sect. 5. The "tactless" person is called in the original ἄκαιρος (*Characteres*, xii.) ; the "vain" man μικροφιλότιμος (xxi.).

Page 487 (Bottom). "A scion of Melite : " κλάδος Μελιταῖος. Those who, like the Leipzig editors, think κλάδος must be the dog's name, overlook the fact that the kindred words, ἔρνος, θάλος, and κλάδος itself, appear in sepulchral inscriptions with quite similar application. Cf. the list of words in Kaibel's *Epigrammata Græca*. This use of poetical words is expressly intended to bring out the character of the vain person. (Cf. also the representation of a Melitean dog with the inscription Μελιταίη in the *Bulletino dell' Istituto*, 1851, pp. 55 and 58 ; reproduced in O. Keller's treatise on dog-breeds in antiquity, Österr. Jahreshefte, viii. 243.)

Page 488 (Top). The "fate-reviler" (μεμψίμοιρος) is the subject of character-study xvii., the boaster (ἀλαζών) of xxiii.

Page 489 (Bottom). Eduard Zeller : ii. 2, p. 855 (ed. 3). I have the satisfaction of knowing that he was converted by my treatise referred to above, as appears from an expression of his in the Archiv. f. Geschichte d. Philosophie, iii. 317 : "The prevailing view that they [the *Characters*] are a mere collection of extracts from one or more Theophrastean writings is convincingly refuted by Gomperz." —La Bruyère : *Les Caractères*, iii. 60 (Brussels edition of 1828). The question as to the date of composition of the *Characters* has not been decided beyond dispute (cf. Cichorius in the Leipzig edition, p. lvii. *seqq.*, and Franz Rühl in the Rhein. Mus., 1898, p. 324 *seqq.*). The last-named scholar has well remarked that "the composition of

the separate descriptions may belong to very different times;" so that
the question itself is hardly framed correctly.

BOOK VI.—CHAPTER XLII.

Page 490 (Top). The references on Ariston, Lycon, and Satyrus
are given in the author's treatise mentioned above, p. 9. (Middle)
"On Manners," "On Conditions of Life:" Περὶ ἠθῶν and Περὶ βίων.
There were also works with the same titles by Clearchus (cf. Weber,
De Clearchi Solensis Vita et Operibus, Breslau, 1880, p. 17; the
fragments are given by Müller, *Fragmenta Historicorum Græcorum*,
ii. pp. 302 *seqq.*), and by Heraclides, and again by Straton (cf. Diog.
Laert., v. 3, 59, and v. 6, 87). Zeno the Epicurean's Περὶ ἠθῶν καὶ βίων,
was at least in part devoted to descriptive individual ethics. We learn
this from the part preserved in *Voll. Hercul. Collectio, prior.* v., with
the separate title, Περὶ παρρησίας. (Bottom) "Wealth of its historical
contents" in Theophrastus' Περὶ ἠθῶν: this is plainly indicated by the
statement of Athenæus (xv. 673 e), that the Commentator Adrastus
devoted *five* books to the "historical and linguistic difficulties"
occurring in this work; while he found *one* such book enough for the
Nicomachean Ethics. There is a fair number of fragments of the
βίος Ἑλλάδος by Dicæarchus; they too have been collected by Müller,
op. cit., ii. 233 *seqq.*
   Sect. 3. Page 491. Phanias or Phainias (the latter spelling seems
to me to be rendered certain by its occurrence in the *Hercul. Voll.*,
cf. my essay, *Die Herculanischen Rollen*, Zeitschr. für Öst. Gymn.,
1866, 10 Heft, p. 701). His historical fragments have likewise been
collected by Müller, *op. cit.*, ii. 293 *seqq.* (Bottom) "A collection
of historical materials:" Ἱστορικὰ ὑπομνήματα.—The "comprehensive
chapter" of the "Law-lexicon:" preserved in the *Florilegium* of
Stobæus (xliv.; ii. 166 *seqq.*, Meineke), treated by Franz Hofman,
with the collaboration of the present author (*Beiträge zur Geschichte
des griech. und röm. Rechts*, pp. 46–62). I dissent from Usener's
contention (Rhein Mus., xvi. 470 *seqq.*) that the work referred to by
Diogenes Laertius as Νόμων κατὰ στοιχεῖον κδ′ was not really a lexicon
of law or politics. The "remarkable addition κατὰ στοιχεῖον" signifies,
according to Usener, "that in the Νόμοι, the number of whose books
was equal to that of the letters of the alphabet, these letters were used
in the numeration of the books." That is to say, Ζ stood for 6 instead
of 7, 10 was represented by Κ instead of I, and so forth; the mode of
designation, in fact, which is universal in the works of Aristotle was
applied to this particular work of Theophrastus. This trivial circumstance, then, was embodied, so we are to suppose, in the title of the
work itself; and for the sake of this supposition we are to place an
unnatural interpretation on the words κατὰ στοιχεῖον. Usener, indeed,
calls the natural interpretation an "hypothesis." But it is a case of

an established usage. I quote the instances which lie readiest to hand : Hesychius, in the preface of his dictionary, writes : πολλοὶ μὲν καὶ ἄλλοι τῶν παλαιῶν τὰς κατὰ στοιχεῖον συντεθείκασι λέξεις. The patriarch Photius entitles his dictionary: Λεξικὸν κατὰ στοιχεῖον. Similarly we read in the lexicon of Timæus, *in.* : τάξας δὲ ταῦτα κατὰ στοιχεῖον καὶ μεταφράσας, κ.τ.λ. See also Dioscurides, *Materia Medica*, i. 3: οἱ δὲ κατὰ στοιχεῖον ἀναγράψαντες διέζευξαν τῆς ὁμογενείας τά τε γένη, κ.τ.λ. In face of these instances what do Usener's objections amount to ? " How could general notions like those in the Συμβολαῖα [the title of the large fragment in Stobæus] be treated connectedly with so great detail if the special subjects of πρᾶσις, συγγραφαί, παρακαταθῆκαι, etc., had to be discussed again in their separate places ? " We answer that Theophrastus, like any other author who arranges his matter in dictionary form, had the resource of cross-references. Nor do the inferences drawn from the few extant fragments seem to me very cogent. Usener himself admits that according to the " quotation in Harpocration, p. 141, 28 Bekker," the chapter Περὶ συμβολαίων belongs to the eighteenth book, that is, to the very place required by an alphabetical arrangement, since Σ = 18. But suppose the superscription had been lost : then the words for " sale " and " purchase," πρᾶσις and ὠνή, might have suggested objections against alphabetical arrangement quite similar to those which Usener raises in respect of a few other quotations of which the content is known to us, but not the heading.

" On Statecraft or Applied Politics : " I thus translate Πολιτικὰ πρὸς τοὺς καιρούς, a title which in another place (Zeitschr. f. Öst. Gymn., 1865, p. 816, note 3) I rendered otherwise, namely as " on political opportunism." Neither of these translations fully corresponds to the idea of the work which we form from the fragments (cf. Usener, *Analecta Theophrastea*, 7). " Political casuistry " might be suggested ; but the implied connexion with ethical casuistry would be misleading. The contents were chiefly historical, perhaps most nearly comparable with the collection of financial *coups* in Aristotle's *Economics*. The evidence of Cicero (*De Finibus*, v. 4, 11) seems to prove that the work was in part of a normative character. After referring to Aristotle's *Polities* and the possibility of learning from that work "qui esset optumus reipublicæ status," he proceeds : " Hoc amplius Theophrastus quæ essent in re publica inclinationes rerum et momenta temporum, quibus esset moderandum utcunque res postularet." And in a letter to Atticus (*Ad Atticum*, ix. 2) he writes, in reference to the political situation and the means of meeting it : " Nihil me existimaris neque usu neque a Theophrasto didicisse," etc. Here we see the book of Theophrastus set side by side with experience the preceptress.

Page 492 (Middle). " It is only quite recently . . . " This remark on the influence on the rhetorical works rests on private communications kindly made to me by a young fellow-countryman, the author of a recently published book, *Theophrasti* Περὶ λέξεως *Libri Fragmenta collegit, disposuit, prolegomenis instruxit Augustus Mayer.* Eudemus : cf. the collection of fragments, *Eudemi Rhodii quæ supersunt Collegit Leonardus Spengel,* Berlin, 1866.—Aristoxenus : son of Spintharus, of Tarentum. The fragments of this prolific pupil of Aristotle are to be found (with the exception of those on rhythm and technical music) in Müller, *Fragmenta Histor. Græc.,* ii. 269 *seqq.* The "harmonic fragments" have been edited by Paul Marquard, Berlin, 1868 ; reference may also be given to *Aristoxenos von Tarent, Melik und Rhythmik des Klassischen Hellenentums,* 2 vols., by R. Westphal (Leipzig, 1893).—"Joy, mourning, and enthusiasm : " according to Plutarch, *Quæst. Conviv.,* i. 5, 2 = *Moralia,* ii. 754, 23 *seqq.* Dübner. An extensive fragment from his two books on music (preserved in Porphyrius' commentary on the *Harmonics* of Ptolemæus, iii. 291, Wall.) has been treated by Brandis, *op. cit.,* 366–369. Besides those two books Περὶ μουσικῆς, the ancient lists also mention a book *Harmonics,* and an obviously historical work *On Musicians.* (Below) " The history of religion : " six books Περὶ τὸ θεῖον ἱστορίας and three books Περὶ θεῶν (*De Diis Epicherematum*), cf. Usener's *Analecta Theophrastea,* 11.

Page 493 (Top). " Inhabitants of Mount Athos " (Acrothoitæ) : cf. Jakob Bernays, *Theophrastos' Schrift über Frömmigkeit,* Berlin, 1866, pp. 36 *seq.,* and 56, 57.—Ancient criticism : Clemens *Protrept.,* 66, 58, Potter.—Cicero : *De Natura Deorum,* i. 13.

Sect. 4. Cf. Bernays, *op. cit.,* pp. 51 *seqq.*—Human sacrifices in Arcadia, their continuance to the time of the Roman Empire : cf. Farnell, *Cults of the Greek States,* i. 41 *seq.*—Greeks on the Carthaginian sacrifices to Baal : *ibid.,* i. 33. On this and on what follows, cf. Bernays, p. 86 *seq.,* where he relies on Theophrastus as quoted by Porphyrius.—Theophrastus and Clearchus on the Jewish nation : cf. Bernays, *op. cit.,* pp. 84 *seq.,* 111 *seqq.,* and 187. The fragment from Clearchus Περὶ ὕπνου is preserved by Josephus, *Contra Apionem,* i. 22 = vi. 200 *seq.,* Bekker (in *Fragmenta Histor. Græc.,* ii. 323 *seq.*).

Page 495 (Top). " Kinship . . . of man and beast : " cf. Bernays, *op. cit.,* 96 *seqq.* (Bottom) " On the intelligence and disposition of animals : " Περὶ ζῴων φρονήσεως καὶ ἤθους. It is clear that Plutarch in his *De Sollertia Animalium* (*Moralia,* 1174 *seqq.,* Dübner) defends the same thesis as Theophrastus. His opponents, who deny animals a share in Logos, or higher intelligence, are Stoics. Cf. ch. 11, 5 ; also 10, 1, and 4, 10 ; there is another allusion in 3, 11. That Plutarch levied contributions on Theophrastus' apology for animals seems to us highly probable, though no one, as it seems, has so far made public a conjecture to that effect, not even the author of the monograph *Über die Tierpsychologie des Plutarchos* (by Adolf Dyroff, Würzburger Gymn. Progr., 1897). It is hardly by chance that Plutarch's language, where he treats of differences in degree between the psychic functions of living beings, echoes that of Theophrastus. Compare *De Sollertia Animalium*, ch. 4, 1, 2 (= 1177, 28 *seqq.*, Dübner): ἀπορῶ πῶς ἡ φύσις ἔδωκε τὴν ἀρχὴν αὐτοῖς, ἐπὶ τὸ τέλος ἐξικέσθαι μὴ δυναμένοις . . . (l. 42) εἶτα τῶν θηρίων αἰτιᾶσθαι τὸ μὴ καθαρὸν μηδ' ἀπηκριβωμένον πρὸς ἀρετὴν, κ.τ.λ., with Theophrastus as quoted by Porphyrius (p. 97, Bernays): αἱ γὰρ τῶν σωμάτων ἀρχαὶ πεφύκασιν αἱ αὐταί... πολὺ δὲ μᾶλλον τῷ τὰς ἐν αὐτοῖς ψυχὰς ἀδιαφόρους πεφυκέναι ... ἀλλ' ὥσπερ τὰ σώματα, οὕτω καὶ τὰς ψυχὰς τὰ μὲν ἀπηκριβωμένας ἔχει τῶν ζῴων, τὰ δὲ ἧττον τοιαύτας.

Page 496 (Top). "The sacrificer's purity of heart :" cf. Bernays, *op. cit.*, pp. 66–68 and 76. (Middle) On the ethics of Theophrastus, cf. Brandis, *op. cit.*, pp. 347 *seqq.* The unduly high value which he places on friendship is common to him with the other representatives of the Hellenistic age, which attached greater worth to private than to public life. Nor did he omit the casuistry of friendship; cf. Aulus Gellius, *Noctes Atticæ*, i. 3, 9 *seqq.*—The theory of the mean applied even to justice: cf. Stobæus, *Eclogæ*, ii. 7, 300 = ii. 140, 6 *seqq.*, Wachsmuth. (Bottom) "Reproached for having lowered the worth of virtue :" Cicero, *Tuscal.*, v. 9, 24 *seqq.*; *Acad. Post.*, i. 9; *De Finibus*, v. 5, 26. The line quoted by Cicero (*Tusc.*, *loc. cit.*): "Vitam regit fortuna, non sapientia " is the Latin translation of the Greek: Τύχη τὰ θνητῶν πράγματ', οὐκ εὐβουλία; *Menandri Monosticha*, 725. It may be added that Callisthenes, so far as we can judge, did actually show a lack of εὐβουλία; cf. my essay *Anaxarch und Kallisthenes* in the Commentationes Mommsenianæ, pp. 471, *seqq.*

Page 497 (Top). "Callisthenes, or on Mourning :" of the other dialogues of Theophrastus, we know by name the Μεγαρικός, the dialogue-form of which appears chiefly from the similarity of its title to the Τρωικός of Hippias (cf. vol. i. p. 433; further information is given by Hirzel, *Der Dialog.*, i. p. 311), also the *Symposium*, the Ἐρωτικός, and the Προτρεπτικός (cf. Hirzel, *ibid.*, 345).—"Criticism of Theophrastus as an author :" Cicero, *Brutus*, 31, 121 ("Quis Aristotele nervosior, Theophrasto dulcior ? ") and *Tuscul.*, *loc. cit.*

BOOK VI.—CHAPTER XLIII.

Straton is treated of by Diogenes Laertius in v. 3. He states (v. 4, 68) that Straton died in the course of the 127th Olympiad, "thus in 269-8 at the latest, so that his first year of headship, even by inclusive reckoning, could not be later than 286-5 . . . Straton ruled the school for eighteen years, from 287-6 or 286-5 to 270-69 or 269-8 " (Beloch, *Griech. Gesch.*, iii. 2, 469). The fragments of Straton have not yet been collected. The monograph by C. Nauwerck, *De Stratone Lampsaceno*, Berlin, 1836, is now out of date.

Page 499 (Top). On Strato at the Egyptian court, see Mahaffy, *The Empire of the Ptolemies*, p. 166. There is no ground for attributing his departure thence to jealousy on the part of the *literati*. A sufficient explanation is furnished by the accession of his royal pupil and by the death of Theophrastus. (Middle) "Curators of the school:" as we find a board of ten mentioned in the wills both of Theophrastus and of Lycon, this number would seem to have been customary, and it may be assumed that in Diog. Laert., v. 3, 62, where only nine names appear, one must have dropped out. (Bottom) Menedemus : Straton's remark about him is given by Plutarch, *De Tranquillitate Animi*, 13 = *Moralia*, 573, 15 Dübner.

Page 500 (Top). Verdict of Polybius : xii. 25 c. = iii. 211, 14 *seqq.*, Büttner-Wobst. (Middle) "On Dizziness and Numbness :" the title as recorded is Περὶ λιμοῦ καὶ σκοτώσεων. Reiske conjectured ἰλίγγου for λιμοῦ. Ad. Wilhelm suggests δίνου. (Bottom) A special work "On the Philosophic King :" it is a question whether there is documentary evidence for this title, which is only found in Cobet's edition of Diogenes Laertius, while earlier editions gave Περὶ φιλοσοφίας (Zeller, ii. 2, 903, ed. 3). Something of an enigma is presented by the title or titles, Περὶ τοῦ προτέρου γένους, περὶ τοῦ ἰδίου, περὶ τοῦ μέλλοντος. Perhaps what is meant is a work consisting of three books or sections : on the past, the special (present), and future generation. Of what nature could the contents of such a work be ?

Page 501. Straton as a physicist has been treated by G. Rodier (*La physique de Straton de Lampsaque*, Paris, 1890), and in a penetrating manner by Diels (*Über das physikalische System des Straton*, Berliner Sitzungsberichte, 1893, ix.), whom in the main we follow. Diels has proved that Straton was laid under large contribution in the preface to Hero's *Pneumatics*. The proof rests principally on the exact agreement between the quotation from Straton in Simplicius' commentary on Aristotle's *Physics*, iv. 9 (693, 11 *seqq.*, Diels) and Hero's preface, now i. 24, 20 *seqq.*, W. Schmidt (*Heronis Opera*, Leipzig, Teubner, 1899). Still, "this entire Heronic digression, περὶ τοῦ κενοῦ (Diels, p. 15), ought not, we think, to be called "an abridged extract from the similarly entitled book of Straton." Even Diels can hardly have supposed that there is an entire absence of added matter, since there is a reference to the much later Archimedes and his treatise *On Floating Bodies* (*ibid.*, p. 24, 11, Schmidt). More weight may be attached to the fact that a particular passage (pp. 10, 19 *seqq.*) closely echoes the Aristotelian doctrine of natural places : τὰ μὲν γὰρ λεπτότερα τῆς φθορᾶς εἰς τὸν ἀνωτάτω χωρεῖ τόπον, ἔνθαπερ καὶ τὸ πῦρ. But this echo is in contradiction with the authoritative statement of Simplicius in his commentary on Aristotle's *De Cœlo*, i. 8 (pp. 267, 268, Heiberg), that Strato revived the Democritean doctrine of displacement (ἔκθλιψις). I should be glad to see this contradiction removed, and with it the obstacle which prevents me from accepting the result arrived at by Diels unqualified by this limitation. A word in passing : at p. 26, l. 21 (ed. Schmidt) of the preface the words (τὸ θερμὸν) ought probably to be inserted after σωμάτων. Cf. p. 24, 24 : τὸ φῶς οὐδὲ ἡ θερμότης. Without these words Hero, or Straton, would be made to say that light (τὸ φῶς) passes "through copper, iron, and all other bodies," that is, he must have been acquainted with Röntgen rays! (Middle) "A dream or phantasy:" cf. Cicero, *Acad.*, ii. 38, 121.

Page 503 (Top). "Qualities:" ποιότητες. Cf. Sextus Pyrrhon., iii. 33 = 126, 26, Bekker: Στράτων δὲ ὁ φυσικὸς τὰς ποιότητας—that is, ἀρχὰς λέγει. We have here a cardinal distinction between the fundamental doctrine of Straton and that of Democritus. In order to mark this distinction and the absence of a fanciful elaboration, on Straton's part, of the atomic theory (see above), it is perhaps well to avoid the *expression* "atoms" in describing the natural philosophy of the latter. But it would be a mistake to suppose that there was an essential difference between the atoms of Democritus and the ultimate particles, corpuscles, or elements of mass conceived by our philosopher. The primary bodies of Democritus, with their manifold variety of form, were not mere points or centres of force, but possessed extension just as much as those of Straton. And if the latter are spoken of as infinitely divisible (Sextus, *Adv. Math.*, x. 155 = 508, 22 *seqq.*, Bekker), this is to be understood (as rightly remarked by Diels, *op. cit.*, p. 12, note 3) not of actual, but merely of ideal division (according to Simplicius on the *Physics, Corollarium de loco*, 618, 24, Diels).— If motion was not to be unintelligible, time would need to be an infinitely divisible *continuum*, just as space and bodies were for him (Sextus, *loc. cit.*). Thus we are certainly justified if, with Zeller (ii. 2, 912, ed. 3), we regard the addition of Sextus, κινεῖσθαί τε τὸ κινούμενον ἐν ἀμερεῖ χρόνῳ ὅλον ἄθρουν μεριστὸν διάστημα καὶ οὐ κατὰ τὸ πρότερον πρότερον as a misunderstanding, and give the preference to the statement of Simplicius (commentary on the *Physics, Corollarium de tempore*, 789, 2): ἀριθμὸν μὲν γὰρ κινήσεως εἶναι τὸν χρόνον οὐκ ἀποδέχεται, διότι ὁ μὲν ἀριθμὸς διωρισμένον ποσόν, ἡ δὲ κίνησις καὶ ὁ χρόνος συνεχής, τὸ δὲ συνεχὲς οὐκ ἀριθμητόν. (Bottom) "Set Nature in the place of the Deity:" this rests chiefly on the authority of Cicero, who makes Velleius the Epicurean say: "Strato . . . qui omnem vim divinam in *natura* sitam esse censet," etc. (*De Natura Deorum*, i. 13, 35), with which we at once compare *Acad.*, ii. 38, 121 : " Negat opera deorum se uti ad fabricandum mundum : quaecumque sint, omnia effecta esse *natura*."

Page 504 (Par. 2). " High esteem paid to the 'physicist:'" Diog. Laert., v. 3, 58 : ἀνὴρ ἐλλογιμώτατος καὶ φυσικὸς ἐπικληθεὶς ἀπὸ τοῦ περὶ τὴν θεωρίαν ταύτην παρ' ὁντινοῦν ἐπιμελέστατα διατετριφέναι. Simplicius on Aristotle's *Physics*, vi. 4 (965, 7 *seqq.*): Στράτων . . . ἐν τοῖς ἀρίστοις Περιπατητικοῖς ἀριθμούμενος.—Aristarchus and Straton: Stobæus, *Eclogæ Physicæ*, i. 16, p. 98, 6, Meineke = i. 149, 6, Wachsmuth. See also Bergk, *Fünf Abhandlungen*, p. 141, note 3, and Diels, *op. cit.*, p. 19. (Middle) Eratosthenes: his selection from Straton is mentioned by Strabo, i. 3, p. 49 = i. pp. 64-66, Meineke. A recently discovered book of Archimedes: Hermes, xlii., Biblioteca Mathematica, 1907, with German translation by Zeuthen, English translation in the *Monist*, April, 1909, recently discussed by Heiberg in the periodical *Das Weltall*, ix. 11, 12. (Bottom) Ctesibius and Erasistratus: cf. Diels, *op. cit.*, p. 10 *seq.*, and 11 *seqq.*; Wellmann in Pauly and Wissowa's *Encyclopædia*, *s.v.* "Erasistratos," and *Zwei Vorträge zur Geschichte der antiken Medicin,* pp. 20 *seqq.*, in the separate reprint from the Neue Jahrbücher f. d. Klass. *Altertum*, xxi.

Page 505 (Top). "A twofold argument:" cf. Simplicius on *Physics*, vi. 4 (975, 10 *seqq.*, Diels), where Straton's book on motion is referred to. Cf. Poppelreuter, *Zur Psychologie des Aristoteles, Theophrast, Strato*, pp. 46 *seq.*, where also a reference is given to the second passage bearing on the subject, Plutarch, *De Sollertia Animalium*, 3, 6 = *Moralia*, 1176, 15 *seqq.*, Dübner. Here is the weighty saying: ὡς οὐδ' αἰσθάνεσθαι τὸ παράπαν ἄνευ τοῦ νοεῖν ὑπάρχει, with the illustration appended. The comparison with the striking of a clock was suggested by Grote. (Par. 2) "Seat of the psychic functions:" the μεσόφρυον; cf. Diels, *Doxographi Græci*, 391, 5. Straton's attack upon the proofs of immortality in the *Phædo*: cf. *Olympiodori Scholia in Platonis Phædonem*, ed. Chr. Eberh. Finckh (Heilbronn, 1847, pp. 150 *seqq.*).

INDEX TO VOL. IV.

N.B.—*As in former Volumes, the references to the text are intended to carry with them references to the corresponding portions of the Notes and Additions. As much the greater part of this volume deals with Aristotle, his name is often omitted from headings of which it would otherwise have formed part.*

END OF VOL. IV.

PRINTED IN GREAT BRITAIN BY WILLIAM CLOWES AND SONS, LIMITED, LONDON AND BECCLES.